WORSHIP AND THEOLOGY
IN ENGLAND

WORSHIP AND THEOLOGY IN ENGLAND

WORSHIP
AND THEOLOGY IN
ENGLAND

THE ECUMENICAL CENTURY,

1900-1965

BY HORTON DAVIES

PRINCETON, NEW JERSEY
PRINCETON UNIVERSITY PRESS
1965

HORTON DAVIES is currently the Henry W.
Putnam Professor of the History of Christianity at Princeton University. He was born
in Wales, became an honors graduate in both
Arts and Divinity at Edinburgh University,
and obtained his Doctorate of Philosophy at
Oxford University. Mr. Davies has served successively as minister of an English Congregational Church in London, Dean of the Faculty
of Divinity at Rhodes University in the Union
of South Africa, and Head of the Department
of Church History at Mansfield and Regent's
Park Colleges at Oxford University.

Printed in the United States of America by
Princeton University Press, Princeton, New Jersey

ACKNOWLEDGMENTS

THE SCALE of the indebtedness of the writer of contemporary history forbids its adequate acknowledgment. He needs to consult the participants and observers of events. In writing religious history he must also be scrupulously fair to members of traditions other than his own and seek their interpretations of theology and worship. Above all, when he deals with the two hand-maids of worship, religious art and music, he requires expert guid-ance. I have not hesitated to avail myself of much advice, gener-ously proffered in interviews and correspondence, most of which is acknowledged in the footnotes of relevant chapters or in the de-scriptions of the illustrations.

My special thanks are due to those who have assisted me far beyond the call of duty. I wish to thank Lady Kathleen Epstein for three interviews on the work of the late Sir Jacob Epstein; the Right Reverend B. Christopher Butler, O.S.B., the Abbot of Downside, who invited me to be the guest of the Benedictine Com-munity which has contributed so generously to spirituality and scholarship; the Reverend Dr. Ernest A. Payne, the Secretary of the Baptist Union of Great Britain and Ireland, for helpful correspond-ence; the Reverend Dr. John Marsh, Principal of Mansfield College, Oxford, in whose home I stayed during Michaelmas Term 1964; the Reverend Dr. Erik R. Routley of Edinburgh, a former Oxford colleague, for his advice in that field which he has made peculiarly his own—Sacred Music; the Reverend Dr. E. C. Ratcliff, Regius Professor Emeritus of Divinity in the University of Cambridge, England's leading liturgiologist, for many kindnesses; the Rev-erend R. Aled Davies of Croydon, Convener of the Presbyterian Church of England's Assembly Committee on Public Worship, for an unusually full report on the state of worship in that Communion; and the memory of the late Dr. Mortimer Rowe, former General Secretary of the Unitarian and Free Christian Churches of Great Britain, for both letters and the loan of rare books. These and numberless others have been my benefactors in scholarship. It is also a pleasure to thank Mrs. Dan Crawford who typed the manu-script so efficiently, and Mrs. Polly Hanford of Princeton Univer-sity Press for her careful editorial work on a 'mid-Atlantic' manu-script which was neither wholly English nor American in its spelling or use of idiom. I am also deeply indebted to the considera-tion shown me by Mr. Herbert W. Bailey, Jr., and Miss R. Miriam

Brokaw, respectively the Director and the Managing Editor of Princeton University Press. My gratitude to my wife is beyond all reckoning.

The Research Committee of Princeton University deserves my gratitude for the award of two grants which made it possible to spend two summers in English libraries. The Trustees of the John S. Guggenheim Memorial Foundation of New York by the award of two Fellowships have accelerated the progress towards the completion of this five-volume project. I am greatly cheered by their encouragement as I press on to complete the two final volumes, I and II.

To all these persons and institutions I express my deep gratitude.

HORTON DAVIES

Easter 1965
Department of Religion,
Princeton University

viii

CONTENTS

PART TWO: THE NARROW FOCUS

CONTENTS

ILLUSTRATIONS

Following page 60

Christians driven together for protection against the forces of modern secularity, and in the Chapel of Christ the Servant which, with its plain glass and cylindrical shape, shines like a welcoming lighthouse through the dark of industrial Coventry at night. His artistic sensitivity is seen in the invitation of artists of the calibre of Graham Sutherland (whose tapestry of Christ in Glory dominates the East wall), John Hutton, John Piper, Lawrence Lee, and Sir Jacob Epstein to contribute their unfettered talents to glorify God's house.

5. COVENTRY CATHEDRAL: ROOF OF CHAPEL OF UNITY
This Chapel is used for joint devotions by members of the various Christian Churches in Coventry and is owned jointly by the Cathedral and the Free Churches of Coventry. The stained glass set in concrete was the work of Margaret Traherne.

6. COVENTRY CATHEDRAL: CHAPEL OF CHRIST THE SERVANT
This symbolizes the industrial mission of Christianity and has an impressive pendent cross over the central mensa. This cross, resembling four vast twisted anvils, is entirely appropriate.

7. COVENTRY CATHEDRAL: JOHN PIPER'S BAPTISTRY WINDOW
Designed by John Piper and executed by Patrick Reyntiens, this is a vast window of 198 lights of abstract design. There is a golden pool hovering over the font; above it are the celestial colours purple, ultramarine and other shades of blue, and below are the earthy reds, browns, and greens, shimmering in splendour.

8. LIVERPOOL (ROMAN CATHOLIC) CATHEDRAL: THE MODEL
Frederick Gibberd, the architect of the Metropolitan Cathedral of Christ the King in Liverpool, has produced a symbolic shape entirely appropriate to the twentieth century, as well as being liturgically functional. His cathedral, now rising, is a circular tent shape surmounted by a glass cylinder with pinnacles suggesting a crown of thorns. The tent is the perfect symbol of the Church in pilgrimage and beneath it is a vast central altar which will enable 2,000 worshippers both to see and hear the Mass and thus to participate fully. The glass in the cylinder is to be designed by John Piper. The model shows

the general view from the south. (His Eminence Cardinal John C. Heenan, Monsignor T. A. Turner, and Mr. Frederick Gibberd were most helpful in providing information.)

9. IBADAN (ANGLICAN) CATHEDRAL, NIGERIA: THE MODEL (and photographs)
This photograph is included to show the most original work of George Pace of York who has built many churches in England, but whose major work is the University Chapel at Ibadan and the impressive cathedral planned for the largest indigenously African city on the continent. It is a liturgically controlled plan for a cathedral which is unmistakably Christian, yet by its delicate grilles and lattice-work windows seems appropriately located in the heart of a considerable Moslem population, as well as ensuring a cool escape from the brilliant sun of Africa.

10. GREAT CHAPEL OF THE HOUSE OF THE SACRED MISSION, KELHAM
Built in 1927-28 by Charles Clayton Thompson, this is the main chapel of the Anglican Society of the Sacred Mission, which, through the leadership of the late Father Gabriel Hebert, has done so much to acclimatise the fruits of the Liturgical Movement in England. The rood is the work of Sargent Jagger, perhaps better known as the sculptor of the Artillery Memorial at Hyde Park Corner. (The photograph was taken by Mr. Albert Alspach of Mansfield College, Oxford, a Lutheran ordinand and friend.)

11. ST. MARY, WELLINGBOROUGH: COMPER'S BLENDING OF GOTHIC AND CLASSIC
This is perhaps the most notable proof of Sir J. N. Comper's thesis that beauty may be created by inclusion—blending Gothic and Classic. Only a colour photograph could do justice to the brilliance of the gold and blue decor which shine all the more resplendently against the background of cold grey. The most brilliant example of his decoration is probably the Lady Chapel of the Great Abbey Church at Downside. An instance of Baroque splendour is the Church of the Good Shepherd, Carshalton, Surrey, with gold and whitewash.

12. ST. GEORGE'S CHURCH, LETCHWORTH
A striking altar with a Christus straining upward in a great

shaft of light dominates the Church built by Peter Bosanquet and Partners of Oxford. It reflects in dramatic fashion the trend towards making new churches liturgically functional. (Photograph by Colin Westwood.)

13. WILLIAM TEMPLE MEMORIAL CHURCH, WYTHENSHAWE: PLAN
   This Manchester Anglican Church is the work of that fertile architect, George Pace of York. It is notable for dramatic altar, centrally located font, and choir adjacent to both blocks of the congregation.

14. WILLIAM TEMPLE CHURCH: SW AND SE ELEVATIONS
   As always, the fenestration is the sign-manual of George Pace's work.

15. TRINITY PRESBYTERIAN CHURCH, NORWICH
   The triangulation of the beams of the roof both symbolize the dedication of this Presbyterian Church and emphasize the worship centre. The latter is unusual in refusing to give either pulpit or communion table precedence. It thus stresses the co-ordinate importance of Sacrament and Sermon. (Photography by courtesy of the Minister, the Rev. E. Francis Jones.)

16. PUNSHON MEMORIAL METHODIST CHURCH, BOURNE-MOUTH
   This impressive Church is large, but light and airy. It would have delighted the late A. E. Whitham, a Bournemouth Methodist minister who instructed Free Churchmen in the importance of the cultivation of the devotional life. (Photograph by courtesy of Mr. Arthur H. Skippenoe, the Church Steward, and the Rev. Oliver Phillipson of Manchester.)

17. GUILDFORD CONGREGATIONAL CHURCH
   This octagonal church, with central illuminated cross, canti-levered pulpit, and solid communion table has been ingeniously designed by Barber, Bundy, and Greenfield, the Guild-ford Architects, to allow the sanctuary to be extended on two sides for Family Church festivals. On regular Sundays the extra areas are enclosed for graded religious instruction. (Photograph by courtesy of the Minister, the Rev. Nigel G. Porter.) It should be noted that in the last three photographs the Free Churches have re-appropriated the central symbol of the Cross for worship.

18. CHRIST CHURCH AND UPTON (BAPTIST AND CONGREGA-
TIONAL)

This Church in South-East London is notable as a venture in
Christian unity. The Church is gathered about the central
Lord's Table which is raised upon a dais. Invisible is a large
stained-glass window emblematic of the Communion of Saints
and the theme of Christian unity. (Photograph by courtesy of
the former Minister, the Rev. P. G. Saunders.)

19. JOHN HUTTON: MADONNA AND CHILD (COVENTRY CA-
THEDRAL)

Instead of the usual West wall of stone there is in Coventry
Cathedral a wall of glass. On this John Hutton, a brilliant
glass engraver, has incised a series of angels and saints, of
which the dominating figure is this Madonna and Child.

20. JACOB EPSTEIN: MADONNA AND CHILD (CAVENDISH
SQUARE, LONDON, W.1.)

This is perhaps the greatest of all Sir Jacob Epstein's religious
masterpieces. This thirteen-foot-high group depicts the mantled Madonna shrouded in pity as she bends over her young
Son, with arms outstretched to greet the world and, prolep-
tically, to meet the Cross. It hangs on a bridge connecting the
two parts of the Convent of the Holy Child Jesus in the small
square, Cavendish Square, close to the large West End department stores. (Photographer Hans Wild.)

21. HENRY MOORE: MADONNA AND CHILD (NORTHAMPTON)

This masterwork of Henry Moore, sculpted of Hornton stone,
is to be found behind a delicate wrought-iron grille in a
transept of St. Mathew's Church, Northampton, opposite a
Crucifixion painting by Graham Sutherland (Fig. 22). The
Christ Child sits enthroned on the Madonna's lap. She is the
figure of eternal Pity, and He of eternal Wisdom. (Photograph by courtesy of Mr. Henry Moore, O.M.)

22. GRAHAM SUTHERLAND: THE CRUCIFIXION (NORTHAMP-
TON)

Mr. Graham Sutherland despises sentimental renderings of
the Crucifixion. This Crucifixion, painted with emaciated
body, broken legs, and skewered fingers, is a moving image
of the Man of Sorrows and appropriate for an era of agony

like ours. The almost casual cross or kiss marks are the tributes of everyman to the Saviour.

23. GRAHAM SUTHERLAND: THE CRUCIFIXION (EAST ACTON)
This Crucifixion, while of the same type as the Northampton one, shows increased interpretative power. The contorted arms which bear the weight are gnarled, the gaping mouth seems to cry "I thirst," and the red curtain seems to thrust the blanched body towards the attention of the worshippers, while the electric globes are twentieth-century reminders of torture in condemned cells. Like Rouault's, this is a powerful and distinctive twentieth-century image of Christ "afflicted in our afflictions." It is found in St. Aidan's Roman Catholic Church, East Acton, and is reproduced by the kindness of the parish priest, the Rev. James Ethrington. (Photograph by Kirwan.)

24. STANLEY SPENCER: CRUCIFIXION (ALDENHAM SCHOOL)
This painting hangs over the altar of Aldenham School, Ellstree, Hertfordshire and is reproduced by kind permission of the Headmaster. Painted by that eccentric genius, Sir Stanley Spencer, in the throes of his mortal cancer, it is a powerful image of pain rather than of faith in darkness. The fiendish ferocity of the carpenters is reminiscent of a Bosch, and the angle of the viewpoint is as ingenious as that of Salvator Dali.

25. JACOB EPSTEIN: ST. MICHAEL AND THE DEVIL (COVENTRY CATHEDRAL)
This superb contrast between the lithe athletic St. Michael and the gross and pendulous Devil hangs on an exterior wall of Coventry Cathedral. (Photograph by The Times of London.)

26. JACOB EPSTEIN: THE ASCENDING CHRIST, MAQUETTE
This maquette, now in the possession of the author, was Sir Jacob's model, made during the last year of his life, for a large statue to be hung behind and above the altar of the Church of the Ascension, Crownhill, Devonport. This lithe Christ, victorious over death, seems by a sheer sculptural legerdemain to gyrate upwards as the wind presses his garments against his ascetical body. The maquette is merely the first draft of what would have been another masterwork. (I am indebted for information to Lady Kathleen Epstein.)

27. "WOODBINE WILLIE" (STUDDERT KENNEDY)
This cartoon of Studdert Kennedy by Ronald Sinclair is from St. Martin-in-the-Fields where he was, for a while, on the staff of the "parish church of the British Empire." He was a courageous and utterly unconventional padre in the first World War and he helped to change the image of the Anglican parson from a personage to a companion.

28. DEAN INGE
The famous "gloomy Dean" was the most quotable of English ecclesiastics during his tenure of the Deanery of St. Paul's Cathedral, London. A mystic, scholar, and wit, he spread his independent views in pulpit and in the press. (Photograph of portrait in the National Portrait Gallery.)

29. BISHOP H. HENSLEY HENSON
His 3-volume 'Retrospect of an Unimportant Life' is the most lively interpretation of the progress of the Church of England during this century. Independent, honest, witty, and courageous, like his friend Dean Inge, his sermons were models of sensible and succinct preaching.

30. ARCHBISHOP WILLIAM TEMPLE
He was the most significant Anglican leader of the present century. An able philosopher, a superb chairman of theological commissions, an ecclesiastical statesman of great vision, his concern for social justice earned the title "The People's Archbishop."

31. FATHER GABRIEL HEBERT, S.S.M.
By preaching, writing, and example, Fr. Hebert, of the Society of the Sacred Mission, was the pioneer of the Liturgical Movement in England.

32. DR. LESLIE D. WEATHERHEAD
A clerical pioneer in the realm of psychology, Dr. Weatherhead was probably the most widely known preacher in England, especially during his long tenure of the pulpit of City Temple, sometimes called "the Cathedral of the English Free Churches." He is a Methodist minister.

WORSHIP AND THEOLOGY

INTRODUCTION

THE SERIES, *Worship and Theology in England*, of which this volume is the fifth, is being written in the conviction that the study of the cultus of the Christian Churches offers the deepest clue to their interior life, as well as an index to their state of health. Theology and ethics are the conscious faces which the Churches show to the world; worship is the unposed face of the Church turned towards God in adoration and aspiration. Since worship is essentially *common* prayer, it might be argued that it is more truly representative of the life of the Christian community than theology (which is predominantly the work of thinkers operating as individuals within the tradition) or ethics (which vary with changing contexts). Its importance, however, is better judged when worship is seen as an inclusive category; for, being the adoration of the Body of Christ responsive to revelation, it necessarily includes both the knowledge of God (theology) and the strongest motives to fulfill the Divine will (ethics). The value of the cultus as an expression of the dynamic ethos of a community has long been acknowledged by social anthropologists; yet it is far from being recognized as significant by the majority of church historians.

Nonetheless its worth has been recognized by two distinguished English historians, John Selden (the seventeenth century antiquarian) and Professor Herbert Butterfield, Master of Peterhouse, Cambridge. In his *Table Talk*, it is recorded that Selden observed: "To know what was generally believed in all ages, the way is to consult the liturgies, not any man's private writing. So, if you would know how the Church of England serves God, go to the Common Prayer Book, consult not this nor that man."[1] Professor Butterfield observes that serious students, like Lord Acton, have been greatly interested in Church history, but that in considering its institutional impact on an age they have "tended to overlook that more intimate thing, the inner spiritual life of the Church." He adds, perhaps selecting the spiritual low point of 1800:

"The ordinary historian, when he comes, shall we say, to the year 1800 does not think to point out to the readers that in this year, still, as in so many previous years, thousands and thousands of priests and ministers were preaching the Gospel week in and

---

[1] *Table Talk, 1689*, under "Liturgy."

3

week out, constantly reminding the farmer and the shopkeeper of charity and humility, persuading them to think for a moment about the great issues of life, and inducing them to confess their sins. Yet this was a phenomenon calculated greatly to alter the quality of life and the very texture of human history; and it has been the standing work of the Church throughout the ages—even under the worst of popes here was a light that never went out."[2]

The present volume, then, brings the comparative history of Christian worship in all the major denominations in England up to the present. Like its two predecessors,[3] worship is studied both in a theological and in an aesthetic context. The changes of theology are reflected directly in the preaching of the age and more directly in freer than in liturgical types of worship. This is evident in the comparative neglect of worship when social witness is accorded imperative interest (as in the depreciation of the Lord's Supper in the Free Churches during the predominance of the "Social Gospel" emphasis), or when intellectual and moral discourses freeze the springs of devotion (as in Latitudinarian Anglicanism).

Worship is also greatly influenced by the prevailing modes of architecture, art, and music. To take a single example, one may cite the contemporary struggle between church architects who stand for the principle of *numinosity* and symbolism and those who emphasize the principle of *community-feeling* and functionalism. Since England has in the twentieth century witnessed an artistic and musical renaissance, the wider implications of aestheticism on worship have received fuller treatment in this volume.

This book has proved, in fact, to be the hardest to write of the three so far attempted in this series. The poet Horace rightly observed that to treat of current events is like walking on ashes beneath which the embers are still glowing.[4] Many experiments which excited a passing interest in their day are known to be unimportant to later investigators only because they were rapidly covered by the dust of oblivion; but the historian of current events has to do the sifting for himself. How can he tell whether a liturgical experiment which seems promising is a dangerous *ignis fatuus*, or a mere flash in the pan, or a guiding light? Another difficulty is the sheer bulk of reports, monographs, and periodical

[2] *Christianity and History*, p. 131.
[3] *Worship and Theology in England*, Vol. III: *From Watts and Wesley to Maurice, 1690-1850* and Vol. IV: *From Newman to Martineau, 1850-1900*.
[4] The third ode.

articles printed in our overproductive century on the theme of worship, a theme which has been brought into prominence by the success of the Modern Liturgical Movement. Merely to read them is difficult enough: to digest them calls for a Gargantuan appetite.

In facing these problems, I have had to rely more than in previous volumes on the official reports of the liturgical commissions or worship committees of the English Churches, and on their denominationally sponsored liturgies or service-books, and less on the often brilliant writings of individual interpreters, however creative. Furthermore, my judgment has been confirmed in many cases, but also contradicted in others, by the advice of experts in the fields of worship, art, architecture, and music whom I have interviewed or with whom I have corresponded. Yet, even in a century remarkable for its passionate concern for the establishment of Christian unity which, as Archbishop Temple insisted, was "the great new fact of our time" which argues for a stress on the unity of achievement in worship, I have also tried to do justice to the contributions of individual scholars, preachers, and artists precisely because this has been a period of liturgical experiment and artistic ferment.

My sub-title—"The Ecumenical Century"—has been selected to emphasize the fact that for Christian life in England as elsewhere this marks the decisive difference between the *competitive* character of nineteenth and the *cooperative* character of twentieth century Christianity. The term "Ecumenical" does not merely evoke a nostalgia for the first five centuries of the Christian era, when the Fathers of those Ecumenical Councils declared the apparently[5] unanimous mind of the Church against the heretics and schismatics in a moving demonstration of unity. Rather it points to the undoubted fact that attempts have been made, with renewed vigour by Protestants and Orthodox, on the one side, and more recently by Roman Catholics, on the other side, to heal the wounds of Christendom.[6]

Two events in recent ecclesiastical history symbolize this pas-

[5] See S. L. Greenslade, *Schism in the Early Church*, an important revisionist study.

[6] For a reliable series of accounts of the development of the ecumenical outlook since the Reformation see Ruth Rouse and S. C. Neill, eds., *A History of the Ecumenical Movement, 1517-1948*. Roman Catholic interpretations of Ecumenism are M. J. Congar, Divided Christendom (London, 1939, a trans. of *Chrétiens désunis*, Paris, 1937) and *Aspects de l'oecumenisme* (Bruxelles, 1962) and Hans Küng, *The Council in Action: Theological Reflections on the Second Vatican Council* (trans. C. Hastings, New York, 1964).

sionate concern for reunion. One was the foundation in 1948 at Amsterdam of the World Council of Churches, which had been prepared for by the Faith and Order and the Life and Work Commissions of cooperating Protestants, Anglicans, and Orthodox. The other is the epoch-making first session of the Ecumenical (or Second Vatican) Council of the Roman Catholic Church which was convoked in 1962, and which spoke of Orthodox and Protestants not as heretics but as "separated brethren" and whose representatives were invited as official observers to the Council. This rapprochement of a divided Christendom is most clearly mirrored in worship. In no period since the Reformation but our own would it seem natural and wholly right for an English Free Church minister, E. Romilly Micklem, gratefully to affirm his devotional indebtedness to "his mother the Church of England, his grandmother the Church of Rome, and his great-grandmother the Jewish Synagogue."[7]

At the same time, the success of the Pentecostalist Movement, which has been called Christianity's "Fourth Force" is a warning to the historic churches that Christian Reunion—if it be envisaged as an organization with a vast and impersonal super-structure, blissful only in the eyes of bureaucrats—could be too dearly purchased, at the cost of fellowship, variety, and freedom at the grass-roots level.

This book falls into two parts. The first, termed "The Wide-Angle View," presents a picture of the unparalleled agreement in worship in England of which the Ecumenical Movement in general, and the Modern Liturgical Movement in particular, are both stimulus and expression. The second part, "The Narrow Focus," shows that while there are elements of unity, there are also significant differences in worship. It presents the claim that the techniques of liturgical, free, and silent prayer, hitherto the separate treasures of different traditions, may be regarded as ultimately complementary approaches to the Divine in the Coming Great Church. It is thus hoped that both unity and difference have been given their accurate places in the reconstruction of the worship of the past six and a half decades.

Chapter i provides an account of "The Continental Liturgical Movement and its Influence," as it recounts the successive phases of the Movement in Solesmes, Mont-César, and Maria-Laach, and the appropriation of these insights by Lutherans and Reformed in

---

[7] *Our Approach to God*, p. 148.

Europe, and by Anglicans, Roman Catholics, and Free Churchmen in Britain. What is so fascinating about this Movement is that it has enabled Protestant Churches to recover in part the Catholic liturgical heritage, while the Catholics seem to have appropriated the Protestant valuation of preaching, of shared worship in the vernacular tongue, and the importance of the laity as the people of God. It is an appropriate index of the decreasing insularity of English theological interest.

Chapters II and III are studies in religious aesthetics. The second chapter documents "The Rebirth of Religious Architecture and Art" from neo-Gothic to functional liturgical architecture (exemplified, in part, in Scott's Anglican Cathedral and Gibberd's projected Roman Catholic Cathedral in Liverpool), and assays the contribution of Jacob Epstein, Henry Moore, Graham Sutherland, and others, to religious art. Chapter III records "The Development of Church Music" from Vaughan Williams to Benjamin Britten, and considers anthems, hymns, chants, and psalmody, in the classical and modern manners.

Chapters IV and V describe the changing fashions in English theology, using 1933 as the watershed year. The movement from a revelational to a redemptional and finally to a radical secular-oriented theology is charted. In Chapter IV—"The Early Development of Theology"—particular attention is paid to the theologians of the "social Gospel" (R. J. Campbell), of mysticism (Inge, von Hügel, Underhill), of Incarnationalism (Gore and Temple), and of the *Holy* Fatherhood of God (Forsyth and Oman). In Chapter V attention is given to the influence of Karl Barth, to the schools of "Realized Eschatology" (Hoskyns and Dodd), and of neo-Orthodoxy, and finally to the Cambridge Radicals. The impact that each theological change had on the role of worship in the Church is then analysed.

The first part concludes with Chapter VI, "Trends and Types of Preaching." This mirrors the theological changes in four major types of preaching: apologetical, charismatic, exegetical, and liturgical, as seen in the leading preachers—Anglican, Roman Catholic, and Free Church. Among the vivid figures encountered in this chapter are Monsignor Ronald Knox, Bishop H. Hensley Henson, Drs. Leslie Weatherhead, and W. E. Sangster, not forgetting "Woodbine Willie" and "Dick" Sheppard. They, and especially the two latter, complement the objectivity of worship with the passionate subjectivity of preaching. Other preachers are objective

7

exponents of the Scriptures or of Christian revelation reflected in the Liturgy.

The second part of the book consists of seven chapters, detailing the progress of theory and practice in worship in five traditions. Chapter VII, on "Roman Catholic Worship," tries to show why the Liturgical Movement has made tardy progress in this Communion in England, but also records the liturgical scholarship and spirituality of the English Benedictines, the importance of popular instruction given by some of the English Jesuits, and the liturgical promise of the Second Vatican Council. Chapter VIII, on "Anglican Worship to 1928," attempts to account for the rejection of the 1928 Revised Prayer Book by Parliament. Chapter IX on "Anglican Worship after 1928," tries to assess the consequences, including a closing of party-ranks within the Church, a deeper and more united understanding of the nature of the Eucharist, and a recent remarkable efflorescence of liturgical experiments. Chapter X, on "The Worship of the Free Churches," shows the major revaluations of their traditions of worship undertaken by the English Baptists, Congregationalists, Methodists, and Presbyterians, and questions whether the decline of free prayer is to be considered entirely a gain in worship. Chapter XI, on "Quaker Worship," takes account of modern Quaker defences of corporate silent prayer and considers the contribution this might make as an important ingredient of liturgical worship. Chapter XII, on "Unitarian Worship," notes the liturgical fertility of this denomination, and claims that its radical honesty of thought, its ethical integrity, and its deep understanding of the doctrine of Creation are greatly needed by the more orthodox Churches. Both Chapters XI and XII raise the question whether Quakerism and Unitarianism will pull up the Christological anchor and move out into the wider sea of interreligious theism, or re-establish their basis on historical Christian foundations and come more fully into the Churchly orbit.

The book ends with Chapter XIII, a "Concluding Critique," the purpose of which is to assess the gains in worship achieved during this century and to point to the remaining critical issues which have to be faced.

As I come to the end of this introduction I wonder whether in the pages that follow I have sufficiently stressed that Christianity was, on any statistical analysis, weakening its hold on the life of the nation to the point of feebleness. This century has been for the Church, as for all the British people, a desperate time—a period of crises, of wars, of scepticism, of secularism, and of stupendous scientific advance in technology in inverse proportion to the drastic decline in Church attendance and worship. Twice the lights have gone out in Europe and left a spiritual black-out which did not vanish when the electric lights were switched on again. In nihilistic days when the winds of change swept like hurricanes through the land, the torches of Christians were fewer, less luminous, and more flickering. But if Christ's companies were smaller, they were also more committed and far more united than in the past. The same winds of change have helped to winnow the chaff from the grains of wheat: there is little pride or prestige in Church membership for the natural man in contemporary England. For a remnant, man's extremity has proved to be God's opportunity, and the challenges of society were found to be answerable only in grace. In the call to contemporary faith, the appeals to respectability, to a merely aesthetic experience, to a nominal or half-hearted attachment, are mercifully minimal. So worship is less an escape than an encounter with the living God and a demand to witness in daily life and social service that *hurts*—that is compassion, a sharing in Christ's passion, and a *scandal*.

Even if sensitive English Christians share the sense of being witnesses to a twilight with no earthly promise of dawn, a realistic theology tells them that Western Christianity has failed because it failed to evangelize or only half evangelized. God needed men and men exploited God. For myself, I share this diagnosis of François Mauriac's and with him would affirm: "Whatever happens, even in a world three-quarters blotted out by a weapon of destruction, there will always be in the back part of some cellar a small group crowding around a table and a man anointed who breaks and distributes the Living Bread."[8] As in the earliest days of the Church, its present day worshippers are "perplexed, yet not unto despair."

8 *What I Believe* (trans. with an introduction by Wallace Fowlie, New York, 1963), pp. 80-81.

9

PART I: THE WIDE-ANGLE VIEW

CHAPTER I

THE CONTINENTAL LITURGICAL
MOVEMENT AND ITS INFLUENCE

ENGLISH INSULARITY is often mocked by retelling the fable
that a London newspaper once printed the headline: "Fog in
the English Channel: Continent Isolated." If England ever
was so insular, culturally or spiritually, it is no longer so today.

The English Churches, especially since 1914, have increasingly
reflected the four inter-related concerns of European and American
Christianity. They have played a notable part in the Ecumenical
Movement[1] for the reunion of a divided Christendom. They have
shared in the recovery of a Biblical and Patristic theology of depth
and relevance.[2] They have, with less theoretical success, been
trying to develop a more sophisticated Christian social ethic in the
modern technocratic context. Finally, and this is the particular
concern of this chapter, they have been greatly influenced by the
Continental Liturgical Movement and have made some considerable contributions to the newer understanding of worship as the
renewal of the people of God.

1. *The Importance of the Liturgical Movement*

A provisional definition of a tentative character will provide a
skeleton on which the flesh and muscle of the Liturgical Movement
(its history, principles, and practices) can later be laid. The
Liturgical Movement may be defined as an interconfessional renewal of Christian worship and life which sees in the self-offering
of the Eternal Son of God on the Cross a Sacrifice which is both
the descent of Divinity and the ascent of the Perfect Humanity, and
therefore as the type and pattern of Christian worship in the
Eucharist, the nexus of Christian unity, the inspiration of all
human talents and labour, and the supreme means of grace. In the
narrower sense "Liturgy" refers to the Eucharistic rite (as both
Revelation and response in which the Sacrament of the Word is

---

[1] N.B. In this chapter the contributions of a multitude of scholars are mentioned,
sometimes without listing all the relevant titles. In most cases the latter can be
found in the Bibliography.

The fullest and most authoritative study of the subject is Ruth Rouse and
S. C. Neill, eds., *A History of the Ecumenical Movement, 1517-1948.*

[2] For a study of the parallel course of the Liturgical and Biblical Movements,
see K. Federer, *Liturgie und Glaube; eine theologie-geschichtliche Untersuchung.*

linked with the Sacrament of the Holy Communion), and the restoration of the Eucharist to its central place in truly corporate worship has been the primary concern of the Liturgical Movement. In the wider sense "Liturgy" has been used to refer to the whole round of the official public worship of the Christian Church, in the Daily Office, and in authorized forms. In this wider sense, moreover, the Movement has been concerned with such major issues as the theological basis of worship, its sincerity and relevance to modern life.

It must be insisted that the Liturgical Movement has been encouraged by the researches of learned liturgiologists as well as by the severely practical concerns of parish priests and ministers. It is not only an organization within the single largest Communion of Christendom (the Roman Catholic Church), but also an inter-denominational reformation of Catholic and Protestant import. It may quite properly be regarded as a movement of the Holy Spirit, since its effect has been to increase the holiness, charity, social witness, and ecumenicity of Christians in a tragically divided world. Its outstanding mark is increasing vitality. Its impact was first felt in a significant manner in Europe in 1840 and its influence on Britain and North America has been considerable, especially in recent decades. If Protestants have led in the theological revival of our times, then Catholics have clearly pioneered in the Liturgical Movement. More important, however, is the fact that the vitality of each movement has had a marked influence on its hitherto opposing ecclesiastical tradition.

A preliminary pointer to the significance of the Continental Liturgical Movement is the assessal of its importance made by non-Roman Catholic scholars in recent years. Between the First and Second World Wars there was the pioneering appreciation of the Movement in the work of the Swedish Lutheran (later Archbishop) Yngve Brilioth in his *Eucharistic Faith and Practice, Evangelical and Catholic* and of the Anglican priest, A. G. Hebert, in *Liturgy and Society*. More recently, however, there have been a series of important studies of the Continental Liturgical Movement, each of which manifests an amazing empathy from the Protestant side. Jean-Daniel Bénôit, of the University of Strasbourg, a French Reformed theologian, has published *Liturgical Renewal: Catholic and Protestant Developments on the Continent* (1958), which was originally given as a series of lectures to Anglican clergymen in the diocese of London. This is an important indication of the interaction of Catholic and Protestant theory and practice in worship. The Anglican liturgiologist and former Dean of Lincoln Cathedral, J. H. Srawley, has produced a suggestive account of the principles of the most recent phase of the Liturgical Movement in *The Liturgical Movement* (Alcuin Club, 1954). Two American clergy, both Episcopalians, Massey H. Shepherd, Jr.[3] in *The Living Liturgy* and in the volume he has edited, entitled *The Liturgical Renewal of the Church*, and Alfred R. Shands in *The Liturgical Movement and the Local Church* (1959), show how deeply sensitive and appreciative is right-wing Protestantism to the new developments of worship on the continent of Europe. Furthermore, an American Lutheran scholar, Ernest B. Koenker, has produced the fullest theological appraisal of *The Liturgical Renaissance in the Roman Catholic Church* from the Protestant side.

An even more impressive testimony to the impact of the Continental Liturgical Movement is to be found in the growing recognition on the part of Protestant Communions (in some cases this is a *recovery* of an earlier tradition) that Holy Communion or the Lord's Supper is the central and climactic act of the corporate worship of the Christian community. This is to be found in certain movements within the Protestant Churches of Britain and America. Many of these movements, though not all, have an official character. These are: the "Parish and People" Movement within the Church of England and the "Associated Parishes" of the American Episcopal Church; the "Church Service Society" and the Iona Community Movement within (and also beyond) the Church of Scotland; the "Methodist Sacramental Fellowship" in England and the newly founded "Wesley Society" in the United States; and the "Church Order Group" among the ministry of the Congregational churches in England and Wales. Moreover, the denominations to which these movements belong have been engaged in important liturgical experiments, some of which have been incorporated in their official books of worship. Lutherans and Episcopalians, of course, already have an honoured Liturgy. That such interconfessional liturgical borrowing and lending which has crossed the Catholic, Orthodox, and Protestant lines is a significant fact of our times can be seen from the most cursory survey of the pages of acknowledgments which preface the texts of most modern liturgies, denominational handbooks or manuals of worship, and devotional compilations.

[3] Professor Massey H. Shepherd, Jr. has also written a notable ecumenical liturgical volume, *The Reform of Liturgical Worship: Perspectives and Prospects.*

Besides, a rain-shower of liturgical pamphlets in ecclesiastical journals, and a hail-storm of books, pelting from the presses, ought by now to have drenched the literate minister and thoughtful laymen in the new liturgical climate of our times. Though many are high, few are dry. Possibly only the most Tridentine of Roman Catholics and the most dissident of Protestant Nonconformists remain dry in this deluge, merely because they are stranded on the arid sands of a sixteenth century controversy.

If it be erroneous to refuse to acknowledge the impact of the Liturgical Movement, it is equally so to claim too much for it, as two considerations will bear out. In the first place, far from the influence having been all one way, and the Roman Catholics the donors and the Protestants merely recipients, there has been reciprocal giving and accepting. At first glance the claim that classical Reformed worship has influenced the liturgical thought and practice of the Roman Catholic Church would seem improbable to the point of absurdity; it seems less so when some of the more revolutionary principles of the Continental Liturgical Movement are considered. Many of these principles were once the convictions and are now the commonplaces of Reformed celebrations of the Holy Communion or Lord's Supper. Such principles are: the insistence upon a rite translated from the Latin into the vernacular for the edification of the common people; an insistence upon participation rather than passivity on the part of the communicants, with its correlate of corporate Communion rather than any private Eucharistic devotions (such as the "Forty Hours" or "Benediction"); the manducation of *both* the consecrated Bread and Wine, rather than Communion in *one* kind; liturgical preaching, for which a parallel can be found in the "Communion Discourses" in the Reformed tradition; and the so-called Western or Basilican posture for celebration, in which the priest or minister faces the people across the Holy Table (possible only when the Altar is brought forward from the usual position immediately beneath the East wall and window). All of these principles and practices, for which a pre-Reformation precedent can be found, even if arbitrarily and unconvincingly, are more easily and naturally found as legitimate Reformed protests against abuses of the Sacrament as celebrated in the later mediaeval Western Church, and they have been customary in most Reformed Churches during the past four centuries. Thus it is not necessary to claim Roman Catholic influence for practices which have been characteristically those of classical Protestantism in its worship.

Furthermore, it has been characteristic of English and American life (and not less of English and American theology) to adapt, modify, and mould its borrowings to suit its own needs. While the insularity and moderation of English theology[4] is not as prominent in the twentieth as it has been in the three prior centuries, it is itself a factor which would urge the pragmatic English to be suspicious of Continental importations until they have been thoroughly tested and Anglicized. On the positive side, England can claim that she made her own contributions of singular importance to the renewal of worship. If France urges the claim that the origins of the Liturgical Movement are to be found in a Romantic protest against Rationalism made vivid in the mediaevalism of the novels of Victor Hugo and J. K. Huysmans, or if Germany urges the priority of Schlegel, then Britain demands the palm for Sir Walter Scott's "Waverley" series of novels, or, if the debate is desperate, for the architectural mediaevalism of William Beckford and Horace Walpole. In these "Gothic Games" (if the international competition to discover the earliest pioneers of neo-mediaevalism may be so termed) France can claim that Rohant de Fleury, with his study of the Mass in art, Didron's iconographic monographs, and Viollet-le-Duc's architectural researches and restorations, were at least as significant as the mediaeval restorationism of Pugin, Barry, G. G. Scott, Street, and Butterfield[5] in Victorian England, even though an English nationalist might find it convenient to cite the German Reichensperger's tribute to Pugin that "he was the hero in the fight for Christian art."[6] Though the Oxford Movement was not without Continental influences, it would be an injustice not to regard it as predominantly an indigenous and successful English attempt to renew liturgical and sacramental worship. Thus the ambiguities of origins and the multiplicity of cultural influences, as well as the pragmatic character of English religion, are restraints on exaggerated claims for the impact of the Continental Liturgical Movement on English ways of worship. It must, however, also be insisted upon that English theology became increasingly dependent upon European theology in the twentieth century and that the

[4] See C. C. J. Webb, *A Century of Anglican Theology*, pp. 20-25.
[5] See B. F. L. Clarke, *Church Buildings of the Nineteenth Century.*
[6] Olivier Rousseau, *L'Histoire du Mouvement Liturgique*, p. 132.

impact of the second phase of the Continental Liturgical Movement has been considerable.

What has been said of English theology is also largely true of American theology and worship, which has been profoundly influenced by the free and spontaneous techniques of evangelism in the "Great Awakenings" and on the western-moving frontier, making the very concepts of Liturgy and Church traditions matters of suspicion. Here, too, pragmatism prevails. The "Continental" or European character of the Liturgical Movement will be considered as reference is made to its most important contributions, which came from France in the nineteenth and from Belgium, Italy, the Rhineland, and Austria in the twentieth century.

2. *The First Phase: Solesmes*

Since worship, which he termed the *opus Dei*,[7] was for St. Benedict of Nursia the primary privilege and duty of monks (although both contemplation and manual labour played their important but subordinate parts), it is not surprising that the restoration of the Benedictine order in France was accompanied by an intense renewal of liturgical life. The pre-eminent pioneer in the Liturgical Movement in France was Dom Prosper Guéranger (1805-1875), an ardent disciple of Lamennais. The latter had wished to bring France back to the political and social order of the days of Pope Gregory VII by means of the revival of the Roman Catholic Church. However roseate Lamennais' view of the eleventh century was (and this is a common characteristic of mediaeval religious restorationists), it is understandable. After the political unsettlements of popular revolutions succeeded by dictatorships in nineteenth century France, it was inevitable that an idealized image of the conjoint rule of the Orb and the Cross (of godly emperor and holy pontiff) in the eleventh century, in which Chartres—the sublimest symbol of French Catholic faith—was erected, should glisten enticingly in the minds of devout Frenchmen. It was a case, not of *reculer pour mieux sauter* (for to advance beyond Chartres was unthinkable), but only *reculer pour sauter*. For Guéranger, as for St. Francis of Assisi, the command was to rebuild God's house in ruins.[8] Guéranger's ruins demanding restoration were those of the ancient Abbey of Solesmes, left desolate by the image-

---

[7] There are two instances in the *Regula* of Saint Benedict where this term is employed, once notably in *Caput* LXIII, where it is stated: *Ergo nihil operi Dei praeponat* ("Nothing is to take precedence of the worship of God").

[8] G. Cozien, *L'oeuvre de Dom Guéranger*, p. 43.

breakers of the French Revolution. If Lamennais desired a revival of the mediaeval politico-social order, Guéranger longed for the restoration of the Church life of the Middle Ages. His own vocation, he was convinced, was to return to the Church those now desolate sanctuaries of prayer which had nourished saints. The restored abbey of Solesmes would be the type and forerunner of such ecclesiastical renewal.

Solesmes, widely known for its restoration of Gregorian chanting, was the first power-house and dynamo of liturgical renewal, and its Daily Office and its celebration of the Festivals were widely admired and frequently imitated. While relatively few were able to make their pilgrimage to Solesmes and share in its worship, two publications of the greatest influence carried the principles and the scholarship of the abbey to the remotest corners of Catholic Christendom. These were the *Institutions liturgiques* of 1840 and *L'Année liturgique*, issued from 1841 onward. Within sixty years of issuing the first imprint over half a million copies of the *Année liturgique* had been sold and it had been translated into the major European languages. Though Guéranger was the director of this scholarly work, much of the credit for the Greek and Patristic erudition must go to Dom Pitra, one of his monks, who edited classical works on the Greek Liturgy and hymnology and was created a Cardinal in 1863.

The entire aim of Guéranger was the rejuvenation of liturgical piety in an age that was increasingly secular, rationalistic, and individualistic. He believed that the restoration of the Benedictine rule and worship would build up Christian faith to combat secularism, that Christian mysticism was the antidote to rationalism, and that the disciplined community life in the Church would defeat undisciplined individualism. For him the Church was most truly herself in worship, an offering of adoration to God linked with the perfect Offering of the God-man and High Priest, Jesus Christ, with and for humanity. The Divine Liturgy, being the Spirit-prompted response of the Church at worship, was regarded as the essential means of human sanctification and therefore of humanity's renovation and redemption. The conception is romantically conveyed in the preface to his *L'Année liturgique*:

"It is in Holy Church that the Divine Spirit dwells. He came down to her as an impetuous wind, and manifested Himself to her under the expressive symbols of tongues of fire. Ever since that day of Pentecost, He has dwelt in this His favoured Bride. He is the principle of everything that is in her. He it is that prompts her prayers, her desires, her canticles of praise, her enthusiasm and even her mourning. Hence her prayer is as uninterrupted as her existence. Day and night her voice sounds sweetly in the ear of her divine Spouse, and her words are ever finding a welcome in His heart."[9]

Guéranger believed that the temporal cycle of the Liturgy was a providentially inspired means of accommodating in time the eternal mysteries of the Creation of man, his re-creation and restoration through the Incarnation, and his sanctification in the Church by the Holy Spirit. The sanctoral cycle he interpreted as the proof of the Divine renewal, from the first century of the Christian dispensation to his own. Rome was for him the mother of saints and the traditional Roman rite was the path to perfection. Utterly faithful to the Roman *magisterium*, he approved all devotions officially sanctioned by the Roman Church, whether it were the cult of the Blessed Sacrament or of the Sacred Heart.

Although he was deeply concerned to instruct the laity in the meaning of the Liturgy, and, indeed, had translated several parts of it into French (always excepting the Canon of the Mass), he never deviated from the conviction that the Mass must be said in Latin, the "sacred tongue." As a keen Ultramontanist (and therefore the sworn enemy of any attempt to retain or introduce any national variants or "Uses" in the Liturgy), he might be expected to prefer the use of the Latin language, but it was due in part to his excessive antiquarianism and in part also to his view that a partially understood language would preserve the essential element of mystery in Christian worship. (He seemed unaware that such a thesis makes mystery and ignorance equivalents, whereas mystery and transcendence are more properly correlated.)

His profound spirituality (which made him so admirable an expositor of the Liturgy) was nourished upon a love of the Scriptures, themselves illuminated by Patristic examples of exegesis, and upon a high respect for the continuity of tradition. Father Louis Bouyer, critical as he is of the sentimentalism and archaeologism of Guéranger's restoration of the Liturgy, yet acknowledges that his reforms made the monastic worship at Solesmes "one of the most impressive types to be found in modern times."[10] Such devotion and erudition in general, and in particular, the restoration

[9] Vol. I, pp. 1-2, trans. and cited by Dom Olivier Rousseau, *op.cit.* Chap. 1.
[10] *Life and Liturgy* (republished as paperback, 1962), p. 11.

of the Gregorian mode of chanting, austere and yet haunting; a scrupulous observance of all rubrics and ceremonies of the Roman rite; and above all, a sober, uncluttered, untheatrical celebration of the Liturgy, were his abiding contributions to the renaissance of Catholic worship.

Guéranger's importance can also be gauged in his stimulus to others to maintain and to improve upon his own work. His own religious order, the Benedictines, made excellent use of his initiative and example by the prosecution of liturgiology in France, England, Belgium, and in the Rhineland. The first prior of Farnborough, England (itself a daughter house of Solesmes), was Dom Fernand Cabrol, who in the very year of the foundation of the house had published a study of the liturgy of Jerusalem in the fourth century based upon his edition of the *Peregrinatio Silviae* (1895). In 1903 he began to publish the monumental *Dictionnaire d'Archéologie chrétienne et de Liturgie*, with the help of the learned Dom Henri Leclercq. Two other distinguished Frenchmen also promoted the scientific study of liturgies. One was Louis Duchesne, the author of a work translated as *Christian Worship: its Origin and Evolution*, which went into several editions, and the other was Pierre Batiffol, author of the *Histoire du Bréviaire Romain* (1893) and of the popular *Leçons sur la Messe*. In Southern Germany the first centre of revived Benedictinism was the congregation of Beuron, founded in 1863. Its founders had stayed with Guéranger in Solesmes and were greatly attracted by his liturgical ideals, as was evident in the writings of Dom Maurus Wolter.[11] The Belgian Solesmes was the Abbey of Maredsous, a great liturgical centre of Benedictinism which has attained even greater fame in our own day as the promoter of Mont-César near Louvain, a daughter house which had its own profound modification of the Guéranger tradition to offer under Dom Morin and Dom Lambert Beauduin. The second great twentieth century Benedictine liturgical centre is Maria Laach in the Rhineland, renowned for the work of Abbot Herwegen and Dom Odo Casel, which complemented and corrected the work of Guéranger, and was itself complemented by the practical concerns of Abbot Pius Parsch of Klosterneuberg in Austria. A most distinguished English contribution to liturgics was made by the Benedictine lay brother, associated with Downside, Edmund

[11] See his *Gertrudenbuch*, St. Gertrude's sixteenth century *exercitia spiritualia* patterned on the liturgical cycle, a massive commentary on the psalms, and the *Praecipua Ordinis Monastici Monumenta* which devotes a chapter to the value of the Divine Office.

Bishop. All these, however much they might and did differ from Prosper Guéranger, were sons that could rise up and call him blessed.

Admirable, even epochal, as was Guéranger's work, it was not flawless. The flies in this liturgical amber were romanticism and Ultramontanism. The sober worship of Solesmes was, indeed, a relief after the theatrical posturings and the dramatic *mise-en-scène* of the Baroque period, but Baroque was a genuine expression of the spirit of its age whereas Solesmes was an artificial and antiquarian reconstruction of a long buried past, if indeed that past had ever existed in such an idealized form. The mediaevalism it sought to revive was a fancied mediaevalism, as irrelevant as the manufacture of a modern gargoyle in concrete, even if much lovelier. In brief, this was only a splendid fossil, not the contemporary expression of a living tradition of Divine worship. Moreover, it was essentially monastic worship, the "shadowy image of Cluny."[12] It had no direct relevance to the worship of the masses in city or rural congregations in the nineteenth century; it was an idyllic, aesthetic, and disciplined escape for monks.

It was romantic, not only in its roseate reconstruction and apparent irrelevance, but also in its sentimentality. The real focus of the Eucharist for Dom Guéranger was the "miracle" of the Divine Presence of Christ, not the sacrificial Action. To put the point directly: Guéranger was impressed by the descent of Christ in a moment of time in the Mass, rather than by the Church's ascent with Christ and inclusion in His perfect and eternal Offering which consummates the whole drama of redemption for the people of God. It was an irruptionist and individualistic conception of the action of God in the Sacrament of Holy Communion, and could naturally accommodate such modern cults as that of the Sacred Heart and the Exposition of the Blessed Sacrament, which suffer from the same excessively subjective emphasis.[13] Different considerations may help to establish the justice of this criticism: notably, the radical revision of the Eastern liturgies demanded by Guéranger in *Les Institutions liturgiques* in order to make them conform to the Roman rite of 1570; the disproportionate emphasis given by his successors to the Feast of Corpus Christi in *L'Année liturgique* (an entire volume is devoted to the theme), and the fact that the

---

[12] Bouyer, *Life and Liturgy*, p. 12.
[13] See E. Dumoutet, *Le désir de voir l'Hostie*, for a penetrating criticism of sentimental subjectivism in mediaeval worship.

most genuinely communal worship at Solesmes, celebrated with the most impressive ceremonial, was Benediction rather than the Community Mass.

Guéranger's Ultramontanism (also a legacy from Lamennais) accounted for the liturgical inflexibility that made him consider the 1570 Missal of Pope Pius V as inalterably sacrosanct, assuming it to be the final development of Western worship. He was, therefore, prevented from considering that earlier forms of the Roman liturgy might have been worthier of preservation. Moreover, he was almost as blind to the intrinsic glories of the Eastern rites as he was to the importance of ancient French usages, as distinguished from the neo-Gallican liturgies of the seventeenth and eighteenth centuries on which he poured the vials of his scorn.

The very deficiencies of a Guéranger, however, were to be corrected by his own order, especially in the work of Dom Lambert Beauduin of Mont-César and of Abbot Ildefons Herwegen and Dom Odo Casel of Maria Laach. The Belgian Benedictine saw that the right locus for the liturgical revival was a properly instructed parish congregation; the German Benedictines were the constructive critics of the idiosyncratic and romantic tendencies of revived mediaevalism, and they had their own positive *mysterientheologie* to expound. Both Mont-César and Maria Laach were daughters of the Solesmian revival.

3. *The Second Phase: Mont-César and Maria Laach*

It is during the second phase, that is in the twentieth century, that the Liturgical Movement has made its most impressive contributions, and its influence is far from being spent. The greatest impetus the Movement received was the strong support of Pope Pius X, who became the official propagator of the liturgical apostolate.

The beginning of the second phase of the Continental Liturgical Movement is usually dated from a speech made in 1910 at Malines by Dom Lambert Beauduin. In this he urged that the Liturgy should be understood as the action of the Church as a whole, bringing the whole individual man in the whole community to God. The idea of lay participation in the Eucharist was, however, put forward by another Belgian Benedictine, Dom Gerhard Van Caloen, as early as 1883 at the Eucharistic Congress of Liége; he had given proof of his conviction by the publication in 1882 of a small missal in Latin and French, the *Missel des Fidèles*. It was

23

the Abbey of Mont-César, however, founded in 1897, which became the chief centre of liturgical renewal in Belgium and Beauduin was its leading luminary.

Lambert Beauduin was professed as a Benedictine monk in 1906, after eight important years of experience as a parish priest devoted chiefly to social work. Here was a man who knew the supreme importance of worship, but also the extraordinary difficulty of maintaining the life of devotion in the crowded tenements of the industrial cities of present-day Europe, and with the apparent lack of any nexus between worship and daily work. Realizing that the Liturgy in the Church is the central and integrating act of all parish life, he became convinced of the paramount need for parish priests to instruct their flocks in the meaning of the supernatural life as mediated by the rites and Sacraments of the Church. Thus a parish worship in which an instructed laity shared in the prayers as well as in the praises of the Mass would mean spiritual renewal.

Partly as a result of Beauduin's passionate and intelligent advocacy of these convictions, the Catholic Congress at Malines (1909) resolved on a programme of liturgical reform, which was fully approved by Cardinal Mercier. There was complete agreement, in the first place, on the need to emphasize the use of the Roman missal as a book of popular piety (instead of the usual private devotional manuals), and therefore on the need for a wide dissemination of the complete text of at least Sunday Mass and Vespers in a vernacular translation. It was also proposed to give a definitely liturgical character to popular piety. This aim was to be accomplished by encouraging the laity to recite Compline as evening prayer, to attend parish High Mass and Vespers, to use the prayers of the Missal as both a preparation for and a thanksgiving after receiving Communion, and to restore the ancient liturgical traditions in their homes. It was also agreed to work for a wider and more worthy use of the Gregorian chant, according to the wish of Pope Pius X. Finally, it was agreed to provide annual retreats for parish choirs at a liturgical centre, and thus again fulfil the wish of the Pope, who had founded a *schola cantorum* in Salzano, where he had been parish priest, and who had declared in the frequently cited sentence in *Motu Proprio* (1903): "We must not sing or pray during Mass, but we must sing and pray the Mass."[14]

14 *Motu Proprio* insisted that the public worship of the Church is the principal

In order to give effect to these reforms Dom Beauduin published *La Vie liturgique,* of which 50,000 copies were sold during its first year of publication (1909). After two years his series of pamphlets had developed into the review, *Questions liturgiques,* which was intended exclusively for the clergy.[15] At frequent gatherings of parish priests in retreat at Mont-César Abbey, the ardent monk and former secular priest instructed them in the meaning of liturgical spirituality. Thus the treasures of Solesmes, instead of being hoarded in monasteries, were prodigally scattered to become the common possession of the parochial clergy, and through them of the laity.

Beauduin's teaching was admirably condensed in *La Piété de l'Eglise, principes et faits* (1914), which demonstrated the theological basis of true piety, based upon the Divine action in the life of the faithful. Writing from within the context of a bitter-sweet remembrance of a parish ministry in which he found labouring men and women to be mere driftwood caught by the impersonal industrial maelstrom, "hands" to be used if skilled, and discarded if ailing, old, or redundant, Beauduin insisted that the liturgical revival would enable men and women to know the dignity of human nature. This reality was made known in the Incarnation, which had made possible the lifting up of our callous, sinful, and lonely humanity to God, and the Liturgy was the recalling and renewal of the Incarnation's effects upon the faithful by the power of the re-creating and sanctifying Holy Spirit. Recalling the acrimonious class feuds of his parish, the disdainful patronage of employers, the sullenness or servility of employees, and the desperate need for a charity that would work for social justice and go beyond it, Dom Beauduin maintained that the Liturgical Revival would foster brotherhood by a profound understanding of the Church as the Body of Christ, in which He lives and works, organically uniting the members to Himself and to each other. Furthermore, Dom Lambert insisted that the Eucharistic Sacrifice evoked the spirit of renunciation in the faithful, for here again the Incarnate Christ

---

means of sanctifying the people of God, that worship should be purged of profane music, and that Gregorian chanting should be encouraged. In the Bull *Divino Afflatu* (1911), Pius X insisted on the reform of the Church Calendar, the Psalter, and the Breviary.

15 See Lambert Beauduin, *Mélanges liturgiques recueillis parmi les oeuvres de Dom L. Beauduin, O.S.B.,* which contains his most important articles.

and High Priest makes the perfect Offering of His life to the Father and the "Offertory" requires the participants to offer themselves with Christ for the world. The rich appositeness of Beauduin's teaching was a genuine integration of the liturgy as adoration in the Church and witness in the world.

The stronger theological and historic undergirding of the Liturgical Movement was to come from the German Benedictines of Beuron and especially of Maria Laach. As the historical studies of Guéranger had been applied to the practical needs of parish congregations by Beauduin, so the liturgical researches of Maria Laach were applied to the parishes by Abbot Pius Parsch and the Augustinian canons of Klosterneuberg.[16]

The leadership of Maria Laach in the second phase of the Liturgical Movement coincided almost exactly with the abbacy of Dr. Ildefons Herwegen (1913-1946). The exact beginning of Maria Laach's influence may perhaps be traced to Holy Week in 1914, when a group of Catholic university teachers, doctors, and lawyers asked the Abbot of Maria Laach to advise them on how to encourage the faithful in more active participation in the Mass. It was the research undertaken and promoted by Herwegen and his most able henchman, Dom Odo Casel, which taught the clergy and the more cultured laity the revolutionary implications of the Liturgy for life. This corporate scholarly enterprise included the commencement of the series "Ecclesia Orans" in 1918, with the appearance of Guardini's *Vom Geist der Liturgie*;[17] in the same year the monks of Maria Laach and of other Benedictine foundations in the Rhineland edited and issued *Liturgiegeschichtliche Quellen und Forschungen*, and three years later in 1921 there began to appear the important annual, *Jahrbuch fur Liturgiewissenschaft*. The third of these monuments of scholarship, and the most penetrating, is a memorial to Dom Odo Casel, the outstanding theologian of the entire Movement. In 1931 Herwegen established the important Institute of Liturgical and Monastic Studies at Maria Laach.

It is profoundly significant that this spiritual and intellectual renewal of worship was promoted during a time when Europe was prodigally expending the blood of its manhood in the mud and barbed-wire entrenchments of Flanders, where there were

---

[16] See Pierre Mesnard, *Le Mouvement liturgique de Klosterneuberg.*
[17] Translated into English by A. Lane and published together with an additional work under the title *The Spirit and the Liturgy.*

No passing bells for those who die as cattle
Only the monstrous anger of the guns
Shall patter out their hasty orisons.[18]

Our own century was and is peculiarly in need of the integration
and wholeness that divided man can recover in the Liturgy by
understanding his destiny in the purpose of God, as a part of the
people of God, fortified by the grace of God. Maria Laach's task
was to demonstrate the "Christification" of man in community.

Many aspects of the Liturgical Movement are illustrated in the
researches of Maria Laach and its associated Benedictine monasteries. These include the return to the Biblical and Christ-centred
tradition of the Early Church; the recognition of the importance of
the vivifying Word proclaimed in the lections and sermons of the
Synaxis as well as in the *Verbum visibile* of the Eucharist; the need
for an objective and corporate, as contrasted with a subjective and
individualistic, liturgical piety; an emphasis on the *communal* offering of the Eucharistic Sacrifice, as well as a complementary stress
on the Holy Communion as a commemorative repast; and also the
strongly social implications of the Liturgy for the overcoming of
class divisions and its potential consecration of Christian art. Maria
Laach's chief contribution to the understanding of the Liturgy,
however, has been the systematic exposition of it as the efficaciously
sanctifying representation of the Christian Mystery of salvation.
This is the so-called *mysterientheologie*.[19]

Its chief exponent, Dom Odo Casel, distinguishes three correlated aspects of the *mysterium*.[20] First of all, the supreme Mystery
is God in His own Being, the utterly Holy and Unapproachable
One. Secondly, the revelation of God in Christ is the personal
Mystery of God the invisible revealed in the flesh, and in His
humiliation, Incarnation, Sacrificial death upon the Cross, as in
His Resurrection and Ascension, God marvellously reveals Himself in a way that far surpasses all human capacities. The third
mystery is that of the cult, which is defined as a liturgical action
"in which the redemptive act is rendered present in the rite,"[21] and

[18] Wilfred Owen's *Anthem for Doomed Youth*, recently popularized by Benjamin Britten's *War Requiem*.
[19] See the over-high evaluation of Casel's work in Alphonse Heitz's article in
La Maison-Dieu, VII (1946), where (p. 51) he describes as mere "tid-bits"
(*amorces*) the contributions of the predecessors of the Maria Laach School.
[20] See *Das Christliche Kultmysterium* (3rd edn., Regensburg, 1948).
[21] *Repraesentatio* or *gegenwartigsetzung* are the words used.

"since the cultic community accomplishes the rite, it shares the saving rite and through it attains redemption."[22]

It must, however, be emphasized that for Casel not only the Passion of Christ but the entire work of redemption is made present again in the Liturgy, from His advent to His second advent. Moreover, this is declared and believed to be not a psychological or subjective reality but an ontological and objective reality, which, though veiled in symbol or image, actually shares in the reality of God's redemptive action of grace for His people.

Related to "mystery" is the term "transfiguration," and these are seminal terms for the Eastern Church as for Maria Laach. The purpose of the Liturgy, as of the Christian religion, is to sanctify, even to deify mankind, bringing transfigured Christians to the Christ of the Transfiguration. Through the bestowal of grace in the Liturgy, man is raised to the supernatural order and therefore into sharing the Divine existence, light, and glory. Not for Maria Laach any individual meditations on the crucified Christ or devotions to the Christ "imprisoned" in the Tabernacle, but a proleptic sharing of the life of the glorified Christ. The focal centre is the Christ in Glory, but with the constant remembrance that this Christ went "from God to God" by the route of the humiliation and the *via dolorosa*.

It will be no surprise, therefore, recognizing the Eastern Patristic provenance of the central theological concepts of Maria Laach's expositors, that the art of Beuron and Maria Laach is Byzantine, not Baroque in character. It is a simplified stylized art in which the symbols point to the universal divine reality that intersects time, rather than the dramatic, tortuous, psychologism (and even naturalism) that characterizes Baroque. The art of the German Benedictines is closer to the Christ in Glory of the tympanum of Vézelay than to the El Greco Christ in the agony of the Garden of Gethsemane. This, indeed, might have been expected from Abbot Herwegen's sharp disjunction in *Kirche und Seele* (Munster, 1928) between the sentimental, subjective, and individualistic piety[23] of the later mediaeval and post-Tridentine Mass and the objective and corporate liturgical piety of the Fathers. In the same book he had also argued that mediaeval romanticism (which, by

---

[22] *Das Christliche Kultmysterium*, p. 121.

[23] Gallican worship found such floridity attractive (see Gregory Dix, *The Shape of the Liturgy*) and the neo-Platonism of the Pseudo-Dionysius reached its most bizarre and idiosyncratic heights in symbolical interpretations of Gulielmus Durandus.

implication, had been rejuvenated by Guéranger) had shifted the emphasis in the Eucharist from the union of the whole Church with God to a concentration on individual benefits to be derived from the Mass. By such a misplaced emphasis, Herwegen maintained that a Christocentric action of the Church had degenerated into a pious or moralistic passivity of the laity, as individual spectators, who were no longer participants in the Eucharistic action. It is clear that the liturgical work of Maria Laach was as much a revolution as it was a restoration.

The scholarly researches and recovered insights of Maria Laach were made available to the parishes by the Augustinian canons of Klosterneuberg in Austria, chiefly through the work of popularization undertaken by Pius Parsch, which was later to be taken up by the pastor Pinsk in Berlin and the Jesuit scholar Jungmann in Innsbruck.[24] Parsch's deepest insight was to join in promoting the union of a Biblical movement with the Liturgical Movement through the review, *Bibel und Liturgie*, thus uniting the Liturgy with its main source, the record of God's revelation. The Bible itself came alive for many thousands of Catholics perhaps for the first time since the Reformation of the sixteenth century, and in the true context of the Liturgy.

Further developments in the second phase of the Liturgical Movement, accelerated by the work of Maria Laach, are to be found in France. Here the important *Centre de Pastorale Liturgique* was founded in 1943 by a remarkable act of continuing cooperation between Benedictines, Jesuits, Oratorians, and secular priests. This centre has concentrated on making the Liturgy the centre of the mission of the Church in a secularized nation. Elsewhere in France a limitation of the mission of the Church by focussing on the new intellectual pagans or almost exclusively on establishing social justice have aroused more opposition than is inevitable on the introduction of innovation. The critics have argued that such an approach has led to the denial of the importance of the parish as the traditional unit of the Church, that it has disregarded the traditional Liturgy in favour of "para-liturgies" as half-way houses between the outsider and the insider, and that social justice may be a by-product of Christian concern elicited by

[24] Joseph Jungmann, S.J., is the author of a masterly historical study, *Missarum Solemnia; eine genetische Erklärung der romischen Messe* (2 vols., 4th impression, Vienna, 1958). This has been translated into English as *The Mass of the Roman Rite, Its Origins and Development*, by F. A. Brunner.

the true fraternity created by the Holy Spirit, but can never be the main end of the Liturgy or the mission of the Church.

Even more significant, as a proof of the pre-eminent importance of Maria Laach's contribution to the second phase of the Liturgical Movement, is the remarkable number of Roman Catholic theologians and liturgiologists who have endorsed, or partly endorsed, the theological and practical insights of Herwegen and Casel. Among these may be mentioned Dom Anscar Vonier, O.S.B., Henri de Lubac, S.J., Jean Daniélou, S.J., P. Doncoeur, S.J., Pié Duployé, O.P., Eugène Masure, and Louis Bouyer, Cong.Orat., all of whom expound the *mysterientheologie*. It is accepted, with some reservations, by François Diekamp, J. Butler, Karl Adam, and Sohngen. It is, however, severely criticized by Joseph Jungmann and Theodore Klauser, as well as by certain members of the hierarchy.

The *mysterientheologie* has been criticized as denigrating the scholastic and mediaeval interpretations of the Mass, as Greek antiquarianism, and as denying the once-for-allness of history in claiming the re-enactment of the crucial historic event in the Liturgy. The debate continues, but it is undeniable that the theology of the Mystery has brought freshness and vigour and, most meaningfully, a sense of the rediscovery of the saving work of Christ, into the worship of scholars and of simple people. Its ecumenical significance is profound. Not only does it provide a bridge between Eastern Orthodox and Western Catholic theology, but it offers a third alternative to mediaeval scholastic and post-Tridentine Eucharistic interpretations, and this has met with an interested response on the part of Protestant theologians. Its revivification of parish life, through emphasis on the Divine initiative and the action of grace in the Liturgy, is its most impressive fruit.

The *mysterientheologie* has many other important implications. Faith, in its view, is more than assent to intellectual propositions, since it requires the commitment of the whole life of the whole man to God. Man is no longer envisioned atomistically, but as a part of the people of God, mystically incorporated into the *Corpus Christi* in the action of the Mass, sharing the life, purposes, and divine energy of God. This theology, furthermore, views man's daily work as worship, the offering which the Christian in the world brings to the company of the transfigured, to be presented in the Offertory of the Liturgy, together with the Perfect Offering of Atonement renewed. The Eucharist itself is transformed also: it is no longer merely a hierarchical offering in which the laity are passively present, but an action of grace in which the general priesthood of the people of God is exercised in response to the gracious Offering and Sacrifice of the Great High Priest, Christ Himself.

4. *A Theological Consensus for Practical Reform*

Despite differences of emphasis in the various countries in which the Liturgical Renaissance has been experienced, there is a broad, general theological agreement which has been sufficient to warrant a platform for liturgical reforms.

If one comprehensive category is sought which may be sufficiently inclusive of the many aspects of the Liturgical Movement, it might well be "Social Salvation." It is a reminder that in our time the rediscovery has been made of the Church as the people of God, the saved and saving society. In its worship the Church reaffirms its utter dependence upon the grace of God as it rehearses the mighty acts which have created and re-created the people of God—the Creation, the Restoration after the Fall in the Incarnation, the Passion and Sacrifice, the Resurrection, the Ascension and continual Intercession of Jesus Christ, the bestowal of the Spirit of renewal and integration (the Holy Spirit), and His witnesses (the saints)—and as it looks forward in hope to the Consummation of the Divine purpose in the Second Advent and the Final Judgment of Christ and the gathering in of the nations. As part of the Church militant on earth the people of God rejoices, even amid its trials, with the veteran victors of the Church triumphant. The Body of Christ offers a *symphonic* sacrifice of praise.

From this conception of social salvation which is the being and the end of the Church, several important liturgical corollaries may be drawn. It follows that true Christian worship can never be an individualistic, idiosyncratic search for personal merit or advantage ("O it will be glory for me") but must be the communal action of the entire *Corpus Christi*. Here there should be no passive performance of an empty, if aesthetically pleasing, rite in which mere spectators are dumb while the priest consecrates the sacred elements in a language of great dignity, mystery, and unintelligibility (such as Latin is for the great majority of the faithful), with his back turned to the people of God. Neither should there be a concentration upon one special moment of time (as at the elevation of the Host) to the comparative neglect of the rest of the action, nor should there be private meditation at the Exposition of the

Mass in a monstrance, as if this were the height of devotion; both are excluded because the Eucharist is a communal and continuously significant rite.

The Liturgical Movement in its variously important emphases teaches the social nature of salvation. That is why it is concerned with a vernacular rite[25] (or, in many parishes also with a Dialogue Mass) to encourage common participation and joint understanding. The sense of the general priesthood of the laity (who are the λαος τοῦ θεοῦ) is made more visible when the priest celebrates in the Western or Basilican posture, facing the people from behind the altar—which is placed centrally in the new churches inspired by the Liturgical Movement—and when provision is made for the faithful to take part in the Offertory procession to demonstrate that their own life and work is to be consecrated with the Perfect Offering of Christ Crucified for their salvation and the world's. It cannot be too frequently emphasized that the Liturgical Movement expresses in all its teaching and reforms the demand that the people of God shall take their full part in Divine worship and that a central altar, vernacular translations of the Roman rite, and the closest relationship between priests and the faithful shall express a common status (though differentiated liturgical functions) of the redeemed and renewed of Christ all participating in the Eucharistic action.

The social nature of salvation is also expressed by the Liturgical Movement in its ecumenical thrust. In delving behind post-Tridentine and mediaeval scholastic Eucharistic interpretations, the leaders of the Movement have recovered the Biblical and Patristic roots of theology and thus opened up a conversation between Catholic, Orthodox, and, to some extent, Protestant Christians. There is renewed appreciation for the hitherto divided insights of a fragmented Christendom. The objective and communal piety of the Church Fathers in East and West is again acclaimed for its profundity and relevance. The understanding of the Liturgy as the representation in time of the eternal action of God mysteriously revealed in the Incarnation, and the adoration paid to Christ the King of Glory, are grateful appropriations of the treasures of spirituality of the Eastern Church. The emphases on the efficacy of grace through the mediatorship of Christ, the importance of edification of the faithful in vernacular rites and liturgical preaching, the

[25] See C. Korolevskij, *Liturgie en langue vivante; Orient et Occident,* and C. R. A. Cunliffe, ed., *English in the Liturgy; a Symposium.*

growing sense of the priesthood of all believers shown in the liturgical apostolate, and, above all, the return to vigorous Bible study, all have parallels in classical Protestantism. The increasing openness[26] to such diverse Christian traditions is a manifestation of ecumenical zeal of some protagonists of the Liturgical Movement in working for the better visible expression of the *Una Sancta*. Even more remarkable evidence of ecumenical interchange is provided by the recent foundation of religious communities by Protestants at Taizé and Pomeyrol in France, and at Grandchamp in Switzerland, in which a primary concern is for the restoration of liturgical worship and prayer for the unity of Christ's Church. Such ecumenical reciprocity is at least partly attributable to the growing impact of the Liturgical Movement.

In yet another sense, and a very significant one, the Movement has stressed the social nature of salvation by integrating worship and work, *orare* with *laborare*. Not only have many of its churches, expressing the glory of Creation and Incarnation in modern techniques of art and architecture, been placed in the ugly milieu of industrial slums, but their worship has enabled men and women to discern a purpose in their daily labour as co-workers with Christ the carpenter, whose yoke then becomes easy. Particularly in the Offertory have they learned to lay the products of their labours on the altar, that they and their work and their associates may be hallowed. Moreover, the inspiration for social justice has often been stimulated by their worship of God, the beneficent Creator, the gracious Redeemer of the whole human race, and Sanctifier and Judge. They have learned penitence, forgiveness, and charity—those Divine lenitives for the inevitable abrasions caused by industrial relationships—in the Liturgy. The Liturgical Movement has shown that the Divine Action in the Liturgy provokes corporate human action in and after worship. It is, therefore, the nexus between adoration and sacrificial service.

5. Lutheran, Reformed, and Orthodox Contributions to the Liturgical Movement

As we have seen, the Roman Catholic contribution to the Liturgical Movement was important. So was the less easily defined—

---

[26] As evidence of such openness on the Roman Catholic side one has only to recall the researches of Herwegen and Casel into the Eastern rites or Louis Bouyer's *The Spirit and Forms of Protestantism*. On the Protestant side the openness to Roman Catholic liturgy is evidenced in the works of Y. Brilioth, Hebert, Koenker, Bénoît, Thurian, Massey Shepherd, Shands, and many others.

because inter-related—contribution to liturgical understanding and practice made by the Lutheran, Reformed, Orthodox, and other Communions associated in the Faith and Order Commission[27] of the Ecumenical Movement, in what became officially established as the World Council of Churches in Amsterdam in 1948.[28] The Faith and Order Conferences at which official representatives of these different Churches met to discuss their common convictions and to explore their differences in the understanding of the nature and function of the Church, the Ministry, the Sacraments and forms of worship, gave an immense stimulus to the Liturgical Movement. This may be recognized readily by consulting the symposia which were issued by the Commission or its subdivisions. Two of the most notable symposia which before Lund stressed the differences (for after Lund in 1955 the emphasis was to be on the Biblical and Patristic unity underlying differences in the hope of overcoming them) were: *The Ministry and the Sacraments* (1937) edited by R. Dunkerley and A. C. Headlam, and *Ways of Worship* (1951).[29] Such conferences and their conclusions indicate the growth of a common concentration on the worship of the Church of considerable moment and value. Since, however, they are joint reports of committees they are inevitably compromises.

They must, therefore, be supplemented by the significant investigations of individual writers of the various non-Roman Communions. Their contributions to the philosophy, psychology, history, and theology of worship have been considerable, and have helped to stress the primacy of worship in the on-going life of the Christian Community.

The names of Rudolf Otto, Friedrich Heiler, Nathan Söderblom, and Yngve Brilioth are themselves an index of the magnitude of the Lutheran contribution. The first three were phenomenologists who explored the distinctive dimensions of religious experience among many religions in different historical contexts, and par-

[27] See the following official reports: H. N. Bate, ed., *Faith and Order*—the Lausanne Conference proceedings; Leonard Hodgson, ed., *The Second World Conference on Faith and Order*—The Edinburgh Conference proceedings; Oliver S. Tomkins, ed., *The Third World Conference on Faith and Order*—The Lund Conference proceedings.

[28] See W. A. Visser t'Hooft, ed., *The First Assembly of the World Council of Churches*—report of the Assembly held in Amsterdam in 1948. Accounts of later Assemblies of the World Council of Churches are: W. A. Visser t'Hooft, ed., *The Evanston Report* and S. M. Cavert, ed., *The New Delhi Report*.

[29] *One Lord, One Baptism* (Faith and Order Paper No. 29, Minneapolis, 1961) contains a Faith and Order Report on "The Meaning of Baptism."

ticularly in the Christian religion. The fourth was a distinguished Church historian.

Time will permit only the sketchiest account of their work, selecting *Das Heilige* (translated as *The Idea of the Holy*) as typical Otto, *Das Gebet* (translated as *Prayer*) as typical Heiler, and *The Living God* as typical Söderblom. It should be noted that Otto and Heiler even produced rather academic liturgical forms as practical fruits of their researches. The concern of all three phenomenologists was to treat the religious experience as *sui generis*, in the tradition of Schleiermacher, and all three were erudite philosophers and historians of religions. While Otto and Heiler were attracted by mysticism, Söderblom was equally concerned with the institutional aspects of religion (as was the case with von Hügel). Their importance for our purpose is that they refused to subsume religion under either philosophy or morals, though recognizing that the experiences of awe and adoration necessarily issue in intellectual statements and moral practice.

The core of religion, however, according to Otto, was itself *felt*, and in the first encounter with the divine (God or gods) it was experienced as a polarity of attraction and repulsion: a *mysterium tremendum et fascinans*. The fact that it was a mystery indicated that it could not be rationally comprehended because the Divine transcendence exceeds human grasp. It attracts because it is love, but it repels because it is Holy love. Such an analysis, combined with Heiler's study of different religious types of prayer and of mysticism, inevitably encouraged an investigation of worship which is the corporate expression of the affectional response to God. Moreover, all rites of Christian worship explore the alternate rhythms of attraction and repulsion, of adoration and thanksgiving, on the one hand, and of confession, on the other. Furthermore, the work of anthropologists was making abundantly clear that all peoples have practised religious community rites and used ceremonial signs, thus again emphasizing the importance of ritual and ceremonial.

Yngve Brilioth's work as a church historian contributed even more directly to the impetus to ecumenical and liturgical renewal. In 1930 there first appeared in the English translation by A. G. Hebert (himself the pioneer Anglican promoter of the Liturgical Movement), Brilioth's *Eucharistic Faith and Practice, Evangelical and Catholic*. In a wide geographical and historical survey, Brilioth showed that any adequate rite for Holy Communion must contain four basic elements (with the ecumenical complication that every Christian Communion must examine itself to see if any of these complementary elements were missing in its celebration of Mass, Holy Communion, or the Lord's Supper). The first element was *Communion*, which makes the Eucharist the sharing of a community meal. The second was *Sacrifice*: the concept that the Church is pleading the eternally efficacious Atonement and Reconciliation accomplished by the death of Christ now the Ever-living Eternal High-Priest, with which is linked the Church's own offering of its members with the Head. The third essential element was the *Eucharist*, the joyous thanksgiving of the Church which finds its chief expression in the Lord's Prayer offered by him who presides at the worship. The fourth and final element was the *Memorial*, chiefly of the Cross as the culmination of the overflowing of the Divine love, but, in addition, a recalling of God's mighty acts before and after this pivotal event in Sacred history. This was a capital work of ecumenical analysis and synthesis and has been influential in Protestant and even Roman Catholic circles.[30]

Among many Reformed scholars who have contributed significantly to the understanding of worship in our time, one of preeminent importance would be Gerhardus Van der Leeuw, a phenomenologist and distinguished historian of religions. His *magnum opus* was translated as *Religion in Essence and Manifestation* (1938), and gave significant place to the importance of rites in religion. A more recently issued posthumous volume, now in an English translation, *Sacred and Profane Beauty* (1963) has important implications for worship. Perhaps his lasting memorial is the foundation of *Studia Liturgica*, "an international and ecumenical quarterly for liturgical research and renewal" which first appeared in 1962. It is significant that Wiebe Vos, its editor and founder, is introduced by the Bishop of Bristol as "a pupil and disciple of the late Professor G. Van der Leeuw [who] has inherited a deep concern for an ecumenical approach to liturgical matters, in the spirit of that great and gifted pioneer."[31] Numerous other Reformed scholars have been concerned with the Biblical

[30] The importance of this analysis can be seen by the fact that it was accepted by Fr. Louis Bouyer, the Oratorian, in *Life and Liturgy*. Subsequent scholarship would, however, add an additional element, the *Eschatological*, by which the Church at the Communion Service lives, in anticipation, in the completed Kingdom of God, at the end of the ages. This is a dimension of the life of pre-Constantinian Christianity much emphasized in the early Fathers and the importance of which Dom Gregory Dix has shown in *The Shape of the Liturgy*.

[31] *Studia Liturgica* (Rotterdam), Vol. I, No. 1, March 1962, p. 1.

basis of worship, its structure, and its historical development; and the relationship of worship to architecture. They have particularly stressed the coordinate importance of Word and Sacrament.[32]

The contribution of the Orthodox churches to the understanding of worship has been far from negligible. Some indication of this has already been given in the way that this understanding fertilized the Maria Laach mystery-theology. The refugee scholars from the Russian Revolution such as Berdyaev, Zernov, and Florovsky, in their peregrinations in France, England, and the United States have given the West a far deeper understanding of Eastern liturgies and spirituality than was possible before. A symptom of this desire for rapprochement in England was the foundation of the Society of St. Sergius and St. Alban, with a membership from the Orthodox and the Anglican Communions. A desire for closer relationship between the Roman Catholic and Orthodox Communions in England led to the foundation of the Society of St. John Chrysostom in 1926 and to the editorship of the *Eastern Churches Quarterly* by Dom Bede Winslow, O.S.B. The purpose of both societies was to encourage the understanding of the doctrines and liturgy of the Eastern Christians.

Three strong emphases of Orthodox theology and spirituality have had important implications for the theology of worship. As against any atomistic individualism, the concept of *Sobornost*— the Christian life as incorporation in Christ and his Community— has been stressed. According to this view, the mystical Coinherence in Christ is supremely manifested by the worshipping community. Furthermore, the therapeutic view that idiosyncrasies and alienations are overcome in the salvificatory community under its Head is another important correlate of this conception. A second important emphasis has been Solovyev's recovery of the Patristic concept of God-Manhood, so that the purpose of the Incarnate Christ is to take up our humanity to God, in a word, to deify humanity, and this proceeds through the sanctification effected in the Liturgy. Finally, the recovery of the eschatological emphasis owes much to the inspiring writings of Nicholas Berdyaev, in which he empha-

---

[32] Among these would be: J-D. Bénoît, author of *Initiation à la Liturgie*; Jean Cadier, author of *La Cène*; Max Thurian, a prolific writer of Taizé, the French Reformed Church Community; W. D. Maxwell, A. A. McArthur, William M'Millan, A. L. Drummond, T. H. Keir, Howard Hageman, P. Carnegie Simpson, André Biéler, and the important work of the distinguished German church historian, Hans Lietzmann, especially his *Messe und Herrenmahl* (Engl. trans., *Mass and Lord's Supper: A Study in the History of Liturgy*, by Dorothy Reeve, with introduction and supplementary essay by R. D. Richardson, appearing in nine fascicules).

sizes that eternal life is a quality of existence that begins here and now and is not postponed to the hereafter. There again, the Liturgy is where Christians become what they are intended to be and share in the powers of the age to come. Apart from these important theological convictions, the Western world has come to recognize the Biblical basis of worship, the intricate symbolism in the mysteries of the Orthodox Eucharist, and to appreciate as never before the stylistic qualities of their icons as pointers to Eternal qualities. Who can estimate the impact of the visual and musical glory of the worship of the Orthodox Churches—particularly those of the Russian and Greek Churches, and their impressive festivals—on Protestant visitors?

6. *The Influence of the Liturgical Movement in England*

Since the rest of this volume is a testimony to the impact of the Liturgical Movement in England in the present century, our immediate concern is merely to provide the briefest sketch of those who were the leaders of liturgical renewal in the Anglican and Free Churches.[33] Members of the Roman Catholic Church in England have not made a contribution to liturgical renewal comparable with that of Roman Catholic scholars in France, Germany, Belgium, or Italy.[34] Their contributions to worship are considered later in Chapter VII.

Anglican interest in the development of the Liturgical Movement was, as might be expected, close and continuing. In the first place, the Church of England is unique among Protestant Communions in having retained substantially unchanged its vernacular revision of the late mediaeval Western Rite from the mid-sixteenth century to the present day. Furthermore, the Oxford Movement of the nineteenth century reaffirmed the primacy of the Liturgy. It has, therefore, never ceased to be a *liturgical* Church and, moreover, it finds its nexus of unity, its spiritual regimen, its tradition and way of life in the Book of Common Prayer. In addition, the first Book of Common Prayer was an attempt to revise worship on the basis of Scripture and the practice of the Early Church (for

[33] A. H. Couratin in "Liturgiology 1939-1960" (*Theology*, Vol. LXIII, No. 485, November 1960, pp. 451-458) begins with the monitory statement: "In no other branch of theology has interest increased in the last twenty-one years as it has in Liturgy."

[34] This is probably because in a predominantly Protestant country any Roman Catholic stress on a vernacular liturgy, on the table aspect of the altar, and on the active cooperation of the laity, would seem like imitating Protestantism. The pioneers of the Liturgical Movement in English Roman Catholicism were Monsignor O'Connor of Bradford and Eric Gill.

these are its twin foundations as the Elizabethan apologists, Jewel and Hooker, ever maintained).

The Church of England has ever had a succession of scholars researching in the area of the early development of liturgies in East and West. The succession has been maintained in the present century, as the names of F. E. Brightman, W. H. Frere, J. H. Srawley, Gregory Dix, and E. C. Ratcliff will indicate. Furthermore, the services of Anglican liturgical scholars have been required in advising the other Provinces of the Anglican Communion when revisions of the Book of Common Prayer began in India, South Africa, Canada, and in the Caribbean.[35] The very set-back suffered by Parliament's refusal to approve the "deposited" Prayer Book, in 1927 and 1928, released the services of liturgists for overseas recommendations where the other provinces were free from the limitations (and advantages) of Erastianism, and even for the exciting ecumenical revisions being prepared for the United Church of South India. Finally, the consecration of several Anglican religious communities to the primacy of worship and spirituality has benefitted the entire Anglican Communion. It is significant that Father Gabriel Hebert and Dom Gregory Dix belonged, respectively, to the Society of the Sacred Mission at Kelham and to the Anglican Benedictine Community at Nashdom.

The earliest Anglican interpreter of the Continental Liturgical Movement was Father Gabriel Hebert. Learned in the Swedish tongue, he considered it part of his mission to introduce important Swedish theological works into English by his translations. He translated Anders Nygren's *Agape and Eros* and Gustaf Aulen's *Christus Victor*, and also Brilioth's important *Eucharistic Faith and Practice, Catholic and Protestant*. Having undergone this ecumenical work of translation, Hebert showed his own mettle as an interpreter of the Continental Liturgical Movement in *Liturgy and Society: The Function of the Church in the Modern World* (1935). As stimulating as it was profound, the book went through five impressions in nine years, and was the subject of keen theological debate far beyond the confines of his own Communion.

The Preface indicated the strength and breadth of Hebert's outlook. It averred that this "is an essay on the Church and her message, particularly as embodied in the actual order of the Church

[35] For these Rites see Bernard Wigan, *The Liturgy in English.* A fine study of the South African Rite is P. B. Hinchcliff's *The South African Liturgy.* The more experimental English liturgies will be discussed later in Chapter IX.

and her liturgy, in relation to the problem of belief and a true social life in the confused order of today."[36] Here was no merely antiquarian or aesthetic approach, but a plea to consider that the Church in her worship was living her theology, and renewing her spiritual life. Here was the claim that the Church was expressing the will of God in a redeemed society which already transcended in principle and partly in reality the divisions of race, nationality, and class that tear the outside world asunder, and was also commissioned to demonstrate this integrating life in the world.

In this pioneering volume, Hebert wrote urgently from a threefold conviction. First, he intended to show that the Church, far from being a collection of individuals or a quasi-legal entity, had its own organic life as the mystical Body of Christ, of which He is the Head and all Christians are members.[37] Secondly, he was concerned to demonstrate that a diluted liberal and accommodating theology had made too easy terms with the times. He opposed the *Zeitgeist* with the Holy Spirit in Bible and Liturgy. Positively he wished to claim that only a reassertion of the Gospel, as recorded in the Bible and witnessed to in the historic Creeds, was both critical and consoling enough to meet the desperate need of man in difficult days, together with the adequacies of Divine and supernatural grace as communicated through Christ and His Church. Thirdly, he was attempting to show that "the Church in England is as much a missionary Church as the Church in India or Japan."[38]

Hebert believed that the Liturgical Revival offered a way of presenting Christianity as more than a system of belief (which a purely theological approach would imply), and as more than an individual way of holiness (as piety had often previously regarded spirituality). Christianity could now be presented "as a way of life for the worshipping community"[39] which was a corporate renewal of faith (through the theology proclaimed in Sermon and Sacrament), of commitment and consecration (through the Offertory), and an incentive to serve and transform the fragmented society outside, as the very mission of the Church. Thus the evangelical, liturgical, and sociological are seen to be three correlated aspects of Christian life focussed in the corporate Christian cultus.

This theoretical programme was to find its practical expression in the Parish Communion, and more popularly in the *Parish and People* movement and magazine. It is a tribute to Hebert's per-

---

[36] *Liturgy and Society*, p. 7.   [37] *Ibid.*, pp. 12-13.
[38] *Ibid.*, p. 14.   [39] *Ibid.*, p. 64.

suasiveness that his advocacy wrought a fundamental change in many Anglican parishes, so that Communion at eight o'clock in the morning and Matins at 10:30 or 11:00 A.M. were less well attended than the Parish Communion at 9:00 or 9:30 A.M., followed by a Parish breakfast.[40]

The master-work in the interpretation of the history and the significance of Liturgy from an Anglican viewpoint was *The Shape of the Liturgy* (1948), the work of Dom Gregory Dix, the witty, erudite, and very original monk of the Anglican Benedictine house at Nashdom. The work of fourteen years of study and fourteen months of writing, it follows the development of the pattern of the liturgy from its two-fold origin as a combination of the Synaxis (or Liturgy of the Spirit), deriving from the Synagogue, and the Eucharist, deriving from the Upper Room, through its Patristic, mediaeval, Reformation and Counter-Reformation, as well as modern developments, as it takes on the characteristic colouring of different peoples and centuries. Essentially he claims it has a "Four Action" shape: the "taking" of bread and wine (the Offertory); the "giving of thanks" or "blessing" (the Eucharistic prayer with its preliminary dialogue of invitation with its parallel in the Preface of the Prayer of Consecration); the "breaking" or Fraction; and the sharing or "Communion." The most important chapters are the ninth ("The Meaning of the Eucharist" with its stress on the Eucharist as Action, as manifestation, and Eschatology and the Eucharist),[41] and the eleventh ("The Sanctification of Time"), where Dom Gregory shows that in the fourth century worship, since Christianity under Constantine became a *religio licita*, is public and not private, less eschatological and more conscious of time. The worldly contempt for Christianity in several countries may indeed cause the twentieth century to rediscover the pre-Constantinian characteristic of its worship as a mystery which is focussed on eternity; but while the social implications of the Liturgy are recognized there need be no withdrawal except for return, and gathering only for scattering.

The contemporary implications of the Eucharist are finely described in the prefatory account of the concepts of man and society implicit in the Eucharist, which speak to modern man's relation to

[40] This is described as worked out in different city, suburban, and rural parishes in the volume Hebert edited, *The Parish Communion.*

[41] "The Eucharist is nothing else but the eternal gesture of the Son of Man towards His Father as He passes into the Kingdom of God" (*The Shape of the Liturgy*, p. 266).

society and his need to obtain a sufficiency of material things. "There is," says Dom Gregory, "a Christian pattern of a solution which is expressed for us and by us at the Eucharist."[42] The individual's need of material things even for the good life is emphasized and met, yet the needs are met from the resources of the whole society, which are offered by each of its members for all. This analysis culminates in a *tour de force* which must be cited in full:

"Over against the dissatisfied 'Acquisitive Man' and his no less avid successor the dehumanised 'Mass-Man' of our economically focussed societies insecurely organised for time, Christianity sets the type of 'Eucharistic Man'—man giving thanks with the product of his labours upon the gifts of God, and daily rejoicing with his fellows in the worshipping society which is grounded in eternity. This is man to whom it was promised on the night before Calvary that he should henceforth eat and drink at the table of God and be a king. This is not only a more joyful and more humane ideal. It is the divine and only authentic conception of the meaning of all human life and its realization is in the eucharist."[43]

Though particular parts of Dix's reconstruction and interpretation may be criticized,[44] the extraordinary sweep of the perspective and the verve of the writing, and the perceptiveness and contemporary relevance of this invigorating study are undeniable. In consequence the volume was widely studied in many Christian Communions, more especially as it is a summary of liturgical research for the previous half-century.

A scholar of at least equal erudition and greater caution is Professor E. C. Ratcliff. At Oxford where he was University Lecturer in Liturgiology and Fellow of Queen's College, at London where he was Professor of Ecclesiastical History, and at Cambridge where he was Ely Professor and subsequently Regius Professor of Divinity, Dr. Ratcliff's influence has been considerable. His lectures on early Christian liturgies and on the Book of Common Prayer, which are masterpieces of compressed and lucid

---

[42] *Ibid.*, p. xviii.
[43] *Ibid.*, pp. xviii-xix.
[44] Exception has been taken to the following features in the work: an over-emphasis on the Hellenistic contrast between the eternal and the temporal with insufficient recognition of the Biblical conception of time as fulfilment and *dénouement*; a supposed caricature of Reformed doctrines of the Church and of the Lord's Supper as, respectively, atomistic and memorialist (forgetting Calvin's understanding of the Church as the Communion of the elect and the sacraments as *Sigilla Verbi*), and the presumption that, contrary to Jeremias, the context of the Last Supper was a *chaburah*, not a Passover meal.

erudition, his careful tutorials on the liturgical texts, and his supervision of research students (or examination of their completed dissertations) now holding scholastic posts in different countries,[45] have been impressive. His advice to revisers or makers of liturgies in other lands, and his membership of the Liturgical Commission of the Church of England, are also indications of a quiet but deeply pervasive and continuous influence. His written works are a mere fraction of his hidden resources. They include an admirable chapter on "Christian Worship and Liturgy" in K. E. Kirk's *The Study of Theology* (1939), another in Nuttall and Chadwick's *From Unity to Uniformity, 1662-1962*, on the Savoy Conference preceding the 1661 revision of the Book of Common Prayer, and yet another assessing Cranmer as liturgist, in *Three Commemorative Lectures delivered in Lambeth Palace* (1956). His books include the magisterial *The Booke of Common Prayer of the Churche of England: Its making and revisions. M.D.xlix—M.D.clxi* (1949) and a superb rationale of the English Coronation Rite.[46]

In our own time, largely because the Church is no longer an established or privileged institution in the secular state, liturgics has come to be a study of the Church's self-understanding, intelligible both to the church member and the interested enquirer. To this necessary task of popularization the Anglican Evelyn Underhill, student of mysticism, devoted disciple of Baron Friedrich von Hügel (a Roman Catholic with strong Anglican sympathies), contributed admirably by her interconfessional study, *Worship*, which appeared in 1936 and which has, in paperback, a continuing widespread influence. Other Anglican exemplars of *vulgarization haute* are: Colin Dunlop in *Anglican Public Worship* (1953); J. A. T. Robinson in *Liturgy Coming to Life* (1961) and a controversial chapter in his iconoclastic volume, *Honest to God* (1963); Basil Minchin in his series *Worship in the Body of Christ* (which

[45] Four may be mentioned: A. H. Couratin, now the Archdeacon of Durham, formerly Principal of St. Stephen's House, Oxford, and Ratcliff's successor as University Lecturer in Liturgiology at Oxford; C. W. Dugmore, Professor of Ecclesiastical History in the University of London at King's College; Professor James F. White, of the School of Theology at Southern Methodist University, author of *The Cambridge Movement*, and Professor P. B. Hinchliff of Rhodes University, Grahamstown, South Africa. Other liturgical scholars who would acknowledge his direct influence are Bernard Wigan, A. Elliott Peaston, C. J. Cuming, and the present writer.

[46] Reference should also be made to two important articles by E. C. Ratcliff, "The Sanctus and the Pattern of the Early Anaphora" in *The Journal of Ecclesiastical History*, Vol. I (1950), pp. 29-36; 125-34, which claim that the primitive consecration prayer was a prayer of thanksgiving culminating in the Sanctus and excluding invocation and oblation.

began in 1958); and the work of the Birmingham trio of J. Gordon Davies, Gilbert Cope, and D. A. Tytler, as well as many others.

Father Lionel Thornton's massive and detailed Biblical and theological studies of the nature of the Church have also had a considerable indirect influence on the understanding of the liturgy.[47]

Nor should the careful scholarly researches into liturgy, spirituality, and hymnody by many other Anglican scholars be forgotten. Two outstanding volumes were Bishop Kenneth Kirk's *The Vision of God* (1934) and G. W. O. Addleshaw and F. Etchells, *The Architectural Setting of Anglican Worship* (1950). Important studies of Anglican liturgical revisions were made by R. C. D. Jasper and G. J. Cuming, A. C. Don and G. Donaldson. The chief researchers into the history of psalmody and hymnody in the English language were John Julian and M. Frost. A. M. Allchin, Martin Thornton, and G. J. Stranks studied the history of English spirituality. Moreover, E. Milner-White and A. H. Couratin were admirable composers of litanies and collects. T. S. Garrett wrote illuminating studies of the Worship of the Church of South India.

A significant feature of this century has been the increasing interest of the "Low Church" or Evangelical wing in the history and theology of worship. Its representatives have made notable contributions in this field, among them C. F. D. Moule, C. W. Bowles, A. B. MacDonald, G. F. Bromiley, D. E. Harrison, and F. W. Dillistone. In its cumulative impact the concentration of so many Anglican scholars in the field of worship has been most impressive.

In the Free Churches the signs of an appreciation of the Liturgical Movement are more difficult to discern[48] because they are discovered more easily in the ferment of discussions on worship in the denominational quarterlies and newspapers, or in the denominational revisions of manuals of worship, than in books that drew widespread attention. One book, however, was a notable contribution to the Free Church reappraisal of worship in the light of the long Christian tradition. It might be regarded as a Free

---

[47] The following of Lionel S. Thornton's books are pertinent: *The Common Life in the Body of Christ; The Dominion of Christ; Christ and the Church*, as well as his organic and Whiteheadian conception of the nature of Christ's union with the Father, the Universe, and the Church, in *The Incarnate Lord*.

[48] Cf. *A Free Church Book of Common Prayer*, anonymously edited by J. M. Lloyd Thomas, had already appeared in 1929. It is perhaps one of the few significant contributions of the moribund but fascinating "Free Catholic Movement," of which Lloyd Thomas and W. E. Orchard were the leaders. This movement is studied in Chapter x, Section 3.

Church counterpart to the Anglican compilation *Liturgy and Worship*, edited by W. K. Lowther Clarke. Planned by Dr. Nathaniel Micklem, then Principal of Mansfield College, Oxford, it was entitled *Christian Worship, Studies in its History and Meaning* (1936). The foreword claimed that the book, written by members of Mansfield College, was "A Systematic Study of Public Worship," and hoped that "our historical studies may be accepted as a serious contribution to this great subject and that our later chapters in particular, may serve as an interpretation, and in this sense as a vindication, of the common tradition of our Reformed Churches." The first part dealt with Biblical Studies in which H. Wheeler Robinson, T. W. Manson, W. H. Cadman, and C. H. Dodd contributed chapters. The second consisted of historical studies with chapters by J. V. Bartlet, R. S. Franks, James Moffatt, C. J. Cadoux, J. S. Whale, and A. G. Mathews. The third and concluding part contained contemporary studies by E. R. Micklem, Edward Shillito, Kenneth Parry, and the Editor. It was the first time that as notable a group of Free Church Scholars (Congregationalists, Presbyterians, and a Baptist) had surveyed the history of the great Christian tradition of worship and indicated its primary importance for their Communions, which hitherto had been thought by others (and perhaps even by neglect among themselves) to emphasize preaching to the derogation of prayers and sacraments. Apart from its intrinsic importance, the volume was a portent.

It was not long before several authors in the tradition of the English Free Churches were stressing the importance of worship in their books. Apart from further works by the members of the Mansfield College symposium, contributions made by other Congregationalists were: Bernard Lord Manning (notably in *The Hymns of Wesley and Watts* and *Essays on Orthodox Dissent*); John Marsh (both in his historical introduction to *A Book of Public Worship compiled for the use of Congregationalists*[49] and in his important essay in *Ways of Worship*, edited by Edwall, Hayman, and Maxwell in 1951); James Todd in *Prayers and Services for Christian Festivals* (1951), a companion volume to *A Book of Public Worship*; and Raymond Abba in *Principles of Christian Worship with special reference to the Free Churches* (1957). Erik Routley wrote several important books in the area of church music and the theology of hymnody. The Congregationalists may, indeed,

---

[49] Edited by John Huxtable, John Marsh, Romilly Micklem, and James Todd.

be regarded as pioneers in England of the Free Church renewal of worship in the present day.

Among English Presbyterians the name of Dr. P. Carnegie Simpson, with his concern for a Catholic Evangelicalism, was pre-eminent. But, of course, the splendid influence of the larger sister Communion, the Church of Scotland, should not be forgotten. There was no Communion during this period to which the English Free Churches turned with greater admiration and respect in the area of theology and worship than the Church of Scotland. The 1940 edition of the *Book of Common Order*, with its splendidly comprehensive First order for Holy Communion was taken as the pattern of Reformed worship. The writings of its liturgiologists such as Millar Patrick, William M'Millan, W. D. Maxwell, Allan McArthur, and D. H. Hislop were as widely read in England, and especially among Free Church ministers, as were the works of its distinguished theologians.

The Methodists contributed to the revival of interest in worship with several interesting historical studies. Many of them seemed to imply that they wished the umbilical knot linking them to the Church of England in the eighteenth century had never been severed. As there were "High Church" Genevans among Presbyterians and Congregationalists, so there were several "High Church" Methodists. R. Newton Flew, Principal of Wesley House, Cambridge, produced a most erudite study of *Christian Perfection* through nineteen centuries in East and West. J. E. Rattenbury wrote *Vital Elements in Public Worship* (1936), *The Eucharistic Hymns of John and Charles Wesley* (1948), and *Thoughts on Holy Communion* (1948), and stressed that John Wesley never ceased to be a high churchman in his evaluation of Holy Communion. In two careful works John C. Bowmer wrote of *The Sacrament of the Lord's Supper in Early Methodism* (1951) and brought the story more succinctly up to the present in *The Lord's Supper in Methodism, 1791-1960* (1961). John Bishop wrote of *Methodist Worship in relation to Free Church Worship* (1950). Perhaps the most popular of all exemplars of the Catholicity of this branch of Protestantism was A. E. Whitham. Three volumes of his which were correlated collections of articles with a wide sale were *The Pastures of His Presence*, *The Culture and Discipline of the Spiritual Life*, and *The Catholic Christ*. They stressed that Catholic and Protestant saints were united in the *imitatio Christi*, and moreover, of the Incarnate Christ. More recently A. Raymond

George has combined a Biblical and a liturgical interest in *Communion with God in the New Testament* (1958), and is co-editor with J. Gordon Davies of a series of volumes entitled *Ecumenical Studies in Worship*. Gordon S. Wakefield's *Puritan Devotion: its place in the development of Christian Piety* (1957) was a choice of topic unusual for Methodist writers and important in seeing the clear parallels between Puritan and Methodist forms of piety. Geoffrey Parrinder made a welcome contribution to comparative religion in *Worship in the World's Religions* (1961).

Although the Baptists share the same type of polity as the Congregationalists and have shared with them the social indignity and the spiritual rigour of espousing orthodox dissent, yet their differences on the issue of believers' baptism as contrasted with paedo-baptism have tended to keep them apart and to the left of the Congregationalists in their frequent iconoclasm in worship. "High Church" Baptists have had a difficult path to tread. All the more creditable for their courage, therefore, have been the contributions of H. Wheeler Robinson, D. Tait Patterson, Neville Clarke, Stephen Winward, and Ernest A. Payne. No more liturgically advanced directory of worship in any of the Free Churches has been prepared than *Orders and Prayers for Church Worship*, by Ernest A. Payne and Stephen F. Winward (1962). While they do not jettison the flexibility of the Free Church tradition, they undergird it with a traditional theological and liturgical structure. Thus they keep the essential elements of the traditional liturgy of the Word and of the Upper Room, while refusing to become liturgical literalists insisting on sacrosanct and inalterable words and phrases. This achievement is all the more striking as this denomination in England has traditionally, since the time of John Smyth, the first Cambridge don to become a "Se-Baptist," insisted on the priority of the untrammelled Holy Spirit in worship and denigrated the priestly in order to exalt the prophetic. That prophet and priest join hands in this manual is the most striking proof of the triple and interrelated impact of the Biblical, Ecumenical, and Liturgical Movements—in crossing denominational boundaries and overcoming even hard and fast and almost un-examinable denominational traditions which were no longer guides but chains.

7. An Appraisal

It is abundantly clear that the England of the twentieth century has manifested a remarkable interconfessional renewal of worship.

47

However, when full appreciation is given to the Liturgical Movement as one of the major signs, and indeed a major medium, of the "Twentieth Century Reformation," like all mixed Divine-human institutions it is in danger of claiming too much for itself. Two chief dangers must be guarded against: the first is aestheticism and the second is antiquarianism. It might be thought that Guéranger rather than his successors was in greater danger of falling a victim to these tendencies, particularly as his pioneering work was out of touch with parish life, whereas the Liturgical Institutes, Liturgical Weeks, and Liturgical Years of the present time have in mind the needs of secular priests and their flocks as well as of members of the religious communities. Certainly the dangers are minimized by the emphatic concern in the present phase of the Liturgical Movement for the restoration to the laity of their privileges as participants in the Liturgy; but the dangers are not entirely eliminated.

The danger of antiquarianism is great, although the exponents of the Movement have objected to the fossilization and petrifaction of the Tridentine Liturgy and even to the roseate view of the mediaeval rites, because the repristination of the Patristic ideal without a consideration of the changed circumstances of the present century could be a more dangerous, because a more remote, form of antiquarianism. Furthermore, while the Eastern Church in the early centuries of the Christian era undertook much eleemosynary work for "the household of faith," it was not distinguished for any prophetic attempt to remould the conditions of society into a more just and Christian order. In fact, it was ethically nearly static, so that in the Byzantine Church–State the chosen people became almost the frozen people. A contemporary expression of the Liturgy, while being faithful to the Christian tradition, must apply itself creatively to stimulating the twentieth century's paramount concern for establishing social justice and winning the artisan, in a way that was beneath the contempt of the Byzantine theocratic rulers.

The danger of aestheticism is the greater in the Catholic and Orthodox areas of Christendom because they have ever inspired the visual and plastic arts with the sacramental principle deriving from the Incarnation, whereas Protestantism (with some great exceptions such as Dürer and Rembrandt) has been afraid of absolutising the finite in art and of confusing the Creator with the created (idolatry). The tendency of the Catholic and Orthodox branches of the Church to equate the Church with the Kingdom of God (not to see the Church as the main but not exclusive agent of the Kingdom), and their assumption that the Church is the extension of the Incarnation, leads them into the danger of sanctifying the social *status quo*. Protestantism's danger, on the contrary, is that of a too ready response to the new currents of thought in the world and therefore of contemporary relevance at the cost of diluting the historic faith.

Both Catholicism and Orthodoxy, on the one hand, and Protestantism, on the other, need the criticism of the Gospel, with its prophetic role of exposing the easy conformities and blind idolatries of institutionalism and its aesthetic trappings. The faithful proclamation of the Gospel in its fulness will not permit the making of the finite absolute, or the equation of the symbol with the reality it represents and also veils. The Gospel proclaimed in its freedom and fulness is the countervailing correction of the supposedly inherent efficacy of the most perfect and lovely liturgy, the necessary distinguisher between the Creator and the works of men who are only derivatively creators. While the Liturgy should and often does proclaim the Gospel, it can also mute it, particularly in so-called liturgical preaching where the unbound Word of God is thought sometimes to be a subjective element in an objective rite, and collects and sequences, not the written record of God's revelation, are made the basis of liturgical homilies.

It should not be forgotten, moreover, that even when the term "priesthood" is interpreted to include the laity in the Liturgy, the entire *Sacrificium laudis* is only a human response inspired by the Sacrifice of Him who, besides being the Great High Priest, is also a Prophet and King. His prophetic authority and His kingly rule are made known in the preaching of the Word, witnessed to by the interior action of the Holy Spirit. The ultimate restraint, then, on any aestheticism and antiquarianism in the Liturgical Movement, is the giving of a coordinate place to the Word and the Sacrament. In this way the Liturgy of the Word will reinforce the Liturgy of the Upper Room, and ensure that from worship shall spring mission and the more just re-ordering of the life of the world in its political, economic, and social aspects. Today as never before Liturgy is correlated with Life.[50]

[50] Perhaps the most promising feature of the latest phase of the Liturgical Movement is that in the Roman Catholic Church, accelerated by the Second Vatican Council, "a new period in the history of the Roman Liturgy is coming under our eyes, and that *The Epoch of Changelessness or Rubricism* is over." In this judgment Archdeacon Couratin (*Theology*, Vol. LXIII, No. 485, November 1960, p. 452), referred to the Roman decrees of 1947 and 1955 which introduced the simplification of the rubrics of the Breviary and the Missal, and also the new Paschal Vigil for Holy Week.

CHAPTER II

THE REBIRTH OF RELIGIOUS ARCHITECTURE AND ART

THE BUILDING or embellishment of churches was a marginal activity for most leading architects and artists during most of our period. There were good reasons for this. The chief one was that worship and religious instruction were the fringe concerns of the minority of the nation's population after the First World War. Also, a nostalgia for the past blinded many church building-committees to the needs and the technical opportunities of the present. Hence the creative architects and artists learned to expect abuse instead of encouragement. Inevitably, the result was that most churches erected in the first four decades were tame clichés, mere regurgitated Gothic. The more exotic churches were chaotic evocations of a Byzantine or Baroque past that had only existed overseas, or a gallimaufry of all styles. In the two most recent decades, however, there has been a genuine rebirth of religious art and architecture that is functionally contemporary.

But the reluctance of that rebirth mirrors the confusion of our times. Artists of the twentieth century have had their imaginations sometimes liberated, but more often cluttered, with the artifacts of many civilizations, centuries, and countries. Thus, in the confused consciousness of the modern artist, Japanese colour-prints and icons from Constantinople jostle with Aztec monuments and Melanesian masks, Benin bronzes and Bushmen rock-paintings, T'ang horses with swords recovered from sunken Viking ships, Icelandic animal carvings with mediaeval illuminated manuscripts and ivories from France. El Greco's "Agony in the Garden" vies for attention with Picasso's "The Bombing of Guernica," and the gods of Praxiteles with the Christ and the clowns of Rouault.

Confusion was worse confounded by the successive radical changes of style: post-impressionism, symbolism, vorticism, cubism, naturalism, functionalism, and abstractionism followed fast upon one another's heels to dizzy the pursuer. New materials and new techniques (plastics, pre-stressed concrete, and light alloys) have revolutionised and dazzled the architects and artists of today.

In these circumstances it is not surprising that twentieth century religious architecture and art in England is marked successively by timid traditionalism, blundering syncretism, and pragmatic functionalism. The wonder is rather that England can boast that from this chaos have arisen architects and artists of the finest calibre, whose religious work will engage our detailed attention. The architects are Sir Giles Gilbert Scott, Sir Edward Maufe, Sir Basil Spence, Sir Ninian Comper, and Mr. Frank Gibberd. The sculptors are Sir Jacob Epstein, Eric Gill and Henry Moore. The painters are Sir Stanley Spencer, Graham Sutherland, and John Piper.

1. *Cathedrals and their Functions*

The largest, though not always the most impressive, of modern ecclesiastical edifices are cathedrals. In the nineteenth century they tended to be diocesan museums and their Chapters the fussy custodians of an archaic dignity, despite the vigorous protests[1] of a Pusey or a Howson, and, of course, St. Paul's and Westminster Abbey were great preaching centres. They have had a remarkable renaissance in the twentieth century. The pioneer in their revival was Dean Bennett of Chester, who changed Chester Cathedral from a museum for curious visitors into a home for pilgrims. His pioneering example, in domesticating a cathedral, was widely but not quickly followed.

That is the inference to be drawn from the observation of the anonymous editor of *Crockford* in 1943 that cathedrals were admired more highly as architectural monuments than as religious institutions. "As the latter," he added, "we believe them to be of unique and supreme importance to the whole Church, as the principal repositories of the Anglican faith and worship in a dark and cloudy day."[2]

The functions of a modern cathedral were defined in the Report of the Cathedrals Commission of 1961 as follows:

"These are the visible counterparts of the episcopal system. Just as there has to be a Bishop to ordain and confirm, so there must be a Church which outwardly symbolises the organisation of the family life around a Mother-Church. The Cathedral is the natural centre for ordinations and some other episcopal functions. Besides

[1] See E. B. Pusey, *Remarks on the Prospective and Past Benefits of Cathedral Institutions*, and J. S. Howson, ed., *A Week in Chester Cathedral*. Also, Frank Bennett, *The Nature of a Cathedral* and Roger Lloyd, *The Church of England in the Twentieth Century*, Vol. II, Chap. 8.
[2] In a supplement of 1943 reprinted in *Crockford Prefaces: The Editor Looks Back*. In 1929, however, he had remarked on "the resurrection . . . of Cathedral Churches which has taken place within living memory" (*ibid.*, pp. 83-84).

this, the traditional arrangement whereby the worship of the Cathedral is entrusted to a Dean or Provost and Chapter, provides a ministry of depth and variety which is beyond that normally available in a parish church. The worship offered there is often of an artistic quality higher than is normally possible. Its corporate nature, in which Dean and Canons all participate, preserves in miniature what was good in the monastic tradition of a corporate devotion to the *opus Dei*. . . . Far from being outmoded the Cathedral Churches of England have never before served as living centres of worship for such a variety of ordinary Church members."[3]

The modern Anglican cathedral is thus seen primarily as a "living centre of worship" in which the service of Holy Communion is the climax, but in which also the preaching of the Word, the musical settings of chants, anthems and masses, and the art of the architect, the stone-mason, the glazier, the metal-worker, the weaver, the embroiderer, and not least the sculptor, all assist the people of God to join in His praise, to bless Him for His works of nature and of grace. The cathedral is, therefore, both liturgical centre and home of the diocese.

From this twin concept of its functions are derived important ancillary activities and interests: theological study and scholarship; the improvement and extension of Christian education, as of social and industrial evangelism;[4] and the glorification of God through music, drama, and the plastic arts.[5] Its pulsating life as a dynamo of spiritual power can be appreciated by contrasting a present-day cathedral, such as Coventry or Southwark, with the life of a cathedral a century ago as described by two Broad Church Canons, Sydney Smith and Charles Kingsley.[6] Compassion has replaced petrifaction in most cathedrals, if not yet in Royal Abbey Churches.

3 Pp. 21-22.

4 Sheffield, Manchester and Coventry specialise in the industrial mission of the modern Church, as also Southwark.

5 Canterbury and Chichester Cathedrals are renowned for their work in presenting religious drama of high quality, while Coventry and Chichester are distinguished patrons of painters, sculptors, and glaziers.

6 In 1841 Smith gave the following evidence before the Select Committee on National Monuments: "The whole Cathedral [St. Paul's], excepting the choir and those assembled in it for divine service, is converted into a lobby for fashionable loungers; hundreds of persons come together for no other reason than to make an exhibition of this description; so that what with the pacing of feet, the murmur of voices, the gadding to and fro of figures, every Church-like notion is driven from their minds; the whole thing resembles more a promenade in a ball-room than a congregation in the house of God" (cited by C. K. F. Brown, *A History of the English Clergy, 1800-1900*, pp. 64-65). Charles Kingsley wrote of an afternoon service in the same cathedral in Chap. XVII of his Christian-Socialist novel *Yeast*: "The organ droned sadly in its iron cage to a few musical amateurs. Some nursery-maids and foreign sailors stared about within the spiked felon's

2. *Five New Cathedrals*

The predominant impression left by the new Anglican cathedrals of Liverpool and Guildford and the Roman Catholic cathedral of Westminster is one of traditionalism. The first two are neo-Gothic and the third is neo-Byzantine. Coventry (Anglican) Cathedral, though lacking a central altar, is in most other respects modern.

The Roman Catholic Metropolitan Cathedral of Christ the King being erected in Liverpool is modern through and through. This can be seen both in its polygonal shape with circular sanctuary, and in its tent-shaped exterior, surmounted by a crown (a cylindrical tower with pinnacles of alternating crosses and spikes). By means of ingenious planning the external space is internally reflected, so that the most dominant object, the tower, is over the most significant space, the sanctuary. In the designing, the liturgical concern was paramount: to associate the congregation ever more closely with the celebrant of the Mass in order that the ministers at the altar should be clearly in the sight of the people. The central altar, made of a single block of white Carrara marble, is surrounded on three sides by the congregation, and two thousand people can be within sixty feet of the Sanctuary steps.[7] The problem of a circular plan, that it lacks direction, was solved by forming a principal north to south axis through the building by placing an entrance porch at one end and the most important chapel (that of the Blessed Sacrament) at the other. The east and west entrances form a secondary axis. The Chapel of the Blessed Sacrament and the Lady Chapel project from the perimeter of the cathedral to form extensions of the nave. The eight other smaller chapels are individually designed to contrast with and yet support the vast central space. Some will be secluded spaces for meditation and others will open out into the nave.

Frederick Gibberd, the architect, was selected in an open com-

---

dock which shut off the body of the cathedral, and tried in vain to hear what was going on inside the choir. As a wise author—a Protestant, too—has lately said: 'the scanty service rattled in the vast building like a dried kernel too small for its shell.' The place breathed imbecility and unreality and sleepy life in death, while the whole nineteenth century went roaring on its way outside. . . . Coleridge's dictum that a cathedral is petrified religion, may be taken to bear more meanings than one."

[7] Other dimensions of interest are: external diameter, 288 feet; diameter of Sanctuary, 54 feet; width of base or podium, 315 feet; and height of centre line of cathedral to the top of the pinnacles, 324 feet. This information was supplied by Monsignor Thomas Turner of the Metropolitan Cathedral.

petition for which the assessors were the Archbishop of Liverpool (now Archbishop of Westminster), the architect of Coventry Cathedral, and David Stokes. The architect had to face formidable problems. How was the new building to be related to the massive crypt of Lutyens? How could it best express the aims of the modern Liturgical Movement? Could so vast a space be covered with a cathedral enclosing ten chapels and providing a huge car park at a price estimated in 1959 at no more than a million pounds sterling? Could a symbolism be devised which was authentically Christian, yet recognizably modern? It is, of course, too early to judge the ultimate effect from the architect's model; but already it can be seen that here is an intriguingly imaginative, functional, and elegant design. The crowned tent image is a powerful image of the nature of the Church in the twentieth century as the pilgrimage of faith of the people of God nourished with the iron-ration of the Liturgy.

Gibberd (as was the case with Spence at Coventry) is making use of the talents of distinguished modern artists. John Piper and Patrick Reyntiens are to fill the spaces between the ribs in the cylindrical tower with coloured glass. The cone of the lantern will form three bursts of light, symbolizing the Trinity, set against a background of the colour progression of the spectrum. David Atkins has designed the nave floor with white and grey marble as the foundation, with black and dark grey marble for the intricate motifs. The massive ninety-feet high entrance porch (echoing Marcel Breuer's bell-tower shields of the Benedictine Abbey at Collegeville, Minnesota) and the sliding doors will bear designs of William Mitchell, symbolizing respectively the three crosses and crowns and the four evangelists. These are wholly appropriate for a cathedral dedicated to Christ the King.[8]

In each of the traditional neo-Gothic cathedrals the ideal of liturgical primacy and dignity predominates over the concept of a diocesan family home for the people of God. The very monumentality of the design prefers ultimacy to intimacy. Moreover, a distant altar, as in the cases of Westminster Cathedral and the Anglican cathedrals of Liverpool and Coventry, encourages a passive, not a participating type of worship, and this is contrary to the trend of the modern liturgical movement which stresses a

---

[8] Most of the information in the three previous paragraphs is contained in a kind letter from the architect (December 30, 1963), to whom I was recommended by the courtesy of the Most Reverend John C. Heenan, now Archbishop of Westminster. See Fig. 8.

"domestic" rather than a "theatrical" kind of worship, though discouraging any over-familiarity with God.

Liverpool Anglican Cathedral was built from the designs of Sir Giles Gilbert Scott, the grandson of the eminent nineteenth century Gothic revivalist and restorer, and is one of the most splendid edifices of that nostalgic mode. St. James' Mount, with its commanding view of the mouth of the Mersey and the great ocean-going liners, was the site chosen for the building which began to arise in 1904, and which was unfinished at the architect's death in 1960. Other new cathedrals, such as Sheffield or Blackburn, began their life as adaptations of existing parish churches, with the advantage of possessing vigorous congregations. Liverpool Cathedral, on the other hand, forfeited the advantage of a ready-made congregation for the benefit of an elevated site. It seems that the twenty-two-year-old architect planned on too grand a scale for the financial means of the diocese, though he could hardly have foreseen the disruption created by two World Wars.[9]

Its dimensions fully warrant the literal use of the much-abused epithet "colossal." When completed, it will be the second largest cathedral in Christendom, exceeded only by St. Peter's in Rome. Its great eastern arm (liturgically, not geographically considered) is 138 feet long; its spacious central area at the crossing, which runs the entire width of the building, is 200 feet long, is surmounted by a tower 308 feet high, and constitutes a vast preaching space which can accommodate a mighty throng whose vision is uninterrupted by piers. The aisled nave of three huge bays will terminate in a western narthex. The total length of the completed cathedral, excluding buttresses, but including nave, central preaching space, choir and Lady Chapel, will be 560 feet.[10]

The exterior massing suggests a mighty ship or fortress of the Spirit, while the interior is reminiscent of immemorial cliffs against which the tides of time will batter in vain. No fussy or redundant detail distracts the attention. Such decoration as there is is the more impressive for its restraint, and leaves the walls to speak for

[9] George Pace (*Anglican World*, Vol. I, No. 6, 1961) writes that each new stone added to Liverpool costs twelve times what it did when the building was started, and that Guildford Cathedral was expected to cost £250,000 when the designs were approved, had cost £540,000 at the date of the article and another £200,000 was still needed. Sir Edward Maufe had "nursed his scheme through five episcopates" (p. 23). See Fig. 1.

[10] Information about dimensions from G. H. Cook, *The English Cathedrals through the Centuries*, pp. 337-40.

themselves.[11] The piers of the choir are intricately moulded; there is a traceried parapet atop the central space and immediately below the central tower; there is arcading in the vast bays; but all serve to stress the massive simplicity of the warm stone cliffs of the walls and to accent the symmetry. The reredos, carved in the most discriminating detail, the font with its delicate and soaring cover, the subtle organ case, and the aspiring lines of the Lady Chapel with apse, recall the inspiration of French and Spanish, as well as English Gothic masterpieces. The windows of the cathedral are large and simple, with the exception of the east window with its four lights, huge central mullion, and flowing tracery. Of particular interest is the recently installed Scholars' window, commemorating the scholarship of distinguished Anglican divines, among them the chief author of The Book of Common Prayer, Archbishop Cranmer, and the apologists, Hooker and F. D. Maurice.

Liverpool's notable Consecration Service (of 1924) was based on the sermon of St. Bernard, "On the Consecration of a Church," and was the work of Dean Dwelly, who also designed the unusual and appropriate vestments and robes of clergy and choir.[12]

Another great edifice built in the archaeological manner was Westminster Roman Catholic Cathedral, commissioned by Cardinal Vaughan and designed by Bentley in the Byzantine style, it may be assumed, so as not to compete with the former Benedictine Abbey, Westminster Abbey, its near Gothic neighbour. Its vast brick exterior, with striped campanile tower, discloses the shapes of a huge nave and sanctuary covered with four shallow domes. The interior is, however, far more appealing. The vault of the nave rises to 109 feet (exactly four feet higher than Westminster Abbey vault), and the arches of the nave are 90 feet high. The aisles are sacrificed to the demands of several heavy side chapels. The interior columns of *verde antico* from the Thessalian quarries of Larissa lead the eye towards the central dome, under which is glimpsed first the huge pendent crucifix and beyond it the impressive high altar beneath a *baldachino*, with eight columns of onyx bearing a marble canopy. In the sanctuary the jewelled effect is maintained by the columns of red jasper granite and pavonazza, although the

11 George Pace, *ibid.*, p. 27, refers to "the juxtaposition of starkness with small intricate areas of detail."

12 See E. H. Short, *The House of God*, p. 289. At the invitation of Dr. F. W. Dillistone (then the Dean of Liverpool), the present writer visited the cathedral in 1960 and perused a copy of Dwelly's superb Consecration Order, a model of its kind.

mosaic work on the central cupola seems timid and uninspired compared with the simple mosaics of San Apollinare in Classe or the more splendid and rich mosaics of Ravenna's San Vitale basilica. In justice it should be said, however, that much more decoration remains to be done.[13]

In this cathedral that evokes memories of Roman Baroque and much earlier basilical models, the English simplicity of Eric Gill's Stations of the Cross carved in limestone low relief strikes a welcome, if incongruous note.[14] Particularly impressive are the first station with its contrast of the bound hands of Jesus and Pilate's hands free only to wash them of concern, the fifth depicting Jesus and Veronica, the seventh contrasting the vigour of the stalwart centurion with the bent back and head of Jesus as He falls a second time, and the thirteenth where the sagging body of Christ is taken down from the cross, while Mary, with folded hands and furrowed cheek, watches. The unsentimental but deeply felt clarity of technique, the variety of the postures, the different angles from which the cross is shown, the changing of the border design for each station, and the hieratic stylization of the whole, not forgetting the fine lettering, is cumulatively most impressive. Perhaps the most haunting single work of religious art in the cathedral is a black metal wall plaque in bas relief depicting a plain nun, with an appealing angularity of design that conveys the meaning of sacrifice more impressively than the rest of the basilica. Spiritually and aesthetically considered, she might well have been one of the sisters commemorated in Hopkins' unforgettable "Wreck of the Deutschland."

The second Anglican cathedral to be built in the present century was Guildford in Surrey, the foundation stone of which was laid in 1936, four years after Edward Brantwood Maufe had won the competition for the best design. Among his earlier experiments in church architecture were St. Saviour's, Acton, and St. Thomas the Apostle, Hanwell. It is possible that the able but unheralded architect, Temple Moore, may have influenced the work of both Sir Giles Gilbert Scott and Sir Edward Maufe, for Scott was apprenticed to Bodley and Moore, and the latter's Middlesborough Church of St. Cuthbert and St. Columba was outstanding in its use of brickwork. Other probable influences on Maufe were the new

[13] Most of the information in the above paragraph was obtained from E. H. Short, *op.cit.*, p. 280, supplemented by a visit in July 1963. See Fig. 2.
[14] This work was commissioned in 1914, a year after Gill had been received into the Roman Catholic Church, and was completed in 1918.

churches in Scandinavia and Germany built in the twenties and thirties.[15]

The site of the new Cathedral of the Holy Spirit, which was consecrated in 1961, was Stag Hill, which offers a commanding view of the neighborhood. The cathedral is a simple modern derivative of the Gothic tradition, but the interpretation is severe and restrained, and the effect is much lighter than in Liverpool. Maufe is well aware that he can be charged with traditionalism, in which he glories, but he stoutly maintains that this is not antiquarianism. The latter, he asserts, "is merely a modern feeling [for] it is traditional to be modern; that is to say our forebears built as well as they knew how to suit their own conditions and did not attempt to copy the past—in fact they thought they could build better than the past. They were the modernists of their day."[16] Maufe further claims that the modernism of today is seen in the use of modern materials, and in new methods of construction which are able to provide larger spans and to reduce fire hazards. While recognizing the importance of functionalism, Sir Edward insists that the religious mind "seeks the infinite—the in-finite. Churches must not strike the eye with finality; we should not see everything at once—there should be a certain mystery—there should be spaces in which the imagination can play."[17] Furthermore, he warns that there is a danger that the artists employed to embellish a cathedral or church will almost certainly be specialists and individualists, unused to subordinating their personalities to produce a co-ordinated effect. Therefore there is a need for an architect of "sympathetic and benevolent mind" to direct a team of artists and craftsmen and to maintain the organic unity of the whole. These precepts seem to have been practised first at Guildford before the architect recommended them to others.

The cathedral, of cruciform shape, is 365 feet long, with a great central tower which rises, at the crossing, to a height of 175 feet. It has an eastern choir-arm which is enaisled; its extension is the Lady chapel. The unaisled transepts are shallow. The wide nave has seven bays, with narrow aisles at each side which lead to a narthex at the west end with north and south porches. A forecourt or garth is being added on each side of the western end of the cathedral. The garth is also to be enclosed by an arcaded cov-

---

[15] See George Pace's article, "Modern Power Houses of Faith," in *Anglican World*, Vol. I, No. 6 (1961), p. 27. See Fig. 3.

[16] Sir Edward Maufe's *Modern Church Architecture*, p. 4.

[17] *Ibid.*, p. 6.

ered way leading to the porch. The five-sided apse of the Lady chapel is raised above a crypt chapel.

In comparison with Liverpool Anglican Cathedral, where the worshipper is lost in the vastness, there is a feeling of sublimity and also of intimacy, the latter probably because the congregation is close to the choir, and the shallow transepts at Guildford contrast with the dwarfing central space at Liverpool. In comparison with Coventry, where individual artistic brilliance (as in the green and gold tapestry and in the coruscating Baptistery window) detracts from the organic unity, the art in Guildford is almost mediaeval in its near anonymity. It is significant that the uncoloured and incised glass of John Hutton is equally effective in both Coventry and Guildford, although the treatment of the angels in the former is freer and in the latter tightly formal. In short, if the danger of Coventry is that of becoming a brilliant showcase of modern religious art, and the danger of Liverpool is that it may reduce man to the measure of an ant, the wonder of Guildford is that it combines a sense of God's majesty with a feeling of the intimacy of His people. Of the three modern Anglican cathedrals Guildford seems most conducive to *common prayer*.

3. *Coventry: Deo Adjuvante Resurgo*[18]

There is no question, however, but that Coventry is the most exciting modern English cathedral to visit. This is attested by the constant flood (even deluge) of week-end visitors, both eager pilgrims and informed aesthetes, and perhaps some looking for a *new* curiosity shop. Many problems and their attempted architectural solutions combine to stimulate and hold the interest.

What kind of cathedral is appropriate for a rebuilt mediaeval city which has become the roaring workshop of the modern automobile industry, and from which cars and buses emerge to cross the English Channel and the Atlantic Ocean? How are the gaunt ruins of the old cathedral to be related to the new one? For the former has a superb mediaeval tower and spire still standing, a gutted nave with sightless windows, and a charred cross with the legend "Father, Forgive," as poignant reminders of Coventry's ordeal by fire in the Second World War, and of that greater agony of Christ's. How are the old essential symbols of the Christian faith and life to be repristinated by the architect and his team of out-

[18] The arms of the new Coventry Cathedral bear this Latin legend, which may be translated, "With God's help I rise again."

standingly brilliant artists, such as Epstein, Sutherland, Piper, and Hutton, so as to be relevant without being idiosyncratic? How can one great edifice express the purpose of the Church in the modern world, giving due place to the liturgical and evangelistic, the ecumenical and diocesan tasks? Can the right combination of tradition and experiment be found? Above all, how can these theological affirmations be made in an age in which they are no longer organic to the culture? It is questions such as these which raise the highest expectations of the visitor or pilgrim on the way to Coventry.[19]

The year after the ending of the Second World War the Cathedral Council of Coventry appointed a reconstruction committee charged with the duty of rebuilding the cathedral. They authorized the holding of a competition open to all the architects of Britain and the Commonwealth, which the three assessors appointed by the President of the Royal Institute of British Architects (including Sir Edward Maufe) declared in 1951 to have been won by the designs submitted by Mr. (later Sir) Basil Spence of Edinburgh and London. Their report stated: "In selecting this design we do not only feel that it is the best design submitted, but that it is one which shows that the author has qualities of spirit and imagination of the highest order. He lets the conditions grow under his hand to produce a splendid cathedral, and as the conditions are unusual, the resulting conception is unusual, revealing the author's ability to solve the problem of designing a cathedral in terms of contemporary architecture."[20] The new cathedral was completed in 1962.

Spence has made the ruins of the old cathedral an imposing forecourt to the new, which is at right-angles to it,[21] and has used the module of the old Church of St. Michael in the new. Links between the old and the new are forged by the use of the same pink-grey sandstone colouring in the new walls, as by the slender

[19] See the partly perceptive, partly ingenuous, and wholly enthusiastic book written by Coventry's architect on his cathedral, Sir Basil Spence's *A Phoenix at Coventry*. See also Figs. 4-7.

[20] Citation from the brochure *The New Coventry Cathedral* (Coventry, edn. of September 1959, p. 5), from which, together with Basil Spence, *op.cit.*, much of the ensuing factual information is derived. Several "angry young" architects were displeased that a more modern design (reproduced in Peter Hammond's *Liturgy and Architecture*) offered in the competition was not accepted, although the assessors recommended it in high terms.

[21] As the architect has planned the main axis of the new cathedral in a north-south direction, the high altar is geographically at the north end of the cathedral. All subsequent references to the new Coventry Cathedral will, therefore, be liturgical (not compass) directions.

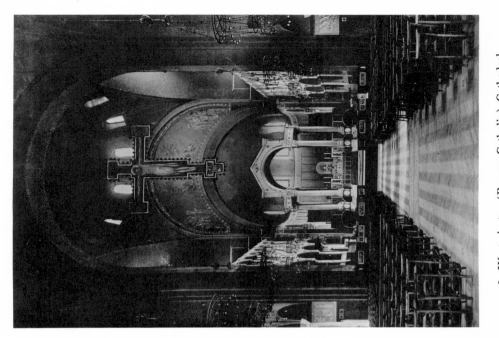

2. Westminster (Roman Catholic) Cathedral

1. Liverpool (Anglican) Cathedral: the Crossing

3. Guildford (Anglican) Cathedral: the Chancel

4. Coventry (Anglican) Cathedral: the Nave

6. Coventry Cathedral: Chapel of Christ the Servant

5. Coventry Cathedral: Roof of Chapel of Unity

8. Liverpool (Roman Catholic) Cathedral: the Model

7. Coventry Cathedral
John Piper's Baptistry Window

10. Great Chapel of the House of the Sacred Mission, Kelham

9. Ibadan (Anglican) Cathedral, Nigeria: the Model

12. St. George's, Letchworth

11. St. Mary, Wellingborough
Comper's Blending of Gothic and Classic

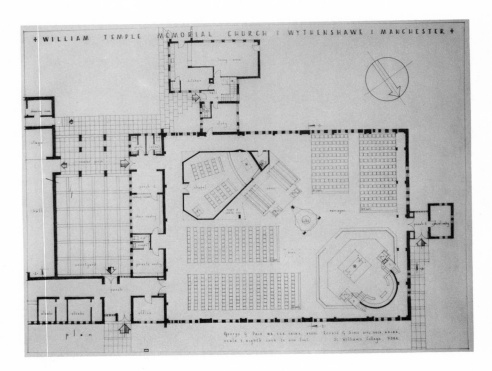

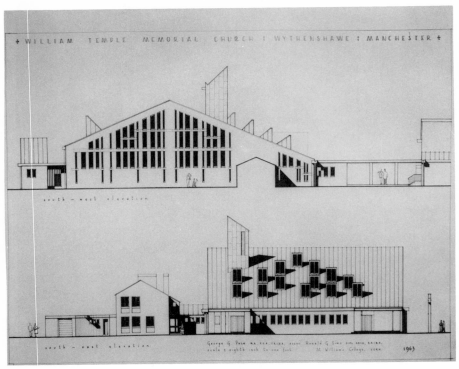

13. William Temple Memorial Church, Wythenshawe: Plan

14. William Temple Church: SW and SE elevations

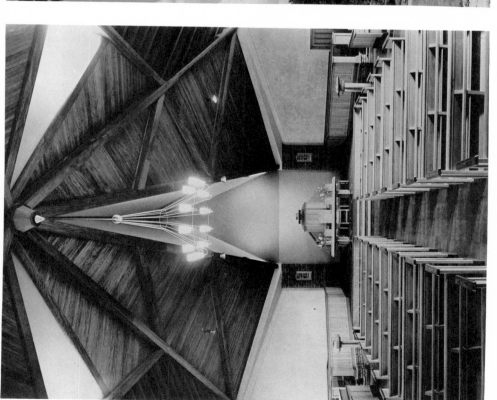

16. Punshon Memorial Methodist Church, Bournemouth

15. Trinity Presbyterian Church, Norwich

17. Guildford Congregational Church

18. Christ Church and Upton (Baptist and Congregational), S.E. London

21. Henry Moore: Madonna and Child, Northampton

19. John Hutton: Madonna and Child (Coventry Cathedral)

20. Jacob Epstein: Madonna and Child, London

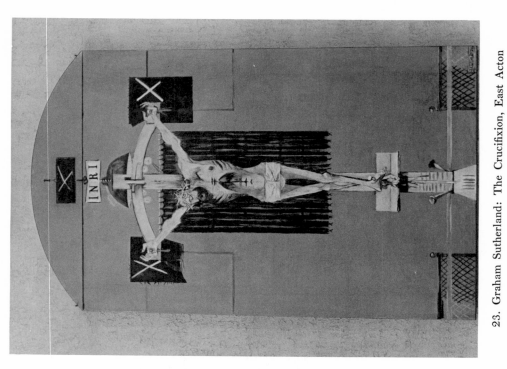

23. Graham Sutherland: The Crucifixion, East Acton

22. Graham Sutherland: The Crucifixion, Northampton

24. Stanley Spencer: Crucifixion, Aldenham School

25. Jacob Epstein: St. Michael and the Devil, Coventry Cathedral

26. Jacob Epstein: The Ascending Christ, Maquette

28. Dean Inge

27. "Woodbine Willie" (Studdert Kennedy)

29. Bishop H. Hensley Henson

30. Archbishop William Temple

31. Father Gabriel Hebert, S.S.M.

32. Dr. Leslie D. Weatherhead

flèche atop the crossing of the new cathedral, recalling in miniature the mightier thrust of the old spire above its tower, which
reaches to 295 feet. A colossal arch leading to the porch joins the
new and old cathedrals.

Apart from the internal arrangement of the nave and aisles with
the high altar at the liturgical east end, the break with traditional
cathedral building is complete.

The vast nave, 270 feet long, has walls planned in zigzag
fashion, so that in each angle of the zigzag there is one wall which
is a solid cliff of masonry, while the other is a mullioned and
transomed window of multi-coloured lights rising from base to roof
height. All the dappled light from these windows is directed
towards the high altar. Thus the visitor entering the doors of the
great western window-wall, on which John Hutton has engraved
thirty-five angels and thirty-one saints,[22] is confronted with an
uninterrupted vista of the high altar, and beyond and above it the
green and gold tapestry of Graham Sutherland's design representing Jesus Christ the Redeemer in the Glory of the Father. The
Aubusson tapestry covers the entire east wall of the cathedral and
dominates, if it does not overdominate, the altar. The ceiling is a
huge wooden prismatic canopy, supported by two columns of seven
slender pillars each, which are star-shaped in section and which
taper towards the base. The floor of the nave is of black and white
marble with insets of maple leaf motifs to commemorate Canadian
generosity.

Other powerful centres of focus are the massively solid "Crusader's Tent" which is entered from the north-western corner of
the nave and serves as a chapel of Christian unity. Directly opposite it, in the south-western corner, is the resplendent Baptistery
window, designed by John Piper. The south-eastern corner of the
nave (immediately adjacent to the south wall of the Lady chapel)
has a small chapel for private meditation, named the Chapel of
Christ in Gethsemane, affording a glimpse, through a striking
metal frame of a crown of thorns, of a gilded mosaic mural of an
angel holding a bejewelled chalice. Then, passing this on the left
hand, the visitor approaches the steps to the cylindrical Chapel of
Christ the Servant, the centre for the cathedral's work for industry.
On its black marble floor there is a wide disc or plinth of white

[22] Particularly impressive are the designs for the Madonna and Child, the long-
necked Abbess Hilda of Whitby, and an angel practically bursting his cheeks in
blowing the trumpet of praise, like an ethereal version of Louis Armstrong. See
Fig. 19.

marble, on which rests the *mensa* or table-altar which is supported by four conic shapes. The plinth is inscribed in large golden letters, "I am among you as one that serves." Above the table is a long pendent white cross to which is attached a rough metallic sculpture of hammer, spikes, and nails, which simultaneously suggests the crown of thorns, the nail-making guild for which ancient Coventry was famous, and modern industrialism. The plain windows of the chapel, with the light streaming out from within, is inviting by day and reassuring as a lighthouse by night.

The most striking characteristic of the building has yet to be mentioned. This is the approach along the accordion-shaped nave from west to east, so arranged that the worshipper sitting in the congregation or the visitor walking towards the altar will see no window, unless he turns or looks back, for every window is masked by the portion of the wall behind it. The ten large nave windows, which have been designed by Lawrence Lee, with the help of Geoffrey Clarke and Keith New, and executed by a team of artists and students at the Royal College of Art, are planned on the basis of colour-symbolism representative of the successive stages in life. According to the architect's interpretation, a rather subjective one in this case, the first pair of windows composed in tones of green and yellow symbolizes youth; the next pair, in pink and red, represents adolescence and the age of passion; the next pair, multi-coloured, represents the age of experience; then the next pair, in deep blue and purple, represents the age of wisdom; and the final pair, nearest to the altar, is of golden hues. In Spence's words: "As in life, the colour of the windows is revealed only as you reach each stage—the past is known, the future is not. Only when the altar is reached the whole range of colour is seen for the first time."[23] The plan of the fenestration is thus extremely ingenious, if somewhat contrived, and it results in the walls and the floor of the nave being stencilled and dappled with a myriad dyes, varying with the position of the sun and the intensity of its rays. In the ultra-modern nave there are, stylistically considered, two incongruously primitive or "Stonehenge" features. One is the roughly scooped-out Bethlehem boulder-basin which serves as a font at the foot of the shimmering Baptistery window, and the other is the series of stone tablets, with New Testament inscriptions, attached to the walls of the nave.

[23] Citation from the brochure, *The New Coventry Cathedral*, p. 18. For fuller description see Basil Spence, *A Phoenix at Coventry*, p. 119.

Coventry is the most truly modern, and therefore the most controversial cathedral to have been completed in England in the twentieth century. It is on the whole a striking rebuttal of the charge that English religious architecture is excessively tame and traditional. In this great centre of worship and art, there are powerful reminders of the ecumenical, sociological, and missionary concerns of the present Church of Christ in a modern industrial milieu. It links the centuries in Coventry with the Christ of the ages and of the contemporary world. It has encouraged the distinctive gifts of England's major artists, with the notable exception of Henry Moore. The daring ambition of the architect, as it has brought considerable achievements, was also almost bound to produce a few failures.

There seem to be four weaknesses. The first is in the structural dichotomy, by which there is no suggestion that the inner structure (of the prismatic ceiling supported by seven slender pairs of concrete piers) is related to the outer (the pair of ten massive wall panels of local masonry). As a distinguished American architectural historian (himself an Episcopalian) has written, in a predominantly appreciative review of the building, "unquestionably there should be a visible separation and statement here."[24]

A liturgical critic could rightly draw attention to the over-attenuation of the nave and to the lack of a more centrally positioned high altar, in keeping with the sense of God's people renewed about His board. Incidentally this possibility was seriously considered by Sir Basil and the former Bishop of Coventry, and rejected.[25] As it is, there is now a "theatrical" altar for spectators rather than sharers in the Eucharist.

A third criticism might justifiably question whether the brilliant individualism of certain artists had been sufficiently subordinated to the unity of the cathedral. To be specific: do not the brilliance and size of Piper's Baptistery window and Sutherland's tapestry dominate the attention and thus distract it from the organic unity of the whole edifice? And, in this way, are not ancillary emphases (respectively the reredos and the sacrament of initiation) through their aesthetic brilliance overshadowing the primary emphases of the altar and the pulpit, where the Eucharist is celebrated and the Word preached? Or, to put the question in another way: have the

[24] G. E. Kidder Smith, *The New Architecture of Europe*, p. 66.
[25] *A Phoenix at Coventry*, pp. 41-44.

needs of the regular worshippers been sacrificed by the desire to dazzle fascinated pilgrims?

A fourth criticism is that while the Chapel of Christ the Servant seems admirably adapted to its purpose of welcoming the outsider by its illuminated invitation, yet the Chapel of Unity, original as its design undoubtedly is, by its forbidding fortress-like exterior seems to frustrate the ecumenical purpose for which it exists. The strong and even menacing treatment seems ill-fitted to represent a crusader's tent, for such surely was essentially transitory and mobile in character. A possible rebuttal of this criticism would be that the various branches of Christ's Church are being pushed together by the pressures of an increasingly secular world and that ecumenism is best symbolized by such a fortress. In that case, it is still relevant to ask why the rest of the cathedral, with its emphasis on triumph and glory, is so optimistic a portrayal of the role of the Church in the world.

In justice to the architect, however, it must be recognized that it is his generosity which has not only allowed but encouraged distinguished individual artists to compete for attention in the cathedral, and that this may well be inevitable in the twentieth century where the artist is not a part of a guild, as his mediaeval counterpart was.[26]

The place of the traditional cathedral reredos and east window is in Coventry filled by the largest tapestry in the world, 74 feet 8 inches high and 38 feet wide. It was designed by Graham Sutherland and woven at Aubusson by the firm of Pinto Frères under the artistic direction of Mme. Marie Cutolli.[27] Sutherland was asked to design a Christ in Glory and to select his colours to fit in with the general decorative scheme. (It may be recalled that the nave windows nearest to the high altar are of a golden colour, and the tapestry is chiefly in pale gold and variegated greens.) The choice of Sutherland was particularly fitting, for besides being the most eminent modern painter in England, he is a devout Roman Catholic deeply moved by the mysteries of the Christian faith, as

[26] The warning of Sir Edward Maufe may be recalled: "One wishes that the best artists and craftsmen of our day were employed quite simply and naturally in our churches and not brought in as specialists." He continues (referring to the painter): "He has for so long thought that the aim is to compete with others in galleries that he is losing his power to relate his work to the rest of the building" (*Modern Church Architecture*, p. 7). The problem in Coventry was not cooperation, but *size*; Piper and Sutherland worked with the architects' colour-scheme.

[27] Coventry Cathedral has an international quality, both in the sources of its support (the West German government paid for the windows of the Chapel of Unity and Canadians for the organ) and in its artistic contributions: French weaving, some Swedish glass and mosaic, and the "Tablets of the Word" inscribed by Ralph Beyer of distinguished German parentage.

his poignant and stark Crucifixion at St. Matthew's (Anglican) Church in Northampton (Fig. 22) had already shown.

The tapestry, in fact, contains two designs, ingeniously separated and yet related. The upper design, occupying approximately four-fifths of the space, is technically described as "The Christ in Glory in the Tetramorph." The last term refers to the four panels, symbolizing the writers of the four gospels, which are laterally related to the central ovoid panel representing the glorified Redeemer. This part (the upper) is clearly visible to the congregation in the nave, since the lower panel is obscured at least in part by the high altar. The lower panel is a most moving representation of the Crucifixion, exhibiting a pallid, emaciated, and tortured Christ, and it becomes the vivid "reredos" of the Lady Chapel "space."[28] Its blacks and greys strike the right sombre notes for the Christ who passed to His glory through the anguish and desolation of the Cross. It also bears, in a smaller tetramorph, the four casual chalk-marked crosses (or kisses) which make it an expression of contemporaneous love and sacrifice, and which were seen in Sutherland's Northampton Crucifixion painting.[29] This crucified Christ also evokes memories of Grünewald's Eisenheim Christus, of the victims of Belsen, Buchenwald and Auschwitz, and of the preoccupation of the painter with thorns and their effects.

The Christ in Glory represents the vision of a serenely young and compassionate Christ, with both hands raised in blessing. Yet the nail-prints are shown in his feet, between which stands typical man, erect, in that position to which he was raised by Christ after the Fall. Christ's simple white, monk-like garment, swells out in egg-like shape, accented by yellow tints on the white from waist to knees, suggesting that He is the re-creative principle.[30] Beside the central ovoid panel are the four excited witnesses to the Gospel of the crucified and exalted Christ, and their iconography owes much to the Book of Revelation 4:6-8.[31] The theme of redemption is

---

[28] The term "space" is used to designate the fact that no wall divides the 48 feet separating the high altar from the Sutherland tapestry, and that the Lady Chapel is merely the area of the nave behind the high altar terminated by the Crucifixion panel.

[29] For fuller explanation see Sutherland's article, "Thoughts on Painting," in *The Listener* (issue of September 6, 1952, pp. 376-78) and *The Work of Graham Sutherland*, text by Douglas Cooper, p. 34. See Figs. 22 and 23.

[30] Here the iconography is overweighted. Cooper indicates the subtlety of Sutherland's imagination by citing a letter to him in which the painter states: ". . . I wanted to do a large figure like a Buddha or one of the Egyptian figures in the Valley of Kings" (*ibid.*, p. 36). There are also evocations of Byzantine images and a reflection of early Patristic interpretations of the cosmic regenerative role of the Logos. Not all symbols are, however, compossible, without some confusion.

[31] ". . . and round about the throne were four beasts full of eyes before and

repeated in the small chalice below the feet of the Christ, in which the serpent of evil writhes as it drowns. The symmetry of the oval rectangle and the four rectangles containing the evangelical "beasts" is subtly broken by the figure of St. Michael, the patron saint of Coventry Cathedral. Above the mandorla behind the head of Christ is an effulgence of rays, and right at the very top of the tapestry the dove, symbol of the Holy Spirit, is shown in a small blue triangle, evoking the Holy Trinity. The Glory of the Father in which the exalted Christ lives is suggested by the vigorous rays which develop into an intense bar of light, and by the pale yellow or gold lines that define and link the central oval and the side rectangular panels. The background of the tapestry is green, predominantly a cypress shade but merging into the hue of the first shoots of fern in springtime. The space between the Christ and the oval outline is coloured in greys that vary from pale to gunmetal shades. The background of the beasts in their rectangular boxes varies from sepia to lavender blue. There are significant splashes of blood-red in the upper parts of the panels of the four evangelists, which spill over into the green outside them and provide a link with the theme of the underpart of the tapestry. The variegated colours, however, make verbal description more than usually inadequate, and they are equalled only by the complex richness of the symbolism.

The second great work of art in the cathedral is, of course, the immense, glowing, jewelled wonder of John Piper's Baptistery window.[32] The colour is so daring, and so interpenetrating and merging are the variegated hues, that it defies anything but the baldest description in words. Moreover, since the work is entirely abstract, it defies exact interpretation, while at the same time provoking the most intensely subjective reactions from its beholders. It is made up of 198 lights spaced between the carved mullions. It is flanked by crimson hues, but the eye is first caught by the central circle of pure white light, ringed with gold, which

behind. And the first beast was like a lion, and the second beast like a calf, and the third beast had a face as a man, and the fourth beast was like a flying eagle. And the four beasts had each of them six wings about him: and they were full of eyes within: and they rest not day and night, saying, Holy, holy, holy, Lord God Almighty, which was, and is, and is to come." We may note that Sutherland's is one of the few interpretations of the "beasts" to give them the multiplicity of eyes which the text demands.

[32] The coincidence may be noted that Sutherland and Piper were both born in 1903 and both educated at Epsom College. Thereafter their paths diverged: Sutherland studying art at Goldsmith's College, London University, and Piper at the Royal College of Art in London. Sutherland is a Roman Catholic and Piper an Anglican.

leads above into bands of a dark sepia that merge into an irregular rectangle of the bewitching butterfly-winged blue, deepening into purple at its edges, in turn leading to the crimson of the border. Here and there the lights are flecked with brilliant gold. Below, the white circle ringed with gold merges into fresh bracken green, then into a light sepia, and reaches the base in aquamarine tints.[33] There, on an octagonal plinth of black marble, rests the hollowed out primaeval bowl (or font) of Baptism.

For some, the central white circle edged with gold will resemble a pool, fitting symbol of the cleansing of Baptism, and the impact of Christ in life's fever will seem as exhilarating and freshening as a plunge in a Cumberland lake. Others, like the poet Traherne, may interpret the white circle as a symbol of the perfection of eternity and the high blue as a celestial symbol, representing the eternal dimension of Christian living. Yet others, again, will link the blue and white as the virginal colours of chastity and perfection. And some, like the architect, will refer to the earthy colours in the lower half of the panel and the celestial or spiritual colours in the upper half. The sheer brilliance of the window is open to almost any Christian or associational interpretation on the part of the delighted viewer.

The third great work of art appears on the outside of the cathedral. It is the late Sir Jacob Epstein's impressive sculpture of St. Michael and the Devil, his last completed religious work. This bronze group weighs four tons. The figure of St. Michael is 19 feet 6 inches high and the span of his wings extends to 23 feet. In the dedication service, Dr. C. K. N. Bardsley, the Bishop of Coventry, said of the representation of the Devil: "Here is no stupid melodramatic portrayal of an unreal entity—here is a man—fallen man —man as we see him today—man who has missed his mark, man who has cast himself out of heaven." The Bishop went on to describe Epstein (Sir Jacob had died in 1959, the year before the unveiling) as "a very great artist, a man much misunderstood, a giant who had to face the jibes and jeers of the little men."[34]

This bronze group is, indeed, a strong image of the struggle between good and evil. It may perhaps be interpreted more specifically as the struggle between the "athlete" of the Spirit, ever

[33] The glass was made by Patrick Reyntiens, who interpreted Piper's design with sympathetic subtlety. See Fig. 7.

[34] The sculpture was unveiled by Lady Kathleen Epstein, the sculptor's widow, who said: "I am so glad that it is on an outside wall, where the people can see it as they go to their work." The citations from the speeches at the unveiling are taken from the report of *The Times* (of London), issue of January 25, 1960.

vigilant to do the Divine bidding, and the heavy, paunchy, grovel-ling indulgence of the Devil who once was enormously strong. It bears many of the distinctive qualities of Epstein's major religious works. There is the superb moulding of hands and feet, as of the knotty torso muscles of the lithe St. Michael, with his intense and pointed face. There are also the brilliant feathering of the wings; the subtle wind-blown drapery, emphasizing the bone structure of the ascetical spirit; even the spear, with its triangular tip in Michael's right hand, stressing determination, as does his clenched left hand, calling attention to the spire of the old cathedral.

The chief force of the group derives from a major contrast and a minor correlation. The major contrast is between the vertical *up-thrust* of the angel, with pillar-like body and upright spear, all austerity and aspiration and freedom—as the extended arms and feet indicate—with the cramped horizontal *down-drag* of the proud and sensual Devil with heavy thighs and paunch, barrel-chest, arrogant bull-like head, who is writhing though bound, still pro-testing with jutting chin and the splayed fingers of the hands twisted behind his back. This embodiment of the double paradox of the freedom of God's servant and the enslavement of the libertine is admirable. Though the figures are separate (presumably for eternity, since there is here no hint of ultimate reconciliation),[35] they are linked, not only as victor and vanquished, but by the correspondence of the anklets of St. Michael and the chains cramp-ing the Devil's feet. It is an exceedingly powerful statement of a significant myth. Even so, it is not perhaps in the very top rank of Epstein's religious works, as are the *Madonna and Child* in Cavendish Square, or the *Christ in Majesty* of Llandaff cathedral.

While Coventry Cathedral is not as convincing an expression of the twentieth century understanding of the nature of the mystery of God as the pioneer pilgrimage chapel of Ronchamps by Le Corbusier, yet the edifice (and the works of art of which it is the brilliant casket) represents an exciting and distinguished achieve-ment and a portent for the future of English Church architecture and art. It comes not very far short of fulfilling the final petition of "A Prayer for the New Cathedral" that "in the end there may come forth from Thee the building of Thine own good pleasure, which may speak to us and to generations to come of Thy majesty and

---

[35] Had the faces of the devil and the angel borne any resemblance at all, it would have been natural to interpret this powerful group as a symbolic statement of man's inner civil war, the dichotomy that rages within. See Fig. 25.

love in Jesus Christ our Lord."[36] The difficulty for modern man is how to find in threatening and torturing times any immediate relevance in Byzantine-style mosaics and glories, or in mythological angels, or, indeed, in the blazing beauty of the Baptistery window, or in the green and gold of the tapestry (except at its sombre base, largely hidden from the congregation).[37] The stark grey and black Sutherland Crucifixion panel, the overpowering whirl of that high dungeon (the Chapel of Unity), the struggle in the Epstein sculpture, and the vast poignancy of the burned-out old cathedral—these alone speak to many of Christ as our contemporary and of the agony of a despised and rejected Church, and of a bewildered populace, and of what may prove to be the redemptive pain of the present in God's own inscrutable designs. Coventry Cathedral is ingenious, exciting, novel: it is only rarely disturbing. Its serenity and optimism may seem to have been too easily purchased in our day. Yet, and this is its chief importance, it marks the beginning of a technical, if not iconographical, break with the recent past, so dominated by Gothic nostalgia and, therefore, by escapism. It is an important, if only partly successful, experiment, but a welcome portent.

4. Other Churches[38]

Even though domination by neo-Gothic continued to enthrall

[36] *The New Coventry Cathedral* (brochure, edn. of November 1958), p. 28.

[37] See, for example, the strictures of A. C. Bridge on the irrelevance of angels in this century in *Images of God*, p. 28, and of Ian Nairn, the architectural correspondent, in *The Daily Telegraph*, issue of May 18, 1962. The latter writes of Coventry Cathedral and its architect: "Sir Basil is an ebullient optimist designing in what is, in religious terms, a deeply pessimistic century. More than that, he had for Coventry a deeply sombre theme—Christ of the Passions and Sorrows, the hard way of persecution and atonement." Nairn does, however, praise the Chapel of Unity (which he thought would make a better Baptistery) as "a haunting, disorienting room worth matching with the great architectural discordances."

[38] In this section of the chapter it would be impractical, as it is unnecessary, to describe the different styles employed by several denominations for their church architecture in the three periods of the present century as divided by two World Wars. Hence a summary sketch is provided which can be supplemented from the following sources: A. L. Drummond, *The Church Architecture of Protestantism*; Martin S. Briggs, *Puritan Architecture and its Future*; Edwin Maufe, *Modern Church Architecture*; Edward D. Mills, *The Modern Church; Sixty Post-war Churches* (Incorporated Church Building Society, London, 1957); John Betjeman, *Collins Guide to English Parish Churches*, with its admirable introductory historical essay and its accounts of judicious restorations; Peter Hammond, *Liturgy and Architecture* and the same author's *Towards a Church Architecture*; and the general architectural history, Henry Russell Hitchcock, *Architecture—Nineteenth and Twentieth Centuries*. The following periodicals should also be consulted: *Architectural Design, Architectural Review, The Journal of the Royal Institute of British Architects*. A comprehensive interdenominational history of British church architecture in the twentieth century is greatly needed.

most church building committees and ecclesiastical architects throughout the period, there were occasional signs of dissatisfaction. Incongruous as they appeared on the English scene, Byzantine revival churches began to challenge the hold of Gothic.[39] Between the First and Second World War architects of the Free Churches in new housing areas devised the "dual-purpose" edifice, intended to serve as a sanctuary on Sunday and as a social and educational centre during the rest of the week. While often architecturally undistinguished, they represented a serious questioning of the basic functions of churches in the twentieth century, and marked a further dissolution of Gothic nostalgia.[40] Even Gothic itself began to be stream-lined, as in the impressive Baptist Church at Sutton, Surrey, locally and wryly christened "Gaumont-Gothic,"[41] probably because of its superficial resemblance to a cinema, in its functionalism and raked floor.

The first English swallow of the long-delayed summer of the Continental Liturgical Movement's impact on architecture made its appearance in Bradford, Yorkshire. Here, it was the influence of the hero of G. K. Chesterton's "Father Brown" stories—Father John O'Connor—which inspired the architect, J. H. L. Langton, to design the Church of the First Martyrs in 1935. It admirably fulfilled O'Connor's intention to create a building which would express the essential character of the liturgy as a corporate action in which celebrant and laity have their own parts to play. The plan was octagonal, the altar central, and the pulpit was placed behind

[39] Two very simple, dignified adaptations of the basilical style in Surrey, produced in the inter-war period, were the Church of the Peace of God (Congregational) in Oxted and the Ewell Congregational Church. Immanuel, Southbourne, in Hampshire, was also a simple and dignified sanctuary of the same denomination. Examples of "stream-lined Gothic" Free Churches included Purley and Leatherhead Congregational Churches, and St. Andrew's Presbyterian Church, Cheam—all in Surrey.

[40] "Dual-purpose" or "Community" churches were also built in considerable numbers by the Free Churches to replace the over 200 sanctuaries destroyed in World War II. This situation "gave the architects an opportunity to build functionally and economically and, with a great housing shortage, it was often necessary to provide significant social amenities in churches." (E. D. Mills *The Modern Church*, pp. 31ff. See also p. 27 for the author's drawings of Mitcham Methodist "Community Church" which he designed.) Some recent Anglican dual-purpose churches are discussed, with reproductions of several varied plans, in Peter Hammond, *Liturgy and Architecture*, pp. 124-28. See also L. A. Brown and L. T. Moore, *The Dual Purpose Church*. N. Cachemaille-Day, Henry Braddock, and D. F. Martin-Smith have been perhaps the most successful architects of Anglican churches of this type.

[41] Sutton Baptist Church was notable for the strong central communion-table behind which was set a semi-circle of seats for minister and deacons, for its impressive pulpit and sounding-board, and for the unfussy lines of its brick and wood.

the altar on the dominant axis of the church. The Baptistery was located on the left of the church as the congregation of the faithful entered the porch.

Eric Gill was entranced by it, writing: "The altar is right in the middle and the result is very remarkable. The sacrifice is offered not only for the people but by and in the midst of them."[42] Indeed, so impressed was Gill that he designed a Roman Catholic church for Gorleston-on-Sea, Norfolk, in 1939 to embody his conception of "Mass for the Masses." The altar was central because, in Gill's words, "it began as a table around which people sat and partook of the consecrated bread and wine. It remains that thing."[43] Unfortunately these examples were not followed for another two decades, although at the time of writing the Roman Catholic church at Wythenshawe, near Manchester, is one of several recent churches admirably adapted for the purposes of the "Dialogue Mass."[44]

The impact of the Continental Liturgical Movement on Anglican architecture was not felt in any significant way until the closing years of the sixth decade of the century. The determination of advanced theologians and architects to press for genuinely contemporary liturgical churches was marked by the foundation of the "New Churches Research Group" in 1958. It aimed at promoting the cooperation of theologians and architects in various regions to provide direction for diocesan architectural projects.[45]

The Chapel of Queen's (Anglican) Theological College, begun in 1938, interrupted by the war, and dedicated in 1947, was the first Anglican attempt—under the inspiration of its Principal, J. O. Cobham—to build a sacred edifice expressive of the new liturgical concerns. The architect, H. W. Hobbis, was persuaded to erect a church like an early Roman basilica, with rectangular nave and an apse. The impact of the liturgical movement is also evident in the

---

[42] Walter Shewring, ed., *The Letters of Eric Gill*, p. 351. See also G. K. Chesterton, *Autobiography*, pp. 322-28.

[43] See Gill's *Sacred and Secular*, p. 351. I owe this reference to Peter Hammond's authoritative volume, *Liturgy and Architecture*, and am greatly indebted in particular to the account of liturgy and architecture in the Church of England since 1945 (Chap. 7).

[44] Other interesting Roman Catholic churches were built at Pershore in England and in Glenrothes New Town in Scotland, the architects being Gillespie, Kidd, and Coia. See also new churches in Oxford and East Acton.

[45] See Robert Maguire, *Program and Idea* ("New Churches Group Papers," No. 2); also J. Gordon Davies, who has written widely on theology and architecture and is the founder and director of the Institute for Liturgy and Architecture at Birmingham University—see *Studia Liturgica* (Rotterdam), Vol. I, No. 4, December 1962, p. 265. Nor should the educational value of the influential "Parish and People" Movement, founded in 1950, be forgotten, as it helped to create a climate favourable to architectural change in the Anglican Communion.

Chapel of St. Aidan's (Anglican) Theological College in Birkenhead, where there is a central Communion-table.

Neither of these buildings, however, was the harbinger of theological and liturgical re-assessment in the Church of England. D. F. Martin-Smith, architect of John Keble Church at Mill Hill (1936), had given considerable thought to the location of the choir. Some effect of the "Parish Communion" Movement, associated originally with Fr. A. G. Hebert of Kelham, is probably to be seen in the planning of a nave wider than it is long, in which there was a central space for clergy and choir, surrounded on three sides by the congregation. The altar was, indeed, easily visible, but it was placed against the east wall. Another church in the modern mode—apart from its lack of a central altar—was the star-shaped St. Michael and All Angels, Wythenshawe (1937), designed by a notable innovator, N. F. Cachemaille-Day. It used the diagrid system of reinforced concrete construction, based on a grid of squares "tilted" into diamond shapes. The slender columns do not impede the view of the altar, to which the congregation seems close. A third modern church was the work of J. N. (later Sir Ninian) Comper. St. Philip's, Cosham (1938), is both simple and functional. It is significant that Comper, this brilliant exponent of "unity by inclusion," who so admirably designed Baroque chancels and roods for ancient Gothic churches, here planned a functional church as "a building to house an altar." The fourth century plan, so Comper believed, having a short rectangle with a free-standing altar beneath a ciborium, "is most suitable for the needs of the modern parish, with the altar in the midst of the worshippers," as contrasted with the "mediaeval plan to which we in England still adhere" which is unsuitable, "developed as it was for monastic use."[46]

The influence of the European Liturgical Movement on Anglican architecture is most clearly seen in several fairly recent buildings. All of them emphasize a dominating and easily visible altar, which seems to draw the congregation to itself as to a magnet, despite the fact that the ground-plans are of many different shapes. The basilical or Romanesque plan is employed in All Saints, Bawdesley (1955), whose architect was J. Fletcher Watson, and in St. Cuthbert's, Peterloo, County of Durham (1957), which was designed by the firm of Cordingley and McIntyre. In each case a rectangular nave leads to an apsidal sanctuary.

[46] *Of the Atmosphere of a Church*, p. 21. See Fig. 11.

Cachemaille-Day at All Saints, Hanworth, Middlesex (1951-1957), has designed a church that is an eucharistic room, with a subordinated structure for all ancillary purposes. As his plans for Bishop Gorton Church, Allesley Park, Coventry, and for St. Columba, Bannersgate, Birmingham, show, he has a strong preference for a square in his designs. The Church of St. Michael, Hatfield Hyde, Welwyn Garden City (the architects of which were Denis Clarke Hall, Sam Scorer, and Roy Bright), is also based on a square, but the altar is sited on a diagonal line. Perhaps the most brilliant use of a square is that of Robert Maguire's design for St. Paul, Bow Common, London (1958-1960), "a church of outstanding promise."[47] The major entrance for the congregation forces the people to pass the Baptistery (thereby it is an indication that Baptism is the initiation into the Christian life) and a processional path round the central altar is subtly marked by thin and therefore unobtrusive piers on all four sides. A small supplementary rectangle houses a secondary altar.

Octagonal designs were prepared for the Church of the Holy Cross, Doncaster, by its architects, Henry Braddock and D. F. Martin-Smith, as also for the Church of St. Francis, Locklease, Bristol, by the architects T. H. B. Burrough and F. L. Hannam. The former is remarkable for its exterior shape—that of a vast concrete tent.

A circular plan dominates the project for a housing-estate church at Ronkswood, Worcester, devised by Maurice W. Jones. It features a dais that projects into the circle with a dominating altar, a bishop's seat on the east wall, and twin ambos flanking the altar. The first two rows below the dais are reserved for the choir.

Thus the flexibility of pre-stressed concrete is being increasingly exploited in a fecund variety of plans in modern Anglican churches. It is equally clear that some exciting new architects find liberation from the Gothic thrall a spur to build churches expressive of the understanding of the congregation as the Body of Christ, not the passive watchers of an impressive clerical or choral performance.

Several architects belong to this new school concerned to make relevant "theological affirmations" with ideas, materials, and techniques appropriate to our day. Among them are the partners, Robert Potter and Richard Hare, who designed the Church of the Ascension, Crownhill, Plymouth;[48] St. George, Oakdale, Poole,

[47] P. Hammond, *Liturgy and Architecture*, p. 111.
[48] Sir Jacob Epstein had prepared a maquette for an impressive sculpture of

Dorset; and St. Mary, Peckham, London. Another lively and imaginative architect is George G. Pace, architect of the brilliant interdenominational Chapel of the Resurrection in University College, Ibadan, Nigeria, of the Church of St. Mary, Newby, Scarborough, Yorkshire, and of many other churches.[49] He collaborated with Sir Jacob Epstein in designing the cylindrical organ-case, supported by the delicate double concrete bridge, in Llandaff Cathedral, on which is suspended the superb *Majestas*. He is also a most perceptive interpreter of the new liturgical architecture in his writings.

Another interesting partnership is that of Alison and Peter Smithson, who submitted an intriguingly functional design for the new Coventry Cathedral which was referred to earlier in this chapter. This highly praised plan aimed "to place the congregation equidistant from the altar rather than progressively away from it," included ancillary chapels open to the central altar instead of separated from it, and designed "a single block of translucent stone at the heart of the cathedral" as its altar. The latter would have been placed in the diagonal forming the east-west axis of the square plan. The entire space would have been covered by a huge concrete vault, forming an "anti-elastic shell," which was to be tilted up at the east and down at the west.[50] Other church architects in the new mode are Robert Macguire, R. E. Enthoven, and the enduringly fertile Cachemaille-Day, Martin-Smith and Bosanquet (Fig. 12).

The architecture of the Free Churches has greatly improved in the course of the century, but it cannot show a comparable inventiveness nor an ability to attract the talents of gifted painters, sculptors, or designers in glass, metals, and tapestry to work with architects. For this there are many reasons. There is, first, the continuing Puritan suspicion of aesthetics as a substitute for ethics. Another reason is a theological overemphasis on the doctrine of the

---

the Ascending Christ and half of the designs for the twelve hexagonal windows of the east wall of this church, when his death in 1959 prevented their completion. The windows, using a different iconography, were completed by Geoffrey Clarke. This information was supplied in a personal communication (dated August 1, 1963) to the writer from the Rev. Eric Turnbull, Vicar of St. Margaret's Church, King's Lynn, formerly the Vicar of the Church of the Ascension, Crownhill, and a great Epstein enthusiast. I am indebted to him for much information about the religious interpretation of Sir Jacob's work. See Fig. 26.

[49] Pace was architect also of the Church of All Saints, Intake, Doncaster, of the Chapel of St. Michael's College, Llandaff, of the Church of SS. Leonard and Jude, Doncaster, and of St. Mark, Sheffield. He favours single eucharistic rooms and free-standing central altars. See his designs for Ibadan Anglican cathedral, Fig. 9; also Figs. 13 and 14.

[50] P. Hammond, *Liturgy and Architecture*, pp. 135-36.

Atonement to the detriment of the doctrines of Creation and Incarnation. Allied to the latter is a high estimate of the audible Word (as proclaimed from the pulpit) and an insufficient appreciation of the visible Word (in the Sacraments of Baptism and Holy Communion). It should, however, be noted that in several of the Free Churches there is, especially among the younger ministers, a recognition that pulpit and holy table must play complementary, not competitive roles.

There is also a curious reason why the Continental Liturgical Movement, while influential on Anglicanism, which proudly claims to be in the Catholic and the Reformed tradition, cannot in the nature of things have more than a superficial impact on the Free Churches: it is that the English Baptists, Presbyterians, Congregationalists, and the non-Wesleyan parts of the Methodist Church have always adopted the Basilican posture at the Communion, and stressed the maximum participation of the people of God in their sacred ordinances. Thus what was being contended for in terms of sharing and intelligibility by the Roman and Anglo-Catholic protagonists of the Liturgical Movement was a privilege never forfeited by the Churches stemming from the Reformation, except possibly on the part of a few wealthy suburban Free Church communities who aped Anglican "spectator-worship" and the use of the remote altar, in the latter years of the nineteenth and the first three decades of the twentieth century.

Other important non-theological factors which also play their part in the slower renaissance of Free Church architecture are matters of taste and of finance. While historically the Unitarians with their elegant eighteenth century meeting-houses, with exquisite chandeliers, silver goblets for the Communion, and finely carved mahogany, and the present-day Quakers with their "scrubbed simplicity" are proof that different interpretations of taste have been given by the well-to-do, nevertheless there is a close correlation between wealth, culture, and architecture. The plain fact is that for a long part of their history the Baptists, Congregationalists, Methodists, and Presbyterians of England sacrificed generously of their pounds and pennies to build their churches, being unestablished Churches, but what might have been spent on elegant sanctuaries or their enrichments was given to the maintenance of the ministry and of missionaries in foreign lands. Such a tradition, with a sound recognition that it is the people who constitute the Church, not a building, and that ethical obedience and charity to the needy are the proofs of their covenant-relationship to God and to the wider Body of Christ, is rightly cherished. But in recent years, in most cases, it has been realized that a functional building need not be a stark one and that while colour-blindness may be an asset for inter-racial relationships, it is not an essential mark of sincerity in worship.

Setting aside the curious imitations and syncretisms of the earlier half of the period, one of the most hopeful recent developments has been a return to the central concept of the meeting-house tradition in Free Church architecture.[51] Two very different examples of this trend are Christ Church and Upton Chapel, Kennington Road, London, S.E. 1 (1959) and Bromley Congregational Church, Kent (1955-1958).

The architect of Christ Church, Peter Darvall, had an unusual assignment: it was to build on a partly ruined corner site (where Westminster Bridge Road and Kennington Road intersect) a five-storeyed office building (Lincoln House) and a modern church, while retaining the corner Gothic Revival tower and spire of the old church, half the cost of which had been contributed by Americans. The exterior amalgam, apart from a stone lattice screen, is a jarring syncretism of styles. The chief interest, however, is the planning of the simple sanctuary, which is to serve a united congregation of Baptists and Congregationalists. A central dais, with three steps, supports a simple Communion-table and benches. It is surrounded on three sides by rising banks of pews, which clearly emphasize the fact that the people are gathered about God's table. The central space between the pews gives an important and slightly subordinate role to the pulpit, some six feet away from the edge of the dais to the west, but what it lacks in siting it gains in elevation over the table. At the eastern end of the central space is a very small font (small comfort to Congregationalists), and behind several pews a Baptistery of ampler dimensions (a great consolation to Baptists), and an eastern window with a central cross towards which there marches an ecumenical procession of "the named and unnamed saints of the Church Universal" (making everyone happy).[52] There is a suspended ceiling of wood and

---

[51] See my *Worship and Theology*, Vol. III, *From Watts and Wesley to Maurice*, Chap. II.

[52] The phrase is taken from a letter from the Rev. P. G. Saunders, the minister, who sent me his own impressions of this worshipful church, along with a descriptive brochure and an excellent photograph. When he wrote (October 17, 1960) his single criticism was that the light from the latticed stone openwork on the

plaster to carry concealed fluorescent lighting and to outline the central area, serving—tell it not in Gath—the purpose of a baldachino. There will be spotlights on the table and pulpit. Perhaps the chief significance of this church design is that primacy has been given to the Communion-table as the focal point of worship about which the Christian community is gathered, and this in a Baptist-Congregationalist merger.

The Bromley Congregational Church, formed in 1790, had its third sanctuary and adjacent buildings destroyed by enemy action in 1941, and the present modern buildings were erected between 1955 and 1958. The architect, R. R. Wilkins, is a deacon of the Bromley Church, and he and the minister, the Rev. Eric Shave, a gifted musician, cooperated in planning the shape and uses of the new buildings.[53] "Its shape," the latter writes, "is a modification in modern materials of our forefathers' Meeting Houses of the post-1689 period—domestic architecture, usually rectangular, with pulpit and table on the long side and pews around the other three sides. Norwich Old Meeting was in some senses the pattern and inspiration for our architect." Architect and minister were "as concerned as our forefathers to emphasize the centrality of the Word and Sacraments by placing the Pulpit and Table in the centre, and the Church as a fellowship gathered around. We also stress the 'audibility' of the Word." There is no gallery, despite the fact that in the time of William and Mary, and afterwards, galleries were often added to accommodate the enlarged congregations worshipping in the meeting-houses. The historic precedent was rejected because "a gallery manifestly divides a worshipping community into two sections."[54]

Other special characteristics of the sanctuary are worthy of note. The floor is ramped, indicating the importance of visibility as

---

back of the preacher's head makes it difficult for the congregation to concentrate on the sermon. See Fig. 18.

[53] The Rev. Eric Shave has provided all the information and the citations are from a letter written by him, dated August 22, 1963, giving an account of the theological and practical principles which were expressed in the architecture. Mr. Wilkins, the architect, was good enough to send me a copy of the plans.

[54] It should be noted that Trinity Congregational Church, Poplar, also designed as a modern meeting-house, uses a three-sided gallery, in contrast to Bromley, but attempts by its low elevation above the floor below to give it a close association with the body of the sanctuary. This church, built to the designs of C. C. Handisyde and D. R. Stark, was part of the "Live Architecture" section of the 1951 Festival of Britain. See Edward Mills, *The Modern Church*, pp. 94-95. An unusual composition, it combines exterior nobility with interior intimacy. Ultimacy and intimacy are also combined in a fresh way in the polygonal plan of Guildford Congregational Church, Surrey (1964). The latter is a most ingenious modern building, mirroring the "Family Church" conception. See Fig. 17.

well as audibility; the organ pipes are concealed in a special chamber behind the pulpit, and the entire wall is set in a simple mahogany screen containing rectangular frames of "sonic twine" to permit the sound to enter. The organ console is at the front of the pews and slightly to the side, sunk 18 inches, and immediately before the four ranks of choir seats. The stepped dais can be cleared of furniture (pulpit included) for festival occasions and for the presentation of religious drama. An entrance vestibule 35 feet long provides a meeting-place of fellowship on all occasions, especially on Sundays, and is a simple solution of the Free Church dilemma—"the need for silence in Church and for fellowship between the worshippers." As a result, "our church is always a quiet place, but the vestibule is always noisy with conversation." The lighting, too, is of a special character. There is "a flat ceiling, a deep-blue in colour, in which 12 perspex circles are placed through which light is thrown at night. Forty 18 inch lancet windows 30 feet high give white 'sky' light but the long walls on the pulpit side are plain and windowless and face south, so sunlight does not enter to dazzle." Finally, it should be noted, that the buildings "form an integrated whole, designed to reflect in theory and in practice the principles of 'Family Church'[55] and to incorporate the total social life of a Christian community with the place of worship in the centre."

In general, then, it may be said that Free Church architecture, when it was not merely syncretistic and chaotic in its borrowings and imitations, followed three styles from 1930 onwards. First, and most common, was "streamlined Gothic" or simplified Gothic, which was particularly popular among prosperous middle-class "dormitory" communities in outer London or on the fringes of the larger provincial cities. It was highly favoured by Presbyterians and Congregationalists and, in some cases, by Baptists, but most of all by the Methodists, who, because of their eighteenth century

[55] The reference is to the book of the Rev. H. A. Hamilton, *The Family Church*, and to the author's inspired leadership in the attempt to cross the abyss between Church and Sunday School (which previously had met in different buildings). He insisted upon including children in the common worship in the sanctuary at the beginning of Sunday morning worship, and throughout the service for the four great "Festivals of Family Church." He also advocated the provision of "Church friends" with whom children might sit, if their own parents were disinterested in their spiritual progress. This renewed familial concept of the Church also provided many other features to offset the usual sectional weeknight activities in churches. It involved a revolution in Christian education for adults as well as children and was exceedingly influential among the Congregational Union of Churches as well as among individual congregations of other Free Churches.

links with the Church of England, are particularly characterized by Anglican nostalgia.

In the second place, "dual purpose" edifices were widely used by all the Free Churches in new housing estates and in extension charges. The Methodist architect, Edward D. Mills, was outstanding in erecting this type of building. Many dual function buildings were put up immediately after the end of World War II on bombed sites because they were, at the time of a national housing shortage, the most economical way of meeting religious and social needs. Moreover, these very needs had always been strongly stressed by the "gathered church" type for which worship, fellowship, and social obligations have been correlated.

The third and most recent type of Free Church sanctuary has been a return to origins, not in any slavishly antiquarian way, but as a rediscovery of their authentic tradition. Churches in the Puritan tradition, whether Congregationalist or Baptist, have rediscovered the significance of the meeting-house. They are again valuing its simplicity and intimacy, with its central Communion-Table and elevated pulpit, about which the congregation gathers to share in the Lord's Supper, and to receive the lively oracles of God. For their part, the Methodists have most recently recovered a forgotten part of their inheritance from John Wesley—that is, his preference for churches of octagonal shape. The most recent striking example of such a rediscovery is Sale Methodist Church in Cheshire.[56]

As the largest Free Church denomination in England, the Methodist Church exceeds the others in the total number of new buildings erected since the Second World War, and they are far too many to allow for particularisation. A vivid impression of their number and variety may be obtained from the plans and photographs in Edward D. Mills' *The Modern Church*, and especially in E. Benson Perkins' *The Methodist Church Builds Again*, as from the published annual reports of the Department of Church Affairs of the Methodist Church.[57] Methodists may justly be proud of the new Punshon Memorial Church in Bournemouth, with its glass, steel, and brick verticality (Fig. 16).

[56] See *The Manchester Guardian*, issue of September 20, 1963, brought to my attention by the Rev. Kenneth W. Wadsworth, minister of the Congregational Church, Heaton Moor.

[57] The address of the Department of Chapel Affairs of the Methodist Church is Central Buildings, Oldham Street, Manchester, which has been operative since the Methodist Union of 1932. For bibliographical information I am much indebted to the Rev. Professor Frank Baker, now at the Duke University Divinity School, Durham, N.C.

The Baptists, according to Dr. Ernest A. Payne, their General Secretary, have produced several sanctuaries of unusual interest since the last war. These include: Westbourne Park, Paddington; Mare Street, Hackney (both of which were destroyed in the blitz and their successors designed by the same architect, Arthur Bailey); Chatswood, Norwood; Amersham Free Church (where the building was almost entirely planned by the Rev. Neville Clark, notable liturgiologist of his denomination); and New George Street, Plymouth.[58]

The English Presbyterians have built sixteen churches between 1949 and 1960. Many of them were extension charges and such buildings are rarely distinctive, being hampered by the compromise decisions of committees and the limitation of funds. So far as reproductions of the exteriors of a small sample of these provide basis for judgment, the Presbyterian Churches at Rugby (1956) and Gosport (1956), as at Wythenshawe (1959), seem less hackneyed in conception than the run-of-the-mill Free Churches.[59] The most notable recent churches of this denomination are to be found in Lockleaze, Bristol, and in Norwich (Fig. 15).

The Congregationalists, too, have added their quota of interesting churches.[60] The three outstanding churches they have built since the end of the Second World War are, as has been previously mentioned, Trinity in Poplar, Bromley, and Guildford. Others worthy of consideration are Lewes (1954), Goring (1961), and Ifield (1963)—all in Sussex—Grindon, Sutherland (1962), and Henningthorpe, Rotherham (partly completed) in Yorkshire. They are notable for shape, the imaginative use of new materials such as multi-coloured bricks, the mixture of external textures (brick and hardwood), for the impressiveness of the fenestration, and for their Congregational emphasis on the community as the family of God.

In the best of the new Free Churches, however, the table-fellowship aspect of the gathered Church, sustained by the Communion-

---

[58] This information, with the comments slightly abbreviated, was contained in a most helpful letter of Dr. Payne's written from Washington, D.C., on August 17, 1963. See Chap. x for evidence of the ecumenical and liturgical renewal in the life of the English Baptists.

[59] This information was supplied by Miss R. A. Eyles, secretary to the Rev. A. L. Macarthur, General Secretary of the Presbyterian Church of England, in the latter's absence. Her letter was accompanied by a copy of the *Presbyterian Messenger* (No. 1297—114th year, issue of March 1959), which included photographs of the exteriors of some of the new Presbyterian edifices, which are generally simple, unpretentious, and functional. Some are, frankly, dull.

[60] This information I owe largely to the kindness of a friend, the Rev. Kenneth W. Wadsworth, Minister of the Congregational Church, Heaton Moor.

Service and obedient to the Living Word of God and expectant for the inspiration of the Holy Spirit, is fitly expressed by functionalism in architecture and the absence of fussy, distracting decoration or of any striving for social prestige by imitations of styles alien to their past and irrelevant to their present task. Above all, their twin foci are the central Communion-table and dominating Pulpit, illuminated by the clear light of day, unobfuscated by mimic Gothic windows or made mysterious by the ambiguity of distant, half-hidden sideboards which are neither table nor altar. Their clear functionalism, unpretentious use of modern techniques, and clean lines are re-invigorating in their assertion of relevance both of God and to the demands and needs of the twentieth century.

5. Artists in the Service of the Church

The mutual suspicion of creative artists and churchmen which has befogged their relationships over many years will not easily be dissipated. It is, however, significant that several Anglican clergy have been enthusiastic supporters[61] of creative artists and that two Anglican societies have been founded to further cooperation between architects, artists, clergy, and laity.

Reference has already been made to one of them: the "New

[61] Readers may well be able to supply their own additions to this list of clergymen who have worked to cross the abyss separating "artists who love God . . . and Christians who love the arts" (see the dedication of A. C. Bridge's *Images of God*). One of the pioneers was Conrad Noel, vicar of Thaxted, and another is the present Dean of Chichester (the Very Rev. Walter Hussey), who vigorously championed and commissioned Henry Moore and Graham Sutherland in their more controversial days, when he was Vicar of St. Matthew's, Northampton. A great Epstein enthusiast is the Rev. Eric Turnbull, formerly Vicar of the Church of the Ascension, Crownhill, Plymouth, who had persuaded Sir Jacob to sculpt a fifteen-feet high "Ascending Christ" (which reached the stage only of an exquisite maquette), a project defeated by the artist's death in 1959. The Rev. Frank J. Glendenning organized an admirable festival of the arts at Hull in 1957 (see his account of it in *The Church and the Arts*). The Rev. A. C. Bridge, formerly a professional artist, has written engagingly and persuasively about the problem of finding suitable *Images of God* for the twentieth century, and Dr. F. W. Dillistone (lately Dean of Liverpool) and Dr. Gilbert Cope have also concerned themselves with the same problem. (See Bibliographical Index for details.) A former architect, the Rev. Peter Hammond, has written with insight and conviction on the new functional, liturgical architecture in *Liturgy and Architecture*, and edited an important volume, *Towards a Church Architecture*. The Rev. Professor J. Gordon Davies, founder and director of the Birmingham University Institute of Liturgy and Architecture, has written widely and eruditely on the theme. The Rev. Gerald Irvine was notably successful in St. Anne's, Soho, in correlating the Christian faith with contemporary culture in its dramatic, poetic, musical and artistic expressions. Nor should the important contribution of such Anglican laymen as Sir John Betjeman, John Piper, and George Pace be forgotten. These names are only a distinguished fraction of those who are urging the correlation of Christianity and Art in the Church of England.

Churches Research Group."[62] The other important organization is the long-established Council for the Care of Churches which came into being shortly after the end of the First World War, primarily to coordinate the work of the advisory committees in each diocese. Today it conceives its task in a three-fold manner. It exists, first, for the prevention of ruthless church restoration; secondly, to encourage good artists and craftsmen in their work for the churches; and, thirdly, as a centre for the dissemination of education. To fulfil these aims it has provided at All Hallows on the Wall, the headquarters of the Council, a library of church art and architecture, a photographic record which will eventually depict all the churches of the nation, and a collection of colour-slides illustrating church architecture and furnishings which may be hired for lectures. Thus, it is proposed to extend the aesthetic education of the Church of England.

Of particular interest is the fact that under the Guild Churches Act of 1952 sixteen of the churches of the City of London were set aside as centres for some specialized branch of the ministry of the Church of England to daily workers in the metropolis. All Hallows on the Wall was designated a Christian Arts Centre. The eighteenth century church, designed by George Dance the Younger, was damaged by air attack in 1941; it was restored and reconsecrated in 1962 to provide in the unfurnished nave a space for lectures and artistic exhibitions and, in the chancel, daily services of worship. Its aesthetic usefulness is enhanced by its unbroken wall surfaces, and the good illumination which comes from the windows set high in the walls. The exhibitions seek to "preserve a balance between the fine arts and the crafts, between the 'modern' and the traditional, and between treasures we have inherited from the past and the work of living artists and architects." In addition, an attempt is made to exhibit good design in everyday products, and to balance the tribute paid to established artists with the encouragement of those who have yet to win renown.

The sponsors declare: "Not all the exhibitions will be concerned with 'religious art' in the narrower sense; for we recognize no hard-and-fast division between the sacred and the secular. Work of sincerity and depth by an artist not specifically committed may be of more value to the Church than a facile and superficial treatment of conventional themes."[63] This Christian Arts Centre is one

[62] See footnote 43 *supra* and the paragraph to which it refers.
[63] The citations are from a pamphlet entitled "All Hallows on the Wall, a

further promising sign that the Church of England is grappling basically with the problem of communicating the Christian faith in a contemporary idiom, without jettisoning the appreciation of a great tradition of Christian iconography. Its establishment, with open-mindedness towards the future, is an act of faith in the potentialities of modern architects, artists, and craftsmen, as well as in the capacities of the office-workers and shop assistants of the immediate neighbourhood to appreciate lively art.

The last consideration, in this chapter, must be an attempt to sketch, although with the baldest brevity, the contribution that some twentieth century painters and sculptors have made in England to the understanding of the Christian faith and life in our time. The ensuing and concluding sections will be restricted to the most considerable artists of established reputation, with only passing mention of artists of promise, and it will also attempt to indicate the variety of media in which they have worked to the glory of God and for the delight and instruction of men.

6. Three Painters: Spencer, Sutherland, and Piper

There are three pre-eminent painters who have essayed Christian themes: Sir Stanley Spencer, Graham Sutherland, and John Piper. Other painters of religious interest are: Roy de Maistre (born 1894), David Jones (born 1895), Ceri Richards (born 1903), and Hans Feibusch (born 1898).[64]

Christian Arts Centre," on sale at the church, which is to be found in the vicinity of Liverpool Street Station. When I visited the Arts Centre in July 1963, an admirably representative exhibition of Epstein's sculptures, drawings, and designs for stained-glass windows was showing. It had been well selected and mounted.

[64] Roy de Maistre is a friend of Francis Bacon (the latter a brilliant technical painter who is haunted by the horror of a dysteleological universe) and his paintings are cubistically shaped in sombre colours. A Roman Catholic "convert" of deep conviction, his moving Pietà (of 1950) is now in the Tate Gallery, and a Crucifixion painting by him is in the City of Leicester Art Gallery. (See Sir John Rothenstein, *Modern English Painters*, Vol. II, pp. 254ff.)

David Jones is another "convert" to Roman Catholicism, and a disciple of the late Eric Gill. His painting consists of profusely detailed essays in symbolism, depicting other rites as anticipations of the Christian Liturgy and Sacrifice. His *Aphrodite in Aulis* and *Vexilla Regis* are practically pictorial equivalents for the allusive dramatic poems of Charles Williams, though each was independent of the other. (See Rothenstein, *ibid.*, Vol. II, pp. 302ff.)

Ceri Richards is a distinguished abstract painter, who painted the striking altarpiece of the Last Supper for the Chapel of St. Edmund Hall, Oxford, in which Christ is depicted as the contemporary guest in what is perhaps a working-man's home. His paintings are in the permanent collections of the Tate, the National Museum of Wales, and the Canadian National Gallery. (See *Who's Who in Art*, Eastbourne, 12th edn., 1962.)

Hans Feibusch is best known as a muralist, and the author of *Mural Painting*. His representations of Biblical scenes are to be found in many Anglican churches, notably in Chichester Cathedral, St. Elizabeth's Eastbourne, St. John's Waterloo

Stanley Spencer (1891-1959) is considered by many to be an eccentric, and by a few to be a genius.[65] Certainly he was a visionary painter who peopled his native village of Cookham on the Thames with the personages of the Old and New Testament whom he thus makes contemporary. His apocalyptic experience in the First World War in Macedonia fused with his meditation on Christian symbols to produce the series of oil paintings in the Oratory of All Souls, Burghclere, in Berkshire. The most remarkable altarpiece vividly illustrates the meaning of the Resurrection by depicting a huge central mound of white crosses which tired soldiers have thrown down in token of their liberation from mortality. Its weakness is the relative insignificance of the figure of Christ, who is presumably the key to the event. His final works were a series of paintings for a Temple of Love, of which the inspiration was human rather than Divine love, *eros* not *agape*, and which pose the problem of whether his inspiration was Christian in the narrower and traditional sense, or pagan. But of the brilliance and originality of his compositions, the immediacy of their impact, the sheer clarity of his brushwork, there is no question.

It appears that his earlier religious paintings derived their inspiration from the simple evangelical faith of his mother, with whom he attended the Methodist Chapel in Cookham at the turn of the century. It was "in chapel-religion he came to know what it felt like to believe in God and in Christ, without intellect perhaps, but intensely and emotionally, and with a form of imagination to which the events of the Bible were literally and indeed rhetorically ever present."[66]

Of this baptism of the imagination, Spencer himself wrote: "I loved the gentle atmosphere that belonged to the poor slummy people who came to the chapel. I remember Mr. Francis the baker, and think of the years I sat and listened to his sermons, which though a little insipid and sanctimonious, were homely. The comfortable atmosphere of this chapel stimulated me as a painter. Being 'Sanctified' was the way they had of expressing themselves. When they fell in that state, they would go and flop down, just

---

Road, London, and in the parish churches of Southwark, Harrow, Battersea, Bermondsey, Wembley and Exeter. His works are, on the whole, formal, conventional, reverent representations in pastel shades of incidents from the Gospels.

[65] See *Stanley Spencer* by Elizabeth Rothenstein and *Stanley Spencer: A Biography* by Maurice Collis.

[66] Elizabeth Rothenstein, *Stanley Spencer*, p. 2a.

under the auditorium.[67] I felt I should not look, but though my eyes were down I was trying to imagine what shape they were on the sacred piece of ground where they were 'coming to the Lord.' It was a patch of hard linoleum, with room for only one man at a time. It seemed to me the taking off place for a Wesleyan heaven. When I heard someone pass by my pew and get down there, I felt it was a sort of apotheosis of the grocer or confectioner or whoever it was." Yet Spencer imagined them in their apotheosis to be more wholly themselves than before. A grocer, he insisted, would be "more intensely a grocer," as he lay, "crumpled, his face turned up in a wonderful ecstasy, expressive of the Wesleyan conception of goodness."[68]

Thus Cookham and a vivid evangelical, Biblicistic Christianity are the twin sources of the inspiration of Spencer's early religious paintings. In 1915 he painted *The Centurion's Servant*, depicting a bedside scene where four simple villagers are praying beside a brass bedstead on which lies a sick child. They are portraits of four Cookham villagers, himself included, linked by anxiety commingled with faith. In 1919 and 1920 he produced twenty paintings, among them the famous *Christ Carrying the Cross*, now in the Tate Gallery, and *The Last Supper*. The former depicts Christ passing by on the way to the Cross, as Spencer would have viewed the event from the front window of "Fernlea," his Cookham home. The villagers look out from their windows, not in compassion so much as in curious surprise, and the Spirit-blown curtains flanking each of the onlookers suggests that they are angelic witnesses to the scene of cosmic significance. The end of the sacred procession is brought up by two workmen with ladders that form a St. Andrew's cross. The iron railings, each segment of which is topped by a blunt diamond-shape, evoke the memory of spears. The onlookers are all typical villagers, only the Christ, almost hidden by the Cross he carries, and the imagined soldiers are phantasms of Spencer's invention. The mood is not tragedy, but calm wonder that Christ is seen in the Cookham of "England's green and pleasant land."

The same sense of naïve wonder dominates *The Last Supper*.

[67] Spencer probably refers to the rostrum or platform where he writes "auditorium."

[68] The citations are from Spencer's voluminous journal, excerpted in the biography of Maurice Collis, *Stanley Spencer*, p. 29. The naïve but deeply impressive Biblicism of Spencer's boyhood is remarkably similar to that experienced by the relations of James Baldwin, so movingly recorded in his novel, *Go Tell it on the Mountain*.

The austere brick room may be the interior of one of the Cookham malt-houses, but it might be anywhere. The thirteen figures are not based on the villagers Spencer knew, being entirely invented on the basis of the New Testament narrative. The climactic moment is the recognition by the disciples that the bread broken by the Christ is *His flesh*, and as St. John eagerly examines the divided loaf his mouth is open with stupefaction. The impression is of simple, gentle faith, responding to a miracle.

After the Burghclere murals, already referred to, the next important work was *The Cookham Resurrection* of 1927. The eschatological awe traditionally sensed in this earth-shaking event as envisioned by the New Testament and the great religious masters in painting is entirely lacking in this picture. What Spencer records is happy Cookham villagers, for whom death has been merely an incorruptible interval of interruption, resuming their calm pleasures. The euphoric scene is Cookham churchyard viewed from the vicarage gate. In the upper left corner there is a Thames excursion steamer filled with trippers. In the centre is the porch of the church, with two vague figures, who are supposedly the Father and the Son. Below are tombstones and headstones, from which the unperturbed dead are rising. Almost all of them are well-known figures in the village, some of them Spencer's relations and friends. His patron Henry Slesser, a distinguished lawyer who had become Solicitor-General in 1924, rises in wig and gown from a flowery tomb in the foreground. Hilda Carline, Spencer's wife, is pictured in five different attitudes. Three of them show her smelling a rose, climbing over a stile, and lying on a central ivy-covered tomb. Her brother Richard appears thrice. Spencer himself is shown twice, once as a nude figure in front of the porch, and a second time as a clothed figure lazily viewing the scene from the bottom right-hand corner.[69] The detail is brilliantly captured, and the entire scene resembles an earthly paradise rather than any apocalypse.[70] As in *The Christ Carrying the Cross*, there is only

[69] For identification, see Collis, *ibid.*, pp. 85-87.

[70] On the evidence of Spencer's journal, Collis argues that this picture is largely the transcript of Spencer's joy in marriage to Hilda and the consequent experience of fatherhood. Further, Collis points out that for the Divine figures in the porch Spencer merely reworked a previous sketch he had made of Hilda and himself, adding, "The presiding deities of *The Cookham Resurrection* are Hilda and Stanley" (*ibid.*, p. 87). Spencer later came to think of this as the first of his sexually motivated pictures, believing that in depicting an awakening to love it also depicted an awakening to the divine. The comment of H. D. Ziman, who knew Spencer, seems apt: "Nor was there any decline in the pantheist ardour—an ardour expressed neither in prayer nor in Christian belief—that he developed

a shadowy and unconvincing representation of the important figures of God the Father and Christ, but the sense of human fellowship and bliss is marvellously conveyed.

What Elizabeth Rothenstein has called Spencer's "pictorial garrulity" is even more pronounced in his Port Glasgow *Resurrection* series, which was done between 1947 and 1950. Spencer had come to love the Clydeside ship-builders and their families, and conceived of producing an immense Resurrection on the cemetery on the hill above Port Glasgow peopled with the Scottish townsfolk. Of this series only *The Resurrection: Port Glasgow* and the *Hill of Sion* (1946) were completed on the vast scale he had originally planned. There is here a fantastic and bewildering fecundity of figures, from angels blowing the good news on their trumpets, to embracing lovers, mothers dandling babies on their knees, daughters combing their mothers' hair, to entire groups waving handkerchiefs, or raising their arms in greeting, or dancing with joy. The prodigality of the inventiveness is staggering, but this is even less of a religious picture than the *Cookham Resurrection*. "There is in it," says Elizabeth Rothenstein, "no sense whatever of the unfolding of a tremendous eschatological destiny or of human beings in the immediate presence of their Creator." This Resurrection only shows "a cosmic euphoria in which, with lighter hearts and greater gusto, people continue to do what they have always done, especially to gossip."[71]

Almost all sense of the transcendental has disappeared in the later pictures, in the riotous exuberation of his frolicking fancy. Not surprisingly, only one religious edifice (excepting the Burghclere Oratory, which is more a consecrated art museum than an oratory) contains a Spencer painting. That is Aldenham School Chapel in Hertfordshire, which has a striking *Crucifixion* (Fig. 24) as an altar-piece. It was painted while he was mortally sick and it shrieks with a violence uncharacteristic of the rest of Spencer's painting. All the energy is concentrated on the Bosch-like brutal figures who drive the nails into Christ's hands. It may elicit a sense of pity for the "King of the Jews," with his bearded, crowned, and

as a boy. It was heightened some years later into a permanent identification of divine love with physical love, which gave it an embarrassing force." (*Daily Telegraph*, issue of May 18, 1962. I owe this reference to my sister-in-law, Mrs. G. H. A. Cordwent of Milverton, Somerset.) It is significant that Spencer delighted in the painting and poetry of the visionary William Blake who made a similar identification (see Collis, *ibid.*, p. 54).

[71] E. Rothenstein, *Stanley Spencer*, p. 5a.

lolling head, but there is no mystical sense of redemption found through suffering or of devotion to the *salvator mundi*, such as are found in the crucifixions depicted by Rouault or Graham Sutherland. Pictorial possibilities rather than religious sensitivities are exploited and it is most probably, as was so often the case with Spencer, a passionate transcript of his own experience. Gone is the calm of the early religious pictures, but none of the brilliance of invention or the original angularity of viewpoint. It was given to this strange and immensely gifted visionary painter to transform Cookham into a happy, if not always a holy, suburb of heaven.

Graham Sutherland, a convert to Roman Catholicism, is a deeply religious and a far more reflective painter than Sir Stanley Spencer was. Born in 1903, he attended Epsom College, was apprenticed for a time at the railway-engineering workshops of Derby, and studied at Goldsmith's College of the University of London. Successively, he was an etcher, a poster artist, and a designer of fabrics and ceramics. During the Second World War he was an official artist, producing paintings of devastated buildings, which, as Eric Newton expresses it, revealed "a wild crucified poignancy that gives the war a new meaning,"[72] or studies of steel-workers and miners "who have the anxious and tense look of creatures in thrall to some monster."[73] The most moving emblem of the agony of the war was his *Blasted Oak*, which has "roots as vicious as a vulture's claw," and the top of the trunk has an open formation "which at one moment suggests the fearsome beak of a bird about to tear at its prey, and at another a human head screaming in agony."[74]

From 1945 onwards he has given much of his time to religious themes. His best known works, commissioned for churches, are the altar tapestry of *Christ in Glory* at Coventry Cathedral,[75] the *Noli me tangere* altar-piece painting in the Chapel of St. Mary Magdalen in Chichester Cathedral, the *Crucifixion* in St. Matthew's Anglican Church in Northampton, and the mural of the *Crucifixion* at St. Aidan's Roman Catholic Church, Acton East.[76]

[72] See *In My View*, p. 117.
[73] *The Work of Graham Sutherland*, p. 26, text by Douglas Cooper.
[74] *Ibid.*, p. 27.
[75] Previously considered in section 3 of this chapter. See Fig. 3.
[76] I am indebted for information on the interpretation of these works to several sources: to Douglas Cooper's monograph; to a sermon by the present Dean of Chichester (the Very Rev. Walter Hussey) subsequently printed; Sutherland's article, "Thoughts on Painting" (*The Listener*, issue September 6, 1952, pp. 376-78), and my own observation of his work—with the single exception of the Chichester altarpiece of which I have a transparency sent by courtesy of the Dean,

Sutherland was invited by the then Canon (now Dean) Walter Hussey in the autumn of 1944 to paint an Agony in the Garden for a wall on the south transept of St. Matthew's Church in Northampton, as a companion piece to the noble sculpture of the Madonna and Child by Henry Moore in the north transept. Because the painter was reluctant to undertake an ecclesiastical commission, he hesitated, and, being profoundly moved by his experience of war, suggested a Crucifixion as an alternative subject. Sutherland has written:

"The Crucifixion idea interested me because it has a duality which has always fascinated me. It is the most tragic of all themes, yet inherent in it is the promise of salvation. It is the symbol of the precarious balanced moment, the hair's breadth between black and white. It is that moment when the sky seems superbly blue—and when one feels it *is* only blue in that superb way because at any moment it could be black—there is the other side of the mirror—and on that point of balance one may fall into great gloom or rise to great happiness."[77]

Sutherland himself meditated for twelve months before attempting the painting into which he put these meditations, fused with his brooding on the Grünewald altar-piece at Eisenheim[78] which he had only seen in an illustration at that time, on the flesh-ripping power of thorns (then and since an absorbing subject for him), and the photographs he had seen of the horrific victims of the concentration camps of Nazi Germany. The result was a disturbingly stark image of the Crucifixion. The spread-eagled arms of the Christ, his open hands with clutching fingers, the heavy, sagging body whose weight tears the shoulders, and the brute strength of the Cross itself—all create a terrible pathos and an "universal monitory symbol."[79] The symbolic crosses chalked on the wall, apparently by an unknown hand, bring the scene into our vicinity and century.

This unforgettable image of Divine suffering has been criticised for two defects: for the weakness of the lower half of the body and

---

who also despatched a copy of the Address given by Sir Eric Maclagan at the unveiling and dedication of the Northampton Crucifixion. The latter declared of Sutherland's painting: ". . . the painting of the Crucifixion is a worthy match for the [Henry Moore] statue of the Virgin and Child with which you have now grown familiar." See Figs. 22 and 23.

[77] *The Listener*, Sept. 6, 1952, pp. 376-78, "Thoughts on Painting."

[78] Sutherland was, of course, familiar with Picasso's drawings after Grünewald, published in *Minotaure*, No. 1 (1933).

[79] D. Cooper, *The Work of Graham Sutherland*, pp. 34ff.

limbs in comparison with the strength of the upper part, and for the often arbitrary suggestions of shadow.[80] Neither defect is repeated in the vast mural of the Crucifixion which Sutherland has painted on the unbroken east wall of the Roman Catholic Church of St. Aidan in East Acton. The Cross itself is shaped like a Greek letter $\tau\alpha\upsilon$ (the upright terminates in a drooping bow form), as contrasted with the Y-shape of the Northampton Crucifixion, from which hangs an emaciated Christ with the head supported by his right arm. The ribs are clearly delineated, and the thin legs form a diamond shape. At the four corners, adjacent to each arm and leg, are small rectangles placed slightly asymmetrically, each bearing a rudely scrawled criss-cross. This entire space, with the exception of the Cross and the pendent body, is painted in crimson, contrasting with the chill grey of the rest of the east wall. The effect is a complete contrast with the all too common sentimental versions of the crucified Christ: for steel and sacrifice (grey and crimson) are the dominant symbolic colours. This mural, too, is an austere symbol of the costliness of sacrifice and, therefore, of the profound love of Christ, the crucified Redeemer.

Sutherland's originality is even more strikingly demonstrated in the *Noli me tangere*, in which the artist interprets the Gospel incident (John 20:17) where the risen Christ forbids the eager Magdalen to touch him as he is about to ascend to the Father. The entire picture is a study of the mystery of how faith penetrates the lowly incognito of Christ. A stubble-faced Jesus, in a white tunic, with a labourer's maize-coloured hat (suggestive of a halo) is ascending an outdoor staircase or fire-escape. His left hand points heavenwards along the line of the rising balustrade, and his right hand is raised in an ambiguous gesture, which seems both to fend off Mary Magdalen and to bless her. The Magdalen appears to be rising from her knees in a frantic attempt to grasp her Saviour, and the carnal green of her pendulous body contrasts with the ascetical strength of Christ's firm limbs and determined step. The whole is a study in vermilion, with a rectangle of turquoise defining the Christ figure; and a flourish of palm leaves symbolizes his victory over death. Other palm trees behind a metal grille, which the topmost branches escape, emphasize again the note of liberation. An oval aperture in the top right of a castellated wall, with a hint of deep azure, is a token of the ultimate destination and glory of the ascending Christ. The iconography is almost entirely Suther-

[80] *Ibid.* Compare Figs. 22 and 23.

land's own and shows a profound mind meditating on a deep religious mystery.

The third of the trio of outstanding painters of religious themes is John Piper, born in 1903. He is a brilliant and subtle colourist, as shown (to select a few examples) in the threatening sombreness of his Druidic landscapes of Wales, in the variety of his topographical and architectural studies, and in the splendour of his sunburst of a Baptistery window in Coventry.[81] He is a master of many styles: naturalistic, symbolical, and abstract. In recent years he has specialised in designs for stained-glass windows which have been executed by Patrick Reyntiens. The Emmaus window at Llandaff Cathedral admirably fits a modern style into the three lights of a mediaeval window frame. Here the ethereal figure of Christ is evoked as a *stranger's* presence dimly recognized by the companions of the way. The semi-abstract technique which he has evolved marvellously divines the awe induced by spiritual presences freed from the limitations of the corporeal. In this window translucent colours are mingled with solid blocks of colour; substance merges into shadow; interpenetrating curves and broken lines as well as vertical shafts of light—all are powerful hints of the transcendental temporarily immanent.

Piper's largest interpretative work, not in the abstract mode, is the group of three windows, each of three lights, designed for Oundle School Chapel.[82] The nine lights contain nine Christological interpretations, and in each of them the Christ figure is more than life-size. These are not nine attempts at realism, but nine essays in catching the abstract and eternal qualities of the Son of God. This is achieved by the different shapes of the Christ figure and by stressing the different objects each Christ figure holds in his hands. Thus the left-hand window exhibits Christ as the Way, the Life, and the Truth, respectively with a star, a cross, and a book. The central window exhibits Christ as the Vine, the Bread of Heaven, and the Water of Regeneration, by means, respectively, of a cup, a wafer, and a bowl. In the right-hand window Christ is exhibited as Judge, Teacher, and Shepherd, holding, respectively, a flail, a rod, and a crook. The effect is as delightful as it is theologically instructive.

[81] The Coventry window was considered previously in the third section of this chapter.

[82] Full information on these windows was obtained from a commemorative, illustrative publication, entitled *The John Piper Windows executed for Oundle School Chapel by Patrick Reyntiens dedicated in the presence of her Majesty Queen Elizabeth the Queen Mother, May 26, 1956.*

Reyntiens has devised new methods to enable him to interpret the subtlety of Piper's lines and colours. For example, he has combined the processes of etching and staining glass, with the superimposition of one piece of glass upon another. Thus the effects are magically translucent, and "gold gleams through green and brown; reds and blues shine through one another as well as merging into radiant purples so sombre as to be on the very confines of black."[83]

Piper's importance consists, therefore, partly in his technical variety and virtuosity, and partly in his capacity to suggest the ambivalent fear and fascination of spiritual presences. He is a supreme colourist.

7. Three Sculptors: Gill, Epstein, and Henry Moore

The Renaissance of religious art in England is demonstrated as clearly in sculpture as in painting or stained-glass. Three very different sculptors have made significant contributions in this area. Eric Gill (1882-1940) was a brilliant typographer, a controversial propagandist of Christian art and Christian socialism, and a sculptor in wood and stone. This ardent Roman Catholic "convert" was the head of a large family and a passionate believer in social justice and the enemy of mass-production of *objets d'art*. He was also an amateur architect. Sir Jacob Epstein (1880-1959), a Jew born in New York City, was haunted all his life by the greatest Jewish religious figure in history, Jesus of Nazareth, of whom he made the most moving and monumental images in our time, with the possible exception of Georges Rouault. This fecund sculptor of the great men of his day and also of the unconsidered poor was passionately interested in religious dimensions and their representation, although belonging to a people that had emphasized the transcendence of God by considering all representations

[83] *Ibid.* Other brilliant designers in glass are John Hutton (whose work is to be found in Coventry and Guildford Cathedrals) and Geoffrey Clarke, also a sculptor (whose work is to be found in Norwich, Chichester, and Coventry Cathedrals). The latter has designed the 12 hexagonal windows of the east wall in the Church of the Ascension, Crownhill, Plymouth, in a semi-abstract form, symbolizing the twelve "I am" sayings of Christ. Raw aluminum, rather than lead, is used to bind the designs, which harmonise with the grey and blue stones of the wall in which they are set. The colours of the glass are often doubly glazed and carry their own symbolical associations. The Rev. Eric Turnbull offers the following interpretation of the third window ("I am the Resurrection and the Life"): "Coming out of the ruins, the fallen columns of death, is a shaft of blue, symbolising the risen and living Lord of the Church. On the sculpture of this shaft is a mark as though to remind us of the strife through which the battle was won" (from a typescript of the Rev. Eric Turnbull enclosed in a letter of August 1, 1963). Clarke also designed the strong and simple wrought-iron and free-standing candle-stands for the altar of the Chapel of St. Mary Magdalen in Chichester Cathedral.

of Deity as idolatry. Henry Moore (born in 1898), the son of a Yorkshire miner, has by his strange drawings of cocooned sleepers in the Tube shelters of London during the Second World War, and by his towering archetypal sculptures in metal and stone, imposed his brooding imagination on the retina of the modern world.[84] Both Gill and Epstein have left many works in the religious genre, but Moore only one—the hieratic triumph of the Madonna and Child in St. Matthew's Church, Northampton. Each sculptor is compellingly contemporary, concerned with the sociological and psychological problems of our day,[85] yet each is memorably individual and original in attitude and expression.

Gill's importance was that of a pioneer who protested on behalf of the goodness and truth of the Roman Catholic Church that it required a beauty of comparable magnitude, and should not be satisfied with the banality of so many ecclesiastical furnishings, which were merely the mass products of a crudely materialistic and commercial civilization. In him William Morris seemed reborn as a Catholic. "The Church," he argued, "which has the spending of so much money, might at least employ the best artists even if they be few and eccentric."[86] He set himself to destroy two aesthetic fallacies, as he conceived them to be: the view that a work of art is essentially an imitation of an object in Nature, and the claim that the Beautiful necessarily represents the Good. He insisted that verisimilitude to Nature was exalted only by a people who had lost religion, but that genuine art was not imitative, since "in such activity man cooperates with God in creating it."[87] Beauty, he averred, is absolute, and independent of ethical considerations, whereas loveliness is merely relative. "The Madonna of Cimabue is beautiful with an absolute beauty. The Madonna of Sassoferrato is lovely because it portrays that kind of woman who is lovable to those who love that kind of woman, and in that kind of attitude which is charming to those who are charmed by it."[88]

[84] Moore was awarded the International Sculpture Prize at the 2nd Sao Paulo Biennale and at the 24th Venice Biennale, and his works are in the permanent collections of the leading museums of the world. A Henry Moore group adorns the UNESCO headquarters building in Paris and several may be seen in the Metropolitan Museum of Art in New York City, in the Battersea Open-Air Sculpture Park in South London, and in the Tate Gallery.

[85] Gill's membership of Communities (Llanthony and Ditchling) and his concern for "Mass for the Masses," Epstein's *Social Consciousness* group in Fairmount Park in Philadelphia, and Moore's preoccupation with the basic family unit (whether as mother and child or, later, as father, mother and child) give point to this generalization.

[86] *Christianity and Art*, p. 10.

[87] *Ibid.*, p. 30.

[88] *Ibid.*, p. 27.

It will be apparent that, in preferring Cimabue's Madonna to Sassoferrato's, Gill has introduced a theological-ethical criterion into what purports to be a purely aesthetic judgment. His writings are full of stimulating judgments, frequently perceptive and occasionally wrong-headed. Certainly his whole-hearted devotion to religion was like horse-blinkers: it gave him direction but made him tread too narrow a path.[89]

Eric Gill's woodcuts and carvings almost always reflected the Christian doctrine of creation, the belief that "the natural world is God's present to Himself."[90] It was entirely characteristic of him to write of the Stations of the Cross that he had carved for Westminster Roman Catholic Cathedral: "But I was really the boy for the job, because I not only had the proper Christian enthusiasm, but I had sufficient, if only just sufficient, technical knowledge combined with a complete and genuine ignorance of art-school anatomy and traditional academic style." His patrons, so he believed, "thought I was carving in the Byzantine style on purpose. Certainly I was carving in what might be called an archaic manner; but I wasn't doing it on purpose, but only because I couldn't do it in any other way."[91] In fact, here was a recapturing of a simpler stylized and hieratic Byzantine mode which stressed the dignity of the Son of God and tried to snare the permanent in the passing moment. The lines are clean and streamlined.

One of Gill's most moving major works is the *Crucifixion* of 1910, a stone bas-relief of 37 inches by 31 inches, now in the Tate Gallery. Absolutely naked, this flattened and blood-drained Christ, with the long oval face, domed head and high-arched eyebrows, and vast eyelids closed in death, is most eloquent in his appealing silence. The raised Greek and the incised Latin inscriptions are also masterly. Had Gill lived to see the renascence of Christian art in England, of which he was the forerunner, he might have felt that his writing and carving were worth all the labour, misunderstanding, and criticism that they cost him.

The lot of the creative and controversial artist is hard, and the misprision[92] which Jacob Epstein faced in his early years is a

[89] See Sir John Rothenstein, *Modern English Painters*, Vol. II, pp. 299-300, where he states that Gill's religion "led him into some contradictions, absurdities, and even uncharities."

[90] Section II: "Creation—After God," p. 19 of *Christianity and Art*.

[91] *Autobiography*, pp. 200ff.

[92] The information on the religious sculptures of Sir Jacob Epstein I owe chiefly to three informative and gracious interviews with his widow, Lady Kathleen Epstein, in late June and July of 1963, and to the following printed sources:

left-handed tribute to his vitality, prodigality of output, and originality of concept and technique.

Manhattan's teeming East Side stimulated his curiosity about human beings, for there the Irish, the Jews, the Negroes, and the Chinese lived in close juxtaposition. An orthodox Jewish upbringing left him with little interest in ritual and ceremonial, but the imagery of the Old Testament had undoubtedly left its mark upon him, since he returned to it in his drawings illustrating Old Testament incidents and in the alabaster sculptures of Adam and of Jacob wrestling with the angel. It also provided his abiding interest in ethical and social attitudes and opened the way for the appreciation of the foundational figures of the New Covenant, Jesus and Mary of Nazareth. In Paris he met Brancusi and Modigliani, as a result of a commission he received to carve a tomb for the remains of Oscar Wilde. Moving to London, where he made his permanent home, he was for a time greatly influenced by T. E. Hulme, philosopher and art critic, in the direction of abstractionism, and he had a brief "vorticist" phase, of which the *Rock Drill* (1913), which welds man and drill into one romanticized machine, is the token. This abstract impersonalism did not hold him long in its thrall, but some of the residue of deliberate distortion remained in the larger stone carvings and gave his works an important accent and a thrusting emphasis.

The religious works followed one another in rapid succession and with astonishing variety. *The Risen Christ*, begun in 1917, was completed in 1919. In 1926 that daring but tender evocation of the Virgin's humility and trust, *The Visitation*, was completed, and is now in the Tate Gallery. In 1927, using an Indian woman and her small son as models, Epstein completed his first group of *The Madonna and Child*, which is now in Riverside Church, New York City. Between 1929 and 1931 he made a series of drawings of Old Testament incidents and sculpted a *Genesis*, a primordial image of age-long travail. Because it was the antithesis of the sentimental, it brought upon him the revilings of the ignorant and a notoriety that was hardly exceeded by the immoral Rector of Stiffkey, for both *Genesis* and the Rector were exhibited on the

Epstein: An Autobiography; Geoffrey Ireland, *Epstein: A Camera Study of the Sculptor at Work*, containing a valuable introduction by Laurie Lee the poet. Lady Epstein has assisted in the preparation of definitive studies, *Epstein: Drawings* and of *Jacob Epstein: Sculptor*, both edited by Richard Buckle. I also found Sir John Rothenstein's introduction to *Epstein: Arts Council Memorial Exhibition* quite invaluable.

sands of Blackpool beach for the titillation of the gaping holiday-makers. In 1935 the Romanesque-style carving of *Behold the Man* was exhibited; this dolorous thorn-crowned Christ, flattened by pain, was a powerful image of suffering, the appearance of which coincided with Hitler's pogrom against the Jews.[93] In 1937 the *Consummatum Est* was completed, and in 1939 the powerful, up-straining *Adam*. In 1941 the dynamic struggle of *Jacob with the Angel* was finished and in 1945 *Lucifer*, that proudly sensual angel.

In 1949 *Lazarus* in his cerements, reluctantly coming back to life, and seeming to topple over, was completed, and is now to be found in the ante-chapel of New College, Oxford. Here it is superbly situated, with its heavy feet towards the west door and its head looking towards the reredos with the multiple images of the saints in the beatitude which Lazarus has left. In 1951 one of the supreme works, the Cavendish Square *Madonna and Child*, commissioned by the Convent of the Holy Child Jesus, was begun; it was unveiled in 1952. In 1953 *Social Consciousness* was completed in clay, and the commission to undertake the Llandaff Cathedral *Majestas* (Christ in Glory) was given. The latter was unveiled in 1957 and is another of Epstein's major works. In 1955 he was commissioned to sculpt the *Smuts Memorial* in Parliament Square and also the *St. Michael and the Devil* for Coventry Cathedral; the former was unveiled in 1956 and the latter was completed a year later. In 1957 the *William Blake* memorial bust was unveiled in Westminster Abbey, and is a fitting tribute from one visionary to another.

A severe thrombosis interrupted several commissions in 1958, and thus Epstein's single attempt to depict *The Ascending Christ* was frustrated, leaving only an exquisite maquette as a hint of a great statue that might have been, ethereal in its face upturned to the Father, its elongated limbs and thin up-pointing hands, and with a rotating action hinted by the wind-blown gown.[94] In 1959 portraits of Dr. Geoffrey Fisher, Archbishop of Canterbury, and of Sir Basil Spence were completed, as well as the two last child portraits (in which Sir Jacob also excelled). The Bowater House Group plaster cast was finished on the morning of August 19,

[93] Lady Epstein told the writer that Sir Jacob intended this as an image of "suffering that never ends." This *Ecce Homo* is now in the possession of Canon C. B. Mortlock. Epstein himself wrote of it: "I wished to make an *Ecce Homo*, a symbol of man, bound, crowned with thorns, and facing with a relentless and overmastering gaze of pity and prescience an unhappy world" (*Autobiography*, p. 144).

[94] In the author's possession. See Fig. 26.

1959, and the casting instructions were given to the bronze moulder. The same night that great sculptor whose large studio had given an aesthetic extension of life to hundreds of famous and little known people and who had revitalised our understanding of the Judaeo-Christian saga, lay dead.

Amid God's plenty space can only be found for the briefest consideration of three religious masterpieces.[95] *The Visitation* (1926) is an arrestingly tender but daring treatment of the Virgin in bronze, which is 65 inches high. The head, with frank and open eyes and slightly parted mouth, is inclined forwards and the two long plaits of hair emphasize the submissive line of the neck. The forearms are raised upwards and forwards from the elbows and the left hand rests upon the back of the right, forming from the front a bridge and from the side a further suggestion of forward inclination. The frontal view of the bridged arms provides, as it were, a pedestal upon which the head and neck seem to rest, and the upthrust of the arms is continued, in slightly asymmetrical fashion, by the plaits. Innocence, gentleness, and the humble submissiveness of "Be it unto me according to thy Word" are expressed in a figure literally bent to the bidding of the divine messenger.

Sir Jacob wrote of the *Madonna and Child* (1951-52): "No work of mine has brought so many tributes from so many diverse quarters."[96] So triumphant a work, sculpturally and emotionally, requires the discriminating praise of a poet to do it justice. This Laurie Lee has attempted in the following tribute:

"The siting is perfect; the design complex and monumentally simple. The two figures float above us with no apparent artifice of support and their relationship to each other and to us is profoundly moving. The Christ child is not the customary babe but a lean lad of some five or six years. The mantled Mother with open hands reveals and offers him to the world. And the child both in expression and design is all prophecy: the robe that wraps his narrow body is also the robe of the tomb; the arms outstretched to embrace the world also assume the attitude of crucifixion; and the face with its large wide eyes and serene brow, looks out with love and knows what that love will cost him. This is one of the finest, most subtle,

---

[95] The *St. Michael and the Devil* on the exterior of Coventry Cathedral was considered in section 3 of this chapter. See Fig. 25.

[96] This 13½ feet high group was cast in lead. It is placed above an arch designed by Louis Osman which connects two Palladian-style buildings on the north side of Cavendish Square in London's West End. Sir Jacob gave it his concentrated attention during six months (*Autobiography*, p. 235). See Fig. 20.

most affectionate of Epstein's works. It is also one of the most original conceptions of this theme."[97]

Only one other contemporary sculpture equal to the theme deserves to be compared with it—Henry Moore's *Madonna and Child*. The latter is, however, a great hieratic archetype, while this is majestically merciful. Moore suggests Deity above us, Epstein Deity for us.

Perhaps the subtlest of all Epstein's religious images is the moving *Majestas*[98] of Christ in Llandaff Cathedral (1953-57). This, too, is superbly sited and mounted, with the collaboration of George G. Pace. When mediaeval Llandaff Cathedral was severely damaged by a land-mine in the Second World War, Pace was placed in charge of the reconstruction, working closely with the then Dean of Llandaff, now the Bishop, Dr. Glyn Simon. It was decided to invite Epstein to sculpt a vast representation of Christ in Glory, which would hang on a great cylinder, bearing the organ pipes, and would be most elegantly raised on the delicate arms of two curving concrete bridges. The Epsteins, accompanied by Sir Stanley Spencer, visited the roofless and window-shattered cathedral in 1953. Discerning its dim outline as the dusk was falling, and making out the dark forms of two cassocked canons with black cloaks, Sir Jacob was impressed by the poignancy of the scene and enthusiastically devoted himself to preparing a symbol of the glorious rebirth of the Church.[99]

This eventually became the 14½ feet high *Majestas*, which was cast in aluminium. In the words of Laurie Lee: "It is a transfixing figure, floating, with pointed hands and feet, the sleeves in flat folds, like wings. The whole vacant column of the body annihilates the carnal world and leads one's eyes inexorably upwards to the face. And here again is one of Epstein's personal creations, a face transfigured, remote, supernatural, yet a face of suffering and love."[100] What is so astonishing about the *Majestas* is that it harmoniously combines three Christological concepts: the impassible Byzantine Christ enthroned in glory, the Semitic suffering Christ with sharp nose and agonising eyes, and the contemporary Christ whose hands plead *Shalom, Shalom*, to a world that does not know

[97] Citation from the unnumbered pagination of the introduction to Geoffrey Ireland, *Epstein: A Camera Study of the Sculptor at Work.*

[98] A photographic reproduction of the *Majestas* appears on the dust-jacket of the present volume and of each other in this series.

[99] Information from Lady Kathleen Epstein's notes in the exhibition brochure *Epstein at King's Lynn* and in a conversation with her.

[100] Ireland, *Epstein . . . ,* introduction.

the secret of its peace. In Sir Jacob Epstein we salute a Jew who understood the Biblical faith with profundity and relevance and whose religious works continually renew their claims on imagination and belief.

The last of the trio of sculptors is the most original of all, Henry Moore (born 1898).[101] If a profound concern for man's role in the universe and his relationships with society, or a capacity to evoke feelings of awe and ultimate concern, are what is intended by the term "religion"—then Moore is profoundly religious. If, however, we hold to a more traditional and narrower as well as more explicit definition of allegiance to a historic faith (and in particular to Christianity as a religion of redemption), then only his *Madonna and Child* can be considered, thematically, as Christian art.[102] Moore's *Madonna and Child* (1943-1944) reposes behind a delicate wrought-iron grille in the north transept of St. Matthew's Anglican Church, Northampton. It is magisterially carved in Hornton stone and rises to a height of 59 inches. Its serene and quiet dignity entirely fulfils the sculptor's intention: "I have tried to give a sense of complete ease and repose as though the Madonna could stay in that position for ever (as, being in stone, she will have to)."[103] The Madonna presents her Son to the world on which he gazes with calm benevolence and preternatural wisdom, suggesting that he is, indeed, the *Logos* or Divine Wisdom incarnate.

The image has also profound psychological meaning for Henry Moore, who has concerned himself in a whole series of works with the feminine archetype, as if to redress the balance of a destructive, one-sided, and patriarchal culture. As Erich Neumann has written: "The birth of the feminine archetype in modern man signifies at the same time the development of human relatedness, of his social

---

[101] See *inter alia* the following: *Henry Moore, Sculptor*, by Herbert Read; *Henry Moore*, by Geoffrey Grigson; *Shelter Sketchbook, London* (1944); *Henry Moore: Sculptures and Drawings* introduced by Herbert Read; *Henry Moore: Portfolio of Forty Drawings*; *Henry Moore*, by James Johnson Sweeney; *Henry Moore*, by Guilio Carlo Argan; *Henry Moore, Schriften und Skulpturen*, by Werner Hofman; *The Archetypal World of Henry Moore* (Bollingen Series LXVIII) by Erich Neumann; *Henry Moore*, by J. P. Hodin; and *Heads, Figures and Ideas: A Sculptor's Notebook*, by Henry Moore. See Fig. 21.

[102] This is not the place to go into the important theological question of whether works of art may be called "Christian" if their creators repudiate any formal association with any branch of the Christian Church, because they are, willy-nilly, done in the providence of God and by the gift of imagination through which man is a cooperator with the Creator. The present writer would, however, prefer to err on the side of theological and aesthetic latitude, especially as the art works of so many committed Christians can be so conventional, flat, and uninspired.

[103] Herbert Read, *Henry Moore: Sculptures and Drawings*, Vol. I, p. xxv.

capacity, and the growing consciousness of the unity of mankind on earth."[104]

8. *Summation*

This summary survey of the slow and reluctant rebirth of religious art in England has tried to do justice to the unimaginative traditionalism, mingled with the stirrings of syncretism, of the first four decades of the present century, in which the pioneer voices of Eric Gill and of Jacob Epstein were either unheard or vilified (as in the case of the latter).[105] During this time English ecclesiastical architecture seemed to be unaware of the liturgical and architectural revolution achieved in Audincourt and Ronchamps, at Vence and at Cologne, or in remoter Finland or Brasilia. In such circumstances, the most that could be hoped for was the inspired conservatism of Guildford or Coventry, though Sir Basil Spence's cathedral became a frame for many artists of compelling distinction, and is more than a frame, and Gibberd's Liverpool "tent of pilgrimage" is functionally, liturgically, and symbolically modern.

The value and the danger of religion is its conservative clinging to the past, a clinging that is all the more passionate when it is challenged by the unparalleled rate of contemporary change. It was, indeed, inevitable that a country with a great historic tradition, compelled to play a secondary political role, should seek for solace in its past, and that churchmen should—for the most part—stress what they believed to be the eternal verities of the Christian faith and look for artists with a traditional iconography and architects who would build in the grand Gothic manner. Moreover, a religion such as Christianity bases its hope for the future on the climactic revelatory acts of God in Christ, believing that B.C. and A.D. form

104 *The Archetypal World of Henry Moore*, p. 129. This is a fascinating Jungian interpretation of the powerful symbols of Henry Moore, which makes the perceptive criticism (p. 89) that "this Madonna figure and other sketches of the kind lack that drastic contemporary element that makes their eternity *our* eternity. This does not detract from the beauty of these sculptures so much as from their 'aliveness,' which is otherwise the most revolutionary quality of Moore's work."

105 See Sir John Rothenstein's introduction to *Epstein: Arts Council Memorial Exhibition*, where he elaborates the paradox that the man considered to be an "anarchist" and a "barbarian" was one of the most traditional of the major sculptors of his time. The even greater paradox is that Epstein, who came from a people forbidden to make representations of Divine beings or human beings, created some of the most impressive and moving Biblical images of his time, as did Chagall. See Cecil Roth, ed., *Jewish Art, An Illustrated History*, pp. 17ff., for a discussion of the prohibition of "graven images" and the ways in which this was interpreted in the history of Judaism.

the very hinge on which history turns. There can, in the nature of things, be no new Christianity, but only new forms in which the relevance of the Divine saga or *heilsgeschichte* is made known and contemporized. All this, and the lack of any great master of architecture since Wren, or any great sculpture at all, and indeed the want of a visual tradition that can compare with the most brilliant achievements of Italy, France, the Netherlands, Germany or Spain, makes the traditionalism and the weak syncretism intelligible. But it also makes all the more remarkable the emergence of modern masters like Henry Moore and Graham Sutherland and of a new and passionate interest in art and architecture. Truth further compels the admission that for the most part Eric Gill's strictures have not lost their validity because in too many sanctuaries mass-produced *bon-dieuserie* continues to insult God and real artists.

But equally it must be insisted that there is a growing sense of grave dissatisfaction with this situation, and that the new functional liturgical architecture and the symbolical and abstract religious art of the fifth, sixth, and seventh decades will continue to gain ground. It is not too much to hope from the evidence already present, of which only the most striking examples have been studied in this chapter, that increasingly architects, sculptors, painters, glaziers, metal-workers, weavers, and embroiderers will join with the musicians and poets and the whole people of God in a paean of *contemporary* praise, in a veritable twentieth century *Benedicite*.

101

CHAPTER III

THE DEVELOPMENT
OF CHURCH MUSIC

T HE RENAISSANCE of religious art is paralleled by the vigorous growth of religious music. "In church music," writes Erik R. Routley, "there has been no age so full of surprises, and so full of creative promise, as our own."[1] While this seems a perilous judgment, it is supported by several important considerations. The first is that never since the sixteenth century have so many distinguished musicians in the secular field attempted to write sacred music. This is true of such varied composers on the European continent as Stravinsky, Webern, Poulenc, Krenek, and Messiaen. On the English scene it applies with particular force to such twentieth century composers as Elgar and Vaughan Williams, Bliss and Walton, Howells and Britten. Some of the more popular English Victorian composers, like Sullivan, also wrote church music, but their ecclesiastical work was a kind of "writing down" to the church level, a species of amateurishness. The twentieth century composers, by contrast, use their professional standards and techniques to the full in their church music.

The point is that some of the most distinguished modern music in England is written for the Church and that has not been the case since the golden days of Tallis, Byrd, and Purcell. Furthermore, in the recent decades of the twentieth century any temptation for English church music to be romantically escapist or merely cathedrally sonorous and antiquarian has been rejected by the realistic recognition that the Church is *in* the world. Therefore the Church in its music must be involved in the problems of modern life, including the struggle for faith against the inroads of secularism. The outward prosperity of the Church is a thing of the past, and this has forced the Church into a living encounter with the world. Church music, in the vivid phrase of Routley, must now travel second-class. The most hopeful sign of all is that the most

[1] *Twentieth Century Church Music*, p. 5. I here wish to express my deep gratitude to my friend, Dr. Erik R. Routley, for his great kindness in allowing me to read this volume in proof. It is a superb survey of the period, written in the most engaging style, by this witty and erudite musician, church historian, and expert hymnologist, to whom I am greatly indebted. This chapter has been supervised by Dr. Routley and also by Mr. Myron McLellan, a young composer now a doctoral candidate in the Department of Religion at Princeton University.

recent church music is radically experimental both in high-brow and in low-brow directions. This factor alone accounts for the hazardous as well as the promising condition of modern church music in England.

In the past six and a half decades, three major trends can be discerned in the development of English church music, each of which warrants consideration. First, there was the period in which church music attained to professional standards, and was marked by the work of outstanding craftsmen, most of whom were the organists of the English cathedrals. It was, moreover, a time when several eminent musicians, previously not in the sacred field, turned to composing sacred music. It was also the period of distinguished musical teaching, and of important historical research. The foundations of the highest standards of English church music were then laid down. The second phase of development was a move away from traditional music in both the sacred and secular spheres to music that was radically experimental in character. The most recent phase, though it has not eliminated either of the two earlier trends, shows the Church coming to terms with the social revolution and attempting to produce highly controversial "popular" music, for the missionary purpose of relating to the experience of the modern adolescent influenced by the "Hit Parade."

1. *Raising the Standards of English Church Music*

This, the earliest phase in the century's development, may be said to have reached reasonable fulfilment with the establishment of the Royal School of Church Music in 1927. With the achievement of a highly professional tradition in English church music, it was possible for Commissions appointed by the Archbishops of Canterbury and York to publish in 1922 a report entitled *Music in Worship* and in 1951 another entitled *Music in Church* (revised edition, 1960). But it is significant that the latter looked back to 1906 and the founding of the Church Music Society, as the pioneer period in which musical standards were raised in church to a genuinely professional level.[2]

The attainment of professional standards involved a serious break with the cult of mediocrity and amateurishness, and with the rather pretentious vulgarity and crude sentimentality which had marked the compositions of some of the most famous Victorian composers, such as Sullivan and Stainer.

2 *Music in Church*, p. 7.

103

The pioneers were two close friends, who both honoured and criticized each other, Ralph Vaughan Williams and Gustav Holst.[3] Each won distinction in the wider field of music, orchestrally and vocally. Holst's *Planets* was his single greatest work, but Williams won the greater fame with more compositions. Holst disseminated an appreciation of English music by his lectures, while Vaughan Williams by his musical editorship of English hymnals, his organization and writing for the Three Choirs Festivals, and his researches into English musical history, helped to set the highest standards.

Vaughan Williams proved in the *Sancta Civitas* (1925) that he could combine the strains of the ancients with modern harmonic devices. He also produced superb hymn-tunes, as in his "Sine Nomine" to accompany "For all the saints" or his "Down Ampney" for "Come down, O love divine." He was capable, also, of dramatic composing, as his *Dona nobis Pacem* and *Hodie* (1954) demonstrated. His *Mass in G Minor* showed how this versatile musician could fashion a sensitive setting to the requirements of the Anglican liturgy. Holst's church music is not as well known, nor on so large or varied a scale, but it is exquisite. Two examples are the charming anthem, "This I have done for my true love," based on the Cornish carol, "Tomorrow shall be my dancing day" (published by Augener, 1922), and the music to the Mystery Play, *The Coming of Christ* (1928). Holst also contributed valuable hymn tunes to *Songs of Praise*. Both Vaughan Williams and Holst have the power of evoking religious awe and mystery with a great economy of resources.

Vaughan Williams' importance as the musical editor of two important hymnals, the *English Hymnal* and *Songs of Praise*, will be considered later. What it is important to stress immediately is those qualities in music for which Vaughan Williams and Holst were looking, in their dissent from the harmonic and contrapuntal orthodoxy of the eighteenth and nineteenth centuries and which they found, in part, in Tudor England, in both folk and church music. They dissented from four-part writing, and Williams often preferred two-part and three-part writing. They preferred modal scales to the customary diatonic scale with its regularity. They also delighted in highly melismatic melody, both in the original

[3] See their correspondence in U. Vaughan Williams and I. Holst, eds., *Heirs and Rebels.*

sense of using graceful and florid vocalization, and in the narrower sense of having several notes sung to one syllable.

Important as they were, they were by no means alone. The standards of music were also raised by more conservative craftsmen, such as Charles Wood, Edward Bairstow, and Basil Harwood. This group was succeeded by another group of excellent craftsmen, almost all cathedral organists, which included Sydney Nicholson, William Harris, Harold Darke, H. K. Andrews, Thomas Armstrong, Herbert Sumsion, George Oldroyd, Sydney Campbell, and Ernest Bullock. The only comparable national figure representing Dissent was Eric Thiman, the musical editor of *Congregational Praise* (1951). By their compositions, as by their education of church musical taste among choirs and worshippers, they also helped appreciably to raise the standards.

Among the great teachers was Sir Walford Davies, who popularized good vocal music through the medium of the British Broadcasting Corporation as effectively as Sir Henry Wood popularized orchestral music through his "Promenade Concerts" at the Albert Hall. Two other admirable teachers of music in the period were the brothers, Martin and Geoffrey Shaw, instructors and inspectors in the English day schools.[4]

The Free Church musicians had far the greater leeway to make up because Nonconformity had neither the Liturgy nor the Cathedral tradition behind it. It had to overcome its own Victorian customs, in which heartiness rather than discrimination was characteristic of congregational singing, and which insisted on congregations singing the anthems as well as the hymns. It was also hampered by the fact that little time or money was spared for music because the high point of worship was the intellectual sermon, and money had already been expended on the impressiveness of the building or the preacher's salary. In these circumstances, the work of Eric Thiman in raising standards was extraordinarily important. He was helped by the contributions of other less distinguished, but still notable, Free Church musicians, including the Methodists, Luke Wiseman, F. D. Westbrook, and George Brockless[5] (the latter being organist of Westminster Central Hall), and the Congregationalist, Richard Aldridge.

It was a further proof that English church music had come of

---

[4] Routley, *Twentieth Century Church Music*, p. 52, claims that "they made the world safe for music to sail on past them."

[5] The son of George Brockless, Brian, is an experimental composer who wrote the anthem "Now blessed be Thou, Christ Jesu" (1960).

age professionally when composers whose chief experience was outside ecclesiastical music produced church music, knowing that it would be appreciated and worthily interpreted. Herbert Howells, Sir Arthur Bliss, and Sir William Walton are professional musicians who paid this compliment to the improved musical standards in churches.

Howells had written in a vein which was reminiscent of Vaughan Williams in his use of Tudor idioms and in an alternation of romanticism and astringency. His *Four Anthems* (1941-1943) are frequently heard, particularly "O Pray for the peace of Jerusalem" and the vigorous "Let God arise." But his most remarkable work in church music is an ingenious series of cathedral or collegiate services dedicated to particular choirs, bearing in mind their history and their acoustical contexts and resources. The series began with the *Collegium Regiale* setting of the Evening Canticles written for King's College, Cambridge, in 1947. Other settings were composed for Worcester (1953), St. Paul's, London (1954), Westminster Abbey (1956), St. John's College, Cambridge (1958), and in 1958 he composed a Communion setting for Christ Church, Oxford, entitled *Missa Aedis Christi*. A very remarkable Requiem is his *Hymnus Paradisi* (1950). In the main, Howells' work is in the traditional vein.

It was no less remarkable that two symphonists should also have written church music in our period. Sir Arthur Bliss composed the long anthem, "Stand up and bless the Lord," as part of the consecration service for Llandaff Cathedral in 1960, and a large cantata, "The Beatitudes," was part of the consecration celebrations for Coventry Cathedral in 1962. Sir William Walton is "the finest example of a composer not naturally a churchman whose contributions to church literature are remarkable."[6] In 1953 he provided the ceremonial setting for the *Te Deum* at the Coronation of Queen Elizabeth II in Westminster Abbey. His greatest work, a massive *Gloria* for choir and orchestra, was composed in 1961 for the 125th anniversary of the Huddersfield Choral Society. It is full of inventive surprises and splendours. He brings to ecclesiastical music the passion and the irony of the world.

Distinguished musical teachers who have written church music must also be mentioned, however briefly. They include Edmund Rubbra, who has written three liturgical Masses, a setting of *Lauda Sion*, and two ceremonial settings of the *Te Deum*; Egon Wellesz,

[6] Erik R. Routley, *ibid.*, p. 64.

the historian of Byzantine music and biographer of Schoenberg, who composed a *Mass in F minor* (1949); and Arthur Hutchings, who composed a *Communion service in G* (1957). Nor should it be forgotten that Herbert Howells was a distinguished teacher of music.

2. *Experimental Music*

What Henry Moore is in the world of art, Benjamin Britten is in music—unquestionably an international figure who has explored the musical possibilities of the human voice as Moore has explored the plastic possibilities of stone and metal. While his reputation is chiefly due to his operas, he has written church music of undoubted originality and depth, even if his is not as advanced a technique as many in the *avant garde*. These important ecclesiastical works include a *Ceremony of Carols*, *Rejoice in the Lamb* (both published in 1943), *Festival Te Deum* (1945), *St. Nicholas* (1948), *Hymn to St. Peter* (1955), *Noye's Fludde* (1958), *Missa Brevis* (1959), and the splendidly indignant *War Requiem* (1962). These works are astonishing in their invention and variety, the brilliance of their technique, and in their humanity. To look for parallels one has to compare him with Purcell in the English tradition for the exploitation of voice and instrument, and to Verdi for the originality of his Requiem, but he is all the time distinctively Benjamin Britten, and no man's imitator.

If his influence is to be seen in those who experiment in new vocal possibilities, dissonance, and economy in rhetorical devices, then Nicholas Maw, Mansel Thomas, and John Joubert, though not disciples, have felt his impact. John Joubert, the composer of *Missa Beati Joannis* (1962) is possibly the most distinguished of those for whom Britten blazed the experimental trail.

Other experimenters are more advanced radicals. The influence of Schoenberg is seen most clearly in Michael Tippett, who composed a *Magnificat* and a *Nunc Dimittis* for St. John's College, Cambridge, in 1961. Messiaen's influence can be discerned in the music of Peter Maxwell Davies, whose most impressive work up to now is a carol sequence, *O magnum mysterium* (1961). Webern's impact is most clearly seen in Harrison Birtwhistle's *Monody for Corpus Christi*. Another experimentalist who is a disciple of Messiaen is Malcolm Williamson, who essays both the high-brow and low-brow manner. *Planctus* (1962) is a contemplation of death in which tenors and basses share alternately in a single vocal line, the two voices only occasionally overlapping. *Wrestling Jacob* (1962) is an ingenious setting of three verses of Charles Wesley's hymn, "Come, O thou Traveller unknown." The mere mention of these experiments is an indication of the liveliness of English church music and its openness to the idioms of the secular music of its age, which have blown rhetorical posturing and every other kind of complacency to the four winds.

3. *Church Light Music*

A much more controversial development in the modern Church has been an attempt to write "popular" music in order to attract the teen-agers who would otherwise reject church music as entirely "square." It is a deliberate "writing-down" of contemporary church music, which is defended by those who write it or use it as a missionary accommodation, a kind of pre-conversion music in a modernized Sankey mode. It is also defended as a fracturing of the Church's image as bourgeois. It is ridiculed by its critics as an unwarrantable perversion of the standards of the Gospel in terms of a sensuous, superficial, and sentimental musical appeal, and as a failure in its attempt to turn juvenile delinquents into juvenile disciples.

The movement commenced with Father Geoffrey Beaumont's *Folk Mass*, published in 1956. In a Preface to it, Beaumont stated that this setting of the Anglican Liturgy was written at the request of a vicar in the East end of London, who claimed that church music was utterly foreign to most people and that nothing had been written since the time of the Elizabethans which could properly be called a *Folk Mass*. Beaumont asserted that in its title "the word 'Folk' is used literally to mean the normal everyday popular kind of music." The work is commonly, but inaccurately, termed the "Jazz Mass."

While the priest is expected to sing his part of the Liturgy to the familiar Merbecke setting, the congregation's part is sung by "dictation"—that is, each phrase is sung first by the cantor and repeated by the congregation. Thus it can easily be learned by the people, and even sung without rehearsal. The style of the music is that of a revue, and the "catchy" tune that is most easily remembered is that of the "Sanctus." It resembles so-called pop music only in the dull and repetitive bass: it is not saccharine enough, nor sufficiently re-iterative, to compete with popular hits. Nor, it may be suggested, is the musical comedy or revue type of music likely to succeed without those lavish embellishments of stage, costuming, orchestra, and widely advertised personalities, which are characteristic of its secular context.

One can hardly imagine a more unsuitable setting for such a type of music than the rather bare church hall in which this kind of musical mission is attempted.

It is, however, as a portent rather than as an achievement that the *Folk Mass* is significant. It was the incentive for the founding of the *20th Century Church Light Music Group*, which has produced much church music in a style imitating Beaumont's. Perhaps its best known works are Patrick Appleford's *Mass of Five Melodies* and a *Festival Te Deum* by John Alldis. Appleford learned from Beaumont's experiment that the services of a cantor should be dispensed with. Neither musician succeeds in writing truly popular music. It seems that the group is more successful with hymn tunes, for some of them can produce tunes that go with a swing. Beaumont's "Chesterton" is a good example, as also his "Gracias," and it is interesting that these have been included in the *Baptist Hymn Book* of 1962. Others associated with him are less able to produce the "Oklahoma!" type of melodies than he, and often succeed only in sounding like re-activated Gilbert and Sullivan or antiquated "Tin Pan Alley." The two publications of the group in this genre are *Thirty 20th Century Hymn Tunes* (1960) and *More 20th Century Hymn Tunes* (1962). The group has not, however, proved as successful in trying to write words to match its tunes.

In *Rhythm in Religion* (1960) there is a serious attempt made to write popular lyrics which will match "popular" music. The eight songs are all the work of clergy, and one can admire their intentions rather than their achievements. These lyrics are marked by a paternalism which attributes to young people a sense of alienation and a search for direction—perhaps what the clergy hope for rather than find in their charges.

There appears to be only one writer of religious verse in England who is able to produce appropriate lyrics for the new popular music. He is Sydney Carter, an authentic folk-singer, who is unusual in being also a Christian. A record of his collected songs has been made, entitled *Songs of Faith and Doubt*. His expertise may be judged from the fact that his song-writing was added to Donald Swann's repertory in "At the Drop of a Hat." He can use irony and satire in a deeply religious fashion, as in the ballade beginning,

"I danced in the morning when the world was begun." Two of its stanzas go thus:

> I danced on the Sabbath and I cured the lame
> And the holy people said it was a shame:
> They whipped and they stripped and they hung me high,
> And they left me there on a Cross to die.
>
> I danced on a Friday when the sky turned black;
> It's hard to dance with the devil on your back.
> They buried my body and they thought I'd gone.
> But I am the dance, and I still go on.

This has the true character of folk music, and its refrains bring in the important community element. Furthermore, it points to the possibility of twentieth century carols, mingling the sacred and the secular as the mediaeval carols did. There is no doubt that irony and satire can be used in the twentieth century Church as a potent weapon for detecting Pharisaism, and that new carols can convey as the old did the authentic Christian *joie de vivre*.

4. Hymnody

The higher professional quality of craftsmanship in church music in the present century is clearly reflected in the improvement in the hymnals that the various communions have produced. This has been accompanied by a more serious and widespread discussion of those qualities in words and music that constitute a good hymn.

This pedagogical concern is reflected in a distinctive type of twentieth century writing on praise—the hymnal companion or handbook. As in so much else in the period, Percy Dearmer was the pioneer, writing his *Songs of Praise Discussed* in 1933. Kenneth L. Parry and Erik R. Routley produced their *Companion to Congregational Praise* in 1953, and Hugh Martin edited *The Baptist Hymn Book Companion* in 1962. A more historical approach to an important hymn book was W. K. Lowther Clarke's *A Hundred Years of Hymns Ancient and Modern* (1961). The greatest historian of hymnody was, of course, Dr. John Julian, the compiler of the monumental *Dictionary of Hymnology*, the first edition of which appeared in 1891. Other important and informed writers on hymnody were Winfred Douglas,[7] Louis F. Benson,[8]

---

[7] *Church Music in History and Practice.* Both Douglas and Benson were American ministers whose work was well known in England.
[8] *The Hymnody of the Christian Church.*

and the prolific Erik R. Routley.[9] Their work, as well as that of the writers of hymn book companions, was to educate ministers, organists, and interested laity in the appreciation of the literary, musical, and theological values of hymns.

A typical discussion of the qualities, both musical and literary, to be desired in Christian worship, is to be found in the Anglican report of 1951, *Music in Church*, prepared under the chairmanship of Noel T. Hopkins, Provost of Wakefield. Four general canons are laid down as to the music. It is to be "a fitting expression of the words; the words matter most." As music, it must be good, which is further defined as having "life without levity, and dignity without heaviness," the avoidance of discords, and the keeping to simple harmony. It is further to be thoroughly "in keeping with the spirit of the liturgy." This, again, is defined as music which exhibits nobility and restraint, and freedom from sensationalism and mawkishness. Finally, this music should be "fitted to the conditions existing in the church for which it is designed."[10] This means that a rustic parish church choir should not attempt cathedral-type music, for true worship should aim at the glory of God (rather than that of the choir) and the assistance of the congregation.

These canons are applied to the selection of hymns and hymn tunes in more detail. It is insisted that worth rather than popularity should be the first criterion. It is strongly stated that "the emphasis on sincerity and strength in religion is more than ever apparent in an age that is peculiarly critical of pretence and sentimentality."[11] The need of the hour is for austerity. A succinct definition is given of a good hymn tune. It is "one of which the emotional content is appropriate to its plan and occasion; the harmonized parts, especially the bass, should be interesting and distinctive; the melody should be well drawn, not made up of notes which bear no close relation to one another, nor insisting with a wearisome reiteration on a recurrence of the same note; so that it sounds clear, decided and convincing when sung without harmonies." It is then added that "the rhythm must fit closely to the words, but must be neither trivial nor obtrusive nor dull."[12]

These abstractions are given point by contrasting tinsel tunes with genuinely golden ones. "Maidstone" with its hurdy-gurdy rhythm, and the tawdriness of "St. Bees," are set over against the

<hr/>

[9] See *The Church and Music*; *Church Music and Theology*; *The Music of Christian Hymnody*; *Hymns and Human Life*; and *I'll Praise My Maker*.
[10] *Music in Church*, p. 4.   [11] *Ibid.*, p. 35.
[12] *Ibid.*, p. 37.

beautiful simplicity of Gibbons' "Canterbury" or "Song 13." The feeble melody of Barnby's setting of "For all the Saints" is contrasted with the vigour and triumphant ring of those by Stanford and Vaughan Williams.[13]

What have been the distinctive contributions of the twentieth century to hymnody? As might be expected, the sense of comradeship in a world-wide Church,[14] as stimulated by the Ecumenical Movement, has been expressed in such hymns as John Oxenham's "In Christ there is no East or West." One hymn from the Liturgy of Malabar and another moving hymn on discipleship translated by Nicol Macnicol from the Indian original are becoming increasingly prized by English congregations. The pre-Kraemer[15] confidence that Christianity is the culmination rather than the criticism of other major religions is fittingly expressed in George Matheson's "Gather us in Thou love that fillest all."

The impact of the "social Gospel" is also strong on twentieth century hymnody,[16] resulting in the importation of many hymns on the subject of the Kingdom of God from the United States, such as "Rise up, O men of God" by William Merrill, a Presbyterian clergyman of Pelagian tendencies. Two written by Englishmen, which bid fair to become classics, are Canon Scott Holland's "Judge Eternal, throned in splendour" and G. K. Chesterton's "O God of earth and altar." Less successful were the hymns purporting to be Christian humanism, like that of Clifford Bax: "Turn back, O man, forswear thy foolish ways," which were, in fact, purely humanistic in their orientation.

Another feature of twentieth century hymnody was the composing of children's hymns which did not treat children as little men and women, or religion as renunciation, as had so many Victorian hymns. Two admirable examples are Percy Dearmer's "Jesus, good above all other" and Charter Piggott's "In our work and in our play."[17]

[13] *Ibid.*, pp. 37-38.

[14] Percy Dearmer in the preface to *Songs of Praise* commented: "The hymns themselves show how Catholic we have become in spite of ourselves." Even churches using the same language, however, are still a long way from considering a denominational hymnbook an anachronism.

[15] The reference is to Hendrik Kraemer's work, *The Christian Message in a Non-Christian World*, written from a strongly Barthian standpoint, affirming Christianity's finality, in preparation for the Madras Conference of the International Missionary Council.

[16] See the present author's article, "The Expression of the Social Gospel in Worship," in *Studia Liturgica* (Rotterdam), Vol. II, No. 3 (September 1963), pp. 174-92.

[17] Cited in full in H. A. L. Jefferson, *Hymns in Christian Worship*.

The lead for improved hymnody was given by five important Anglican hymnals. Two were works of scholarship, but three had much wider popularity. Of the first type was the *Yattendon Hymnal* of 1899, compiled by Robert Bridges for the village church of Yattendon in Berkshire. Containing only 100 hymns, it was a selection distinguished by the highest devotional, literary, and musical quality.[18] It clearly enunciated and exemplified a new principle—that the most suitable words must be matched to the most adequate tune. Of the same order was *The Songs of Syon* compiled by the Reverend G. R. Woodward. This collection of 414 hymns indicated a tendency towards authenticity in the choice of words as well as in the music of the finer hymn tunes of the European countries. It has proved to be a rich mine for later musical editors.

The widely influential hymn books were *Hymns Ancient and Modern*[19] (which had first appeared in 1861, but was revised in 1904 and appeared in an important revision in 1950), the *English Hymnal* of 1906 (musically revised in 1933), and *Songs of Praise* of 1925 (enlarged in 1931). The two latter volumes had as their musical editor the incomparable Ralph Vaughan Williams (assisted by Martin Shaw for *Songs of Praise*), and as literary editor, Dr. Percy Dearmer.

The importance of Vaughan Williams for hymnody is three-fold. He researched widely into the psalmody of Geneva, the folk-songs of Britain, the classics of early English hymnody and the tunes of the French Counter-Reformation, and raided these treasures for both *English Hymnal* and *Songs of Praise*. Moreover, when texts had been corrupted, he often restored them. For the earlier volume he contributed three excellent tunes of his own composition: "Sine Nomine," "Down Ampney," and "Randolph," and to the later one "Mantegna," "Marathon," and "Guildford," among others. In addition, he introduced Arnold Bax's "Wonder," Darke's "Cornhill," Patrick Hadley's "Pembroke," and borrowed John Ireland's "Love Unknown" from the *Public School Hymn Book* of 1919.

Dearmer's concern was to publish the hymns as their authors wrote them (not as they had been bowdlerized), to introduce hymns of social service and national reformation, and to make genuine poetry serve the cause of congregational piety. He was responsible for widely popularizing a hymn based on Bunyan, "He

[18] See Winfred Douglas, *Church Music in History and Practice*, p. 220.
[19] See W. K. Lowther Clarke, *A Hundred Years of Hymns Ancient and Modern*.

who would valiant be"; as also the following: Donne's "Wilt Thou forgive"; Milton's "The Lord will come and not be slow"; Christina Rossetti's "In the bleak mid-winter"; G. K. Chesterton's "O God of earth and altar"; Bridges' "Rejoice, O Land, in God thy Might"; and Scott Holland's "Judge Eternal." Some of his more novel selections were, however, anticipated by the catholicity of Garrett Horder's *Worship Song* of 1905.[20] According to Canon Roger Lloyd, Dearmer's *English Hymnal* did more to improve the worship of the Church of England than his *Parson's Handbook*.[21]

Although these three major Anglican handbooks aspire to catholicity in the breadth of their choice, they have acquired partisan associations. The green covers of the *English Hymnal* are linked with the expectation of "Catholic" worship in the churches in which they are used. The dark blue or maroon binding of *Hymns Ancient and Modern* suggests the Anglican *via media*. The light blue covers of *Songs of Praise* hint at a liberal and even modernist outlook in the theology of the contents. In truth, however, the *English Hymnal* has catholicity as well as being Catholic in churchmanship, and is admirably fitted to be a companion to the Anglican Liturgy. *Hymns Ancient and Modern* is rather unadventurous and staid. *Songs of Praise* was deliberately conceived as being "national, in the sense of including a full expression of that faith which is common to the English-speaking peoples today, both in the British Commonwealth and the United States."[22] Each has, of course, been subject to criticisms. The *English Hymnal* has been faulted for the chill of its devotional spirit and for an insular narrow-mindedness.[23] *Hymns Ancient and Modern* has been considered stuffily high-brow and musically tame. *Songs of Praise* was musically adventurous, so it was thought, but doctrinally diluted. Nevertheless, all three greatly enriched the vocabulary of English praise in both words and music.

Yet there was also needed, particularly among Anglicans, a revival of interest in congregational singing. This was a task superbly fulfilled by Sir Walford Davies and Sir Hugh Allen. The former, who came of a Welsh Nonconformist background, used broadcasting for this purpose, and the latter invented the "Hymn Festival" as a device for introducing new hymns. As early as 1912 he collected large congregations in the Sheldonian Theatre in Ox-

---

[20] See William Jensen Reynolds, *A Survey of Christian Hymnody*, pp. 76-77.
[21] *The Church of England in the Twentieth Century*, I, p. 163.
[22] Citation from Dearmer's Preface.
[23] See Dom Anselm Hughes, *The Rivers of the Flood*, p. 137.

ford and provided them with specially printed hymn-sheets to encourage their participation in new hymn tunes.[24]

Hymn-singing had always been popular among the congregations of the English Free Churches, but the quality of their hymns (excepting those of Watts and Wesley) was no match for the cordiality of their singing. Both in theological content and in musical accompaniment there was a great need for the improvement that the century was to mark in their official hymn books.[25] The most recent of them to appear show that they have learned the lessons of Bridges and Dearmer, Vaughan Williams and Martin Shaw.

The unreformed state of things was clearly revealed in A. J. Klaiber's article[26] on a hymn ballot taken among Baptists in 1926, in which votes were cast for 235 hymns, though 112 received only one vote each. A few hymns many would call great were omitted. Those included: "Now thank we all our God"; "Let us with a gladsome mind"; "Glorious things of thee are spoken"; and "Awake my soul and with the sun." Ten per cent of the selections were children's hymns. The most popular in the order of choice were: "O Love, that wilt not let me go"; "Lead, kindly Light"; "Jesus, Lover of my soul"; "Still, still with Thee"; "Rock of Ages"; "Beneath the Cross of Christ"; "The day Thou gavest"; "Dear Lord and Father of mankind"; "At even ere the sun was set"; and "Abide with me." What is common to these choices is an individualistic piety (the persistence of the first personal pronoun singular is striking), romanticism in mood (descending to the eroticism of "Still, still with Thee when purple morning breaketh"), and swooping tunes. What was true of the preferences of the Baptists was almost certainly equally true of those of the Congregationalists, the Methodists, and, to a limited extent, the Presbyterians, whose Calvinistic austerity preserved them from too great a liking for syrup.

By the forties, however, *English Hymnal* and *Songs of Praise* had had their salutary influence on the Free Churches. *The Church Hymnary* (Presbyterian) of 1927 went overboard in its desire to

24 See Erik R. Routley, *Twentieth Century Church Music*, p. 99.

25 Many Anglican congregations were also addicted to Victorian sentimentality in words and music. Dom Anselm Hughes writes amusingly about the religious folk-songs of the period, "one of which—'Erbide with me'—is used as the official hymn at football cup-ties, while another—'Eternal Father, strong to save'—much beloved for the saccharine semitones of its tune ('Melita') is sung at 11 a.m. on all our ocean liners in the first-class saloon, quite regardless of the state of the weather" (*ibid.*, p. 136).

26 See *The Baptist Quarterly*, Vol. III (1926-27), p. 312.

imitate the *English Hymnal* in a dive for status symbols. The *Methodist Hymn Book* of 1933 borrowed less from the same source. The *Congregational Hymnary* of 1916 included "Coutances" and "Deus tuorum militum," but resolutely refused to use Vaughan Williams or to follow his principle of authenticity. Similarly, the compilers of the *Baptist Church Hymnal* (1933) were motivated— in Routley's ribald phrase—by "ignorance-by-decision."[27] But the reformation is clearly in evidence in both *Congregational Praise* of 1951 and the *Baptist Hymn Book* of 1962. *Congregational Praise* had Eric Thiman as musical editor (with Erik Routley as the Secretary of the Committee). They helped to make this the finest of the Free Church hymn books for literary and musical quality. The *Baptist Hymn Book* had Hugh Martin as chairman of its editorial committee and E. P. Sharpe as chairman of the music advisory committee. This hymnal was the first to include two of Geoffrey Beaumont's "pop" tunes, but was quite conservative in its retention of some Sankey gospel songs, in which it was perhaps influenced by the evangelistic crusades of Billy Graham in England. No such concessions to popular taste were made by the editors of *Congregational Praise*, for they argued that the congregations whose churches preferred Sankey would use that selection on week-nights. This was all to the good, as some hymns seem rather to corrupt than commend the Gospel. Dr. Routley argued this in his study, *The Gift of Conversion* (1957) which was a sustained critique of attempts to manipulate the personality in revivalistic services. More recently his views have been incisively summed up as follows: "I contend that it is wrong to reduce evangelism to an operation on the soul of the individual, leaving out his brains and his aesthetic sense and his social sense; that it is wrong to represent salvation as one long rest in bed with an automatically re-heated hot-water bottle; that it is contrary to the Gospel to represent 'peace' of the heavenly kind as a long silence broken only by the drone of a harmonium. . . ."[28]

The least satisfactory people's book of praise to be produced in the twentieth century is the *Westminster Hymnal*, prepared for English Roman Catholics. This is the case despite the fact that its first issue had the benefit of the musical advice of Sir Richard Terry, who had published admirable editions of ancient psalters, and the revision committee, in the preparation of the edition of

---

[27] Communicated in a letter, dated April 18, 1964.
[28] *Music, Sacred and Profane*, p. 139.

1940, had the literary advice of Monsignor Ronald Knox, a master of English prose and of translation. It is partly attributable to the fact, as admitted by Evelyn Waugh, that "many adult English Catholics do not hear a hymn from one year's end to another."[29] It is possible also that those who miss hymns the most are converts, and therefore their advice is probably suspect. A further dissuasive may be the rather wooden translations from the Latin of some of the hymns. Finally, there is almost certainly a feeling that hymns are an accommodation to the sentimentality of the simpler laity and their love for a catchy tune, as contrasted with the professional preference for Gregorian chants. Routley hardly exaggerates in referring to the music of the day echoed in the unrevised *Westminster Hymnal* as "treacly, instrumental, café-orchestra stuff."[30] Monsignor Knox persuaded the committee for revision to introduce the work of comparatively modern poets such as Francis Thompson, Chesterton, Lionel Johnson, Canon Gray, and "Michael Field." He made 47 translations from the Latin out of a total of 106, and composed four hymns of his own. Even so, the final result of the revised *Westminster Hymnal* of 1940 was the attainment of higher professional standards in both words and music, but at the cost of a decline in popularity. Fortunately, English Roman Catholics have a much better record in the field of popular psalmody.

5. *Psalmody*

Three different communions in England have three distinctive contributions to make to the use of the psalms in praise. The Presbyterians, following the lead of the Church of Scotland, prefer metrical psalmody sung to the simple and solemn accompaniments of the high Genevan days.[31] The Roman Catholics chant in the Gregorian manner and are learning the Père Joseph Gélineau mode of psalmody. The Anglican chant is a harmonized and stylized development from plainsong, which has been interpreted and performed as emphasizing "speech rhythms," particularly under the aegis of Sir Walford Davies, Dr. Thalben-Ball,[32] and the Royal School of Church Music. The pioneer in the reform of Anglican chanting, who avoided the text-mangling and the four-beat bars of

[29] See Evelyn Waugh's *Ronald Knox*, p. 253.
[30] *Music, Sacred and Profane*, p. 129.
[31] See Miller Patrick's *Four Centuries of Scottish Psalmody* and Maurice Frost's *English and Scottish Psalm and Hymn Tunes.*
[32] See his *Choral Psalter* (1940), which should be compared with the *Parish Psalter* (1930) and the *Oxford Psalter* (1929).

"Hellmost Helmore,"[33] was Madeley Richardson of Southwark Cathedral, just prior to 1908.

Despite the notable improvement in Anglican chanting which the "speech rhythm" school has brought in and which is excellently performed in most cathedrals, and the exquisite austerity and ideational quality of Gregorian chanting, especially as heard in Benedictine Abbeys, such music is too difficult for the purposes of congregational singing.[34] And, while metrical psalmody is simple enough, yet all too often it is doggerel rather than poetry, for the rhymes are false and the syntax is forced. Hence, with one exception, no present method is likely to lead to that full participation of the laity in worship which is one of the central aims of the modern Liturgical Movement.

The promising exception is associated with the work of the Jesuit, Père Joseph Gélineau of France.[35] Gélineau tried to render in French the basic rhythm of the Hebrew text, which had in each line an equal number of stressed syllables but an irregular number of unstressed syllables. As he translated the Psalms into French he arranged the lines of each psalm in its original stanza structure.[36] As Leonard Ellinwood has pointed out, this Hebrew rhythmic system which Gélineau tries to preserve in French, and which is now being adapted to English, has a curious analogue in the "sprung rhythm" of the English poet, Gerard Manley Hopkins, himself also a Jesuit priest.[37] The following illustration will make the principle plain, using Psalm XCII: 11 in Hebrew, French and English, and marking the stresses in italic print:

Sad-*dik* kat-ta-*mar* yif-*rah*
Le *juste* poussera comme un *pal*mier.
The *just* man shall *flour*ish as a *palm* tree.

Ke-'*er*-es Ba-le-ba-*non* yis-*geh*
Il grandira comme un *cèd*re du *Li*ban.
He shall *grow* as a *cedar* on *Le*banon.[38]

[33] See Dom Ambrose Hughes, *The Rivers of the Flood*, p. 132.
[34] See the discussion of the relative advantages of Gregorian and Anglican chanting in *Music in Church*, pp. 32-33.
[35] See the entire Psalms in Père Gélineau's translation in *La Sainte Bible traduite en français sous la direction de l'Ecole biblique de Jérusalem.*
[36] See Dom Gregory Murray's article, "The Psalms, a rhythmic restoration leads to a popular revival," in *The Downside Review*, Vol. LXXIV (April 1956), pp. 95-102.
[37] See Winfred Douglas, *Church Music in History and Practice*, p. 235.
[38] *Ibid.*

Having completed his translations, Père Gélineau composed melodies to which they might be sung by a congregation. They are characterized by the utmost simplicity, with a change of pitch only on accented syllables. For this reason they are well suited for congregational use. They are being used by the Protestant Community at Taizé in the Daily Offices, and have been heard at the High Kirk of St. Giles in Edinburgh. It is ironic that in the Roman Catholic Church, for which they were intended, they may be used generally only on non-liturgical occasions. Such popularity as the Gélineau method of chanting has achieved in Britain is chiefly due to the sponsorship of Dom Gregory Murray of Downside Abbey, who is also an expert in Gregorian chanting.

6. *Conclusion*

Looking back over sixty-five years of the present century, one can see that, while the congregations were larger at its start, the quality of the hymnody, the psalmody, and the anthems[39] was inferior to what it is today. Piety was often sentimental and individualistic, instead of objective and corporate, and church music was not merely insular and complacent, but it had lost touch with the English past and was unrelated to the European Continent. Vaughan Williams was to reawaken ecclesiastical England to its classical heritage in church music and folk music, and to make it empathetic to the strong simplicity of Genevan psalm-tunes and the richness of Catholic baroque music in seventeenth and eighteenth century France. In due course most of the leading composers of the age were to write church music, so that it was no longer a synonym for tamely conventional echoes of the past reiterated *ad nauseam*. Finally, church music, under the influence of Benjamin Britten and composers of the *avant garde*, became highly experimental in English adaptations of Webern and Messiaen. In a more controversial manner, there were pastoral experiments in popular music.

So lively is the experimentation now proceeding in England in the writing of anthems, hymns, carols, and psalm-settings that this brief survey is fittingly concluded on a note of interrogation. Will modern church music, in becoming secular (that is, in speaking

---

[39] In the first part of the chapter consideration was paid to some of the most memorable anthems of the period. In a brief chapter a section devoted to them would have become inordinately long if it had attempted to be comprehensive. For further information see Edmund H. Fellowes, *English Cathedral Music*, and Erik R. Routley, *Twentieth Century Church Music*.

with the authentic idiom of its time), rightly cease to be *church* music while becoming in a more relevant sense *religious* music? Will it meet the deeper needs of humanity through raising existential questions to which a contemporary, not a second-hand faith, is the living and hard-won answer?

CHAPTER IV

THE EARLY DEVELOPMENT OF
THEOLOGY (1900-1933)

HABERE DEUM EST COLERE DEUM, said Luther. An abstract principle may be considered, but a living God must be worshipped. Yet the quality of worship in every religion is determined by the worshippers' conception of the nature of their deity.

If Christian theology in a given period isolates one of God's major attributes or activities, to ignore the rest, the change will be felt in the worship. If, for example, his Creatorship alone is emphasized, worship will be pantheistic in character and the Harvest Festival will become the supreme day of the Christian Year. If Divine Judgment predominates in theology, then worship will be characterized by legalistic and scrupulous fear. If the Divine Saviourhood alone is stressed, then worship becomes pietistically sentimental and mawkish. If Sanctification predominates over the other attributes and activities of God, then the Christian life becomes a moral activism and dispenses with worship, except as a didactic reminder of duties to be done. For this reason one cannot hope to understand the developments of twentieth century worship without first engaging in a study of the changing theology of our period.

Furthermore, since theology is not carried on in a vacuum, but is ever sensitive to the currents of the national life, we must first sketch in the background of the dramatic changes which modified the ethos of Britain in the twentieth century.

1. Changes in the National Ethos

Three cataclysmic factors have radically changed optimistic imperialistic Edwardian England into the sober, realistic, country of today. The first was the horrifying impact of two World Wars. The second was the change from an opulent centre of empire spanning the seas to the leading partner of a freely associated British Commonwealth of Nations, with the passage of the Statute of Westminster in 1931. The third is the institutionalization of the concept of social justice in the development of the Social Welfare State. In consequence of this searing and apocalyptic revelation of the two World Wars, the humanists committed themselves to a greater humaneness, and the optimistic liberal Christians began to think again about that destructive selfishness in man which an older theology had called original sin, and of man's desperate need of the transformation of Divine grace.[1] Theology, as we shall see, became more realistic, knowing from bitter experience that man is both crucifier as well as redeemable.

The second great change in British life—Britain's reduced political and economic role as the Empire became a Common-wealth—had spiritual results more difficult to calculate. Among them was the desire to seek for a new political and economic grouping in an United Europe with a Common Market, with parallel overtures in which the British Churches renewed contact with their European ecclesiastical cousins in denominational as well as ecumenical conferences. A sense of European spiritual soli-darity is growing apace.

The third, and certainly the most significant, change in twen-tieth century Britain is the establishment of the Social Welfare State. The old England of the two nations, the haves and have-nots, is dying rapidly and is being accelerated by the proliferation of new universities. The fact that this social revolution has been accomplished without bloodshed and in silence is a tribute to the cooperation of humanists and political reformers, on the one hand, and to the impact of Christian socialism and liberalism on the other hand. Many of the more cautiously hopeful Britons look with pride on the establishment of the Social Welfare State as not only the half-way house between the excesses of totalitarian Communism in the East and of relatively unbridled Capitalism in the West, but also as the pattern of the future. On the other side, the baffled look to tradition as their guide in a desperate attempt to create a "Second Elizabethan Age." It is significant that the latter view-point is typical of the middle classes (and often of the elderly members of that class) who are the chief support of the Churches, and that it is the Churches with traditional creeds, liturgies, sacra-ments, and church order (Roman Catholic and Anglican) which are making the greatest strides in contemporary England.

What has been the effect of the Welfare State on English Christianity? There have been advantages and disadvantages. Among the former are the fact that there is a greater awareness of the tenets of Christian faith and ethics in the schools and conse-

---

[1] See D. R. Davies, *On to Orthodoxy*, p. 27.

quently, as educational levels have arisen, so has the quality of Christian proclamation in pulpit, television and broadcasting. Furthermore, as the State has relieved the Churches of most of their ancient responsibilities for education and social welfare, it has liberated them to concentrate on the preaching and living of the Gospel as the answer to the perennial desperateness of the heart of man faced with his three ancient enemies: the egotism of sin in all its personal and anti-social manifestations, the bitterness of physical and mental suffering, and the tragedy of death. One further advantage is that it has eliminated almost all those nominal Christians who attend worship for the sake of respectability or social prestige. Hence the Church of Christ has been freed to become the more fully committed Church of the remnant, when previously it had been what our forefathers called, with curled lip, a "mixed multitude." Furthermore, although the protection of the State is real and important, it is also very impersonal; so the Churches exist in part to be living centres of community life. In all this there is clear and unmistakable gain. Where, then, is there loss?

A Church no longer allowed to express its love for its neighbour in education and social welfare might degenerate into moralistic pietism, sitting at ease in Zion. Irrelevant on the social questions of the day, or muzzled because of its dependence upon the State's sustentation of its members, it could easily lapse into an euphoric type of worship which was no more than escapism from the here into the hereafter. That fate can alone be avoided by a Church whose preachers will be the watchdogs of the nation's conscience, and the critics of the arrogance, the secularism, the chauvinism, and the unfinished tasks of the State. Happily there are signs that the contemporary Church does not lack men of courage and charity to speak the prophetic Word of God. Such preaching is undoubtedly needed in a period when West Indian and African ghettoes are being established in London and Birmingham, and when fear takes the form of advocating massive retaliation and "overkill" in military strategy.

The cumulative effect of these three significant changes in British life has been to re-establish conviction in the centre, while demolishing the outworks of theology. The latter part of our period has seen the demise of Liberalism in politics and in theology. Moreover, the Christian faith and life have been subjected to the most relentless attacks from Darwin's day to Freud's. In addition, the rapid changes in the political and social maps of Europe, Africa, and the East, not to mention the seismic shock to the conscience caused by Hiroshima and Nagasaki, all counsel caution and moderation, not optimism. Interim judgments and shortened horizons are definitely the order of the day. The dominant note in Christian theology is realism, and the clue for that is found not only in the spirit of the times but in the very centre of the Christian saga. For there the cross of Christ cautions against all facile optimism, and the resurrection of Christ against all desperate pessimism. As we shall see, the development of Christian thought in the first three decades of this century is from theologies of explanation and experience to theologies of redemption, from confidence in man's automatic progress to perfection to confidence alone in God who wrought victory from the apparent disaster of the Cross, from secular utopianism to the rule of God, from the horizontal to the vertical dimension. In short, it is a journey from immanence to transcendence, from general revelation to Biblical redemption.

2. Immanentalism: The "New Theology"[2]

Immanentalism was given impetus from both theological and sociological pressures at the very beginning of the century. Harnack's influential *Das Wesen des Christentums* (1900) appeared in English translation in 1901 as *What is Christianity?* Suspicious of dogma, as the unwarrantable Hellenization of the Gospel, Harnack stressed the religion *of* Jesus, not the traditional religion *about* Jesus, and came to the conclusion that it was essentially the proclamation of the Fatherhood of God and the brotherhood of man. On this analysis, religion was less mystical than moral in character. This very emphasis was the more gladly accepted because it implied that it was the duty of Christians, along with all

[2] The following are the major re-statements of theology in an extreme immanental and experiential direction: K. C. Anderson, *The Larger Faith*; R. J. Campbell, *The New Theology*, *New Theology Sermons*, and *Christianity and the Social Order*; J. Warschauer, *The New Evangel*; T. Rhondda Williams, *The New Theology—An Exposition*; C. H. Vine, ed., *The Old Faith and the New Theology*; and the work of an American theologian, W. L. Walker, *What about the New Theology?* A similar movement in America was termed "The Social Gospel" and its leading exponent was Walter Rauschenbusch. For the impact of this movement on American Protestant worship, see the present writer's article, "The Expression of the Social Gospel in Worship," in *Studia Liturgica* (Rotterdam), Vol. II, No. 3 (September 1963), pp. 174-92. The term "new theology" was first used in a precise sense by the American theologian, Theodore T. Munger, in *The Freedom of Faith* (1883) in which the view was traced through Horace Bushnell to S. T. Coleridge.

men of goodwill, to bring in the Kingdom of God. This notion harmonized perfectly with the demands of Socialism for the establishment of the classless society. Essentially the New Theology was a moral awakening within the Protestant Churches, in which the conception of social justice was expounded as an imperative of the Gospel in contradistinction to the ruthlessly impersonal ethics of competitive industrialism. It had, of course, other characteristic liberal features, including a stress on evolution rather than Divine irruption as God's method. It rejected verbal inspiration of the Scriptures and materialistic ideas of future punishment, and generally accepted the conclusions of modern science which laid stress on the education of character as opposed to revivalism. It made little of the Church, and everything of the Kingdom of God which it interpreted as utopianism.

Its most distinguished, if controversial, English exponent was R. J. Campbell, minister of City Temple, the most influential Free Church pulpit in London, who had been brought up as an Anglican and who, after lamenting the chaos his new iconoclasm had created, returned to the Church of England.[3] But although the leader of the movement defected, its popularity remained undiminished in the Free Churches until the middle of the third decade of the century.

It was born from a belief in the necessity of re-articulating the Christian faith in terms of the indwelling of God in the universe and in mankind. It was conceived that the older orthodoxy had presented the doctrine of the divine transcendence in such a way as "to amount to a practical dualism, and to lead men to think of God as above and apart from His world instead of expressing Himself through the world."[4] The older conception of Deity had indeed fitted God into the Procrustean bed of Greek philosophy, with its stress upon His immutability and impassability. The result was that this distant, almost Aristotelian, Deity was pictured as an absentee God, not as the Biblical God "who visits and redeems His people." Moreover, His infrequent visits were conceived as miraculous irruptions into the natural order, as in the crossing of the Red Sea to deliver the people of Israel or in the Resurrection to deliver the Crucified Leader of the new people of God. Apart from these quite unpredictable incursions, the older evangelicalism believed that He made an equally unpredictable descent into the human soul once in a life-time, at conversion. The new immanence emphasized, in however exaggerated a way, that God's dealings

[3] See *A Spiritual Pilgrimage*.   [4] *The New Theology*, p. 4.

with men were continuous, not occasional; that His influence was known in the provident over-ruling of the universe in its constancy and order; that He was the Creator of the moral law that bound human households, societies, and nations together; and that His constant inspiration was the fountain of truth, beauty, and goodness in the universe and in mankind. This countered the old supernaturalism, revivalism, intellectual Philistinism, occasionalism, and individualism. It was undoubtedly a formidable case that the New Theology was able to make against the old orthodoxy.

The New Theology became a crusading theology precisely because it was believed that the significant drift from the Churches already apparent at the beginning of the century was due to anachronistic statements of theology, including dogmatic beliefs about "the Fall, the scriptural basis of revelation, the blood-atonement, the punishment of sin, heaven and hell" which Campbell believed to be "not only misleading, but unethical."[5] Where churches were full, and thus meeting the needs of modern men, Campbell asserted that it was not because of the doctrines they preached, but because of their deep human sympathies. "Religion is necessary to mankind," said Campbell, "but churches are not."[6] Furthermore, the new anti-authoritarianism of the immanental theology was not a revolution in Protestantism alone, it was already being embraced by brave souls within Roman Catholicism. Campbell pointed to Father Tyrrell, the Jesuit and Modernist, to Archdeacon Wilberforce in the Church of England, to the Frenchman Auguste Sabatier, and to T. Rhondda Williams, a Congregationalist—all were swallows of the new theological summer.

Furthermore, Campbell argued that the new theology was essentially a more spiritual Socialism. "The great social movement which is now taking place in every country of the civilised world toward universal peace and brotherhood and a better and fairer distribution of wealth is really the same movement as that which in the more distinctly religious sphere is coming to be called the New Theology." Indeed, the term theology is almost a misnomer for a "moral and spiritual movement" which recognizes that "we are at the beginning of a great religious and ethical awakening."[7]

Why was this form of liberal Protestantism so greatly attracted to Socialism? It was due to a sense of the radical contradiction between the Christian standard of conduct and the impersonalism and ruthless competition of a commercial and industrial society.

[5] *Ibid.*, p. 9.   [6] *Ibid.*, p. 12.   [7] *Ibid.*, p. 14.

Thus "to that end we must destroy the social system which makes selfishness the rule and compels a man to act on his lower motives, and we must put a better in its place. . . . In a word we want collectivism in place of competition; we want the Kingdom of God."[8]

Campbell, in the same year in which *The New Theology* appeared, devoted another book exclusively to the social question. It was entitled *Christianity and the Social Order*. It was a vigorous attempt to demonstrate the correspondence between the principles of Christianity and those of modern Socialism. It began by showing that nearly 75 per cent of the adult population of Britain was permanently out of touch with organized religion. The artisans, as well as the professional and upper classes, had rejected Christianity as irrelevant, leaving the Churches as the haunts only of the respectable bourgeoisie. What was so disturbing to Campbell was the thought that such other-worldliness, as presently taught in the pulpits, was not merely irrelevant, but it was also "totally absent from primitive Christian thought."[9] He recognized that the High Church clergy of the Church of England and the members of the Salvation Army were exceptions to the rule, for both served the poor with distinction. Nonetheless he felt this was to deal with symptoms, not with causes. Charity demoralized the poor; social justice would elevate them. Socialism was welcomed for two reasons: it was a concern for a genuinely international fellowship and the message of hope for the oppressed and unprivileged everywhere. Campbell documents his indictment of the callousness of the ruling classes and the indifference of the middle classes with telling statistics, of which two typical examples may be given. The first makes full use of the fact that "about one-seventieth part of the population of the United Kingdom owns far more than one-half of the entire accumulated wealth, public and private."[10]

The other chilling example is cited from Charles Booth's *Life and Labour of the People of London*, the volume that lifted the manhole lid from the obnoxious sociological sewers of Edwardian London, to the effect that "the classes on or below the poverty line of earnings not exceeding a guinea per week per family number 1,292,737 or 30.7% of the whole population."[11] It was a damning exposure of the hypocrisy of a supposedly Christian nation's failure to fulfil the second Christian commandment to love its neighbour as

[8] *Ibid.*, p. 249.
[9] *Christianity and the Social Order*, p. ix.
[10] *Ibid.*, p. 160.   [11] *Ibid.*, p. 171.

itself. The book concluded with a peroration on Socialism, which must be quoted because it expresses so completely the coalescence (and confusion) of Christian and collectivist hopes which was typical of the new theology:

"The normal life should be the life of brightness and joy. And this is the life which is in the gift of that greater day which is already on the horizon, when the motives of greed and fear will have passed away for ever by the coming of a social order in which there shall be no longer any room for them. The rich man will lose nothing that he has now, and he will gain immeasurably in the joy of seeing everywhere around him a contented and happy people, his brothers and equals. To the poor it will mean the fulfilment of the promise uttered in the name of Jesus: 'I am come that they might have life and have it more abundantly.' To all alike it will be the fulfilment of the prayer of Jesus, 'That they may all be one.' "[12]

It must be remembered that the more Catholic theologians in the Church of England were also convinced of the compatibility of Christianity and Socialism. Had not Charles Gore confessed as much in the wry epigram: "Each for himself and God for us all, as the elephant said when he danced among the chickens"?

Was the new theology, then, the historic Christian faith with the substitution of collectivist and this-worldly ethics for the individualistic and other-worldly ethics of orthodoxy and pietism? It was this, but also much more than this. The new ethics required a radical reformulation of the historic theology for its support, and the reconstruction of theology was as controversial as the political colour of the ethics. The new theology involved a new Christology, a new interpretation of sin, a new eschatology with a revised view of man's destiny, and a radical ecclesiology, with profound consequences for the understanding of worship.

In Christology the deity of Christ was repudiated, because it was believed that the Council of Chalcedon was guilty of dualism in defining the historic Christ as a personality in whom were united two different natures, divine and human.[13] Campbell insisted that all Christians accepted in practice the identity of the divine and human in Jesus and potentially in themselves. To the objection that this was to make Christ only a man, he replied: "I make Him the Only Man! . . . We have only seen the perfect manhood once and that was the manhood of Jesus. The rest of us have to get

---

[12] *Ibid.*, pp. 283-84.　　　　[13] *The New Theology*, pp. 77, 81.

there."[14] Yet the unity between Christ and God was posited exclusively in moral, not in metaphysical terms. This alone could guarantee that Jesus would be humanity's exemplar. Hence the new theology's emphasis was all on the humanity of Jesus. "All honour," Campbell wrote, "to those who have called us back to the real Jesus, the Jesus of Galilee and Jerusalem, the Jesus with the prophet's fire, the Jesus who was so gentle to children and erring women, and yet before whom canting hypocrites and truculent ecclesiastics slunk away abashed."[15] Campbell seemed to be unaware, until the fact was pointed out to him by Bishop Charles Gore, that his virtual denial of the Incarnation of Christ was to remove the only lever great enough to raise humanity from its acquisitiveness, for Divine grace is needed even more than a perfect exemplar of altruism.[16]

Campbell's most scandalous statements, however, were his redefinition of sin as a blundering search for God, as contrasted with the Biblical conception of rebellion against God. He was, perhaps, unfortunate in the examples he chose. He wrote: "The man who got dead drunk last night did so because of the impulse within him to break through the barriers of his limitations, to express himself, and to realise more abundant life." As if this were not a Dionysiac enough interpretation of religion, Campbell continued: "The roué you saw in Piccadilly last night, who went out to corrupt innocence and wallow in filthiness of the flesh, was engaged in his blundering quest for God."[17]

There was more justification for Campbell's reinterpretation of the Atonement in terms of the vicarious principle operative in daily life than for his euphoric interpretation of sin. But this, too, gave offence because of his choice of illustration. "Go," he wrote, "with J. Keir Hardie to the House of Commons and listen to his pleading for justice to his order, and you see the Atonement."[18] Campbell's chief point was to stress that Christianity should not confine itself to a devotional attitude to Christ's sacrifice on the Cross but should issue in atoning action to overcome the inequalities of society. His mistake, however, was to reduce the work of Christ to an illustration from being the act that inaugurated the new relationship between God and men.

[14] *Ibid.*, p. 77.   [15] *Ibid.*, pp. 80-81.
[16] Gore's critique was *The New Theology and the Old Religion*.
[17] Both citations are from a sermon on "More Abundant Life" preached in City Temple on March 18, 1906, and republished in *The New Theology*, p. 151.
[18] *Ibid.*, p. 169.

The radical revision of the orthodox conception of man's destiny as well as the redefinition of the role of the Church is fully contained in the exposition of the key concept of the new theology—the Kingdom of God. This was the characteristic concept of Liberal Protestantism throughout the present century, and none was held more tenaciously by Christian laymen in our time who found in it the sanctification of their secular vocations as service for Christ in the world. And this, despite the fact that Schweitzer's *The Quest of the Historical Jesus*, appearing in English translation in 1910, had entirely shattered the view that the Kingdom of God was the earthly establishment of a kingdom of social betterment by insisting that it was a supernatural and world-denying kingdom to be inaugurated imminently by the Messiah.

The proponents of the new Theology were attracted to the interpretation of the Kingdom of God as the central motif of the teaching of the Synoptic Gospels, for several reasons. They reacted against the Rabbinical and metaphysical subtleties of Paul and held the view that the apostle to the Gentiles had corrupted the simplicity of the Gospel of Jesus, transforming an association for righteousness into an institution with sacraments that bore more likeness to the Graeco-Roman mystery religions than to the preaching of Jesus. They protested against the complacent and other-worldly piety, the restrictive credal and confessional forms, the top-heavy institutionalism, and the bourgeois respectability of the Churches, all of which they believed were responsible for alienating artisans from a commitment to true Christianity. Here, in the Kingdom of God, was a concept profound and simple enough to unite all men of goodwill, and one authentically stamped with the example and teaching of the founder of Christianity, prophet and carpenter. Here was an escape from "cold Christs and tangled Trinities." Here, too, was the basis of the new ethical revolution that the world needed.

The two chief characteristics of the interpretation of the Kingdom of God were its corporate and utopian nature. It chimed with both the collectivistic thinking of the age and the confident belief that universal education and the beneficent impact of the natural, social, and technological sciences were about to usher in an era of unrivalled progress and peace. It was a rigorous attempt to show that Christianity had a here-and-now relevance which orthodoxy had wilfully obscured. Orthodox Christianity had been in error in transferring to a future life the concepts of judgment, heaven, and hell. The so-called "Last Things" could be demonstrated to be operative in the present. "The aim and object of salvation are not the getting of a man into heaven, but the getting of heaven into him."[19]

What, then, becomes of the Church on this view? Campbell maintained that there were two views of the Church held in history, which he described as the *sacerdotal* and *evangelical* concepts. The sacerdotal view was that Jesus founded a religious society to represent Him on earth, which was the ark of salvation, and only members of this Church were saved by being called from a ruined world to a blessed immortality. The gateway was Baptism, the continuing source of grace the Holy Communion, and the essential form of government was by bishops, priests, and deacons, authenticated by an apostolical succession. However influential such a view has been in history, Campbell believed it was founded upon an error: "I am quite sure He [Jesus] never thought of such a thing, and historical criticism of Christian origins does not leave the sacerdotalist much to stand on. Jesus appointed neither bishop nor priest, and never ordained that any mechanical ceremony should be the means of admission to the Christian society or be necessary to the eternal welfare of anyone."[20]

The evangelical view denies that Jesus founded a fixed or rigid organization for His society. On this interpretation the Church is "the totality of the followers of Jesus" and now "most sensible men are satisfied that forms of government matter much less than the kind of life that flourishes in the society itself."[21] It is the strictly functional and instrumental view of the Church as the agent for the Kingdom of God which Campbell preferred, and he and his followers rejected the hierarchical and sacramental view.

They also rejected the view that the function of the Church was to pluck brands from the burning and save them for a future heaven. For them the world was not a city of destruction, as for Bunyan. By contrast they held that the "work of the Church is to save the world and to believe that it is worth the saving."[22] Campbell is sure that, for Christ, "the purpose of the *ecclesia* was to help to realise the Kingdom of God by preaching and living the fellowship of love."[23]

Such, then, was the new theology preached by Campbell and by many other ministers, especially in the Free Churches. Among

[19] *The New Theology*, p. 224. [20] *Ibid.*, p. 242.
[21] *Ibid.*, pp. 242-43. [22] *Ibid.*, p. 244.
[23] *Ibid.*

them the best known were the Rev. C. Ensor Walters, the Methodist crusader who had sat with Bernard Shaw as a vestryman of the St. Pancras ward of London; the chivalrous Silvester Horne, minister of Whitefield's Memorial (Congregational) Church and a member of Parliament in the Liberal interest; the doughty John Clifford, Baptist divine of London, leader of the Passive Resistance Movement against the levy of an education rate to support parochial schools in 1903—that last gasp of the Nonconformist Conscience—and supreme democrat[24] and social reformer. They were a dauntless company and did much to prepare the way for the coming in due time of the Social Welfare State. Certainly they sensitized the consciences of the churchly middle classes to the needs of working men and women. Certainly they insisted that pious attitudes must be translated into social actions and they banished a self-regarding and valetudinarian pietism. But in their main object, to entice the alienated artisans into the Church, they failed and failed miserably. The working-man who played billiards or darts in the settlement churches, or attended lectures on social problems, felt no compulsion to attend the worship or join the membership of the churches. Perhaps this was because apostles of the new theology had taught the lessons of the equivalence of Christianity and Socialism, and the reduction of theology to ethics, and the other-worldly to the this-worldly, only too well. The artisans took them at their word.

The effects of the new theology on worship may easily be imagined. If all sacraments were merely the vestiges of sacerdotalism, and sacerdotalism was an erroneous conception of the nature of the Church, then both Baptism and Holy Communion were merely antiquarian trappings. There was, in any case, little point in baptizing a child into the name of the Holy Trinity, for carpenter Christology had removed the halo of Divinity from Christ, and His Community was merely a human association for the betterment of human relations like any other Ethical Culture society, with perhaps a capacity for generating more sentiment. Holy Communion could not remain, in the traditional sense, a means of grace; it could survive only as a useful social ordinance recalling the vows of fidelity made by the community committed to honouring the ethical standards of Jesus. Hymns, indeed, would be composed

---

[24] He always travelled third class, he explained, "because there is no fourth class, and it enables me to see the class from which I sprang." See Sir James Marchant, *Dr. John Clifford, C.H., Life, Letters and Reminiscences*, pp. 78-79.

joyously to proclaim the advent of the Kingdom of God—and this was the abiding contribution to worship of the new theology movement. Prayers would confess the corporate sins of anti-social behaviour and intercessions would meaningfully recall the under-privileged children who had previously been conveniently forgotten. Sermons, above all, would ring like bells—the chime of compassion for the poor alternating with the clangour of prophetic denunciation of the callously opulent. But the real thrust of the movement was ethical action. The adoration of God lost its priority and holiness its ultimacy, and the earthly paradise obscured the home of the saints contemplating the vision of God and enjoying the love of God. The tragedy was that worship, on this analysis of priorities, was inevitably regarded as an evasion or postponement of social duty, and the love of neighbour was not thought to require as its absolute prerequisite the love of God. The equation of religion with ethics, of the other-worldly with the irrelevant, of liturgy and sacraments with insincerity, and of piety with the picayune, was to lead to the most appalling triviality, formlessness, and even the glorification of the gauche in Free Church worship for the best part of three decades.

Where there is evident such a weakness in worship it is ultimately traceable to a defective theology. What were the defects of the new theology? The ultimate defect was the utter dominance of the immanental over the transcendental concept of God, so that the mystery, the majesty, and the judgment of God were dissipated. As a consequence there were three other major defects. The imperatives of corporate ethics were aggrandized at the expense of the need for personal transformation and discipleship. The key category—the Kingdom of God—was interpreted in too evolutionary and temporal a manner, ignoring both the Divine initiative in the crisis that brings in the Kingdom and in its transhistorical fulfilment. Finally, the new theology confused the secular utopianism of the day with the historical hope of the Kingdom and grievously undervalued the institutional Church with its corporate discipline and its sacramental life.

The Anglican social reformers wisely chose to make the Incarnation of Christ, rather than the concept of the Kingdom, the fulcrum for social leverage.[25] This safeguarded the divinity of Christ, against the carpenter Christology, provided a high (pos-

[25] See M. B. Reckitt, *From Maurice to Temple: A Century of the Social Movement in the Church of England.*

sibly idolatrously high) doctrine of the Church as the "extension of the Incarnation," as contrasted with the social gospellers with their instrumentalist approach. It founded the sacraments on the "incarnational principle" and ensured that they remained a perpetual reminder and channel of God's renewal of mankind by grace, as Augustinian conceptions continued to prevail in the Book of Common Prayer against the dilutions of Schleiermacher, Ritschl, and Harnack elsewhere in Protestantism, and they spoke both of a transfigured social order on earth and of the everlasting Communion of the Saints.

The Kingdom of God did offer two advantages, however, for the new theologians: one was the possibility for all men of goodwill to unite in social action, whether inside or outside the Churches. The other was an insistence upon the sovereign freedom of God's Holy Spirit which ceremonialism, sacerdotalism, and an exclusive and hierarchical ecclesiasticism were in danger of forgetting. But these advantages were negatived in part by the double weakness of the concept of the Kingdom of God.[26] It was easily confused with utopian humanism and lent itself to the Pelagianism which sang in a typically popular hymn during this period:

Rise up, O men of God!
The Church for you doth wait,
Her strength unequal to her task;
Rise up and make her great![27]

3. *Immanentalism: The Rediscovery of Mysticism*

While the rediscovery of mysticism is, from one standpoint, another indication of the early twentieth century's interest in immanentalism and experience in religion, it is also a deeper because a more authentically *spiritual* phenomenon than the "New Theology" and one that had more enduring influence on the theory and practice of worship. For this evaluation five reasons may be given.

The first is that mysticism locates religion neither in the brain nor in the will (though it is often accompanied with asceticism and

[26] In fairness to Campbell's memory, it should be stated that he bought out the rights of *The New Theology* to prevent it being re-issued and admitted, in *A Spiritual Pilgrimage*, p. 165, that "it was much too hastily written, was crude and uncompromising in statement, polemical in spirit, and gave a totally wrong impression of the quality of the Sermons delivered week by week from the City Temple pulpit." Certainly the 1903 edition of *City Temple Sermons*, Nos. III, IV, XXI, and XXII, all of which are concerned with prayer and its relation to service, bear out the truth of Campbell's contention.

[27] Composed by William Merrill in 1911.

rigorous self- and world-denial), but in the heart. Religion is, for the mystic, essentially the adoration of God and worship is the corporate expression of adoration. In the second place, in an increasingly ecumenical century thoughtful Christians were less interested in the discriminatory theological labels that divide, and more in the experience that unites both Catholic and Protestant. There came to be a renewed interest in the mysticism of Walter Hilton and Dame Julian of Norwich, of St. Bernard and St. Bonaventura, of St. Catherine of Genoa and St. John of the Cross, as representing the Catholic side, and in the mysticism of Boehme and Luther, of Wesley and William Law, of George Fox and John Woolman, as representing the Protestant side. Moreover, the recognition that there had been distinguished mystics in Islam and in Hinduism encouraged the thought that here was indisputable evidence of the universality and of the objective validity of religious experience. Fourthly, the exponents of mysticism in England were not intemperate enthusiasts or hotheads, but historical and critical scholars of intellectual, moral, and spiritual depth and discernment. This was particularly true of William Ralph Inge (1860-1954), for a quarter of a century the famous "Gloomy Dean" of St. Paul's Cathedral; of Baron Friedrich von Hügel (1852-1925), an Austrian Roman Catholic layman of the deepest culture, with many Modernist friends, who settled in England in 1867 and had a long and deep influence on the Church of England; as also of his disciple, Miss Evelyn Underhill (1875-1941), the writer of two classics, *Mysticism* and *Worship*. Finally, each of these authors insisted as strongly on the transcendence of God as on His immanence, and thus corrected the inevitable subjectivity of an exclusive assertion of Divine immanence.

There were special circumstantial reasons for the mystical renaissance.[28] A century of blood-letting was profoundly interested

[28] The immense flood of studies of mysticism may be gathered from the following selection of titles printed in London. The Catholic mystics were translated *en masse*. The three volumes of Fénelon's *Spiritual Letters* were translated by Sidney Lear in 1880, 1892, and 1906. The same author translated the *Spiritual Letters* of St. François de Sales in 1892, while the Salesian *Treatise of the Love of God* was translated by W. J. Knox Little in 1901, and the *Introduction to the Devout Life* by A. Ross in 1925. Madame Guyon's *A Short and Easy Method of Prayer* appeared in English translation in 1901 and her *Autobiography* was translated by Alpen in 1897. Brother Lawrence's *The Practice of the Presence of God* appeared in English in 1906. E. K. Sanders published the following series of studies of Catholic mystics: *Fénelon, His Friends and Enemies* (1901); *Angélique of Port Royal* (1905); *Vincent de Paul* (1913); and *St. Chantal* (1918). Jacob Boehme's *The Way to Christ* was translated in 1911; his *The Aurore* in 1914; his *Six Theosophic Points* in 1919; and his *Confessions* in 1920. William Law's *Liberal*

in the way to achieve interior peace. Grasping materialists were intrigued by those who despised the world and all its successes.[29] Historians turned sceptical by the impossibility of attaining the quest for the historical Jesus, when Harnack and Schweitzer produced such varying reconstructions, preferred the pragmatism of mysticism. Tortured amateur philosophers, weary of idealism's abstractions, turned to the tried and trusty *philosophia perennis* of Christian Platonism. In short, men looked for an exposition of religion to the experts—the saints—after trying the unsatisfactory reconstructions of the philosophers, the historians, and the social scientists. It was the hardest as well as the surest source of religious renewal to be found in a feverish and iconoclastic era.

The three most significant English exponents of mysticism filled three roles. Dean Inge was the pioneer. Baron von Hügel was the philosopher-historian who wisely saw that the institutional and intellectual elements in religion were necessary to undergird the primary mystical element, thus guaranteeing its stability. Evelyn Underhill was the popularizer.

Inge was one of the great and paradoxical personalities of the period. It is possible that he was the most quoted clergyman of his time, for as well as being wise he was witty. Bernard Shaw regarded him as "the greatest intellectual asset of the English Church."[30] It is curious that so urbane and witty a personage should have been attracted to mysticism: yet it was precisely because this witty personality and polymath believed that mysticism was the heart of religion that he gained a hearing for it.

---

and Mystical Writings was edited by W. Scott Palmer in 1908 and John Woolman's *Journal and Essays* was edited by A. M. Gummere in 1922. George Fox's *Journal* was edited from the MSS by N. Penney in 1911 (Cambridge), while two admirable accounts of spirituality from Quakers were Rufus Jones's *Spiritual Reformers in the 16th and 17th Centuries* (1914) and Braithwaite's *The Beginnings of Quakerism* (1912). Dom Cuthbert Butler's study, *Western Mysticism*, appeared in 1922, and the greatest volume in the field, Baron von Hügel's *The Mystical Element of Religion*, appeared in the same year as Brémond's superb *Histoire Littéraire du Sentiment Réligieux en France* (6 vols., Paris, 1923). These are but trickles of what was a torrent of works on mysticism which appeared in the first quarter of the present century. It should also be noted that William James in his *Varieties of Religious Experience* (1902) gave a spur to phenomenology and pragmatism, as well as making popular the new study—the psychology of religion.

29 One recalls the assertion of Chesterton that an age is attracted by the saints that contradict it most, as his explanation of the attraction of the Victorian industrialists for St. Francis the mystic of nature and of the attraction of our contemporary relativists for the massive objectivity of the *Summa* of St. Thomas Aquinas.

30 Sidney Dark, *Five Deans*, p. 211. Archbishop Temple, however, outshone Inge in constructive intellectual capacity and his influence was more widespread. For an admirable biography, see Adam Fox, *Dean Inge*.

Inge believed in the ultimate coincidence of philosophy and religion: "The goal of philosophy is the same as the goal of religion—perfect knowledge of the Perfect."[31] It was, however, only in a single chapter of the long history of philosophy that Inge found the confluence of rational thinking with a mystical apprehension of God. This was neo-Platonism and its leading exponent was Plotinus. Inge, in fact, became the chief expositor of the Plotinian system and produced the results of his studies in the Gifford Lectures, published in 1918 as *The Philosophy of Plotinus*. In the introduction he stated: "I have steeped myself in his writings, and I have tried not only to understand them as one might try to understand any other intellectual system, but to take them as a guide to right living and right thinking. He must be studied as a spiritual director, a prophet and not only as a thinker. We can only understand him by following him and making his experience our own."[32] For him Platonism was the perennial philosophy and consequently he concluded: "We cannot preserve Platonism without Christianity, or Christianity without Platonism, or civilization without both."[33] The value of thus combining philosophy and mysticism was that the dual search would deliver the modern world from both shallow rationalism and emotional irrationalism.

Inge's pioneering contributions to English religion were, however, made in two earlier volumes, the Bampton Lectures published as *Christian Mysticism* (1899) which excited considerable interest in the University of Oxford, and *Studies in English Mystics* (1907).

Inge began *Christian Mysticism* by defining mysticism as "the attempt to realise the presence of the living God in the soul and in nature, or, more generally, as *the attempt to realise, in thought and feeling, the immanence of the temporal in the eternal and of the eternal in the temporal.*"[34] He claimed that it rested on four basic propositions or articles of faith. These were: the soul is the organ of spiritual truth; man in knowing God is a partaker of the Divine nature; sensuality and selfishness are absolute disqualifications for spiritual knowledge; and "the true hierophant of the mysteries of God is love."[35] He concluded the general discussion of mysticism by asserting that the mystic makes it the aim of his life "to be transformed into the likeness of Him in whose image

[31] *Contemporary British Philosophy*, Series I, p. 191.
[32] I, p. 7.   [33] *Ibid.*, II, p. 227.
[34] *Christian Mysticism*, p. 5.   [35] *Ibid.*, p. 9.

he was created." The ladder of perfection, the commonest image for this process, is usually marked by three steps or stages of ascent: the purgative, the illuminative, and the unitive life.

The second chapter deals with the mystical element in the Bible, stressing its great importance for Paul and the author of the Fourth Gospel, the latter being "the charter of Christian Mysticism."[36] The third and fourth chapters describe Christian Platonism and Speculative Mysticism in the East and in the West, respectively. Scholasticism is criticized as "philosophy in chains" and the *via negativa* of the Pseudo-Dionysius as "mysticism blind-folded."[37] The fifth and sixth chapters treat of Practical and Devotional Mysticism. Inge regards the introspective, negative, and quietistic mystics of the Counter-Reformation as being more important historically than intrinsically, believing that "the spiritual Christianity of the modern epoch is rather called to the consecration of art, science, and social life than to lonely contemplation."[38]

The most important seventh and eighth chapters on Nature, Mysticism, and Symbolism show the importance both of the Incarnation and of the sacramental system in Christianity and of the necessity of mysticism for the apprehension of their meaning. "I do not shrink from expressing my conviction," asserts Inge, "that the true meaning of the sacramental system, which in its external forms is so strangely anticipated by the Greek mysteries, and in its inward significance strikes down to the fundamental principles of mystical Christianity, can only be understood by those who are in some sympathy with mysticism."[39] He is equally convinced that the abstract mysticism of the negative way is dangerous to Christian faith and worship, for it insists that all symbols are veils between our eyes and reality and must be done away with.

The final chapter has some significant constructive suggestions to offer. Like von Hügel after him, Inge insists that every religion must have an institutional as well as a mystical element. "Just as, if the feeling of immediate communion with God has faded, we shall have 'a dead Christ,' as Fox the Quaker said of the Anglican Church in his day; so, if the seer and prophet expel the priest, there will be no discipline and no cohesion."[40] Nonetheless, as the older seats of infallible authority, the infallible Church and the infallible Book, are so fiercely assailed, the only alternative authority is that of spiritual religion experienced in life. Thus a renais-

---

36 *Ibid.*, p. 44. 37 *Ibid.*, p. 148. 38 *Ibid.*, pp. 244-45.
39 *Ibid.*, p. 260. 40 *Ibid.*, pp. 329-30.

sance of mysticism is the primary need of Christianity in the twentieth century.

Studies of English Mystics is a slighter volume, but its importance lies in the fact that it recalled the pragmatic English to their sober, yet tender traditions of mystical piety. The introductory chapter on the psychology of mysticism warned against the two dangers that come from too entire a dependence upon feeling in mysticism: the antinomianism that holds that the sins of the body cannot stain the soul, and the quietism that ends in purposeless passivity. In its day the studies of the *Ancren Riwle*, Julian of Norwich, Walter Hilton, and William Law, were new. That they are now commonplace is a tribute to Inge's instruction and evocation of interest. The inclusion of studies of Wordsworth and Browning, while unusual, was a stroke of genius, for no poets were more popular among the preachers of the day and therefore likelier to win Inge an audience for a more thorough-going consideration of traditional mysticism.

The conclusion of the volume is an admirable analysis of the attractions of mystical religion for thoughtful people. It is precisely those persons who crave for a basis of belief that will not rest on tradition or authority or historical evidence, but on the ascertainable facts of human experience, who find the study of mysticism alluring. For the mystics are the only thorough-going empiricists. "They guide us to the perennial fresh springs of religion, and present it to us as a living and active force, as palpable and undeniable as the so-called 'forces of nature,' though less easy to explain and control. . . . The religions of authority are tottering to their fall; but the religion of the Spirit is still near the beginning of that triumphant course which Christ foretold for it on the last evening of His life: 'When He, the Spirit of Truth is come, He will guide you into all truth . . . He will glorify Me; for He will take of Mine, and will show it unto you.' "[41]

Baron Friedrich von Hügel had a mind of less brilliance, but of more balanced profundity than Inge. Moreover, although he was a layman, no priest was ever a more dedicated director of the souls of the intelligent than he. His religious loyalty to the Roman Catholic tradition was joined to an almost universal charity which could sympathise with the Roman Catholic Modernists such as Loisy and

[41] *Ibid.*, pp. 238-39. In view of the next paragraph it is interesting to read Inge's tribute to von Hügel in *God and the Astronomers*, p. 120: "There is no writer on the philosophy of religion with whom I am more in general sympathy and from whom I have learned more than Friedrich von Hügel."

Tyrrell, on the one hand, and with the mystics of the Islamic and Hindu traditions, on the other. No other religious thinker of the period insisted more strongly than he on the necessity for a triple rope to make religion strong: with mystical, intellectual, and institutional strands. No other thinker of his day was more aware of the fructifying contribution religion has made to culture, nor of the importance of all the intellectual, moral, and spiritual disciplines in their contribution to human culture and well-being. Although a great phenomenologist, as his classical study of *The Mystical Element of Religion as studied in Saint Catherine of Genoa and her Friends* (1909, 1923, and 1961) abundantly demonstrates, the emphasis on the transcendent reality of God increased steadily in the books that followed it. *Eternal Life* (1912); *Essays and Addresses in the Philosophy of Religion* (1st Series, 1921; 2nd Series, 1926); *The Reality of God* (1931) and *Selected Letters* (1933) are overwhelming testimony to this gifted layman's concern to express the mystery and grace of the spiritual life in its historical, theological, and practical dimensions in all his writings.

He analysed the three elements which he believed were disclosed in Western civilization.[42] There is Hellenism, the thirst for richness and harmony; there is Christianity, the revelation of personality and the depth of existence; and there is Science, the apprehension of fact and law. All three of them are necessary to the fulness of human life.

Religion is the apprehension of the reality of God. God is revealed to us in experience, though by no means is the meaning of God exhausted by our experience of Him. Von Hügel lays the strongest emphasis on the Divine transcendence. Yet although God Himself transcends space and time, the religion in which we apprehend Him lies within the context of our life in this world. Consequently von Hügel warns, "There is no such thing for man as a complete escape from history and institutions."[43] Religion, therefore, must manifest itself in historical forms—in institutions like the Church, and through sensuous media such as rituals and sacraments, art and music, and the like. In these the Divine is incarnated, so that the transcendent reality becomes immanent in earthly forms. The finest expression in history of the religious spirit is, for the Baron, the institution of the Catholic Church, with all the

[42] *The Mystical Element of Religion* . . . , Vol. I, Chap. 1. For von Hügel's relations to Catholic Modernism see M. D. Petre, *Von Hügel and Tyrrell*, and A. R. Vidler, *The Modernist Movement in the Roman Church.*
[43] *Essays and Addresses*, Series I, p. 15.

richness of its worship and symbolism. At the same time he will be the last to deny value to any way by which the genuine understanding of God has been historically mediated in any religion. From this all-too-compressed summary of his views, it will be clear that Baron von Hügel's contribution to mysticism has profoundly important effects for worship, for he recognizes it as the corporate expression of adoration, penitence, petition, intercession, and consecration. Moreover, he knows how the liturgy with the subtle aid of repeated ritual, with the harmony of praise, with the visually dramatic actions of the sacraments, together with the great expectations it arouses in the hearts of believers on the great festivals of the Christian Year, is a potent teacher of the Christian faith and a powerful channel of Divine grace.

The chief importance of Baron von Hügel, however, was the great influence of his wise and judicious understanding of many aspects of religion, including mysticism. This was particularly valuable in an age of febrile change, when the latest fashion was apt to jettison the traditional values. He was the great synthetist of the early part of the century. This is finely exhibited in the famous second chapter of *The Mystical Element of Religion.*[44]

Von Hügel argued that a retrospect of man's religious life would show that each individual has been shaped religiously by three modes of apprehension. As a child, sense and memory were the chief means of apprehending religion and at this stage "the External, Authoritative, Historical, Traditional, Institutional side and function of Religion are everywhere present."[45] The youth, however, approaches religion in terms of question and argument, so that "Religion here becomes Thought, System, a Philosophy."[46] The mature man has emotional and volitional, ethical and spiritual powers, and these are fed by the experimental and mystical side of religion. "Here Religion is felt rather than seen or reasoned about, is loved and lived rather than analyzed, is action and power, rather than external fact or intellectual verification."[47] Hence in the religious development of man three essential elements come into play: the institutional, the intellectual, and the mystical.

Von Hügel then demonstrates that each element in the triple strand has special motives for suppressing the other two. The

[44] Von Hügel notes (p. viii of the Preface to the 2nd edn., 1923) that Bishop Charles Gore had asked for a separate publication of the 32 pages of Chapter II, concerning the "Three Elements of Religion."
[45] *The Mystical Element of Religion,* Vol. I, p. 51.
[46] *Ibid.,* p. 52.   [47] *Ibid.,* p. 53.

historical and institutional element is spatially and temporally exclusive in asserting the finality of the revelation and the institution that guarantees it, thus demanding surrender, not analysis, and in the process starving or cramping science and literature, art, and politics. How is this to be avoided? Von Hügel answers: "Through dependence upon the living God cooperating with the living soul!"[48] By this he means relying on the inexhaustible self-interpreting illumination of God. Similarly, there will be the tendency on the part of the newly awakened soul experiencing interior freshness to despise the external aids of religion and to refuse the concrete yoke of the institutional discipline, but only at the cost of the soul becoming unconsciously weak or feverish. But, he warns, "The Church's insistence upon some vocal prayer, upon some differentiated specific acts of the various moral and theological virtues, upon sacramental practice . . . is a living commentary upon the difficulty and importance of the point under discussion."[49]

Furthermore, there will be an attempt on the part of the emotional element, either alone or in combination with the institutional element, to suppress the analytic and speculative elements. The danger will be that it will cling to historical facts and elude critical examination, or will feed intensely on its own emotions, opposing all slow discrimination or mere approximation. Here, again, "the true solution will ever be found in an even fuller conception of Personality and of its primary place in the religious life."[50] The intellectual element of the personality will be able to provide rest, expression, and purification for the moral and spiritual side of human nature. The rest comes from the intellect's neglect of emotions, actions, and persons, to concentrate on abstractions and things. The expression comes from the restating by the intellect of the results of the moral and spiritual activities so that they may be understood by civilization and culture. "Above all, they can help to purify these moral-spiritual activities, owing to their interposing . . . a zone of abstraction, of cool, clear thinking."[51]

Finally, von Hügel anticipates and answers the criticism that this three-fold analysis of religion is excessively intellectual, Pelagian, and Epicurean. He argues that Christianity is not a religion for intellectuals only, while all Christians use their intellects. He splendidly claims that some intellectual virtues, such as moral courage, intellectual honesty, chivalrous fairness, manly renuncia-

48 *Ibid.*, p. 73.   49 *Ibid.*, p. 74.   50 *Ibid.*, p. 76.
51 *Ibid.*, p. 77.

tion of popularity and easy honours, "bear upon them the impress of God and His Christ" as profoundly spiritual qualities. He utterly rejects Pelagianism, claiming that "Every one of our acts, our very physical existence and persistence, is dependent, at every moment and in every direction, upon the prevenient, accompanying and subsequent power and help of God, and still more is every religious, every truly spiritual and supernatural act of the soul impossible without the constant action of God's grace."[52] Yet the actions from without are seen as our volition and are known within as God's energies. Nor is his understanding of religion Epicurean: for it is in the mystical life that the Cross and Renunciation are imitated most deeply.

Although much interested in the Divine immanence in history, von Hügel was even more insistent on the importance of the Divine transcendence. His greatest importance lies in his philosophical balancing of the intellectual, institutional, and mystical elements of religion, as in his ever-repeated stress on the priority and pre-venience of Divine grace and on the significance of eternal life as a present possession and an everlasting hope. The mystics are, for him, ultimately important because they dramatically fulfilled the two necessary conditions for living a fully mature religious life. They are filled with "the vivid, continuous sense that God the Spirit upholding our poor little spirits, is the true originator and the true end of the whole movement" and they possess "the con-tinuous sense of the ever necessary, ever fruitful, ever bliss-producing Cross of Christ—the great law and fact that only through self-renunciation and suffering can the soul win its true self." These are "the two eyes of religion and twin pulse-beats of its very heart" and "have been realized, with magnificent persistence and intensity, by the greatest of the Inclusive Mystics."[53]

Reconsidering his views on religion in the Preface to the second edition of 1923, von Hügel claimed that he now saw with greater clarity that the "Givenness" of all religion worthy of the name is its central characteristic. "The Otherness, the Prevenience of God, the One-sided relation between God and man, these constitute the deepest measure and touchstone of all religion."[54] This prophetic recognition amid the flux of competing immanentalisms is the measure of the greatness of the man, as of his continuing influence after the demise of both Protestant Liberalism and Catholic Mod-ernism and during the resurgence of theologies of revelation and

[52] *Ibid.*, pp. 79-80.   [53] *Ibid.*, II, p. 395.   [54] P. xvi.

redemption. He had prepared the way to reintegrate transcendence with immanence, and thus opened up a path which later phenomenologists such as Van der Leeuw, Söderblom, and Otto were to follow. In Evelyn Underhill he was to find, in England, the disciple who would make his insights known to the wayfaring pilgrim who could not be expected to grapple with his philosophical profundity and complexity, but who needed his balanced insight into the nature of the religious life.

We turn to Evelyn Underhill,[55] not only because she was a distinguished popularizer (for she was a poet, scholar, and expositor of mysticism in her own right before she met von Hügel), but because she it was who combined an abiding interest in personal mysticism and in public worship and educated the religious public to understand the primary significance of both for the contemporary Church. This educational task was accomplished not only in her published writings but in the many religious retreats of which she was the skilled director, and through her perceptive letters which have been edited with an introduction by Charles Williams.

She wrote thirty-three books, almost all of them concerned with spirituality. Three of them deserve careful attention. These are *Mysticism, A Study of the Nature and Development of Man's Spiritual Consciousness* (1911); *The Mystics of the Church* (1925); and *Worship* (1936). They reveal a mind that found neo-Platonism congenial (as did Dean Inge) in its earlier phase, but which (with the friendship of Baron von Hügel, who had taken the place of Father R. H. Benson as her spiritual director) became increasingly incarnational and more appreciative of the institutional aspects of religion. By 1922 she had become a practising member of the Church of England and belonged decisively to its Catholic wing. The change can be noted in the fact that the first book published after the transition, *The Life of the Spirit and the Life of Today* (1922), included a chapter on "Institutional Religion and the Life of the Spirit," while the next book carried the institutional emphasis in the title, *The Mystics of the Church* (1925). She thus expressed in her own pilgrimage the religious movement of the whole period as it proceeded from immanentalism to transcendentalism, from Liberal Protestantism to Orthodoxy,

[55] See Margaret Cropper, *Evelyn Underhill*, for the facts of her life, and Lucy Menzies, ed., *The Collected Papers of Evelyn Underhill*, for an evaluation by Lumsden Barkway, Bishop of St. Andrews, and for a bibliography of Evelyn Underhill's writings, pp. 37-38. A useful anthology of her writings has been compiled by Thomas Kepler, *The Evelyn Underhill Reader*.

from private mysticism to public worship, from the individual to the institutional expression of allegiance, and from Theocentric to Christocentric faith.

Her first great work was *Mysticism* (1911). It attempted in two parts, the first historical and the second psychological, to "set out and justify a definite theory of man's mystical consciousness."[56] Mysticism was defined as "essentially a movement of the heart, seeking to transcend the limitations of the individual standpoint and to surrender itself to ultimate Reality; for no personal gain, to satisfy no transcendental curiosity, to obtain no other-worldly joys, but purely from an instinct of love."[57] Four basic statements are made about the nature of mysticism: it is practical, not theoretical; it is entirely spiritual; its business and method is love; and true mysticism is never self-seeking.[58] As a definite psychological experience it has two sides: "the Vision or consciousness of Absolute Perfection" and "the inward transmutation to which that Vision compels the mystic, in order that he may be to some extent worthy of that which he has beheld. . . . He has seen the Perfect; he wants to be perfect, too."[59]

Two most important chapters are those on "Mysticism and Theology" and on "Mysticism and Symbolism." The distinction is made between transcendental and immanental mystics and Christian theology provides the best theoretical background, according to Evelyn Underhill, in the doctrine of the Trinity, since it combines the unknowable God with the Wisdom of God (the Son) in a personal principle, while in the doctrine of the Incarnation it explains the nature of the inward and mystical experience where the soul resumes the life history of the race. She wisely adds: "In the last resort, the doctrine of the Incarnation is the only safeguard of the mystics against the pantheism to which they always tend. The unconditioned Absolute, so soon as it alone becomes the object of their contemplation, is apt to be conceived merely as Divine Essence; the idea of personality evaporates and loving communion is at an end."[60]

[56] *Mysticism*, p. ix.
[57] *Ibid.*, p. 84. A more precise definition was supplied in *The Essentials of Mysticism and other Essays*, pp. 4-5: "this adoring and all-possessing consciousness of the rich and complete divine life over against the self's life, and of the possible achievement of a level of being, a sublimation of the self, wherein we are perfectly united with it, may fairly be written down as a necessary element of all mystical life."
[58] A summary of statements made on pp. 97, 100, 101, 107, 109.
[59] *Ibid.*, p. 108.
[60] *Ibid.*, p. 145.

The chapter on "Mysticism and Symbolism" studies three groups of mystical symbols: the image of pilgrimage as the symbol of the Divine transcendence; the image of the lover seeking the Beloved; and the image of the saint seeking purity and perfection. It is strongly asserted that no spiritual experiences are capable of direct description, but they must always be expressed in a symbolic, allusive, and oblique mode, suggesting rather than telling the truth. The importance for worship of the following citation is immeasurable: "The greater the suggestive quality of the symbol used, the more answering emotion it invokes in those to whom it is addressed, the more truth it will convey." Furthermore, a good symbol will use to the utmost "the resources of beauty and of passion, will bring with it hints of mystery and wonder, bewitch with dreamy periods the mind to which it is addressed. Its appeal will not be to the clever brain, but to the desirous heart of man."[61]

The second part of the book is wholly concerned to describe the Mystic Way. Evelyn Underhill elaborates instead of the usual three-fold path a more precise five-fold way. The first stage is awakening or conversion. The second stage is self-knowledge or purgation. The third stage is illumination. The fourth stage is surrender or the dark night of the soul. The fifth and final stage is union.

The novelty of the book consisted in its careful analysis of the five stages of the mystical experience, with many illustrative excerpts from mystics of many religions and centuries, and in the insistence that the state of mystical union does not mean a withdrawal from social duty, but rather that the inclusive mystic is the most active citizen of the Kingdom of God.[62] For the author herself the chief importance of *Mysticism* was that it gained her the friendship of Baron von Hügel.[63]

She granted a positive and educative role to the institution of the Church[64] in her next important volume, *The Mystics of the Church*, conceding that mysticism needs to be tested and corrected by the good sense of the Church, otherwise it grows feverishly emotional, lacking in genial appreciation of other persons, or even narrowly

[61] *Ibid.*, p. 151.

[62] See Margaret Cropper, *Evelyn Underhill*, pp. 46-47.

[63] *Ibid.*, p. 5, indicates that von Hügel liked the book but felt it did not do justice to the importance of "liturgical acts, of the Sacraments, of the Visible, of History."

[64] In *The Essentials of Mysticism and other Essays* she had regarded the Church as a necessary nuisance for mystics and was critical of the conservative crudity of the cultus. See esp. pp. 27-28.

intense, combative, and intolerant.[65] In this book she shows for the first time a deep appreciation of Christocentric mysticism. She acknowledges that "Christianity is unique among the world's great religions in this: that its Founder is to His closest followers not merely a prophet, pattern of conduct, or Divine figure revealed in the historic past, but the object here and now of an experienced communion of the most vivid kind." She adds that "Christians claim that this communion has remained unimpaired for nineteen hundred years and is the true source of the Church's undying energy."[66] The persons who have most vividly experienced this communion are, of course, the mystics, and they have been the instruments of making the Church's loyalty to her Master a living thing. Whereas earlier Evelyn Underhill had regarded the Transcendental mystics more highly than the incarnational mystics, now she gives the latter sustained and appreciative treatment.

The fullest recognition of the theological, historical and liturgical role of the Church is provided, however, in her last great book, *Worship* (1936). No book on this theme, treating all its varieties with ecumenical fairness, has been as widely read or as influential in our time in the English-speaking world.[67] Its perspective was that of a "mountain-top view of the longing adoration of man for God."[68] The book was divided into two parts, treating the theory and practice of worship. The first part dealt with the nature of Worship, Ritual and Symbol, Sacrament and Sacrifice, and with the Characters, the Principles, and Liturgical Elements of Christian Worship, as also with the Eucharist and the principles of personal worship. The second part was historical and descriptive, tracing the development of Jewish worship, the beginnings of Christian worship, Catholic worship in East and West, the worship of the Reformed Churches, Free Church worship, and the Anglican tradition. The book demanded careful and objective scholarship, open-mindedness in willing to learn new things, and a capacity to

---

65 *The Mystics of the Church*, p. 16.

66 *Ibid.*, p. 24. It had an interesting concluding chapter on modern mystics, including cameo studies of J. W. Rowntree, Charles de Foucauld, and Sadhu Sundar Singh.

67 Yet she accepted the invitation to write it with great reluctance. See Margaret Cropper, *Evelyn Underhill*, p. 197.

68 *Ibid.*, p. 197. In a review in *The Christian Century*, Dr. Henry P. Van Dusen declared that "here may be discovered the inner genius of whole branches of Christendom," and *The Times* reviewer acknowledged *Worship* to be "a masterpiece of the spiritual life, free from all professional partisanship and the prejudices of the sacristy—a book that will bear fruit for many years to come among men and women of many different communions."

penetrate beyond labels to realities. Among those whom Evelyn Underhill consulted were Bishops W. H. Frere and Leslie Owen, and Drs. W. Russell Maltby and Nicholas Zernov.

The fine spirit in which it is written may be illustrated from the Preface. She wished to show all traditions, sacramental and non-sacramental alike, "as chapels of various types in the one Cathedral of the Spirit," for each great form of the Christian cultus has as its object "to lead human souls, by different ways, to that pure act of adoration which is the consummation of worship."[69]

For those of the non-sacramental tradition its great value was that it introduced them to the reasons why the Catholic tradition stressed the importance of the sacraments. The universality of sacraments was not, she insisted, as is commonly believed, a witness to the Divine Immanence, but a proclamation of the Divine Transcendence. It is due to man's acknowledgment of the chasm between Creator and creature and "the need of a bridge, an ordained path along which the Eternal Perfect may penetrate time and the things of time." Thus "Here man is pressed by God immanent to prepare the matrix; but it is God transcendent who pours into it His quickening love to cleanse, feed, and transform."[70] Typical also is Evelyn Underhill's pithy distinction between a symbol and a sacrament: "A symbol is a significant image, which helps the worshipping soul to apprehend spiritual reality." On the other hand, "a sacrament is a significant deed, a particular use of temporal things, which gives to them the value of eternal things and thus incorporates and conveys spiritual reality."[71] In consequence sacraments are the expression of an incarnational philosophy. This was a word in season, but only by implication, to the non-sacramental traditions of worship which had lost so much of the sense of wonder, beauty, and mystery in worship by their iconoclasm with reference to symbols and sacraments and by their dry didacticism.

In similar ecumenical fashion, she showed that the Protestant elevation of the Word and the Catholic elevation of the Eucharist were not intended to be alternatives, but are essential and complementary aspects of the Liturgy. She showed that the Christian Year (and it is significant that subsequent to her exposition it became more common for the Free Churches to discard their Puritan opposition to the great Christian festivals) lights up all phases of human experience with the radiance of eternity. Thus, "the helplessness and humility of infancy, the long hidden period of disci-

---

[69] *Worship*, p. viii.   [70] *Ibid.*, p. 46.   [71] *Ibid.*, p. 43.

pline and growth, the lonely crisis and choice of the temptation, above all the heart-shaking events of Holy Week, Easter, and the Forty Days—all these become disclosures of the Supernatural made through and in man, and therefore having a direct application to man's need and experience."[72]

The book concludes by insisting that ultimately the way of devotion and the way of sacrificial service to others is one way, for both are signs of "Creation's response to its Origin and Lord."[73] The hope for the future is that the true meaning and message of the Incarnation will come to be more perfectly understood, when the demand on man's worshipping love and total self-offering will receive a more complete response—"a response stretching upward in awestruck contemplation to share that adoring vision of the Principle which is 'the inheritance of saints in light,' and downwards and outwards in loving action, to embrace and so transform the world."[74]

After completing *Worship*, Evelyn Underhill gave much time to reflecting on the significance of the Eucharist in another volume, *The Mystery of Sacrifice* (1938). She believed that the Liturgy had become the supreme ritual act of the Christian Family because every aspect of the response which the created order makes to its origin and Lord finds there its sanction and expression. The fully Christian life was, for her, a Eucharistic life. "That is, a natural life conformed to the pattern of Jesus, given in its wholeness to God, laid on His altar as a sacrifice of love, and consecrated, transformed by His inpouring life, to be used to give life and good to other souls."[75]

By her writings Evelyn Underhill taught thousands for whom religion had been ethical idealism, or a set of orthodox opinions, that it was the adventure of holiness, the search for the Perfect Who alone is truth, beauty, and goodness, with the aid of the great guides of the mystics, and with the liturgical and sacramental helps of the Church, and that the greatest bridge between God and men had been thrown across the abyss by the Incarnation.

The concentration on mysticism in the work of Inge, von Hügel and Underhill, and their countless disciples and imitators, was to prove fertile ground for the later growth of orthodoxy in doctrine, the reassertion of the doctrine of the Church as the Body of Christ that was to be recovered in the Ecumenical Movement (both

[72] *Ibid.*, pp. 76-77.   [73] *Ibid.*, p. 343.   [74] *Ibid.*
[75] P. xv.

Protestant and Catholic), and in the renewal of theologies of revelation and redemption in the latter part of the third decade of this century. It cannot have been easy to believe in the ultimate victory of a transcendental concept of God or in a revived ecclesiology when immanentalism was so popular in the Catholic Modernism, the Liberal Protestantism, and the Social Gospel Movement of the first twenty years of the century.

4. *The Incarnationalists*: *Gore and Temple*

In Charles Gore (1853-1932) and William Temple (1881-1944), the two leading theologians of the Anglican Communion in the twentieth century, there was to be found the strength of immanentalism. Both emphasized the continuity between the divine operations in providence and grace, and in the consentient witness to God in nature, in history and in conscience, as well as in the recognition of social duty. There was also in both a conviction that faith and truth were ultimately one as guaranteed by the same God who is their originator, and hence they were theologians of revelation and explanation rather than of crisis and redemption. But they also differed very significantly from the extreme Liberal Protestants of the day, or Modernists as they were sometimes called. This can be seen in the significance they gave to the doctrines of the Incarnation, the Church, and the Sacraments. Moreover, such an emphasis strongly undergirded the importance of the cultus, which had been minimized in the ethical and social concerns exaggerated by the Social Gospellers.

This difference is manifest in the devastating critique of immanentalism provided by Gore's *The New Theology and the Old Religion*, which shook Campbell's confidence in his own reconstruction and eventually brought him back to the Anglican fold with the confession that "This poor sad world of ours needs a more strenuous gospel than the assurance that our sins are merely wrong turnings on the upward road, and that all must inevitably come right at the last."[76] The new emphasis is concentrated in Temple's assertion that the Incarnation was the supreme instance of "the immanence of the transcendent."[77]

Our reason for grouping Gore and Temple together, despite the fact that Gore was the leader of the Anglo-Catholics in the Church

[76] *Spiritual Pilgrimage*, p. 173. W. E. Orchard, an early supporter of Campbell, also repented and became a Roman Catholic priest. See his *From Faith to Faith*.
[77] *Nature, Man and God*, p. 290f.

of England and that Temple was not clearly affiliated with any party, is that both were strong incarnationalists and Temple admitted his indebtedness to Gore as a paramount influence. In his dedication to *Studies in the Spirit and Truth of Christianity* (1917), Temple acknowledged his gratitude to Gore as "one from whom I have learnt more than any other now living of the Spirit of Christianity." On many occasions in Temple's public life, when he had to decide whether or not to accept preferments or appointments, Gore was consulted as a second father.[78] While stressing their close affinity, however, it must be emphasized that Temple was far from being an echo of Gore, since he was a brilliant, profound, and independent thinker. Moreover, there were considerable differences in approach between Gore and Temple. Gore was a Biblical and historical scholar by training, while Temple was a philosopher in his approach to the theological task. Furthermore, while each believed in the centrality of the Incarnation and denied any adoptionist Christology, Gore was persuaded to adopt Kenoticism, of which Temple was exceedingly doubtful. Furthermore, while Gore treated the purpose of the Incarnation as the rectification of a fallen world, Temple saw it more positively as the fulfilment of the purpose of creation.[79] Then, again, Temple's experiences brought him into touch with a wider world than Gore's, and he exercised more onerous public and ecclesiastical responsibilities. Finally, Gore was attracted by the Pauline and Temple by the Johannine elements in the New Testament; so that Temple was more sympathetic to mysticism than Gore. This incarnational theology (which Gore preferred to call "Liberal Catholicism") included three essential elements. It combined a deep spiritual devotion mediated by the Liturgy, with an emphasis on candour in Biblical and theological scholarship, together with a passion for social justice. It was, therefore, a subtle combination of devotion, critical independence, and compassion, in which the sacramental devotion of the Tractarians was linked with the Maurician concern for social justice, and both with the Liberal conviction that faith and truth were indissoluble.

In Gore the first element was seen conspicuously in the founda-

[78] F. A. Iremonger, *William Temple, Archbishop of Canterbury, His Life and Letters*, pp. 89, 131, 133, 194-95, 262-63, 283, 332. Prestige in his life of Gore (p. 538) credits Temple with the following tribute to Gore: "Though I have had many tutors in Christ, he was perhaps above all others my father; and so far as I can picture Jesus Christ, I picture him as not unlike the father I have lost." [79] See Joseph Fletcher, *William Temple, Twentieth Century Christian*, p. 34.

151

tion of the Community of the Resurrection in 1887 and in his study of Eucharistic doctrine, *The Body of Christ* (1901).[80] In Temple it was worked out in the sacramental view of the universe in *Nature, Man, and God*, in the two volumes of *Readings in St. John's Gospel*, and in the brilliant account of the Eucharist as the transcript of a redeemed social order on earth in *Hope of a New World*.

The second element of Liberal Catholicism, the correlation of Christian faith with the world's culture, was first seen in Gore's daring essay on Inspiration contributed to *Lux Mundi* in 1889, and the volume was significantly subtitled "a series of studies in the Religion of the Incarnation." Both Biblical criticism and the doctrine of evolution forced him to admit that the knowledge of the Incarnate Lord was limited by the conditions of the first century. He later developed the implications of this acknowledgment in a "Kenotic" view of Christology, by which he meant that the Eternal Logos in becoming man "emptied himself" of the metaphysical attributes of Deity while retaining the moral and spiritual attributes. The approach brought great relief to Christians whose intelligence had hitherto to be strait-jacketed in the confines of unnecessary dogmas. Thereafter Gore aimed at being as open-minded as possible, and often jocularly referred to himself as a "Free-thinker."[81] In fact, however, he held tenaciously to the positions he had maintained in this early period, and so "while in the 1890s he was looked upon as the pioneer of a liberal and progressive theology, thereafter he appeared more in the role of a resolute defender of orthodoxy."[82]

Temple's whole approach, as a philosopher, was to show the rational implications of faith in the spirit of Anselm's *credo ut intelligam*. He claimed in *Mens Creatrix* (1917) and in *Christus Veritas* (1924) that if Reality is sought by the different paths of philosophy, science, and art, they will never meet unless there be a God in whom these values eternally exist. He clearly contends that the most satisfactory explanation of the universe is the hypothesis of its creation by intelligent purpose. Life is seen to have

---

[80] S. C. Carpenter in *Prophet and Priest, A Lecture given on the Charles Gore Memorial Foundation on 13 November 1952 at Westminster Abbey* writes (p. 15): "Finally, those who knew him, knew also that he was in every fibre of his being, priest of God. His concentration at the altar was amazing. The first time I ever saw him celebrate Holy Communion (it was in a College Chapel), I had the sensation that he was gathering the congregation of young men with a sweep of his arms, and drawing them towards God. And many have testified that it was a revelation to hear him say the Litany."

[81] *Ibid.*, p. 14.

[82] A. R. Vidler, *The Church in an Age of Revolution*, pp. 193-94.

four gradations: matter, life, mind, and spirit, and man is seen as the crown of creation, resembling God, dimly but truly, in his mental and spiritual sensitivities, as in the capacity to understand, to make conscious moral choices, and to live in fellowship. God's intelligence and power are shown in creation and his supreme revelation of Himself is in the Incarnation, which Temple expressed as the concept of the Supreme as servant, and which he believed to be a uniquely Christian insight.

In contributing to the third element of Liberal Catholicism, the concern for social justice, both were equally eminent. Sometimes the fiery words of Bishop Gore as prophet would emerge when they were least expected. When at a formal civic dinner he had pronounced the episcopal blessing, he added, "God forgive us for having all this to enjoy, of which many of our neighbors know nothing."[83] At the age of twenty-six he was the most conspicuous of the university socialists at Oxford, and he was fond of citing A. H. Clough's couplet:

> Thou shalt not covet: but tradition
> Approves all forms of competition.[84]

H. D. A. Major rightly affirmed that Gore had revolutionised the public's concept of the political colour of Church of England clergymen, so that "she who had been aptly described as the Conservative party at prayer, became, as the result of Gore's influence, at least in the person of her Anglo-Catholic clergy, the Socialist party at Mass."[85] Although the son of an Archbishop of Canterbury, and later to attain this highest office in the Anglican Church himself, William Temple showed his concern for the underprivileged by accepting the presidency of the Workers Educational Association, a post which he held from 1908 to 1924. His view was that there was a mental slavery as real as any economic bondage and that "If you want human liberty you must have educated people."[86] His fullest thought on the matter appeared in *Christianity and the Social Order*, a Penguin paperback issued in 1942 which had unusually large sales and earned for him the sobriquet of "the pink Archbishop." It insisted on the Church's

[83] I am unable to trace the exact source of this information, but I believe that the narrator of it was Dr. W. F. Lofthouse in reminiscences recorded in *The Methodist Recorder*, ca. 1960.
[84] G. L. Prestige, *The Life of Charles Gore, a Great Englishman*, p. 71.
[85] *The Modern Churchman*, Vol. XXI (February 1932), p. 583.
[86] F. A. Iremonger, *William Temple*, p. 80.

right and duty to "interfere" in social questions, proved that the right was readily conceded in the past, and expounded the primary and the derivative principles by which any social order is to be judged.

Thus both Gore's and Temple's interpretations of Christianity were heeded precisely because they gave their due weight to the spiritual, the intellectual, and moral-social aspects of man's nature. At the same time they acknowledged the truth of immanentalism in both its Social Gospel and Modernistic forms,[87] while going beyond it to assert that it was the *transcendental* God who was immanent.

It is time to turn to the interpretation of the Incarnation in Gore and Temple, as this was their key category and their distinctive theological contribution. They were, of course, in the main Anglican tradition in stressing the Incarnation, in their loyalty to Patristic thought, their exaltation of reason, and their fidelity to Scripture. But there were three other factors which forced them in this direction. One was that the Incarnation was central in the Biblical and theological researches of Westcott and Hort. In the second place, since the Incarnation stressed the advent of the Logos or Wisdom of God in the flesh, it provided a principle of rationality and coherence, whereby the Christ was the clue both to the ultimate purpose of the Creator and the unique example of the perfect human life. In the third place, the Incarnation as the supreme Sacrament was the authority for the "Sacramental principle," and so for the belief that the Sacraments of Baptism and the Eucharist ministered to the spiritual-physical nature of man.

There was much in common between Gore's *The Incarnation of the Son of God* (1891) and Temple's *Christus Veritas* (1924). Both saw the Incarnation as not only the hinge of history, but also as the climax and crown of Divine revelation. Gore showed that there was a progression in nature from the inorganic to the organic and from the animal to the rational, and this he maintained was a "progressive revelation of God." Temple, too, acknowledged the significance of the same ascending series. Each confessed that the ultimate revelation of God was to be found in the Divine personality

---

[87] Gore was, however, an unrelenting foe of Modernism, which he conceived to be immanentalism in the most extreme form. The Modernists shared a number of R. J. Campbell's views, but were far better informed on the scientific criticisms of contemporary religion. For Anglican primers on Modernism, see H. D. A. Major, *English Modernism: its Origin, Methods, Aims*; M. G. Glazebrook, *The Faith of a Modern Churchman*, and R. D. Richardson, *The Gospel of Modernism*.

of the Incarnate Lord, who in manifesting the order, moral character, and loving personality of God is thus *Christus Consummator*.
But He was more than the exemplar; He was also the Divine force
by which Christian character could be realized.

Temple, too, insisted on the necessity of the Incarnation. "It
is," he wrote, "the only way in which divine truth can be expressed,
not because of our infirmity, but because of its own nature. What is
personal can only be expressed in a person."[88] The rationale for the
Incarnation is God's own nature as love and man's endowment of
spiritual freedom, so that God can attract but never compel men
by His love. Also, according to Temple, God did not become a man
at the Incarnation, but the Man. Thus there is the assertion of
Christ's solidarity with humanity. Furthermore, Temple saw the
great importance of the combination of the spiritual and the physical in the Incarnation, as challenging the common belief that the
spiritual and the material are mutually exclusive. In consequence
Christianity, far from encouraging an asceticism which attempts to
flee from the body, or a pietism which escapes the obligations of
citizenship, is more this-worldly than most other great religions.
This insight he expressed in striking fashion: "Christianity is the
most materialistic of all the great religions."[89]

Gore's view of the Church was higher than Temple's. This arose,
in part, from the polemical need to counteract Hatch's Bampton
Lectures of 1881, which had maintained that the Church was the
company of the elect, and therefore invisible. Such visibility as it
had, said Hatch, was due to the natural attraction of people with
the same aims and beliefs. Gore, on the other hand, argued that
the Church was both a supernatural creation and a visible organization. He popularized the idea that the Church is the extension of
the Incarnation, a concept he borrowed from Jeremy Taylor who
had found it in the early Fathers.[90] To enter the community of the
Church is, for Gore, to be incorporated into the life of Christ which
is perpetuated by the Spirit in the Church, and the Eucharist is the
chief means for perpetuating the life of Christ. His summary of
the sacramental principle is that the communication of the life of
Christ is done by means of material and social ceremonies. This is,
he affirms, analogous to what man knows of the relation of the
human spirit to bodily conditions, and of the relation of the indi-

[88] *Readings in St. John's Gospel: Second Series*, p. 231.
[89] *Nature, Man, and God*, p. 478.
[90] James Carpenter, *Gore, A Study in Liberal Catholic Thought*, p. 224f.

vidual to society, and of "the principles of the pre-eminently human and social religion of the Son of Man."[91]

Yet highly as Gore valued the Eucharist, as the chief means of grace, he was far from encouraging, with some High Churchmen, the practice of the exposition of the Reserved Sacrament, since he believed that the main end of the Eucharist was communion and *participation*, and that the true indwelling of Christ was in the members of His Body. He was highly critical of the subjectivism, psychologism, and clericalism that marred the mediaeval celebration of the Mass, some fifty years before Dom Gregory Dix drew attention to these faults in *The Shape of the Liturgy.*[92] Gore himself held that there was no renewed surrender of Christ in the Eucharist. The term "sacrifice" in the Eucharist was appropriately used only in view of its relation to the heavenly altar of Christ's perpetual self-presentation as eternal High Priest. All that the Church can do "is to make thankful commemoration, in His way and in His Spirit, of His redemptive sufferings, and to unite ourselves to His perpetual intercession, where He presents Himself for us in the heavenly places, or as He makes Himself present among us in our eucharistic worship."[93]

By philosophical inclination, by ecumenical mediation, and as Archbishop first of York and later of Canterbury, Temple was to keep much freer from party affiliations in the Church than Gore, the leader of the High Church party. Yet he held the conviction "that the visible order of the Holy Catholic Church of Christ is part of its essence as a sacrament of the Incarnation."[94] Moreover, he deeply valued the Sacrament of Holy Communion, holding it to be a ritual expression of the dialectical unity of spirit and matter in the redemption of the world and of mankind effected by the unity of divinity and humanity in the Incarnation. He wrote: "We usually think of the Holy Communion in association only with God's act in *Redemption*; we must also think of it in connexion with His act in Creation. Then the power that guides and sustains us will be indeed the Holy Spirit proceeding from the Father and the Son."[95]

---

[91] *The Body of Christ*, p. 47.

[92] This point is made by E. L. Mascall in *Corpus Christi*, pp. 151-52.

[93] *The Body of Christ*, pp. 183-84.

[94] This is a summary taken from Archbishop A. M. Ramsey's account of Temple's ecclesiology, in his fine analysis of the development of Anglican theology entitled *From Gore to Temple; the Development of Anglican Theology between Lux Mundi and the Second World War, 1889-1939*, p. 153f.

[95] *The Hope of a New World*, p. 69. In the same volume Temple gives a splendid account of the Eucharist as a design of the new world order intended by

Enough of the work of Gore and Temple has been discussed to show how they improved upon the immanentalism of their day by insisting that the only significance of the immanental was that it was the immanence of the *transcendental* God, and that it was not immanence in general that mattered, but the supreme instance of immanence, the Incarnation. By so doing they returned theology to its central basis in the historical witness of the Scriptures and the Creeds, in the ongoing testimony of the Christian community that spans the continents and the centuries, and asserted—for the great benefit of the study and practice of the devotional life—that the Incarnational principle justified the use of the Sacraments as central in the Christian cultus. At the same time they vindicated the place of philosophy, science, and art in the Christian theme of things, without accommodating Christian theology to the beckonings of culture. And they decisively showed the inadequacy of the immanentalism of their day.

It was a great service, but, like all human endeavours, imperfect and incomplete. Even within the tradition of Liberal Catholicism another generation was to question the emphases of Gore and his followers. They were to ask if the concentration on the Incarnation would not inevitably lead to a theology of explanation instead of a theology of atonement, and whether a theology of revelation and explanation did not undervalue the place of faith in the Christian life, and, finally, whether the Biblical categories of crisis, judgment, idolatry, rebellion, forgiveness, and reconciliation had been given their decisive role in Christian interpretation?[96]

5. From Immanence to Transcendence: Forsyth and Oman

As the most extreme supporters of immanentalism as expressed in the New Theology were Free Churchmen, it is gratifying that the most radical correction of these errors were made by two creative theologians in the same tradition, Peter Taylor Forsyth (1848-1921) and John Oman (1860-1934). Both were emigrants from Scotland to England and Forsyth became Principal of Hack-

---

the Creator and thus stresses an eschatological element missing in Gore's account of the Eucharist.

[96] The newer Liberal Catholicism used less a historical approach, like Gore, than an analytical. See the work of its leader, E. G. Selwyn, in *An Approach to Christianity* and the admirable symposium edited by Selwyn, *Essays Catholic and Critical*, with the brilliant essays by A. E. Taylor on "The Vindication of Religion" and Hoskyns on "The Christ of the Synoptic Gospels." The terms "Catholic" (in reference to sacramental religion) and "Critical" (in reference to radical approaches to Bible and tradition) were taken with equal seriousness.

ney (Congregational) Theological College in London, while Oman became Principal of Westminster (Presbyterian) Theological College in Cambridge. Just as the Anglican Church by its attraction to the Patristic age tends to found its theology on the Doctrine of the Incarnation, which forms the basis of its liturgical and sacramental life, so the Reformed and Puritan Churches founded their systems on the Protestant Reformers and the *theologia crucis*. Thus the Free Church theologians were in a stronger position to commend Christianity as the criticism of culture rather than its crown, stressing the Biblical discontinuity of judgment and justification by grace, as distinct from the Catholic stress on grace as perfecting rather than destroying nature. Their central category for interpreting Christianity was Atonement rather than Incarnation, and the proclamation of the Cross, as St. Paul well knew, has ever seemed folly to the worldly-wise.

Their importance is that in differing ways they protested against the immanentalism of the age in which God and man, the supernatural and the natural, the Kingdom of God and secular utopianism, were confused. Forsyth began as a liberal, and in the acceptance of Biblical criticism and in the correlation of Christianity with culture and society, continued a liberal, but his thought became increasingly critical of liberalism as it recovered the distinctively Biblical categories. Oman never ceased to be a liberal in theology, but he was a chastened liberal who considered it to be his task to rescue the older and discarded theological terms and to fill them with contemporary relevance. Of the two, Forsyth was the more original and prophetic, so much so that he has been considered a "Barth before Barth."[97] Most of his works are being republished so that they are more widely read forty years after his death than they were in his own day, when their "fireworks in a fog" style and their criticisms of liberal theology caused them to seem brilliantly obscure and irrelevant. Oman was perhaps not as great a theologian, but he was an abler philosopher of religion, capable of sustained systematic exposition, where Forsyth's genius was to provoke, suggest, and stimulate rather than to explain.

In three respects they contributed significantly to the correction

[97] Notably by MacConnachie in the foreword to F. W. Camfield's *Revelation and the Holy Spirit*, p. vii. See the catena of tributes to Forsyth's major importance in W. L. Bradley, *P. T. Forsyth, The Man and His Work*, pp. 259-68, and Robert McAfee Brown, *P. T. Forsyth: Prophet for Today*, pp. 9-10. They include tributes from Barth himself, and his son Markus, J. K. Mozley, R. W. Dale, A. R. Vidler, F. W. Dillistone, Theodore Wedel, J. S. Whale, H. F. Lovell Cocks, James Denney, and Nathaniel Micklem.

of the current vapid immanentalism. Each came to feel that religion had been so sentimentalized that it was essential to moralize dogma to give it backbone. In particular, they brought back into the theological domain the concept of "grace," which had been superannuated by liberalism in favour of the weaker and more anthropomorphic term of "love." In the second place, they countered an excessive immanentalism with the restoration of the complementary and more ultimate emphasis on the Divine transcendence. In Forsyth transcendence was moralized in terms of the holiness of God, to include the element of judgment that is essential to the Divine love and which distinguishes it from sentimentality. In Oman's case, there was a deep dissatisfaction with psychological theories of religion which, in explaining religion, explained it away, and a determination to show that the environment of man was as supernatural as it was natural. Thirdly, in reaction from the depreciation of the Church in favour of the all-inclusive concept of the Kingdom of God then current among liberal theologians, Oman showed that the Church rested on the Divine order and Forsyth demonstrated that it was a Divine-human society founded on and sustained by the Gospel of the Redeemer. In brief, both asserted that the Church was called into being by Divine creation, not by human association. Forsyth's originality was seen, ecclesiologically, in his understanding of Catholic claims even where he dissented from them, and in his insistence upon the centrality of the Sacrament of the Word, whether audibly manifested, as in the preaching, or visibly, as in the Sacraments of Baptism and the Lord's Supper. A single citation from Forsyth's greatest book will make plain his profundity and balance, and the correction he made of a one-sided immanentalism:

"God and man meet in humanity, not as two entities or natures which coexist, but as two movements in mutual interplay, mutual struggle, and reciprocal communion. On the one hand we have an initiative, creative, productive action, clear and sure on the part of the eternal God; on the other hand we have the seeking, receptive, appropriating action of groping, erring, growing man. . . . All spiritual action is history. History is action and reciprocal action. It is commerce, and even conflict, with the transcendent."[98]

Oman's greatest success in the recovery of the concept of grace and in the moralization of dogma was achieved in his modern classic, *Grace and Personality* (1917). Here he sought to solve the persistently troubling question that had vexed St. Augustine and

[98] *The Person and Place of Jesus Christ*, p. 336f.

Pelagius, Luther and Erasmus, namely, the relationship between Divine grace and human freedom. His solution was found in a conception of grace as personal, whereby God appeals to human insight and decision. In short, in place of *irresistible* grace Oman put *persuasive* grace. The problem was posed in the following terms: "The essential quality of a moral person is moral independence and an ideal person would be of absolute moral independence. But the essential quality of a religious person is to depend on God; and he must be as absolutely dependent as a moral person must be absolutely independent."[99] Here Oman knew he must do justice both to his Calvinistic inheritance in accepting the sovereignty of God and to his ethical inheritance from Kant in insisting upon the independence of the moral agent. The antinomy can only be solved by recognizing that grace is "neither overriding omnipotence guided by omnipotence" nor as "a sort of love philtre" impersonally conveyed through the Sacraments, but only as "a gracious personal relationship" between God and the human personality through which God persuades us to choose our own good. Grace thus becomes the common basis of religion and ethics, for we "accept God's will, as, by insight, we discover it to be our own."[100] Just as there was a Catholic Liberalism in Gore and Temple and their school, to be distinguished from both Catholic Modernism and Liberal Protestantism, so in Oman and Forsyth we see the lineaments of a Liberal Evangelicalism to be distinguished from Liberal Modernism.

As early as 1892 we find the great Congregational theologian, R. W. Dale, writing to a friend: "Forsyth said a good thing the other day—he thought that 'the time had come to get back the word *Grace* into our preaching'; word and thing have too much disappeared."[101] No term describes more concisely the central concern of the thrusting theology of Forsyth. His subsequent writings are all variations on the theme of "the gracious God," a term he greatly preferred to the more common reference to the "grace of God," as less subject to impersonal interpretation. Forsyth was eager to distinguish his understanding of the term from two other current interpretations of its meaning.[102] He denied, as Oman had done, the Roman Catholic view of grace as an infusion into the individual, as a substance or power "piped" into the individual through the hierarchical administration of the Sacraments. He equally dissented

---

[99] *Grace and Personality*, p. 58.
[100] *Ibid.*, Chap. X, with citations from pp. 80-90.
[101] A. W. W. Dale, *The Life of R. W. Dale of Birmingham*, p. 636.
[102] *The Person and Place of Jesus Christ*, pp. 331-32.

from a left-wing and sectarian view of grace as a cordial benevolence of God, apparently oblivious to sin, as sheer sentimentality. He accepted the Reformation's rediscovery of the Biblical concept of grace as the Divine mercy, never earned but freely given—in short, grace to the malignant in granting forgiveness and the power to become "a new man in Christ Jesus." It is nothing less than the reconciling action of God in Christ. It is all of the Divine initiative. "The gospel descends on man; it does not rise from him. It is not a projection of his innate spirituality. It is revealed, not discovered, not invented. It is a gift to our poverty, not a triumph of our resource. It is something which holds us; it is not something we hold. It is Christ sent to us and not developed from us, bestowed on our need, and not produced from our strength, and He is given for our sin more than for our weakness."[103]

Grace was, indeed, a profound experience for Forsyth; after serving many years in the ministry as a liberal he was converted by grace to a theology of grace. "I was," he confessed, "turned from a Christian to a believer, from a lover of love to an object of grace. And so, whereas I first thought that what the Churches needed was enlightened instruction and liberal theology, I came to be sure that what they needed was evangelization. . . . Religion without an experimental foundation in grace readily feels panic in the presence of criticism."[104]

It was Forsyth's perceptiveness to realize a generation before the rest of Europe's theologians that the true centre of theology was the Atonement, not the Incarnation, so that theology is the challenger of human culture, not at all its agent and instrument. He saw that religion is often misconceived as an achievement by man, instead of being, what the work of Christ showed it to be, wholly the gift of a gracious God to undeserving humanity. Thus for Forsyth the Atonement is the medium through which the Incarnation is to be understood, for the essential nature of revelation is that it is redemptive. It is not the transmission of information primarily but the transformation of personality. Consequently he affirmed, counter to the predominant emphasis of the Liberal Catholics like Gore, that "our faith has much more directly to do with the benefits of Christ than with the nature of Christ . . . it is through the work of redemption that I know the person of the Redeemer."[105] To place

[103] *Positive Preaching and the Modern Mind*, p. 144.
[104] *Ibid.*, pp. 193-94.
[105] *The Person and Place of Jesus Christ*, pp. 278-79.

the Incarnation before the Atonement was a reversal of values, to give to explanation the priority before reconciliation.

Theologies of immanence postulate God's identification with the world in such a way as virtually to deny the abyss between Creator and created, and to identify human discovery with Divine revelation and human ideals with Divine deliverances. Oman by his insistence upon the supernatural environment of the personality and Forsyth by his emphasis on the holiness of God accented the discontinuity between God and the world, as between infinite and finite, eternal and temporal, righteous and sinful. This was their second contribution to the correction of the theology of their day.

Oman wished to rescue the term "supernatural" from the opprobrium in which it had fallen in the eighteenth century, when it was thought to involve an arbitrary conception of miracle as the lawless caprice of Deity. He felt that the necessity for its restoration, with a restricted meaning, lay in the fact that Liberal Protestantism in discarding it was inevitably involved in the assumptions of a naturalistic philosophy. Moreover, the latter denied the existence of any transcendent spiritual reality and reduced the meaning of "natural" to either "mechanical" or "material." This act of repristination was performed in *The Natural and the Supernatural* (1931). The first part argues that the experience of the sacred and the holy is not a distinctive or abnormal reaction of the human organism to the natural environment, but a response to the Supernatural Environment overflowing the natural and *regularly open* to experience. Thus for Oman "the Supernatural means the world which manifests more than natural values which stir the sense of the holy and demand to be esteemed as sacred."[106] Experience is partly natural in that its values are comparative and to be judged as fulfilling practical needs, whereas "part of it is Supernatural, in the sense that its values are absolute to which our needs must submit."[107]

The second, or epistemological, part challenges the current naturalism as being due to a failure to recognize that there is any other kind of knowledge other than the abstraction inherent in scientific explanation. In a central chapter on "Awareness and Apprehension" he argues that for the understanding of our environment as a whole, in balance and richness, if not in precision, the

[106] *The Natural and the Supernatural*, p. 71.
[107] *Ibid.*, p. 72.

162

poet's awareness and the child's naïve perception are more reliable guides than scientific measurements or analyses.

The third part attacks the naturalistic world-view with its idea of a mechanically fixed sequence of cause and effect. He holds that this nineteenth century dogma oversimplifies reality more than the Buddhist concept of retribution or *karma* or the Hebrew assertion of the correlation of sin and suffering. Indeed, the two latter concepts are important summaries of aspects of our universal environment. This section ends with an appeal to the richness, variety, and resourcefulness of life as postulating the reality of human freedom and the personality of God.

The fourth and final section of the book deals with the problem of the relation of the Supernatural to the natural. He finds two major contrasting trends in the history of religion: the pantheistic and the monotheistic. The former affirms the absorption of the many into the One and monotheism affirms the victory of the many. The consequence is that for monistic religion the world is ultimately unreal and mystical world-flight is its corollary; while for monotheistic religion the natural world remains real and sacred as a partial embodiment of supernatural values. The natural consequence of the latter view is a hopeful life and an attempt to create a better natural world through the indwelling power of the Supernatural. In his evaluation of religions he places acosmic pantheism and negative mysticism at the bottom of the ladder; above them, Persian dualism and Jewish legalism; and on the topmost rung he puts the ethical religion of the prophets, with its climax and culmination in the life and teaching of Jesus. Thus by positive and negative arguments he claims a place for the Supernatural in a monotheistic religion of strongly ethical type. It was perhaps as far as a philosopher could go, but it sounded very like Schleiermacher's definition of religion,[108] with a substitution of the ethical value-judgments of Ritschl for the sense of dependence in Schleiermacher. At any rate when the current was running strongly for naturalism, Oman argued well for the place of the Supernatural, by which he intended God.

Forsyth was not so much concerned for the Supernatural in a trans-spatial or trans-temporal sense, as in the ontological sense.

[108] The referen.e is to the English translation of Schleiermacher's *The Christian Faith*, para. 11: Christianity is "a monotheistic faith, belonging to the teleological type of religion, and is essentially distinguished from other such faiths by the fact that in it everything is related to the redemption accomplished by Jesus of Nazareth."

That is, he was concerned for that dimension or depth in the Divine Being by which God is qualitatively different from man, and this he termed "holiness." In this the influence of the great Danish philosopher, Kierkegaard, is to be discerned. It was characteristic of Forsyth that when he considered the problem of human sin his first concern was not the damage sin did to men (as with most other theologians), but what it meant to God and how it affects Him. In framing a satisfactory concept of holiness, Forsyth had to beware of two extremes. He could not permit the cynicism or sentimentalism which affirmed, *Dieu pardonnera, c'est son métier*, nor could he resuscitate the Augustinian, Anselmic, or Calvinist conception of the Divine holiness, which equated it with honour or justice, reducing mercy to an exception for the elect. The Liberals in theology stressed love without justice, but the orthodox stressed justice without love. That was the dilemma.

By the idea of "holy love" Forsyth takes the truth from each view, while avoiding the excesses. Correcting the orthodoxy of the day, he substitutes "holiness" for "justice." In this way he escapes any tendency to legalism because holiness embraces within it the idea of love, whereas justice does not. By the same definition he protects his theology from the dangers of sentimentalism, since he qualifies the idea of love with holiness. The following passage admirably illustrates his meaning: "The holiness of God is His self-sufficient perfection, Whose passion it is to establish itself in the unholy by gracious love. Holiness is love morally perfect; love is holiness brimming and overflowing. The perfection speaks in the overflow. It is in redemption. Love is perfect, not in amount but in kind, not as intense, but as holy. And holiness is perfect, not as being remote, not as being merely pure, but as it asserts itself in redeeming grace."[109]

Forsyth was never tired of insisting that only a holy God takes sin seriously and that His love takes the form of wishing the sinner to be holy. Thus he wrote: "The holiness of God is a deeper revelation on the Cross than His love; for it is what gives His love divine value. And it is meaningless without judgment. The one thing He could not do was simply to wipe the slate and write off the loss. He must either inflict punishment or endure it."[110] God's moral transcendence, His holy love, was always to be found by Forsyth at the Cross. In the older views of the Atonement God was thought to

[109] *Positive Preaching and the Modern Mind*, p. 145.
[110] *The Cruciality of the Cross*, p. 98.

judge by penalising either men or Christ; in Forsyth's view God judges by self-reconciliation, and by the *objective* act of the Cross He changes man's relationship to God by the offering of forgiveness through Christ and the power of transformation. Finally, Christ is Mediator because of His dual office, facing God and facing man. As Lord, Christ confesses God's holiness; as Man, Christ confesses man's guilt. In this manner He fulfils the requirement for a lasting reconciliation.[111] Forsyth's genius is to have recovered the sense of the Otherness of God, which was missing in Liberal theology, yet to have purged its definition from any arbitrary, legalistic, or penal substitutionary accretions, and shown its relevance both to soteriology and to the need for a vertebral Christian ethic.

The third contribution of both Oman and Forsyth is in the field of ecclesiology. Both wrote books on the doctrine of the Church, when it was highly unusual for Free Church theologians to do so. Oman's, the slighter of the two volumes, was entitled *The Church and the Divine Order* (1911). Forsyth's substantial and challenging volume was called *The Church and the Sacraments* (1917).

Oman's book had a three-fold importance. It was the first significant book on its theme to have been written by a minister of the revived Presbyterian Church in England, until it was supplanted by P. Carnegie Simpson's *The Evangelical Church Catholic* (1934) which did greater justice to the Catholic tradition, the Sacraments, and the needs of ecumenism than did Oman. It recalled Free Churchmen to the objective authority of the Divine order in the Community of Christ, and warned them that theirs was a freedom within the Gospel and not outside it, or, as Forsyth would have phrased it, a "founded freedom." Thirdly, it presented in forthright fashion his defence and explication of the Reformed doctrine of the Church as a fellowship of believers united personally to Christ and to each other.

The Church had a double aspect for Oman. Viewed in relation to God it is the embodiment of the Divine order, in which the Father rules. On the human side it is the fellowship of those who have responded to God's rule which has respect for men's freedom. Oman entirely rejected the view that the Church can be defined in terms of its organization. While other Free Churchmen criticized the sacerdotalism of the Catholic concept of the Church denying the priesthood of all believers, Oman trained his guns on the

---

[111] For a fuller elaboration of this theme see W. L. Bradley, *P. T. Forsyth, The Man and His Work*, pp. 118ff.

concept of hierarchical authority, since he believed that "the essence of Catholicism is the reintroduction of the law,"[112] and the denial of the relationship of love and trust which was most characteristic of life in the Gospel. The authority of the Church rested on the supernatural Divine order initiated by God Himself and was contrasted with the current liberal conception of God's Kingdom as "the progressive amelioration of humanity."[113] Authority was, however, as in all the writings of Oman, of a personal nature—persuasive, not coercive. Thus God had dealt with men in Christ, and thus they must cooperate with each other. On the face of it this smacks of nominalism, but Oman was not unaware of the importance of tradition and of the need for visible ordinances. He urged that the Christian "will not think it necessary before he can serve the Church to cut himself off from its failures and to endeavour to create a new fellowship corresponding in everything with the ideal, before he can begin."[114] Even more strongly had Forsyth insisted on the danger of the isolationism which cuts off the modern religious community from God's work in history through His Church. "We cannot," he wrote, "just clear two thousand years by a huge somersault and land with a splash in the New Testament, with its polity, practice and habit of mind. . . . It denies historic providence. It repudiates the Kingdom of God in history. It robs us of most of the sainthood, sacrifice, and devotion of the whole Church, and often leaves our public prayers to be but pious journalese."[115]

Oman believed that there was a substantial truth in the Reformed distinction between the "invisible" and the "visible" Church, in that human judgment can never be equated with the Divine judgment and ultimately only God knows who are His. But since the Church is in the world, its existence, though not its purity, must be manifested by institutions, and needs some representative authority. But in principle for the Catholic the *institution* is primary, with its priesthood, bishops, councils, and Pope; while for the Protestant it is the *fellowship* that is primary, with its succession of believers gathered in the bond of love.[116] Moreover, in Protestantism such authority is to be exercised as servant, not master, and is not to appeal to any other motives than for love's sake. "The Church must

---

[112] *The Church and the Divine Order*, p. 107.
[113] *Ibid.*, p. 42.
[114] *Ibid.*, p. 313.
[115] *Congregationalism and Reunion*, p. 10.
[116] *The Church and the Divine Order*, pp. 207ff.

live and work as a corporation, but she must not magnify herself as a corporation."[117]

Oman asserted, as a true Protestant, that the institutions of Christianity are secondary to the faith and experience on which they are based. But he gravely underestimated the importance of external authority, and in this respect was not abreast of the most advanced ecumenical thinking of the day. The truth in his view was that no external unity can be expressive of the Christian spirit and that a giant corporation created by the merger of many smaller institutions may be the product of compromise, not of conviction. While the realism of the following citation has relevance for the present, yet its concluding phrase has long been outmoded: "When airs of social superiority ill-becoming those who claim to be the only true successors of the fishermen of Galilee, and resentment and bitterness ill-becoming those who claim to be blessed with the highest ideal of the Church's freedom, pass away, we shall either have outward union, or be so united in heart as to be able to do without it."[118] As over against the political collectivism of his day, and the dangers inherent in the Catholic hierarchical definition of the character of the Church, Oman made a salutary protest in the interest of freedom, fellowship, and "persuasive grace." His weakness was that he was prepared to go to such exaggerated lengths to preserve these values as to declare an external union of the Church to be unnecessary. He had, however, rightly insisted that the Church of Christ is not a merely voluntary organization, but founded firmly upon the rule of God the Father.

Forsyth's ecclesiology was profounder, partly because in reacting from theological liberalism he retained its values while adding to them; partly because he had a much stronger sense of the importance of the historic traditions of the Church, and of the witness of its liturgy and Sacraments; and partly because he did greater justice to the Roman Catholic tradition from which he dissented. It was, to give one famous example, characteristic of his attitude towards a contemporary Protestant cheapening of Holy Communion that he held "a mere memorialism to be a more fatal error than the Mass, and a far less lovely."[119] In the same catholic spirit he wrote: "We have starved ourselves of the rich treasury of Christian devotion in the profound and lovely liturgies of the long past, and of the wealth of example, inspiration, and guidance in the calendar of

[117] *Ibid.*, p. 326f.   [118] *Ibid.*, p. 315.
[119] *The Church and the Sacraments*, p. xvi.

167

Christian sainthood."[120] It was Forsyth's genius that he combined intellectual insight in his theology with a moral passion and—in a way that has been rare in the Reformed tradition—with a deep appreciation of aesthetic values. The latter was seen in the two perceptive volumes he wrote on art,[121] in his publication of *Intercessory Services for Aid in Public Worship*, and in his important contributions to the *Book of Congregational Worship* (1920), the first to be prepared officially by that denomination.

Forsyth held a very high doctrine of the Church. Occasionally he termed the Church the Body of Christ, but he preferred the image which characterized it as the Bride of Christ, because "it is not only His organ but the object of communion by the Spirit."[122] He would not, however, like Gore, speak of the Church as the "extension of the Incarnation," for that was in his view to commit the idolatry of making Christ and Church equivalent. "The Church is not the continuation of Christ, but His creation and response."[123] Forsyth ever stressed not only the radical dependence of the Church on Christ, but also its continual renewal by the Holy Spirit. Hence it could not be a continuation or extension of Christ, but only a new creation by Christ.

Like Oman, he denied that the Church was constituted by the hierarchy. The true succession of the Apostolate was not the bishopric, as the Roman Catholics and Anglo-Catholics maintained, nor the saints, as Inge declared, but the Bible. "The apostolic succession is the evangelical succession,"[124] he wrote, because the canon of Scripture was written to prolong the voices of the apostles and to replace their vanished witness. But if he was critical of the Catholic conception of the nature and authority of the Church, he was critical of certain Protestant ideas of the Church. He denied the older evangelical view which regarded the Church as a society for saving souls from the Devil, and the view of the social gospellers for whom it was merely an agency for social improvement. He criticized both a Churchless Gospel and the Social Gospel. In the authentic Maurician tradition he claimed "it was a race that Christ redeemed, not a mere bouquet of believers," and thus he admitted the evangelical emphasis on redemption while denying its atomism.

[120] *Ibid.*, p. 37.
[121] These were: *Religion in Recent Art* and *Christ on Parnassus, Lectures on Art, Ethic, and Theology*.
[122] From a symposium, *Different Conceptions of Priesthood and Sacrifice*, pp. 32-33, cited in W. L. Bradley, *P. T. Forsyth . . .* , pp. 221-22.
[123] *The Church and the Sacraments*, pp. 82-83.
[124] *Ibid.*, p. 139.

He insisted that the "same act which sets us in Christ sets us also in the society of Christ. To be in Christ is in the same act to be in the Church. . . . The act of faith which saves us from self would only have a negative meaning if it did not save us at the same time into a society which is a centre of service and sympathy."[125] He warned the protagonists of the social gospel that "the great Church must always be more dogmatic to the social eye than accommodating. . . . It must consent to be unpopular with men that it may be faithful for man's God."[126]

Forsyth was peculiarly perceptive in his understanding of authority. He criticized the Roman Catholics for having set the Church up as equal to or even higher than the Gospel, and his fellow Protestants for having denied the very existence of the Gospel by vindicating their institutions through an appeal to the good works they accomplished. Authority in the Church could only be "the moral holy power of redeeming grace."[127] He recognized the authority of the Bible as primary, but in no literal fashion, and insisted that the Gospel of grace in Christ crucified which produced both Bible and Church was the authoritative principle for interpreting the Bible and testing the life of the Church in every age. He understood why Protestants, with the collapse of the external authorities of Bible and Church, rushed to claim the authority of the individual religious experience. He acknowledged that its value, as a witness to the Spirit, was considerable in delivering the Church from formalism, confessionalism, and literalism. At the same time he insisted that it must never be divorced from the witness to the Word.

Individual experience could never, not even the witness of the conscience, be an adequate authority for the Christian Church. It has, so he maintains, five inherent weaknesses. Experience is judged by intensity, whereas objective facts and the faith they elicit—the contents of belief—are supremely important. Impression becomes more important than regeneration when experience is normative. Its supporters forget that religious experience is sin-distorted and ignore the fact that conscience can condemn but not redeem. A religion of experience casts off the anchors of history and tradition, with the result that such religion degenerates into a

---

125 *Ibid.*, pp. 61-62.
126 *The British Weekly*, issue of October 9, 1913, p. 43.
127 Address as Chairman of the Congregational Union in 1905, published in *The Congregational Union Year Book*, 1906, p. 59.

reverie. Finally, a religion of experience is not strong enough, because of its subjectivity, to carry a Church.

The authority of the Church is the Gospel of grace. It creates human nature anew, providing forgiveness for estranged man, moral direction and drive leading to conversion and sanctification in the committed company of Christ's people nourished on the Word and Sacraments, and experiencing here and now the assurance of life everlasting. In a remarkable amalgam Forsyth had restated the doctrine of the Church so as to preserve the strengths of the high Anglican and Reformed views, without the tendency towards the idolatry of the institution in the one, and the atomistic individualism of the other.

More deeply than any other Free Church theologian of his day Forsyth understood the significance of the Sacraments, without depreciating the proclamation of the Word. He returned to the Augustinian understanding that the preaching is the *audible* Word and the Sacraments are the *visible* Word. He would not accept any merely symbolic interpretations of the Sacraments. He was scathing about contemporary Congregational practice, with the resulting impression that only the Anglican and Roman Churches took the Sacraments seriously. He wanted to bring the Sacraments to the place that was currently held by clubs as the centre of the social life of the Free Churches. He desired to counteract the cult of the popular preacher, with the reminder that the "chief function of the Church is worship, not preaching, and it is in the supreme and most universal act of worship that we have to show our unity—viz. in Communion."[128] He insisted so strongly on the objectivity of the Sacraments that he did not scruple to write of a Sacrament as an *opus operatum*.[129] By this, however, he did not intend to imply that the objectivity of the Sacrament was due to any change in the bread and wine. Rather, he believed that the gifts of forgiveness and regeneration were conveyed by the real presence of Christ at His Table. Baptism communicates regeneration in title, but the gift has to be appropriated before it becomes actual regeneration. Baptism means that the "stamp of being God's property has been put on the child in a public way" and that "he is born to be born again" and "will be false to his best antecedents and his social committal if he do not become regenerated in the

[128] Letter cited in full in W. L. Bradley, *P. T. Forsyth* . . . , pp. 277-78.
[129] *The Church and the Sacraments*, p. 216.

Holy Ghost."[130] He could not believe that Christ was sacrificed afresh in each celebration of the Lord's Supper, but he most certainly held that Christ re-presents His finished sacrifice to His Father on His people's behalf at each Holy Communion.[131] He wrote: "A Church may survive with power errors about its Sacraments as tremendous as those of Rome, but neglect, starvation, and renunciation of Sacraments it cannot survive."[132]

Forsyth insisted upon the theological basis of Churchmanship, on the objective character of the Sacraments as real means of grace; and upon the historic continuity of the Church and the inspiration of its ancient prayers and the witness of the saints. In so doing he led the Free Churches of his own day and a later grateful generation to prize their inheritance in the Gospel and in the Reformation. He also helped to mediate the Catholic tradition to Nonconformity. Anglicans were then in the grip of a Patristic antiquarianism and Free Churchmen extolled the spirit of Christianity oblivious of the need for forms; he taught them to understand each other, and thus accelerated the impetus of the ecumenical movement.

What impact did the teachings of Oman and Forsyth have on the theory and practice of worship? There is no question that their stress on the Divine authority and empowering of the Church served to emphasize the importance of the spiritual discipline of the Christian community, and the immense benefits of gathering for the proclamation of the transforming Word. Forsyth went further in showing that the Sacraments were equally the conveyors of grace, channelling the forgiveness and the regeneration of God. He realized the significance of liturgies as teachers of a reverent approach to God and witnesses to the devotion of the Communion of saints through the long Christian centuries. In due time his emphasis on the objectivity of the Sacraments would lead to their more frequent and more cherished celebration. But, above all, his re-iterated emphasis on the primacy and ultimacy of the supernatural—and it is significant that his last book was entitled *This Life and the Next* (1918)—and on the majestic mercy of a holy God, consummated in the sacrifice of Christ, could only issue in recommending a grateful response to grace. It is in that atmosphere, not in the congratulatory and optimistic mood of immanentalism, that worship thrives.

[130] *Ibid.*, p. 168.   [131] *Ibid.*, p. 256.   [132] *Ibid.*, p. 166.

6. *Conclusion*

We have seen that the history of the English people in the first three decades of the century began with high optimism, but that the balloons of inevitable progress were pricked on the barbed wire of the First World War trenches.[133] Britain's place in the world and her power were reduced, as the British Empire became the British Commonwealth of Nations. The establishment of the Social Welfare State was a proof of the inevitability of collectivism, but also it was an index of social justice, and an achievement of political radicalism and the Christian conscience. The theology of the period is, in part, a reflection of the spirit of the people. Immanentalism was a theology of excessive optimism. We have seen it expressed in the "New Theology" of R. J. Campbell and his followers, which, like Liberal Modernism, was a theology in rebellion against the traditional and historical Christian faith at almost all points. The Bible claimed that salvation came by faith in God's power, but liberalism trusted chiefly in man's own effort.

So liberalism persuaded the Church to seek for popularity by working for social renewal, and by eliminating the other-worldly horizon to concentrate on creating the Socialist utopia on earth. The consequence, as we have seen, was that worship seemed irrelevant to the very artisans whom the new approach hoped to attract. The work in the slums seemed important; the working of the Sacraments seemed antiquarianism and superstition.

Attempts were, indeed, made to dam the floods of theological liberalism. It was hoped that a study of mysticism, as a phenomenon common to many religions besides Christianity, would persuade the world of the universal reality and the reliability of the Christian life. But its techniques were too exotic and strenuous for the common man and it appealed only to the faithful few, despite the sensitive advocacy of Dean Inge, Baron von Hügel, and Evelyn Underhill. But the two latter, in particular, showed that it was an essential part of Christianity and witnessed to the centrality of adoration in public worship, supremely in the Eucharist, as the impetus to the Christian life. They, too, were prophets ahead of their time in witnessing to the faithful. They never let it be for-

[133] C. C. J. Webb believed that World War I had three theological effects. It encouraged the revolt against Christian ethics. It "dealt a mortal blow to . . . optimistic religious immanentalism." It "promoted a revival of interest in the quest of a revelation from without of values which men despaired of finding within a process of civilization which had issued in so tremendous a catastrophe" (*Religious Thought in England from 1850*, p. 149).

gotten that a great abyss, uncrossable on man's part, separates proud man from Almighty God, and that Christ was the bridge and Mediator between the holy and the unholy. They insisted that true religion involves renunciation as the price of immeasurable joy, and is not served by a frantic activism. At least in an era of acute secularism they persuaded the faithful to re-appreciate their heritage in the devotional discipline of the saints and in the supreme corporate act of Christian worship, the Liturgy. Moreover, better than they knew, they were preparing Christians to recognize that they were already one in Christ, however divisive their denominational labels might be.

Neither Gore nor Temple was a particularly mystical man, but each insisted on demonstrating the centrality of the Incarnation, as the supreme example of the immanence of the Transcendent One, with Christ as both the revelation of the Divine design and the perfect exemplar. Both found the Eucharist to be a stimulus to social justice, and Temple, in particular, discerned in it the pattern for the creation of more equitable re-ordering of God's gifts for the creation of true community. For both of them worship was the central need of a truly human life, as the creature's acknowledgment of the Creator and the channel of transforming grace.

Oman affirmed that the supernatural was known through the natural and was, whether man recognized it or not, his background. The Church was a pointer to that Divine order of love, rather than law, which God wills for His earthly children and which manifests His own character. Forsyth went beyond any theologian of his day in realizing that God must be a *holy* Father, and that it is because he hates sin He must judge it, so that judgment is the yonder side of costly and caring love. Further, Forsyth restored the forgotten word "Grace" to the Protestant theological vocabulary, and Oman made it personal again. In concentrating on the Atonement, rather than the Incarnation, as the decisive act of a holy God to redeem the world, Forsyth provided a much needed criterion by which all human aspirations and societies could be judged, and insisted that the Church must be not democracy's tribune, as liberal theologians believed, but its censor. He had a deep understanding of the Catholic and Anglican traditions in their strengths and weaknesses. He particularly valued their devotional and sacramental riches. In so doing he not only prepared Nonconformity to appreciate anew its earlier Reformed sacramental heritage, but also to

173

be in empathetic dialogue with the Catholic tradition. He even prepared the Free Churches to consider the merits of liturgical worship by his teaching and example.

But what Inge, von Hügel, Underhill, Gore, Temple, Oman, and Forsyth had in common, if in differing degrees, was the wit to see that an excessive immanentalism, the apparent friend of religion, was really its enemy. Until they had exposed its pretensions there was no hope for men to return to the recognition of the transcendental God's claim on men, proven by the revelation of His purpose in the Incarnation, sealed by His reconciliation through the Cross, and helped by the Church as the Body and Bride of Christ to inherit eternal life, through the preaching of the Word and the celebration of the Sacraments, and the loving service of humanity prompted by the gratitude of the redeemed. True religion and true worship awaited the recognition by the majority of theologians and ministers that immanentalism was not leading them and their flocks to the earthly paradise, but through the enticing and illusory mists of utopia to the quagmires of despair. The importance of the prophetic seven was to be recognized—if not in their own time—in the latter part of the third decade of the century, when the bitterness of unemployment was followed by the despair of totalitarianism. Then it was that their influence came into its own. They had found their way to the truth by running against the stream.

Four others came by the rocky way of disillusionment with liberal theology, as evinced by their published spiritual biographies. R. J. Campbell recorded the journey in *A Spiritual Pilgrimage* (1917). W. E. Orchard moved from Presbyterianism and Congregationalism to Roman Catholicism as chronicled in *From Faith to Faith* (1933), and C. S. Lewis found his way from an inherited Anglicanism into atheism and back into the fold with many divagations, as retold in *Pilgrim's Regress* (1933). The most enthusiastic devotee of a liberal theology, and also the most excited convert to neo-Orthodoxy was D. R. Davies, whose *On to Orthodoxy* (1939) is the most damaging *exposé* of the shallowness of liberal theology.[134]

[134] Davies, a Congregational minister who left the ministry to devote full time to educational activities on behalf of the Labour movement, and finally became an Anglican vicar, analysed his disillusionment with liberalism in theology as follows: "Christian Liberalism has had four consequences in the social and religious life of our time: (1) a false estimate of human nature; (2) the practical banishment of the other-worldly element in the Christian Ethic; (3) the denial of the uniqueness of Christianity; (4) the secularisation of life and religion" (*On to Orthodoxy*, p. 13).

It seems that a penitential piety becomes credible only when the doctrines of original sin and the holiness of Divine love are stressed. It is only when the Incarnation is stressed that the importance of Sacramental practice is acknowledged. Only when the doctrines of The Cross and Resurrection are emphasized is it felt by faith that "the sufferings of this present world are not to be compared with the joy that shall be revealed." It is a theology of grace alone that elicits the adoration which is the heart-beat of corporate Christian worship and the joyful song of souls in pilgrimage. This was to be more fully appreciated by the theologians of the second three decades of the century.

CHAPTER V

THE LATER DEVELOPMENT OF THEOLOGY[1] (1933-1965)

IN THE first thirty years of this century theology, with the exception of the exponents of mysticism and the incarnationalists, tended to weaken the role of worship in the life of the Church. In fact, the proponents of immanentalism and of the social gospel virtually equated religion with social duty. In contrast, the theology of the next thirty years strongly supported the centrality of worship in the corporate life of Christians.

It was certainly the case with the first three of the four trends in theology, though dubiously so for the fourth. Successively, these trends were: the return to a Biblical theology which brought with it a revival of orthodoxy in belief; the new ecclesiology which insisted that the Church, far from being a convenience of organization, was part of the gift of the Gospel; and the search for a distinctively Christian Sociology deriving from the incarnational and sacramental nature of the Church. The fourth, and most recent, trend of theology, Cambridge Radicalism, represents the fusion of Bultmann, Bonhoeffer, Tillich, and Freud as filtered through English minds. In its prophetic and critical emphasis it is likelier to stimulate preaching than sacramentalism, but it is significant that all its exponents are Anglicans (and most are clergymen), and they are likelier to demand the reformation of worship than its abolition. The first three theological trends, however, being clearly based upon the uniqueness of the Christian revelation as proclaimed in Word and Sacrament, manifestly strengthened the Liturgical Movement in our time.

[1] There appears to be no comprehensive published account of the interconfessional development of English theology from 1933. Limited help is, however, provided by the following volumes. A good account of Anglican theology up to 1939 only is Archbishop A. M. Ramsey's *From Gore to Temple*. E. L. Allen provides two useful chapters on British theology up to 1950 in G. Stephens Spinks' *Religion in Britain since 1900*. John W. Grant's *Free Churchmanship in England* provides a good account of British Free Church theology until about 1948. John Macquarrie's *Twentieth Century Religious Thought* is an admirable survey of European philosophical and religious thought, but gives little space to British theology. Daniel D. Williams' *What Present-day Theologians are Thinking* treats British theologians, both Anglican and Free Church, with great insight, but too briefly for our purpose. A valuable study is J. K. Mozley, *Some Tendencies in British Theology, From the Publication of "Lux Mundi" to the Present Day*.

1. *The Return to Biblical Orthodoxy*

The date given for the beginning of the demise of liberal theology and for its replacement by Biblical theology is 1933. This may seem the less arbitrary when it is remembered that Karl Barth's *Commentary on the Epistle to the Romans* appeared in the English translation by Clement Hoskyns in 1933. That event signalizes the impact on British theology of both Europe's greatest twentieth century theologian and a great English Biblical scholar. Barth was then described variously as a theologian of crisis, a dialectical theologian, and as the theologian of the Word of God. Barth was a Protestant, while his translator, Hoskyns, was an Anglican High Churchman with a deep attachment to Catholic order. Yet both were inveterate foes of any attempt to subordinate the revelation of the living God to the philosophical, scientific, or cultural demands of the spirit of the age. Each in his way was concerned to repristinate the Biblical categories.

Barth's Commentary on Romans waged war upon evolutionary conceptions of the Kingdom of God (that favorite example of liberal doctrinal accommodation), claiming: "Whenever men claim to be able to see the Kingdom of God as a growing organism, or— to describe it more suitably—as a growing building, what they see is not the Kingdom of God but the Tower of Babel."[2] The Divine revelation was not accommodating, nor superficially comforting, but cruelly critical of man's egotism. Hence, thundered Barth, "Religion, when it attacks vigorously, when it is fraught with disturbance, when it is non-aesthetic, non-rhetorical, non-pious, when it is the religion of the 39th Psalm, of Job, and of Luther, and of Kierkegaard, when it is the religion of Paul, bitterly protests against every attempt to make of its grim earnestness some trivial and harmless thing." On the contrary, "Religion is aware that it is in no wise the crown and fulfilment of true humanity; it knows itself rather to be a questionable, disturbing, dangerous thing."[3] Barth emphasized, with Sören Kierkegaard,[4] the infinite qualitative difference between God and man. Hence "the Gospel is not a truth among other truths. Rather it sets a

---

[2] *Commentary* . . . , p. 432.   [3] *Ibid.*, p. 258.

[4] The first English book on Kierkegaard was Dr. E. L. Allen's *Kierkegaard, His Life and Thought*. Existentialism was mediated also by Martin Buber's important *I and Thou* which had a profound influence on H. H. Farmer's thought, and also through a recovery of Pascal and Kierkegaard. See Denzil Patrick's *Pascal and Kierkegaard*. The *Life* by Walter Lowrie and his translations and those of his colleagues made Kierkegaard available to the English-speaking world.

question-mark against all truths."[5] Like Kierkegaard, too, Barth affirmed that faith was existential commitment, and spoke in paradoxes: "for all it is a leap into the void. And it is possible for all, only because it is equally impossible."[6]

The almost forgotten or, at the least, diluted, Biblical terms of Grace and Sin, Justification, Forgiveness, and Resurrection, were interpreted dynamically by Barth. Sin was defined as "that interchanging of God and man, that exalting of men to divinity and depressing of God to humanity, by which we seek to justify and fortify and establish ourselves."[7] "Grace, however, is the fact of forgiveness."[8] Moreover, Grace is not given without a prior judgment of God. Thus "Grace is not grace, if he that receives it is not under judgment. Righteousness is not righteousness if it be not reckoned to the sinner. Life is not life, if it be not life from death. And God is not God, if he be not the End of men."[9] The sole hope for trapped man is the Resurrection of Jesus Christ: "We have seen the old world as a completely closed circle from which we have no means of escape. But, because we have perceived this, we are able to recognize—in the light of the Resurrection of Jesus from the dead—the power and meaning of the Coming Day: the Day of the New World and of the New Man."[10] Here was the return to a strongly Biblical theology, speaking with the existential concern of a Luther and with the magisterial authority of Calvin. "Theology," claimed Barth, "is *ministerium verbi divini*. It is nothing more or less."[11] In Barth's favourite illustration the theologian was like John the Baptist in Grünewald's painting of the Crucifixion, pointing an elongated finger to God the Transcendent in his ineffable majesty. Barth's is a theology of *Krisis* because every human achievement stands under the judgment of God and the Church itself is in constant need of reformation. It is a dialectical theology because it says *Nein* to all attempts to solve human problems apart from God, Creator, Judge, and Redeemer.

Barth's theology did not receive an immediate welcome, and his impact on English theology was never widespread. His paradoxes sounded strange in English ears. His re-assertion of Biblical truth was sometimes misinterpreted as a neo-fundamentalism. His Theology of the Word was thought to be merely the rejuvenescence

---

5 *Commentary* . . . , p. 35.   6 *Ibid.*, p. 99.   7 *Ibid.*, p. 190.
8 *Ibid.*   9 *Ibid.*, p. 187.   10 *Ibid.*
11 *Ibid.*, preface, p. x. The *Römerbrief*, it is interesting to note, has nine references to Luther, five to Calvin, and nineteen to Dostoievsky, as well as seven to Nietzsche and two to Feuerbach.

of Calvinism, though he did not affirm the doctrine of double predestination, and his later exposition of election has strong universalistic overtones. The more serious objections to his earlier theology, however, were his denial of the validity of any natural theology and hence the restriction of revelation to Holy Scripture, and his apparent denigration of man below the level of responsible personality. Nor was there a serious attempt on the part of his critics to follow the brilliant development of his thought in the lengthy volumes of *Die Kirchliche Dogmatik*. But even when Barth's theology was more congenially filtered for English readers through the writings of Emil Brunner, it gave a strong propulsion to the emergence of a Biblical theology in England.

This was provided chiefly by New Testament scholars, of whom the most significant were Sir Edwyn Clement Hoskyns and Professor C. H. Dodd. Both reacted strongly against the futurist eschatology of liberalism which had sometimes been indistinguishable from a future utopia to be brought into being by men. They substituted a "fulfilled" eschatology (the term of Hoskyns) or a "realized" eschatology (in the terminology of Dodd). By this, they meant that the Kingdom of God had been inaugurated by the teaching, the life, death, and resurrection of Jesus Christ, in whom God's new day had dawned.

Hoskyns (1884-1937) had begun a new era in English studies of the New Testament by his brilliant essay, "The Christ of the Synoptic Gospels," in *Essays Catholic and Critical*, edited by E. G. Selwyn (1926). This he followed up with an essay on "Jesus the Messiah" in *Mysterium Christi*, edited by Deissmann and Bell (1930), and *The Riddle of the New Testament* (1931), written in collaboration with F. N. Davey, his pupil at Corpus Christi College, Cambridge. He also left two posthumously published works: the important study, *The Fourth Gospel*, and the volume of *Cambridge Sermons* (1938).

Hoskyns argued in "The Christ of the Synoptic Gospels" that the Gospels were the sacred writings of the infant Christian community; he employed the technique of "Form criticism" to undo the damage created by historical criticism which, as Schweitzer said, had left the reader with "only a tattered copy of the Gospel of Saint Mark" in his hand. The New Testament Epistles were, on this approach, the records connected with the process of building the religious community, and the Gospels should be read in the light of the Epistles, rather than the other and customary way

179

round. The Cross and the Resurrection was the double event that gave them shape. The supernatural element was at least as primitive as the moral element, concluded Hoskyns, and hence "exclusiveness . . . may have its origin in the teaching of Jesus rather than in the theology of St. Paul."[12] His conclusions in this study were revolutionary and warrant extensive citation:

"From this reconstruction it will be seen at once that a whole series of contrasts underlies the Synoptic tradition. . . . The contrast is not between the Jesus of history and the Christ of faith, but between the Christ humiliated and the Christ returning in glory. . . . The contrast is not between a reformed and an unreformed Judaism, but between Judaism and the new supernatural order by which it is at once destroyed and fulfilled: not between the disciples of a Jewish prophet and an ecclesiastically ordered sacramental cultus, but between the disciples of Jesus, who, though translated into the sovereignty of God, are as yet ignorant both of His claims and the significance of their own conversion, and the same disciples, initiated into the mystery of His person and of His life and death, leading the mission to the world, the patriarchs of the new Israel of God. The contrast is not between an ethical teaching and a dreamy eschatology, or between a generous humanitarianism and an emotional religious experience stimulated by mythological beliefs, but between a supernatural order characterized by a radical moral purification involving persistent moral conflict and the endurance of persecution, and a supernatural order in which there is no place either for moral conflict or for persecution."[13] Clearly the Bible and the Church belonged together and Hoskyns had reinterpreted their relevance with new vigour.

More quietly than Barth, but with equal conviction, Hoskyns was preaching to his Corpus Christi students in Cambridge a Christo-centric faith founded on Christ as the inaugurator of God's new regime. In 1926 and 1927 he proclaimed Christ as the fulfilment of the promises of God. He thought it a woeful misunderstanding to conceive of Christianity as awaiting a catastrophe which will overwhelm the present world and usher in the Kingdom of God. "To be a Christian is, rather, the recognition that the great catastrophe lies in the past, that God has acted and is acting energetically, that righteousness has been attained by men and women and is attainable by us through the grace of God."[14]

[12] *Essays Catholic and Critical*, p. 169.
[13] *Ibid.*, pp. 177-78.   [14] *Cambridge Sermons*, p. 27.

Christian discipleship involves, not dreaming, but "plunging head first into the Christian faith and fellowship, believing that the Ecclesia of God is the visible expression in the world of His love and His mercy."[15]

While Hoskyns acknowledged the importance of believing in the role of God in the long history of the human race and in the ordering of Nature, yet "far more important than this is the belief that God acts catastrophically in human affairs, that He works miracles, that men are transformed from sin to righteousness, that prayer calls for an act of God, that it does not merely effect an adaptation to the laws of nature. The God of the Christian religion is a God of miracles."[16] Eschatology, in the view of Hoskyns, exposes, as with a lightning flash, the simplicity of ultimate beliefs, for it "crudely and ruthlessly sweeps away all our little moral busyness, strips us naked of worldly possessions and worldly entanglements, and asks what survives the catastrophe. It is only then that the ultimate moral duties stand alone in their luminous simplicity: Love of God, and Charity to those who, like us, are bereft of that in which they have confidently trusted."[17]

The bracing vigour of Barth's and Hoskyns' Biblical theology can be understood only if we recall the background of European totalitarianism (Nazi, Fascist, and Communist), in which human leaders were claiming an allegiance which belongs only to God, and if we also remember that this theology was making a counter-claim for Christ. This is why Hoskyns preached in these words: "The Church and theology know that they can only sing the glory of God over their own graves and at the place where they have died. . . . And can you wonder that those who know this secret tremble when they see scientists, economists, psychologists, Hitlerites, leaders of the Group Movement, Communists, and all those other confident advisers of men marching with flags flying into the abyss where the Church has already stumbled and fallen?— can you wonder that the Church lifts up its tired, weary warning against human ὕβρις, arrogance?"[18] Like a prophet Hoskyns gives this final warning: "Once again, my brothers in Christ, may I warn you that, as Christians and as men, you are moving along a path narrow and sharp as the edge of a razor, for on one side of you lies the blasphemy of human idolatry, and on the other side yawns the

[15] *Ibid.*, p. 28.　　　[16] *Ibid.*, p. 35.　　　[17] *Ibid.*, p. 37.
[18] *Ibid.*, pp. 147-48. For two studies of the Biblical revival, see William Neil, *The Rediscovery of the Bible* and J. E. Fison, *The Faith of the Bible*.

chasm of detachment and cynical aloofness. Between the two walked the Christ."[19] Biblical theology was clearly the iron-ration of the Christian soldier for Hoskyns. And this theology of fulfilled eschatology called the Christian from the balcony view of life into the blood and dust of commitment in the arena, as Barth's theology was to summon the German Confessional Church into being at the Synod of Barmen. In each theologian it was clearly a case of "Choose ye this day whom ye will serve!" The trumpets of liberalism had been muted; those of Biblical orthodoxy gave forth no uncertain sound.

What Hoskyns was accomplishing as an Anglican, Professor C. H. Dodd was achieving as a Free Churchman, and he was later to be assisted by the work of T. W. Manson, R. Newton Flew, and Vincent Taylor. Dodd's *Apostolic Preaching* of 1936 distinguished the basic pattern of apostolic preaching as the *heilsgeschichte*, or history of salvation, the proclamation of the mighty acts of God, as contrasted with moral instruction. The early Christian sermon was *kerygma*, a proclaiming of the Gospel, as contrasted with topical or hortatory preaching which "is teaching, or exhortation (*paraklesis*), or it is what they called *Homilia*, that is, the more or less informal discussion of various aspects of Christian life and thought, addressed to a congregation already established in the faith."[20] The primitive Church was both the creation and the verification of the proclamation of the mighty acts of God: "The primitive Church, in proclaiming its Gospel to the world, offered its own fellowship and experience as the realization of the Gospel. That is the essence of the matter."[21] Thus the Church was created by the proclamation that Jesus Christ crucified was the Messiah of God, as vindicated by the Resurrection, and the Spirit-filled Community—the new Israel of God—in His Name now offered to baptize all who repented of their sins and desired to share their worship and witness to God's new age. Here, again, was a Biblical theology which stressed the interdependence of the Gospel and the Church.

What the New Testament scholars were teaching was soon reflected in the thought of the theologians. A notable restatement of the faith in terms of orthodoxy, on the part of a former distinguished liberal, was Dr. Nathaniel Micklem's *What is the Faith?* (1936). He argued that the Faith is not to be defined by ration-

---

[19] *Ibid.*, p. 149.　　[20] *Apostolic Preaching*, p. 5.　　[21] *Ibid.*, p. 135.

alism for "the Christian faith is what it is, not what any modern rationalist may like to think it ought to be."[22] Nor is the Faith to be defined in terms of experience, for this assumes "the Christian faith is what I happen to believe."[23] The Incarnation is pivotal, for it is "the recognition that, in Jesus Christ, God has in some way condescended to our low estate and come amongst us."[24] The Trinity is the "only all-comprehensive Christian dogma."[25] He maintained that Protestants should realize that the Blessed Virgin "might be regarded as the patron saint of the Protestant Confession," as the prototype of humble faith.[26] After a discussion of Adoptionist and Kenoticist Christological doctrines, Dr. Micklem decided in favour of the classical Chalcedonian doctrine of the two natures, human and divine. It is also significant that this theological revaluation by a Congregationalist included, as its eleventh chapter, a consideration of "The Church Catholic and Apostolic." Two other events in the life of Dr. Micklem provide surprising evidence of the power of orthodoxy in a Nonconformist theologian. The first is that Dr. Micklem, as Principal of Mansfield College, Oxford, regularly lectured on the theology of St. Thomas Aquinas from the Latin text, and the second, that he was invited by Dr. William Temple, when the latter was Archbishop of Canterbury, to write a Lenten book, which was issued as *The Doctrine of our Redemption.*

It might be supposed that the Free Churches would be readier than Anglicans to devote themselves to the study of a genuinely Biblical theology, since their roots were in the Reformation according to the Word of God, whereas the Anglicans since the days of the Venerable Hooker had insisted that their authority was the three-fold cord of Scripture, Tradition, and right Reason. This supposition would, however, be untrue. Not only the work of Hoskyns, but also the important Biblical and theological studies of Father A. G. Hebert[27] of Kelham and of Father Lionel Thornton of the Community of the Resurrection,[28] are a standing refutation of this view. In fact, the theological faculties at Oxford and Cambridge included many unusually competent Anglican Biblical

[22] *What is the Faith?*, pp. 31-32.   [23] *Ibid.*, p. 32.
[24] *Ibid.*, p. 120.   [25] *Ibid.*, p. 133.
[26] *Ibid.*, p. 146.

[27] Notably his typological study, *The Throne of David* and *Fundamentalism and the Church of God.*

[28] Notably the series of studies which includes *The Common Life in the Body of Christ, Revelation and the Modern World, The Dominion of Christ,* and *Christ and the Church.*

scholars, among whom would have to be included Dr. J. A. T. Robinson,[29] before he became Bishop of Woolwich.

The return to orthodoxy took many forms, all witnessing to the inadequacy of liberalism's attempt to accommodate revelation and churchmanship to contemporary culture. The Roman Catholics, after the expulsion of Modernism from their midst, naturally turned for inspiration to the massive synthesis of philosophy and revelation of St. Thomas Aquinas. In this they were supported by the *Aeterni Patris* of Leo XII and the *Doctoris Angelici* of Pius X, as well as by the *Studiorum Ducem* of Pius XI (1923), confirming the primacy of that Doctor of the Church for Christian theology. Maritain and Gilson, the leading French neo-Thomists, concerned themselves with the tragic disunity of modern society which they diagnosed as due to a lack of direction through the divorce of the natural from the supernatural. Their slogan was, in effect, "Back to Thomas Aquinas and from Thomas forward." Widely read in England, they believed that philosophy and art, as well as social justice, had flourished best and could only flourish as the allies of religion. They believed that the Christian faith, with the backing of the Roman Catholic Church, alone provided a world-view in which all these cultural and social activities now atomized could be united, a collectivist ethics such as the times called for, and a source for progress. In England the leading neo-Thomist was the historian Christopher Dawson. But neo-Thomism also appealed to certain Anglican philosophers, notably Austin Farrer and E. L. Mascall, though each was a theologian of considerable independence.

The English Methodists returned to Biblical orthodoxy in part by the rediscovery of Luther's Gospel of Grace, and appropriately so, for John Wesley's heart was strangely warmed by the proclamation of justification by faith through grace when an unknown person read out Luther's Commentary on the Epistle to the Romans in the Aldersgate Society Meeting on what is now regarded as the Methodist Red-letter Day. Luther's stance *coram Deo* was finely recovered in Philip S. Watson's *Let God be God*, as also in Gordon Rupp's *The Righteousness of God*, and a theocentric theology expelled any lingering traces of anthropocentricism among the younger Methodist theologians.

Among both Congregationalists and Baptists there was a return

---

[29] See especially his study of ecclesiology, *The Body*, and of eschatology, *In the End, God*.

to their Calvinist heritage. This "Genevan revival"[30] of the Reformed tradition was strong in Congregationalism because the liberalism against which it reacted had been extreme in this denomination. The leaders of this new trend were Dr. Nathaniel Micklem (formerly Principal of Mansfield College, Oxford), Dr. J. S. Whale (formerly President of Cheshunt College, Cambridge), and the late Bernard Manning, Senior Tutor of Jesus College, Cambridge.

Dr. Micklem, as Chairman of the Friends of Reunion, was particularly successful in mediating to the Free Churches the devotional heritage of the Universal Church, and appropriately was the editor of *Christian Worship*[31] (1936), while his *A Book of Personal Religion* (1938) showed the continuity of the evangelical tradition in devotion in Bunyan, Calvin, Doddridge, John Newton, Isaac Watts, John Knox, Richard Baxter, and Matthew Henry. Dr. Whale stressed the links of Congregationalism with the Continental Reformed tradition in his chapter on ecclesiology in *Christian Doctrine* (1941), and more fully in *The Protestant Tradition* (1955) which is an admirable assessal of Luther's rediscovery of the Gospel and Calvin's recovery of Churchmanship and discipline. B. L. Manning exhibited the continuity of the Reformed tradition in English Nonconformity with great distinction, in his *Essays in Orthodox Dissent* (1939), in which he showed conclusively that Nonconformists were orthodox in doctrine but dissenters only in churchmanship, refusing any Erastianism that would have compromised their freedom to obey the Gospel. He also wrote *The Hymns of Wesley and Watts* (1942) to demonstrate that the Free Churches sang their orthodox divinity, even if they did not recite it in creeds or confessions. All three insisted in season and out of season that Genevan churchmanship was founded upon the ministry of the Word and Sacraments, which were not to be divided, any more than Gospel and Church were to be divided. This is superbly expressed in Dr. Whale's ecclesiology:

"Christians have never known the Church as a society of man's contriving, and expression of human idealism like a mutual improvement society or a club for recreation, fellowship and goodwill, with the minister of the Word and Sacraments as its competent and salaried secretary. Christians know the Church evangelical and catholic as the sacred gift of God, which no merely naturalistic or evolutionary categories can explain; it is a wonderful and sacred

[30] The term of John W. Grant in *Free Churchmanship in England*, p. 330.
[31] This book is considered in Chap. x *infra*.

185

mystery, the great company of the elect of God stretching beyond the sight of any man across the centuries and the continents; the host of the living God sharing His very life in all places and in all ages, on earth and in heaven; the Church which God loved, Christ purchased, and the Holy Ghost sanctified, and which Christ will present to Himself a glorious Church."[32]

The new insights in Reformed theology and churchmanship were popularized in a series of "Forward Books" under the general editorship of Dr. John Marsh, as well as in the regular meetings of the Congregational "Church Order" Group. Other Congregational theologians who took their Genevan heritage with the utmost seriousness were Principals H. F. Lovell Cocks, H. Cunliffe-Jones, and John Huxtable, and two younger scholars, Daniel T. Jenkins[33] and W. A. Whitehouse.

Among the Baptists, Principals H. Wheeler Robinson, the distinguished Old Testament scholar, and A. C. Underwood, and Dr. Ernest A. Payne,[34] were also protagonists of an orthodox theology combined with Genevan churchmanship. R. C. Walton represented the same trend in the younger generation in *The Gathered Community* (1946). Neville Clark,[35] a young Baptist minister, devoted himself to the task of mediating the Catholic tradition in worship to his denomination.

It was not too much to say that the return to Biblical orthodoxy in England meant the recovery of the Church's soul. The authority of the Biblical revelation, which was both doctrine and life, replaced the uncertainties of human ideals and experiences. The Bible became the source, not the confirmation of religious experience. Theology stressed the objectivity of the Divine deeds for the salvation of the human race. Man learned that the tragedy of his inner civil war was not due to mere ignorance so much as to a Titanism that was the product of human arrogance and self-sufficiency, manifested in rebellion. In the humility of faith, learned after the Divine judgment in history and in the self, God's grace proved effectual for his renovation. His maturation in Christian faith and witness was accomplished in worship, through the preaching of the Word and the celebration of the Sacrament of Holy Communion. His view of life was no longer to be that of

---

[32] *What is a Living Church?*, p. 28f.

[33] See *The Nature of Catholicity, Tradition and the Spirit*, and *Congregationalism*.

[34] See his *The Fellowship of Believers* and *The Free Church Tradition in the Life of England*.

[35] See *The Call to Worship*.

the bystander, but one of commitment in Christ's mystical Body the Church. Biblical theologians had learned in T. S. Eliot's words that "the way forward is the way back."[36]

A proof of the important impact of the return to orthodoxy in doctrine was that it was far from being the concern only of professional theologians or ministers of religion. This movement caught the imagination of lay apologists for Christianity, among them some of the most distinguished literary figures of the day.

G. K. Chesterton gained a widespread hearing for the traditional Christian faith in his witty essays in *Orthodoxy* and *Heretics*, while *The Everlasting Man* was a devastating polemic against the evolutionary concept which formed the credo of the secularist. Dorothy L. Sayers wrote an intriguing exposition and defence of orthodoxy in her brilliant pamphlet, *The Greatest Drama ever Staged*, and expounded Christian morality in another entitled *The Other Six Deadly Sins*. Her longer book, *The Mind of the Maker*, was an admirable study of the Christian doctrines of the Trinity and of Creation, illustrated from the consideration of artistic creativity. Her *Zeal of Thy House*, written for the Canterbury Festival, was a convincing account of the nature of pride. Her radio cycle, *The Man born to be King* (1953), which is presented by the British Broadcasting Corporation annually, may well be considered the most successful public presentation of the relevance of the Christian drama of salvation in our time.

Another exceedingly successful apologist and Oxford don, also a lecturer in English literature, was Clive Staples Lewis. His most successful broadcast talks were published as *Mere Christianity*, while *The Problem of Pain* and *Miracles* provided answers to the major problems of belief. *The Screwtape Letters* are an exceedingly ingenious imaginative attempt to show the subtlety and demonic nature of evil. Charles Williams, though less well known, was a poet and novelist whose work was a manifestation of traditional theological insights, and whose Oxford lectures on Milton were hammer blows against secularism. He succeeded in making the Christian virtue of chastity exciting,[37] and he also wrote a most perceptive history of the Christian Church, in terms of the attractions of orthodoxy and heresy, entitled *The Descent of the Dove* (1949).

[36] *The Four Quartets: The Dry Salvages*, III, line 6.
[37] See his essay on *Comus*, republished as the introduction to the World's Classics edition of *The English Poems of John Milton*.

The most impressive of the poets, Thomas Stearns Eliot, became a convinced Anglo-Catholic, and his theological insights were subtly expressed in *Ash Wednesday*, *the Ariel Poems*, and more directly in the play, *Murder in the Cathedral*, and in his apologia, *The Idea of a Christian Society* (1939). He presented Christianity by indirection in the plays, *The Family Reunion* and *The Cocktail Party*. Where Eliot led, other poets have followed—W. H. Auden, Dylan Thomas, Norman Nicholson, Edwin Muir,[38] and Anne Ridler—in appropriating the Christian symbols in their verse.

All these rediscovered the enchantment of orthodoxy and the wonder of the historic Christian faith, communicating it in essays, myths, drama, and poetry.

2. *The Rediscovery of the Church*

The "Back to the Gospel" movement also turned out to be a "Back to the Church" movement. While the Church of England had rediscovered the apostolicity and catholicity of the Church in the Oxford Movement, it did not become fully aware of the world-wide scandal of disunity until its representatives participated in the Ecumenical Movement of the twentieth century, when the "Bridge Church" discovered that its mixed Protestant-Catholic heritage expressed in miniature the whole tension of a Christendom in schism. For the Free Churches which had customarily elevated the Gospel only to depreciate the Church, as a merely convenient organization readily adaptable to the differing demands of different centuries or cultures, the sense of the Church as itself a gift of God, along with the Gospel, was a new and at first a painful discovery.

Perhaps the most exciting aspect of contemporary Church life is that the "Protestant" Churches are emphasizing that they really share in the Catholic character of the Body of Christ; and the "Catholic" Churches are finding that they must stress aspects of faith and worship for which Protestants stand.[39] But this situation has not merely happened, it has been prepared for by the cooperation of Protestants and Orthodox in the World Council of Churches, which was inaugurated at Amsterdam in 1948, and by the unpredictable liberal trends in the Second Vatican Council of the Roman Catholics. Much prejudice on each side of the ecclesiastical divide

[38] Muir deserves to be much better known. See *Collected Poems: 1921-1958* (1960), especially "The Transfiguration" and "The Killing."
[39] Daniel D. Williams, *What Present-Day Theologians are Thinking*, p. 152.

had to be overcome before the present *rapprochement* was reached. Moreover, on the Protestant side there were several conflicting conceptions of the nature of the Church. Some held the Pietist view that the true Church consisted of sincerely warmed hearts. Some held so strongly to the Calvinist view of the Church as the invisible number of the elect, and were so critical of the Catholic equation of the Kingdom of God with the Church, that they denied the need of a visible Church, exhibiting an apostolic continuity and a Catholic unity. Others, again, insisted on the local autonomy of the local congregation, as they stressed the importance of "gathered churches."

Inevitably the question arises: What were the forces which compelled the Protestants in general and Free Churchmen in particular to return to a more Catholic understanding of the Church? Undoubtedly, the primary influence was the ecumenical experience itself. The Free Churches, conscious of the scandal of reunion, had been engaged in closing their own ranks. In 1907 the Bible Christians, the Methodist New Connexion, and the United Methodist Free Church were all united. In 1932 the Primitive, the United, and the Wesleyan Methodist denominations were merged to form the Methodist Church. In 1929 the United Free Church joined the established Church of Scotland. Even more significant for the re-understanding of the nature and task of the Church of Christ were trans-denominational unions, such as the establishment of the United Church of Canada by the union of the Methodists, the Congregationalists, and a substantial number of the Presbyterians. Even more remarkable was the creation of the United Church of South India, after thirty years of maturation, which combined Anglicans, Methodists, Congregationalists, and Presbyterians. Furthermore, the Anglican Church was making tentative approaches to the Free Churches, as in the famous Lambeth Quadrilateral proposals of 1920, and to the Roman Catholic Church at the Malines Conversations of 1921 and 1926. All these mergers, attempted or concluded, concentrated attention on the essential character of the Christian Church, and led to discussion of the *esse*, the *bene esse*, and latterly, the *plene esse* of the Church. Moreover, in such a volume as *The Ministry and the Sacraments* edited by Dunkerley and Headlam (1937), representatives of different traditions were learning how much they held in common on even the thorniest issues.

A second factor tending towards the rediscovery of the Church

189

was the conclusion of "Form criticism" that the attempt to reach a "Jesus of History" behind the primitive traditions was quite impossible, since the Gospels and the Epistles are missionary literature, not biography. On this view no distinction was possible between the words and actions of Jesus himself and what was produced by the faith of the Apostolic Church. Hoskyns, as we have seen, insisted that the Gospels must be viewed through the lens of the Epistles. A more radical form critic, Professor R. H. Lightfoot of Oxford, concluded: "For all the inestimable value of the Gospels, they yield us little more than a whisper of his voice; we trace in them but the outskirts of his ways. Only when we see him hereafter in his fulness shall we know him also as he was on earth."[40] If there would have been no Church apart from the Gospel, there would clearly be no Gospels apart from the Church. Therefore, Church and Gospel could not be separated.

Old Testament scholarship was also pointing in the same direction, as Dr. H. Wheeler Robinson and others drew attention to the importance of the concept of "corporate personality" for the Hebrews. According to Professor T. W. Manson, the "Son of Man" is a corporate figure. The Old Testament knew almost nothing of solitary religion, but only of God's covenanted people, or, in days of widespread apostasy, of the "faithful remnant." These were the Old Testament analogues of "the Body of Christ."

In the third place, the political lesson of the need for community was being bitterly learned in these years, as the conflict with totalitarianism let the democracies realize that freedom must be mated with social responsibility, and that any sound interpretation of freedom is based upon tradition and order. The very anxieties of the times called for an authoritative system of belief, a faith communally believed for which to live and to die, if necessary. The very defence of a civilization in time of war demands that its spiritual values shall be made plain, and this undoubtedly spurred the passing of the Butler Education Act of 1944, one of the provisions of which was to provide religious education in all the State-aided schools in Great Britain.

The most considerable attempt on the Anglican side to justify a Catholic form of Church order as required by the Gospel itself was Dr. A. M. Ramsey's *The Gospel and the Catholic Church*. Its underlying conviction was "that the meaning of the Christian Church becomes most clear when it is studied in terms of the

40 *History and Interpretation of the Gospels*, p. 225.

Death and Resurrection of Jesus Christ."[41] The conclusion was reached that "the structure of the Catholic Church has great significance in the Gospel of God, and that Apostolic succession is important on account of its *evangelical* meaning."[42] Ramsey declared that in the conception of the Church, not as an institution, but as the Body constituted by Christ's Passion and Resurrection, he hoped to see the reconciliation of the Catholic conception of an institution with Creeds, Sacraments, and Episcopacy (which seems legalistic) with the Protestant concept of a gift of the Gospel and justification by faith (which seems individualistic).

Ramsey utterly repudiated individual experience as an adequate norm for the Church, for "the faithful Christian will not draw attention to himself, as an interesting specimen of life in Christ, but dying to all interest in himself and his 'experience' he will focus attention upon the redeeming acts of Christ in history."[43] To insist upon the authority of an individual experience is to commit a double fault—to deny the adequacy of Christ's deeds and to isolate one's self from the redemptive community of the Church. "In later language, the Church is called 'Apostolic' (sent by the one Redeemer in the flesh), and 'Catholic' (living one universal life); and both notes of the Church are essential to its existence as expressing the Lord's death and resurrection, wherein its 'Holiness' consists."[44]

The importance of the apostles, in Dr. Ramsey's view, is that they represent unity and continuity, "being sent by our Lord who Himself was sent by the Father, and declaring, in effect, 'He came, He died, He rose, we are sent and the Body is One.' "[45] "Apostolic succession" is understood in three ways. The succession of bishop to bishop secured a continuity of Christian teaching and tradition in every see. The bishops also succeeded the apostles in the sense that they performed the apostolic functions of preaching, ruling, and ordaining, and this is summed up by the bishop celebrating at the Eucharist, and interceding for his flock and family. Finally, "apostolic succession" is further used to signify "that grace is handed down from the Apostles through each generation of Bishops by the laying on of hands."[46] In the present the bishop sets forth the Gospel of God as the guardian of teaching, as performing the apostolic functions, and as "an organ in the one Body's continuous life in grace."[47]

[41] *The Gospel* . . . , p. vi.   [42] *Ibid.*, p. vii.   [43] *Ibid.*, p. 44.
[44] *Ibid.*, pp. 44-45.   [45] *Ibid.*, p. 74.   [46] *Ibid.*, p. 82.
[47] *Ibid.*, p. 83.

Denying the distinction made by Heiler in *Das Gebet*, which divides prayer into prophetic and mystical, Dr. Ramsey insists that in the New Testament prayer is *liturgical*. "It is the sharing by men in the one action of Christ, through their dying to their own egotisms as they are joined in the one Body with His death and resurrection."[48] The Liturgy, as the Ministry and the Creeds, all point to the Gospel and the Church.

The rest of the volume is a penetrating re-examination of Christian history, culminating in the conclusion: "Hence while Catholicism must face the issues of the Gospel and examine itself as to its Pelagianism, Protestantism must ask whether, after all, the historic Church order has not something to do with the Gospel of God. It will not deny its own experience, nor the power of its own ministries; it needs to own, in common with all Christendom the need for one Apostolate, as the organ of unity and continuity, to be made universal for all Christians. At present we are all incomplete: 'In him ye are all made full.' "[49]

The ecumenical approach is all the more impressive because in the final chapter, "*Ecclesia Anglicana*," Dr. Ramsey criticizes three ways in which some Anglicans have obscured the Catholic meaning of Church Order, by the "Three Branch" theory which claims unity but rationalizes schism; by an Erastianism which regards the Church of England as the moral organ of the nation; and by the clericalist view of some Anglo-Catholics who have conceived the ministry as a channel of grace isolated from the life of the Body. This was an impressive Biblical and theological treatment of its theme, deserving of thorough consideration.

The most systematic analysis from the Free Church side of the meaning of Catholicity was the book of Daniel Jenkins, *The Nature of Catholicity* (1942). Jenkins recognizes that there must be both unity and continuity in the life of the Church, but he believes that the Church's Catholicity or wholeness is its fidelity to God's present, active and demanding Word in Jesus Christ. The foundation of the Church is Jesus Christ, the Word of God, as the Bible bears witness to the Word. The Bible is, indeed, the Church's book, but it holds before the Church that which stands over it in judgment and mercy, God's redemptive grace. It is not necessary for bishops to be guardians of the apostolic testimony, for "the Apostles themselves took care to ensure that we should

48 *Ibid.*, p. 94.   49 *Ibid.*, p. 201.

be left in no doubt as to the nature of their testimony. They left us the Holy Scriptures."[50]

Jenkins does recognize, however, without any lessening of the authority of the Scriptures, that the creeds and traditions of the Catholic Church are also necessary: "the very fact that the Scriptures need exegesis demands such an authority and we can refuse to recognize it only by refusing to admit that the Spirit has been at work in the Church before us, that is, that the Church of our Fathers has been a true Church and our own Baptism a true Baptism."[51] That there is a need for an apostolic ministry is not contested, but only that apostolicity can be guaranteed by any form of ministry. It is contended that it is the Gospel, as mediated and confirmed by the Holy Spirit, which guarantees the continuous life and therefore the unity of the Church, and therefore it cannot be authenticated by anything extraneous to itself.

Free Churchmen were urged to "take episcopacy into their system" by Archbishop Fisher in a Cambridge sermon of 1946, and many of them might be prepared to do so, since for reasons of history and geography this is the likeliest form of Church Order to win the approval of most of Christendom in a fully united Church. Some would concede that episcopacy is an excellent way of fulfilling the necessary function of *episcope* or oversight in the Church. But since there have been heretical bishops and *episcopi vagantes* in history, they could not put their hands on their hearts and state that episcopacy has always guaranteed, to the faithful, continuity in apostolic faith and practice. How can it then be regarded as of the *esse* of the Church of Christ? B. L. Manning expressed this conviction with characteristic pungency: "It is with salvation by bishops, not government by bishops that we quarrel."[52] For our purpose, to note that Free Churchmen were seriously considering the necessity of the Church as a gift along with the Gospel itself is perhaps more important than to be disturbed about the differences in the continuing debate on the essential form of Church order.

Nonetheless, the Anglican claims have forced the Free Churches to consider both the Biblical nature of the Church and the nature of Church order. Dr. R. Newton Flew and Rupert Davies, at the request of Archbishop Fisher, prepared an interesting and valuable report on *The Catholicity of Protestantism* (1950). They insisted,

50 *Ibid.*, p. 28.   51 *Ibid.*, p. 44.
52 *Church Union: The Next Step for Congregationalists*, p. 6.

after a close study of Luther and Calvin, that "it should now be sufficiently clear that belief in the one Holy Catholic and Apostolic Church is integral to the faith of Protestantism. We believe that incorporation into the Church of Christ, the new Israel of God, is not an optional extra which can be dispensed with by those who possess a high degree of spirituality but takes place in the very act of personal faith in Christ."[53]

The crux of the problem of the essential form of Church order is reached in the sixth chapter on "The Ministry and the Sacraments." Here they refer to the Anglican claim, as reasserted in the work *The Apostolic Ministry* edited by Bishop K. E. Kirk, that the "essential ministry" is the Apostolic Ministry, represented by the episcopate in the apostolical succession, as distinguished from all other ministry which is "dependent." They are satisfied that Professor T. W. Manson, the English Presbyterian scholar, has refuted the validity of this distinction between essential and dependent ministry. His words are: "There is one 'essential' ministry, the only ministry that is unchallengeably essential. That is the ministry which the Lord Jesus Christ opened in Galilee after John the Baptist had been put in prison, the ministry which He carried on in Galilee and Judaea, the ministry which He continues to this day in and through the Church, which is His Body. . . . It is in virtue of this presence that it is possible to call the Church the Body of Christ."[54]

Thus, the only conclusion that can be drawn is that the ministry of the Apostles themselves is derivative and dependent. The Apostles were in no sense the "plenipotentiaries" (much play was made by Dr. Kirk's associates with the term *shaliach*,[55] translated "plenipotentiary"); Christ is God's plenipotentiary and the Holy Spirit sent by Christ is His plenipotentiary. Flew and Davies conclude: "To speak of anyone else, or any body of men, as the plenipotentiary of Christ is not only false but blasphemous; for it is virtually to deny, or at least to discount, the continuous activity of the Holy Spirit in the Church."[56]

Hitherto consideration has been limited to the more problematical aspects of the doctrine of the Church; it is now appropriate

[53] P. 91.   [54] *The Church's Ministry*, p. 22f.
[55] Bishop R. R. Williams in *Authority in the Apostolic Age*, p. 139, wrote: "It is hard to believe that the very basis of the Church's life—the 'Essential Ministry,' as Kirk calls it—can be established only by a prolonged and finally ambiguous argument among Rabbinic and Patristic scholars."
[56] *The Catholicity of Protestantism*, p. 105.

to turn to the more positive aspects as exemplified in the studies of a Free Churchman, Dr. Newton Flew, and of an Anglican, Dr. F. W. Dillistone.

Newton Flew's important study was entitled *Jesus and His Church, A Study of the Idea of the Ecclesia in the New Testament* (1938, second edition, 1943). Five main arguments are supplied for the assertion that Jesus intended to found a Church.[57] Jesus directed His preaching to the re-constitution of Israel in view of the advent of God's rule, and the "little flock" which He addresses is the New Israel. The ethical teaching of Jesus can be rightly understood only as directed to this nucleus of the New Israel, and as involving a promise of God's power to enable the disciples to translate the teaching into life; thus the ethical teaching points forward to the gift of the Holy Spirit promised for the Last Days. The very concept of Messiahship, especially as employed by Jesus, implies the gathering of a New Community. The terms "Gospel" or "Word" or "Mystery" employed in the preaching of Jesus refer to the entity which is constitutive of the New Community. (Those who receive the divine "Word" know it as "good news"; for those who reject it, it is a "Mystery" not yet revealed; and the "Gospel" includes the idea of the New Covenant to be established with the newly constituted People of God.) Finally, the Mission of the New Community is declared when Jesus sends forth His disciples. Thus, Flew establishes that the New Community, Ecclesia, or Church, was an original part of the Gospel, and lays to rest the older view that Paul was the real founder of the Church who complicated and institutionalized the "simple" ethical teaching of a Galilean prophet.

Moreover, the Sacraments are seen by Flew to be essential ordinances of the Church. He maintains that there were three decisive moments in the actions of Christ in constituting the Ecclesia. These were: the calling and instruction of the disciples; commissioning them to proclaim the good news that the new era had dawned in both word and deed; and, at the Last Supper, the institution of the new covenant with the disciples as representing the New People of God.

Flew arrives at four conclusions about the nature of the Church. "1. It is God's own creation. . . . The Ecclesia of God is the People of God, with a continuous life which goes back through the history

---

[57] These are conveniently summarized in the second edition on p. 14 of the Introduction.

of Israel . . . to Abraham . . . to the purpose of God before the world began."[58] "In the second place, the Word of God which called the Church into being has been verified in human experience. . . . The Church . . . has been constituted through the work of the Incarnate Word of God, by sharing in the Spirit, the preaching of the Word and the administration of the Sacraments."[59] Finally, "the principle of authority in the New Testament Church is closely connected with the Word."[60] His point here is that the Apostles were such only as they were eyewitnesses of the Word and witnesses to the Resurrection, and the implication follows that, important as Church order is, it is not as important as the faith.

Among Free Churchmen the acceptance of the authority of a historical Gospel has led to a renewed consideration of the authority of the Church, as God's on-going community of redemption. The Sacraments are no longer regarded as moving spiritual experiences, but as seals of the covenant of promise. The ministry is not a means of self-expression for spiritual philosophers or social reformers, but it is acknowledged unequivocally as "of the Word and Sacraments."[61]

One of the most helpful ecumenical attempts to see the complementary character of the differences between Catholic and Protestant conceptions of the Church is F. W. Dillistone's *The Structure of the Divine Society* (1951). In an exceedingly fresh and clearsighted survey of church history Dillistone isolates six main types of Christian community. The first three of them are Catholic conceptions: the monastic, the imperial, and the organic. The next three are Protestant: the covenantal, the contractual, and the sectarian. Both the monastic and the sectarian types are regarded as tangential to the main concern. The imperial and the contractual concepts are criticized as too static, in that they have become prematurely rigid in their historical formation. The organic and covenantal types, however, are more dynamic, and bear within themselves a vital principle for the on-going life of the Church. Dillistone regards them as the essential types of Catholic and Protestant churchmanship.

The organic conception of the Catholics stresses the common life of Christians in the Body of Christ. It emphasizes the social character of existence. We are born into a family and nation and

---

[58] *Jesus and His Church* . . . , p. 181.
[59] *Ibid.*, p. 182. [60] *Ibid.*
[61] J. W. Grant, *Free Churchmanship in England, 1870-1940*, p. 397.

from these given relationships we receive the very possibility of personal identity and worth. So it is with our Christian life, for the Sacraments in Catholicism hallow the various stages of our life and are essentially social in character. The covenantal conception of Protestants emphasizes those relations into which we enter voluntarily through personal commitments to God and to one another as we look forward to some common purpose in the future. The organic concept implies that Christians are born, and the covenantal concept that Christians are made. Dillistone believes that both are valid analogies for interpreting the nature of the Church, and that the Christian Church can incorporate and reconcile them. The importance of his study is, indeed, to have recognized that these competitive concepts are ultimately complementary. He believes that "Heirs of the Covenant in One Body" is the most apt expression for the complementary view, since this unites the organic-ontological element with the covenantal-eschatological emphasis.[62]

The thorough-going consideration of the nature of the Church in various reports of the Faith and Order Commission of the World Council of Churches, in which British representatives took part, and of the detailed contributions of individual Churchmen of different ecclesiastical traditions in England, is impossible within this limited space. But enough has been said to indicate that this is a very lively part of contemporary theological conversation, likely to become livelier with the new Catholic-Protestant dialogue. It is of the greatest importance that, despite continuing problems in the sphere of Church order, a considerable consensus has been arrived at between the once mutually suspicious Anglican and Free Church traditions, and this has been made possible by the return to a Biblical theology and by the ecumenical enterprise. On both sides of the divide, it is now recognized that the Church, far from being the club of the religious minded, or the moral uplift department of the nation, or the *ecclesiola* of the pietists, is the Body of Christ, founded by the Messiah through His sacrificial Death and Resurrection and empowered by the Holy Spirit. It is commonly acknowledged that its life is fed by the Word and the Sacraments, and that its two-fold function is "to glorify God

[62] This bald summary does not do justice to the complexity and criticisms of Dr. Dillistone's important monograph. A fuller study of Anglican ecclesiology would also have to consider the contributions of Lionel Thornton and E. L. Mascall on the High Church side and the work of F. J. Taylor and others on the Evangelical side. Brief reference to Abbot Christopher Butler's ecclesiology has been made in Chap. VII *infra*.

in adoration and sacrificial service."[63] It is also confessed that the Church must be Apostolic, continuing in the teaching and practice of the Apostles (though there are differences about the nature of the "Apostolic succession"), that it must be Holy, and there is a longing such as has not been felt for centuries that its Catholicity may be made visible and that thus may be fulfilled Christ's High-Priestly Prayer *ut omnes unum sint.*

No further proof of the new consensus on ecclesiology is needed than to cite the following statement from the Report, *Doctrine in the Church of England* (1938), with the assurance that it would be entirely acceptable to all the English Free Churches. The instrumental definition (on p. 112) reads: "The Church exists to worship God made known in Christ, and bears His commission in this world to bear witness to His Gospel, to bring all mankind within the membership, range, and fellowship of the redeemed Society, and to gain for the principles involved in the Gospel application to the conditions of human life from time to time."

This rediscovery of the necessity of the Church has, it need hardly be said, helped to strengthen the conviction of the crucial importance of worship, liturgical and sacramental.

3. *Towards a Christian Sociology*

The third trend during the most recent period of theology has been an attempt, chiefly on the part of High Church Anglicans, to elaborate a distinctively Christian Sociology. Since this is the concern of a very limited group of theologians it warrants only the briefest consideration, especially as the most recent developments of the welfare state in Britain have taken much of the momentum from the movement for the expression of social justice in British society.

The concern to establish a Christian Sociology is no recent phenomenon in the Church of England, which can proudly lay claim to have considered this need as far back as 1848, when F. D. Maurice, Charles Ludlow, and Charles Kingsley cooperated to found the Christian Socialist Movement.[64] This was done as a result of their conviction that unsocial Christians and unChristian Socialists were equally dangerous in that year of revolutions in Europe and the publication of the *Communist Manifesto* by Marx and Engels. The same tradition, based upon the Incarnation and

[63] Leonard Hodgson, *The Second World Conference on Faith and Order*, p. 233.
[64] See M. B. Reckitt, *Maurice to Temple.*

its sacramental implications for human society, was taken from the founding Broad Churchmen by the Anglo-Catholics, in the persons of Stewart Headlam, Charles Gore, and Conrad Noel, and a legion of priests in slum parishes who proved to be the protectors of the poor. Its importance in the present century was signalized by the leadership given to the movement by William Temple, successively Bishop of Manchester, Archbishop of York, and Archbishop of Canterbury, who wrote the most popular presentation of its theme in a paperback entitled, *Christianity and Social Order* (1942).[65]

It was Temple's chairmanship of the 1924 Conference on Politics, Economics, and Citizenship (C.O.P.E.C.) in Birmingham, which convinced him of the importance of ecumenical consideration of the reconstruction of society through the social thinking and witness of Christians. In the summer of 1937 Temple was inevitably the leader in the Oxford Life and Work Conference on "Church, Community and State." His most dramatic role, however, was played at the Malvern Anglican Conference of 1941, when England was subject to ruthless bombing, and there was much consideration of the "social reconstruction" which should follow this war in which sacrifices were democratically equal. Papers were to be read by members of the "Christendom group"[66] who, in general, accepted the highly sacramental theology of W. G. Peck and his friends. They included the impressive names of Dorothy L. Sayers, Maurice Reckitt, T. S. Eliot, Middleton Murry, Donald M. Mackinnon, H. A. Hodges, and V. A. Demant.

The most inflammatory papers were, however, given by Sir Richard Acland and Kenneth Ingram. Acland argued that the common ownership of the means of production was a fundamental principle, which received considerable support, and the headlines of the newspapers in England and the United States asserted that the Archbishop and his advisers had capitulated to socialism. In fact, however, Temple got the Conference to agree only that the ultimate private ownership of the resources of the community *may be* a stumbling-block to a just society.[67] The purpose of emphasizing Temple's leadership in this field is simply to demonstrate

---

[65] A brief summary of this book is provided in Chapter VI. More than 150,000 copies had been sold by 1958 (Joseph Fletcher, *William Temple, Twentieth Century Christian*, p. 282).

[66] See M. B. Reckitt, ed., *Prospect for Christendom*, V. A. Demant, *The Religious Prospect* and W. G. Peck, *An Outline of Christian Sociology*. See also *Malvern, 1941, Proceedings of the Archbishop of York's Conference*.

[67] Fletcher, *William Temple . . .* , pp. 276-79.

that an important body of Anglican thinkers were attempting under his guidance to elaborate a Christian sociology.

What, then, is meant by a Christian sociology? Peck, Demant, and Reckitt have been greatly concerned to develop principles for the Christian interpretation of man in society, and of these the Incarnation is most central. This was made the basis of all Christian evaluation of culture. The foundation of this view is that in Jesus Christ the divine and human natures are united in one person, and Christ represents men before God and incorporates them into a new society of which He is the Head. Thus, in the Incarnation are united the personal and the social principles, which are essential to a true human society. All the positive values of culture are derived from the incarnational principle and judged by it. Art, philosophy, and the socio-political order are all potential values to be incorporated in the new life in Christ.

The Incarnation is, however, to be understood in the light of Christ's Passion, Atonement, and Resurrection. In this way all human values are exposed to the light of the perfect love which judges, forgives and redeems. The redemptive deed of Christ transforms all the partial values of temporal existence by bringing them into a new order of life whose principle is the Divine love in all its depth and inclusiveness.

It could be argued that this approach lacks the definiteness of the Roman Catholic ethical guidance, but it might be retorted that the flexibility possible in the Anglican approach avoids legalism and is free to employ middle axioms and temporary solutions without supposing that they are final. It is clear that no single Christian social philosophy can be derived from this Anglican standpoint, but it provides a dynamic synthesis of faith and human thought. In fact, Anglican social thinkers urge the necessity for both economists and sociologists to supply the scientific data upon which Christian evaluations are founded. These judgments tend to favour a society which combines the maximum of personal freedom compatible with responsible sharing. Generally speaking, Anglican moralists have supported the attempt to find collective solutions for the problems of social security, health, labour conditions, and participation in the decisions of industry and government. As Daniel D. Williams has remarked: "We may appreciate something of the theological integrity and profundity of this school by noting how the doctrine of the Trinity is brought into a new relevance for social problems."[68] The Trinity, in their view, is the Divine Society of Father, Son, and Holy Spirit, which in its own depth understands the mystery of giving and receiving.

In contrast to the liberal "social gospel" teaching of the first two decades of the century, which laid great stress on the "Kingdom of God" as its central concept, the "Christendom group" finds its historical anchorage in the Incarnation, which it makes the paradigm of Divine love and the basis for the sacramental ordering of society. It is, therefore, prepared to see in the Eucharist the pattern for a reconstructed order of society, in which the interdependence of the human society is recognized in its dependence upon God, from whom it receives its human and divine life, a life to be shared.[69]

4. The Thought of the Christian Radicals of Cambridge

The latest development in English theology is the most iconoclastic and therefore the most difficult to evaluate.[70] It is all the more important, therefore, that it should be expounded as far as possible in the words of its proponents, who are less a school than a group of individual theologians in conversation with each other as Cambridge University dons or ex-dons. They are deeply disturbed by the ineffectualness of official Christianity in England, which seems to their view respectable, supine, intellectually irrelevant, and apparently complacent. They are anxious to fracture this stereotype and to present a new image of Christianity, involving a radical recasting of the theology, the piety, and the moral attitudes of the Church.

The new "Christian radicalism"[71] has chiefly found expression

[68] *What Present-day Theologians are Thinking*, p. 95.

[69] No further explanation of these ideas is necessary in view of the social implications of the Eucharist, as expressed by Temple and Dix, which are considered in Chap. IX.

[70] Professor E. L. Mascall has provided a pointed critique of *Soundings* in his *Up and Down in Adria*, and Dr. A. M. Ramsey, the Archbishop of Canterbury, a short evaluation of Bishop John A. T. Robinson's *Honest to God* in *Image Old and New*. While the issues raised by the Cambridge radicals have hit the newspaper headlines, they are by no means alone in these concerns or approaches in Britain. Professor R. Gregor Smith provided a pioneer attempt to domesticate Bonhoeffer's thought in *The New Man: Christianity and Man's Coming of Age* and the Rev. Daniel T. Jenkins essayed a similar task, with cautionary qualifications, in *Beyond Religion*. For the Bultmannian approach reference may be made to Professor John Macquarrie's *The Scope of Demythologizing*. Professor Alan Richardson (now Dean of York) and three Nottingham University colleagues have also prepared a brief critique of the movement, *Four Anchors from the Stern*. See also Erik R. Routley, *The Man for Others*, for a more sympathetic approach.

[71] The term is used by the Rev. David L. Edwards, co-editor with Bishop

in three very recent and unconventional volumes. One, *Honest to God* (1963) is a general and fairly popular account of the re-formulation of Christian faith and life necessary to commend Christianity to the thoughtful agnostic of today and is the work of Dr. John A. T. Robinson, Bishop of Woolwich and former Dean of Clare College, Cambridge. The other two, both of which were edited by Dr. A. R. Vidler, Dean of King's College and former Editor of *Theology*, are *Soundings* (1963) and *Objections to Christian Belief.*[72]

Bishop Robinson of Woolwich is convinced "that there is a growing gulf between the traditional orthodox supranaturalism in which our Faith has been framed and the categories which the 'lay' world (for want of a better term) finds meaningful today."[73] His book is the effort to bridge that gulf. Although this became a best-seller and something of a *succès de scandale*, he ended his introduction with the words: "The one thing of which I am fairly sure is that, in retrospect, it will be seen to have erred in not being nearly radical enough."[74] Dr. Alec Vidler introduces *Soundings* with the declaration, "We can best serve the cause of truth and of the Church by candidly confessing where our perplexities lie, and not by making claims which, so far as we can see, theologians are not at present in a position to justify . . . it is a time for making soundings, not charts or maps."[75] Here then is an exceedingly realistic assessal of the place of Christianity in an age of increasing secularism. Here, too, is an honest, self-critical, tentative and modest essay in re-translating the essentials of Christian belief and practice in a way that will make them relevant in the technocratic age.

How is it proposed to recast the traditional structure of theology? Here the first great problem is to find a modern equivalent for the Divine transcendence that does not involve an antiquated cosmology. Robinson inveighs against the survival in theology of a physical conception of a pre-Copernican God "up there" in the sky or a metaphysical idea of a post-Copernican God "out there." In his view an image employing the metaphor of "depth" is better than the customary one of "height" since the latter suggests

---

Robinson of the *Honest to God Debate*, who writes (p. 21): "If I had to put a label on this movement . . . I would call it Christian radicalism."

[72] Originally delivered as four open lectures in Cambridge University in February, 1963. The American edition (J. B. Lippincott and Company, Philadelphia and New York), on which I am dependent, appeared in 1964.

[73] *Honest to God*, p. 8.   [74] *Ibid.*, p. 10.   [75] *Soundings*, p. ix.

remoteness, superficiality, and the lack of profound concern. He is persuaded by modern psychological usage and by the philosophical theology of Paul Tillich that the categories of "ultimate concern" and the "Ground of Being" are preferable.[76] Furthermore, Robinson is convinced that the traditional arguments for the existence of God presuppose that God is an object to be arrived at when man's search or argument is concluded. That, however, would be to conceive of God as a being among beings instead of Being-in-itself, which is the very pre-condition of the search.[77] The Ground of Being is further defined as Love: "Belief in God is the trust, the well-nigh incredible trust, that to give oneself to the uttermost in love is not to be confounded, but to be accepted; that Love is the ground of our being to which ultimately we 'come home.' "[78] Furthermore, God is to be met, not by withdrawal from the world, but "in unconditional concern 'for the other' *seen through to its ultimate depths*."[79] The Rev. G. F. Woods in his "The Idea of the Transcendent,"[80] in presenting a learned philosophical argument, arrives at a similar solution, contending that this essential concept in relation to God is arrived at analogically and is better conceived in personal than in impersonal analogies.

An equally radical attempt at "demythologizing" in theology is applied to the Chalcedonian Christology which affirms that Christ is the union of two natures, divine and human, in the one person. Robinson argues that this implies that God's Son is an intruder into humanity, since "it conjures up the idea of a divine substance being plunged into flesh and coated with it like chocolate or silver plating."[81] He prefers the image of Christ as a window showing God at work,[82] and asserts that Jesus "reveals God by being utterly transparent to him, precisely as he is nothing 'in himself.' "[83] The Rev. Hugh W. Montefiore in "Towards a Christology for Today"[84] finds three difficulties in the Chalcedonian Christology. The Definition assumes that Godhead and manhood are fully known, that they are comparable natures to be juxtaposed, and disregards the functional and dynamic terms in which Jesus spoke of himself. The paradox of grace, which assures man that he is accepted and loved as he is because of God's identification with man in Jesus and by Jesus' loving acceptance of the worst that man can do to him, is the best analogy whereby we can conceive of the union

[76] *Honest to God*, p. 23.   [77] *Ibid.*, Chap. 2.   [78] *Ibid.*, p. 49.
[79] *Ibid.*, p. 61.   [80] Chap. 3 of *Soundings*.   [81] *Honest to God*, p. 67.
[82] *Ibid.*, p. 71.   [83] *Ibid.*, p. 73.   [84] Chap. 7 of *Soundings*.

of the divine and human in Jesus. The Rev. J. S. Bezzant in "Intellectual Objections"[85] claims that the traditional doctrines of the Trinity and the Incarnation are assailed because we do not know a complete human nature which is not a person and Christ is said to combine two natures in his single personality, while the term "person" is unacceptable in reference to the Trinity for it is an entity "which is neither noun nor adjective."[86]

Traditional explanations of the Atonement also come under considerable fire. Professor D. M. Mackinnon in "Moral Objections"[87] objects to the sadistic implication of the penal substitutionary theory, and the fact that this has sometimes led to a daughter's hope of marriage and personal fulfillment being wrongly "sacrificed" to her aged parents on the analogy of following the Cross. The Rev. Professor G. W. H. Lampe in "The Atonement: Law and Love"[88] similarly criticizes all legalistic conceptions of the Atonement that stress man's attempts to make himself acceptable in God's sight, as a misunderstanding of the Gospel which rightly stresses God's love for men at their worst and their most unacceptable. J. S. Bezzant simply states that the substitutionary concept of Christ's Atonement offends the moral sensibilities of today.

What, then, is to be affirmed as the modern equivalent? Bishop Robinson, taking a leaf from Dietrich Bonhoeffer's book, thinks of the redemptive act of Christ as the work of "The Man for others" who challenges men "to participation in the sufferings of God in the life of the world."[89] For the Rev. H. A. Williams in "Theology and Self-Awareness"[90] the principle of Incarnation is essentially the principle of involvement.[91] The practical implications of this revised creed are stated by the Rev. J. S. Bezzant: "I think it is entirely reasonable for any man who studies the spirit of the facing of life as Christ faced it, and his recorded teaching, to decide that by him he will stand through life, death or eternity rather than join in a possible triumph of evil over him."[92]

These attempts to refashion traditional theology have, of course, come under heavy fire, and this criticism should be considered before going on to review the proposed radical revisions of the

---

85 Chap. 4 of *Objections to Christian Belief*.   86 *Ibid.*, p. 103.
87 Chap. 1 of *Objections to Christian Belief*.   88 Chap. 8 of *Soundings*.
89 Cited *Honest to God*, p. 82, from Bethge, ed., Bonhoeffer's *Letters and Papers from Prison* (2nd edn., 1956), p. 166.
90 Chap. 4 of *Soundings*.   91 *Ibid.*, p. 73.
92 *Objections to Christian Belief*, p. 110.

traditional Christian ethic. Archbishop Ramsey believes that Bishop Robinson's preference of the "depth" image is open to the charge that it hardly does justice to the central element of grace in the Gospel, and he asks: "If there is ultimate reality which is love and personal, does not the initiative come not from us but from thence?"[93] Dr. R. P. C. Hanson believes that transcendence is not adequately interpreted, insisting that for the Bible transcendence is not "metaphysical abstraction or separation, but control."[94] The Rev. Professor H. E. W. Turner is doubtful whether the Atonement can be satisfactorily defined in terms of the acceptance of the unacceptable, since it recalls the old subjectivist interpretation of Justification by Faith "or a Lutheranism run to seed." He insists that the "full formula of 'Justification by Grace through Faith' includes precisely what Tillich and Robinson leave out" and thus there is missing "the powerful action of God in Christ which is the ground . . . of the transforming and liberating experience which Tillich describes."[95]

The second major concern of the Cambridge radicals is to rescue Christian ethics from a perfectionistic escape from the world or from a legalism which caricatures the Christian way as "life-denying rather than life-affirming or life-enhancing."[96] Furthermore, it is exceedingly difficult to appeal with confidence to the three historic authorities which formed the grounds for Christian moral choice: the Bible, a system of theological ethics, and the Natural Law.[97] Dr. Robinson is particularly severe on the old supranaturalist ethics which spoke magisterially of the "sanction of Sinai" or "the clear teaching of our Lord."[98] The Sermon on the Mount, he insists, is not a new Leviticus; rather it provides "illustrations of what love may at any moment require of anyone."[99] He favours a "radical 'ethic of the situation,' with nothing prescribed—except love,"[100] but emphasizes that this will make the most searching demands on the depth and integrity of one's concern for the other on the analogy of the "utterly unselfregarding *agape* of Christ."[101]

This "new morality" is, in fact, an attempt to return to the morality of the New Testament, with its command of love, and to

[93] *Image Old and New*, p. 8.
[94] *The Honest to God Debate*, pp. 108-09.
[95] *Ibid.*, p. 151.
[96] D. M. Mackinnon in *Objections to Christian Belief*, p. 15.
[97] See the careful analysis of these difficulties in G. F. Woods' "The Grounds of Christian Moral Judgments" in *Soundings*, pp. 196ff.
[98] *Honest to God*, p. 109.   [99] *Ibid.*, pp. 110-11.
[100] *Ibid.*, p. 116.   [101] *Ibid.*, p. 119.

St. Augustine's *dilige et quod vis fac*. It will require a revaluation of the conservative ecclesiastical attitude to divorce and remarriage. Mackinnon believes that many of these second unions "have been more abundantly justified by their fruits than the frequently tragic human distress they have replaced."[102]

The most radical interpreter of the new morality is the Rev. H. A. Williams, who believes from his studies in psycho-analysis that much conventional Christian morality is a Pharisaic masquerade and a mockery.[103] On this view, if love is self-giving much of what Christians have called virtue is only cowardice. *Per contra*, much apparent immorality may be genuine self-giving. Williams suggests that the prostitute with the golden heart in the Greek film, *Never on Sunday*, who restores confidence to a troubled young sailor by her physical union with him, performs "an act of charity which proclaims the glory of God."[104]

The third area in which a radical reformation is called for is in the institutional life and especially in the cultus of the Church. Here there is considerable difference of opinion, ranging from some theological revisions desirable in the Book of Common Prayer, which are listed by Professor John Burnaby, to the Rev. H. A. Williams's wholesale condemnation of it as "our incomparably unchristian Liturgy."[105]

It is clear, however, that theological revision of the Prayer Book is required by some of the Cambridge radicals. Professor Burnaby claims that many of the Psalms used in the Liturgy are of the type of *klage-lied* complaints and expostulations which are dominated "by a temper which even the most reckless allegorizing can scarcely baptize into Christianity."[106] He finds that the confession of sins seems "inspired rather by fear of God's implacable justice than by sorrow for the wounding of Divine love."[107] He is not less critical of the sentences ("Man that is born of woman . . .") in the Order for the Burial of the Dead which accompany the committal to the grave—he considers them an offence against the Gospel. Yet he believes that the sacrament of Communion rectifies many theologi-

[102] *Objections to Christian Belief*, p. 14, where he adds, ironically, that "it is impossible to escape the impression that, to certain sorts of clergy, the effective exclusion from sacramental communion of divorced persons who have remarried is the highest form of the Church's moral witness."

[103] See his "Theology and Self-Awareness" in *Soundings*, Chap. 4.

[104] *Ibid.*, p. 81. Mr. Williams uses extreme instances and citations. See also *ibid.*, p. 82, and the Blake citation in *Objections to Christian Belief*, p. 51.

[105] See H. A. Williams, "Unchristian Liturgy," in *Theology* (October, 1958), pp. 401-04.

[106] *Soundings*, p. 236.   [107] *Ibid.*

cal errors, since "the significance of the sacrament is to represent and realize that oneness of life into which the taking of our nature by the Son of God, its bearing through cross and resurrection into the heavenly places, and the coming of the Holy Spirit to be its strength and stay have brought the Creator and his creatures."[108] Clearly Professor Burnaby has a minimal revision in mind.

Although expressed with moderation, Bishop Robinson's views on worship are more revolutionary in their reinterpretation. He is greatly concerned for a "worldly holiness" which will express the holiness in the communal relationships of life. The real function of worship is "to make us sensitive to these depths [meeting Christ in common relationships]; to focus, sharpen and deepen our response to the world and to other people beyond the point of proximate concern (of liking, self-interest, limited commitment, etc.) to ultimate concern; to purify and correct our loves in the light of Christ's love; and in him to find the grace and power to be the reconciled and reconciling community."[109]

It seems that he wishes to apply an ethical test to worship, and thus to minimize its importance as mediating a sense of the glory of God, as instructional in faith, and creative of loyalty to God and to his Church. What he says is: "The test of worship is how far it makes us *more sensitive* to the 'beyond in our midst,' to the Christ in the hungry, the naked, the homeless, and the prisoner."[110] Nonetheless, Robinson advocates the abolition of worship no more than he advocates the abolition of bishops. He is, in fact, urging that even the reforming of worship will be inadequate unless the correlation of the sanctuary with society is made far more explicit. He deplores an unholy escapism, a withdrawal into another world of the spirit, which is often perpetuated by liturgical worship, even of the most dignified or aesthetic type.

He protests with all his command of language against the idea that "the sacramental moments of communion with God are to be expected in the periods of withdrawal, which, like the camel's water, are to see one through the deserts of the day that must otherwise drain one dry."[111] He even wonders, while recognizing that there must be a rhythm of engagement and disengagement in any active life, "whether Christian prayer . . . is not to be *defined* in terms of penetration through the world to God rather than withdrawal from the world to God."[112] It can be expressed most vividly

108 *Ibid.*, p. 237.
110 *Ibid.*, p. 90.
112 *Ibid.*, p. 97.

109 *Honest to God*, pp. 87-88.
111 *Ibid.*, pp. 91-92.

as "preparing in the telephone to meet our God"—that is, to be always open to personal invasion knowing that "persons matter," aware that in our unconditional concern for them we encounter Christ. Such an approach may expose liturgical worship to the most radical revision, provide a prophetic relevance in preaching, and establish a two-way traffic between the Church and the world, as well as encourage much extra-liturgical experimentation in worship and evangelism that would be more natural and less contrived than the present expressions of these perennial tasks of the Christian Community.

All this re-structuring of theology, ethics, and worship, will demand another reformation of the Church of England. Many certainties will have to be given up which were confidently asserted to have been demanded by Christ or the Christian tradition.[113] It is, indeed, a more chastened and charitable Church of England which Dr. Vidler envisions when he speaks of the possibility of a more comprehensive ecclesiastical settlement, which will attempt to satisfy the spiritual, moral, and psychological needs which the state is not competent to meet, and which will "stimulate and defend all those agencies—however little ecclesiastical or ecclesiastical they may be—that minister to the freedom and fulness of man's spiritual life." He concludes his essay on "Religion and the National Church" with a question-mark: "For the Church of England the great question is whether it can be transformed into such a church or is doomed to sink into the position of a religious denomination?"[114] No Church, whether established or disestablished, is likely to gain the loyalty of twentieth century men unless it sees itself in the role not of a master, but of a servant. That clearly is the way the Cambridge Christian radicals visualize the task of the contemporary Community of Christ.

5. Conclusion

As we view the development of theology in England from 1900 to 1965 it may appear to be cyclical rather than linear. For, in the most striking way, the Cambridge radicals are reasserting many of the objections to orthodoxy that Liberal Protestants made at the end of the last and the beginning of the present century. The parallels can be found in the stressing of immanence rather than of transcendence in the doctrine of God, and in the necessity for the Church to be deeply engaged in the struggle for social justice. Dr.

[113] See *Soundings*, pp. 138-39.   [114] *Soundings*, p. 263.

Alec Vidler has rightly paid a belated tribute to the earlier liberals: "Christians in the twentieth century, who on the whole have been less adventurous than the nineteenth century 'liberals' whom they affect to have surpassed, have still much to learn from them."[115] These parallels, however, if alone considered significant, would fail to do justice to the genuine innovations on the theological scene which are distinctive of twentieth century theology in England.

Never has English theology been less insular than in the twentieth century. While it has its own distinctive pragmatism, consonant with the British temper, and in contrast with the more purely theoretical emphasis of non-existential types of theology in Germany, it has been receptive to important foreign influences. German, Scandinavian, French, and American theologians have been read with appreciation. For the point to be appreciated it is necessary only to mention the names of Harnack, Schweitzer, Barth, Otto, Brunner, Bultmann, Bonhoeffer, Kierkegaard, Söderblom, Brilioth, Nygren, Cullmann, the two Niebuhrs, and Paul Tillich. In the process of domestication some of these theological viewpoints lost their sharp and occasionally extreme edges, but the point is that they were taken with very great seriousness and they proved fertile.

In the second place, theology in England has never been so ecumenical as in the present century. This, too, helped to break its insularity, a historic characteristic of English theology, though never of Scottish, which has maintained its links with the Continental Reformed Churches. Thus theology, hammered out in encounter between representatives of different traditions of churchmanship, and published in the form of symposia, has provided a consensus on many major issues that was quite impossible in the nineteenth century.

The third characteristic of the twentieth century in theology, which is true for many other countries besides Britain, is that there is a new-found correlation of Bible, Church, and Liturgy. This is the most significant as well as the most startling phenomenon of the age. It is as if the prodigal intellectual sons who had gone into the far country of culture, and had been dissatisfied with the husks of religious philosophy or the mush of syncretism, returned to appreciate the theocentric faith of the Bible. In rediscovering the Bible, they found it to be the Book of the People of God, and they

[115] *The Church in an Age of Revolution*, pp. 270-71.

learned that their intellectual and critical study of it needed to be nourished by devotion through worship. Whatever the explanation, it became clear that Bible, Church, and Liturgy are three witnesses to the re-creating Word of God, Jesus Christ, and that they belong together.

This has been the century when Christian worship has come into its own, although not without a struggle against the supporters of the "social gospel" who found God better served in the slums than in the sanctuary, or the cultivators of "spontaneity" who would have made their own experience the substitute for the richness of Liturgy's testimony to God through twenty centuries as mediated through many cultures and a variety of theologies. There is no question but that the Liturgical Movement has strengthened theology in the service of the Church, and, through drawing out the social implications of the Liturgy, in service to the world. The importance of the organic conception of the Church and of the social sacraments of its life has never been better understood, nor has the instructional and prophetic practice of preaching and the need for a covenanted commitment to Christ been better appreciated. And, equally important, the sense that both Liturgy and witness require the full participation of the laity is recognized in Catholic and Protestant circles as never before. Not least in importance is the dialogue between Catholic and Protestant which has replaced the shouting across a vast abyss of misunderstanding, and which has been made easier by the "new look" and, indeed, new spirit of Roman Catholicism made evident in the Second Vatican Council. In a period when Christian theology has been subject to powerful intellectual attacks and when almost every Christian Communion in England has declined in numbers and influence these are signs of hope in a crepuscular future.

CHAPTER VI

TRENDS AND TYPES OF PREACHING[1]

I F THE Victorian preacher ascended a pulpit as a crown prince
his throne, the modern preacher quietly enters it as if it were
a witness-box. The era of spellbinders is over. Christianity is
the faith of a minority group in contemporary England.

The modern sermon is twice as quiet and half as long as the
Victorian pulpit discourse. This can be explained partly by the
restriction of the function of the modern pulpit to the communication of the Divine will for men, which eliminates the duty to
provide adult education and entertainment in the pulpit; it is also
partly explicable from the concision and colloquial directness of
speech encouraged by the example of radio and television communication. The tone of the modern sermon, too, is conversational
and confidential. Disraeli's approach to Queen Victoria, not Glad-
stone's, has won the day in pulpit as in Parliament, with the notable
exceptions of Sir Winston Churchill's noble war-time eloquence and
the verbal jousts between him and Aneurin Bevan.

1. Changes during the Century

In the era of the "New Theology"[2] ministers tended to act as if
they were social prophets, alternating between compassion and
indignant denunciation. In consequence their preaching often owed
more to Socialism than to the sacred Scripture. In the succeeding
period there was a revulsion from liberalism to neo-orthodoxy.[3]
No longer was the Church a social settlement, but a colony of
heaven. The Kingdom of God was reconceived, not as a future
utopia towards which all decent men and women were striving,
but as the rule of God, inaugurated by the Apostolic preaching and
in the breaking of bread. This gave a distinctive and elevated
status to the preacher, as he became again the herald of God's
good news, the announcer of the mighty acts of God accomplishing
human salvation. But the preacher also recognized that the Word
of God was mediated by the Sacraments, so that he did not become
too proud.

---

[1] Those who desire a much fuller treatment of this topic are referred to my
Varieties of English Preaching, 1900-1960 (S. C. M. Press, London, and Prentice-
Hall, Inc., Englewood Cliffs, New Jersey, 1963) of which, by the kind permission
of the publishers, this chapter is substantially a condensation.
[2] See Chap. IV *supra*.　　　　　　　　[3] See Chap. V *supra*.

In the most recent period of our century it became increasingly clear that the highest activity of the Christian Church is worship. This recognition brought three consequences in its train. First, worship was hardly ever, as in Victorian days, conceived as a mere preliminary to preaching; as, so to speak, the fruit-cup before the good red steak or "strong meat of the Gospel." It was valued in its own right as a corporate act of loyalty and renewal. Secondly, the Sacraments—as *verba visibilia*—were seen to be, equally with the Word preached, the iron-rations of the pilgrim rather than the truffles of the unusually pious. Finally, there was in recent years a rediscovery of the social imperatives, not only of the Gospel, but also of the service of Holy Communion. The Eucharist was thus seen to be the stimulus to social service,[4] because it re-enacted the Sacrifice of the Eternal Son of God for all humanity and required the members of Christ's Body to offer themselves for others as "a living sacrifice which is your reasonable service." Thus, for the first time since the sixteenth century both Anglicans and Free Churchmen saw preaching and worship as complementary, not competitive. It is peculiarly in this century that the concept and the practice of "Liturgical Preaching" has been revived, although it was well known in the Patristic Age, as the examples of St. Cyril of Jerusalem, St. John Chrysostom, and St. Ambrose amply prove.

2. *The First Type of Preaching*: *Apologetical*

It is inevitable that many of the leading preachers in an age when Christianity is under heavy critical fire or even ignored should become apologists. Such clergy and ministers are necessary to expound and defend the tenets of the Christian faith in the light of modern knowledge. Their essential task is to remove the errors and doubts that stand as barriers to belief, whether these be intellectual, moral, or psychological. Thus they can demonstrate that the Gospel as transforming truth fulfils man's nature and destiny. There is, in consequence, hardly a preacher of note in this century who has not, at least in some of his sermons, either recommended the Christian faith as congruent with reason, or attempted to refashion it semantically or in substance in terms acceptable to the modern mind. To preach otherwise would be to play the part of an ostrich.

This apologetical type of preaching, aiming at stilling doubt

---

[4] *The Second World Conference on Faith and Order* (1938), in the report edited by Leonard Hodgson (p. 233) declared: "The function of the Church is to glorify God in adoration and sacrificial service."

and awakening faith, of which Bishop Butler and F. W. Robertson[5] of Brighton were such admirable exemplars in their times, has attracted the talents of many unusual minds. Among them were the following distinguished Anglicans: William Temple,[6] Archbishop of Canterbury, a considerably better lecturer than preacher; Dean Inge[7] of St. Paul's Cathedral (whose matter was as lively as his manner was deadly); Bishop H. Hensley Henson; Dr. Alec Vidler,[8] Dean of King's College Chapel, Cambridge, and formerly Canon of Windsor; and Professor C. S. Lewis,[9] the inspired layman and littérateur, whose sermons were few but profound in thought and imaginative in expression. Two outstanding Roman Catholic apologetical preachers were Fathers C. C. Martindale and M. C. D'Arcy of the Society of Jesus. The distinguished Free Church apologetical preachers include two Methodists, Dr. Donald Soper, famous for his Tower Hill question and answer sessions, and Dr. Leslie D. Weatherhead; Dr. Townley Lord of Bloomsbury Baptist Church; the Congregationalist, Dr. J. S. Whale,[10] formerly President of Cheshunt College, Cambridge; and Dr. H. H. Farmer, a Presbyterian minister, who occupied the Norris-Hulse Chair of Divinity at Cambridge University.

Of this galaxy of apologetical preachers, three have been chosen for more detailed treatment. Bishop Henson is an example of a keenly independent and trenchantly candid mind, with the broad perspective of an historian,[11] who took great care over the writing of his sermons. Dr. Leslie Weatherhead, apart from being the minister of London's City Temple for a quarter of a century, is a pioneer in correlating Christianity and psychology. Dr. Farmer is a distinguished philosopher of religion, who has been acutely aware of critical attacks on the Christian faith and life from many quarters and of theology's need to grapple with them, as well as being a perceptive writer on the art of preaching.

[5] See my *Worship and Theology in England*, Vol. IV, *From Newman to Martineau*, 1850-1900, pp. 311-22, for an estimate.

[6] Temple's theology is discussed in Chap. IV above, and his preaching in my *Varieties of English Preaching*, pp. 235-47.

[7] Inge's preaching is discussed in my *Varieties of English Preaching*, pp. 80-91, and his theology in Chap. IV of the present volume.

[8] See, in particular, Vidler's *Windsor Sermons*.

[9] Lewis's sermons are discussed in my *Varieties of English Preaching*, pp. 164-78; 186-93.

[10] See Whale's *Christian Doctrine* for a superb series of doctrinal addresses which, like Vidler's *Christian Belief* (1950), were delivered to large gatherings of Cambridge undergraduates.

[11] See the three volumes of his *Retrospect of an Unimportant Life* for a religious critique of our century. His shrewd comments on preaching will be found in Vol. III, pp. 15, 114, 312, 327f., and 331.

3. *The Warrior Bishop*: *H. Hensley Henson*

Herbert Hensley Henson was successively Fellow of All Souls College, Oxford, Head of the Oxford House Settlement in Bethnal Green, Vicar of the vast industrial parish of Barking in Essex, Canon of Westminster and Rector of St. Margaret's (the parish church of the House of Commons), Dean of Durham, Bishop of Hereford, and, finally, from 1920 to 1939, Bishop of Durham. Possessed of a mind of singular independence, which he expressed in the clarity of consummate English prose, he gave himself during a long and distinguished career to the perfecting of his preaching. In consequence, his sermons read better than those of any of his episcopal contemporaries, including William Temple and Charles Gore.

No man was more critical than he of cant and rant in the pulpit. He liked sermons to be lucid demonstrations of central Biblical themes, illuminating the will of God for human duty to which any person of common sense and spiritual insight would immediately respond. Here is sound, solid, clear, reasonable, and practical preaching at its best. Its originality consists in penetrating judgments expressed in pithy and lucid prose.

His sermons are the index of a manly and honest temper, the foe of pretentiousness in Church or State, whether expounded by overweening prelate or arrogant politician. For him the proof of the reality of the creed was the deed done in Christ's name. As Dr. C. A. Alington wrote of him:

> Here, with the warrior bishops of the past
> We lay in peace of that long line the last;
> Unresting soul, predestined from his youth
> To ceaseless combat for the cause of truth . . .
> Still ready to unsheathe against his foes
> The stainless steel of perfect English prose,
> Or launch barbed shafts of epigram and wit
> Which stung to laughter even those they hit: . . . .[12]

His liberality of mind was honoured beyond the confines of the Church of England. He delivered the Lyman Beecher Lectures on Preaching at Yale University in 1909, with the characteristic title, *The Liberty of Prophesying*. In 1935 he delivered the Gifford Lectures at St. Andrews University on Christian Morality.

[12] *Retrospect of an Unimportant Life*, Vol. III, p. vi.

His delay in accepting the yoke of ordination was due to a fear of losing his independence by subscribing to the views of an ecclesiastical party. In this state of mind, he walked to the Norman church of Iffley, stood at the altar of the empty church, and there vowed "that I would never let considerations of my personal reputation and advantage influence my public course." Many years later, reflecting on this decision, he commented: "I was then poor and unknown; I knew that independence, which is the *heritage* of the powerful and wealthy, must be the *trophy* of the poor."[13] Honesty marked every stage of his life. When it was usual to camouflage the acceptance of the principles of Biblical criticism in the pulpit, Henson nailed his colours to the mast, and published the results in *The Creed in the Pulpit*. While fully accepting the Incarnation, he would neither assert nor deny the Virgin Birth, even when the Archbishop of Canterbury pleaded with him to make some statement which would palliate the criticism of his appointment as Bishop of Hereford.

His sermons were prepared with the Greek New Testament open before him. Every word was written out in a careful hand. Even when he preached an old sermon, he almost always rewrote the introduction to make it uniquely applicable to the church he was visiting.[14] In his later years Bishop Henson wondered if, in the midst of his busy administrative life, he had not spent too much time polishing and repolishing his sermons, especially as he had the gift of extemporary speech. His conclusion was that he had no alternative: "Should I be able to face the Judge with a less troubled spirit? Or should I have degenerated into the type, so familiar in the religious world, which is not unfairly described as a WIND-BAG?"[15]

His formidable honesty is tellingly shown in an anecdote. As a retired bishop, Henson was shown to a pew immediately under the pulpit of a fashionable seaside church. Here he had to endure a rhapsodical sermon on the theme that the first Pentecostal experience could be renewed in exact detail, down to experiences of cloven tongues of fire and the gift of speaking in different languages. As Henson left the church, the preacher asked him, "Was I too unorthodox for you?" The bishop replied: "It was not its unorthodoxy which disturbed me, but its incredibility." Later the

[13] *Retrospect*, Vol. I, p. 76.
[14] See the preface by C. J. Stranks to Henson's *Theology and Life*, pp. 7-8.
[15] *Retrospect*, Vol. III, p. 312.

following comment appeared in Henson's journal: "I came away from church with a vivid realization of the chasm that separates popular Christianity, whether Catholic or Protestant, from reasonable religion."[16] Henson, and his friend Inge, were the most eminent representatives of "reasonable religion" in the twentieth century English pulpit.

In his view a good sermon has four essentials: interest, intelligibility, relevance and edification.[17] Interest grasps and holds the attention; intelligibility ensures that the message is understood; relevance is a necessity for effectiveness; and edification assures that the hearer is improved. Henson's own sermons are admirable illustrations of his teaching.

A superficial observer might assume from Henson's brusqueness of manner, and occasional asperity, that he was an intellectual snob. The very opposite was the truth. He simply could not stand pretentiousness, but he had a great affection for natural people. He rightly judged of himself that "Nature had endowed me with a sceptical intellect, a sensitive conscience, a considerable power of self-expression in lucid and incisive speech, and a warm heart."[18] How warm that heart was may be gauged from his observation, after he had attained to the highest offices of the Church of England, that "the happiest years of my ministry were those in which, as the vicar of a great industrial parish, I was nearest to the people. Faces look out at me from the past—toil-worn faces radiant with love and confidence. Nothing of what men foolishly call success is worth comparison with the experiences which those faces recall."[19]

Henson had the intuitive capacity of the great preacher to identify himself with the capacities and interests of his hearers, but without playing down to them. He used quite different approaches when preaching at a great commemorative event in a cathedral or university pulpit, when delivering a "political" sermon to the members of Parliament attending St. Margaret's Church, Westminster, and when preaching to a city or country congregation.

His outstanding qualities as a sermon-maker are evident in every sermon. First he would select a text that aptly summarized his message. Then he would fashion a clear plan for the sermon, making two, three or four firm points. The sentences were almost always brief, and the diction was ever lucid. Every now and then

16 *Retrospect*, Vol. III, pp. 326-27.
17 *Church and Parson in England*, p. 140.
18 *Retrospect*, Vol. I, p. 21.   19 *Ad Clerum*, p. 210.

an incisive statement, frequently barbed, would etch itself on the hearer's memory. Occasionally he offers a startling admonition to the clergy: "If a slumberous habit of almost unconscious indolence is the besetting sin of the largely unemployed rural incumbent, a futile and fussy multiplication of engagements which rather obscures than interprets spiritual duty is the besetting sin of his urban brother."[20] On another occasion he stalked bigger game, as when the bishops assembled for the Fifth Lambeth Conference in 1908 were to receive Holy Communion in Westminster Abbey. In his sermon on that occasion, Henson reminded the congregation: "Our prayer for those Bishops at Lambeth will be the prayer that they may be given grace of denominational self-suppression, that is, the power of a true spiritual perspective, the insight which distinguishes between the essentials and the non-essentials of religion, which recognizes the truth even in novel and unwelcome forms and rises to obey the truth it sees."[21]

Even when his theme is Easter, there is no temptation in Henson to smother the message with lilies. A sermon for Easter Day was entitled, "Easter, the Festival of Other Worldism." Its first two points were the enfranchisement and aspiration that Easter releases, but his third was responsibility. "There is," he wrote, "in the Easter message the note of solemn warning. Beyond the grace stands the Judge, and before Him must be laid open all the secrets of human lives."[22] He was shrewd enough to see the dangers of the "Social Gospel" advocated by partisan parsons, while at the same time recognizing that Christianity brings the gift of social hope, and emphasizes that social service is a religious duty and personal righteousness is the prerequisite for performing effective social service.[23]

Henson was not always the austere prophet. He preached as one who could offer consolation and encouragement. He was also a tutor in spirituality, as his ordination charges published in *Church and Parson in England* demonstrate. For the extraordinarily high quality of his average and incidental sermons, a recent admirable collection, edited by C. J. Stranks and entitled *Theology and Life* (1958) should be consulted.

The analysis of one of these, with the rather unpromising title of "Disinterested Service," may be preferred to further general

[20] *Retrospect*, Vol. III, p. 15. [21] *Westminster Sermons*, p. 95.
[22] *The Creed in the Pulpit*, p. 162.
[23] See *Bishoprick Papers*, p. 180, and *Westminster Sermons*, No. XVIII, "The Social Influence of Christianity."

observations. The text is I Peter 1:8: "Whom not having seen ye love." Henson starts with a reference to a *Hibbert Journal* article by Claude Montefiore, entitled "What a Jew thinks about Jesus." The article relates that Jowett of Balliol said that he could not understand how Thomas à Kempis could feel a personal attachment to a Jesus who had died many centuries previously. It seems odd to Henson that an ordained minister of Christ should find any difficulty in this respect. The transition is then made to St. Peter, who is also intrigued that thousands who have never seen the earthly Christ can love him even through persecution. The secret of the Master's posthumous influence, experienced through all the Christian centuries, is the Resurrection. "Indeed, nothing else can explain it. For the only condition under which personal influence can survive is contact." The proof of the contact is that Christ stamps on his followers the likeness of his own character, so that men cannot "but take knowledge of them that they have been with Jesus."

The Christian character is therefore fully revealed in Christ and derivatively in his followers. His title is a servant and humility is its hall-mark. Public service appeals to the patriotism and pride of men who receive the homage of their contemporaries. But personal service may be unnoticed, and is often unattractive and even repulsive among the poor, the sick, and the unfortunate. It only appeals to those who are filled with disinterested and serviceable love which perpetuates on earth the spirit of Jesus. Religion cannot be presented as a way of gain, otherwise it is deeply secularized, as has happened in America (as de Tocqueville noticed), and is happening in England. Religion is most fitly symbolized by the Cross. Henson closes by retelling an episode recorded in Joinville's *Life of St. Louis* of France, which Joinville heard of when a prisoner among the Moslems. A religious brother saw an old woman carrying a chafing dish of fire in one hand and a cruse of water in the other. She said that she wanted to burn up heaven with fire and quench hell with water so that no one would do right for the reward of heaven or the fear of hell, but just for the love of God. The concluding words of the sermon are: "May God bless this Church with an unfailing succession of loving, devoted men and women who, in face of all difficulties and discouragements, will witness in character and service to the Presence with them of Jesus Christ, 'Whom not having seen, they love.' "

This is a twenty-minute masterpiece on Christian ethics, inspired by Christ's own example. And how typical the breadth of the reading, from mediaeval and modern historical sources, and encompassing the consideration of both Judaism and Islam, if only incidentally.

Henson's dedication to the truth was total, but he made enemies: his truth sometimes could sting like iodine on an open wound. He offended High Churchmen by his criticism of Tractarian exclusiveness and Low Churchmen by his dislike of their heresy-hunting, which he used to describe as the work of the "Protestant underworld." Both the wily ecclesiastical diplomat and the mealy-mouthed time-server regarded Henson as a dangerous prelate. Sometimes it must be acknowledged that he seemed to equate irritability with inspiration, and that the truth was not always spoken in love. But in an age of religious drift, here was a man who swam against the tide and who never mistook *vox populi* for *vox Dei*. For him Christianity was always light and leaven, the illumination of Divine revelation and the transformation of character through Christ.

4. *The Psychological Preacher: Leslie D. Weatherhead*

Dr. Leslie D. Weatherhead, who was born in London in 1893, attained his widest fame as minister of City Temple in the same city from 1936 to 1960. One of England's most popular preachers, he is unrivalled as a ministerial physician of souls and preacher of the integration of personality through Christ and the Beloved Community, the Church. He has pioneered in establishing psychological clinics at Brunswick Methodist Church, Leeds, and at City Temple. His experience as a religious psychologist is based upon thousands of case-histories which have laid bare to him the frustrations, fears, anxieties, and civil wars in the human psyche. He has also made a thorough study of all the scientific and spiritual techniques of healing. His crowning work in this area is *Psychology, Religion and Healing* (1951).[24] As preacher, writer and psychologist Weatherhead has exerted a wide influence.

Weatherhead was perceptive in responding positively to the challenge of what was called the "New Psychology." This took considerable courage, since the founder of psycho-analysis, Sigmund Freud, had written of the prospect for religion as *The Future*

---

[24] It is, as the sub-title indicates, a critical survey "of all the non-physical methods of healing, with an examination of the principles underlying them and the techniques employed to express them, together with some conclusions regarding further investigation and action in this field."

of an Illusion, as if a belief in the Heavenly Father was a symptom of man's unwillingness to stand on his own feet and was only the projection of the comforting illusion of a God on the empty screen of the heavens. Moreover, the assertion of Freud that the sexual instinct was the great driving force in humanity, and the deterministic concepts of the Behaviourists, seem to eliminate the role of religion. Among distinguished psychologists only Jung made place for God. Weatherhead's insight was to turn this potential foe of the faith into an ally.

He has recognized many fruitful insights in psychology with a direct bearing on the Christian life. Both theology and psychoanalysis recognize the paralysing effect of guilt and the unusual importance of confession, but Christianity offers more than acceptance: it offers the forgiveness of God and the restoration of a confident relationship with God and His Church. Weatherhead realizes the positive importance of Christian worship because "in worship, when we express the emotion of admiration for those qualities which God personifies, we are remade in His image, and the more we look away from ourselves to Him, the more we can benefit, paradoxical as it may sound."[25] In true worship the constant emphasis on the unconditional and unchanging love of God to men (as opposed to the hatred that breeds neuroses), the sheer generosity of His grace in Christ (compared with the envy of the sick soul), and the radiant confidence of trust which is faith (contrasted with the suspicion and fear that suppurate in the mind), combine to activate a therapeutic process.

The Christian Church provides a community of altruism as well as a community of appreciation, both of which are essential to the rebuilding of an integrated personality.[26] In sharing the social and missionary work of the Church the introvert becomes outward-looking and the extrovert uses his gifts for the benefit and satisfaction of the needs of others.[27] Weatherhead believes in the great value of intercession for the sick, but complains that this has been exercised in a half-hearted way in the Churches, without imagination and without the confidence of faith.[28] He also holds that preaching aims at providing the very conditions in which a transformation and integration of personality can take place. The Christian com-

[25] *Psychology, Religion and Healing*, p. 453.
[26] *Ibid.*, p. 466. "One of the greatest needs of personality is to be loved."
[27] *Ibid.*
[28] See *ibid.*, p. 241, for the conditions in which this work of the Church in worship can be successfully carried out.

munity hearing God's Word of challenge, consolation, and consecration is the best context for conversion. Here the preacher is enabled by the power of the Holy Spirit to make real the transforming friendship of Christ.[29]

Finally, Weatherhead is not under any illusion that psychologically trained ministers can become little Christs, for "we shall not be able to do the things He did by becoming cleverer psychologists."[30] For Christ's was the supernatural power of the eternal Son of God. In Weatherhead's view the supreme healing power is the Person of Christ himself, which has not been withheld, but unappropriated. His conclusion is: "When the Church returns to her early devotion to Christ and creates united fellowships, even faintly like the small body of men who went out in the power of the risen Christ and His Spirit to turn the world upside down, then a power more potent to heal than any atomic bomb to destroy will once more surge through sick souls and minds and bodies. It will be His own power and recognised as such."[31]

It should be made clear that Weatherhead does not often preach psychological sermons, in the sense that he uses case-studies in the pulpit. *That Immortal Sea* (1953) is an attractive demonstration of his versatility in theme and treatment. Four sermons are concerned with practical problems: acquisitiveness, worry, true and untrue selves, and the confidence necessary to face old age. Four are acute apologetical sermons, one dealing with the forbidding topic of "Foreknowledge, Free Will, and Fate" in which a subtle distinction is made between the direct and the permissive will of God, and another, titled "Is Life a Matter of Luck?" giving the reasons for a belief in a superintending Divine providence. A third is the ironically named "The Advantages of Atheism," which is superbly argued, and the fourth, "Whose Voice shall I Trust?" examines critically the counter-claims of the cynic and materialist in comparison with the claims of the theist. Another group of sermons are movingly evangelical in character, concerned with the unconventional love of Christ, the power of Christ risen who was crucified, and the contrast between human callousness and Christ's total identification with humanity's needs. Other sermons are devotional in character, such as the mystical "This Haunted World."

Another volume of collected sermons, *Over His Own Signature* (1955), was exclusively devoted to sermons of the devotional

---

[29] *Ibid.*   [30] *Ibid.*, p. 78.   [31] *Ibid.*, p. 495.

type. Yet in *The Key Next Door and Other City Temple Sermons* (1960), there are eleven doctrinal sermons, six apologetical sermons, and only two sermons on the spiritual life. Dr. Weatherhead is, therefore, a preacher of many different types of sermon, and he proves himself to be a master-craftsman in every one.

His art conceals art. An analysis of citations, references, and illustrations in his sermons reveals the great breadth of his experience, observation, and reading. In *That Immortal Sea*, for example, there are thirty-one references to personal experience and to encounters with a variety of human callings. They range from boyhood memories of the conversation of "dear old ladies" in a boarding-house to army memories of India where he was a padre. The same volume discloses thirty-seven references to twenty-seven different authors, the most frequent being to Tennyson, Browning, Vaughan and Shakespeare. It is entirely appropriate that a preacher who believes that admiration and reverence are at the heart of worship should return so often to the poets who evoke these very qualities. The third largest class of illustrative material consists of anecdotes, of which there are nineteen in this volume. They open up a horizon to the world that prevents worship from being too introverted, and their subjects range from a Hebridean seaman and sacrificial coal-miners to aeronautical pioneers, an American journalist, and a famous artist. The fourth class of references is to foreign lands, of which there are seventeen. These fulfil a double purpose: as traveller's tales they hold the interest and they keep a local congregation alive to the world. Palestine and India have the priority, because Dr. Weatherhead spent three years in the former and visited the latter. The other groups of references are less important, but also interesting. There are nine references to theologians from Augustine to C. H. Dodd, ten to thinkers as different as von Hügel and Bertrand Russell, nine to ministers and preachers, and three to psychologists.

Like Bishop Hensley Henson, Dr. Weatherhead tries to interpret the New Testament from the Greek text. His exegetical carefulness and philological interest are marked. For example, in his book on the parables, *In Quest of a Kingdom* (1934), there are twenty-eight references to sixteen different Biblical commentators.

What is the secret of success in Britain's most popular preacher? One element is certainly his attractive personality, for the preacher of the primacy of Christ's "transforming friendship" (a favourite term) is himself an excellent example of the candid compassion of the disciple. He is and looks friendly, and can "project" this quality in his preaching in several ways. It may be by the conversational casualness with which he introduces the topic of his sermon, or by the vast number of references to his own personal experience, or by the refusal to use technical theological terms without translation. It may be the use of homely analogies, of colloquial English, and the rare employment of a slang term. It may be the ecumenicity of the man, which is wide enough to admit that God uses religions other than Christianity as avenues to Him.[32] It could be the candour with which old prejudices are dismissed. It is certain that his tenderness, combined with a whimsical humour, play a large part in his appeal. Quite typical is his dislike of the offensive pietist with the bland assurance that he is covered by a Divine insurance-policy, as expressed in the following limerick:

> There was a young lady of Ryde,
> Who was carried away by the tide,
> A man-eating shark
> Was heard to remark,
> "I knew that the Lord would provide!"[33]

Another element in his success is surely his deep sympathy for the difficulties of modern life, his conviction that the dullest lives can have significance through the ennobling grasp of Christ's handshake, and the concentration on understanding and forgiving rather than criticizing. Then, again, Weatherhead has a distinctive quality in his ministry, the insights of the physician of souls, the expert in religious psychology.

His sermons attract in part because they have a clear and memorable structure, and their patterns are very varied. One may be a simple contrast.[34] Another may have a three-fold structure.[35] Yet another will have four points.[36] One, greatly daring, has no less than twelve different conclusions to drive home.[37] This is, whatever the structure, *vertebral* and flexible planning.

[32] *The Key Next Door*, pp. 152ff. It may be observed that Dr. Weatherhead in a letter to the author (dated June 19, 1961) kindly indicated that he thought his best sermons were to be found in *The Key Next Door*, *That Immortal Sea*, and *Over His Own Signature*.

[33] *Ibid.*, p. 114.

[34] As in "Babel or Jerusalem?" contrasting the chaos of Babel with the unity of the primitive Christian community at Pentecost.

[35] As in "Whose Voice shall I Trust?" elaborating three competing viewpoints.

[36] As in "Master and Lord" which has four arguments to establish the Divinity of Christ.

[37] "The Advantages of Atheism," where the twelve "incredibles" for the atheist are twelve questions unanswerable on this hypothesis, but credible on the Christian hypothesis.

Another quality of Weatherhead's is a great gift for putting abstract thought into direct speech and into concrete images. Allied to this is his possession of a strong visual imagination, romantically inclined. Almost every book-title of his conveys a clearly defined image. He has an almost Wordsworthian delight in landscape. The attraction (and danger) of this gift may be appreciated by citing one of his passages, describing the vision of the exiled John of Patmos watching the dawn by the seashore:

"Above him the stars flashed like gems in the splendour of the velvet night, at its darkest just before the dawn. It was early on the Lord's day and he longed to worship with those he had been compelled to leave. He turned towards Jerusalem far in the east, and behold the darkness was breaking. He had had his back to it, gazing mournfully at the black, hostile sea as yet unillumined by the dawn. But now the great splendour had begun. The colour spread across the sky. Daffodil first with gleams of pale green and primrose light, then the faintest pastel pink deepening to crimson and gold. John thought of the temple in Jerusalem catching the gleams in its golden dome as God's day of worship began. As a great wave crashed behind him, he turned at the noise and it seemed to shout to him, in a trumpet voice of majesty and assurance, 'I am Alpha and Omega, the first and the last.' "[38]

He is happier in less ambitious effects, and has a talent for vivid, homely analogies. For example, he translates the urgent relevance of the term "Gospel" as follows: " 'Good news,' said a friend of mine, 'is that which can be shouted across a street.' Thus—The war's over! The baby's born! Susan's out of danger! The strike's settled! Here is my bit of good news for you: *God will receive you—Now!*"[39]

Most important of all the secrets of Weatherhead's success is that he selects the central Christian themes and relates them to the daily needs of men and women. Thus psychology's diagnosis and theology's message complement each other perfectly. Weatherhead never fails to see the striking generosity of God's seeking and saving love in Christ for the least and the lost. The Atonement receives full treatment in both *Personalities of the Passion* (1942)

[38] *Over His Own Signature*, pp. 142-43. This is all-too-artificial "Vistavision" writing, but suitable for popular purposes. More sensitive writing would have avoided the archaism of "behold," the ugly repetition of "had had," and the commonplace "gazing mournfully," and would have toned down the more blatant "gorgeous Technicolor" effects. But it is thoroughly in line with the Madison Avenue manner of television advertising.

[39] *In Quest of a Kingdom*, p. 73.

and *The Plain Man Looks at the Cross* (1945). It is chiefly as Friend, Healer, and Saviour that Weatherhead interprets Christ, though occasionally as Guide, Revealer, Pioneer, and Teacher.

Despite his undoubted qualities, an honest appraisal of Dr. Weatherhead would have to take into account his occasional falls from tenderness to sentimentality and mawkishness.[40] There is little that is prophetic in his preaching, and almost nothing in the way of announcing a coming kingdom of social justice, or any realization that the very structures of classes and nations and institutions are infected with group egotism. There is, in fact, too much consolation and too little criticism in his preaching.

His greatest achievements are to have pioneered in the religious use of psychology, and to have gathered, held, and sustained so scattered and socially variegated a congregation as that of the City Temple[41] through unusually testing times, and to have commended to them the Gospel with singular freshness, clarity, compassion, and relevance for a quarter of a century.

5. The Preacher as Philosopher and Theologian: Professor H. H. Farmer

Like Bishop Henson, Professor Farmer had the rare distinction of being appointed to a Gifford Lectureship and to the Lyman Beecher Lectureship on Preaching at Yale University. Thus, it is widely acknowledged that he has a profound mind, combined with an enviable gift for terse and vivid expression. His developing thought has mirrored the transition of the century from a philosophical to a Biblical theology.

In his *Servant of the Word* (1941), Professor Farmer has shown how theology in its more recent developments has magnified the responsibility and the privilege of preaching. The importance of the "Christ-event"—the unguessable, historically given, Church-creating event of the advent of Jesus Christ which transforms alienated men and women into the people of God's own purpose—has been re-emphasized by modern theologians. The re-telling of

---

[40] In a Christmas sermon he speaks of the strangeness of the gifts of the Magi for the Christ-child and asks: "I do not mean to be in the least irreverent, but did no one give Him a soft, woolly, cuddly toy, the ancient equivalent of a teddy-bear? Did no one give Him a rattle? Did no one treat Him as a little baby thing?" (*The Key Next Door*, p. 213).

[41] In the preface to *The Significance of Silence*, Dr. Weatherhead writes that his congregation includes "a cabinet minister, and others of rank, position and authority, and also the lowliest and the poorest—people who have been unemployed, people who have been in prison." In days of peace it was not unusual to find fourteen different nationalities represented at one service.

that event, or series of events, accompanied by the power of the Holy Spirit, re-creates the new community, the Church. Such is the recognition of both Bultmann and Tillich.

A second modern emphasis has been on "realized eschatology" and is particularly associated with Dr. C. H. Dodd. This stresses that God's mighty saving act began in Christ's coming, and God's campaign was won in principle in the Cross and Resurrection. In this view all preaching is apostolic, and bearing witness to Christ's saving act is itself part of the act of salvation.

The third modern emphasis is on religion as "encounter" between the "I" of God and the "Thou" of man addressed by God. This has been central to the thought of the distinguished Jewish philosopher, Dr. Martin Buber, and its impact on the thought of Professor Farmer has been deep.[42] Farmer insists that God confronts men as "absolute demand" and "final succour." The necessity of preaching, therefore, is to confront men with God's absolute claim on men whom He has destined to live in eternal fellowship with himself in holy love, and to declare his grace available for their help. Moreover, this assistance comes to human beings, not as isolates, but as interdependent persons, and through the agency of others.

This radical personalism carries notable consequences for the practice of preaching. In the face-to-face encounter between preacher and congregation, the reading of sermons and the use of rhetoric, as of superfluous adjectives and quotations, are to be rejected. And because God's supreme Word to man was the *Word-made-flesh*, who went about doing good, concrete language and vigorous verbs are necessary in preaching, in lieu of cloudy abstractions. The manipulation of personality is wholly to be rejected.

No one has stressed more strongly than Farmer the need to correlate the Gospel to human need.[43] Preaching must awaken men out of their dispirited sense of the futility of human existence by affirming "a divine purpose in history which a man is called to serve here and now and yet which transcends history in its final consummation." Men feel that they are ciphers in the depersonalized industry of today and in the vast ant-like aggregations of apartments and new housing developments. They need the assur-

[42] See Farmer's *The World and God, Towards Belief in God, God and Men*, and *Revelation and Religion*.
[43] See Chap. 5 of *The Servant of the Word*.

ance of Christ's promises that the eternal purpose is a design of love for the individual. In the third place, modern men long for security and this is satisfied by the Christian doctrine of providence. They also know of the tremendous powers of evil and irrationality. The Christian message asserts that there is a Cross at its heart and yet Divine love wins its way through the horrors of sin and suffering. Finally men need an absolute in conduct and they find it in the call to loyal discipleship by Christ. Farmer rightly concludes that "our preaching has to be strongly doctrinal . . . in such wise that doctrine and life are seen to be inseparably bound up together."[44] But equally "the strongest apologetic, so far as teaching and preaching are concerned, is always a sound dogmatic."[45]

As an apologist there are admirable qualities in Professor Farmer. He never misrepresents the views which he criticizes. He faces with the utmost candour the criticisms levelled against Christian doctrine. But equally he expects his opponents to take Christian views with basic seriousness. He has little time for the critic of Christianity who only brings with him a "casual, flippant, feet-on-the-mantelpiece attitude." The latter attitude, states Farmer, is as irresponsible as if a man should "set up as a judge of dramatic art on the basis of once having seen in his youth a Punch and Judy show."[46]

The value of Professor Farmer's books and sermons is that they take cognizance of the criticisms of Christianity from the side of the physical and social sciences, as well as from the field of the comparative study of religion. These criticisms are elaborated and answered to the full in *Towards Belief in God*. Since God is ultimate reality which is the source and ground of all being, His existence does not admit of *demonstrative* proof. He is always "Eternal Thou" and therefore always "subject" and never "object." Moreover, God is disclosed not in abstract argument but in action and decision.[47] The arguments which he offers in reply to a multitude of criticisms of Christianity are too many to be capable even of summary treatment. It must, therefore, suffice to say that no modern theologian has looked more thoroughly and honestly at the case against Christianity before attempting to state the case for it. Apologetics of this kind enable Professor Farmer to rid the ground of the chief obstacles to faith, and his two vol-

---

[44] *The Servant of the Word*, p. 143. [45] *God and Men*, p. 14.
[46] *Ibid.*, p. 17. [47] *Towards Belief in God*, pp. 31-38.

umes of sermons express his positive convictions as to the nature and content of the Christian faith.

The first volume, *Things Not Seen* (1927), reveals the theocentric approach of a religious philosopher, and the second, *The Healing Cross* (1941), the Christocentric approach of a Biblical and systematic theologian. In the first volume religion is considered in terms of adjustment and integration, in the conviction that Christianity "can make men more poised, more harmonious, more strong, more dignified, more hopeful, more at peace with themselves, even in the present restricted and inadequate world."[48] The second volume, however, considers Christianity in theologically pragmatic terms. As the Preface indicates, the Christian message consists in setting forth the Christian way "in the life of individual discipleship, in the faith and hope that those given a new or renewed understanding of that way may be moved by the Spirit of God to make, or remake, their choice to walk therein come what may."[49] The later volume also contains a new, astringent note, calling "to adventure, to danger, to heroic and costing enterprise."[50] The difference between the two volumes corresponds to the change from a revelational and philosophical centre to a redemptional and theological foundation, characteristic of the most thoughtful religious minds of the day.

Farmer, like Inge and Henson, has the gift for incisive statement and he can mint memorable epigrams. As samples, the following may be cited from *Things Not Seen*. "A dumb God spells a dead faith." "Without religion morals easily become manners." "A good character is just as likely to get crucified as to get a peerage." "The Cross was . . . a parable in flesh and blood."[51] *The Healing Cross* includes the following epigrams as true as they are brilliant. "Christ's work is not merely to satisfy need, but to show us what our needs are." "Suffering must be a vocation before it can be a victory." "The Kingdom of God is love, it is not gush." "The temple of faith . . . is only well-built when it is built on the very edge of the pit of self-distrust." And there is the contrast between the Incarnation and the Cross: "The Babe symbolizes the weakness of divine love as it were in repose; the Cross is the weakness of divine love in action."[52]

---

[48] *Things Not Seen*, p. 23.   [49] *The Healing Cross*, p. x.
[50] *Ibid.*, p. ix.
[51] The citations are to be found, respectively, on pp. 36, 67, 102, and 161.
[52] The citations are to be found, respectively, on pp. 117, 140, 146, 9 (twice), and 100.

It will be recalled that Farmer urged preachers to use concrete and vivid language. Not only his epigrams, but also his metaphors and similes are proof that he keeps his own precepts. There are seventeen images in *Things Not Seen*, and twenty-six in *The Healing Cross*, some of them strikingly original. One of them conceives of God as some transcendent customs officer bidding the soul for the common good to hold nothing back and declare everything, while immortality is distinguished from the radical re-creation involved in Resurrection by being termed a mere "roof-garden" idea, and the Kingdom of God is said to be misconceived as a garden city.

One sermon ought to be analysed to show the depth of thought and admirable expression in Professor Farmer's preaching. It is the eleventh sermon in *The Healing Cross*, and its title is "Justice and the Gospel." The text is Isaiah 45:21, "A just God and a Saviour." The theme is a comparison of the functions, the moods, the directions, and the agents of justice and love and their need of one another.

The sermon begins by a reference to two images on the London skyscape: the great cross surmounting the dome of St. Paul's Cathedral and the figure of Justice, eyes bandaged and scales in her hands, which tops the Central Criminal Court on Ludgate Hill. Both cathedral and court are concerned with sin, but while detection and punishment is the aim of the law, forgiveness is the aim of the Gospel. Justice is coldly impartial in mood, whereas the Gospel is warmly personal. Justice looks to the criminal's past and the Gospel to the sinner's future. Justice compels, while the Gospel persuades.

The second part of the sermon argues that the distance between law and Gospel is too great. It is bad for justice. Justice, separated from the Gospel, isolates the sinner too much from his fellows and the criminal knows that justice is not done. Justice also isolates the guilty man's act from himself, and all his hopes, struggles, and inner bent.

The third section of the sermon insists that the separation is bad for the Gospel. Apart from justice the Gospel is apt to speak of love both divine and human as ignoring and overlooking sin. This is to forget that the divine forgiveness "searches and pursues and tears out and exposes all the evil in us every bit as ruthlessly as the detectives and the prosecuting counsel of the Central Criminal

Court."[53] An admirable illustration follows from G. K. Chesterton's criticism of Jerome's *The Passing of the Third Floor Back* as presenting the Redeemer not as a divine detective, but as a divine dupe. The conclusion is that while the Gospel is always the declaration of the utterly gracious and undeserved goodness of God to us, equally it is an affirmation of the severity of God, eradicating evil from men, "severe because it is good" and "good because it is severe."

This sermon is a model of clarity in profundity and of the making concrete of highly abstract concepts by the use of the two architectural images as symbols. The divisions are clear and logical, and the conclusion is eminently reasonable. It is quite typical of Dr. Farmer's preaching that it nobly fulfils the canons to which he believes modern preaching must conform. The message of the Gospel must have cosmic dimensions or it will be "too small to be true." It must be expressed with a strong agnostic note running through it to emphasize the mystery of God or it will be "too confident to be true." The note of austerity must be heard in challenge and demand or it will be "too easy to be true." Finally, it must be presented in the context of social solidarity and as the Gospel of the Universal Church.[54]

Two relatively minor criticisms are suggested by Dr. Farmer's sermons. The first is that in his determination to avoid all artificiality in diction and in his disdain for rhetoric, he is hiding under a bushel a poet's gift for creating original images. This quality, so evident in his first volume of sermons, is suppressed by a Calvinist hand in the second volume.[55] The same austerity may also be responsible for the marked concision and terseness of his second volume, which hardly allows time for his points to be taken in by the congregation.[56]

The abiding qualities of Professor Farmer's sermons are their explication of a vertebral Biblical theology, their candidness in accepting the pressure of modern day intellectual difficulties, and their relevance in presenting the Gospel to the modern mind.

6. *The Second Type of Preaching: Expository*

If the most typical twentieth century type of preaching is that

[53] *The Healing Cross*, p. 111.
[54] The points made in this paragraph are elaborated by Farmer in the Preface of *The Healing Cross*.
[55] See *Things Not Seen*, p. 53.
[56] This is probably due to the fact that his first volume came from years of experience in the ministry, while the second emerges from the professor's study.

of the apologist, who states the case for Christianity in the light of the criticisms brought against it, the most traditional type of preaching is expository, a sustained exposition of the sacred Scriptures. Its aim is to awaken and confirm faith. It requires of the preacher a disciplined subjection to the authority of revelation so that he may declare the mighty acts of God for the liberation of the human race from its slavery to egotism, anxiety, futility, frustration, suffering, and the fear of death. Through a large part of the present century this type of preaching fell into abeyance, partly because it was associated with an older view of Biblical inspiration, and partly because liberal accommodations of the faith found it more convenient to take a text as a pretext, than to pretend to expound a passage of Scripture. Apologetical, ethical, or topical sermons were the rage. Hence the expository sermon was, for the most part, considered *passé*.

The great exception to the rule was George Campbell Morgan, an autodidact, whose Biblical sermons and lectures were extraordinarily popular on both sides of the Atlantic. First in Westminster Congregational Chapel from 1904 to 1914, and from 1943 to 1953, Campbell preached to crowded morning and evening services, and at his Friday Night Bible School he lectured to between 1,500 and 2,000 eager students of the Scriptures.[57] His conviction was that "the preacher is not merely asking a congregation to discuss a situation, and consider a proposition, or give attention to a theory. We are out to storm the citadel of the will and to capture it for Jesus Christ."[58] He knew the supreme source-book of the Christian faith better than most men of his day. For example, he would never attempt to expound a book of the Bible until he had read it in the original language and in English at least fifty times.[59] He proved conclusively the varied spiritual wealth that is at the disposal of the preacher who mines the deep lodes of the Scriptures. Dr. J. D. Jones, a more gracious preacher, exercised a long and distinguished ministry at Richmond Hill Congregational Church, Bournemouth, by strong exegetical preaching.

What is of special interest is the general return to expository preaching in the last two decades of the period as a result of the Biblical and theological revival. There is no question that this

---

[57] See John Harries, *G. Campbell Morgan, The Man and His Ministry*, p. 91.
[58] *Ibid.*, p. 245. The alternatives which he rejected were precisely those offered by many a minister in the Liberal Protestant tradition.
[59] *Ibid.*, p. 199. The fruits of these lectures were gathered in a series of volumes, collectively entitled *The Analysed Bible* (10 vols.).

is not only deeply necessary but also that it is widely appreciated. At the present time the two largest congregations in London have been gathered by expository preachers. One is the congregation of Westminster Congregational Chapel under the ministry of a former Harley Street physician, Dr. Martyn Lloyd-Jones,[60] and the other is All Souls', Langham Place, where the Rector is the Rev. John R. W. Stott.[61] It is also significant that a College of Preachers was recently established by the Church of England under the directorship of the Rev. D. W. Cleverly Ford, the author of *An Expository Preacher's Notebook* (1960). The latter, indeed, provides a strong justification for the return to expository preaching on the grounds that the Bible is the Church's primary sourcebook, that liturgical worship is essentially Biblically informed, that Biblical preaching "sustains the Pulpit" and the people, and enables the minister "to speak with an authority without which his preaching is insipid."[62]

7. *Evangelical Greatheart: Dr. W. E. Sangster*[63]

As might be expected, it is the preachers of the evangelical tradition, both in the Anglican Communion and in the Free Churches, who have been the most faithful expository preachers. It is fitting that an outstanding Methodist preacher, Dr. W. E. Sangster, should be selected as a representative of this tradition, because the Methodist Church has a special concern for evangelism. This concern has found splendid expression in the Central Halls of the larger English cities, and Dr. Sangster was from 1939 to 1955 the minister of the Methodist Central Hall, Westminster.

His preaching method was not like that of Campbell Morgan, the running exposition of lengthy passages of Scripture. Rather he explained the central Biblical themes in a breathtakingly rapid and succinct way. He differs from Morgan as telegrams from treatises; his sermons are very like "greetings telegrams," admirably embroidered with imagery which does not detract from the urgency of his communication of the good news. If theologically conservative, he is well read in philosophy, history, and literature.

Born in 1900 of working class parents in the east end of London, he became a local preacher while serving in the British Army dur-

---

[60] See Lloyd-Jones' *Studies in The Sermon on the Mount.*
[61] See Stott's *Basic Christianity* and *Preacher's Portrait.*
[62] P. 14.
[63] See the excellent biography, *Doctor Sangster*, written by his son, and the vivid pamphlet *W.E.S., A Daughter's Tribute* (1960).

ing the First World War, where his hobby was boxing. The Army taught him admiration for the courage of the average British Tommy and developed his natural gift for friendship. After taking theological training at Richmond Methodist College, affiliated with the University of London, he served various circuits in North Wales, and was called to succeed Leslie Weatherhead at Brunswick Church, Leeds. His most responsible charge was at Westminster, where he succeeded another evangelical preacher, Dr. T. Dinsdale Young. He came to Westminster in the inauspicious month of August, 1939, and exercised a memorably courageous ministry during the Second World War, when London experienced a mass evacuation of population and the ordeal of air-bombardment. He continued in Westminster Central Hall until 1955, when he was appointed to direct the Home Mission Department of the Methodist Church. He died in 1960 after two years of suffering, with exemplary courage, the inexorable approach of muscular atrophy. One Easter Day, at the end of his life, being unable to walk or even to speak, he wrote to his daughter: "It is terrible to wake up on Easter morning and have no voice with which to shout, 'He is risen!'—but it would be still more terrible to have a voice and not want to shout."[64]

Only a few months after Sangster began his work in London the bombing began. Central Hall's vast basement was reinforced and it was then thrown open to the homeless folk from the slums of Pimlico, hundreds of whom were to have no other home for the duration of the war. Sangster and his family insisted on making their home there also and in occupying only one cramped room. This they shared for five long years. It was typical of Sangster's compassion and his realism. His wife organized a canteen and thus supplied economical food each night. Sangster himself moved in and out among the shelter-dwellers, with unfailing zest and interest, telling his anecdotes with incomparable verve. "Service before services" was his motto. He refused to cram religion down the throats of a captive audience. Soon, however, he was asked to conduct evening prayers, and these, with a weekly lecture on current affairs and a Sunday concert, were the highlights in the life of that vast basement shelter.[65] On Sundays Sangster preached to enlarging congregations representative of almost the entire social spectrum. Most surprising among the achievements of these years

[64] W.E.S., A Daughter's Tribute, p. 13.
[65] Ibid., pp. 8-9.

was the successful preparation of a doctoral dissertation for the University of London, subsequently published as *The Path to Perfection*, mirror of Sangster's absorbing and catholic interest in spirituality and his conviction that life's supreme quest is for holiness.

If Dr. Sangster was a pietist, he was one with three differences from most others. He knew well enough that men and women needed to be reformed, but he also recognized that economic and social disabilities stunt personality's growth. He had an infectious gaiety and no one could consider this perfect mimic a spoil-sport. Moreover, the range of his reading and hobbies (hill-climbing and visiting ancient abbeys and castles) were those of a man of culture.

He was happy to accept Bernard Manning's definition of a sermon as "a manifestation of the Incarnate Word, from the Written Word by the Spoken Word."[66] He wished to sustain expository preaching because so much of the preaching of the day was marginal, receiving its direction from the daily newspapers rather than from the eternal Good News. He recognized the importance of Christian instruction in doctrinal preaching, but believed that the ultimate task of the preacher was to capture the will. Often his doctrinal sermons ended with an appeal for commitment; but he would be the last to suggest that a preacher should, like an evangelical alarm clock, always be striking for decisions. His most notable sermons fall into two categories: doctrinal and devotional, and, because he used the Christian Year to the full, he was easily able to combine these qualities, as his two volumes of *Westminster Sermons* (1960, 1961) clearly manifest.

One who has read other expository preachers cannot but contrast the crisp, urgent brevity of Sangster's sermons. Other expository preachers, as Pope's characterization of the Alexandrine, are like a wounded snake dragging its slow length along. Sangster's dart, like the snake's tongue, goes directly to the target. He has no prolonged introductions (a failure of that otherwise superb Scottish evangelical preacher, Professor James S. Stewart), or concluding perorations (like the Victorian pulpit orators). Hardly less striking are the vividly fresh and apt illustrations. A New Year sermon, intriguingly titled "Remember to Forget," bids his congregation

---

66 Sangster cites this definition in his *Craft of the Sermon*, p. 25. It is derived from B. L. Manning's *A Layman in the Ministry*, p. 138.

forget their tactlessness, their sins, and the insults they have received during the past year. It ends thus:

> It was Christmas in my home. One of my guests had come a couple of days early and saw me sending off the last of my Christmas cards. He was startled to see a certain name and address. 'Surely, you're not sending a greeting to *him*,' he said.
> 'Why not?' I asked.
> 'But you remember,' he began, 'eighteen months ago.'
> I remembered, then, the thing the man had publicly said about me, but I remembered also resolving at the same time, with God's help, that I would remember to forget. And God had 'made' me to forget!
> I posted the card.[67]

Sangster has only to announce his text, 2 Corinthians 5:8 (RV), "At home in the Lord," when he immediately captures the hearer's interest with a rapid account of the homing instincts of birds, beasts, fish, and (by analogy) of men. His rich apparatus of references and illustrations derives from such varied sources as biographical incident, visits to antiquities or foreign lands, natural science, classical and romantic English poetry, the great saints of the Christian centuries, and his own observations and experiences. He can comb recondite sources for his illustrations: when he is insisting that the State cannot legislate people into goodness, he cites Bernard Bosanquet's *The Philosophical Theory of the State* with its conclusion that all the State can do is "to hinder the hindrances to the good."[68] A distinctive quality of Sangster's is the frequent citation of a verse from the hymns of Watts or Wesley as an apt summary of belief or avowal of loyalty. This lyrical note is rarely absent from his preaching.

His concentrated sermons are always marked by a clear and memorable structure. In a sermon on Christ as the Master of Time, for example, the sub-divisions and lessons are: the past is not dead; the future is not ours; now is the acceptable time.[69] Another excellent sermon, "Four Judgments on Jesus," is based on four New Testament records of evaluations of Jesus, as devil-possessed, a good man, the Christ, and culminating in the confession of Thomas, "My Lord and my God."[70]

Another quality in Sangster's sermons is the frequent appear-

[67] *Westminster Sermons*, Vol. I, p. 10.   [68] *Ibid.*, p. 29.
[69] *Ibid.*, p. 136.   [70] *Ibid.*, Vol. II, sermon 3.

ance of an inspired phrase, vivid word-picture, or striking epigram. Referring to the parable of the Good Samaritan, Sangster observes, "Jesus took that term [Samaritan] from the vocabulary of the brothel and made it adjectival of the saints."[71] One sentence is all the space he needs to sum up the folly of materialism, describing the man whose skeleton was found in Pompeii's volcanic ash clutching trinkets: "He ran back for the bangles and lost his life."[72] There is also his moving title for a sermon on Christ's going up to Jerusalem: "His Destination is on His Face." Equally characteristic is his terse comment on the right response to the Lordship of Christ: "It isn't cheer; it's discipleship. It isn't admiration; it's consecration."[73] He had a genius for finding a profound message in most unpromising texts.

Considering the gaiety and courage of his life, and the magnetism of his affectionate personality, it is no surprise to read his tribute to his Westminster congregation: "They sit without intellectual pride and their faces light up as your points register in their mind. To serve such people—and God through them—is a privilege of which no man is worthy."[74] Sangster served his people splendidly in his vigour, compassion, and consecration. His weaknesses were an occasional tendency to use highly technical language, without translating it, and on the rarest occasions an insensitive reference.[75] Nor did he always resist the temptation of the popular preacher—sensationalism.

These faults are trivial in comparison with the basic integrity of this preacher of a universal Gospel, his Christian spirituality, and his deep compassion, who in his final illness trod the most difficult steps of the path to perfection. He knew that if he did not submit himself to the Word of God he would be overreaching himself.

8. *The Third Type of Preaching: Charismatic*

The third function and type of preaching is to teach the holy love of God as to elicit the response of adoration. Many varieties of preaching can be included in this type. Some preachers, like the Congregationalist, Dr. J. H. Jowett,[76] are first and foremost

---

71 *Ibid.*, Vol. I, sermon 5.   72 *Ibid.*, Vol. II, p. 40.
73 *Ibid.*, p. 43.   74 See *ibid.*, Vol. I, preface.
75 *Ibid.*, Vol. II, p. 94 for an unexplained reference to the fourth dimension. See also Vol. II, p. 19, for the reference to "mankind crucified on a clock."
76 For an appreciation of Jowett, see my *Varieties of English Preaching*, pp. 35-63.

exponents of Christ-mysticism. While other ministers noisily debated the reconstruction of doctrine and the so-called "New Theology," or the reconstruction of society according to the imperatives of the "Social Gospel," Jowett emphasized the central importance of the culture and discipline of the spiritual life. His remarkable volume of sermons in this genre, *The Transfigured Church* (1910), was fifty years ahead of its time, for it diagnosed the weakness of the Church as due to a lack of awe in the conception of God, and to a severe limitation in its understanding of the nature of brotherhood which had led to the loss of the artisans. His claim that the Church needed a theological, liturgical, and social reformation showed astonishing foresight. In his way he was a forerunner of Otto and Casel.

Another fine preacher in the same tradition was the Methodist minister, A. E. Whitham, who had a feeling for the Incarnation, the Sacraments, and a Catholic Christianity that was rare in the English Free Churches. Both Jowett and Whitham knew that Christianity has to be caught as well as taught, and they succeeded in conveying some measure of the grace of God in Christ, by the graciousness of their manner.

9. Very Human Divines: "Dick" Sheppard and "Woodbine Willie"

The two most notable charismatic[77] preachers of the twentieth century in England were, however, "Dick" Sheppard, the famous Vicar of St. Martin-in-the-Fields, called "the parish church of the British Empire,"[78] and Geoffrey Studdert Kennedy, the most popular British padre of the First World War, known as "Woodbine Willie."

If Bishop Phillips Brooks' definition of preaching as "truth through personality" is accepted, it follows that the charismatic preacher is a man of absolutely transparent candour, and a striking personality almost wholly subordinated to God. These were, in fact, the outstanding characteristics of Sheppard and Studdert Kennedy. After the fearful disillusionment that set in after the

---

[77] In the Greek of the New Testament the term *Charis* and its various derivatives refer to the "Grace" of God in Christ and, in a secondary sense, to those persons who are "gracious," because grace-endued. It is in the latter sense that the term is used in this section to mean more than merely dynamic, though Sheppard and Studdert-Kennedy were dynamic.

[78] So called because it is situated in Trafalgar Square where so many Commonwealth countries have the offices of their High Commissioners, and because the overseas religious broadcasts of the British Broadcasting Corporation originated from St. Martin's.

end of the First World War, a merely traditional faith expounded by a complacent Anglican clergyman would have seemed as irrelevant as episcopal gaiters or mediaeval gargoyles. These two men, with perhaps the addition of the co-founder of Toc H, "Tubby" Clayton, and Canon W. H. Elliott, were the only ones who could win and sustain the trust of the disenchanted masses of Englishmen. The fact that Studdert Kennedy was given the bitter-sweet nickname of "Woodbine Willie" by the privates of the British Expeditionary Force in France, and that Hugh Richard Lawrie Sheppard was generally known as "Dick," was proof of their affectionate acceptance by the common man.[79]

Sheppard and Kennedy were in many respects alike. They were colleagues for a time in St. Martin-in-the-Fields. Both were the sons of Anglican clergy. Both had experiences of living among the desperately poor. And both suffered from asthma, and died before their time, exhausted by the spendthrift outpouring of nervous energy required by their ministry to the poor and perplexed. In temperament also, they were alike. Both scorned pretentiousness. Both were intensely generous in time, money, and possessions to the point of quixotry. Both had an irrepressible joy. Both were men of incandescent integrity, genuine humility, and unshakable courage.

They also held a common understanding of their preaching task. They determined to rescue the pulpit from professional or sanctimonious jargon. They were equally concerned to free the teaching of the Church of England from social and political conservatism. Finally, both were eager to present Christ to their people as the companion of men and women in their hardships and sufferings, and as the inspiration for heroic living. Each was a prophet in presenting the Divine revelation as the antidote to popular lies and delusions. Each was also the true priest and confessor, finding his courage, example, and strength in the Sacrament of Holy Communion.

In other ways they differed. Sheppard might be the author of *The Impatience of a Parson*, but he was not half as impatient and impetuous a rebel as Kennedy. Both used colloquialisms in the pulpit, but "Woodbine Willie" never tamed his language, even

[79] It is only a slight exaggeration to state with Ernest H. Jeffs in *Princes of the Modern Pulpit*, p. 155, that "What saved the Church of England, so far as the respect and liking of the masses was concerned, were the personalities and work of two young rebels against ecclesiastical convention—'Dick' Sheppard and 'Woodbine Willie.'"

for the most exquisite or exalted ears. Kennedy used slang, often expletives, and could be counted on to keep the desultory hearer awake by a barrage of explosive terminology. Kennedy was also the more thoughtful radical. He believed that Patripassionism (the doctrine that God the Father suffers) was less a heresy than the essential meaning of the Gospel. While Kennedy used shock tactics, Sheppard tried to coax his hearers into the Kingdom of God.

Sheppard was the model parish priest in St. Martin's for twelve trying years. Kennedy was also an excellent parish priest, but the interruption of the War gave him opportunities as a chaplain which his virile faith coveted most. Sheppard was the successful pioneer of religious broadcasting and his intimate and confidential technique made his ministry at St. Martin's known to thousands upon thousands whom he would never meet. Kennedy, while personally among the most compassionate of men, believed that social justice was the widest possible expression of compassion, and he devoted his post-war years to work as a "Messenger" of the Industrial Christian Fellowship, lecturing up and down the country on the social, economic, and political imperatives of the Gospel.

Kennedy's mind was more acute and his imagination more fertile than were Sheppard's. Indeed, Kennedy was a scholar of great promise and a poet, if a minor one, who became something of a Christian Kipling. Sheppard wanted to make actual Francis Thompson's vision of a new Divine-human encounter in

>   . . . the traffic of Jacob's ladder
> Pitched betwixt Heaven and Charing Cross.

On his first Sunday in St. Martin's he imagined the kind of church it might become and set his hand to make that dream come true. This was his ideal:

"I saw a great and splendid church standing in the greatest square of the greatest city of the world. I stood on the west steps and saw what this church would be to the life of the people. There passed me into its warm inside, hundreds and hundreds of all sorts of people, going up to the temple of their Lord with all their difficulties, trials and sorrows. I saw it full of people, dropping in at all hours of the day and the night. It was never dark; it was lighted all night and all day, and often tired bits of humanity swept in. And I said to them as they passed, 'Where are you going?' And they said: 'This is our home. This is where we are going to learn of the love of Jesus Christ. This is the altar of our Lord, where all our peace lies. This is St. Martin's. . . .'

"It was all reverent and all full of love and they never pushed me behind a pillar because I was poor. . . . They spoke to me of two words only, one was the word 'home' and the other was 'love.' "[80]

In due course St. Martin's became the church of Christ's family where class and cultural divisions were irrelevant. Like a true home, ready to welcome the prodigal sons and daughters, the lights were always on and the doors always open. There was always a bed in the crypt and meals in the refectory. Sheppard's marvellous capacity for friendship was the magnet that drew in others dedicated to the catholicity of charity. Art-lovers, and enthusiasts for drama and music and literature, were catered for by the vital services, the Fellowship Guild, the *St. Martin's Review*, and the St. Martin's Players.

Sheppard's sermons radiated the same joyous love of the brethren for Christ's sake, always loving people in their distinctive individuality and never as potential ecclesiastical scalps. His style was as unaffected as the approach to his people. It was marked by man-to-man frankness. As Halford E. Luccock remarks: "Sheppard always talked to a person; he never merely sprayed the solar system with words."[81] Max Beerbohm, that ironic expert in detecting the foibles of men, wrote of the impact of Sheppard upon him when they met at Portofino: "He radiated a youthfulness that was less that of an undergraduate than a schoolboy. Nevertheless he made me feel younger than my years. And better than my character."[82] Sheppard's gift was to see, like his Master, the image of the king, which Christ would renew, in every world-soiled human coin, that others would have discarded as too tarnished for use.

His sermon beginnings were not as unstudied as they seemed. A casual joke can prick the bubble of pride more effectively than a declamation, as he knew, for example, when he narrated the following anecdote: "There was once a fashionable lady who went to a photographer. She was plain but thought she was beautiful. Said she to the photographer, 'Young man, mind you do me justice,' to which he replied, 'Madam, it's not justice but mercy you need!' "[83]

[80] R. Ellis Roberts, *H. R. L. Sheppard, Life and Letters*, pp. 44-45.
[81] *The Best of Dick Sheppard*, p. xix.
[82] *Ibid.*, p. 80.   [83] *Ibid.*, p. 27.

Sentimental as Sheppard often seemed to be, he also had his sterner side. He knew only too well the contrast between the values of Christ and the values of society. He observed that men, looking at Christ with prejudiced eyes, found in Him what they were determined to find—"a revolutionary, a social reformer, a miracle worker, a physician, a kindhearted philanthropist, an Oriental potentate, an upholder of the established order, and, sometimes, apparently, even the first Anglican clergyman."[84] Typical is the whimsical self-depreciation of the remark that "any idea that a round collar is a slipped halo must be once and for all abandoned."[85] Sheppard was not the witty and urbane priest, but neither was he the hail-fellow-well-met muscular type. He was simply and sincerely man's best friend for Christ's sake who had changed the baleful stereotype of the stiff and starchy Anglican incumbent into that of the "human parson."

If Sheppard saw the Anglican priest as friend, Studdert Kennedy viewed him as a fighter for honesty in business and for social justice in economic life. He assumed the great burden of trying to demonstrate in word and deed his conviction of the humanity of God. A double first class honours man at Trinity College, Dublin, and a reader of deep and lengthy books by preference, he had a heart as capacious as his mind. How admirably he filled the duties of a military chaplain is disclosed in his letter of advice to another chaplain:

"Live with the men, go where they go; make up your mind that you will share all their risks and more, if you can do any good. You can take it that the best place for a padre . . . is where there is most danger of death. Our first job is to go beyond the men in self-sacrifice and reckless devotion.

". . . There is very little spiritual work—it is all muddled and mixed—but it is all spiritual. Take a box of fags in your haversack, and a great deal of love in your heart, and go with them, live with them, talk with them. You can pray *with* them sometimes, but pray *for* them always."[86]

His courage, for which he was awarded the Military Cross, and his pungent style made his impact quite unforgettable. In his addresses and his popular rhymes there were two constant

---

[84] *The Human Parson*, p. 98.
[85] Luccock, *The Best of Dick Sheppard*, p. 162.
[86] The citation is from pp. 139-141 of *G. A. Studdert Kennedy By His Friends*, ed. J. K. Mozley. See also the recent biography, William Purcell, *Woodbine Willie*.

emphases. One was that God is involved with humanity in its sufferings. The other was that the Church is to be the spur to social, political, and economic reforms, not the sanctifier of social distinctions.

He was anxious to combat the prevalent idea that the essence of faith was submission; rather it was, in Pauline phrase, to enter into the fellowship of Christ's sufferings. He satirized the older view in the lines:

> This is the Gospel of the Christ.
>   Submit whate'er betides
> You cannot make the wrong world right
>   'Tis God alone decides.

By contrast with this false view, Kennedy pleads for a manlier imitation of Christ:

> O by Thy Cross and Passion, Lord,
>   By broken hearts that pant
> For comfort and for love of Thee
>   Deliver us from cant.[87]

He believed that it was necessary to choose between the omnipotence of God and his love, and he had no qualms in denying the omnipotence to preserve the love. As long as history lasts he is convinced that love must be suffering; only in heaven will it be triumphantly vindicated. The glory of the Christian faith for him was that it proclaimed there was a Cross in the heart of God before there was a Cross on Calvary. Therefore, as his *Rough Rhymes* tell:

> Father, if He, the Christ, be Thy Revealer,
>   Truly the First Begotten of the Lord,
> Then must Thou be a suff'rer and a Healer,
>   Pierced to the heart by the sorrow of the sword. . . .

> God, the God I love and worship,
>   Reigns in sorrow on the Tree,
> Broken, bleeding, but unconquered,
>   Very God of God to me.

> On my knees I fall and worship
>   That great Cross that shines above.
> For the very God of Heaven is not Power,
>   But Power of Love.

[87] *Lies!* (n.d.), pp. 132-33.

No man protested more strongly than Studdert Kennedy against an Aristotelian conception of God, alone and aloof above the stars, endlessly surveying His own perfections, heedless of men's prayers or curses. For Studdert Kennedy the agony of God was proof of His commitment to the human cause in the Incarnation.

No Anglican clergyman since Canon Scott Holland had sounded the trumpet call for social justice more clamantly than he. He was withering in his condemnation of all who met plans to reduce or abolish poverty with the stale excuse about the impossibility of changing human nature or the misapplication of Christ's words that "the poor are always with you." "There is," he commented, "more real blasphemy in these words than in the most lurid sergeant's speech that ever turned the air of Flanders blue. It is sheer blank atheism."[88] Too religious a man to think that social planners, unassisted by Divine grace which alone transforms the motives of the individual, could build the New Jerusalem out of the dark, Satanic mills of England, he warned the leaders of the Church that its rigid conservatism was forcing men to turn to socialism in place of an unsocial Gospel. The multitude, he cautioned, were revolting from a Church "which damned souls to build churches, sweated workpeople to endow charities, and manufactured prostitutes by low wages to build rescue homes for fallen women and buy a peerage." Furthermore, he claimed that the common people were nauseated by the religion of the upper classes "who patronised God as the best of all policemen, the power that kept the poor people in their places by threats of hell and promises of heaven."[89] He combined the incisive criticisms of Amos with the tenderness of Hosea. As "Messenger" of the Industrial Christian Fellowship, he applied the radical teaching of Christ to war, slums, class-warfare, industrialism, politics, and the problems of marriage. Everywhere his was "the unrestrained utterance of a soul in revolt."[90]

So unconventional a preacher was bound to have many critics as well as thousands of admirers. There is no question that Kennedy upset the balance of the Gospel, which is both criticism and consolation, by often over-emphasizing the judgment of God. It was, perhaps, inevitable when so many clergymen seemed euphoric. Sheppard's defect was the opposite, with the ever present danger of sentimentality. Kennedy's shock tactics ultimately ceased to shock as men became tired of the shepherd who was always crying "Wolf!

[88] *Ibid.*, p. 37.   [89] *Ibid.*, p. 108.
[90] J. K. Mozley, ed., *G. A. Studdert Kennedy . . .* , p. 167.

Wolf!" His language was too muddied with slang and expletives, so that it distracted from his message. His teaching was lop-sided in another way: he failed to balance sacrifice with hope. Christ was more Victim than Victor for Kennedy. Like the great modern French painter, Georges Rouault, Kennedy's portrait of Jesus depicted a swollen-lipped, blood-smeared and thorn-crowned Christ, against menacing leaden skies. There is suggested only in the faintest golden smudged aureole the risen Christ who tore open the sepulchre and destroyed death. Kennedy was, of course, reacting against the liberal Protestant Christ, the idyllic Galilean teacher of sweetness and light. But the result was that his preaching lacked the serenity of the Christian hope.[91]

The ultimate achievement of Kennedy and of Sheppard was that they enabled thousands of disillusioned men and women to see God, not as a remote and inscrutable Potentate, but as the Father of Christ, who was man's most compassionate Companion involved in their afflictions and agonies and committed to the establishment of a Kingdom of holy love in men's social relationships. And, to the great advantage of the Church of England, they remoulded the image of the Anglican clergyman so that he was seen no longer as a prop of the Establishment, but as a very human and lovable parson.

10. *The Fourth Type of Preaching*: *Liturgical*

Partly in revulsion from the topical sermon which is as up-to-date as the stop-press news in one day's newspaper and out-of-date in the next issue, partly in reaction against the hypothetical discussions of Biblical criticism or social and political issues in the pulpit, our century has pressed for the recognition of the devotional sermon. Dr. J. H. Jowett, the Congregationalist, was the first to recognize the need, for he stated that "When life is a picnic we play with theology: When life is a campaign we grope for a religion."[92] Dr. Russell Maltby and the Reverend A. E. Whitham followed in the same succession in the Methodist Church, as did Dr. James Reid among the English Presbyterians and Dr. F. B. Meyer among the Baptists.

With the recovery of the Christian Year in general among the Free Churches, and of special services for Holy Week, occasions

[91] E. H. Jeffs in *Princes of the Modern Pulpit* wrote that "the wounds and scars of battle were too plainly manifest in the man who stood up, with sad mouth and dark and burning eyes, to tell the people of his hard-won discoveries" (p. 167).
[92] *The Transfigured Christ*, p. 59.

were provided for which devotional preaching was essential and it was deeply appreciated. A proof that even the best Christian minds of the age recognized the limitations of dialectical and even of didactic theology in the pulpit was the mystical quality in Archbishop William Temple's later sermons and particularly in his *Readings in St. John's Gospel.* The final impetus to devotional preaching was, of course, the advent of the Liturgical Movement in all the Churches in England. This made it clear that the Liturgy of the Church is its power-house, at once the focus and dynamo of its unity in Christ, and its impulse to mission and social service.

While other preachers, including Inge, are notable exponents on individual mysticism, the newest type of preaching evokes the corporate mystical response of the congregation. It may therefore justly be termed "Liturgical preaching."[93]

11. *Monsignor Ronald Knox: Wit and Wisdom in Worship*[94]

Donne, Swift, Sydney Smith, Inge, and Knox are all admirable examples of wits in the English pulpit, but Knox's wit is gayer than that of the others. Another master of paradox and whimsy, G. K. Chesterton, has caught the effervescent quality of Knox in his quatrain:

> Mary of Holyrood may smile indeed,
> Knowing what grim historic shade it shocks
> To see wit, laughter and the Popish creed
> Cluster and sparkle in the name of Knox.[95]

Knox's writings are as sparkling as stars on a frosty night.

The son of the Evangelical Bishop of Manchester, he carried all before him at Eton and Balliol College, Oxford. As was to be expected of so nimble a dialectical speaker, he was elected President of the Oxford Union, and had the unique distinction of being quoted in a leading article of *The Times* of London when still an undergraduate. Referring to an inexplicable change in the policy of the government of the day, he quipped: "The honourable gentlemen have turned their backs on their country and now they have the effrontery to say their country is behind them."[96] The same wit,

[93] For an Anglican interpretation, see R. H. Fuller, *What is Liturgical Preaching?*
[94] The official biography is Evelyn Waugh's *Ronald Knox.*
[95] *The Collected Poems of G. K. Chesterton,* p. 15.
[96] Nathaniel Micklem, *The Box and the Puppets,* pp. 34-35.

now at the service of religion (for he had been ordained in the Church of England in 1912 and was appointed Chaplain of Trinity College, Oxford), gained him a national reputation with the publication of his satire, *Absolute and Abitofhell*.[97] This protested against the confusion of the traditional Anglican faith with the vapours of philosophical idealism, and its erosion by the acids of Biblical criticism. He had in mind the seven Anglican authors of *Foundations*, who had not yet published the book when he wrote, but with whose views he was all too familiar. The Primate, who preferred decency to dogma, is pilloried thus:

> When suave politeness, temp'ring bigot Zeal,
> Corrected, 'I believe,' to 'One does feel.'

He flays the Biblical critics who dissipate the Divine authority of Scripture by multiplying hypothetical sources, with a powerful contrast between the forefathers in the faith who

> . . . were content MARK, MATTHEW, LUKE and JOHN
> Should bless th' old-fashion'd Beds they lay upon:
> But we, for ev'ry one of theirs have two,
> And trust the Watchfulness of Blessed Q.

Ever a foe to cordial ambiguity, he satirized a polyreligious ecumenism in *Reunion All Around*, with its engaging sub-title, "Or Jael's Hammer Laid Aside and the Milk of Human Kindness Beaten up into Butter and Served in a Lordly Dish, Being a Plea for the Inclusion within the Church of England of all Mahometans, Jews, Buddhists, Brahmins, Papists and Atheists, submitted to the Consideration of the British Public." The disciplinary confusion in the Church of England is reduced to absurdity, as he describes bishops encouraging all unscriptural doctrines, and forbidding high ceremonial, to enable the disobedient clergy "to snatch a fearful joy" and thus taste the spice of martyrdom lacking since the Roman amphitheatre was abolished.

Knox's literary versatility is prodigious. The writer of astute mystery stories, a felicitous translator of Greek and Latin lyrics and epigrams,[98] gifted historian[99] and novelist,[100] he also produced

[97] It first appeared in *The Oxford Magazine* (November 1912) and was reissued in *Essays in Satire* and *In Three Tongues* (1959).
[98] See *In Three Tongues*.
[99] See his *Enthusiasm*, a study of the vagaries of the Christian religion in the seventeenth and eighteenth centuries.
[100] See his *Let Dons Delight*, in which the reader eavesdrops on the fellows of St. Simon Magus college, as they discuss the issues of the day at half century intervals from the Armada to Munich.

the leading modern English translation of the Scriptures authorized by the Roman Catholic Church. The New Testament version appeared in 1945, the Old Testament version in 1949, and both are marvels of clear, precise and idiomatic English. His sermons, too, exhibit great versatility. Polemical sermons were preached in his Anglo-Catholic days,[101] apologetical sermons during his period as Roman Catholic chaplain to Oxford University (1926-1939), and, during his later years, he composed some superb liturgical sermons.

The earliest sermons are often marred by the partisan spirit and by an over-indulgence in facetiousness. One feels that Knox, while capable of writing passages of great beauty, as of religious insight and ardour, is yet chiefly engaged in a hearty bout of ecclesiastical "gamesmanship."

The apologetical and doctrinal sermons offer more substantial fare. They were published under the titles of *In Soft Garments* (1942) and *The Hidden Stream* (1952). He is more impressive in dealing with the day-to-day problems of the Christian life than with abstract doctrine. Contemporary issues give more scope to his irony and psychological insight. He clinches the argument that a plurality of wives or husbands is atavistic today, by insisting that "it is absurd to follow free love unless you follow free hate." Typically Knoxian is an ironical passage about supposedly altruistic bachelors, whom he castigates as "the unselfish people who want to spare several unborn souls the misery of not being brought up at Harrow."[102]

His finest achievements are as a Liturgical preacher. He is ever aware that the revelation of God in Holy Scripture is proclaimed within the context of worship, which aims at the illumination of the mind, the elevation of the heart, and the consecration of the will. Nor does Knox forget that his sermons are also preached within the context of the cycle of the Christian Year, affording opportunities to study the many facets of the Incarnation of the Son of God and to incite the faithful to imitate the saints, themselves the eminent imitators of Christ. Above all, liturgical preaching never allows the congregation to forget that the climax of the Liturgy is the Sacrifice. In all Knox's wit and inventiveness, in his brilliance and aptness of allusion and illustration, the solemn joy of the Liturgy is never forgotten. These sermons enabled the people of God to see that they must *live* the Liturgy in the spirit of glad obedience.

To call Knox a liturgical preacher is not to infer that he was a

---

[101] See *The Church in Bondage*.   [102] *In Soft Garments*, p. 190.

faddist in matters of ceremonial or vestments. The contrary is the truth: far from feeling that the priest was a very important person, Knox is at pains to insist that the priest is God's *slave* or *tool* in the Mass. One does not decorate a spade or a wrench. It should be recalled that *The Mass in Slow Motion*[103] is a series of meditations on *Low* Mass. Nothing could be more appropriate, since Monsignor Knox might speak like an angel but he sang uncommonly like a rook.[104]

His popular explanation of the Mass ran to nine impressions in eleven years. Not only is it a fresh and moving set of reflections on the successive parts of the Mass, it is also a triumph of communication. For it was, in the form of addresses, delivered to a convent school evacuated from London to Shropshire in time of war. It blends the supernatural sense with a conversational tone and idiom. The measure of the achievement is so great that one is forced to hunt for preposterous parallels to hint at its quality, such as, that this is Ronald Searle supernaturalised, or St. Trinian's sanctified! Theological instruction is inculcated by analogies drawn from ink-stains or laddered stockings. Only Knox could think of Divine revelation and its apparent obscurity as a special kind of hide-and-seek played between God and us.

His profoundest and subtlest liturgical preaching is found in sermons that he delivered to Father Kearney's congregation in London's theatreland each year at the festival of Corpus Christi, which were published as *The Window in the Wall, Reflections on the Holy Eucharist* (1956), and in the addresses which he gave to conferences of priests, published as *The Priestly Life; A Retreat* (1958).

The title of *The Window in the Wall* represents a fine leap of the imagination. Using allegorical exegesis, Knox takes his text from the second chapter of *Canticles* where the lover is said to seek a glimpse of the beloved, "looking through each window in turn." This "brings to mind a fancy which I have often had before now— in looking at the Sacred Host enthroned in the monstrance." The fancy is "that the glittering Disc of whiteness which we see occupying that round opening, is not reflecting the light of the candles in front of it, but shining with a light of its own, a light not of this world. . . ."[105] This is the veiled glory of the Eucharistic

---

[103] Further reference is made to this volume in Chapter VII below.

[104] *The Mass in Slow Motion*, p. x. When he sang the Mass the only thought he entertained was "a vivid hope that I might die before we got to the Preface."

[105] *The Window in the Wall*, p. 2.

Christ, a curtained window, which "lets our world communicate with the world of the supernatural."[106] The call of the Beloved is from the stupefaction of the senses and from anxieties. The medicine of Holy Communion "enables the enfeebled soul to look steadily at the divine light, to breathe deeply of the unfamiliar air," until such time as "God calls us, too, to himself, and makes us glad with the beauty of his unveiled presence."[107] The volume includes a great richness of doctrinal teaching, as the Sacrament is seen successively as the bond of Christian union, the means of Christian renewal, the Bread of the pilgrim, and the channel of Christ's sacrifice and compassion.

The Priestly Life begins with a superb address on "Energy and Repose." It starts with St. Augustine's vivid phrase about the Divine nature, as *semper agens, semper quietus*, always active, yet always at rest. It is mirrored in God's providence in Nature, and still more clearly in the earthly life of Christ, and in his continuing grace in the Sacrament. It is also characteristic of the life of the Church, active in the missionaries, theologians, priests, and great ecclesiastics, yet quietly powerful in the cells of praying celibates. Then there follows a passage of eloquence reminiscent of Cardinal Newman, for its crescendo of rising interest, its dramatic contrast, inevitable images, convincing close, and spiritual penetration:

"For, if you would approach near to the innermost secret of her life, you must go, not to the palaces of Pope or bishop, not to the courts of ecclesiastical tribunals, or the lecture rooms of learned theologians. You must go to the cells of Carthusians and Poor Clares, if you want to know what the Church really is. Shut off from the world and its dusty disputes, sheltered by their protecting walls from public inquisitiveness and from the blare of advertisement, these cloistered souls find a peace which is, if we would but realize it, the breath of the Church's life, the source of her triumphs, the solace of her despair. Look at a man or a horse racing; and then remember that behind all that tremendous display of outward activity there is one tiny valve which beats all unseen, all unheard, within the breast; and if that beating were to cease, all the external activities would cease with it. Something of the same importance belongs to those homes of silence and recollectedness where men and women serve God in holy religion: there lies the heart of the Church. Their restfulness is her secret life; the powerhouse from which all her restless activity must spring. Go elsewhere, and you

---

[106] *Ibid.*, p. 4.　　　　　　　[107] *Ibid.*, p. 6.

will see the rippling of her muscles; it is in the hours of contemplation that you will hear the beating of her heart."[108]

In all his later volumes he expresses the "Eucharistic attitude." This he illustrates from Michelangelo's Adam in the Sistine Chapel frescoes—"that recumbent figure, stretching out one hand, at the full length of the arm, towards the Creator, as if in acknowledgment of its utter dependence, its creaturely reliance, on him."[109]

A consummate stylist, Monsignor Knox always preached from a typewritten manuscript but he had a "vocal legerdemain" by which he gave the impression of talking directly to his hearers, when he was, in fact, reading.[110]

His sermons are a product of many virtues. They show the Biblical translator's deep familiarity with Holy Writ, and his submission to its authority. They exhibit a clear and natural structure, lucidity of thought and originality of expression. They have intriguing beginnings and pointed endings. There is a whimsical humanity in the wit and manliness in the monitions. There is also a flexible adaptation of diction and illustration to suit the needs of such different groups as schoolboys at St. Edmund's, Ware, schoolgirls at Aldenham, Oxford undergraduates and priests, and of such special occasions as panegyrics at Westminster Cathedral or society weddings.[111]

For those who like sermons to be a historical and theological exposition of the Scriptures, many of Knox's sermons are too allegorical. The typological exegesis is abused when foreshadowings of the New Testament are found in the Old where there are sometimes only shadows. Even in the Catholic sermons, the easy but fatal transition is sometimes made from light-heartedness to levity, as when Knox writes: "Eastertide is rich in the feasts of martyrs; it was in Spring, perhaps, you got the best bookings for the amphitheatre."[112] For his original and witty mind such a defect was, of course, an occupational hazard.

Our final impression is of a great Roman Catholic preacher, whose brilliant mind and imagination were liberated by grace to make him a most effective cultural attaché of Christ's court and Kingdom. His chief distinction is to have been the unrivalled exponent in England of Liturgical preaching and of the "Eucharistic attitude."

108 *The Priestly Life*, p. 7.   109 *The Window in the Wall*, p. 34.
110 See Evelyn Waugh, *Life*, pp. 120 and 242.
111 See his twenty-four charming wedding addresses collected in *Bridegroom and Bride*.
112 *Bridegroom and Bride*, p. 69.

12. *A Concluding Survey*

In concluding this survey of twentieth century preaching, two questions must be asked. The first is: What are the distinctive characteristics of the sermons of our day? The second is: What is the effect of contemporary preaching on worship?

In the first place, it is undeniable that the apologetical sermon is more typical of the twentieth than of the nineteenth century. In the last century only the Anglican, Robertson of Brighton, and the Unitarian, James Martineau, spring to mind as pre-eminent apologetical preachers. In the twentieth century reasonable preaching would be a fair description of the sermons of Bishop Hensley Henson, Archbishop William Temple, Professor H. H. Farmer, Dean Inge, and Dr. Alec Vidler, to mention only the most distinguished practitioners of the art. There are several reasons for the popularity of the apologetical sermon. Among them are the increasing secularization of the age; the reduction of the numbers of the Church members of all denominations combined to approximately one fifth of the total population; and the intellectual attacks upon Christianity waged by naturalists, positivists, behaviourists, rationalists, and economists. This meant that a beleaguered Church had to fortify its adherents with reasons for the faith they held.

A second typical twentieth century kind of preaching is the psychological sermon, of which Dr. Leslie Weatherhead has been so notable an exponent. This is likely to be developed with greater sophistication in the future, as it demonstrates how the Gospel relates to the basic psychic needs of the personality, in terms of liberating man from anxiety, alienation, futility, and frustration, and in providing him with a capacity for self-acceptance and transcendence.

In the third place, a clearly distinctive sound of twentieth century preaching has been the ecumenical chorus, as contrasted with the beating of the denominational drum. In this respect the sermons of today mark a great advance over the polemical and partisan philippics that marred many Victorian discourses from the pulpit.

Fourthly, the present century has made an attempt in children's sermons to provide graded religious instruction. It was Dean Inge who observed the educational difficulty involved in the act of preaching to radically diverse individuals in the same congregation, divided by age, temperament, culture, and experience. His term for it was "trying to fill rows of narrow necked vessels by throwing buckets of water over them."[113] One serious twentieth century attempt to lessen this difficulty has been the provision of children's sermons, especially in the English Free Churches.

One of the least satisfactory characteristics of children's sermons is that they seem often to be enjoyed more by the adults than the children. This is possibly because they employ less technical theological terms, but probably because they are better illustrated than sermons for adults. Their most serious defect, however, is that they are often sentimental, and almost always trivial variations on the Pelagian theme, "Be good."[114] Yet, it must be acknowledged that in the hands of such experts as George Macdonald, the novelist, P. T. Forsyth, O. G. Whitfield, and others they have been highly imaginative presentations of the wonder and glory of the Christian Gospel and the exploits of the saints.

In the fifth place, twentieth century sermons have been notably ethical and practical. It was also the perceptive Dean Inge who reminded his hearers of another pressing problem in the communication of Christianity. In a typical epigram he insisted that Christianity "is a way of walking, not talking."[115] It is for this very reason that both in the days of the "Social Gospel" and in the last decade of the present century that "Christian action" sermons have increased in number and significance. It is a recovery of the tradition of the Victorian Christian Socialists, F. D. Maurice and Charles Kingsley, with modern nuances. Theirs was prophetic preaching against the economic exploitation of the artisans by sweated labour. Their successors, like Dr. Donald Soper, Canon John Collins, Bishops Huddleston, Robinson and Stockwood, as well as Archbishop Joost De Blank, have turned their attention to racial discrimination. Several clergymen, notably "Dick" Sheppard, have been notable advocates of Christian pacifism. In these ways the pulpit has often led the people to make practical protests or to give generously to the causes which affirmed the brotherhood of mankind.

Sixthly, the present century has seen a new phenomenon—high quality preaching by laymen. While the Roman Catholic Church has not allowed gifted laymen in its pulpits, several laymen have

---

[113] *Goodness and Truth*, pp. 5-6.

[114] Many that I have heard remind me of the *Punch* cartoon of a harassed mother, shouting to her helper, "Go and find out what Johnny's doing and tell him to stop it."

[115] *Things New and Old*, p. 2.

used books as pulpits for the effective dissemination of apologetics. This was notably the case in the essays of G. K. Chesterton and Hilaire Belloc. Anglicans have been hardly less hesitant to invite their distinguished laymen to preach. This is all the more remarkable in that the three most successful apologists for Christianity in England have all been lay members of the Church of England. They are: T. S. Eliot, the distinguished poet, dramatist, man of letters, and author of *The Idea of a Christian Society*; Dorothy L. Sayers, author of a superb study of the doctrine of Creation entitled *The Mind of the Maker* and of the strikingly successful cycle of radio plays, *The Man Born to be King*; and Professor C. S. Lewis, who held the Chair of Mediaeval and Renaissance Literature in Cambridge University. Lewis seems to be the only Anglican layman whose sermons have been published and are to be found in the volume, *Transposition and Other Addresses* (1949).[116] It is perhaps sufficient to say of Lewis that his *Mere Christianity* was the most successful statement of Christian faith and life ever to be broadcast and that his sermon on "Learning in War-time" was republished as the final and climactic contribution to Ashley Sampson's anthology, *Famous English Sermons*. One has only to recall the preaching of T. R. Glover, the Baptist layman and Public Orator of Cambridge University, and of Bernard L. Manning,[117] the Congregational layman and Senior Tutor of Jesus College, Cambridge, to be aware of the rich contribution that devout and intelligent laymen can make to the pulpit. Such resources will almost certainly be exploited with greater assurance by the Churches in the future.

Our final question as to the effect of preaching on worship can be answered in part by recognizing the importance of Liturgical preaching as practised by Monsignor Ronald Knox, and of devotional preaching as practised by J. H. Jowett and A. E. Whitham. For all three, and for many not as famous as they, preaching was an essential part of the act of worship. As truly as the Sacrament of Holy Communion, preaching was a sacramental communication of the gift of the Gospel mediated by the Holy Spirit to the congregation.

Moreover, the mutual reinforcement of the Biblical and Litur-

---

116 The same volume was published in the United States as *The Weight of Glory* and other addresses. For an appreciation of Lewis as preacher see my *Varieties of English Preaching*, pp. 165-72 and 186-93.

117 See Manning's *A Layman in the Ministry*. *Varieties of English Preaching* evaluates his role as a preacher on pp. 165-86.

gical Revivals has produced two results. Preachers increasingly recognize their true status as servants of the Word, and less and less do they desire to be the purveyors of idiosyncratic ideas which in their originality often exhibit only original sin in the form of pride. Furthermore, they are more fully aware that the Liturgy, in which the Service of the Word and the Service of the Upper Room are the two essential parts, stimulate mind, heart, and will to the obedience of faith which finds its secular expression in mission and compassion in the workaday world. Both preaching and worship have the same function, the contemporizing of Christ. Preaching today, therefore, is not in competition with worship. Rather it is its complement.

PART II: THE NARROW FOCUS

CHAPTER VII

ROMAN CATHOLIC WORSHIP

THE FIRST part of this volume was devoted to the liturgical, theological, and aesthetic renewal as manifested in general in the religious life in England. The second part, now beginning, will be a detailed study of the development of the theory and practice of worship in *particular* Christian Communions, moving through the spectrum from Roman Catholicism to Unitarianism in the chapters which follow. We start with Roman Catholicism.

The Catholic hierarchy was restored in England in 1850. In the succeeding eleven decades the Roman Catholic Church has made a steady advance both in numbers and in intellectual influence, despite the rising tide of secularism. An administrative index of this growth was the raising of the dioceses of Liverpool and Birmingham to the dignity of archdioceses in 1911.

1. Roman Catholicism in the Public Life of England

The most striking advance has been made in the development of an informed and influential Catholic middle and upper middle class in England during the present century. In the last century an influential middle class was needed as the link to bind the older aristocratic Catholic families and the many converts who followed Newman from the Church of England to the Roman allegiance with the thousands upon thousands of impoverished Irish artisans and their families who flocked into Liverpool and Birmingham. Two obstacles stood in the way of the development of such a middle class. The Roman Catholics had not founded Catholic public schools in such numbers and with such academic and social prestige as to compete with the greater Anglican public schools, and the ancient universities, the training ground of most of the nation's leaders, were closed to them by the determinate will of their own hierarchy. Cardinal Manning, the Archbishop of Westminster, though himself an Oxford man, had set his face against the entry of Catholics to Oxford and Cambridge because he believed it would expose them to infidelity. Moreover, he spent the resources of the Church on building parochial schools to retain the masses within the Roman

Catholic fold. In 1895, three years after Manning's death, his successor, Vaughan, was persuaded to agree that Catholics might be permitted, though not encouraged, to attend the ancient universities.

For such an entry into the universities the young Catholics had been prepared at the Catholic public schools. Towards the end of the nineteenth century such institutions as Downside, Douai, Ampleforth, and Stonyhurst, had gained a wide reputation for themselves, which in this century has been considerably increased. The shape of things to come could be seen in the last three decades of the century.

Arthur Conan Doyle was at Stonyhurst and Francis Thompson was at Ushaw. Garner, who was to build the great choir of Downside Abbey, was a partner with G. F. Bodley. Edward Elgar, one of this century's notable composers, was organist of St. George's, Worcester. Richard Terry was at the organ of the English cathedral in Antigua. And, to refer to future converts of distinction, Gilbert Chesterton was a schoolboy at St. Paul's, and Eric Gill was living in the Manse of the Countess of Huntingdon's Chapel in Brighton.[1]

What was lacking in the nineteenth was made good in the twentieth century. The strong and influential English Catholic middle class came into being through the increase and size of the famous Catholic schools, both boarding and day-schools, the latter run chiefly by the Jesuits and the former chiefly by the Benedictines; through the foundation at Oxford and Cambridge of Catholic houses of study for the clergy, who could thus maintain a chaplaincy for Catholic students and fend off agnosticism; and through the vigour of the Catholic literary renaissance. The relevance of these factors for the present chapter is that they helped to promote liturgical and historical scholarship and gained a respect for Catholic culture, which would have been impossible had Catholics been forced to live as in an intellectual ghetto.

At the end of the nineteenth century and in the present century, the Jesuits founded Campion Hall in Oxford and the Dominicans a provincial house of studies in the same university, Blackfriars, while the Ampleforth Benedictines established St. Benet's Hall. In the sister university of Cambridge the Downside Benedictines founded St. Benet's. Their examples were followed by the Capuchins, the Salesians, the Christian Brothers de la Salle, the Irish

---

[1] See ed. G. A. Beck, *The English Catholics, 1850-1950*, Chap. VII.

Christian Brothers, and the Rosminian Fathers, all of whom founded clerical houses for university studies.[2] With this symbolic gesture Catholic scholarship in England came of age. No longer was it the exclusive privilege of those converts to Rome from Anglicanism, like the greatest of them, Newman, who had received an education at the ancient universities as Anglicans, or of those who had been educated abroad, like Lord Acton or Baron von Hügel. It would not be long before the effects of these more generous provisions for higher education would be seen in the publication of learned monographs on Catholic history, liturgy, and spirituality. A welcome and unexpected development, however, would be the resurgence of a Catholic tradition of belles-lettres.

2. *The Catholic Literary Renaissance*

Catholicism has, of course, a very distinguished tradition in English literature from mediaeval times. The roll-call of eminent Catholic men of letters must include Chaucer and Langland, Southwell and Campion, Crashaw, Dryden, and Pope, but it has been greatly increased in the past century. In poetry, sprung rhythms, alliterations, brilliant imagery and passionate religious devotion produced a masterpiece in Gerard Manley Hopkins' *The Wreck of the Deutschland*, which would not have been written without a Jesuit's devotion to St. Ignatius' *Spiritual Exercises*; the poem is a fervent expression of the absolute obedience of faith. Francis Thompson produced another masterpiece in *The Hound of Heaven*, recalling the image of God as the inexorable Divine pursuer, such as St. Augustine had found Him to be in the *Confessions*. Lesser, but far from insignificant poets of the Catholic faith, were Coventry Patmore, the panegyrist of married love, Wilfrid Scawen Blunt, Lionel Johnson, Alice Meynell, Ernest Dowson, Lord Alfred Douglas, Alfred Noyes, and that formidable and antic beast, the "Chester-Belloc."

In the realm of essays G. K. Chesterton proved to be one of the most successful of Catholic propagandists, delighting by his teasing paradoxes and fertile fancy. His religious views were interestingly expressed in *Orthodoxy* (1908) and *The Everlasting Man* (1925), the latter a *tour de force* which presented Christianity as a mystery-novel. Hilaire Belloc, ever a trenchant writer, presumed to antagonize all Protestants by writing a history of the Reformation in which the English variety was written off as "the English Accident."

[2] *Ibid.*, pp. 312-13.

Ronald Knox, another great wit and a Jesuit priest, wrote his *Spiritual Aeneid* in 1918 and later a delightful fable, *Let Dons Delight* (1939), where he allows his readers to eavesdrop on the fellows of St. Simon Magus College as they discuss living issues of the day, at half-century intervals, from the time of the Armada to the Munich crisis. The founder of the "Vorticist" movement in literature and art was the greatly gifted D. B. Wyndham Lewis. And Catholic art-criticism has benefited considerably from the expertise of Sir John Rothenstein, John Pope-Hennessy, and E. W. Tristram.

Perhaps the most signal triumphs have come in the art of novel-writing, the most popular and influential of all literary forms in the twentieth century. Compton Mackenzie is the doyen of English Catholic novelists and his trilogy, *The Altar Steps* (1922), *The Parson's Progress*, and *The Heavenly Ladder*, though not his best work, is a polemical study of Anglo-Catholicism as an external and fanatical imitation of Roman Catholicism. It also includes a satirical portrait of Percy Dearmer, the English Nationalist liturgiologist, as the "Rev. J. Q. B. Moxon-Hughes."

The two greatest Catholic novelists, however, are Evelyn Waugh (born 1903) and Graham Greene (born 1904), both Oxford men and converts. They are the English parallels to the Catholic literary renaissance in France which owes so much to Paul Claudel, Georges Bernanos, and François Mauriac. While Waugh's genius runs to satire, as in the superb critique of the escapism and sentimentality of American funeral customs, *The Loved One* (1949), most of his other novels depict, with affection, the idiosyncrasies of life in Catholic country houses where characters are strongly marked, and the faith is strongly held and unembarrassingly discussed. Graham Greene seems to be England's equivalent to Mauriac, and they both depict the conflict between Divine and earthly loves. Greene's *Brighton Rock* (1938) brought back the dimensions of heaven and hell to the flat and garish landscape of Brighton and added depth to the English novel. *The Power and the Glory* (1940) is an astonishing parable of the labyrinthine ways of God's grace in the Augustinian mode. *The Heart of the Matter* (1940) turns on the question of whether a man may be excluded from heaven because he commits a mortal sin for the sake of his wife and illumines grace in squalour, which seems to be Greene's forte.

As Edward Hutton has shown,[3] the Catholic novel has gone through three stages. In the eighteenth century the Catholic faith was treated as ludicrous in England but exotic abroad. In the nineteenth and early twentieth centuries the Catholic novelists had to make the faith appear mysterious and romantic, as Chesterton's novels and "Father Brown" stories show. With Waugh and Greene, however, the gilding is absent and Catholicism is treated as if it were natural and even inevitable. Greene's lack of propaganda is, indeed, the best kind of propaganda and he and Waugh have gained a wide circle of non-Catholic readers.

It is, then, in a cultural context of increased Catholic education, and on the background of an influential Catholic middle class, and in the midst of a Catholic literary renaissance, that important studies in the history of worship and in the meaning of spirituality have been carried out in the present century. Moreover, because Catholicism was swimming against the stream in an age of materialism, deepening doubt, and moral chaos, it made an increasing appeal in a predominantly Protestant country. Its unyielding fidelity to the fulness of the Christian tradition proved alluring to minds that had seen Protestant orthodoxy capitulate to the blandishments of liberalism. Its proclamation of unaccommodating ethical standards also won the grudging admiration of the weaker brethren outside the fold. Its spiritual discipline, as demonstrated by the religious in monasteries and nunneries, who had given up wealth and the joys of family life for the deeper consecration to Christ, as also in the regularity with which the faithful attended Mass, was a proof of Catholicism's continuing power. Its dramatic worship succeeded in eliciting the allegiance and affection of the poor, as no other Communion in England could. It is surely significant that Masterman, an Anglican clergyman, should have given glowing testimony to the popular appeal of the Mass among London's poor: "I have no hesitation in saying that, for the majority of the poor, our services are as incomprehensible as if still performed in the Latin tongue. The central service of the Roman Church, indeed, with its dramatic and appealing character, is far more intelligible even to the humblest worshipper."[4]

[3] "Catholic English Literature," being Chap. XVII of G. A. Beck, ed., *The English Catholics*, p. 556.

[4] Richard Mudie Smith, ed., *The Religious Life of London*, cited in G. A. Beck, *The English Catholics*, pp. 419-20.

3. *Studies in the History of Worship and Spirituality*

Pius XII in his Encyclical, *Mediator Dei* (November 20, 1947), the chief document of the modern Liturgical Movement, paid tribute to "an unprecedented revival of liturgical studies, due in part to the admirable initiative of a number of individuals, but especially to the devoted zeal of certain monasteries of the renowned Benedictine Order." As was seen in the first chapter of this volume, the initiative undoubtedly lay with the Benedictine Abbeys of Solesmes, Mont-César, Beuron, and Maria Laach. In the same tradition, it is unquestionably the Benedictine Abbey of Downside which has pioneered in the development of studies of the history of the Liturgy and of ascetical theology in England. The names of Edmund Bishop, and his friend Cardinal Gasquet, of Abbot John Chapman and Dom Illtyd Trethowan, of Abbot Cuthbert Butler and Dom David Knowles, as well as of Dom Gregory Murray, are sufficient to stake Downside's claim. Other Benedictines in England also made their important contribution, such as Abbot Anscar Vonier of Buckfast, Dom Benedict Steuart of St. Michael's Abbey, Farnborough, and Bishop Hedley, an Ampleforth monk.

In the popular presentation of the lessons of the liturgy the Jesuits were unrivalled, as in Fr. C. C. Martindale's lively *The Mind of the Missal* (1929) and in Fr. Ronald Knox's sparkling account of *The Mass in Slow Motion* (1948). In the person of Fr. Clifford Howell, S.J., they had an indefatigable exponent, both in his writings and his liturgical lectures and missions, of the lessons of the modern Liturgical Movement, including the necessity for lay participation in the Mass by the greater use of the vernacular and, in particular, by the popularization of the Dialogue Mass and the use of commentators, explaining the meaning of the Mass while it was proceeding. The Jesuits also had notable exponents of Eucharistic theology, such as Fr. Bernard Leeming, in his *Principles of Sacramental Theology*, or Fr. Ronald Knox in the less technical group of addresses, *The Window in the Wall* (1956). Yet, significant as these studies were in their effect on the parishes, the most profound studies of Liturgy and spirituality emerged from the Downside cloisters.

The most erudite and original liturgiologist of the century in England was a lay associate of Downside, Edmund Bishop (1846-1917). But for his ailing body and singularity of temperament, he might have been professed as a Benedictine, and he left his library to the Abbey.[5] He developed the passion for study in the original sources and manuscripts in the British Museum, in such hours as could be spared from his duties as a civil servant employed in the Education Department of the Privy Council Office. In 1890 he collaborated with Cardinal Gasquet in producing *Edward VI and the Book of Common Prayer* and they went on to publish *The Bosworth Psalter* in 1908. Francis Aidan Gasquet (1846-1929) had been schooled at Downside, was professed there in 1862, and became the second Abbot in 1900. He was undoubtedly encouraged in the work of scholarship by Edmund Bishop. His greatest work was *Henry VIII and the English Monasteries* (2 vols. 1888-1889), in which he showed that Protestant charges against the state of the monasteries at that period had been greatly exaggerated, amounting to vilification, and demonstrated how much England had lost in spirituality, education, and charity by Henry's seizure of them. As his responsibilities increased, the carefulness of his research and his conclusions unfortunately diminished, but he had shown that an English Abbot could be a distinguished scholar, and many followed the beacon that he and Bishop lit.

Edmund Bishop, to follow the course of the more eminent scholar of the two, though only Gasquet attained the title of "His Eminence," published an important and definitive *Appendix* to the *Liturgical Homilies of Narsai*. His *magnum opus*, which he had contributed in a series of articles to *The Downside Review* over an extended period, was published in 1918 as *Liturgica Historica, Papers on the Liturgy and Religious Life of the Western Church.* His name was known to German scholars, since, for lack of an English publisher, he had gathered the *Collectanea Britannica* and published this collection of about three hundred papal letters of the fifth to the eleventh centuries with annotations in the *Monumenta Germaniae Historica.* In consequence, his latest and posthumous work received international recognition for its vast range, meticulous scholarship, and striking conclusions which, on reconsideration, appeared inevitable.

The opening essay on "The Genius of the Roman Rite" is an index of Bishop's superlative quality. This was reprinted five times, translated into French and German, and was his best known writing. In it Bishop took issue with the common assumption that the Roman Rite is characterized by sensuousness of ritual and

---

[5] See the admirable biography, N. J. Abercrombie, *The Life and Work of Edmund Bishop*, with its detailed account of this pioneer-scholar's contributions to liturgiology.

ceremonial, arguing that this is precisely the element which is not indigenous to it, having been borrowed and adopted through the centuries. Proving his point up to the hilt, he concluded from a study of the early Roman Mass that "the genius of the Roman rite is marked by simplicity, practicality, a great sobriety and self-control, gravity and dignity."[6] He was driven by the determination to trace back to their origins the most venerable components of Catholic worship. Thus the third chapter describes the Gelasian Sacramentary as "The Earliest Roman Mass Book" which was used in Rome at the end of the seventh century. He concludes that it was widely used in Charlemagne's Frankish Kingdom, as a supplement to the *Gregorianum*. The fourth chapter considers some early Mss of the *Gregorianum* and concludes that one group of Mss preserves the book sent by Hadrian to Charlemagne, and that from this can be constructed the authentic texts of the prayers, as well as the rites and formularies used in the Roman Church at the end of the eighth century.[7]

The spirit in which Edmund Bishop approached his work is clearly not that of an antiquarian or rubrician, for he castigates the sterility of much of the liturgical work of the previous century as having been "a study of ritual rather than a study of religion; as a consequence it has seemed to be in touch with professionalism than with life, and appears in its general character to be predominantly of clerical interest."[8] No mere *laudator temporis acti*, he pays tribute to the new devotions which a living Church produces, recognizing that "the source of new forms of private devotion, which become by and by popularized, is in the religious orders."[9] He traces some of the elements of the *Prymer* back to the inspiration of Benedict of Aniane in the ninth century,[10] and he finds the beginnings of the Feast of the Conception of the Blessed Virgin Mary in the devotions of the English monks of Winchester.[11] He provides a history of the development of the Christian Altar from the holy table of cubic shape of the fourth century to the altar-shrine of the eighth, and on to the great reredos altars of the fourteenth and successive centuries, which have become sideboards for the displaying of church treasure and plate on festival days.[12] He is as interesting on the development of the cope, which originally was not a distinctively clerical vestment, to its

---

6 *Liturgica Historica*, p. 12.   7 *Ibid.*, p. 75.
8 *Ibid.*, p. 166.   9 *Ibid.*, p. 213.   10 *Ibid.*, Chap. IX.
11 *Ibid.*, Chap X.   12 *Ibid.*, Chap. II.

present eucharistic use;[13] or on the origin and history of the requirement of six candles on the altar.[14]

The first part of his book is devoted to liturgical studies, and the second part (Chapter XVI onwards) to antiquarian studies. Even in the second part he is chiefly interested in the quality of religious life. A comparison of Irish and English devotions, arising from a study of ancient prayer books, leads him to describe Celtic devotions as "all heart, fluency, and little mind," and to define the specifically English quality of piety as "strong feeling controlled and penetrated by good sense."[15] He delights in pointing out that the building of Milan cathedral in the fourteenth century was a testimony to the initiative, public spirit, and self-sacrifice of the citizens themselves, from the richest to the humblest, who gave their most precious possessions or promised to undertake hours of manual labour, as did the civic leader of Milan. On this the humane Bishop comments: "Let us try to fancy for a moment the Mayor (or Lord Mayor, as it is now) and Corporation going out for an afternoon's digging on the Manchester Ship Canal; it is easier to imagine this than to imagine them helping to dig out the foundations of a new cathedral."[16] The realistic and utterly unromantic nature of Bishop's historical reconstructions is well illustrated by this reflection on mediaeval life:

"A truce to all attempts to idealize the middle ages. It was essentially a rough-and-tumble time, insupportable perhaps to our more delicate organisms, a time of plenty of salt beef and salt fish for those who could get it, an age of peas and beans for ever, with a scant stock of clean linen, little furniture and less comfort, an age when a brass pot and half a dozen pewter plates were heirlooms among country people; a day of shambles, and gutters, and narrow streets, and odours and smoky rooms with little ventilation or too much, of bad drainage or none, days of hardness and discomfort; a time when gold and silver-plate enough to ransom a province decked the buffet today and went into the melting-pot of tomorrow. But those ages had, at all events, one great virtue: it was a time when men were wholly convinced that in spite of all drawbacks life was thoroughly worth living; and when they seemed to enter (one way or the other) into the meaning of the words, redeeming the time because the days are evil."[17]

Part of Bishop's genius was seen in his ability to make the most

[13] *Ibid.*, Chap. XI.   [14] *Ibid.*, Chap. XIII.   [15] *Ibid.*, p. 385.
[16] *Ibid.*, p. 418.   [17] *Ibid.*, pp. 420-21.

educated guesses, and the accuracy of these was to be confirmed by the researches of later scholars. This volume provides two interesting examples. The floridity and even sentimentality of modern ways of devotion are often attributed to Italian origin, but Bishop made the objection, "I will venture to say that much of what is nowadays called Italian in devotions is really German."[18] The researches of the Anglican Benedictine, Gregory Dix, and of Fr. Thurston, the Jesuit scholar, have amply borne out Bishop's contention.[19] Similarly, Bishop was convinced that the remarkable dedication of the Maurist Congregation of Benedictines to historical scholarship must be connected with Richelieu's support of them and his appointment of Dom Grégoire Tarisse to be their Superior.[20] Only two years after Bishop's paper had appeared in the *Downside Review*, the conclusive confirmation of his guesswork appeared in 1913 in Dom Paul Denis' monograph, *Le Cardinal de Richelieu et la Réforme des Monastères Benedictins*. So brilliant a scientific historian, so acute a critic, and so devout a mind, inevitably led not only Cardinal Gasquet but other Benedictine scholars to follow in his footsteps.

His successors, with the exception of Dom Hugh Connolly, have followed him not in the area of liturgical history but in the history of monasticism. The two most eminent are Abbot Cuthbert Butler of Downside, and Dom David Knowles of the same community, former Regius Professor of History in the University of Cambridge. Butler published his lengthy and vivid account of the history of the Benedictine Order and its contribution to the growth of spirituality, education, and charity in Europe as *Benedictine Monachism: Benedictine Life and Rule* in 1922. Perhaps as a result of the frequent visits of Baron Friedrich von Hügel[21] to Downside, and certainly with the active encouragement of Edmund Bishop, Abbot Butler was stimulated to produce his standard history, *Western Mysticism*, in 1922. Dom David Knowles, in a monumental series of volumes, beginning with *The Monastic Order in England* (1940), and continuing with *The Religious Orders in England* (1948) and later volumes, is resuscitating by his historical scholarship and carefully controlled imagination the entire monastic life of mediaeval England. This, too, was a project

18 *Ibid.*, p. 452.
19 *Ibid.*, see Dix, *A Detection of Aumbries*, pp. 47-60, and Thurston's "Benediction of the Blessed Sacrament" in *The Month*, issues of June-September 1901. Bishop's paper was read in 1893 and published in the *Downside Review* in 1895.
20 *Ibid.*, Chap. XXVII.   21 See Chap. V, *supra*.

Bishop had envisioned for Downside Scholars. It is a noble testimony to the *Gesta Dei per monachos* and a tribute to Catholic spirituality through the centuries. Not least interesting is the use of aerial photographs in attempting to reconstruct plans of now ruined and desolate monastic buildings.

Perhaps the most notable work in Eucharistic theology to be essayed by a Benedictine in England was Abbot Anscar Vonier's *A Key to the Doctrine of the Eucharist* (1925).[22] Its most remarkable characteristic is the attempt made to reconcile the teaching of the great Dominican, St. Thomas Aquinas, with the mystery-theology of the Benedictines of Maria Laach Abbey.[23] Vonier was a great supporter of the modern Liturgical Movement and, monk though he was, insisted in his last work, *The People of God* (1937) that it is "a great gain towards our understanding of the Christian mysteries when we are willing to look upon them as being instituted, not for an *élite*, but for a people."[24] His authority for the fullest lay participation in the Mass came from the Canon of the Mass itself, where the Christian multitudes are described as the servants of God, but also as the holy people of God: *Unde et memores, Domine, nos servi tui, sed et plebs tua sancta.* He offers as the key to the Eucharist the emphasis in the teaching of St. Thomas and the Council of Trent on the sacramental character of the Sacrifice of the Altar.

The problem, as he saw it, was: "How am I to be linked up effectively with that great mystery of Christ's death?"[25] The link whereby the benefits of the atonement of Christ (returning to the Father all the glory He had lost through man's transgression) and His redemption (buying back the spiritual liberty of human beings enslaved to sin) were appropriated by humanity was a combination of the Sacraments and faith. He insists that the Sacraments are not symbols but representative signs with power, and calls to his aid the definition of St. Thomas, that "a Sacrament is a commemorative sign of what has gone before, in this case the Passion of Christ, a demonstrative sign of what is being effected in us through the Passion of Christ, that is grace, and a prognostic sign foretelling our future glory."[26]

[22] This was reprinted and published as the second volume of *The Collected Works of Abbot Vonier* to which references are made in this paragraph.
[23] This, the contribution of Abbot Herwegen and Dom Odo Casel, was considered in Chap. I, *supra*.
[24] P. 207.
[25] *A Key to the Doctrine of the Euchrist*, p. 230.
[26] This is a translation of St. Thomas Aquinas, S. Theol. III, Qu. IX, Art. 3:

Vonier argues that these sacramental signs are "not only power-ful in reminding us of the things of God, they have the power to make them live again." They are, that is, "tools in the hands of Christ 'who worketh until now.' "[27] To the Protestant charge that if the Mass is a sacrifice, it would mean that the Sacrifice on Calvary was incomplete, Vonier replies that the two sacrifices belong to entirely different modes of being, the first being a sacri-fice of Christ's own person and the Mass being a sacrifice in the mode of a sacrament. Vonier maintains, as against the immola-tionists, that the Eucharistic Sacrifice is not directly a mystery of Christ's Person, it is primarily a mystery of Christ's Body and Blood.[28] Thus: "Christ, who gave the Body and Blood to the Apostles at the Last Supper, was whole and entire at the head of the festive board. The Christ whose Body and Blood is on the Catholic altar is whole and entire in heaven. But the Eucharistic Body and Blood are representative of Christ in the state in which He was not whole and entire; when He was broken on the Cross at His death."[29] Thus the Eucharistic Body and Blood are the re-presentation not of the Christ who is in heaven, but of the Christ who was broken on Calvary. This doctrine creates some major difficulties, as can readily be seen. In what sense can it be claimed, on Vonier's view, that Christ is the consecrator of the Eucharist?

The difficulties are not lessened when Vonier goes on to insist that "the sacramental presence and the sacramental offering of Christ are not historical events in His career; they do not form new chapters in the book of His life."[30] Confusion becomes greater when he adds: "If there is a repetition of acts, those repetitions are not on the part of Christ, they are on the part of the Church living here on earth."[31] The dilemma which he cannot resolve seems to be: either the completeness of the act on Calvary is maintained, in which case it can hardly be re-presented, or if it is re-presented it is an act of the Church and, therefore, hardly of Christ's. This, indeed, is one of the difficulties of the Platonizing tendency of the mystery-theology, that it can hardly do justice to history's once-for-all character. If the mystery-theology is seeking for a consistent interpretation it might well employ the theology of the Epistle to

---

"Unde sacramentum est et signum rememorativum ejus quod praecessit, scilicet passionis Christi, et demonstrativum ejus quod in nobis efficitur per Christi passionem, scilicet gratiae, et prognosticum, idest praenuntiativum futurae gloriae."

27 *A Key to the Doctrine of the Eucharist*, p. 242.
28 *Ibid.*, p. 282.   29 *Ibid.*, p. 287.   30 *Ibid.*, p. 294.
31 *Ibid.*, p. 295.

the Hebrews and argue that there is one continual sacrifice offered up by Christ as the Great High Priest in Heaven, of which the individual Mass is the local manifestation, but this is decisively rejected by Vonier,[32] possibly because it is customary with High Anglicans.

The most thorough-going criticism of Vonier's sacramental doctrine is provided by Fr. Bernard Leeming in his *Principles of Sacramental Theology* of 1956.[33] The Jesuit theologian, a little unkindly perhaps, regards Vonier's as merely another "moral cause of grace" sacramental theory. He does, however, acknowledge that the theory draws attention to the essentially mysterious character of the Sacraments and to their fuller religious meanings, and provides a salutary warning against trying to define God's awesome dealings with humanity in terms of mere logic-chopping. Furthermore, the theory has the additional merit of emphasizing the essentially personal action of Christ in them, and that they issue in conformity to Christ. Father Leeming criticizes Vonier for obscuring the difference between Christ's presence in the Eucharist from His presence in the other Sacraments. He also urges a clearer exposition of the theological foundations of the sacramental theory. He remarks that even if Christ's death and resurrection are time-lessly made present, yet it is never suggested how they cause the mystic death and resurrection, or how the recipient (in Baptism) is made free of original sin and given grace. He considers that the whole theory is based upon an idealist philosophy, but that the Christian faith cannot be accommodated to such a view. Finally, he argues that Vonier confuses a sacrament with a sacrifice, for the symbolism of a sacrifice is man turning to God, and of a sacrament, of God turning to man to sanctify him.

In reply, it might be said that much of Leeming's criticism seems more appropriate to Dom Odo Casel's exposition than to Vonier's, which went as far in a Thomistic direction as was possible, and also, perhaps, that what God does for man in Christ through the sacrifice on the Cross, mediated by the sacrament, is more significant than even the Church's offering to God. It is clear that the mystery-theology has not yet met all the criticisms, but it is equally clear that it has a Patristic basis and an ecumenical importance far surpassing the Tridentine theory. It needs to be reconstructed rather than rejected. Vonier's work had at least the

32 *Ibid.*, p. 344.
33 See pp. 305-13 for the critique of Vonier.

benefit of familiarising English theologians with the new accents of sacramental theology of Maria Laach and its plea for an ecclesiology which would do justice to the supreme process of the Christian's mystical incorporation through the Sacraments. The latter was to find an admirable exposition in the work of the present Abbot of Downside, Dom B. Christopher Butler, in *The Idea of the Church* (1962).[34]

It was hardly to be expected that the Benedictines in the present century would produce a spiritual writer of the quality of Augustine Baker, whose *Sancta Sophia* has been a constant source of guidance for their novices from the seventeenth to the twentieth centuries. In actual fact, though more brilliantly endowed than Baker, Dom (later Abbot) John Chapman's spiritual directions, collected in *Spiritual Letters* (1935), manifest the same balance and sobriety and commitment to the hands of God as Baker's. Where they differ is in the expression of true humility, for Chapman's self-depreciation and utter lack of pretension finds its outlet in whimsy and often in the most Carrollian sense of humour. He deflates himself so that God may be the ultimate director of the souls of his correspondents, but, when necessary, he does not hesitate to delineate the stages of the spiritual life with the utmost clarity, concision, cogency, and practicality. Yet so modest is he that no one would judge from his tone that he was a distinguished New Testament scholar and historian.

What are the sources of his understanding of spirituality? To begin with, the vicissitudes of a varied religious pilgrimage. The son of the Anglican Archdeacon of Sudbury, educated at Christ Church, Oxford (where he took a first in "Greats") and Cuddesdon theological college, he had tried a spell as a deacon in the Anglican Church, then eight months as a Jesuit novice, and finally found his true bent as a Benedictine novice at Maredsous, where he became the pupil of Dom Columba Marmion, among the most distinguished Retreat leaders of modern times. He was professed in 1895 at Erdington, where he ultimately became Prior.

Thereafter his varied duties included the delicate task of acting as Abbot of the Caldey Island community of monks which had left the Anglican Church to submit to the Roman obedience, a period

---

[34] Here it is argued that there have been three theories of the Church in history, as an invisible and purely interior entity, as a visible entity which is potentially a single communion, and essentially a single, visible historical society, and that the third is the only option that does justice to the New Testament and the tribunal of history.

as chaplain at the Front in France and with prisoners of war in Switzerland, and the years from 1919 to 1922 in Rome as a member of the Vulgate Commission. In 1919 he was affiliated to Downside, returning as Claustral Prior in 1922, and eventually becoming Abbot. This versatile man, with a razor-sharp mind and the aesthetic sensitivity of an accomplished pianist, had a wide enough experience of the world to know its allurements and temptations, and to counsel others about that life of contemplation which he had sought with all his devout heart.[35]

Dom John Chapman had learned much from Dom Columba Marmion, but his deepest tutor was St. John of the Cross, the Spanish mystical doctor. As an Anglican he had learned from *The Imitation of Christ*, and as a Roman Catholic from St. Francis de Sales' *On the Love of God*, from Scupoli's *Spiritual Combat*, and from Gay's *Les Vertues Chrétiennes*. In his later years he appreciated St. Theresa, later still St. John of the Cross, and, finally, he was particularly fond of the Jesuit Father, Pierre de Caussade, for his doctrine of *l'abandon*.[36]

Prayer is always emphasized as a privilege, and never as a grim duty. How typical in its practicality and wit is the following direction: ". . . give yourself to prayer when you can, and trust in God that He will lead you, without your choosing your path. Mr. Asquith is an excellent model (not for Cabinet Ministers), but for contemplatives: wait for pressure from without; do not act unless you must; let the *Daily Mail* take the initiative."[37] Equally characteristic is the point that our detractors, like St. Theresa's, may do more good than our flatterers for our spiritual life. This point is humorously illustrated, as follows: "It was like Barry Pain's story of the girl who was told by the great artist that her hair was divine, while the little boys in the street called out 'carrots' as she passed. She was so puzzled that she wanted to die—so she dyed. I can't help believing that St. Theresa got more good from her detractors than from her visions!"[38] There is not a trace of sentimentality or luxuriating in emotion in Dom John Chapman: "We *cannot* call up feelings of love and adoration when we want to; and they would be of little value if we could."[39]

[35] For biographical details, see the second enlarged edition of *The Spiritual Letters of Dom John Chapman, O.S.B., Fourth Abbot of Downside*, edited with an introductory biography by Dom Roger Hudleston. For an appreciation of his spirituality, see Abbot B. C. Butler's evaluation, in Chap. XV of *English Spiritual Writers*, ed. by Charles Davis, S.J.
[36] See Dom Roger Hudleston, ed., *The Spiritual Letters. . .* , p. 24.
[37] *Ibid.*, p. 35.   [38] *Ibid.*, pp. 91-92.   [39] *Ibid.*, p. 150.

The theory of abandonment to God, so exceedingly helpful to souls going through a dry period of their spiritual life, is admirably expressed in the following statement: "Therefore the whole point of the 'Sacrament of the present moment' . . . is that it is a (covering, yet revealing) sacrament; it is God's action, God's will, or it is God."[40] Dom John Chapman believed that as surely as a fish lives in water, so does the soul live each moment in the action of God. Once that conviction is accepted, there is every cause for trusting the Divine love that casts out fear, a sense of which is sometimes given at the beginning of the spiritual pilgrimage, but which is later withdrawn. When it is withdrawn, there should be no desire for extraordinary proofs of the Divine care in visions or other assurances, for such desires are the expressions of disbelief. Such was Dom John Chapman's robust and obedient piety.

A pamphlet on Contemplative Prayer, which is printed as an appendix to the *Spiritual Letters*, had a very wide circulation, and is an extraordinarily clear map of the successive stages in the spiritual pilgrimage of the soul. As conceived by Dom John Chapman, the first kind of mental prayer is Meditation, consisting of three parts: realizing a truth and thus making the Faith real; the drawing out of the imagination from pleasures towards God; and the making of various Acts, either as resolutions or affections. This process leads inevitably to the second kind of mental prayer, namely, the prayer of "Forced Acts." In this second stage, according to Father Augustine Baker, there is only a little thinking, but the making of many Acts. (Abbot Chapman, following St. John of the Cross, does not believe that this is an enduring stage of the soul's pilgrimage, seeing it only as a "wobbly transition state.") The third kind of mental Prayer is Contemplative. In this stage the Acts are not forced, nor are they the prayer, but merely an accompaniment to avoid distractions. (Abbot Chapman adds that many modern writers place the Prayer of Simplicity, that is, continued acts and thoughts, as an introductory stage of contemplative prayer, and often see it as coming after or in "The Obscure Night" of the soul.)

It was not rapture, but the steady direction of the self towards God that Dom John Chapman sought for himself and his pupils in the spiritual life. His manly intellect, unsentimental realism, and inward reserve, as well as his respect for the independence of the souls he directed, combined with the irrepressible humour that

40 *Ibid.*, p. 83.

marked his humanity, made him a most invigorating spiritual director.

The last contribution of spirituality from Downside to be considered is more directly linked with the modern Liturgical Movement. It is Dom Illtyd Trethowan's *Christ in the Liturgy* (1952). It attempts to do for England what Dom Odo Casel did for Austria and Germany, and Père Louis Bouyer did for France, that is, make generally available the newer understanding of the Liturgy as the mystery which incorporates Christians as the Body of Christ. He begins by raising the objection that the Liturgy seems to be a routine for escaping the problems of prayer and that essential religion is surely the union of the *solus cum Solo*. His answer is that "the silent prayer of the heart is a flowering of the soul fructified by the Liturgy" and is itself a preparation for a deeper sharing in the Liturgy. He sees the Liturgy as a "solemn game," for it is "fundamentally the praise of God, entering so far as we can on this earth into his joy (Claudel's *le grand rire divin*)."[41]

In the central third chapter, expounding "Christ's Sacrifice and Ours," the author claims that Christ "has given us his sacrifice under a sacrament, so that we too may sacrifice. We enter in his sacrifice; *our* bread and wine actually become it. Through that sacrifice which is himself, we are incorporated with him."[42] In the Liturgy, which is Christ's sign, "Christ puts the entire Redemptive mystery, not only his Passion and Death, but his Resurrection and his Ascension," and this means that "we have our Lord in all his reality in his consummated, but ever-active glorious state."[43] In consequence, "the past is not repeated, but it is not dead: it remains real in the present."[44]

Successive chapters deal with the various parts of the Mass, with the Liturgical Year, the Singing of the Mass and the Modern Problems, and the Divine Office. Of the Liturgical Year Dom Illtyd says: "the mystery is so rich and so far beyond our comprehension in its totality that it must be spread out for us over the whole year, so that we may gradually assimilate it more and more."[45] He refers, with pride, to the contribution to the liturgical movement made by Dom Gregory Murray of Downside in *A People's Mass*, for this is a very simple setting of the Ordinary of the Mass in which layfolk can easily participate.[46] This has

[41] *Christ in the Liturgy*, p. 6.   [42] *Ibid.*, p. 33.
[43] *Ibid.*, p. 34.   [44] *Ibid.*, pp. 35-36.   [45] *Ibid.*, p. 68.
[46] *Ibid.*, p. 109. Dom Gregory Murray has also produced the following important pamphlets: *Accentual Cadences in Gregorian Chant, The Authentic Rhythm of*

won wide success not only in England, but also at Lourdes. He is strongly convinced that it is only by the liturgical use of their own language that the congregation will take their proper part in the liturgical action at Mass. Moreover, "any liturgical culture must be a Biblical culture" and hence "a re-education of the faithful in the Bible must accompany liturgical preaching if our efforts are to produce solid and lasting results."[47]

The strong emphasis on the Liturgy could lead to a depreciation of the role of the Divine Office. This Dom Illtyd Trethowan is anxious to guard against. He strongly recommends that the laity should observe morning and evening prayers, by the use of the Offices for Lauds and Vespers. "These take less than a quarter of an hour to recite with decent reverence, and their general adoption, by the educated laity at least, is something which one can hardly advocate too strongly."[48] The relation of the Divine Office to the Eucharist is finely described: "For the Divine Office is the Church's praise spreading out from its centre, the Mass, over the rest of the day. Properly understood, it is the sanctification of *time*, the drawing of particular periods between the celebration of one day's Mass and the next into the orbit, as it were, of the Eucharist."[49]

The Epilogue, on Christian Perfection and Intellectualism, is all the more impressive because Dom Illtyd Trethowan is an able Christian philosopher.[50] Its conclusion is: ". . . in a decadent age it is easy for us to be infected with the idolatry of scholarship which acts as a substitute for the true culture of the mind. We know that the cure for this and all other disorders is, in a word, the Liturgy, the source of contemplation; the Liturgy is the supreme apostolate; it is the Church herself, whose life is the Liturgy, who is the supreme witness to the Resurrection."[51]

One further Benedictine contribution to thought about the Liturgy needs to be mentioned. That is Dom Benedict Steuart's *The Development of Christian Worship* (1953). It is a sketch or outline of the history of the Liturgy written by a monk of St. Michael's Abbey in Farnborough, Hampshire. It is a most useful attempt "to gather together the results of recent writers on the

---

Gregorian Chant, Gregorian Rhythm in the Gregorian Centuries, and *Plainsong Rhythm*.

[47] *Ibid.*, p. 117.   [48] *Ibid.*, p. 123.   [49] *Ibid.*, p. 120.

[50] His best known writings in this genre are *Certainty, philosophical and theological* and *An Essay in Christian Philosophy*.

[51] *Christ in the Liturgy*, p. 148.

history of the Liturgy—both abroad and in this country—for the sake of those people who, while anxious to know more about the meaning and history of the worship of the Church, are unable . . . to do so."[52] Carefully and unpretentiously written, it exhibits a fine ecumenical spirit which recognizes the importance of Anglican contributions to liturgiology, and, in particular, the significance of J. H. Srawley's *Early History of the Liturgy* and Dom Gregory Dix's *The Shape of the Liturgy.* It has a particularly helpful account in an appendix of "The Restored Easter Vigil."[53]

The frequency with which the name Downside has dominated the preceding pages is testimony to the leadership of that great Abbey in the understanding of the Liturgy, the Divine Office, and of the spiritual and contemplative life in England. Benedictines from other abbeys also made their own contribution, notably Abbot Vonier and Dom Benedict Steuart, but the claim must be upheld that in the renascence of Catholic intellectual life in England there were three dominating influences: "the importance and influence of Newman, the outstanding place occupied by the great Benedictine Abbey of Downside, and the leading position taken by converts in all this transaction."[54] In fairness, however, to other Orders it should be emphasized that in the popularization of the meaning of the Liturgy among the educated laity distinguished contributions were also made by the Society of Jesus, notably by Fathers C. C. Martindale, Ronald Knox, and Clifford Howell.[55]

4. The Progress of the Liturgical Movement among English Catholics

At the outset, it must again be emphasized that the progress of the Liturgical Movement in any country which is predominantly Protestant is bound to be slower than in one predominantly Catholic. It is not a matter of mere numbers, but far more of ethos. The point is that so many features of the Modern Liturgical Movement appear to be so Protestant in character: the emphasis on the vernacular, the importance of Biblical exposition, the aim at greater participation in worship, the central altar around which the people are gathered, have their strong Protestant counterparts. Therefore, it may look as if in a predominantly Protestant

[52] P. xi.
[53] *The Development of Christian Worship,* pp. 273-80.
[54] G. A. Beck, ed., *The English Catholics, 1850-1950,* p. 558.
[55] In the section which follows I am greatly indebted to Father Clifford Howell, S.J., although I take entire responsibility for the statements and judgments there made.

country the advocates of the Liturgical Movement are going to Canterbury or even to Wittenberg or Geneva. This is undoubtedly one factor accounting for the relatively slow progress of the Liturgical Revival among English Catholics. Moreover, a country where Roman Catholicism was reintroduced only a century ago is not likely to be able to allow its Religious Orders to take time off from the task of catechising and evangelising to study such apparently academic matters as the history of the Liturgy. These two reasons would be sufficient to account for the tardiness of the appreciation of the Liturgical Revival in England. It can confidently be supposed that its development will be all the more rapid in the ensuing decade because of the highly important Constitution on Sacred Liturgy which was adopted by the second session of the Vatican Ecumenical Council on December 4, 1963. This important document makes it clear that the Liturgical Revival is not the concern of visionary reformers, but of the whole Church.

Before the Second World War there were several books published on the meaning of the Mass, but extraordinarily few that expressed the view that the laity should be participants rather than spectators. This was, indeed, the era when the dignity and splendour of the Liturgy were chiefly considered, a period of rubrical interest. One of those most influential in spreading the concern for order and dignity was Adrian Fortescue,[56] who published *The Tridentine Missal* in 1916 in an edition, with a prefatory explanation, known as the "Liturgy for Layfolk." Two years later there followed the important book, *The Ceremonies of the Roman Rite Described with Plans and Diagrams*, which had reached a tenth edition by 1958. Father Fortescue also had a deep interest in the Liturgies of the Eastern Church, for in 1908 he had published *The Divine Liturgy of . . . John Chrysostom*, translated into English with introduction and annotation by himself. Liturgy continued to be a matter of the sanctuary and choir-loft, with the people as spectators.

It was beginning to be felt in some quarters, however, that they should at least be intelligent spectators. This was the view of Father C. C. Martindale in *The Mind of the Missal*, in which the distinguished Jesuit expounded the rich piety of the liturgical prayers. A similar concern motivated another brilliant Jesuit, Monsignor Ronald Knox, in his sparkling popular account, *The Mass in Slow Motion*. His Introduction is a breathlessly brilliant

---

[56] See J. W. Fortescue and John G. Vance, *Adrian Fortescue: A Memoir* (1924).

summary of the Mass. On the clause in the Creed "and was made man," he comments, "and the splendid dramatic moment of *Et homo factus est*, with the noise of kicking and scraping behind you, where rheumatic knees are being laboriously bent in honour of God made Man."[57] There follows the brilliant image of the Preface in the Prayer of Consecration, "with the various ranks of Angels flashing past like the names of suburban stations as we draw closer to the heart of the great capital."[58] Then there follows the amazed wonder of the Consecration itself: "You elevate the Host, the Chalice; or are they trying to fly upwards out of your hands? You hardly know, it is so strange."[59] Finally, there is his pointed conclusion: "So much of drama every day of our lives; and we, how little we are thrilled by it."[60] Moreover, the very clarity of Knox's addresses, and the astonishing fertility of his illustrations, frequently hide the penetration of the thought that went into their making. This is particularly true of his fascinating series of Eucharistic addresses, *The Window in the Wall* (1956), in which he expounds the Eucharist as the focus of the spiritual life where eternity breaks through into time, the spiritual life through the material life, and Christ into human nature. He envisions it as the Sacrament of unity and peace, of our thanksgiving for creation and renewal in Christ, and of Christ's continuing humility. It is the iron-ration of the pilgrim, the Sacrament that prepares for life and for death. Supremely, it is the Sacrament of Christ's love, manifesting his unchanging friendship, his compassion for the multitude, and the Sacrament of Sacrifice.[61] Such enthusiastic and informed introductions to the Mass must, at the very least, have made those who heard them devout and intelligent spectators at Christ's Banquet.

Still in the archaeological and rubrical period between the First and Second World Wars was the foundation by the Benedictine monk, Dom Bernard McElligott, of the Society of St. Gregory. This association of priests and laity was devoted to the study and the spread of Gregorian chanting. However, the Society also had in mind the practical aim of getting the people to sing their own parts of the Mass to the Gregorian settings. By means of Summer Schools, and of a periodical called *Music and Liturgy*, there was some infusion of Abbot Guéranger's ideals among English Catho-

[57] *The Mass in Slow Motion*, p. xiii.
[58] *Ibid.*, p. xv.   [59] *Ibid.*, p. xvii.   [60] *Ibid.*, p. xviii.
[61] See especially sermons 12, 15, 18, and 20.

277

lics. On the whole, however, the Society's influence was limited to an educated élite and its chief success has been the introduction of plainsong Masses to schools.

The pioneer in the introduction of the Dialogue Mass was Father Clifford Howell, S.J., who during a study leave in Germany had become familiar with the new Liturgical Movement, but had no opportunity to introduce the Dialogue Mass in England before the Second World War. As a military chaplain, however, he began it among the troops abroad. He had a simple Dialogue Mass booklet printed when in Cyprus, and this proved to be most successful in propagating the idea and the practice of the Dialogue Mass. The idea spread to other chaplains and by the end of the war it was common throughout all the armed forces, and found its way into several parishes.

At about the same time Father Samuel Gosling of Alton, Staffordshire, founded the English Liturgy Society, subsequently renamed the Vernacular Society of Great Britain. Lacking the official support of the hierarchy, it made very slow progress indeed, but its views have slowly spread with the years until they are now very much *à la mode*, though the founder did not live to see this popularity. Another major influence in spreading the ideals of the Liturgical Movement was Count Michael de la Bedoyere, until 1962 the editor of the *Catholic Herald*, author of *The Life of Baron von Hügel* (1951).[62] He welcomed articles on the liturgical renewal and opened his correspondence columns to the discussion of many aspects of its pastoral significance, and this ultimately persuaded publishers that there would be sufficient interest in books on the same theme.

Father Clifford Howell was not content with pioneering in the use of the Dialogue Mass in England. He felt that a liturgical parish mission should be developed to teach the relevance of the Liturgy to the daily life of folk in the parishes. Early in 1947 he gave the first liturgical mission under the title of "Layfolks' Week." It comprised a series of "leaflet services," made up of material drawn from the Liturgy in the vernacular, arranged so that the laity were given an active part in praying and singing together, and thus would gain the experience of corporate worship. He it was also who introduced the practice of Commentators and Lectors, at first against considerable opposition, but this has dwindled

---

[62] Count Michael de la Bedoyere also wrote *Christianity in the Market-Place*, *The Layman in the Church*, and the biography, *Cardinal Bernard Griffin, Archbishop of Westminster*.

since the Instruction of the Sacred Congregation of Rites approved these customs in 1958. In books, pamphlets, and articles, as in lectures and in the multitude of Dialogue Masses and Layfolks' Weeks he has conducted, Father Clifford Howell has been a veritable dynamo of the Liturgical Movement in England.[63] He has never failed to point out that the participation of the laity in the Liturgy is the practical implication of the doctrine that the Church is the Mystical Body of Christ and that through the Liturgy the Christian is incorporated into Christ.

In recent years there have been several notable protagonists of the Liturgical Movement, and of the catechetical and Biblical movements associated with it. Donald Attwater, an authority on Eastern spirituality, theology, and liturgy, argued for the vernacular in 1944 in his book, *In the Beginning was the Word: a Plea for English Words in the Worship of the Roman Church.* Lancelot Shepherd, an authority on the Roman Rite, gave his blessing to the same project. Others who provided momentum to the Liturgical Movement were Fathers James Crichton and William Raftery, Monsignor Joseph Buckley, and Canon Alban Burrett. They have encouraged the intelligent participation of the laity in the Liturgy in their own parishes, and written articles on the subject for various Roman Catholic periodicals. Theological justifications of the Liturgical Movement of high quality are Dom Illtyd Trethowan's *Christ in the Liturgy* (1952) and Father Charles Davis' *Liturgy and Doctrine.* The latter also edited an important historical volume, *English Spiritual Writers* (1961), tracing the contributions of English Catholic writers on spirituality from Aelfric of Eynsham and Richard Rolle to John Chapman and Ronald Knox.

One consequence of stressing lay participation in the Liturgy was the need to provide simpler settings for the singing of the people's parts in the Mass. Dom Gregory Murray of Downside met this need in his *People's Mass*, as did Dom Laurence Benevot in *The Proper of the Mass.*[64] Both found a widespread welcome, with the result that congregationally sung Masses are now to be heard in many parishes throughout England. Furthermore, Eng-

---

[63] Reference may be made to Father Howell's *The Work of Our Redemption,* and his *Mass Commentaries*, both books that sold widely, and to his booklet *Mass Together* (Chelworth, Malmesbury, Wiltshire) which was phenomenally successful. He has also written *Preparing for Easter,* and translated two important works by J. A. Jungmann, S.J., namely, *Public Worship* and *The Sacrifice of the Church.*

[64] The four settings were published in 1948.

lish enthusiasts for Père Gélineau's vernacular psalm-singing have explored the possibility of attempting to provide an English equivalent. Baroness Bosch van Drakenstein of the Grail Community in Pinner, Middlesex, has sponsored this work, under the musical editorship of Dom Gregory Murray, and the results have been published in two volumes, so far, of *The Grail Version of the Psalms*, the first containing twenty-four and the second thirty Psalms. These have been taken up by several schools, but only in a few parishes.

Most important of all is the linking of the Liturgical Movement with the Catechetical and Biblical Movements. Canon Drinkwater of Lower Gornal, Dudley, the founder and editor of *The Sower*, was the catechetical pioneer who always recognized the teaching value of the Liturgy, and he was most appreciative of the pastoral aspect of the Liturgical Movement. Its two chief publicists are Fathers Alexander Jones and Hubert Richards. The former has written *Unless some Man show me* (1951), an interesting exposition of the Old Testament. The latter was one of the translators of Charlier's *La Lecture Chrétienne à la Bible*, in English *The Christian Approach to the Bible* (1958). Father Richards is also one of the literary editors of *The Grail Version of the Psalms*.

In the slow but steady progress of the Liturgical Movement in English Catholicism, it can be seen that Edmund Bishop followed in the footsteps of Guéranger; Vonier, Trethowan, and Davis passed on the heritage of Casel, Beauduin, and Jungmann; Howell, Jones, and Richards undertook the tasks of Pius Parsch; and Gregory Murray the part of Gélineau. Thus, the Continental Liturgical Movement was channelled to English Catholics.

As for the future, it can be confidently predicted that the Liturgical Movement will grow from strength to strength in English Catholic life. This is guaranteed by the text of the Constitution on Sacred Liturgy adopted by the Vatican Ecumenical Council at its second session on December 4, 1963. Here authoritative approval was given to the concerns of the Liturgical Movement in a noble expression. This document is, in fact, the classical statement of those aims for which the protagonists of the Liturgical Movement have been striving amid much misunderstanding and obloquy, or indifference, in the earlier years of this century. The present chapter will conclude by giving a brief account of it, as outlining the future of Catholic worship in England, and elsewhere.

The Liturgy is Christ's act, "an exercise of the priestly office of Jesus Christ" and in the Liturgy "the whole public worship is performed by the mystical body of Jesus Christ, that is, by the head and His members." For this reason it is "a sacred action surpassing all others."[65] As the participation of the laity is strongly stressed, so also is the eschatological reference: "in the earthly liturgy we take part in a foretaste of that heavenly liturgy which is celebrated in the Holy City of Jerusalem towards which we journey as pilgrims."[66] Pastors are encouraged "to insure that the faithful take part fully aware of what they are doing, actively engaged in the rite, and enriched by its effects."[67] Popular devotions are to be drawn up in accordance with the sacred Liturgy and to lead to it, "since, in fact, the liturgy by its very nature surpasses any of them."[68]

The active participation of the people is required both by the nature of the Liturgy, as also by the status of Christian people as "a chosen race, a royal priesthood, a holy nation, a redeemed people."[69] A liturgically instructed people presupposes a liturgically informed priesthood. Therefore "the study of sacred liturgy is to be ranked among the compulsory and major courses in seminaries and religious houses of study; in theological faculties it is to rank among the principal courses."[70] It is also to be taught in its theological, historical, spiritual, pastoral, and juridical aspects. Also, professors of dogmatic, spiritual, and pastoral theology, and of the holy scriptures are to bring out the connection between their subjects and the Liturgy.[71]

With great care a restoration of the Liturgy is to be attempted. "In this restoration, both texts and rites should be drawn up so that they express more clearly the holy things which they signify; the Christian people, so far as possible, should be enabled to understand them with ease, and take part in them fully, actively, and as befits a community."[72] The investigation of the various parts of the Liturgy to be revised should be theological, historical, and pastoral.[73] Experience gained from recent liturgical reforms is also to be considered. But "there must be no innovations unless the good of the Church genuinely and certainly requires them."[74] Furthermore, "to achieve the restoration, progress, and adaptation of the sacred liturgy, it is essential to promote that warm and living

[65] *Constitution on Sacred Liturgy*, § 7.
[66] *Ibid.*, § 8.   [67] *Ibid.*, § 11.   [68] *Ibid.*, § 13.
[69] *Ibid.*, § 14, citing I Peter 2:9.
[70] *Ibid.*, § 16.   [71] *Ibid.*   [72] *Ibid.*, § 21.
[73] *Ibid.*, § 23.   [74] *Ibid.*

love for scripture to which the venerable tradition of both eastern and western rites gives testimony."[75]

There is a highly complex consideration of different norms appropriate for the reform of the Liturgy, those of a general character, and those drawn from the hierarchic and communal nature of the Liturgy, and from its didactic and pastoral character, and those for adapting the Liturgy to the culture and traditions of peoples. Certain principles emerge from these considerations. Communal celebrations are to be preferred to private or quasi-private ones. Provision of rubrics to clarify the people's parts is necessary. The rites "should be distinguished by a noble simplicity."[76] The intimate connection between words and rites is to be made clearer in several ways. There is to be more reading from the Scriptures, and it is to be more varied and suitable. The ministry of preaching is to be fulfilled with fidelity. "The sermon, moreover, should draw its content mainly from scriptural and liturgical sources, and its character should be that of a proclamation of God's wonderful works in the history of salvation, the mystery of Christ, ever made present and active within us, especially in the celebration of the liturgy."[77] Bible services are to be encouraged especially on Sundays and feast days, on some weekdays in Advent and Lent, and on the vigils of important festivals.[78]

While the use of the Latin language is to be preserved in the Latin rites, the limits of the employment of the mother tongue may be extended, especially in the readings and directives, as in the prayers and the chants.[79] It is also hoped that in every diocese there will be appointed a liturgical commission for promoting the liturgical apostolate, and also, if possible, commissions for sacred music and sacred art.[80]

Other important parts of the Constitution on Sacred Liturgy are concerned with the reform, restoration, and adaptation of the Eucharist (Chapter II), the other Sacraments and Sacramentals (Chapter III), the Divine Office (Chapter IV), the Liturgical Year (Chapter V), and Sacred Music (Chapter VI). Throughout the aim is that the worship of God may fittingly celebrate the mysteries of salvation, to permit the maximum participation of God's people and thus their edification and sanctification through incorporation in the mystical Body of Christ. To this end there is to be a simplification, clarification, and purification of the rites.

[75] *Ibid.*, § 24.   [76] *Ibid.*, § 34.   [77] *Ibid.*
[78] *Ibid.*   [79] *Ibid.*, § 36.   [80] *Ibid.*, §§ 45, 46.

Above all, the great mysteries of salvation are to be emphasized in the Christian Year, as over the sanctoral cycle, and only those saints of truly universal import are to be recalled as pre-eminent servants of God. Scripture is to come into its own as the record of the Divine revelation, and preaching is to be magnified, for Christian worship is the response to revelation. Thus, it may be seen that the Biblical and Liturgical Movements are complementary and mutually re-inforcing. They are both profoundly concerned with the intellectual and spiritual renewal of the life of Christ's Church.

CHAPTER VIII

ANGLICAN WORSHIP TO 1928

ROM THE worship of the Roman Catholic Church we turn to
that of the Church of England with its Catholic and Reformed
inheritance. Our two chapters on Anglican worship are divided by an important liturgical watershed—the Prayer Book
Controversy of 1928. Until 1928, when Parliament rejected the
Deposited Prayer Book, against the declared will of the Church
of England as expressed through its Church Assembly, the consideration of worship was marked by acrimonious partisanship
between High Church and Low. After 1928 a sobering armistice
ensued, which was followed by a peace built on mutual understanding. Consequently liturgical experiments flourished in a more
united Church.

It is hardly possible to exaggerate the ceremonial chaos which
characterized the Church of England in the first three decades.
It is wittily detailed in the drawings and commentary of Peter F.
Anson, that ecclesiastical Osbert Lancaster of our time, in his
Fashions in Church Furnishings, 1840-1940.[1] This book is a
veritable Christian Diorama! Indeed, the uninitiated reader, consulting only Anson's illustrations of the furnishings of the altar
and the vestments of the clergy, might readily suppose that there
were three Churches of England, not one. The confusion would
be confirmed as he concentrated on the bare and even bleak
interiors of Anglican Evangelical churches, on the "British Museum" ceremonial and furnishings of the moderate Anglo-Catholics
of the Percy Dearmer school who seemed to think they were living
in the late Gothic age of Edward VI and not in the industrial age
of Edward VII, and on the Baroque and Rococo altars favoured by
the extreme Anglican Papalists of the Society of SS. Peter and
Paul which appeared to transport the beholder into seventeenth or
eighteenth century Spain or France.

Evangelical Anglican churches had a simple oak Communion-
table "either left bare or vested in a stiff frontal of crimson cloth,
sometimes embroidered with lilies or passion flowers, but seldom
with a cross."[2] The Communion was celebrated from the North

---

[1] Published by the Faith Press, London, 1960.
[2] Anson, *Fashions in Church Furnishings*, p. 290.

end. If there was a reredos, instead of the usual unadorned panelling, it often was in the form of Gothic arches with the Decalogue, the Lord's Prayer and the Apostles' Creed painted on the panels. The choir was often composed of women as well as men, and the clergyman would celebrate the Lord's Supper in a surplice with a black scarf. Apart from the surplice and the placing of the Communion-table against the East wall, the service with its well-sung hymns and its unabbreviated sermon might easily be mistaken for the worship of Presbyterians or Congregationalists in a London suburb. It was, in brief, unmistakably Reformed in emphasis.

The moderate Anglo-Catholics took their lead from Percy Dearmer.[3] He, in turn, was trying faithfully to popularize the view of J. T. Micklethwaite as expressed in the first publication of the Alcuin Club in 1897, *The Ornaments of the Rubric*. Micklethwaite, accepting the legal view that all ornaments in use in the sixth year of the reign of Edward VI were perfectly legitimate for continuing Anglican use, surprised the public by the results of his indefatigable researches into Edwardine history. He held that images and pictures, as long as they were not superstitiously abused, were valid ornaments; that curtains, riddels and costers about altars were required by the Ornaments Rubric, and that even a hanging pyx might be used for the reservation of the consecrated elements. He contended that in 1548-1549 there were generally two lights on the high altar and one on each side, but that more might be used for great festivals. All these, therefore, instead of being unwarranted Roman additions to the English Rite perpetrated by Anglo-Catholics, were now declared to be not only authentically Anglican, but to be required by the Ornaments Rubric. Here, indeed, was a turning of the tables on the Evangelicals and Liberals who had hitherto criticized the Anglo-Catholics for disloyalty to the Prayer Book tradition! The triumphant chauvinism of Micklethwaite's conclusion deserves citation: "The substitution of foreign ornaments is mischievous from the countenance it gives to those who profess to see in the present revival in the Church of England only an imitation of the Church of Rome. And we do not want the things, our own are better."[4]

1. *The Popularity of "The English Use"*

Percy Dearmer (1867-1936) publicised these findings both in

[3] See Nan Dearmer, *The Life of Percy Dearmer*.
[4] *The Ornaments of the Rubric*, p. 62.

his immensely popular *Parson's Handbook*, which appeared in 1899, re-appeared in a revised and enlarged edition in 1903, and ran to a more profusely illustrated sixth edition in 1907, and in the ceremonial and furnishings of the Church of St. Mary the Virgin in Primrose Hill, London, the living of which he accepted in 1900. His red brick neo-Gothic church, which had been built in 1873, was entirely white-washed, so that the altar which now had riddel curtains and a dorsal stood out for all to see. Three silver lamps of Venetian workmanship were hung in the choir, and in 1914 a rood beam was installed across the chancel arch and a wooden *corona-lucis* was suspended from the rood. All representations of Christ were vested and crowned. The vestments were full and wide, and coloured "apparels" were attached to albs and amices to add to their interest. The ceremonial was elaborate but entirely faithful to the time of Edward VI. The sentimental melodies of Victorian hymn-tunes were abolished and plain-chant was introduced. After 1906 the congregation was introduced to the *English Hymnal*, of which Dearmer was editor-in-chief, and traditional English sacred poetry and melody became familiar.[5] Good music, good craftsmanship, and the beauty of the setting succeeded not only in filling the Church every Sunday, but in widespread interest and imitation. The result was Percy Dearmer turned the "English Use" into an ecclesiastical imperialism. His wife, Nan Dearmer, has not exaggerated in claiming that as a result of his influence the "English Altar" was recovered as the correct official practice of the Church of England and the choir habit of the clergy was restored, as well as the use of the "Lenten Array."[6] His work was forwarded by the Alcuin Club, which by 1912 had published twenty volumes of its "Collections" and almost a dozen "Tracts."

In 1916 Dearmer left Primrose Hill, but four years earlier he and a group of enthusiasts had founded the Warham Guild. This provided a centre in London where those interested in the "English Use" could find the ornaments recommended in the *Parson's Handbook* and be recommended to artists and craftsmen who worked in the sound English tradition. The Guild was assisted by the advice of liturgical and aesthetic experts such as F. E. Brightman, Walter Frere, F. C. Eeles, Geoffrey Lucas, Christopher Webb, and Martin Travers. Its influence was seen not only in parish

5 Anson, *Fashions in Church Furnishings*, pp. 307-09.
6 *Life of Percy Dearmer*, p. 115.

churches but in every English cathedral, and even in the churches of the Commonwealth. One of the most famous examples of such furnishings was the Thaxted parish church under Conrad Noel.

Influential as Dearmer's work was, it was not without its critics. His *Parson's Handbook* was successful because it appealed to many different temperaments and types of churchmanship. (The "English Altar" eventually influenced both Liberal and Evangelical Churchmen.) The *Parson's Handbook* had three major characteristics: it was legalistic, strongly nationalistic, and thoroughly antiquarian. At the same time it had a valid artistic approach which demanded good craftsmanship rather than shoddy mass-production. Its legalism strengthened the Anglo-Catholic party because its loyalty was no longer felt to be under suspicion, and there is no question that the stability, growth, and acceptance of Anglo-Catholicism is one of the most significant elements in the twentieth century Anglican Church. At the same time "Dearmer-titis" stiffly turned rubrics into laws, and seemed to believe in the plenary inspiration of the Edwardine settlement. Moreover, its nationalism was insecurely founded, for it failed to recognize that the liturgical and ceremonial customs of England in the reign of King Edward VI, far from being distinctively English, hardly varied from the liturgical and ceremonial customs then current in Italy, Spain, and France. Even more serious was the antiquarianism, for this was a freezing of the current of worship which must change if a Church is to be alive to the art and customs of its own century. As Dom Anselm Hughes remarks, it soon came to be known as "British Museum" religion, "for its insularity in place was coupled with an insularity in time, which was seeking to stereotype all material details by the patterns of the sixteenth century or earlier."[7] Moreover, these liturgical views can hardly have been based on a consistent theological foundation, for Dearmer's restless energy was soon transferring itself to Christian Socialism, Faith Healing, and the Ministry of Women.

2. *The Back to Baroque Movement*

The first challenge to the "English Use" of Dearmer and the Alcuin Club came with the foundation by the extreme Anglo-Catholics of the Society of SS. Peter and Paul. This was another indication of the liturgical chaos in the Anglican Church. On

---

[7] *The Rivers of the Flood, A Personal Account of the Catholic Revival in England in the Twentieth Century*, p. 50.

February 24, 1911, a number of Anglican papalists who were convinced that, but for the freezing effect of Protestantism, English ceremonial would have developed as in the Roman Catholic Church on the continent of Europe, determined to form a society to provide an alternative to the arrested development of the "English Use." A well-to-do layman, Samuel Gurney, was the secretary of the Society of SS. Peter and Paul, which included the brothers Ronald and Wilfrid Knox, N. P. Williams, Cyril Howell, and the Duke of Argyll. Their hope was that their work in familiarising Englishmen with the Catholic liturgical developments on the European continent would ultimately lead to corporate reunion with the Catholic Churches of Eastern and Western Christendom. To this end they were committed not only to introducing Roman Catholic ceremonial to counteract "British Museum" Religion, but also to introducing such Roman devotions as Benediction and the Rosary.

The outward indications of this revolutionary attitude were to be seen in the purchase for their churches of monstrances, thuribles, tabernacles, crucifixes, statues, chalices, and fiddle-back vestments of the Baroque and Rococo styles. As Dearmer started the fashion for Edwardian neo-Gothic, so the extreme Anglo-Catholics popularized the fashion for the theatrical style of the Counter-Reformation, and turned their churches into Spanish or Italian outposts of Ultramontanism. The new fashion was excellently illustrated in the drawings of Martin Travers in *Pictures of the English Liturgy—Low Mass*, exhibiting an Italianate priest celebrating Mass at a Baroque altar, assisted by a server wearing a lace-edged cotta. A companion volume by the same author, entitled *The Celebration of High Mass* was even more extreme, for each illustration depicted a different Baroque or Rococo altar. One, indeed, displayed High Mass with a monstrance enthroned beneath a canopy supported by ample *putti*. For those of undeviating tendencies toward Rome an authoritative volume appeared in Adrian Fortescue's *Ceremonies of the Roman Rite Described*, which provided an official guide following the Decrees of the Sacred Congregation of Rites.

The most enthusiastic renovator of Anglican churches in a Baroque or Rococo manner was Martin Travers the architect. His first striking example of renovation was to be seen in the changes he effected in the Butterfield Church of St. Augustine, Queen's Gate, London, in 1928. He succeeded in eliminating almost every trace of the Gothic Revival in this edifice. The polychromatic brick-work, so characteristic of Butterfield, disappeared under a deluge of white-wash. A huge Baroque gilt *retablo* practically enveloped the East wall. The lowest central panel included a crucifix suspended over a tabernacle; on the panel above a dove floated in a shaft of golden rays; and on the uppermost panel was the emblem of the sacred heart. The sides of this three-tiered altar fairly writhed with scrolls, and enough carved fruit and flowers to have provided a harvest festival of the British Empire. In this, it was not to be compared with the more delicate and lighter Baroque work of his master, Ninian Comper, who, incidentally, could combine Baroque and Gothic by a beauty of inclusion unknown to Travers. His happiest work, perhaps, was accomplished in the renovation of the Palladian church of St. Magnus the Martyr, Lower Thames Street, London, where seventeenth century Baroque was most appropriately added to a seventeenth century church. The refurbishing is fittingly commemorated by T. S. Eliot as the church

> where the walls
> Of Magnus Martyr hold
> Inexplicable splendour of Ionian white and gold.[8]

In this single instance, and it is a notable claim, Travers may be said to have improved upon the original architect, who was none other than Sir Christopher Wren.[9]

Perhaps the extreme to which this imitation and even exaggeration of the Baroque and Rococo styles went is provided by the Holy House, Walsingham. Peter Anson's two drawings admirably point up the contrast between the simple "English Altar" of the Roman Catholic shrine, and the cluttered Baroque of the Anglican Holy House, which is a pure imitation of the *Santa Casa* of Loreto.[10] The Anglican shrine has no less than fifteen altars in honour of the mysteries of the Rosary. It has a plethora of votive candles, *ex voto* tablets and other offerings of grateful visitors, while the atmosphere is saturated with stale incense and the thick fumes of the pendant oil lamps. The crowned and richly costumed Virgin has pride of place on the lace-draped altar. Indeed, as Anson remarks, "the Reformation might never have taken place."[11] The

8 *The Waste Land*, lines 263-65.

9 Other interesting examples of Travers' work are to be found in St. Matthew's, Westminster; Compton Beauchamp Church, Berkshire; and the Church of the Good Shepherd, Carshalton, Surrey (1930).

10 These drawings will be found on pp. 325 and 326 of Anson's *Fashions in Church Furnishings*.

11 *Ibid.*, p. 326.

contrast between the Anglican and Roman shrines at Walsingham show how the wheels of fashion had come full circle, for the Roman Catholics had returned to the Gothic simplicity of Edward VI and the Anglican papalists had almost out-Romanized Rome with their Baroque theatricality. We could hardly have a more impressive testimony of the chaos of ceremonial variations and furnishings in the Anglican Church.

3. *Preparation for Prayer Book Revision*

It was precisely the chaos in Anglicanism, from the left to the right wings, which made a revision of the Prayer Book essential. Without a revision, it was impossible to have unity in the Church of England, for the Prayer Book is the very nexus of Anglican unity. Moreover, without agreed rubrics, it would be impossible for the bishops to discipline the clergy; for in the absence of a ceremonial norm deviations could not be condemned as such. These, indeed, were the conclusions that the *Report of the Royal Commission on Ecclesiastical Discipline* had arrived at in 1906. It had established that there were ten practices current in the Church of England which were illegal and "clearly inconsistent with the teaching of the Church of England as declared in the Prayer Book."

Some were: the interpolation of prayers and ceremonies belonging to the Canon of the Mass, the adoration of the Reserved Sacrament, Corpus Christi processions with the Sacrament, Benediction with the Sacrament, and the observation of the festivals of the Assumption of the Blessed Virgin Mary and of the Sacred Heart. The three volumes of the same report provided ocular evidence of the vast variety of liturgical practices in England. Eucharistic vestments were worn in 113 churches in the Diocese of London and in thirty-seven churches in the Diocese of Rochester. About thirty London churches used incense. St. Columba's, Haggerston, and St. Cuthbert's, Philbeach Gardens (both in the London Diocese), had "public reservation" of the Sacrament, but many churches had altar tabernacles, whether for decoration or use was uncertain. Some churches openly heard confessions, but few had confessional boxes. Statues, almost always of the Madonna, were fairly frequently seen. Many Anglo-Catholic churches displayed the Stations of the Cross. Such was the wide variety, and it may be presumed that where there were illegal ornaments, illegal devotions were also practised.

The Royal Commission came to two principal conclusions of great importance:

"First, the law of public worship in the Church of England is too narrow for the religious life of the present generation. It needlessly condemns much which a great section of Church people, including many of her most devoted members, value; and modern thought and feeling are characterized by a care for ceremonial, a sense of dignity in worship, and an appreciation of the continuity of the Church, which were not similarly felt when the law took its present shape. In an age which has witnessed an extraordinary revival of spiritual life and activity, the Church has had to work under regulations fitted for a different condition of things, without that power of self-adjustment which is inherent in the conception of a living Church. . . .

"Secondly, the machinery for discipline has broken down. The means of enforcing the law in the Ecclesiastical Courts, even on matters which touch the Church's faith and teaching, are defective and in some respects unsuitable. . . ."[12]

This provided the impetus for the long, and as it turned out unsuccessful, process of revising a Prayer Book which had not been changed since 1661. At the outset it was thought that a simple liberalizing of the rubrics was all that would be necessary. The theory was that if the maximum liberty were given there would be no lawbreakers. However, the outbreak of World War I changed the situation in several ways. For one thing, the exigencies of chaplains made it a common practice to reserve the Sacrament. For another, the chaplains themselves became increasingly convinced that the unrevised Book of Common Prayer failed to speak to the needs of the men in khaki to whom they ministered in worship. In particular, the Orders for Morning and Evening Prayer were felt to be too penitential in their approach to worship, the prolix exhortations too dull, and many of the prayers out of touch with the practical needs of their charges. Furthermore, the fellowship of the chaplains had led to the ecumenical interchange of ideas, and many of them admired the American Prayer Book and the Scottish Book of Common Order for their relation of prayers to twentieth century conditions. For these reasons they returned from the Army eager for a more radical revision. Then, again, the *Enabling Act* had given the Church of England in its Church Assembly self-government, subject only to the overriding powers

[12] Cited by Alec R. Vidler, *The Church in an Age of Revolution*, p. 163.

of Parliament, and it was felt, particularly by the House of Laity, that Prayer Book revision was a most appropriate subject for discussion by the Assembly.

Furthermore, the two Archbishops had set up Five Committees of Inquiry to feel the pulse of the Church in wartime, and one of these published its report in 1918 under the title, *The Worship of the Church*. This furthered the demand for a thorough reconsideration of worship and for revision of the Prayer Book. The Report began by noting a minatory fact that the instinct for worship had been gravely weakened among the English people. Its causes included the mobility created by the industrial revolution, and the loss of any sense of obligation to attend Divine worship. The tradition of personal prayer and of family prayer was gravely diminished and hence public worship was felt to be less relevant. The Report noted "the spread of materialistic ideals, the overpressure of industrial life, the weakening of home life in general, the denominational differences, and consequent on all these, a deepened reticence about all religious matters."[13]

Further causes of the decline in worship were the lack of any common basis for religious instruction in the national schools, and the failure to bring the laity into the planning and sharing of worship. The Committee of Inquiry emphasized how antagonistic an industrial civilization was to the very values that worship sought to conserve. "The persistent pressure of its competitive processes generated in the people a spirit and temper alien from the very nature of the Church's worship, which, in its turn, divorced from the bitter realities of the people's lives, began to assume in their eyes an artificial character."[14] Aggressive individualism and class warfare militated against the very idea of fellowship in the Body of Christ which is central to worship, and encouraged a rapacity which was in extreme opposition to the simplicity and sacrifice engendered by worship. The same industrialism had alienated the poor from the Church, and hence "the idea of the Church as an institution governed by and administered for comparatively small circles of the well-to-do classes steadily took root in the mind of the people...."[15] This was, indeed, a recognition on the part of the Church of England that the "Social Gospel" was having some impact, not to mention the influence of

13 *The Worship of the Church, Being the Report of the Archbishops' Second Committee of Inquiry* (London, 1918—"Published for the National Mission by the S.P.C.K."), pp. 6-7.
14 *Ibid.*, p. 13.   15 *Ibid.*, p. 14.

the strong Christian Socialism of Charles Gore and his Anglo-Catholic supporters.

But this was far more than a party manifesto: the importance of this Report was precisely that its all-party diagnosis of the situation was so probing. The Committee believed, as will be seen, that Prayer Book revision was essential, but they were under no illusions that this was the nostrum that would bring the people flocking back into the Churches. They would, in fact, probably have agreed with Neville Figgis, who told a Cambridge audience in 1909: "In the last generation men were unable to take Jesus as Lord, and were sad. Now they are choosing other masters, and are glad."[16] This is what made the need for relevance in worship and preaching so obligatory, and why the provisions of an essentially sixteenth century Prayer Book could not satisfy the revolutionary situation of the war-racked twentieth century Church.

The Report then proceeded to consider the Prayer Book provisions for worship in detail. The three chaplains on the Committee of Inquiry reported that the men in the armed services had shown a great appreciation for Holy Communion, whereas the rest of the Committee were disturbed to notice that in the parish churches attendance at Matins and Evensong had come to drive the Holy Communion to the position of an exceptional service for committed Christians.

For two reasons this was felt to be a serious misfortune. "In the first place, the Sacrament of the Lord's Supper is definitely ordained by Christ, and has therefore a greater claim on the observance of Christians than any other service that can be devised. Secondly, there seems to be no doubt that the Communion Service makes less demand for intellectual effort and satisfies more directly the spiritual impulses than such services as Morning and Evening Prayer."[17] In the second reason given, it was clear that all the teaching of Inge, von Hügel, and Evelyn Underhill on the primacy of the mystical approach to God had not been wasted. The Committee felt that two difficulties stood in the way of making Holy Communion central: Morning Prayer already occupied the best time for Communion, and the emphasis on fasting before Communion made it impossible to hold it at night. They went on record as favouring a relaxing of the fasting requirement and

---

[16] *The Gospel and Human Need*, p. 8, cited in Roger Lloyd, *The Church of England in the Twentieth Century*, Vol. I, 1900-1918, p. 49.
[17] *The Worship of the Church*, p. 15.

therefore of celebrating evening Communions in town parish churches, and they particularly praised the ideal of corporate Communions held at 8 or 9.30 A.M. The preference for the latter hour was prophetic, though they could not have foreseen how exceedingly popular "Parish Communion" about the morning hour of nine was to become two decades later.

There was considerable dissatisfaction with the practice of using Morning Prayer, the Litany, and the Communion Service successively, as being too lengthy and requiring too much reduplication. There was also a sense that the Occasional Offices were too archaic in their phrasing and too lengthy in their exhortations for modern taste, and so might alienate the many outsiders who first attended a church service at a marriage or a burial.

The most radical criticism, however, came from the three serving chaplains who knew how great was the lost ground that had to be recovered. Among them was Neville Talbot, later to become the much loved and unconventional Bishop of Pretoria, who used to introduce himself with a chanted jingle, "I'm the servant of the Lord with my Bible and my Ford!" In a separate appendix they pleaded for "bold and wide experiment," and made no bones about the fact that in their experience the Prayer Book services were "uninstructive and misleading to some, irritating and alienating to others." In their view this was because modern man did not believe in the plenary inspiration of the Scriptures, as did the original compilers of the Book of Common Prayer. They believed the Prayer Book services tended "to authorize and perpetuate a view of Scripture (and of the Christian religion) which is untrue and offensive to any lively conscience and intelligence." Then the ironic addition is made: "No doubt Dean Paget and Dr. Bright on either side of Christ Church choir could make intelligent allowance about, and find mystical meanings in, any part of the lectionary and psalter. Not so the vast majority of people."[18]

It was not all criticism that they offered, but also appreciation and constructive alternatives. Of Holy Communion they wrote: "We think all chaplains will return home anxious to make this service the main, corporate, family, congregational act of worship and fellowship."[19] Moreover, they greatly preferred the Communion Office of the Episcopal Church of Scotland to the English Order for its fulness and plainness of meaning. They strongly recommended W. H. Frere's simplification of Morning Prayer in his

18 Ibid., p. 34.   19 Ibid., p. 35.

Principles of Liturgical Reform as avoiding the repetition of four Lord's Prayers, two Confessions and Absolutions, two Creeds, and four Prayers for the King. They also advised shorter and simpler exhortations, a revised Psalter with the retranslation of obscure passages, the use of Bidding prayers, and the provision of prayers on such topics as the Kingdom of God, Missions, Labour, and Parliament. They were particularly anxious to make services more congregational in character by the avoiding of intonation and the introduction of more hymns, for "In hymns there is a really living and popular interest in British Christianity."[20] They wickedly added: "We should like to see experiments made in the suppression of choirs."[21]

They were, however, most anxious to see the provision of new Acts of Devotion of a more popular kind than the Book of Common Prayer provides. They believed that the trouble with most forms and litanies put out by authority is that they solely emphasize petition (rather than meditation, or adoration), lack the sense of the Christian brotherhood cutting away all barriers of class or nationality, omit the context of worship in the Communion of Saints, and have no interweaving of the devotions with the life of Christ. Satisfactory new Acts of Devotion must be provided in which "for introduction to and maintenance in the presence of God, the picture of Christ (as the Son revealing the Father) must be brought before the mind, and interwoven with the whole devotion, which should proceed from the known life and known desires of Christ and concentrate the mind thereon."[22] They also added the caution that silence should be used to grasp and realize the presence and picture of God.

Second only to this primary stress Godward was the need for an emphasis on fellowship, and appropriately fellowship will be meaningful when the Act of Devotion is shared by all. Also, protesting against the overwhelming immanentalism of their time, they recommended that "services and acts of devotion should end with an act of dedication in which all join—should end on a note of faith rather than of need."[23] Their testimony was not less impressive because they had looked beyond the liturgical confines of the Church of England, and recognized "the worth of the Book of Common Order (Scottish Presbyterian) as a source of prayer which connects worship with 'the daily round,'" and they recom-

[20] *Ibid.*, p. 36.   [21] *Ibid.*, p. 37.   [22] *Ibid.*, p. 38.
[23] *Ibid.*, p. 39.

mended the Book of Common Worship of the USA for "the wealth of prayer for all occasions" which it contained.[24]

The Committee of Inquiry also considered the need for improvements in Church Music and they were greatly helped by the presence of Dr. Walford Davies on the Committee. Their recommendations in the matter of preaching were, however, insufficiently radical. They strongly criticized the frequent aberrations of Anglican delivery: inaudibility, dullness, long and unintelligible pauses; but omitted that artificiality of tone which Spurgeon characterized as "steeple-in-the-throat grandeur." They suggested that the place of the sermon in the service might be varied to provide interest. They urged that a ten to fifteen minute sermon might "fix and give precision to the lesson of the particular service on any given day."[25]

They approached the real problem and then ran away from it, by suggesting that because the faith of Christ provides a system of thought as well as a rule of life special preaching services should be held (so far so good), but that they should be given in large towns at special seasons in a series. The need for sustained Biblical exegesis for the systematic presentation of the major Christian doctrines in an articulated way, and for an application of Christian ethics to the problems and temptations of the day was no sooner glimpsed by the Committee than glossed over. It is still the most desperate need of the Church of England, as the need for a richer devotional and sacramental life is clamant in the English Free Churches.

However, the deep diagnosis of the weakening of the instinct for worship in this Report and its determination to make Prayer Book revision more relevant to the times is a proof that the revision could not be much longer delayed. If only that national and ecclesiastical unity which had prevailed in time of war had been carried over into the years of peace, or if the Prayer Book revision had been concluded within a year after the Armistice, then Parliament might have recognized this and approved a fairly unanimous revision. One of the effects of the prolonged delay was that it gave more than ample opportunity for bitter factionalism to arise again. It was ultimately the vociferous disagreement of a minority of the Anglo-Catholics and a minority of the Evangelicals that gave Parliament the erroneous impression that the Revised Prayer Book could never be the bond of liturgical concord.

In fairness to the Bishops, however, who come in for consider-

[24] *Ibid.*, p. 38.   [25] *Ibid.*, p. 21.

able criticism later, it must be acknowledged that a serious attempt was made to push through a revision more rapidly. They were seriously proposing consideration of an Alternative Order of Holy Communion in 1918, and had reached agreement on all other matters for revision. They had therefore recommended the Archbishops to call a special conference to deal with this single issue, but the Archbishops were immediately confronted with a Memorial signed by nine Bishops, 3,000 clergy, and 100,000 laymen protesting against any changes in the Communion Service.[26] The Conference did, however, find a compromise Consecration Prayer which was proposed by Dr. Drury, the Evangelical Bishop, and by Dr. Frere, the Anglo-Catholic Bishop. This was to read, immediately after the Words of Institution:

"Wherefore, O Father, we thy humble servants, having in remembrance before Thee the precious death of thy dear Son, his mighty resurrection and glorious ascension, looking also for his coming again, do render unto Thee most hearty thanks for the innumerable benefits which he hath procured unto us; And we pray Thee of thine almighty goodness to send upon us and upon these thy gifts thy holy and blessed Spirit, who is the Sanctifier and the Giver of Life, to whom with Thee and thy Son Jesus Christ be ascribed by every creature in earth and heaven all blessing, honour, glory and power, now henceforth and for evermore. *Amen.*"[27]

The Canterbury Convocation accepted the recommendations on February 11, 1920, although Archbishop Davidson himself would have preferred to have no alternative service. The York Convocation rejected only the Alternative Order for Holy Communion, but accepted all other proposals for revision. The approved proposals were then submitted for the consideration of the Church Assembly (which had come into being through the *Enabling Act* of 1919) and there most of them were ratified. The lay committee, however, was acutely divided on the proposals concerning Holy Communion and Reservation. Five Evangelicals printed a Note objecting to Reservation, and Athelstan Riley printed a dissenting Note questioning features of the Alternative Order for Holy Communion. Partisanship once again became rife, as the dissentients drummed up support for their followers. In October, 1922, the House of Bishops introduced the *Revised Prayer Book* (*Permissive Use*)

[26] G. K. A. Bell, *Randall Davidson, Archbishop of Canterbury*, p. 1326.
[27] Cited *ibid.*, footnote 3 on pp. 1326-27.

Measure into the Assembly, attaching the measure to the unaltered Proposals of the Committee. General approval was given to the Proposals in all three Houses, sitting separately, with three dissentients in the House of Bishops. From April, 1923, for the next two years the Houses of Clergy and Laity, sitting separately, went steadily through the herculean task of revision. From the moment that their Report was published, the revisers were deluged with a torrent of rival sets of proposals for further revision. It became clear that this was only adding fuel to the flames of party difference.[28]

At this point in history there appeared three major proposals for revision which were known, from the colours of their bindings, as the Green, the Grey, and the Orange Books. The Green Book was the production of the English Church Union, a vigorously and uncompromisingly Anglo-Catholic group led by Dr. Darwell Stone and Dr. B. J. Kidd, which would have liked an alternative for Holy Communion more closely resembling the traditional Western Rite. N. P. Williams, a founding member of the Society of SS. Peter and Paul, and a future Professor of Divinity at Oxford, was the secretary. In fact, Stone and his supporters were complicating the issue by proposing an additional alternative Order for Holy Communion.[29] The Grey Book was the provision of alternative services and prayers from the central and liberal standpoint and contained a preface by Dr. William Temple, then Bishop of Manchester. The Orange Book was a collection of scholarly pamphlets of the moderate Anglo-Catholics of the Alcuin Club who stood for the English type of Catholicism. By October, 1925, when the House of Bishops began their task of revision, the Archbishop stated that he had received more than eight hundred different memorials on the subject, including a plea for no change from Cambridge University, a petition to the same effect organized by Bishop Knox with over 305,000 signatures, and a statement signed by nine diocesan Bishops opposing any change in the Order of Holy Communion and any alternative service.[30] The revision stage began on October 25, 1925, and sittings were held for fifty full days in Lambeth Palace between then and 1927. From the outset the Bishops of Norwich, Birmingham, and Worcester were known to be in opposition to the entire work.

[28] For this paragraph I have relied on the summary of events in Bell, *ibid.*, pp. 1327-29.

[29] See Chap. VI of F. L. Cross, *Darwell Stone, Churchman and Counsellor.*

[30] Bell, *Randall Davidson . . . ,* p. 1329.

The diversity of convictions, the multiplicity of varying proposals, the hardening of party lines, and the canvassing of divergent views in the press and in the local communities, as also the strong conservative opposition to any change which the memorialists had indicated, and the lukewarmness of the Archbishop, presaged a stormy passage for the Ark of the Church of England bearing the Prayer Book Measure through the narrow straits of Parliament. Moreover, even the Church Assembly did not provide that overwhelming vote of confidence in the Revised Prayer Book which might have been expected and which would, perhaps, have impressed Parliament with the firm determination of the Church of England to put its own liturgical house in order. Furthermore, Reservation became an acute problem towards the end of the negotiations. "An Alternative Order for the Communion of the Sick" had attempted to meet the need for those who argued for the necessity of the reserved Sacrament for the sick, while safeguarding it from any attempt at Exposition of the Sacrament leading to the adoration of the consecrated elements. In fact, it satisfied neither the Evangelicals who were dead against reservation in any form and opposed any Alternative Order of Holy Communion, and it alienated the extreme Anglo-Catholics who were entirely opposed to any limitations on Reservation, and the attempt to exclude Tridentine devotions. They, too, were opposed to the Alternative Order of Holy Communion because they regarded the *epiklesis*, or invocation of the Holy Spirit on the elements and on the congregation in the Prayer of Consecration, as an Eastern borrowing and a reversal of the Western tradition of the previous fourteen hundred years. The Evangelicals, led by Sir William Joynson-Hicks, then the Home Secretary, demanded a positive assurance from the Archbishop as to how rigorously the Bishops would treat any clergy who disobeyed the rubrics of the new Revised Prayer Book, supposing it were to become law. The Archbishop would give no other assurance than that he supposed it would work out well, and this sanguine vagueness proved unsatisfactory.

The final debate in the Church Assembly took place on July 5 and 6, 1927, on the measure authorizing the optional use of the Deposited Book. (It should be understood that the 1661 Prayer Book was not superseded and that the Deposited Book was a *composite* Book containing the whole of the existing Book of Common Prayer with the proposed additions and deviations.) No sooner had the measure been moved than it was strongly attacked from the extreme Anglo-Catholic quarter by Dr. Darwell Stone, who alleged that 700 Anglo-Catholic priests were of the same mind as he, in unshakable opposition. From the opposite quarter of the Protestant party, Sir William Joynson-Hicks, Sir Thomas Inskip, and the Bishop of Norwich attacked the measure for the Evangelicals. The final vote was not likely to convince Parliament that the Church Assembly was solidly behind the measure, for the minorities were large enough in each House to presage trouble in enforcing the disciplining of the clergy by the Bishops. The House of Bishops voted 34 for the measure and 4 against it. The House of Clergy voted 253 for and 37 against. The House of Laity voted 230 for and 92 against. In all three Houses 517 positive votes were cast and a formidable 133 negative votes. Thus the minority represented 25 per cent of the opinion.[31] If the ecclesiastical horizon was clouded, the political weather would be tempestuous.

4. *The Revised Prayer Book before Parliament*

The story of the Prayer Book Measure before Parliament is shortly and sadly told, but this blow to the prestige of the Church of England, this frustration of the hopes of liturgical improvement, of a deepened spirituality, and of a closing of the party ranks, was so shattering that opinions differ very greatly as to why it happened and how it might have been averted, and even what it meant for the future of the Church of England. Some objectivity may be reached by the presentation of different viewpoints on this major liturgical controversy of the century.

At the beginning all looked well. The Revised Prayer Book Measure was debated for three days by the House of Lords, beginning on December 12, 1927, and it was approved by 241 votes to 88. The Archbishop of Canterbury (Dr. Randall Davidson) was the mover, who argued that the measure expressed "a united wish officially given by a united Church," representatively arrived at through the Church Assembly, and that it would facilitate the work of the Bishops and "would mean the liberation of the Church from the great mass of those petty strifes which have troubled us up and down the country in the past."[32] He was not conscious of any departure from the Reformed tradition of the Church of England in these proposals, and he reminded the House that the Royal Commission of 1906 had insisted that the law of public worship was too narrow for the religious life of the present generation.

[31] Bell, *ibid.*, pp. 1136ff.   [32] *Ibid.*, p. 1345.

On December 15, 1927, the Measure was considered by the House of Commons. The mover, W. C. Bridgeman, a former First Lord of the Admiralty, was discomposed by interruptions and made the unfortunate concession: "I can imagine those who dislike the Church of England may wish to reject this measure."[33] The Home Secretary, Sir William Joynson-Hicks, a leader of the Low Churchmen, took exception to the Bill as yielding to the Romanising tendencies of the Anglo-Catholics, and admitted (after recalling the Archbishop's written promises to persuade the Bishops to curb illegalities in worship which were not kept) that he found it impossible to trust the Bishops. The most flamboyant speech was that of Mr. Rosslyn Mitchell of Paisley, an ultra-Protestant declamation on the threadbare theme of "No Popery." A quiet but effective speech against the measure was made by Sir John Simon. The Measure was defeated by 238 votes to 205. G. K. A. Bell's laconic comment is: "In a single hectic night the House of Commons had apparently destroyed the work of more than twenty years."[34]

This left the Church in a condition of great confusion. It was thought by the bolder spirits that the chains of Erastian subservience to the State must be broken. In this case their policy would be for the Church to adopt the use of the Deposited Book and let the State terminate the favoured position of the Church if it so desired. At least the Church would then be free to rule its own house as it thought best. The Bishops, however, adopted a temporizing course. If all else failed, then the Church might have to think of asserting its spiritual authority and independence, but for the present they could only assume that Parliament had misunderstood their intentions. They therefore recommended that after some modifications in the measure were made to accommodate Parliament's Protestant fears, the measure should be re-introduced. These were duly prepared.

They consisted chiefly of four changes. The Prayer for the Sovereign, after the third collect in Morning and Evening Prayer, was made compulsory in all circumstances. The statement relating to Fasting Communion was inserted among the Communion Office rubrics. The rules proposed for the regulation of Reservation in the Communion of the Sick were printed in full. Also, the Declaration on Kneeling (the Black Rubric, denying the doctrine of transubstantiation) was reprinted at the end of the Alternative Com-

[33] *Ibid.*   [34] *Ibid.*, p. 1347.

301

munion Office. In fact, these changes failed to remove Protestant suspicions, and succeeded only in further alienating the Anglo-Catholic wing. This was amply demonstrated by the voting in the Church Assembly, where on March 28 and 29, 1928, 396 votes were cast for the amended Measure and 153 against it.[35] Thus the minority vote had increased from 25 to 38 per cent within a year.

If the Church Assembly's increasing minority demonstrated that it was unconvinced by the changes, it was unlikely that a suspicious House of Commons would be convinced. On June 13, 1928, the measure was re-introduced into the House of Commons and defeated by 266 votes to 220.

The Bishops had failed in their purpose to persuade Parliament to accept their amended proposals. The question then was, whether they would have the courage to recommend the disestablishment of the Church for the sake of the freedom of the Church, a possibility they had hinted at earlier? In fact they pursued a compromising policy again, desiring the advantages of the State connection, without its limitations. They proposed to have their cake and eat it. That is, they issued a statement that the Church must retain its inalienable right to formulate its faith and forms of worship, and they later declared that in administering their dioceses in the present emergency they would allow such deviations from the 1661 Prayer Book as were covered in the 1928 proposals. They were therefore quietly defying Parliament while retaining the State connection.

Perhaps the most objective account of the reasons for the failure of the Prayer Book Measure to gain Parliamentary assent is that of Bishop G. K. A. Bell.[36] He places first in the list the fear of Rome, "the deep Protestantism of the English people," which he considered irrational. Bishop Henson concurred, averring that "Englishmen are not inevitably episcopalian as the Scots are inevitably presbyterian and the Irish inevitably papists, but *au fond* they are Erastian, Bibliolatrous, and always fiercely anti-Papal."[37]

The second cause for failure, as Bishop Bell sees it, was the disunity among the Churchmen. This was undeniably an important factor. Bell felt that the real issue was whether the Low Churchmen were willing to give a sure place in the Church to such a vital religious movement as Anglo-Catholicism undoubtedly was, or

[35] *Crockford Prefaces. The Editor Looks Back*, pp. 79f.
[36] *Randall Davidson . . .*, p. 1354.
[37] *Retrospect of an Unimportant Life, 1920-1939*, Vol. II, p. 153.

whether they wished to drive it out of the Anglican Church as the Methodists had been ejected in the eighteenth century? Henson, too, was critical of the Evangelicals, but he reserved his keenest irony for the fervent Presbyterian, Rosslyn Mitchell. Of that speech which was commonly believed to have swayed the House of Commons, Hensley Henson wrote: "It is, perhaps, rather difficult to understand the process of reasoning by which he was led to engage in the effort to Erastianize an alien church, but the logic of fanaticism is quite unfathomable."[38] While recognizing the deep party divisions in the Church as partly responsible for the debacle, Henson also saw that a great gap divided the learned liturgiologists from the clergy and even more from the laity. Moreover, the liturgiologists were divided among themselves, some desiring a return to the pre-Reformation tradition in the West, others arguing for the Eastern Liturgies as patterns for revision. There is, however, no question that the hardening of extreme Anglo-Catholic and extreme Evangelical opposition to the revised Prayer Book was a major contributory factor to the Parliamentary rejection, especially as they were active lobbyists.

Certainly, also, the lack of real interest in the project on the part of Archbishop Davidson was a significant factor in the defeat. This is a judgment in which Bell and Henson concur. Henson averred that "the Archbishop's heart was not in the work, and, while his influence restrained friction in the discussions at Lambeth, his counsel did little to direct them."[39] Further than this, his failure to provide definite pledges to restrain clerical illegality, if the Prayer Book Measure were to be passed, definitely weakened the cause. Henson believed that the vote of the House of Commons might fairly be described as *"a vote of censure on the Bishops,"* representing the exasperation against the law-breaking clergy, "which has been accumulating all over the country for many years, and has at length found an opportunity of expression, and a Cabinet Minister [Joynson-Hicks] to express it."[40] In his ruthlessly honest fashion Henson stated that the immediate reasons were to be found in "the foolish language of the Bishop of London, the ceremonial absurdities of the Bishop of St. Albans and the bitterness of feeling aroused by the Bishop of Birmingham," adding that the lobbying of Bishop Knox and the Bishop of Norwich inflamed the passion of the House of Commons.

[38] *Ibid.*, p. 166.   [39] *Ibid.*, p. 162.
[40] *Ibid.*, p. 167. The italics are Henson's.

It is possible, however, that the inherent defect lay in the attempt to solve two different problems in the Prayer Book Measure, the problem of clerical disobedience and the problem of liturgical revision. Thus two incompatibles were combined: the concern for the spiritual renovation of the Church and the curbing of indiscipline, and the Prayer Book was conceived by the legislators as no more than a more effective stick with which to beat refractory clergy. Henson saw this clearly, arguing that although the restoration of discipline and the revision of formularies were valuable, yet they were irreconcilable, for the former was a popular demand, while the other was chiefly the concern of liturgical scholars.[41] Dr. A. R. Vidler agrees with him and adds: "It might be thought that the right way to revise forms of worship should be by way of experimentation in the parishes rather than as a deal between parties in the Church."[42]

5. The Effects of Parliament's Rejection of the Revised Prayer Book

There is still room for argument as to the long-term effects of the Parliamentary rejection of the Prayer Book Revision Measure, but what its immediate effects were is less controversial.

Unquestionably, as Henson had acknowledged at the time, there was a serious loss of respect for the Bishops. Their scholarship, their pastoral concern, and their administrative abilities were not in doubt, but their sincerity was. They seemed to be politicians rather than prophets, compromisers rather than men of conviction and conscience. Dean Matthews of St. Paul's writing twenty years after the events, felt compelled to criticize their insistence upon the *ius liturgicum* as a piecemeal defiance of Parliament and to "wonder whether calculated and surreptitious illegality is likely to serve spiritual ends."[43] Their policy was even more seriously criticized by Bernard Manning, a Congregationalist historian, in

[41] *Ibid.*, p. 152. But Henson gravely underestimates the desire for revision on the part of chaplains, as indicated in the Report of 1918, *The Worship of the Church*, who were not learned liturgiologists.

[42] *The Church in an Age of Revolution*, p. 167. This also became the official verdict of the Church of England, as may be seen from *Prayer Book Revision, A Memorandum of the Church of England Liturgical Commission*. Its conclusion is: "Finally, we would stress the fundamental lesson of 1927-8 that in all future work of Prayer Book revision *the sole purpose must be the provision of an enriched, worthier and more fitting vehicle for the worship of God in the Church of England.* There is, of course, a rightful place for discipline in the life of the Church, but we do not believe that Prayer Book revision should be taken with disciplinary ends in view."

[43] "The Nation and the Prayer Book," article in *Hibbert Journal*, Vol. XLVII (October 1949–July 1950), p. 22.

giving evidence before the Archbishops' Commission on the relations between Church and State of 1931. He asserted: "We do
not believe that Christ's flock can both enjoy the advantages of an
Erastian Establishment like Henry VIII's and Elizabeth's and
Charles II's *and* ecclesiastical liberty."[44] The clear implication was
that the Bishops were running with the hounds and the hare, or,
to vary the metaphor, making the best of both worlds. Certainly,
as a bench they hardly recovered the respect of the man in the
street until Archbishop William Temple went from York to Canterbury in 1942 and proved that a prelate could also be a prophet.
The feebleness of the Bishops in refusing either to accept the
obedience that an Erastian situation of an Established Church
required, or to break the manacles of the State connection and thus
free the Church to be liturgical master in its own house, made
many think of the advantages of disestablishment. Bishop Hensley
Henson, who had been a strong supporter of the national character
of the Church of England, was persuaded by the ignominy of the
Church's defeat by Parliament to become a supporter of disestablishment.[45] Another loss was of the veneration in which the 1661
Rite had hitherto been held, so vigorous was the argument made
for its need of supplementation.

Some, like Dr. Lowther Clarke, the editor of *Liturgy and
Worship* (1932) evinced an ostrich outlook by maintaining that
there were real advantages in the situation. He was gratified that
there was widespread use of the new Occasional Offices and of the
additional collects and occasional prayers. He was convinced that
"the many years of discussion have not been wasted" because "the
English people have received an education in liturgical matters
which otherwise would have been impossible," and he showed an
incredible chauvinism in believing that continental observers of
the British situation envied Englishmen their controversies.[46] The
sober and realistic note was sounded by Dr. Matthews, who conceded the need for a revision of the Prayer Book which would
leave the main substance of Cranmer's work intact but indicate
permissible variations, yet had to conclude: "It is unfortunately
most unlikely that the Church will face the necessary task for a

---

[44] His evidence is reprinted in *Essays in Orthodox Dissent*, pp. 196ff. Manning
added that "inasmuch as Establishment curbs Episcopacy I wish it well. That
is not the word of a Christian but of an Englishman." For the views of another
Free Churchman on the controversy, see P. Carnegie Simpson, *Recollections*, pp.
87-92. Dom Anselm Hughes (*The Rivers of the Flood*, p. 84) refers contemptuously
to the "Lambeth Front."

[45] *Retrospect*, Vol. II, p. 151.   [46] *Liturgy and Worship*, pp. 790-91.

long time to come, because the memory of the disaster of 1928 stands in the way."[47] It was thirty-three years before Archbishop Ramsey felt able to recommend that the Church undertake the revision of the Prayer Book and with a clear understanding of the consequences. On June 27, 1961, in his enthronement sermon in Canterbury, he said:

"Here in England the Church and the State are linked together and we use that link in serving the community. But, in that service and in rendering to God the things that are God's, we ask for greater freedom in the ordering and in the urgent revising of our forms of worship. If the link of Church and State were broken, it would not be we who would ask for this freedom who broke it, but those—if there be such—who denied that freedom to us."[48]

Dr. Ramsey's promise to re-institute liturgical reform was implemented in May 1962 when a new Liturgical Commission, representative of all schools in the Church, was appointed. It was not possible to do that until three long decades had helped to bury the bitterness caused by 1928.

[47] *Hibbert Journal*, Vol. XLVII, p. 21.
[48] James B. Simpson, *The Hundredth Archbishop of Canterbury*, pp. 5-6. It is significant that Dr. Hewlett Johnson, the Dean of Canterbury, referred to an interview with Dr. Ramsey in which the latter said: "I want to make man aware of God" (*ibid.*, p. 247).

CHAPTER IX

ANGLICAN WORSHIP AFTER 1928

WHAT WAS happening in the interval between 1928 and the present day? Clearly, a considerable breathing-space was afforded the Church of England to reconsider the relations of Church and State. As we have seen, an Archbishop's Commission was devoted to this purpose in 1931. In more recent years a rigorous attempt has been made to revise the Canons of the Church of England, and it is hoped that this may solve the disciplinary problem, possibly independently of any revision of the liturgy. In the same breathing-space it seems that the folly of divisiveness on the part of parties within the Church of England had been acknowledged, and the improved ecumenical climate has made intra-denominational divisions seem the more scandalous. Certainly there is a charity and even a mutual understanding between the High and Low Church far deeper than existed in 1928. These are significant changes of the Spirit which cannot be tabulated in statistical fashion, but they are readily acknowledged by the clergy.

The next three and a half decades show a remarkable advance in the appreciation of the importance of worship in the life of the Church. This is evident in three notable ways. What was lost at home might be gained overseas, and on this basis, apparently, English liturgical experts had a considerable influence in revising the formularies of the Prayer Books of several other Provinces of the Anglican Communion; to that extent the fruits of twenty years of liturgical research and revision in England were not lost. In the second place, there grew a deeper theological understanding of the place of the Liturgy, and especially of the Eucharist, in the life of the Church, as was to be seen in successive treatises.[1] Thirdly, due in part to the growth of the Continental Liturgical Movement, in part to the revival of a vigorous Biblical theology, and in part to the stimulus of the Ecumenical Movement, there was an unprecedented desire to make unofficial, and largely local, liturgical experiments of great fertility and relevance, as well as originality. The result is that there probably has never been in Anglican history such widespread interest on the part of clergy

[1] See *supra* Chap. I for the consideration of the theory of worship.

and people, or such informed knowledge on worship, as has been shown in the last two decades. To these developments we now turn.

1. *Anglican Liturgical Influence Overseas*

This is a subject calling for far fuller treatment. Nonetheless, it is important at least to notice how strong a lead was given by the Anglican revisers to Episcopal Churches overseas. One of England's most distinguished liturgiologists, the Rev. Edward C. Ratcliff, collaborated with the Rev. J. C. Winslow in producing the rich *Bombay Liturgy*, which was first printed in *The Eucharist in India, A Plea for a distinctive Liturgy for the Indian Church*, with the approval of the Bishop of Bombay, Dr. E. J. Palmer, in 1920. In 1923 it was authorized for experimental use in the diocese of Bombay, after certain changes were made. In 1933 it was approved, subject to episcopal permission, for the whole Anglican Province in India. After further revision, it was in 1948 incorporated in *A Proposed Prayer Book* of 1951 as "A Liturgy for India." It is to appear in a Supplementary Book. Clearly, this Liturgy has had an important influence on the development of Christian worship in India and its influence is far from spent. The sustained elevation of its language, its profound sense of the Communion of Saints, the large element of adoration it contains, the frequent opportunities provided for responses in the richly varied intercessions, the beauty of the ceremonial, and the preservation of the indigenous atmosphere are its abiding qualities.[2] It is also significant that Dr. E. C. Ratcliff was consulted in the production of the ecumenical Liturgy of the Church of South India,[3] and that the latter includes as a direct borrowing from the Bombay Liturgy the widely admired response in the Prayer of Consecration: "Thy death, O Lord, we commemorate; Thy resurrection we confess; and Thy second coming we await."

This single example has been given prominence, but the pattern of the "Alternative Order for Holy Communion" in the 1928 Prayer Book has undoubtedly played its part in inducing the majority of liturgical revisers in the Anglican Communion to include in their Prayers of Consecration an *epiklesis*,[4] or petition

---

[2] The texts of the Bombay, the South African, the Indian, the Canadian, and other Anglican Liturgies recently revised are contained in *The Liturgy in English* edited by Bernard Wigan.

[3] See T. S. Garrett, *Worship in the Church of South India*. This former Anglican priest, now a presbyter of the Church of South India, has been the foremost expositor of its ecumenical worship.

[4] The 1928 form of the *epiklesis* was the following: "Hear us, O merciful

for the Holy Spirit's sanctification. It is at least significant that this Eastern importation by way of the Episcopal Church of Scotland, included in the English revision, is a feature of the Liturgies of South Africa[5] (1929), Ceylon (1933), Japan (1953), Canada (1959), the West Indies (1959), and India (1960).

Moreover, there is one other proof of the pervasive influence of Anglican liturgical thought and practice which is so commonplace that it may be taken for granted. That is, that when Congregationalists, Methodists, and Presbyterians have gone into an organic union with Anglicans, as in the Church of South India, or are considering such, as are the Methodists in England, or the three Free Churches in Australia, it is always assumed that the worship will take the form of the Book of Common Prayer. That is, after all, the only Reformed vernacular rite to have remained in continuous use since the mid-sixteenth century in Europe, and is not only an abiding link with the great Western Catholic tradition, but also owes something to the Eastern Church, and in its Psalter goes back to the Hebrew Temple and Synagogue. The denominations that have hitherto united with the Anglican Church have no comparable tradition of worship,[6] important as their theological and pastoral insights are.

2. *The Growing Importance of the Eucharist*

Several reasons may be given for the remarkable witness the Anglican Church has made to the centrality of the Sacrament of the Eucharist in the Christian life. In part it is included in Anglican loyalty to the Patristic tradition both credal and sacramental. It is also allied, at least in the twentieth century,[7] with the strongly incarnational theologies of Charles Gore, William Temple, Lionel Thornton, and O. C. Quick and others. Furthermore, Anglicans have always recognized that there is a deep mystery at its heart,

---

Father, we most humbly beseech Thee, and with thy Holy and Life-giving Spirit vouchsafe to bless and sanctify both us and these thy gifts of Bread and Wine, that they may be unto us the Body and Blood of thy Son, our Saviour Jesus Christ, to the end that we, receiving the same, may be strengthened and refreshed both in body and in soul."

[5] See Professor P. B. Hinchliff's *The South African Liturgy* and *The Anglican Church in South Africa*.

[6] See W. D. Maxwell's *The Book of Common Prayer and the Worship of Non-Anglican Churches*.

[7] Gore and company, however, inherited an incarnational tradition of the nineteenth century based on Maurice, Westcott, and Hort, not to mention the earlier heritage of the Caroline divines and of the Elizabethans, Jewel, and Hooker. Furthermore, the Incarnation was linked with the Atonement in R. C. Moberly's *Atonement and Personality*.

and few have presumed to dissect it (or, what is the same, to define it). They have been content to refer to the "Real Presence." Then, again, their churches have always given a dominant place to the altar, and, in many cases, suggested its numinous quality with altar rails and richly embellished reredos, or given glimpses of it through wrought-iron screens or below massive roods. Even in the newest churches, designed in the light of the Liturgical Movement, the altars may be simpler but they are central and dominating. In many other Communions the altar has been dominated by the pulpit. In Anglicanism this was only true in the eighteenth and rationalizing century, and the Oxford Movement and the Cambridge Ecclesiological Society[8] soon put an end to that. It is hardly to be wondered at, then, that the present century should have produced some admirable Anglican studies of Eucharistic theology. This is so because Holy Communion, for High Churchman and Low Churchman alike, has been the chief means of grace, the application of the benefits of Christ's Passion and Resurrection to His people, and the inspiration and solace of the Christian life.

The century's classic philosophical and theological study of the theme was O. C. Quick's *The Christian Sacraments* (1927) which warrants extended treatment, but this was by no means the only worthy study of its theme. Gore's *The Body of Christ* (1901) attempted to recover the Patristic understanding of the Eucharist for Anglicans, and F. C. N. Hicks emphasized the same understanding in *The Fulness of Sacrifice* (1930). Both stressed the heavenly offering of the great High Priest. A. L. Lilley's *The Sacraments* (1928) was a concise historical study which gave a sympathetic interpretation of the mediaeval understanding of the Sacraments. J. K. Mozley's *The Gospel Sacraments* (1933), while acknowledging its indebtedness to Quick's monograph, was very practical in its emphasis, and in its appreciation of P. T. Forsyth's great book *The Church and the Sacraments* paid a tribute as just as it was unusual from such a quarter on such a theme. Eric L. Mascall's *Corpus Christi, Essays on the Church and the Eucharist* (1953) was another High Church interpretation of its theme, but with singular independence of judgment. It criticized the psychological atomism of mediaeval and post-mediaeval interpretations of the Sacrament, and warned against building upon a sacramental theory of the universe or reducing the meaning of the

---

[8] See James F. White, *The Cambridge Movement: The Ecclesiologists and the Gothic Revival.*

Eucharist to its social implications.[9] It also introduced many readers to the strengths and weaknesses of recent Roman Catholic Eucharistic interpretations, and re-emphasized the need to recover the eschatological dimension of the Eucharist. J. A. T. Robinson produced a very lively interpretation of the relevance of Holy Communion in his lectures, *On Being the Church in the World* (1960) and a more popular account in *The Liturgy Coming to Life* (1961).

It is a significant fact of the period that the Evangelicals in the English Church made their own contributions. That redoubtable Protestant Bishop E. A. Knox of Manchester produced a characteristically provocative study, entitled *Sacrifice or Sacrament* (1914), a theme to which another Evangelical, A. M. Stibbs, returned in *Sacrament, Sacrifice and Eucharist* (1961). Yet Stibbs' volume, while denying that we should think "we can share in offering the sacrifice which He alone could and did offer,"[10] or that Christ's sacrifice is perpetually offered, moves beyond Memorialism and acknowledges that the benefits received are the remission of sins, the life-giving Spirit, and the invitation to share in the eternal feast.[11]

The great Biblical fidelity and historical understanding of the Evangelical school is, however, more representatively expressed in two other volumes. The one is *The Evangelical Doctrine of Holy Communion*, edited by A. J. Macdonald, with a valuable chapter by its editor; it also includes a penetrating essay on "Anglican Eucharistic Theology Today" by V. F. Storrs, in which he asserts that "In the Evangelical wing of the Church a new feeling for sacramentalism is arising,"[12] and claims that the trend is towards dynamic receptionism and away from memorialism. The other important volume is J. E. L. Oulton's *Holy Communion and Holy Spirit, A Study in Doctrinal Relationship* (1951). This is a most careful exploration of the relationship between these two doctrines, in a detailed New Testament study with illustrative references to the doctrinal exposition and liturgical practice of the Early Church. It criticizes Low Church Memorialism as being "merely self-edification: it offers no grace, it contains no Gospel,"[13] it also criticizes High Church beliefs on the Latin model in the efficacy of a consecratory formula, as being further from the New Testament than the Eastern Church's preference for an *epiklesis*. But even here Oulton is critical of liturgies which invoke the Holy Spirit on the

---

[9] Pp. 42, 45-46. [10] P. 30. [11] *Ibid.*, pp. 52-57.
[12] P. 312. [13] P. 128.

311

people as well as on the elements, for this is to pray "as if He were not already with them and abiding in them."[14] The scholarship of such Evangelicals cannot be dismissed lightly, and, what is more significant, there is no longer any desire to serve a party line, as the independence of the conclusions clearly shows.

Perhaps the most dated position on the Sacraments is the Modernist Anglican interpretation of which F. H. Amphlett Micklewright's *Sacraments and the Modern Man: A Modernist Explanation*[15] is an example, more notable for its negations than its affirmations. Nonetheless, while being concerned to cleanse the Sacrament from superstition and from any connotations of substitution and expiation, he recognizes the symbolic value of the Eucharist, as mystical and didactic. "It is this eternal preaching of the message of the Cross, the example of Jesus, which is presented to the worshipper through the symbolism of the broken bread and the pouring out of the wine."[16] Furthermore, "inasmuch as the Christian Gospel is one of Divine Action, the act of communion appears too as a meeting in a mystic sense of the temporal and the eternal, the reception by the believer, under the form of outward signs of the things which are eternal."[17] A recognition is also made of the social significance of Holy Communion.[18] Its gravest weakness, however, is the product of both the underlying idealist philosophy and of the belief in the uniformity of nature, which means that Micklewright dissociates the spiritual and the material instead of uniting them in the Incarnation and in the Sacrament. This is clearly shown in his pejorative references to "magical" views of Ignatius of Antioch and his approbation of the author of the Fourth Gospel as being the "father of all mystics," because in his thinking "the temporal and material universe stands over against that which is eternal, the world of values."[19] The disjunction is fatal to Micklewright's interpretation of the Christian faith, for Hellenism has overwhelmed the Gospel and the Sacraments.

The classic Anglican interpretation of the Eucharist in our period is O. C. Quick's *The Christian Sacraments.*[20] Quick's plan

---

[14] *Ibid.*, p. 133.   [15] No date, but clearly post-1933.
[16] *Sacraments and the Modern Man* . . . , p. 130.
[17] *Ibid.*, p. 132.   [18] *Ibid.*, pp. 142-44.   [19] *Ibid.*, p. 112.
[20] The book was published in 1927; in 1933 A. G. Hebert in *Liturgy and Society* (p. 57) affirmed of Chap. v, "Christ's Life as a Sacrament (2) The Atonement," that it is a classic. J. K. Mozley in the Preface (pp. 9-10) of his *The Gospel Sacraments* wrote of Quick's monograph that it was "the most notable Anglican treatment of the subject within living memory."

was to lay a general philosophical foundation in the first three chapters, and to represent in the fourth and fifth chapters "the historical Incarnation and Atonement as the supreme sacrament and fount of all others,"[21] while subsequent chapters dealt with the operation of the Sacraments, the Church and its unity, and considered Baptism and Holy Communion in detail.

Crucial to his exposition was the distinction between ethical and aesthetic sacramentalism, corresponding to the difference between sacraments as instruments and sacraments as symbols. He contended that each needed the other, "yet no philosophical argument, or carefully drawn analogy, can help the understanding so much as the consideration of the life of Christ in its double aspect as the supreme self-expression of the Godhead within the created world, and as the supreme instrument whereby that world is brought to its fulfilment in eternity."[22] Moving from sacramentalism to sacraments, he affirmed that "for Christians the supreme sacrament, apart from which no other has use or meaning, is the life of Jesus Christ."[23] The fine intervening chapters on the Incarnation, the Atonement, the operation of the Sacraments, the Church and Unity,[24] as well as Baptism, must be ignored in our summary in order to concentrate on his treatment of the Eucharist. It is expressive because all human life, as it realizes its own ideal, is made up of an act of self-offering to God and an act of communion with Him and in Him through Jesus Christ our Lord; yet it is also instrumental as a constantly repeated act from which the soul draws its spiritual food.

The eschatological element is strong in Quick's interpretation,[25] which recognizes that the Messianic Banquet in the Kingdom of God is a central motif but insists that between the Last Supper and its establishment the crucifixion of the Messiah must take place. In the Eucharist Christians "are made partakers of the life offered for them on Calvary, in order that in the end their communion with that life may be fulfilled in the open and glorious vision of their Saviour before the throne of God."[26]

Quick then turns to the two vexed problems of Eucharistic theology, "the problem of the sacrifice offered, and the problem

[21] *The Christian Sacraments*, pp. xi-xii.
[22] *Ibid.*, p. 54.   [23] *Ibid.*
[24] This includes the fruitful idea that practically all the divisions of Christendom should be considered "as being in principle schisms within the Church" (*ibid.*, p. 147).
[25] Quick indicates here his indebtedness to the thought of Hoskyns in *Essays Catholic and Critical*.
[26] *Ibid.*, p. 194.

of the presence communicated."[27] Christ's sacrifice, it is insisted, is representative, not vicarious. How, then, does the Eucharist become a sacrifice? Quick answers that it does so both mystically and morally. That is, "the life of the truly perfect man, being sacrificed once and for all, is sufficient to cleanse and perfect all those to whom it is really communicated," for "Christ died for us that He might live in us."[28] Thus, Christ's life in men exhibits itself in the same activity of self-sacrifice which He in His own person perfectly fulfilled.

Turning to the mode of Christ's presence in the Eucharist, Quick considers the four traditional theories: Transubstantiation, Consubstantiation, Virtualism, and Receptionism. The first two connect the Presence with the consecration of the elements and the second two affirm the Presence in the hearts and souls of faithful worshippers. Yet in assaying the traditional doctrines, two presuppositions are unacceptable to twentieth century minds. These are: the view that material objects possess a substantiality distinguishable from their accidents or sensible properties and from their value or use; and the concept that heaven is a place where Christ's ascended body is extended in space.

Quick is looking for a theory which will do justice to three factors. The Presence is to be sought, first, in elements not as physical objects but as they are within the process of a certain action which uses them as instruments and expresses itself in them. Secondly, such a theory must not imply a "real absence" of Christ elsewhere, but must insist that the Eucharist is the expressive symbol of the entire process by which the world is made to fulfil God's purpose. Thirdly, the "Real Presence" must be so defined as not to leave the communicant at the mercy of his own flickering introversion. Quick believes that these requirements are satisfied in the following exposition of his theory:

"The Eucharist is the self offering of Christ as externalised in human ritual, so that human lives may be incorporated into its living reality through communion with Him Who offers and is offered. The action of every Eucharist begins in the inward and eternal sphere where Christ is seated at the right hand of God. Christ's action then reaches its first stage of externalisation in His Body the Church, which at a given place and time in the person of its priest solemnly offers the bread and wine in memorial of His passion. The action is thus further externalised and extended

[27] *Ibid.*, p. 196.   [28] *Ibid.*

into the consecrated bread and wine as themselves representing the offered Body of Christ's manhood. From this furthest or lowest point of externalisation the action of the living Christ returns back and upwards into the members of His Body the Church as they receive Him in communion. In them it brings forth the spiritual fruits of their own self-offering which raises them towards heaven in Christ's power. So the Eucharistic action returns in the end to heaven which was its source. Thus interpreted it consists of a double movement, first downward and outward, then upward and inward. Thus it embodies in ritual and fulfils through the life of the Church that which was at first and perfectly embodied in fact through the historical life of Jesus Christ."[29]

The value of Quick's theory is that it tries to combine both expressive and instrumentalist elements in a mystical and moral combination. His final chapter, "Worship and Morals," warns against both ascetic rigorism and emotional self-indulgence, and reminds the reader that the reconciliation between worship and ethics is found "in the discovery that the true worship of God and the true service of men are alike possible in the one Holy Spirit of love."[30] Yet, with characteristic fidelity to the Bible, Quick says that this union is not commonly achieved—for the Parable of the Good Samaritan records that it was the men of worship (the priest and the levite) who passed by human need on the other side, and that Jesus gave a singularly cold reception to those who professed a sentimental devotion to Him, as in the case of the woman who cried, "Blessed is the womb that bare thee!" Worship, he concludes, is to be the stimulant of the soul, not its narcotic.

It is not the least of the values of Anglican sacramental teaching that it has often stimulated those who most value the Eucharist to undertake the humblest work for Christ in the slums or in the mission-field. No speech at the Anglo-Catholic Congress in 1923 received a stronger ovation than these simple words of the Bishop of Zanzibar: "You have your Mass, you have your altars, you have begun to get your tabernacles. Now go out into the highways and hedges, and look for Jesus in the ragged and the naked, in those who have lost hope, and in those who are struggling to make good. Look for Jesus in them; and when you have found Him, gird yourself with His towel of fellowship and wash His feet in the fellowship of His brethren."[31]

---

[29] *Ibid.*, pp. 223-24.   [30] *Ibid.*, p. 240.
[31] H. Maynard Smith, *Frank, Bishop of Zanzibar*, p. 302.

The same sense of the social implications of the Eucharist, though expressed in a much more sophisticated way, and with a deeper understanding of the economic and political order, was characteristic of Archbishop William Temple's thinking. In *Personal Religion and the Life of Fellowship* (1926) Temple insisted that the Eucharist was no mystery cult, but the Family Meal where the children gathered round the Table to receive what the Father gives them. Consequently, he insisted, "differences of rank, wealth, learning, intelligence, nationality, race, all disappear; 'we, being many, are one Bread.' "[32]

By the time he wrote *The Hope of a New World* (1940), he saw the Eucharist as also the symbol of a transfigured social order and of the true sanctification of labour for the community. The Holy Communion is, of course, in the traditional sense a means of grace, an effective channel of God's transforming love, but it is also expressive of God's intentions for human community. Bread and wine are the perfect symbols of the economic life of man. Bread is an instance of God's gifts to man made available by human cooperation with God. On God's part there is the gift of seed, soil, sun, and rain. Man's contribution is the labour of ploughing the land, scattering the seed, gathering in of the harvest, threshing the flour, baking the bread and distributing it for the satisfaction of human need. Thus:

"In the Holy Communion service we take the bread and wine—man's industrial and commercial life in symbol—and offer it to God; because we have offered it to Him, He gives it back to us as the means of nurturing us, not in our animal nature alone, but as agents of His purpose, limbs of a body responsive to His will; and as we receive it back from Him, we share it with one another in a true fellowship. If we think of the service in this way, it is a perfect picture of what secular society should be; and a Christian civilization is one where the citizens seek to make their ordered life something of which that service is the symbol."[33] In the Holy Communion so interpreted there is a profound doctrine of man in society. The same theme is most eloquently developed in the

[32] *Personal Religion* . . . , p. 48.
[33] *The Hope of a New World*, pp. 69-70. It is worth recording Temple's notable definition of worship: "What worship means is the submission of the whole being to the object of worship. It is the opening of the heart to receive the love of God; it is the subjection of conscience to be directed by Him; it is the declaration of need to be fulfilled by Him; it is the subjection of desire to be controlled by Him; and as the result of all these together, it is the surrender of the will to be used by Him" (*The Church and Its Teaching To-day*, p. 15).

concluding paragraphs of the introduction to Dom Gregory Dix's *The Shape of the Liturgy* (1948), in which he contrasts "Acquisitive Man" and his successor "Mass-Man" with "Eucharistic Man."[34]

It has been contended that the Anglican Church developed a deepened appreciation of the centrality of the Sacrament of Holy Communion during this period, and the treatises from different schools of thought have borne this out. What is of equal significance, however, is that there has been developing a growing unity of interpretation, in marked contrast with the partisanship of Eucharistic interpretation that characterized the Prayer Book Controversy. The most impressive proof of this assertion is to be found in the remarkable agreement arrived at by a Commission, representative of the chief schools of thought, as it defined in *Doctrine in the Church of England* (1937) its understanding of the hitherto controversial concept of Sacrifice in the Eucharist:

"The Eucharist is a corporate act of the Church towards God, wherein it is united with its Lord, victorious and triumphant, Himself both priest and victim in the sacrifice of the Cross. This connection has been expressed in at least four ways: (1) through stress on the union of ourselves with Christ in the act of communion, and in that union the offering of 'the sacrifice of praise and thanksgiving' and of 'ourselves, our souls and bodies'—a view generally held in the Church of England, many members of which would find here alone the sacrificial element in the rite; (2) through emphasis on the fact that in the Eucharist we repeat the words and acts of Christ at the last supper in words and acts whereby it is held that He invested His approaching death with the character of a sacrifice; (3) through the insistence that the rite is a representation before the Father of the actual sacrifice of the Cross; (4) through the doctrine of the Heavenly Altar, at which we join in the perpetual offering by Christ of Himself and share the life of Christ crucified and risen . . . . There are those who would combine all the views stated, while some of them would be repudiated in certain quarters. We consider that all of them would be regarded as legitimate in the Church of England, and we are agreed in general terms in holding that the Eucharist may be rightly termed a sacrifice—which we have defined as 'an act in which man worships God, the form of the act being an expression of the homage due from the creature to the creator.' But if the Eucharist is thus spoken of as a sacrifice, it must be understood

[34] Pp. xviii-xix, and cited fully in Chap. I.

as a sacrifice in which (to speak as exactly as the subject allows) we do not offer Christ, but where Christ unites us with Himself in the self-offering of the life that was 'obedient unto death, yea the death of the Cross.' "[35]

That statement is an irenic triumph. Even so, there remain important differences of emphasis, as, for example, between those for whom the Eucharist is the Church's supreme *offering*, and those who believe it to be the thankful celebration of God's supreme *gift*.

Archbishop Ramsey has written of the permanent characteristics of Anglican theology as including "the appeal to Scripture and the Fathers, the fondness for Nicene categories, the union of doctrine and liturgy, the isolation from Continental influences."[36] This is a perceptive evaluation, provided that one modification and a significant addition may be made. The modification necessary is that increasingly as the century advanced Anglican theology became subject to Continental influences, both Swedish and French, and the German influence was not negligible.[37] The addition to be made is that Anglican sacramental teaching is inescapably ethical. Holy attitudes must issue in holy actions. One of the glories of the Anglican tradition is that it, like Puritanism, rejected a "cloistered and fugitive virtue." This insistence that the spirit of the sanctuary must be carried into the streets, and that without the humility induced by worship social service becomes mere patronage, is finely stressed by Bishop K. E. Kirk in *The Vision of God*. There he writes: "Yet apart from the atmosphere of worship, every act of service avails only to inflate the agent's sense of patronage. He is the doctor, humanity his patient: he is the Samaritan, his neighbour the crippled wayfarer: He is the instructor, others are merely his pupils. Gratitude (if they show gratitude) only confirms his conviction of his own importance; resentment (if they resent his services) only ministers to the glow of self-

[35] *Doctrine in the Church of England*, p. 162.
[36] *From Gore to Temple: the Development of Anglican Theology between Lux Mundi and the Second World War, 1889-1939*, pp. viii-ix.
[37] Anglican Biblical scholarship was indebted to German thought and the Liberal school was influenced by Harnack, Schweitzer, and Otto. A. G. Hebert was, by his translations and his constructive works, a potent mediator of Swedish scholarship, and the influence of Yngve Brilioth, Gustaf Aulen, and Anders Nygren, in particular, was considerable, as English translations of *Eucharistic Faith and Practice*, *Christus Victor*, and *Agape and Eros* were widely read. In Patristics and Liturgics the influence of such French scholars as J. Daniélou, Louis Bouyer, and Cullmann, and of such German scholars as Bultmann and Jungmann was considerable. Barth was appreciated by such Anglican scholars as Hoskyns, Camfield, and Bromiley.

esteem with which he comforts himself in secret."[38] By contrast, the glory of worship is to elicit the grace of humility.

3. *A Fecundity of Experimentation*

The third characteristic of Anglican worship, particularly evident in the last decade of our period, was the fertility of liturgical experimentation. There could be no more vigorous indication of vitality in the Anglican tradition than this, especially as these experiments are marked by imagination and relevance.

Five experiments have evoked unusual interest and therefore deserve detailed consideration. The first is "Parish Communion," associated with A. G. Hebert of Kelham, which began obscurely in 1913, was given publicity in the book[39] which Hebert edited in 1937, and later was even more widely disseminated by the "Parish and People" movement, with its own magazine of that name. The second is the "House Church" associated with Ernest Southcott, who in 1950 or thereabouts attempted to combine the celebration of Holy Communion with evangelism by taking the Church to the homes of his people in the new housing estate of Halton, Leeds. The third experiment, "The Clare College Liturgy," is a liturgical manual of 1954 produced by two chaplains of this Cambridge College, J. A. T. Robinson and C. F. D. Moule. The fourth is "An Experimental Liturgy" of 1958, which was celebrated on the entire Independent Television network in 1959. The fifth and last is the official Report of the Church of England Liturgical Commission, *Baptism and Confirmation*, published in 1959.

4. *"The Parish Communion"*

"By 'the Parish Communion' is meant the celebration of the Holy Eucharist, with the communion of the people in a parish church as the chief service of the day, or better, as the assembly of the Christian community for the worship of God," wrote Hebert, adding "on Sundays the most suitable hour will generally be not long before or after 9.0. A.M."[40] This concern for a simple major celebration of Holy Communion in which most of the confirmed members of the parish would participate was meant to end the current fracturing of the family life and witness of the Church, whereby some parishes had sparsely attended 8 A.M. Communions

[38] P. 184.
[39] *The Parish Communion, A Book of Essays.*
[40] *Ibid.*, p. 3.

followed by a largely attended service of Matins, while other parishes had a High Mass with large attendance and little participation in the Eucharist. It was also believed that the Holy Communion service should be the chief expression of the *koinonia* or fellowship of the Body of Christ in a particular parish and at a convenient hour for entire families to attend. Furthermore, when the worshippers partook of a "Parish breakfast" following the "Parish Communion," they would naturally get to know each other better and become more truly a community in Christ. These were the practical considerations.

There were also significant theological concerns. The Eucharist demonstrates the real nature of the Church when celebrated in the manner of the Parish Communion with full participation. The Church surrounding the altar rehearses "the mystery of the divine *agape* whereby man has been redeemed and the redeemed fellowship constituted as the Body of Christ. The Eucharist sums up the whole Gospel of redemption as the sacramental showing-forth of the one Sacrifice of Christ and of the offering up of the members of Christ through union with Him to be a reasonable, holy, and living sacrifice to God."[41] The Offertory, therefore, must be shown to have much greater relevance to the worshippers. In the early church the bread and wine were brought to the altar by the people themselves and this act then clearly demonstrated their will to offer themselves with their gifts. The modern equivalent, popularized by the Parish Communion, is for representatives of the people to carry the elements in procession from the back of the church, as well as the alms, "each member of the congregation, in some cases, having placed a wafer in the ciborium or on the paten as they came into church."[42] In other ways, too, an attempt is made to involve the congregation more actively in the worship. The Epistle may be read by a layman; and the entire congregation will be instructed to join heartily in the responses and in such parts of the liturgy as are to be sung, where the settings are appropriate for community singing. "Often babies in arms or small children accompany their parents to the communion rail, to be blessed perhaps by the priest as he moves along administering the sacrament."[43] Such care to involve the congregation actively goes a long way to destroy the old mistaken view that the Eucharist was

[41] *Ibid.*, p. 4.
[42] Martin Pierce, *The Parish Communion* (Alcuin Club Pamphlet, undated), p. 4.
[43] *Ibid.*

a theatrical spectacle performed by liturgical experts in the sight of a largely silent and submissive people.

The custom of holding a Parish Communion followed by a Parish Breakfast originated in 1913 in the rural Warwickshire parish of Temple Balsall,[44] where the Eucharist at 8.45 A.M. was the principal service of the day. The Parish Eucharist was initiated at St. John's, Newcastle-upon-Tyne, in 1927 and by 1937, 170 of 250 communicants attended this service regularly each Sunday at 9.15 A.M. It may be of interest to provide a description of the form the Offertory took in this church at that date:

"During the saying of the Offertory Prayer we now have an Offertory Procession. A credence table is placed at the West end of the church, and on it two vessels containing the approximate number of breads that will be required for the communion of the people, and two wine cruets. When the celebrant returns to the altar after the address, four members of the congregation who have been chosen beforehand (if possible, a man and a woman, a boy and a girl) go to this credence table, and while the congregation are saying the offertory Prayer, carry the people's offerings of bread and wine through the congregation to the altar rail, where the offerings are received by the servers and handed to the celebrant for presentation at the altar. Such a procession helps the people to realize the significance of the offertory by giving it a visible dramatic form. It restores the act of offering to its true importance, and marks it as the foundation of the whole Eucharistic action. It has the additional value of giving a share in the action of worship to a greater number of the laity, who need not all be of the male sex."[45]

The Parish Communion has, in subsequent years, become almost the normative celebration of the Eucharist in the Church of England. It has stressed important values, but it has also raised some serious questions. Clearly it is a great gain that, as in the early Church, the Eucharist should have been re-established at the centre of Sunday worship and that it should be widely attended by a devout and committed people. It is also a considerable boon that it is customary in high as well as in low parishes, for it means that the Sacrament of unity is really accomplishing unification. Furthermore, Parish Communion (whether or not it is followed by Parish Breakfast as a kind of equivalent to the love-feast or *agape* of the early Church) undoubtedly helps the local congrega-

[44] Hebert, ed., *The Parish Communion*, p. 261.
[45] *Ibid.*, pp. 277-78.

tion to understand itself as a true family in Christ. The meaning of Baptism is also more readily apprehended by the people. Not least important is the fact that "the Parish Meeting can discover itself as a fellowship of counsel and evangelism."[46] It has helped to awaken a responsible laity.

Even so, some serious theological questions must be raised by the popularity of the Parish Communion as, indeed, they were by Dr. A. M. Ramsey in his *Durham Essays and Addresses*. The most serious caveat concerns the reduction of instruction inevitable in a service which can allow only about seven minutes for a sermon. Such concision almost compels the preacher to be dogmatic and coercive rather than explanatory and persuasive. Here it is pertinent to recall that one of the attractions of the Elizabethan settlement, according to A. L. Rowse, was the change from the Mass to the sermon which led to "an increase of reflection and edification, a stimulus to education and the active virtues."[47] Is the Parish Communion, then, a second Elizabethan unsettlement? At least, it is a displacement of the Anglican conjoint emphasis on the Word and Sacrament to the advantage of the Sacrament and the disadvantage of the Word.

As Dr. Ramsey has indicated, an exaggerated emphasis on the importance of the Offertory can lead to a Pelagian glorification of man and a forgetfulness that the smaller human offerings are only possible because of the Father's prior acceptance of the perfect sacrifice of the Cross. Dr. E. L. Mascall has also warned that in some circles the idea has gained ground that what makes the liturgy corporate is the fact that many people celebrate it at the same time, yet "whether the communicants be few or many, the liturgy is essentially corporate because it is the act of Christ in the *corpus mysticum*."[48] Moreover, when the note of fellowship is stressed, it must not be forgotten that this is a larger community than the merely local parish community. It is linked with the whole Church militant upon earth and triumphant in Heaven, as the *Sanctus* in the prayer of consecration suggests.[49] The older generation of Churchmen also sense a loss of awe and numinosity in the Parish Communion, which they recall as characterizing the eight

---

[46] Pierce, *The Parish Communion*, p. 16.
[47] *The England of Elizabeth*, p. 485.
[48] *Corpus Christi*, p. 78.
[49] Dr. Ramsey in *Durham Essays and Addresses* (p. 20) suggests this requires a fuller liturgical expression than is provided in the present Communion Office and which was a feature of the First Prayer Book of Edward VI.

o'clock early morning Communions. The provision of a nave altar and the use of the westward posture, not to mention the fidgeting of children, make it harder to concentrate on God and all too easy to focus on man.

It is, of course, possible that the vogue for Parish Communion will pass, especially as for many persons an Evening Communion would be more convenient, and there seems to be little point in Anglican hesitation on such a matter when Roman Catholic permission is readily available for Evening Masses. Moreover, the Evangelical wing of the Church has a long tradition of holding Holy Communion in the evening. Those who will resist such a change are, of course, such clergy as believe that fasting before Communion is an indispensable discipline.

5. The "House Church"

There are two very important features in the worship of the "House Church" as originally developed by Ernest Southcott in Halton, Leeds. The first is that this is an expression of liturgical evangelism, an attempt to supplement the worship and witness of the parish church in the homes of the people. The second is that an appropriate charismatic element enters into the service of Holy Communion when celebrated on the dining-table of a home. This is the interpolation of simple, extempore prayer for or by those in whose home Communion is celebrated.

Southcott's parish comprised some fifteen thousand persons, including the Halton Moor Estate, a slum-clearance area of some six thousand people. His problem was to discover how to make the Church relevant to their daily lives. For this purpose Southcott conceived the idea of *extensive* and *intensive* House Churches.[50] The *extensive* House Churches consist entirely of Bible Study groups of neighbours meeting in a centrally convenient home. The *intensive* House Churches are similar, but more fully instructed and committed cells or groups also meeting in homes, where the Holy Communion is celebrated. The latter is not a substitute for Communion in the parish church, but a supplement to it. It is even an incentive to attend the Parish Communion.

House celebrations have taken place in four different ways.[51] In the case of sick people who were regular communicants, Com-

---

[50] A third occasional type of House Church is interdenominational in character, but this has been little employed. See Malcolm Boyd, *Crisis in Communication: A Christian Examination of the Mass Media*, p. 83.

[51] See E. W. Southcott, "The House Church," in *Theology*, Vol. LVI, No. 395 (May 1953), pp. 169-70.

munion is taken to them from the Reserved Sacrament at monthly intervals where it is requested. In the case of elderly people, house celebrations are held monthly for their benefit in different parts of the parish and are attended by friends and neighbours. Twice a year (in a week during Lent and in a week following the Harvest Festival) the Halton clergy hold house celebrations each morning of the week and people are invited to attend by the family after consultation with the clergy. The lapsed are invited to be present, but not to communicate until they have been confirmed. The fourth method followed a month's mission in October, 1952, where the chief technique was to hold house meetings and house celebrations. For an entire month house celebrations were held each morning at 6, 7, and 9.15, and house meetings each day for a fortnight. Nine hundred attended the house celebrations, five hundred the house meetings and over a thousand people entered each other's houses during that short time. Canon Southcott comments: "Here is the Church being the Church. Certainly it is the Eucharist in action."[52]

This is but a sketch—it needs to be filled in with local colour. An American observer described his impressions as follows: "Early on week-day mornings there are house-church meetings with celebrations of Holy Communion in some of the small houses of the Halton Moor Estate. The lights of the house break through the cold and blackness outside and testify to the gatherings of Christians for the breaking of bread together—a very effective form of communication, one is told by certain men and women who first observed the goings on from outside across the street or way, and who are now inside the fold taking part." The account continues with an inside description: "The kitchen table is set up within the living room in one of the compact slum-clearance dwellings. Used candles from the altar at the parish church are placed upon the table that becomes the altar. . . . Home-made bread, the same bread that the family had eaten for tea the night before is used for the service. The Bible and last evening's newspaper are close together; and they will shortly be in the same conversation, too."[53]

Another observer also conveys a vivid impression: "Let it only be said, therefore, that in Halton men who would never otherwise have dreamt of coming to Communion, not in church, and certainly not on a weekday, are coming—at six in the morning—to Communion in the home." The explanation is: "Because here . . . is Christ abiding in the midst of the family. . . . Here is Christ ex-

[52] *Ibid.*, p. 170.   [53] Malcolm Boyd, *op.cit.*, p. 83.

posed in the midst of bread and wine and crockery and the table-cloth; and 'Jesus has come to our house!' Here they are, there he is, in the Church! Father reads the epistle. Mother offers up prayers for her home and her street, for her husband's works and the children. '. . . and are in love and charity with your neighbours,' says the Invitation."[54]

Southcott himself has remarked that in the house-celebration there is occasionally time for a short relevant sermon and an opportunity for lay people to intercede in a movingly personal way such as could not be done in the formal worship of the parish. It is clearly one of the values of the house church that it can combine liturgical structure and order with free prayer. Here the Catholic and Puritan traditions are meaningfully combined in a way that has not been experienced in the Church of England since the time of John Wesley and George Whitefield.

What then, is the significance of the House Church experiment? Certainly it has proved to be an effective means of bringing the lapsed or the indifferent back to the Christian community and way of life. But has it any deeper theological significance? There is no doubt that it witnesses significantly to the fact that the Church does not consist of bricks and mortar or concrete, but is the *people* of God. Dr. J. A. T. Robinson believes that the House Church is an approximation to New Testament Christianity, representing the "tap-roots of the Vine, the Church under ground, that of the life of the tree most closely in contact with the clinging soil of everyday existence: it is the tree as it is embedded in the deepest crevices and seams of the secular world."[55] Its great advantage in the modern world is that the cell is a part of the Church with great flexibility and mobility, operating in the area of natural community. It meets in a house: it could as easily meet in an office or a factory or, as it once did, in the catacombs.

It is important to recognize, however, that this is never regarded as an end, complete in itself. The house celebrations are intimately related to Parish Communion at St. Wilfrid's Church, Halton. When Southcott was interviewed and asked about the relationship of the House Church to the Parish Church, he insisted that the House Church was giving roots to the Parish Church, for otherwise the latter's congregation was too large and the membership too

[54] Eric James, "What is going on at Halton?", *Theology*, *Vol.* LX, No. 440 (February 1957), p. 63.
[55] "The House Church and the Parish Church," *Theology*, Vol. LIII, No. 362 (August 1950), p. 285.

loosely linked together. In the House Church, it was realized that "We don't go to Church, we *are* the Church."[56] Furthermore, it is at these gatherings in the home that a new relationship is sensed between the holy and the common, and everyday life can be offered to God. He ended the interview with a reminder that the Abbé Michonneau said the parable of the hundred sheep should be retold for our own day: Now there are ninety-nine sheep out in the wilderness and only one in the fold.

As might be expected, the Parish Communion at St. Wilfrid's, Halton, is well abreast of the Liturgical Movement's achievements. The celebration is at a table-altar in the nave and the priest faces the congregation as he offers the consecration prayer. The people take bread and place it in the ciborium. Many of the collects in the Order for Holy Communion are said in common. Laymen lead many of the bidding prayers, speaking from different parts of the nave. A true participation of the people links house celebrations and parish celebrations.

What, then, are the values of the House Church experiment? A powerful means has been discovered for demonstrating the potential sanctification of the common life, of the nexus between Christ the Bread of Life and our daily bread, and of every meal as a miniature Eucharist. Here, too, is a Biblical and liturgical mission allowing for the differing stages of commitment. The interested but uncommitted are reached in the extensive house church, and are observers at the Eucharist in the intensive house church. Then, after instruction and confirmation, they share in the parish and House Church Communions, becoming witnesses in turn to their friends and neighbours. Above all, the Eucharist, whether celebrated with splendour or simplicity, is seen to be the pattern of Christian love and service in the world, empowered by the example and the grace of Christ.

There are two potential dangers in the House Church experiment. The first is that the part may be preferred to the whole. The intimate fellowship and the charismatic service in the home may make the formal parish Communion seem impersonal, theatrical, remote, and to that extent less meaningful. The second is a danger inherent in all aggrandizations of the role of the chief Sacrament in the life of the Church—that is the depreciation of the role of the ministry of the Word. To be sure, the Bible is given

---

[56] The interview is recorded in *Faith at Work* (October–November 1958), pp. 23-27. This magazine is published in Lebanon, Pennsylvania.

a preparatory and instructional role in the extensive house churches. But preaching is reduced to the briefest of talks in the intensive house church; yet the committed Christian needs the iron-ration of Scripture more than the catechumen.

One further hesitation remains. While the example of Ernest Southcott has been followed successfully in a few parishes of the Protestant Episcopal Church of the United States and, with some changes, in a few parishes of the Presbyterian Church of Scotland, it has not been widely imitated in the Church of England. In fact, it has hardly been imitated at all in his own Communion. Is it particularly successful only in the north of England and would it be less successful among the more reserved southerners? Does it only succeed in slum-clearance communities deeply in need of new community roots? Was Southcott unusually fortunate in the sympathy and approval of his diocesan at Ripon and his suffragan at Knaresborough? Or, finally, does the "House Church" experiment need for its successful accomplishment a leader with the courage, drive, imagination, dedication, and warm personality of an Ernest Southcott himself?

6. The "Clare College Manual" for the Liturgy

This experiment in worship attempts to meet the needs of a College House Church. It does not provide a new liturgy. The novelty is to be found in the fact that the Prayer Book Order for Holy Communion is made more meaningful by the use of a specially prepared manual of instruction, with the words of the service on the right-hand pages, and the commentary on the left-hand pages. Furthermore, the ceremonial adds to the relevance of the service in its context in collegiate life, and the exciting preaching of the former Dean, Dr. J. A. T. Robinson, added to the significance of the celebrations.

The manual illuminates the structure of the Liturgy by a helpful introduction and additional preparatory and post-communion prayers, as also by meditations and observations appropriate to the various parts of the Anglican service chosen from the Bible and from several ecumenical sources. Thus the chief gains of the modern Liturgical Movement are transmitted by the manual, which is simply titled, "The Holy Communion, Clare College, Cambridge." In this way members of the College, who comprised a number of Free Churchmen as well as the Anglican majority, became familiar with the coordinate stress on Word and Sacrament, the renewed understanding of the importance of the Offertory, and, in particular, with the "Four Action" pattern of the Eucharist as analysed by Dom Gregory Dix in *The Shape of Liturgy*, and the idea that this is a con-celebration of the whole people of God. In addition, the elements used for consecration consisted of college-baked bread and wine from the college cellars.

The great quality of the manual is that it combines clear theological instruction and spiritual directions with naturalness, and avoids the two commonest perils of manuals of this type, sentimentality and rubrical antiquarianism. A significant sample from the introduction will illustrate the qualities which have been claimed for it. After observing that the service of Holy Communion falls into two distinct parts, it continues:

> The first part, the Liturgy of the Word, has its focus in the Bible, and takes place not at the Table but round the Lecterns. It is a service of prayer, Scripture-reading and preaching, in which the living Christ speaks to his assembled People, as Jesus discoursed with his disciples in the Upper Room, expounding the meaning of his death and promised presence.
>
> In the second part, the Breaking of the Bread, he makes himself known in the Action which he instituted and which ever since has been the central act of the Church on the Lord's Day. In it he makes present to us, through the power of his risen life, all that he wrought on the Cross, till he comes in final victory.
>
> The pattern of this action is four-fold, continuing that of Jesus at the Last Supper, when he took, and blessed, and broke, and gave.[57]

Then there follows a concise exposition of the spiritual meaning of the renewal of these acts in Holy Communion:

> We come, first, to commemorate with thanksgiving that he in his life, death and resurrection offered himself thus to be taken and consecrated, broken and given *for* us;
>
> secondly, to trust his promise that in the bread and wine, taken, blessed, broken and shared as he commanded, he will come *to* us;
>
> thirdly, to let our lives likewise be taken, blessed, broken

[57] Clare College Manual, p. 2. The Clare College Communion Service complete with commentary is published also as an Appendix to J. A. T. Robinson's *The Liturgy Coming to Life*.

and given in union with his, that God's redeeming work and rule may be extended *through* us.[58]

There is special interest in the notes opposite the Offertory. There we read:

> Jesus began by taking the loaf off the supper table. His work now, in us and through us, cannot start until the ordinary material of our lives, just as it is, is turned over entirely to him. In the Offertory we take a loaf baked in the College kitchens and a decanter of wine from the College cellars—symbols of our labour and our leisure, the gifts of God to us as we have worked upon them. They are brought up by laymen, out of the midst of our everyday life, and offered to God, together with our money.[59]

Further interest attaches to a rubric following immediately after the concluding Blessing:

> The ministers go out, a deacon carrying the remainder of the Loaf not set apart for Holy Communion, to be shared at the Breakfast.[60]

The supplementary prayers for private meditation are taken from a wide range of sources, including the Armenian Liturgy, The South India Liturgy,[61] the Liturgy of St. John Chrysostom, the Liturgy of St. James, the Liturgy of St. Basil, the Liturgy of Malabar, and, most interestingly, John Wesley's Covenant Service as used by the English Methodist Church. The citations range from St. Augustine to P. T. Forsyth.

Of the instructional and inspirational value of this unpretentious manual of thirty-one pages there can be no question. But the service must have meant considerably more when Dr. John Robinson was preaching, as may be discovered from his book, *Liturgy Coming to Life* (1960), an account of the Clare College experiment, including some of his Eucharistic addresses. In terms of re-interpreting traditional services with imagination, wit and spirituality, the only parallel I can think of is Monsignor Ronald Knox's *The Mass in Slow Motion* (1948) and that is the highest praise.

The preparation of the Clare College manual was necessary

---

[58] *Ibid.*   [59] *Ibid.*, p. 12.   [60] *Ibid.*, p. 29.
[61] In fact, the citation comes from the Bombay Liturgy used as a source by the South India Liturgy.

because previous ones were the reflection of party ecclesiastical prejudice and of subjective rather than corporate piety, or too obviously written by clergy for clergy. Robinson's manual was prepared in the conviction that "the road to living liturgical reform leads from the bottom upwards, and that is why controlled experiment in the local worshipping community, especially at the sub-parochial or house church level, is so vital to the health of the Body of Christ."[62] There were, of course, serious disadvantages in a college community attempting to live like a church, for it was both an artificial and a highly changing entity; artificial in that there were no women or children apart from those of the teaching and administrative staff, and highly mobile because most undergraduates left after three years. Moreover, the high points of the Christian Year, Christmas and Easter, for example, arrived to find the undergraduates on vacation.

Robinson felt that it was his duty, when Dean of Clare College from 1951 to 1959, to recover the Patristic understanding of the Liturgy as quite literally the *ergon* or work of the *laos*, the people (of God), by which the latter are constituted through the Sacrifice of Christ the very Body of Christ. He was greatly impressed by Gregory Dix's *The Shape of the Liturgy* because it emphasized that the structure of the Liturgy was not based on any pattern of words, but on a four-fold *action*, as performed by Jesus at the Last Supper. He hoped to make it clear in the celebration of the Liturgy that "this is the crucible of the new creation, in which God's new world is continually being fashioned out of the old, as ordinary men and women are renewed and sent out as carriers of Christ's risen life."[63]

He added the preparatory prayers and citations from the great liturgies of Christendom precisely because he felt the exultant note celebrating the mighty acts of God in Christ was missing in the Prayer Book, drowned by the penitential concentration on Calvary, to the neglect of the Creation, Incarnation, and Resurrection. He also magnified the place of the Liturgy of the Word, believing that the sermon is "an indispensable instrument for the regular communication of any through-going theology of the Eucharist and its implications" and that the Word of God must be contemporary, "speaking to every man in his own language, cutting through all

[62] *Liturgy coming to Life*, p. 15. The author adds: "Nothing lasting will be achieved, as 1928 showed, by imposition from the top downwards."
[63] *Ibid.*, p. 23.

that muffles and stifles its impact."[64] He found it necessary to stress the four major actions of Taking, Blessing, Breaking, and Sharing, but this was difficult with the Prayer Book Rite of 1661 where the Offertory is separated from the Thanksgiving or Blessing, and the Fraction has been absorbed into the Consecration Prayer.

He also considered it important to accentuate the fact that the action of the Liturgy is social, not individual. If worshippers come to the Eucharist not merely to feed upon the Body of Christ, but to be created the Body of Christ, then this can be emphasized in the common loaf. It is lost in wafers or "breads." In the use of the common loaf there is a second advantage: the importance of the *Fraction* is demonstrated, with its symbolical reminder that the life of God can be given and shared only if it is broken. Moreover, Robinson wished to make it as plain as possible that the Liturgy was con-celebrated, the work of all the worshippers. For this reason he let it be known that any regular communicant was, in turn, to take his part in the communal action to which all were committed. He might be called upon to read the Epistle, to introduce the biddings or requests for prayer, or to make the offering of the bread and wine representing the common life. The western posture for the celebration was adopted, with the president facing the congregation, because it cut across party divisions, and because its psychological function was "to focus attention on a point in the middle, as the Christ comes to stand among his people as the breaker of bread, and to direct their gaze upwards as they lift their hearts to him as their ascended Lord."[65]

Like Archbishop William Temple, Dr. Robinson regards the Eucharist as the stimulus to sacrificial social action. Speaking of the common bread in the Eucharist, he insists that "we cannot without judgment share bread here and acquiesce in a world food distribution that brings plenty to some but malnutrition and starvation to millions more. We cannot without judgment share bread here with men of every race and tolerate a colour bar in restaurants and hotels."[66]

Dr. Robinson has shown that until the Church of England produces a revision of the Prayer Book more suitable both to the insights of our own day and of the early Church, it is possible by re-interpretation, by significant ceremonial, and by the use of an inspiring manual, to make the Liturgy indeed come alive.[67]

[64] *Ibid.*, p. 24.   [65] *Ibid.*, p. 33.   [66] *Ibid.*, p. 43.
[67] There seemed to be no point in offering a critical evaluation, because we

7. *"An Experimental Liturgy"*

In comparison with the previous experiments we have been considering, here is a more daring enterprise, the construction of a new liturgy, which combines the best of the past and the present to provide a more adequate vehicle of worship for the Church of England in an ecumenical century. Ambitious as the project is, finality is not claimed for it. Its three authors, Professor J. Gordon Davies[68] of the University of Birmingham, and two fellow clergy of the same city, Dr. Gilbert Cope[69] and D. A. Tytler, gave it the modest title of "An Experimental Liturgy." Their hope, when this was published in 1958, was that it might lead others to produce their own experimental liturgies or constructively to criticize this one, and thus prepare the Church of England to study the issues that would have to be considered when full-scale liturgical revision should again be contemplated.

Four basic principles have controlled their thinking. The first was the negative decision to avoid depending too much on any existing rite, since all are either too mediaeval or too Reformed in character. They decided, in the next place, to make a comparative study of liturgies preparatory to devising their own, thus ensuring that their rite would have an ecumenical character.[70] Thirdly, they desired to manifest the Biblical foundation of faith as integrated into the Sacrament, and also to demonstrate the Biblical doctrine through the structure of the rite. Finally, this was to be an attempt to make the Liturgy a truly corporate action, thoroughly understood by the people.

---

have already recognized the criticisms of the house church and the parish communion, and this Clare College service of Holy Communion is something of a combination of both related to the special needs of an academic community. In one respect it improves on both—in giving a larger place to preaching. For a criticism of the theology of the Offertory, see Paul Gibson, "Liturgical Revision and a Theology of Incorporation," *Theology*, Vol. LXIII, No. 486 (June 1960), p. 230.

[68] Professor Davies is the founder and head of the Liturgical Institute at the University of Birmingham, the author of *The Origin and Development of Early Christian Architecture* (1952) and of *The Architectural Setting of Baptism*, and is a former Bampton Lecturer.

[69] The Rev. Gilbert Cope wrote *Symbolism in the Bible and the Church* and edited *Making the Building Serve the Liturgy*.

[70] The Independent Television Authority's brochure publicising the transmission of the Experimental Order for Holy Communion on July 27, 1959, contains the following statement in the introduction by J. G. Davies: "the group responsible for producing this experiment did not take any one Order for Communion as its model, but tried, by a comparison of very many, to discover what features are essential in order that the rite should embody the fulness of Christian belief and practice as it is preserved fragmented in the separate branches of the Church."

They accepted the two-fold traditional structure of the Synaxis and the Eucharist, since the basic structure of the Synaxis came from the Synagogue, while that of the Eucharist derived from the Upper Room. Their only modification was to provide an act of Preparation to precede the Synaxis, and thus their rite has three parts.

Part I is *Preparation* and includes four elements: the Entrance, Chant, Greeting (and Collect for Purity), Confession and Prayer for Forgiveness (said by all the people). Part II is *The Ministry of the Word* (corresponding to the Synaxis) and contains ten elements: the Little Entrance (and Salutation), the Collect for the Day, the Old Testament Lesson, a Psalm or Canticle, the Epistle, a Psalm or Canticle, the Gospel (all standing) with *Gloria tibi* and *Laus tibi* optional, a Sermon, the Nicene Creed (with textual emendations), the Grace said by all (and possibly the Announcements and Special Biddings), and the Litany of Intercession. Part III is *The Ministry of the Sacrament*, which consists of five main elements, and many sub-elements. First there is the Offertory (with the *Pax* and presentation of offerings). Then the Thanksgiving follows, with *Sursum corda* and *Sanctus*, the Great Thanksgiving including an ascription to the Trinity said by the people, and the Lord's Prayer said by the people. The Fraction succeeds, including a Sentence and Response, this to be followed by Silence, and possibly by the Prayer of Humble Access. The fourth element is Communion, including the Communion of the clergy, the Invitation to the people and their response (emphasizing the concept of the Messianic Banquet), the Communion of the people, the Post-Communion Thanksgiving. The fifth and final element is the Dismissal.

Such is this interesting rite in skeletal form. There is a logic in the successive order of the various elements. The Preparation follows the shape of Isaiah's vision in the Temple, as the *Gloria in excelsis*—the sublime expression of adoration—leads naturally to the confession of sin and a plea for forgiveness.[71] The Ministry of the Word fittingly begins with a custom borrowed from the Eastern Orthodox Liturgy, the solemn carrying in of the Bible, known as the Little Entrance. This is followed by the reading of the Old Testament, the Epistle, and the Gospel, and the Sermon which expounds the Word of God, which fittingly elicits the response of

[71] It is not an Absolution, since this is to anticipate one of the benefits of the Eucharist itself.

the Creed (in a revised version adopting the first person plural) said by all the people. This part of the service ends with a prayer of intercession in the form of a litany, to enable all to share actively in it. The second main division of the Liturgy, the Ministry of the Sacrament, begins with the bringing forward by the representatives of the people of the gifts of bread, wine, and alms, as tokens of their self-offering. These gifts are then taken and blessed in a prayer of thanksgiving, which offers God gratitude for creation, redemption, and the institution of the Holy Communion, asks for the fruits of communion—forgiveness, unity, renewal and spiritual strength, and recalls the saving acts of Christ to whom the worshippers are linked by the Holy Spirit. Such a prayer fittingly concludes with the recitation by all of the Lord's Prayer, the prayer of the Christian family. The Fraction, or Breaking of the Bread, is followed by a call to Communion. Then a short prayer of thanksgiving is followed by the Dismissal, which reminds the worshippers of their responsibility as representatives of the Church in the world consequent on their union with the risen and ascended Lord of the Church.[72]

The ceremonial of this rite strongly emphasizes the corporate character of the Church. The celebrant faces the people for all are gathered to make a common spiritual sacrifice and to share a common meal at the same altar-table. Members of the congregation take it in turn to bring the Bible to the lectern and to read the Old Testament Lesson and the Epistle. The Litany of Intercession takes the responsive form, but extempore prayer or silence (with or without biddings) may be used, and in each case a member of the congregation may lead the congregation in these prayers. Representatives of the laity bring up to the table-altar the bread, wine, and alms. A single loaf of bread is used for the Fraction to symbolize the unity of all members in the Body of Christ. The Invitation to the people and their response employs the concept of the Messianic Banquet, in which the world-wide fellowship in the Kingdom of God is acknowledged. In all these ways, and in many responses, psalms and canticles throughout the service, the *koinonia* of the Church is re-affirmed and the people really share in the Liturgy.

"An Experimental Liturgy" is therefore marked by a strong consciousness of the fellowship of the Church of Christ, expressed

[72] This is a summary of the meaning of the service using the words of Dr. J. G. Davies as much as possible.

vividly in the ceremonial. The range of Biblical lessons emphasizes the continuity of the people of God throughout history, and the Messianic Banquet the world-wide extension of the Church. The Prayer of Thanksgiving, in which the people have a large vocal part, provides a summary of the holy acts of God from the creation while the Messianic Banquet looks to the consummation of history, and the emphasis is on the once crucified but now risen and ascended Christ. It is a simple, Biblical, joyful, and ecumenical rite. The only question that remains is whether it is sufficiently comprehensive for its purpose, and perhaps whether God's offering to us is minimized and the Church's offering to God overstressed.

In a cogent reply to criticisms,[73] Professor J. G. Davies readily admits that a master of English prose, such as Cranmer was, would be required to provide better rhythms and cadences in the prayers than his group was capable of doing, and that a smoother transition might be effected between the end of the Preparation and the beginning of the Ministry of the Word. He is, however, unwilling to eliminate the Preparation, as some would wish, since he believes this is psychologically necessary for most modern congregations. He concedes, too, that since it is hoped that the sermon will lead to a deeper penitence, the Confession might be taken from the Preparation and inserted between the Sermon and the Creed. A desire was expressed for an action to accompany the versicle and response of the Pax, as is done in the Liturgy of the Church of South India.

More serious criticisms were made of the Thanksgiving. It was said to present two distinct parts instead of a continuous unity. It was also urged that the contention of Professor E. C. Ratcliff that the earliest prayers of consecration had the *Sanctus* as the climax, not the commencement, should have been heeded. Davies, however, remains unconvinced by the evidence, and even if he were, does not feel "that *there was only one pattern*" or that it should be regarded as an ideal form. While admitting that a good rationale has been given by the Rev. A. H. Couratin for the *Sanctus* as the climax of the prayer of consecration, Professor Davies thinks there is an equally good one for retaining it in its usual position, namely, that the focus and setting of Christian worship is in heaven. The position of the Fraction is criticized as coming after and not before the Lord's Prayer, to which Davies replies that it is much more convenient for distribution to follow immediately after frac-

[73] *Theology*, Vol. LXII, No. 469 (July 1959), pp. 274-79.

tion and it is more emphatic as a central act in its present position. In keeping with the corporate principles of the revisers it is also suggested that all (not merely the celebrant) should say the Post-Communion Prayer. Finally, Davies concedes that a better form of Dismissal would be: "The Lord be with you. And with thy spirit. Let us depart in peace. In the name of Christ, Amen." And his parting wish is: "May the debate continue to a fruitful conclusion."

From the widespread discussion that the experimental rite evoked, from Canada to Australia, and from India to the United States, it is clear that it has fulfilled its primary purpose of stimulating Anglicans to consider afresh in the light of modern liturgical thinking the principles of Prayer Book revision. It has, moreover, stressed the importance of Biblical theology in liturgical reconstruction, and has dared to treat the English Prayer Book as if it were not sacrosanct and inalterable. Furthermore, while it is not likely to be the *last* word in liturgical revision, it significantly stresses the Eucharist in comprehensive fashion as a memorial, a thanksgiving, a sacrifice, a communion, and an eschatological anticipation of the consummated Kingdom of God. And, as we have suggested, it is an important *first* word in liturgical reform, and one of ecumenical interest precisely because of its attempt at Biblical fidelity. Its borrowings from the Eastern Rites (a Little Entrance, without a Great Entrance, and an *epiklesis*) for a Western Rite are, however, perhaps exotic and not entirely consistent.

8. *The Reconsideration of Baptism and Confirmation*

Hitherto our consideration of worship in the Anglican Church has been almost exclusively concerned with Holy Communion, the central and normative Sacrament of the Christian life. Turning to the initiatory Sacrament, Baptism, and its completion in Confirmation, will give us an opportunity both to study the radical rethinking on Baptism that has occupied Anglican theologians for many years, and to consider the work of the Church of England Liturgical Commission which, after the disappointment of 1928, has after thirty years taken up again the official task of Prayer Book Revision. Its first fruits are to be seen in the report, *Baptism and Confirmation*, presented to the Archbishops of Canterbury and York in November of 1958 and published in 1959.

The subject of Baptism has lately become a storm centre of controversy. For this there are many reasons. Much of the practice of Infant Baptism has obviously become nominal, since a pitifully small number of the children who are baptized ever become confirmed communicant members of the Church. Furthermore, a vigorous denomination, the Baptists, exists to combat the very concept of paedo-Baptism, restricting this Sacrament to believers, and yet many of them believe that there is an advantage in holding a dedication of the child to God within the Christian community. It is also significant that two distinguished Reformed theologians, Karl Barth and Emil Brunner, reject Infant Baptism as a declension from the New Testament insistence upon repentance and faith as prerequisites for entry into the Christian community, while Oscar Cullmann and Joachim Jeremias have defended the traditional practice.[74]

The whole historical question of whether Infant Baptism is an early and primitive practice in the Church or a late excrescence is hotly debated. Moreover, theologians in support of the traditional practice assert that Infant Baptism alone stresses the priority of grace, the finished work of Christ, and the import of the Christian Church as the sphere of the operation of the Holy Spirit. Their Baptist critics, however, assert that faith as the conscious human response to grace must be given its proper role, and that Baptism by immersion is the most dramatic symbolic way of marking the death of the egocentric personality and its rebirth in Christ. Finally, there is commonly felt to be the need for a stronger link binding Baptism to Confirmation and first Communion.

The Church of England was driven to a reconsideration of Baptism by its failure to keep in its community the infants brought to the font. In 1939 it was reported to the Upper House of Canterbury that in the previous twenty-four years 67 per cent of all babies born in England, that is 11½ millions, were baptized in the Church of England, yet the Easter communicants in 1937 numbered only 2¼ millions.[75] Moreover, of the 67 per cent baptized, only 26 per cent were confirmed, and no more than 9 per cent became regular Anglican communicants. It was abundantly clear that the act of Baptism initiated but did not incorporate.

[74] See Barth's *Die Kirchliche Lehre von der Taufe* (1953) and Brunner's *Wahrheit als Begegnung* (1938) and the defences in Cullmann's *Die Tauflehre des Neuen Testaments* (1948) and Jeremias' *Hat die Urkirche die Kindertaufe geubt?* (1949). A useful survey of recent ecumenical thinking on Baptism is Ernest A. Payne's contribution to *Christian Baptism, A Fresh Attempt to Understand the Rite in terms of Scripture, History and Theology*, edited by A. Gilmore. See also the Church of Scotland's fine study, *The Biblical Doctrine of Baptism*.

[75] Figures given in Roger Lloyd, *The Church of England in the Twentieth Century*, Vol. II, p. 63.

Dom Gregory Dix in *The Theology of Confirmation in Relation to Baptism* (1946) emphasized that in the Early Church the catechumens underwent a long period of training before Baptism and that after their initiation there followed "Easter Mass in the dawn, and first Communion, as the beginning of Christian life in the exultant Church."[76] He insisted that in those days Baptism, Confirmation and first Communion were three parts of the same rite, and several responsible Churchmen have urged that Baptism should be preceded by instruction and be administered at the age of Confirmation.

On the other hand, two important studies in the early history of Baptism by English scholars supported the view that Infant Baptism was probably known in New Testament times and certainly not later than 80 A.D. W. F. Flemington, a Methodist scholar, made his case in *The New Testament Doctrine of Baptism* (1948). He claimed that "the baptism of infants is a thoroughly legitimate development of New Testament teaching, a practice in full accord with the mind of Christ, and, indeed, one that, rightly interpreted, safeguards certain aspects of evangelical teaching even more effectively than the practice whereby baptism is administered only to 'believers.' "[77] He elucidated the latter point in his claim as meaning that Infant Baptism expresses "the objective givenness of the Gospel."[78]

The other defence of the traditional practice came from the hand of Professor G. W. H. Lampe in *The Seal of the Spirit* (1951). He argued, most eruditely, that in the apostolic Church "Spirit-baptism" and "water-baptism" were indissolubly linked. He concluded that Baptism was the indwelling presence of the Holy Spirit as personal, rather than as a *donum gratiae*, which was given to the believer at this Sacrament of conversion, and that this personal presence would be more fully understood and experienced in the further Christian pilgrimage in the Spirit. This expectation of a fuller apprehension of the meaning of Baptism in the future is clearly as applicable to Infant as to Believers' Baptism. Lampe, however, is critical of some Anglican theologians who associate the special linking of the Holy Spirit with Confirmation and the laying-on of hands, for this denigrates the gift of the Spirit in Baptism.

[76] P. 12. L. S. Thornton, *Confirmation To-day*, should also be consulted, as both Dix and Thornton recognize Confirmation rather than Baptism as the predominant element in Christian initiation.
[77] P. 130.　　　　　　　　　　　　[78] *Ibid.*, p. 131.

Two further studies which influenced the thought of the Liturgical Commission of the Church of England in its thinking were official reports. The first was *The Theology of Christian Initiation*, the result of a theological commission "appointed by the Archbishops of Canterbury and York to advise on the relations between Baptism, Confirmation and Holy Communion." The Commission emphasized the continuity between the three rites, because "the present-day counterpart to the primitive initiation is not Baptism alone, but Baptism, together with Confirmation, followed by first Communion."[79] Baptism and Confirmation were ultimately separated in the West and were linked in the East only at the expense of administering the complete rite to infants. It was emphasized that the classical order of Christian initiatory rites is "1. Preparation and Examination; 2. Baptism; 3. Confirmation; 4. First Communion." But, it was pointed out, "When Baptism is given in infancy, 1. has to be taken in two parts, (a) by sponsors, (b) in person, so that the new order is 1a, 2, 1b, 3, 4."[80] This situation has arisen not only because of the problems related to Infant Baptism, but also because in the earliest days the abyss dividing the Church and the world was clear-cut, whereas the situation is different in the settled life of the Church centuries later.

Four suggestions are made as warranting careful consideration: "(a) The confining of Infant Baptism to those children of whose Christian upbringing there is some assurance. (b) The establishment of a Catechumenate. (c) The more frequent administration of Baptism within the public Services of the Church. (d) The bringing into prominence of the Baptism and Confirmation of adults as an object-lesson on those aspects of initiation which were prominent in the first age of Christianity and now need to be made prominent again."[81]

The second important official study in this area was the final report of the Joint Committee of the Convocations of Canterbury and York, which was published as *Baptism and Confirmation Today* (1954). It was clearly intended to strike a hard blow against the nominalism associated too frequently with Infant Baptism in the Church of England. Its conclusions were substantially in keeping with the earlier report of 1948. It concluded that "Infant Baptism is only in line with the full teaching of the Church if: (i) it is accepted that it points forward to Confirmation

[79] *The Theology of Christian Initiation*, p. 12.
[80] *Ibid.*, p. 19.　　　　　　　　　　[81] *Ibid.*, p. 22.

and Holy Communion; (ii) there is reasonable chance of the child being taught to 'improve his Baptism'; (iii) the instruction of baptized children in the Christian faith and life be regarded as a matter of the utmost importance."

With this growing unity of opinion in the understanding of initiation, the Liturgical Commission of the Church of England was in a happy condition for commencing the task of Prayer Book revision. It turned its attention first to Baptism and Confirmation, and later was engaged on the reform of the Eucharistic Liturgy.

The first and eagerly awaited report of the Liturgical Commission was submitted to the Archbishops of Canterbury and York in November of 1958 and was printed in 1959 as *Baptism and Confirmation*. Representative of both Anglo-Catholic and Evangelical viewpoints, the Commission was remarkable for its many scholars learned in liturgical lore. Many of them, whom it would be invidious to single out for mention, were known to the wider world through their writings. It may, however, be remarked that it was a little curious that there was no layman in the original membership of the Commission, especially as on all hands the modern stress is on the importance of the laity's part in the Liturgy.

One great novelty, though it was an attempt to recover primitive usage, was the printing first of the Order for the Baptism and Confirmation of Adults, as the "archetypal" service. The Order for Infant Baptism was printed next as a separate service, but directions were appended for its combination, when desirable, with Holy Communion or with Morning or Evening Prayer. The intention was clear that Infant Baptism with its solemn promises made by the sponsors was to be regarded as no "hole and corner" affair, but ought to be administered in the context of full congregational worship. Adult Confirmation was printed third, as a corollary of Infant Baptism. "In this way it is hoped," so the report reads, "to relate each part of the pattern to the archetypal service, while at the same time providing for the maximum of flexibility to meet a variety of pastoral occasions."[82]

A second novelty is the provision for the "Ministry of the Word." That is, a new preface to Adult Baptism, Infant Baptism, and Adult Confirmation is provided, of substantially the same type as the introduction to Holy Communion in the Prayer Book, consisting of a Collect, Scripture Lessons, and a Sermon or Homily framed upon them, in conformity with both Patristic and Reformed

[82] *Baptism and Confirmation*, p. x.

tradition. This, again, was an effective way of combatting mere convention and nominalism in these orders of worship.

An attempt was made to frame orders for Infant and Adult Baptism as much alike as possible. In each order the blessing of the water comes first, then the acts of renunciation and faith, and then the pouring of the water. The principal prayer in each service is the blessing of the water, and in this "an attempt has been made to express the whole Biblical doctrine of Baptism."[83] This prayer offers thanksgiving for Christ as the agent of creation and of redemption, who received the Baptism of repentance and was anointed with the Holy Spirit for man's sake, was delivered up to the suffering of death to purify unto himself a people for his own possession, and who on his ascension poured out the Holy Spirit of promise and renewal. It ends by beseeching God "to sanctify this water to the mystical washing away of sin; and grant that all to be baptized herein may be made members of thy Church, which is the Body of thy Son our Lord; that so, being baptized unto his death, and being made partakers of his resurrection, they may die daily unto sin and rise again unto righteousness; and serving thee faithfully with all thy saints, may inherit the kingdom of thy glory. . . ."[84] This is an admirable summary of the *heilsgeschichte* with special reference to Baptism. In the matter of the promises required there is, however, a different requirement for adults and children. The form for adults is the customary one, while that for infants is briefer and simpler, being thought more apt for godparents at Infant Baptism and for children making promises at Confirmation.

Since it was reported that the ceremony of signing with the Cross was thought by some persons to be the outward and visible sign of Baptism, it was thought wise to place it, along with the optional giving of the lighted candle, under a new heading, "The Ceremonies after Baptism." No provision, however, was made for the giving of a white robe or for the permissive use of oil before Baptism or of chrism after Baptism or Confirmation, since such customs were either impractical or did not command widespread interest.

The Confirmation Rite was drafted with the purpose of "emphasizing the centrality of the prayer for the coming of the Spirit."[85] The Bishop is directed to say this prayer facing the candidates with arms outstretched in their direction according to ancient

[83] *Ibid.*, p. xi.   [84] *Ibid.*, p. 12.   [85] *Ibid.*, p. xii.

custom. Great care was taken in employing the term "confirm" in such a way as to exclude neither of the meanings attached to it, as strengthening or completing.

The important prayer of the Bishop includes responsive "Amens" to stress the significance of the gifts of the Spirit:

> Almighty and everliving God, who hast vouchsafed to regenerate *these* thy *servants* by water and the Holy Ghost, and hast given unto *them* forgiveness of all their sins: Send down from heaven upon *them* thy Holy Ghost the Comforter. *Amen.*
> The Spirit of wisdom and understanding. *Amen.*
> The Spirit of counsel and ghostly strength. *Amen.*
> The Spirit of knowledge and true godliness. *Amen.*
> And fill *them*, O Lord, with the Spirit of thy holy fear. *Amen.*[86]

The formula of confirmation is simple, speedy, and sufficient: "*Confirm*, O Lord, thy servant N. [or, this thy servant] with thy Holy Spirit, that *he* may continue thine for ever."[87]

Three General Rubrics are provided. The first indicates the norm for the administration of these services, namely that the whole congregation shall witness the reception of new members into Christ's Church and be themselves reminded of the promises that they (or their sponsors) made at Baptism and which they made for themselves at Confirmation. The second rubric requires the font to be set up in such a place that the whole congregation shall be able to see and hear the Sacrament of Baptism. The third rubric indicates that Confirmation requires of candidates the ability to say the Creed, the Lord's Prayer, the Decalogue, and the capacity to answer the other questions asked in the Church Catechism.[88]

Finally, the Commission expresses the hope that the report will be welcomed as an attempt to equip the Church with flexible liturgical forms adaptable to changing needs in the pastoral situation, and that it will be recognized as an honest attempt to get behind those controversies which arose out of the late mediaeval period.[89]

The members of the Liturgical Commission must be applauded for their irenic spirit, for the strong Biblical basis of their theology and prayers, for clearly indicating by their rubrics that Baptism is most meaningful as a part of a regular service in the face of a congregation (not a private gathering for family and friends), and

[86] *Ibid.*, p. 15.   [87] *Ibid.*, p. 16.   [88] *Ibid.*, p. xvi.
[89] *Ibid.*

for stressing the solemnity of the promises made (which a sermon or homily will make plain). Moreover, the formal unity of the three services may do much to accustom the mind of the people to a sense of their inter-relationship in the development of the Christian life, while the flexibility allowed for so that they may be incorporated in Morning or Evening Prayer or in the service of Holy Communion will be welcomed by the parish minister. All this represents a considerable achievement and augurs well for the consequent responsibility for providing a revised Order for Holy Communion.

Nonetheless, the Orders already published have not escaped criticism. Indeed, two members of the Commission thought the revision was too radical a departure from the present practice of the Church of England, and disliked the flexibility. Others are disturbed that the Order for Infant Baptism includes no mention of the customary "receive this child into the congregation of Christ's flock." Objection has been raised to the elimination of Mark 10:13-16 and the substitution of Matthew 28:18-30 in the Baptism of Infants since it has nothing to do with infants, to which it might be retorted that the alternative has nothing to do with Baptism. Some exception has been taken to the infelicitous English of the prayers. Perhaps the most controversial feature of the report is to have taken the Adult Baptism and Confirmation as archetypal and primary, when, in fact, Infant Baptism is the commoner mode of present day initiation. On the whole, however, the report has been welcomed.

9. *Retrospect and Prospect*

The historian's task is to record and interpret, not to prophesy, especially in such uncertain times as the present. In comparing the ethos of the Church of England in its internal and external relations at the beginning of the century and in the nadir of its fortunes in 1928, with the present situation, some important and hopeful differences can be observed, and these are promising for the development of its worship.

At the beginning of the century relationships between Anglicans and Free Churchmen were embittered, but there is today a common recognition that England is mission territory for all the denominations. Furthermore, it is common in most universities for Anglican and Free Church ordinands to have been taught by some lecturers of confessional loyalties other than their own, and certainly the best contemporary scholarship in theology is far from being exclusively Anglican. The Student Christian Movement at the universities and local ministers' fraternals in towns and cities have broken down the older alienation. It is commonly admitted that Anglicans have the pre-eminence in worship and Free Churchmen the leadership in preaching, and among the younger generation of clergy and ministers there is a deep longing for reunion. The Ecumenical Movement has changed the whole picture.

The old party exclusiveness which characterized internal relationships at the beginning of the century, and which reappeared in the tragic divisions over Prayer Book revision in 1927 and 1928, has now markedly decreased, with the increase of a great sense of common loyalty to the Church. The Anglo-Catholics are now far less likely to imitate Roman Catholicism than they were and they have entered fully into the recovery of a Biblical theology. Their strenuous spiritual regimen once feared by the Low Churchmen is now admired, as well as their splendid record of service in slum parishes, and their stressing of the social implications of the Eucharist. Anglo-Catholics for their part have come to respect the scholarship and devotion of the Evangelical clergy,[90] and the Evangelicals themselves have acknowledged that they did not pay enough attention to the beauty of holiness in worship or to the importance of the corporate nature of the Church manifested and renewed in the Eucharist. This unity is above all seen in the conjoint stress on Word and Sacrament. Thus an united Church of England is far likelier than the quarrelsome Church of 1928 to impress Parliament with the urgent need for the reform of the Prayer Book. The very fact that the Church of England members of a joint Anglican and Methodist Committee appointed to reconsider the reunion of these Churches were unanimously in favour of union could also prove that the Church of England has more right to speak for the nation spiritually than might previously have been supposed. For, after all, the Methodists are the largest of the English Free Churches.

The almost arrogant sacerdotalism of earlier generations of Anglican clergy is now obsolescent and may shortly become obsolete. Contemporary Anglican worship manifests, through the

90 The Evangelicals have established a research centre at Oxford, named Latimer House, presumably as a complement to the High Church centre at Oxford, Pusey House. In 1960, the Evangelicals established a College of Preachers to which some High Church as well as many Low Church clergy have repaired for refresher courses.

Parish Communion, the House Church, "An Experimental Liturgy," and the Clare College Manual for Holy Communion, a desire to recognize the importance of the laity. It is likely that the apostolate of the laity will be even further developed if the Anglicans and the Methodists unite, for a great strength of Methodism has been the thousands of local preachers who have supplemented the work of the ordained ministers, and who have preached the Gospel in terms understood by the common people. The democratisation of the Church is likelier to lead to even greater relevance in its worship.

Furthermore, we have drawn attention to the more influential examples of liturgical experiment in the Anglican Church in recent years as a sign of new life in a community that reveres tradition. These were, however, only a tithe of the experiments that were being tried. No mention was made of the Rev. Geoffrey Beaumont's *Folk Mass*,[91] an attempt to utilise popular melody in the service of the Church, and thus to bridge the gap between the Church and the world, and between the older and the younger generations. Nor were the renewed importance of services of spiritual healing mentioned. Both experiments are likely to become more common in the future. It is very likely also that the Easter Vigil, a recent Roman Catholic recovery of the practice of the Early Church, may become acclimatised in England in the near future.[92]

From time to time the names of members of Anglican religious communities have appeared in these pages, notably those of Father A. G. Hebert and Dom Gregory Dix, the authors respectively of *Liturgy and Society* and *The Shape of the Liturgy*. It is not without significance that these are among the most significant Anglican treatises on worship in our period. The implication is clear that in such communities of celibates, dedicated to the contemplation of God, deep spirituality may be found, and that its gains are made available for the culture of the spiritual life not of the few, but of the entire Church. The same spirituality engenders the courage of faith as manifested, for example, in Father (now Bishop) Trevor Huddleston's fight against *apartheid* in Southern Africa, so modestly recorded in *Naught for Your Comfort* and so movingly described in the character of Father Vincent in Alan

[91] For a critique see Erik R. Routley, *Church Music and Theology*, pp. 104-07. Also see Chap. III *supra*.
[92] See J. T. Martin, *Christ our Passover*.

Paton's *Cry the Beloved Country*. The Church of England's heritage of worship is immeasurably strengthened by the presence in its midst of communities consecrated to the *opus Dei*, in which there is discipline without deadliness, goodness with gaiety, and faith without fear or favour. The Community of the Resurrection, The Society of the Sacred Mission, the Cowley Fathers, and the Anglican Benedictine Community at Nashdom, must not be forgotten for their contribution to the renewal of worship in England.[93]

We have cited Bishop Hensley Henson's judgment that the Parliamentary rejection of the Revised Prayer Book was in fact less a vote of no confidence in the Book than in the Bishops, for they seemed to be men of expediency rather than of conviction. The same charge could hardly be made of the present Archbishop of Canterbury who, in his enthronement sermon, announced a determination to see Prayer Book revision through and an unwillingness to muzzle the Church at the behest of Parliament. No more could it be made against the present Bishop of Woolwich, whose book *Honest to God*[94] has been satirized as an exposition of the paradox that "the creed of the English is that there is no God and that it is wise to pray to him from time to time," but whose worst enemies could not deny him candour and courage. The bench of Bishops is no longer a synonym for vacillating expediency.

Throughout our period, which has been one of increasing gains for secularism, we have yet seen a genuine ecumenical advance, an improvement in the internal and external relationships of the Church of England, a desire to make far greater use of the talents of the laity, an increase in the courage of the leaders of the Church, a new fertility in liturgical and evangelistic experiment, an increase in the appreciation of monasticism, a deepening concern that society shall manifest the justice that God wills for his people, and a desire to correlate religion with visual art and drama. Above all, there has been growing a clearer and more cogent conviction of the Divine origin and empowering of the Church as manifested in the Eucharist. However strong the forces of secularism and materialism, there is great encouragement in the thought that the

---

93 See Peter F. Anson, *The Call of the Cloister* and A. M. Allchin, *The Silent Rebellion* (1958). See also the tribute of an English Presbyterian: "The whole witness of the religious orders is a standing challenge to the values of the present age. The vows to poverty, chastity and obedience are the very opposites of the materialism, sensuality and license which are commonly exalted among us." (Kenneth Slack, *The British Churches Today*, p. 37).

94 This book was discussed in Chap. v.

Church has never lost sight of her calling to adore God and to serve mankind. And it is precisely this calling which has been renewed in the Church of England through more than half a century's concentration on worship.[95]

[95] One is reminded of the words of Reinhold Niebuhr to Archbishop William Temple: "I told him I thought the Prayer-book had saved the Anglican Communion from rationalism and Pelagianism more than Episcopacy had done" (cited in F. A. Iremonger, *William Temple*, p. 494).

CHAPTER X

THE WORSHIP OF THE FREE CHURCHES

IKE THE Anglican Church, the English Free Churches—the collective designation for the Baptist, Congregational, Presbyterian, and Methodist Communions—have experienced a renewal in worship. Anglican worship, as we have seen, is an amalgam of Catholic and Reformed elements, with the former predominating. Free Church worship is predominantly Reformed— an amalgam of the Puritan and Pietist traditions within Protestantism—with a recent recovery of some Catholic elements, notably a higher evaluation of liturgical forms and of the Sacraments of Baptism and the Lord's Supper.

The Puritan tradition contributed a strong stress on the sovereignty of God, the authority of Scripture, the primacy of preaching, and a preference for extemporary prayers over set forms. The Pietist tradition modified the idea of Divine sovereignty with an emphatic assertion of the universality of grace, reinforced evangelism and spontaneity in prayer, and added warmth to the covenanted fellowship.

The Catholic influence has been mediated by involvement in the Ecumenical Movement, by the example of Anglican worship (especially strong on the Methodists who were originally a Society within the Church of England), by the admirable service-books of the Church of Scotland, and by a renewed interest in the study of the primitive Church and of the early Fathers.

The worship of the Free Churches is Biblically-based, unpretentious in its simplicity, and not infrequently austere. It is, however, rarely a fugitive piety. Its architecture may occasionally run to an incongruous imitation of Gothic, but there is nothing antiquarian about its ethics. The very ambivalence of its favourite term for worship suggests that there is no hiatus between the "service" of God in the sanctuary and the "service" of men in the street. Its high evaluation of preaching is due to the conviction that when God's Word is faithfully expounded His people receive the Divine promises for consolation, the Divine warnings for correction, and the Divine example and instruction of Christ for their pilgrimage. Especially in recent years aesthetics have not been

348

thought to be inimical to ethics, and symbolism is no longer equated with idolatry. But, as we shall see, aesthetic dilettantism has its own dangers in worship, no less than its opposite, unbuttoned amateurism or calculated casualness.

1. *Three Major Trends in Worship*

"Change and decay in all around I see" was the despairing cry of a Victorian observer. The kaleidoscopic rapidity and variety of change was, however, even more strikingly a characteristic of the twentieth century scene. Anglican worship, as we have already seen, despite the balance and ballast given by the Book of Common Prayer, displayed some giddy vagaries of fashion in ceremonial, vestments, architecture, and music, as it veered from Gothic to Baroque, and from Rococo to Functionalism. The Free Churches, without any norm such as a prescribed Liturgy, were even more at the mercy of modes of taste and interest. In general, however, there were three major trends corresponding to three different theologies and their three different conceptions of the nature of the Church.

The first trend, anti-historical and anti-authoritarian, is hard to define because so inchoate, but it may not unfairly be called "The School of Spontaneity." It was the longest trend, lasting from the beginning of the first to the middle of the fourth decade. It was particularly strong among Congregationalists, and W. B. Selbie, J. Vernon Bartlet, C. J. Cadoux, and Albert Peel were probably its most notable representatives. That it should have attracted the first, a pioneer in the study of the psychology of religion (and a splendid preacher), is not surprising, but it is more than curious that it should have appealed to the other three for they were all distinguished historians.

The second trend was that exhibited by the self-designated "Society of Free Catholics," who admired Catholic mysticism and sacramentalism but disliked Catholic doctrine. This small but influential body included W. E. Orchard, R. J. Campbell, and J. M. Lloyd Thomas, respectively Presbyterian, Congregational, and Unitarian ministers when they joined the Society. It flourished in the second and third decades and then petered out, as Orchard became a Roman Catholic and Campbell an Anglo-Catholic, but not before they had produced two remarkable liturgies of a comprehensive character.

The third trend may be styled "Reformed Churchmanship,"

since it indicates both a strong sense of the Church's continuity and of its re-foundation on the basis of the recovered Gospel in the sixteenth century. It began about 1936, revealing the impact of Karl Barth's Theology of the Word of God, and has continued with great vigour to the present. Its first generation leaders in Congregationalism were Nathaniel Micklem, John S. Whale, and B. L. Manning; in Methodism, R. Newton Flew; and among the Baptists, A. C. Underwood. Its second generation representatives in Congregationalism include John Marsh, Daniel Jenkins, Hubert Cunliffe-Jones, W. A. Whitehouse, and John Huxtable; in Methodism, Gordon Rupp, Philip Watson, and Rupert Davies; and among the Baptists, Ernest A. Payne, R. C. Walton, Neville Clark, and Stephen Winward.

2. The "School of Spontaneity"

Four very powerful influences combined to produce the strongly pervasive impact of this group on the theory and practice of worship, and they are still influential in helping to create a prejudice against liturgical worship as consisting of only "stinted forms." The first was the strong historical memory of the Free Churches, and particularly of the Congregationalists and Presbyterians, for whom the Book of Common Prayer is less a liturgical treasure than an instrument of oppression. It was because the Puritan ministers of these two denominations could not subscribe to the declaration that the Book of Common Prayer was in all things conformable to the Word of God that in 1662 they lost their livings and went out into the wilderness.

The second factor was the strong conviction that forms of prayer are only crutches for beginners in prayer but that when a man has learned how to speak to God in the freedom and intimacy of the Holy Spirit he will cast away all forms; on this view to retain a liturgy is to remain in the adolescent stage of the spiritual life. Hence the easy equivalent is made of sincerity with formlessness. And in making it there was the long tradition of the Society of Friends to support it. Had not the Quakers proved that the adoration of God needs neither ministers, nor altars, nor prayer-books, nor hymn-books, nor even sacraments? As their favourite Johannine text has it: "the Spirit bloweth where it listeth."

The third influence derived from the reigning philosophy and theology of the age, idealism and immanentalism. The former insisted that all objects are ultimately identifiable with ideas, which meant that concept was far more important than concretion; and, as applied to theology, that it is the Logos that counts, not the Incarnation, and that sacraments are, therefore, pictures for simple people. Immanentalism identified God either partly or completely with the world, and the Kingdom of God became little more than the sum total of human idealism. Hence there was a rigid dichotomy between the spiritual and the material, the ideational and the sensate.

The fourth and final influence was the socialistic version of the Christian faith, called either the "new theology" or the "social Gospel," which interpreted love of God almost exclusively in terms of the love of neighbour. The effect of these four influences on traditional Christian worship may be judged from the opposition of categories which its representatives set up. Freedom was contrasted with authority, contemporary experience with the dead hand of tradition, spiritual insight with the life of the senses, sermon with sacrament, social service with formal worship, this-worldly altruism with other-worldly selfishness, creativity with the creeds, the prophetic with the priestly, conceptual with picture-thinking, the Kingdom of God with the Church, and, the favourite antithesis, Spirit with Institution. It will be abundantly clear that the die was heavily loaded against tradition, history, creeds, liturgy, and sacraments, and even against the Church as an institution.[1]

While the general tendency of the "School of Spontaneity" was to derogate from the orderliness and dignity of worship, and even to degenerate in some cases into informality indistinguishable from gaucherie, it also had its merits. Chief among these was the note of contemporary compassion for the underprivileged and a determination to support all workers for social amelioration. These concerns were reflected in Litanies for Labour, in a variety of intercessions for social workers, doctors, nurses, and teachers, and in the rousing hymns of the social gospel which celebrated the establishment of a coming Kingdom of social justice and international peace. In this respect John Hunter's *Devotional Services*,[2] which appeared first in 1882 and in 1901 in its final and greatly

[1] Quite typical is Henry W. Clark's assertion: "According to the Nonconformist view of the Church it is in the idea and in the inner experience of life one is immersed, the idea being formative in the theory of the Church, and the experience formative on the Church's actual meaning—that one does not begin with organisation, but comes to it . . . as to a thing second both in importance and time" (*History of English Nonconformity*, Vol. II, p. 309).

[2] This was treated extensively in my *Worship and Theology in England*, Vol. IV, *From Newman to Martineau, 1850-1900*, pp. 229-37.

enlarged form, set the Free Church standard for the first three decades. It was as influential in Britain as was its American counterpart, Walter Rauschenbusch's *For God and the People: Prayers of the Social Awakening* (1910).

Three disturbing pictures of the gaucherie in worship induced by the cult of informality will be sufficient evidence for the dangers of the approach. Bernard Manning gives an all too vivid account of how some Congregationalists celebrated the Lord's Supper: "Have you never been at a Communion service where the bread and the wine, handed to us from the Upper Room itself, were treated as tiresome, rather unspiritual adjuncts to a service, *impedimenta* to be disposed of as rapidly and inconspicuously as possible, lest they should hinder us (God forgive us) from spiritual flights on our own account? . . . The bread and wine are sometimes huddled round to us before the service proper begins, or perhaps under cover of some hymn. The bread is not broken. The wine is not poured out. Prayer, thanksgiving and the invocation of the Holy Ghost do not precede the distribution of the elements. . . . Let me not be thought to exaggerate. I bring no general charge against our churches, but I say that in some places and at some times these things are done; and everyone knows that that is true."[3]

H. Wheeler Robinson confessed to a similar repugnance when he considered the worship of the Baptists, his own denomination: "An Anglican, entering a Baptist Church for divine worship might often be alienated by the seeming want of reverence. There is no visible altar, and an obtrusive pulpit takes its place. The choir is too visible, and does not seem greatly concerned with anything but its own function. Deacons walk about unnecessarily, and even come to chat with people in the pews. The secretary gives out notices at an alarming length, and may intersperse a few remarks. The preacher, who wears no distinctive dress, follows no particular order in his prayers, and may be wearisomely long in his sermon. People stay about in clusters talking when the service is over, and the minister may come down and join them, or stand in the vestibule shaking hands with people. As for the Communion Service—!"[4]

Apparently some parts of rural Methodism are in a similar case. A reporter in East Anglia, a headmaster and a Free Churchman (but not a Methodist), who has acted for several years as a Methodist local preacher, writes: "The Methodist Church puzzles

[3] *Essays in Orthodox Dissent*, pp. 61ff.
[4] *The Baptist View of the Church and Ministry* (1944), p. 23.

me; it is curiously bifurcated. It takes the Baptismal and Communion Service from the Church of England, almost unchanged. But in the ordinary service there seems to be no renascence of worship. Even when ministers take the service, the long rambling prayers persist and the formal informality which never says, 'Hymn no. 666,' but 'Shall we sing no. 666?' Yet if anyone replied: 'Might we have 999 instead?' there would be consternation. I have even heard this summer: 'Shall we read a portion of the Old Testament?' "[5] That these experiences are no longer typical, however commonplace they might have been in the first three decades of the century, is a proof of how far the English Free Churches have come on the road to reverence.

The immanentalism of Liberal Protestant theology in these first thirty years shows other characteristics besides gaucherie in worship. Inheriting the strong stress on experience which marked religious thinking from Schleiermacher to Sabatier, it is not surprising that subjectivity and moody introspection should also leave their marks on the worship of the English Free Churches.

This subjectivity is manifested in egotistical and introspective hymns, the products of lyrical spiders forever spinning from their own insides, and in prayers that concentrate on human feelings and moods rather than on divine deeds or demands.[6] It has become a serious matter when subjectivity even intrudes on the objectivity which denominational directories or manuals of worship are supposed to provide. This happens in the Congregational *Manual for Ministers* of 1936 in two outstanding instances. The sentimental emphasis is dominant in the Order for Holy Communion which places, immediately after the Prayer of Humble Access, John Hunter's invitation: "Come to this sacred Table, not because you

[5] I am indebted to the kindness of the Rev. Dr. Andrew L. Drummond of Alva, Scotland, for this report from the headmaster in East Anglia which he copied in a letter to me dated August 20, 1962. Probably the residual austerity of Calvinism has saved the Presbyterian Church of England from an attitude of "cosiness" towards its Creator. W. E. Orchard suggests as much in *From Faith to Faith*, pp. 48-49.

[6] Among the better hymns that overuse the first person singular, those of George Matheson "Make me a captive, Lord" and "O love that wilt not let me go" might be cited, and among the worst is the erotic "Still, still with Thee, when purple morning breaketh." The state of Christians forever taking their own spiritual temperatures is almost ironically expressed in Shairp's hymn of which the first six lines read:

> 'Twixt gleams of joy and clouds of doubt
> Our feelings come and go;
> Our best estate is tossed about
> In ceaseless ebb and flow.
> No mood of feeling, form of thought,
> Is constant for a day.

must, but because you may. . . . Come, not to express an opinion, but to seek a Presence and pray for a Spirit." It also appears in a prayer in the Order of Service for Christmas Day in which familiarity becomes over-familiarity, and fellowship "folksy." "Father of all," it begins well enough, "at this time when the solitary are set in families," then descends to "when children's children gather under the old roof"[7] and ends on a didactic anticlimax. At other times the tenderness is appropriate and restrained, as in the Service for the Burial of a Child. Yet it is a weakness when a Service of Infant Baptism is interpreted to mean, through the Exhortation, that the central fact is that the child is being dedicated to God, not that the Church by virtue of Christ's everlasting Gospel is adding to its membership. This error is contained in the Methodist *Book of Offices* (1936).

In fact the emphasis on children in this period was one of the strongest contributions of an immanentalist theology, presumably as a consequence of its denial of the doctrine of original sin. Here, if anywhere, sentimentality would obtrude, and particularly at Baptist services of the dedication of children or in Congregational "christenings." The minister who refused to make the sign of the Cross on the child's forehead, although this was a venerable custom, was happy enough to plant his own sign, a firm kiss, on the infant's brow. Another proof of the sentimentality of the period and part of its cult of the child was the demand made of Free Church ministers to include a children's sermon as a regular part of the Sunday morning service. This almost inevitably produced a lowering of the seriousness and reverence of worship, when the minister became cute, comic, or painfully condescending. It was even more embarrassing when, in unbuttoned mood, he fell into his anecdotage, recounting the peccadilloes of his youth or of his own children. But, lest we unduly malign one section of the Christian community in England, it should not be forgotten that this was also the period when "Children's Corners" proliferated in Anglican churches. In these would be found miniature chairs and tables, minuscule books, the inevitable Margaret Tarrant picture of an effeminate Jesus surrounded by rabbits, squirrels, and children with perfect manners, but rarely a living child in the Children's Corner!

In this period the sentimentality of children's hymns was so

7 *Manual for Ministers*, pp. 102-03. Yet it was an advance for a Congregational manual of worship to provide prayers for the Christian Year.

treacly that it provoked that sturdy Scottish theologian, A. M. Fairbairn, to the fervent outburst "I am grateful that my childhood was nurtured on the Book of Psalms rather than on the jingling verses that celebrate the 'Sweet Saviour,' or protest how I love 'my Jesus.' "[8] The attitude which Fairbairn criticized led to such astonishing statements as the following, included in an exhortation at a Service of Infant Baptism in a Presbyterian Church: "It has been well said that the most important gospel for a child is not the gospel according to Matthew or Mark, but the gospel according to father and mother."[9] Subjectivity and sentimentality became so strong that Nathaniel Micklem argued that the strongest defence of liturgical forms was that they would rescue both ministers and congregations from being at the mercy of ministerial moods.[10]

Another characteristic of the worship of the "School of Spontaneity" was its near pantheism, to which the wearying didacticism of the "sermons in stones" mentality is closely related. It was as if the Free Churches in their eagerness to run away from the high sacramentalism of the Roman Catholics and the Anglo-Catholics had fallen among Quakers. Certainly the pan-sacramentalism of the Society of Friends was very popular during this period. From this all-spreading root sprang the extempore prayers of thanksgiving that celebrated the scenic wonders of the universe[11] (and the Alps in particular if the minister had just holidayed in Switzerland, or Ben Nevis and Loch Lomond if he were a Presbyterian). It was the origin of the chubby-faced junior choir simpering for the hundredth time through "All things bright and beautiful, all creatures great and small," and because of it the Harvest Festival became the most popular special Sunday of the year, with its annual opportunity for the expression of cupboard love.

Perhaps this pan-sacramentalism was never given a more striking place than in the order for the sanctification of a Church Bazaar in the Congregational *Manual for Ministers* (1936). Such breath-taking liturgical inventiveness should not have been beyond devising a form for the blessing of Bingo or for the concelebration of Canasta. One cannot but admire the ingenuity of the liturgist, however one may suspect his judgment. The order

[8] *Studies in Religion and Theology*, p. 272.
[9] Eric Phillip, *Sacramental and Other Services*, p. 2. Phillip was a minister of the Presbyterian Church of England.
[10] See the article "Extempore Prayer in the Congregational Tradition," *The Congregational Quarterly*, Vol. XIII (1935), p. 330.
[11] See an example of gilded romanticism in D. Tait Patterson's *The Call to Worship*, p. 123.

contains three choice banalities. The first is the Old Testament lesson, with its pointed hint: "And all the women that were wise-hearted did spin with their hands and brought that which they had spun." The second is a specially composed hymn including the apt verse:

> Unveil through deeds which love has wrought
> The Presence wondrous and divine
> That common objects, sold and bought,
> May glow as sacramental sign.

And surely there has never been another liturgical rubric like the one that ends the service: *Then shall follow the Chairman's introduction of the Opener of the Bazaar, the declaration of the opening, and the appropriate votes of thanks.*[12] Bonhoeffer has written of cheap grace, but here were sacraments, glowing ones too, at cut-rates. So pervasive was this pan-sacramentalism that it became necessary for theologians to insist with Archbishop William Temple that if God was everywhere in general then it was difficult to focus on Him anywhere in particular. The sensitive Methodist devotional writer, A. E. Whitham, joined the protest, affirming: "The characteristic truth of Christianity is not that God is everywhere, which may easily mean that he is nowhere, but that God is somewhere—specially, seriously, savingly somewhere—not that He saturates me like a Scotch mist, but that he satisfies me like a warm friend."[13]

The emphasis on the authority of personal experience was retained longest by the Methodist Church. This was not remarkable in view of its Pietistic origins, and of the formalism of the day which John Wesley tried so hard to combat. It is significant that the introduction to the supplementary Methodist book, *Divine Worship* (1935), was most careful to stress that forms were no substitute for experience. Thus: "The glow of a personal experience is necessary to give a sense of reality and the warmth of sincerity to worship, but as the member draws its nourishment from the body, so religious experience finds its strength and renewal as well as its natural expression in fellowship."[14] Indeed, this particular volume demonstrates the very great strengths as well as the weaknesses of Liberal Protestant worship. On the negative side there is the wallowing introversion and self-pity,[15] the

---

[12] *Manual for Ministers*, p. 173.   [13] *The Catholic Christ*, p. 29.
[14] *Divine Worship*, p. 13.   [15] *Ibid.*, p. 198.

almost interminable catalogue of specific sins and failures,[16] the sentimentalities of the child cult,[17] the pantheism,[18] and the excessive horizontal stress on fellowship.[19] The great values are the recovery of the humanity of Jesus as exemplar,[20] the deep compassion for the handicapped,[21] the stress on the civic and social responsibilities of Christians,[22] and, in particular, on Christian concern for the economic order.[23]

Another characteristic of the worship of the "School of Spontaneity" was that ministers could rarely resist the perils of didacticism in their public prayers. This is perhaps most clearly revealed in a telling direction in the *Directory for Public Worship for use in the Presbyterian Church of England* (1921). This reads: "The Sermon may be placed much earlier in the service, and the teaching which it conveys may then find expression in the prayers and praise that follow, whether in thanksgiving for special mercies, in confession, or in intercession. The Sermon may thus be used to guide the people in their worship."[24] This particular defect has been the historic bane of Protestant worship, not merely of Liberal Protestantism. In effect, it turned the potential priest and mediator in prayer into a boring schoolmaster, who might develop the worship as a series of variations on the one-stringed fiddle of his topic for the day. If the provision of a Liturgy is one way to prevent ministerial tyranny in worship, the use of a lectionary is a similar protective device to spare the congregation from the limited anthology of lections which the minister himself finds helpful.

As early as 1919, Sir John McClure warned in his Chairman's address to the Congregational Union Assembly that preaching had pre-empted all interest in prayer. Indeed, the sermon had become "the golden calf of the denomination" with the result that the earlier parts of the service were merely preliminaries to preaching, and "our assemblies are too often looked upon as the lecture-rooms of popular speakers."[25] The real heart of the problem was succinctly expressed in the assertion that "the preachers of today, who

---

[16] *Ibid.*, pp. 184-87.   [17] *Ibid.*, pp. 169-72.
[18] *Ibid.*, pp. 217-19.
[19] Seen in the first part of the introduction and in the use of popular hymns as prayers (pp. 203ff.).
[20] *Ibid.*, pp. 112f., 212, 218.
[21] *Ibid.*, p. 177f. for "An Act of Sympathy with Suffering."
[22] *Ibid.*, pp. 237-38.
[23] *Ibid.*, p. 173f. for "Intercession for Social Life."
[24] P. 12.
[25] "The Public Worship of God," an address of May 13, 1919, published in *The Congregational Union Year Book* (1920), p. 53.

are ancestored in the Puritans know, in the main, how to present an argument, but not how to create an atmosphere."[26]

Finally, in the "School of Spontaneity" there was a serious devaluation of the Sacraments of Baptism and the Lord's Supper. They were, neither of them, primarily regarded as means of grace, as channels of the transforming Holy Spirit, but as affirmations of fellowship and badges of dedication to the work of Christ. For this reason the stress in Infant Baptism was on the dedication of the child and his parents to God, and in the Lord's Supper on a community memorial rite. The first point may be illustrated from the ambiguity—which was probably deliberate—in the single question put to the parents at Infant Baptism in *The Manual for Ministers* (1936): "You have come to present this child for Christian *baptism and dedication*; do you promise that he shall be brought up as a Christian child in the nurture and admonition of the Lord?" It is equally typical that the expected Pelagian answer was: "We do."[27]

The devaluation of the Lord's Supper was indicated not only by a memorialist doctrine, as we have indicated, but by insisting that a layman had as much right to celebrate it as a minister,[28] and, above all, by the substitution of unfermented for fermented wine and the provision of "diced cubes" of bread, which meant that the great acts of Fraction and Libation hitherto deemed central to the Sacrament were no longer performed. The very term "Sacraments" which had formerly been exclusively reserved for Baptism and the Lord's Supper was now eviscerated of its historic meaning. A tell-tale prayer in the same service book expresses thanksgiving to God at the end of the year "for the sacraments of love and service which have made us conscious of Thy presence in our common life."[29] A final proof that Holy Communion was no longer the greatest privilege of the membership of the Church was seen in the promiscuous invitation issued invariably at most Free Church Communions "to all who love our Lord Jesus Christ to be guests at

[26] Fred Smith in an article, "From Principle to Procedure. A Study concerning modes of Worship," *Congregational Quarterly*, Vol. VIII (1930), p. 482.

[27] P. 74. The italics are mine to indicate where the ambiguity may be found.

[28] In 1931 the Congregational Union asked a layman to preside at the celebration of the Lord's Supper in its Autumn Assembly in the presence of perhaps a hundred ordained ministers. See R. Mackintosh, "The Genius of Congregationalism" in Peel, ed., *Essays Congregational and Catholic* (1931), p. 123. And in 1923 the *Directory of Worship* of the Presbyterian Church of England was amended to allow non-ministerial elders to administer the Lord's Supper in exceptional circumstances at preaching stations.

[29] *Manual for Ministers*, "Order of Service for the Close of the Year."

His table." Since the Methodists had long believed that Communion was a converting[30] as well as a communicating Sacrament, they alone had a theological justification for their position.

All in all, this was perhaps the period of which the Free Churches had least reason to be proud in their theology and in their worship. Previously their worship had been simple, possibly even bare, but also august in its consciousness of a solemn rendezvous with God. The structure and authority of Puritan worship was the Biblical basis which rejected the impure inventions and traditions of men and offered God a New Testament worship marked by purity, spirituality, and fidelity to the Divine ordinances. Its freedom was a freedom in the Holy Spirit under the Word, and never the right of private taste, public fashion, or ministerial predilection. In sheer contrast, the worship of the "School of Spontaneity" was formal about its informality, and gloried in its gaucherie. Its most radical critics established another group.

3. The Society of Free Catholics

This Society was never large and it may well have been born fifty years before its time, for it was attempting what then seemed the impossible task of combining Protestantism and Catholicism. Indeed, it never was sure of its objectives. As W. E. Orchard wrote, its comprehensive basis "led to no agreement as to whether 'Free Catholicism' was a new kind of Catholicism, or simply a way of interpreting and commending historic Catholicism, and as a means of preparing for final re-union with Rome."[31] Its founder was the Rev. J. M. Lloyd Thomas, a large-minded and cultivated Unitarian minister who had been greatly influenced by the Modernist Movement on the Continent, and in particular by Loisy and Sabatier, and who gathered about him other Unitarian ministers dissenting from the rationalistic didacticism of their tradition.

His views were publicised in *A Free Catholic Church* (1907). "In a Free Catholic Church," he wrote, "it is believed will ultimately be found an Ideal which, if courageously worked out, will transcend or reconcile the oppositions not merely of Anglicanism and Dissent, but of Romanism and Protestantism."[32] In brief, this was a liberal theology turning back to the devotional and sacramental

---

[30] In June 1740, John Wesley wrote: "But experience shows the gross falsehood of the assertion that the Lord's Supper is not a converting ordinance. For many now present know, the very beginning of your conversion to God . . . was wrought at the Lord's Supper (Wesley's *Works*, Vol. I, p. 262).
[31] *From Faith to Faith*, p. 151.   [32] *A Free Catholic Church*, p. 3.

riches of the historic Church. Its central conviction was that the foundation of the unity of a truly comprehensive Church could never be dogma, but only devotional practice, for it is on doctrine that men are divided, a view which F. D. Maurice had also held. It is only, so they believed, on the basis of symbolic language that men's hearts and imaginations can be brought into unity. Hence, "a Free Catholic Church will accordingly use in its public worship not words of dogmatic precision, but the figurative language of devotional utterance. Its liturgy will not be designed to define opinion like a creed, but to express desire and aspiration like a prayer."[33]

In the course of time, some distinguished recruits from other denominations joined the Society, notably R. J. Campbell, the minister of the City Temple, a controversial Congregationalist, and W. E. Orchard, a Presbyterian minister in charge of the Congregational Church of the King's Weigh House in Mayfair. There were also some Anglican clergy and Roman Catholic laity associated with the Society. Campbell was the first to leave, wholly repudiating his liberalism and becoming an Anglo-Catholic. Lloyd Thomas felt that this desertion was a mortal blow to the Society and that it was quite unnecessary, since devout Free Churchmen were equally sure of the presence of God in their Sacraments. He was constrained to rebuke Campbell with a reminder: "Has he not seen, as I have praised God to see, when Nonconformists have knelt before the altar to receive the Blessed Sacrament how they have sometimes broken down in tears? If that was not the living touch of the living Christ upon their souls and the most holy and real communion—I do not know what it is. I cannot conceive what more even the Roman Mass can be for a sincere and devout Roman."[34] Orchard was to remain the most indefatigable liturgical experimenter of the Free Catholics until he finally submitted to the Roman obedience. Lloyd Thomas alone remained faithful to the Society. He edited its Magazine, and he worshipped with an uncommonly rich ceremonial and ritual borrowed from many Christian centuries in which the very select congregation of the Old Meeting Unitarian Church in Birmingham were privileged to join. But if the Society of Free Catholics did nothing else, it had two accomplishments to its credit. It left behind an intriguing invitation to the ministers of the Free Churches to explore the

[33] *Ibid.*, p. 85.
[34] *Anglo-Catholic or Free Catholic? A Comment on Revd. R. J. Campbell's "Spiritual Pilgrimage,"* p. 11.

liturgies and devotions of historic Christendom as a supplement to their own spare diet of worship, and it provided in the liturgical compilations of Lloyd Thomas and W. E. Orchard brilliant examples of such recoveries.

The Free Catholics disliked the dogmatism of Roman belief but delighted in Roman Catholic sacramental and devotional practice. They were allured by the theological freedom of Protestantism but repelled by the irreverence and unimaginativeness of its contemporary worship. They intended to combine the good features of each tradition, devotional forms with intellectual freedom. In particular, their work was marked by four important characteristics. They proposed to substitute the ardour of mysticism for the chill of didacticism. Instead of the idiosyncratic and all too contemporary prayers of the Free Churches, they proposed to re-establish the historic prayers of Christendom, hallowed by the use of the centuries. In place of the "sacerdotalism" of the single voice of the Free Church minister in his tediously long prayers, they proposed responsive prayers in which the whole congregation could unite with heart and voice. And, finally, the language of their devotions, and the furnishings of their churches, as well as the stained-glass windows and the architecture itself, would be deeply symbolical, and they would restore Holy Communion to the central position it had been given in the earliest age of the Church.

The first fruits of the work of the Society of Free Catholics was Orchard's remarkably comprehensive liturgy, the *Divine Service* of 1919. Brought up as an adolescent in the Presbyterian Church, he was trained at Westminster Theological College in Cambridge, and attained to some local fame as minister of the Enfield Presbyterian Church. Because it was required of him, he prayed extemporaneously, but uncomfortably. At the same time, he was honest enough to admit that it was an apt form of prayer for outsiders and inquirers who might have found liturgical forms artificial and cold, for this kind of prayer "may so strive to interpret the unrealised Godward cravings of others, and give them such expression, as to lead them almost unconsciously into praying themselves."[35] In fact, he produced a superb collection of such prayers in a book called *The Temple*.[36] For the morning service, which was attended by the committed Christian families at Enfield,

---

[35] *From Faith to Faith*, p. 90.
[36] *Ibid.* Of these prayers Orchard records: "They have converted some to faith, taught many to pray, and been the dying companion of not a few."

Orchard occasionally introduced some simple liturgical forms, which were gradually increased and improved. His tolerant congregation permitted him to remove the organ and rostrum at the "East end" of the sanctuary and to make "a kind of chancel, with the pulpit on one side, and the Communion Table in the centre, behind which, on a sort of reredos, I was allowed to place a brass cross with enamel figures of the four living creatures on the arms, and the *Agnus Dei*, the whole flanked by a brass Alpha and Omega." With pride, he adds: "I think this, too, must have been almost the first Presbyterian Church to have a cross in close association with the Communion Table, at least, South of the Tweed."[37]

In 1914 he was called to succeed Dr. John Hunter, the most eminent Congregational liturgist of his day, as the minister of the historic King's Weigh House which, ever since the time of the renowned Binney, had been the laboratory of the most advanced worship in the Free Churches. The architect of this building was Alfred Waterhouse. It did not please Orchard who called it an "oval shaped boilerette." He thought its locale unfortunate, remarking, "Whatever worship Mayfair may patronize, it is not likely to be Congregational."[38] At the outset of his ministry he agreed to use Hunter's *Devotional Services* for the ordinary services, but not his Communion Order, for "in this he had not only broken away from all historic forms, but had prefaced it with a series of affirmations as to what it did not mean, which I could never take on my lips."[39] Orchard's own Communion Service was on the model of the Book of Common Prayer, except that he became increasingly convinced that transubstantiation was the most satisfactory doctrine for the Eucharist, and that it was appropriate to prepare for the reception of the Eucharist with confession.[40]

His views about this time are expressed with admirable clarity (too clearly for the Congregational Union of England and Wales) in a volume with the challenging title, *The New Catholicism and other Sermons*. The tenth sermon, "The New Catholicism," might well have been printed as the manifesto of the Society of Free Catholics, so excellent a statement is it of their aims. The primary principle is its "desire to reappropriate everything of spiritual value in the historic Catholic system" and the first item to be reappropriated is "its mystic worship." By this Orchard means that the Supernatural reached the soul through the senses. The false

[37] *Ibid.*, p. 105. [38] *Ibid.*, p. 117. [39] *Ibid.*, p. 118.
[40] *Ibid.*, p. 131.

spirituality of many Free Church thinkers of this period is shrewdly exposed in the charge that to assert body and soul are antagonistic "not only blames the Creator for uniting them, but makes the Incarnation either unthinkable or a mere condescension to a weak human need."[41] He goes on to argue that it is only the perfect reconciliation of the spiritual and the material that "will inspire us to redeem the body from unchastity and grossness, and rescue the material world from ugliness and exploitation. It is no accident that art has reached its highest attainment through Catholic worship."[42]

He insists that Catholicism alone has taken with full seriousness the real presence of Christ in the Sacrament which others have tried to explain away. As for its pageantry, this is inevitable both because of the reality and primacy of the supernatural and also because positive joy demands pageantry for its expression. "The worst enemy of Catholicism," he adds, "could not say it had been a bad school of mysticism; it has been its most prolific soil."[43]

If Orchard were to have been asked at this stage why he did not then leave Nonconformity, in all sincerity he would have replied that he was seeking a Catholicism wide enough to include what Nonconformity had stood for—especially the freedom of prophesying and praying. His generous hospitality would make room for the Baptists because they made the ordinance of initiation significant, for the Methodists because of their zeal for holiness, and for the Quakers because of their stress on silence and spontaneity.[44] Orchard's dissatisfaction with Roman Catholicism is simply that it is not Catholic enough in its comprehensiveness. "If I could not feel that I belonged to the Church which produced Augustine, Francis and Pascal, as well as Luther, Bunyan, and Wesley, I would refuse to belong to any church at all."[45] With such convictions as to the centrality and depth of Eucharistic worship, and as to the inspiration of the saints of the Christian tradition, it was no wonder that he had to frame a Liturgy for the New Catholicism. This is precisely what *Divine Service* is.[46]

The Preface is an interesting statement of the principles upon which Orchard operated. First, in his desire for comprehensive-

[41] *The New Catholicism*, p. 147.
[42] *Ibid.*   [43] *Ibid.*, p. 149.   [44] *Ibid.*, p. 154.
[45] *Ibid.*, a sermon, "The Church of Three Dimensions," p. 56.
[46] Its full title is: "The Order of Divine Service for Public Worship, the administration of the Sacraments and other Rites and Ceremonies, and a selection from the Daily Offices compiled from ancient and modern devotions together with an abridged and revised Psalter and Canticles pointed for Chanting."

ness, he was proposing these liturgical forms not as alternatives to free prayer, but as supplements to it. He demands "that room shall be left both for freely uttered and for silent prayer, not only as existing alongside liturgical forms, but as their very crown and consummation."[47] He recognizes that there are differences of practice which will make advanced doctrines and customs acceptable in some quarters, while simpler rites would be more welcome in other quarters. In line with the aim to meet the needs of both Catholic and Protestant temperaments, therefore, he has chosen to provide alternative forms rather than "adopting a colourless and concealed compromise."[48] The most striking evidence of this is the provision for both "A Simple Observance of the Lord's Supper" and "The Order for the celebration of the Eucharist."[49] His autobiography indicates that in one respect he thought he was able to improve on the Book of Common Prayer. That was by providing ten services for Sunday mornings and evenings, "which we found much preferable to the sameness of the Book of Common Prayer; especially as it enabled us to use so much more of the rich and glorious liturgical material in existence."[50]

The chief feature of *Divine Service* is, of course, its use of the great historic liturgies and prayers of Christendom. Its chief sources are: the Book of Common Prayer, Bright's *Ancient Collects*, Selina Fox's *A Chain of Prayer Across the Ages*, Hunter's *Devotional Services*, and Charles Plummer's *Devotions from Ancient and Mediaeval Sources*. He has ransacked the liturgical treasures of the ages to recover such gems as the prayers of Archbishop Laud and of Bishops Andrewes, Hickes, Cosin, and Cotton, the Liturgies of the Western and Eastern Churches, and he utilises the devotions of St. Francis Xavier, Bersier, and Martineau. Here is God's plenty. Orchard was, however, no mere scissors and paste man. He

---

[47] *Ibid.*, p. 5.   [48] *Ibid.*, p. 6.

[49] Both these forms of Communion were regularly celebrated as alternatives by Orchard at the King's Weigh House. It may seem surprising, since Orchard's own preference was so clearly in favour of the high Eucharist, that his conscience allowed him to celebrate the low Lord's Supper. Investigation of the latter rite shows, however, that the rubrics allow both celebrant and communicants to add silent directed petitions which could have the effect of making it more advanced than it appears. For example, when the institution narrative is reached, the president reads, "And as they were eating, Jesus took bread, and blessed," at which point a rubric reads, *Here the Holy Spirit should be silently invoked.* After the Fraction, and delivery, the direction is then given for a *Prayer pleading the sacrifice of Christ and making offering of self to God.* Finally, the reading of the High Priestly Prayer of Christ requires at stated intervals in the silence the remembrance of the saints and the departed, the remembrance of the living, and the prayer for the unity of the Church. Hence, though the ceremonial is simple, the doctrine is, in fact, advanced.

[50] *From Faith to Faith*, p. 134.

was a sensitive editor in looking for translations of ancient collects and litanies that provided the most felicitous cadences, in skilful adaptations, in planning each service so that it had clear architectonic, and in making his own original contributions.

No less than twenty-six prayers are of his own composition, including Litanies of Labour, of Missions, of the Church, of the Sick, of the Holy Ghost, and in the tenth Order of Worship. Some of these prayers are worthy to be compared with the great collects in respect of their Scriptural bases, arrow-like directness, and profound simplicity. In three areas of prayer Orchard excelled: on the great festivals of the Christian Year, in petitions for peace, and in compassionate understanding of the exploited, the degraded, and the dying. In the first category he has sublimely jubilant prayers for Christmas[51] and Easter.[52] In the second, "Christ the only Prince of Peace"[53] is a passionate plea such as only this great pacifist could offer. In the understanding of the problems of the working man, he deserves to be compared for his prophetic ardour with John Hunter, and his collect for Labour Day[54] and his Litany of Labour[55] are incomparable of their kind. His sensitive prayer for St. Mary Magdalene's Day[56] reminds one that it was said during the first World War that his was the only church that prostitutes used to attend, because there was no trace of Pharisaism in Orchard's pure and generous heart or in the inclusive gospel that he preached. His prayers for mourners[57] and especially one at the burial service of a child[58] are epitomes of tenderness.

Where so much is excellent, it is tempting to cite inordinately. It must suffice, however, to illustrate Orchard in joyful and in tender moods. Here is the aspiring adoration of his Easter prayer: "O THOU who makest the stars, and turnest the shadow of death into the morning; on this day of days we meet to render Thee, our Lord and King, the tribute of our praise; for the resurrection of the spring-time, for the everlasting hopes that rise within the human heart, and for the Gospel which hath brought life and immortality to light. Receive our thanksgiving, reveal thy presence, and send forth into our hearts the Spirit of the Risen Christ."[59]

By contrast, here is his prayer at the burial of a child: "HEAVENLY Father, whose face the angels of little children do always

---

51 *Divine Service*, p. 73.   52 *Ibid.*, p. 91.
53 *Ibid.*, p. 168.   54 *Ibid.*, p. 162.
55 *Ibid.*, p. 108. This was included in the Methodist Manual, *Divine Worship*.
56 *Ibid.*, p. 163.   57 *Ibid.*, p. 186.   58 *Ibid.*, p. 193.
59 *Ibid.*, p. 91.

behold, and who by thy Son Jesus Christ hast taught us that of such is the kingdom of heaven; we commend unto thy faithful keeping the soul of this little child, whom thou hast gathered with the lambs in thy bosom; beseeching thee that thou wilt accept the innocence of this thy little one, cleansing *him* from all stain of earthly life; that *he* may dwell for ever in thy presence, and find a home in the heavenly Jerusalem, that city which is full of boys and girls playing in the streets thereof; and this we ask through Jesus Christ our Lord."[60]

Subsequent Free Church compilers of worship manuals have learned much from Orchard. In particular, they have followed his comprehensiveness in their borrowings from all centuries and Communions, and benefitted from his gift for expressing contemporary concerns with a strongly Biblical diction in the traditional forms of collect and litany, and, above all, from his genius for collecting a Biblical catena on a particular theme and arranging it responsively as an act of devotion, a declaration of faith, or a reminder of Christian duty.[61] The latter was his most original contribution to liturgical creation.

Ultimately Orchard found that, as his detractors had always prophesied, he had to make his submission to Rome for, despite the naïve belief of the Society of Free Catholics to the contrary, it was impossible to practise Catholic ceremonial and Sacraments without the undergirding of Catholic doctrine on which they rested. Henceforth, as a Roman Catholic priest, he could no longer experiment in compiling revised liturgies, but he did produce a remarkable collection of his own private prayers, the *Sancta Sanctorum: Prayers for the Holy of Holies* (1955). These highly personal meditations recall those of John Henry Newman in their searching self-analysis, deep humility, longing for charity, and in the pruned richness of their imagery. Other themes are Orchard's own, as in a profound prayer that atheists may be delivered from their alluring and evanescent illusions, or in another expressing a prophetic sense of judgment on the Church for its "reluctant yieldings to the pressure of unwelcome truth" and "alliances with worldly powers and the

---

[60] *Ibid.*, p. 193. Each of these prayers shows a tendency to romanticism and sentimentality which is kept in check by the Scriptural citations and the expanded collect form.

[61] Examples are: The Divine Praises or the Declaration of the Divine Nature (2nd Order), the Promises of the Word of God (4th Order), The Commandments of the Lord Jesus (6th Order), New Testament Confession of Faith (7th Order), and Apostolic Exhortations (9th Order).

adoption of earthly armour."[62] They are marked throughout with the deepest spirituality, as of one who sincerely prays "make me like a window of purest glass, which calls no attention to itself by figure, colour, or inscription, but which simply lets the sunshine stream through unhindered and undiminished."[63]

During his controversial ministry at King's Weigh House, when it was said that a Roman Catholic who had been persuaded to attend Orchard's Eucharist expressed the opinion that she much preferred her own simpler services,[64] Orchard was thought to be a peacock. In fact, as his sermons and this last book of personal prayers shows, he was more like a dove, and there was never anything of the pouter pigeon in this deeply spiritual, if impracticable man, ahead of his time.

The last fruits of the Society of Free Catholics was the production of the marvellously comprehensive *Free Church Book of Common Prayer* (1929), chiefly the work of the founder of the movement, J. M. Lloyd Thomas.[65] It was, moreover, regularly in use at his Unitarian Church, the Old Meeting in Birmingham. In many ways it is like Orchard's *Divine Service*, particularly in its raiding of the liturgical treasures of Christendom. However, as the title might suggest, it makes considerable use of Free Church devotional materials, such as Hunter's *Devotional Services*, Orchard's *Divine Service*, and the Unitarian classic in which Martineau contributed some strikingly beautiful prayers, *Common Prayer for Christian Worship*. Furthermore, there is a considerable amount of fresh devotional material composed expressly for the book, including fourteen original prayers. The latter included several prayers to be said with the choir before and after service, and a delicate collect for St. Mary Magdalene's Day. A curious characteristic was the number of prayers for animals.

The book has some unique features, among them the provision in the Fourth Order of a service that could be used by non-Christian

---

[62] *Sancta Sanctorum*, p. 153.   [63] *Ibid.*, p. 69.
[64] Orchard repeats this story in *From Faith to Faith*, p. 139.
[65] A narrative account of this movement is greatly to be desired for it is of considerable ecumenical significance. The Dr. Williams Library has a complete set of the periodical issued by the Free Catholic Society. It is a pity that we do not know definitely which Free Church ministers were associated with J. M. Lloyd Thomas in producing this work of which he was "General Editor." The names of two "High Church" Baptist ministers frequently mentioned in this connection are the Revs. F. C. Spurr, Minister of the Hamstead Road Baptist Church, Birmingham (1922-1936) and G. H. R. Laslett, Spurr's successor in the same church. Spurr's predecessor, R. H. Coats, wrote the admirable *Types of English Piety*, a work on Nonconformist spirituality. (This information I owe to Dr. Ernest A. Payne, General Secretary of the Baptist Union of Great Britain and Ireland in a letter of February 5, 1963.)

theists as well as by Christians, containing adaptations from prayers of the Jewish Liturgy. The First and Fourth Orders of worship were written to promote Christian reunion, as "their use in the Free Churches will enrich their services and promote, through experience of a common devotion, the spirit of re-union and thus hasten the coming of a united Church at home as well as, for example, in South India and the wider mission field."[66] Another characteristic is that allowance is made for periods of silent prayer,[67] for extempore prayer,[68] and for alternatives.[69] Perhaps the chief difference from Orchard's *Divine Service* is in the wider use of modern, post-Reformation prayers. For example, Martineau's *Prayers in Congregation and College*, C. S. Woodward's *The Challenge* (for a children's thanksgiving), Percy Dearmer's *The Sanctuary*, the prayers of the Cambridge Platonists (Whichcote and Norris), Dekker, John Milton, Cardinal Newman, Samuel Johnson, Richard Baxter, Archbishop Benson, John Donne, Robert Nelson, and Bishop Moule, are all laid under debt, in addition to the many authors used by Orchard.

The value of this large compilation of 552 pages, which has the unevenness which might be expected from the work of a committee of individualists, was not that its responsive orders of worship were widely used. In fact, there is no certain evidence that it was used *in toto* anywhere but in Lloyd Thomas's own church. Its value was rather the book's pedagogical importance in introducing to the ministry of the English Free Churches a far wider horizon of devotional practice. The wide sales of the book indicates that it found its way into many ministers' studies and was used as an anthology of devotion. Certainly it proved that the Free Church tradition in Hunter, Orchard, and Lloyd Thomas was making its own contribution to liturgical forms of worship, and that it was employing the classical techniques of the collect and litany, while filling them with modern content. It was, above all, a welcome change from the idiosyncrasies and the dreary didacticism of the school of spontaneity, and it recovered soaring mysticism and sacramental reverence for the Free Churches, and made them part heirs of the Catholic centuries in East and West.

Nonetheless, the Society of Free Catholics was a failure in trying to win the majority of Free Churchmen to its fold. In part, this was because the Society was built upon a flawed foundation—that

[66] *Free Church Book of Common Prayer*, preface, p. ix.
[67] *Ibid.*, p. 11.   [68] *Ibid.*, p. 13.   [69] *Ibid.*, p. 20.

Catholic forms of devotion are meaningful to those who repudiate Catholic doctrine. In part, also, this was due to the fact that ministers trained to consider free prayer the finest form of charismatic spirituality could only consider the liturgies of the past as elegant and anachronistic exercises. They were blooms too exotic to be successfully transplanted into the kitchen gardens of Nonconformity. Finally, the Society's members combined too heterogeneous a collection of individuals. But at least in their expression of the sense of the Great Church of the centuries, they provided a bridge to the future for that ecumenism in prayer which now characterizes every Free Church manual of prayer, and in their brief collects and responsive litanies of intercession, they broke the tyranny of the long didactic and extemporaneous prayers which had been traditional in the Free Churches since the Savoy Conference of 1661. They helped also to regain a reverence for the Sacraments.

The *Rodborough Bede Book*, compiled by the Rev. C. Ernest Watson (1869-1942) in 1930, deserves brief consideration here, although he was not a member of the Society of Free Catholics. Nonetheless, he was a friend of Orchard who made considerable use of *Divine Service* and *The Temple* in his own compilation, and was attempting in a less extreme way to supplement the Puritan tradition with the great liturgical devotions of the primitive Church. What gave the *Bede Book* its distinctive character is that Watson preferred, as the title implies, Anglo-Saxon words to those of Latin derivation in the diction of English prayers, and that this anthology of prayers and services was regularly used in the Congregational church of Rodborough in rural Gloucestershire where he had a long and faithful ministry.

Apart from the artificial restriction of its diction, the work suffers a loss of structure from making a fetish of alternative brief exercises for the beginning and ending of worship (of which there are over a hundred). Its other weakness is its attenuated theology which excluded the very concepts which gave the historic liturgies their life and power, as may be seen in his five all too condensed orders for the Eucharist. Its strength is in its anticipation of the influence of the Modern Liturgical Movement in providing so many responsive prayers for the active participation of the congregation in worship, in the various techniques of prayer so generously illustrated, in the use of agricultural imagery, and in making so notable a protest against disordered spontaneity. Watson's achievement is recorded in A. T. S. James, *A Cotswold Minister* (1944).

4. *The Return to the Reformed Tradition*

As the Free Catholics had rebelled against the apostles of spontaneity, so the school of Reformed Churchmen rebelled against the liberal theology of both, and against the eclecticism of the Free Catholics. For this attitude there are many reasons. The older immanentalism was giving way under the Continental influence of Karl Barth and Emil Brunner to a repristination of Reformed theology. Furthermore, the early twentieth century phase of indiscriminate enthusiasm for Christian re-union was followed in the mid-thirties by a second phase in which each denomination was looking carefully to its own roots, in the hope of discovering what it distinctively had to contribute to the Ecumenical Movement. This had an inevitable impact on worship. Rattenbury,[70] Bowmer,[71] and Bishop[72] wrote valuable studies of classical Methodist worship, celebrating its combination of evangelical preaching with Anglican sacramental practice, while Newton Flew[73] claimed that Wesley's doctrine of Christian perfection was the product of a long line of development in Christian history. Nathaniel Micklem,[74] John S. Whale,[75] and Bernard L. Manning[76] among the Congregationalists recalled the denomination to its high Genevan origins, and Horton Davies[77] produced the first extensive study of Puritan worship. Ernest Payne[78] reminded the Baptists of their birthright in faith and worship. Carnegie Simpson[79] did the same for the English Presbyterians, while a fine series of studies in the history of Scottish Presbyterian worship emerged from the hands of W. D. Maxwell,[80]

[70] Rattenbury wrote *Vital Elements in Public Worship* and *Eucharistic Hymns of John and Charles Wesley.*

[71] Bowmer was the author of *The Sacrament of the Lord's Supper in Early Methodism* and *The Lord's Supper in Methodism, 1791-1960.*

[72] John Bishop wrote *Methodist Worship in relation to Free Church Worship.*

[73] R. Newton Flew also wrote, with R. E. Davies, *The Catholicity of Protestantism.* His major volume is *The Idea of Perfection.*

[74] Micklem was the editor of *Christian Worship,* the compiler of a fine series of Communion meditations in the Reformed tradition from Calvin downwards, entitled *A Book of Personal Religion,* and the author of *Congregationalism and the Church Catholic.*

[75] J. S. Whale wrote *What is a Living Church?* and the often reprinted *Christian Doctrine.*

[76] B. L. Manning wrote *Essays in Orthodox Dissent, Why not Abandon the Church?,* and *The Hymns of Wesley and Watts.*

[77] The reference is to *The Worship of the English Puritans.*

[78] E. A. Payne wrote *The Fellowship of Believers* and *The Free Church Tradition in the Life of England.*

[79] P. Carnegie Simpson wrote *The Evangelical Church Catholic.*

[80] W. D. Maxwell wrote *An Outline of Christian Worship,* and *A History of Worship in the Church of Scotland.*

William McMillan,[81] and G. B. Burnet.[82] In the movement whose slogan seemed to be "Back to the Reformation," the Methodists[83] were chiefly concerned to recover the theology of Martin Luther. This led to a balanced recovery of the Word and Sacrament, and to the preparation of books of worship that were authentically in the Reformed Tradition.

In the return to this tradition in worship, a splendid lead had been given by the liturgists of the Church of Scotland. Ever since the foundation of the Church Service Society in 1865,[84] the Scottish Church Society of 1892, and the Scottish Ecclesiological Society of 1903, there has been a group of Presbyterian clergymen and laity in Scotland deeply interested in and thoroughly informed on the subject of Reformed and Catholic worship. Even more important, they have produced a type of worship which at its best may be termed "Reformed Catholic," for it avails itself of the Patristic heritage in worship, along with the Reformation emphasis on the importance of preaching and the significance of the two Dominical Sacraments. Two books produced by the Church of Scotland have been deeply influential on the development of an ordered and reverential worship in the Presbyterian, Congregational, and to some extent, Baptist Churches of England. One is *Prayers for Divine Service* (1923) and the other is *The Book of Common Order* (1940), with its superb first Order for Holy Communion, which is the glory of Scottish worship.[85]

The denominational service books published at the beginning of the century had little sense of their own traditions. These, with the exception of those produced by the English Presbyterians, were largely imitations of the Book of Common Prayer and poor imitations at that. This is true of the *Book of Congregational Worship*[86]

---

[81] William McMillan wrote *The Worship of the Scottish Reformed Church.*
[82] G. B. Burnet wrote *The Holy Communion in the Reformed Church of Scotland, 1560-1960.*
[83] See P. S. Watson, *Let God be God* and Gordon Rupp, *The Righteousness of God.*
[84] For the nineteenth century influence of the Church of Scotland on English Free Church worship see *Worship and Theology in England*, Vol. IV, *From Martineau to Newman, 1850-1900*, pp. 100-13.
[85] Its fine consecration prayer has an *epiklesis* like the Eastern Church but the posture is Western and in public view; like the Anglican Rite the language is the vernacular, but unlike it, it refuses to incorporate the Words of Institution and to hide the acts of Fraction and Libation in the consecration prayer. See W. D. Maxwell, *History of Worship in the Church of Scotland*, pp. 181-82.
[86] It is to be noted, for example, in the 1920 book that, while the general order of Holy Communion follows the Book of Common Prayer, and the Consecration Prayer has the *Sursum corda*, the *Sanctus*, and a kind of *anamnesis*, yet there is no

of 1920, even though P. T. Forsyth was included on the committee of compilers. When they departed from Anglican models they relied on Hunter, Orchard, and the like. They did not return to the Reformation or to the Scriptures as their sources. The same judgment could more decisively be made of the Congregation *Manual for Ministers* (1936). The Methodist Church may be forgiven for showing less independence of the Anglican tradition than did the other Free Churches, because when *The Book of Offices* was produced in 1936 the three major divisions of British Methodism had only just been united, and, after all, the Methodists have strong Anglican roots.

The effect of the movement to return to the sources of Reformed Churchmanship was an intimation that the era of Anglican imitations was over. The most recent denominational service-books are more directly related to the history of their own denominations than were either the first service books of the century, or the rather strained and exotic compilations of the Free Catholics. The main concerns of this new school were admirably expressed by John Grant in *Free Churchmanship in England*.

He wrote: "An unfamiliar school of churchmanship appeared, valuing not only the freedom of the Free Churches but also the despised Calvinism that had given rise to English Nonconformity, asserting the necessity of dogma and laying a new emphasis upon the Church visible with its ministry and sacraments. What began as a protest of a few men against the dethronement of the Gospel in certain Nonconformist circles has grown into a widespread revival of Reformed ideals of churchmanship."[87] The new understanding of the Church in terms of the historic Gospel and of the Sacraments in terms of the Word was most vigorously expounded in Principal Nathaniel Micklem's pioneering volume of 1936, entitled *What is the Faith?*

5. Recent Congregational Worship

One of the most impressive contributions in the new mode was that of a group of four "High Genevan" Congregationalists, John Marsh, Romilly Micklem, John Huxtable and James Todd. They prepared *A Book of Public Worship compiled for the use of Congregationalists*.[88] Although the book was not an official com-

---

epiklesis, nor a recapitulation of the mighty acts of God, and, which is an astonishing departure from the Puritan tradition, neither Fraction nor Libation.

[87] *Free Churchmanship in England*, p. 325.

[88] The first edition appeared in 1948. Marsh, now the Principal, was then the

pilation of the Congregational Union of England and Wales, it has probably been more widely used by Congregationalists than any other service book. Its First Communion Order had the distinction of being the sole Free Church Eucharistic Order to be included in Bernard Wigan's important volume, *The Liturgy in English*, along with the Liturgy of the Church of South India, and the Communion Order of the Scottish Book of Common Order, in a volume which otherwise consisted of Anglican liturgies.

A Book of Public Worship contains a long and interesting introduction by John Marsh. Here the basic principles are outlined. The first is that Congregational worship is founded upon a structure which links the Sermon with the Lord's Supper, and the Order for Morning and Evening worship is based on dry Mass, not on such mediaeval offices as Matins or Evensong. Secondly, it was thought desirable to provide orders of service "rightly expressing the place and meaning of Baptism, the Lord's Supper, and Church membership in relation to our own polity."[89] Finally, there was a deliberate search for materials in the Puritan tradition, notably in Baxter's Reformed Liturgy and in the Middelburg Prayer Book, as well as from other similar sources.

The conscious pride in the Reformed tradition is a notable characteristic of the introduction and the contents. Other features are the provision of four different orders of Holy Communion, and even of an abbreviated order for the Lord's Supper "for those who have early Communions on such days as Easter Sunday."[90] Two of the orders keep to the "ancient and reformed practice in placing the sermon before the 'long prayer': often the intercessions will come most appropriately after minds have been stirred by the preaching of the Gospel."[91] The Congregationalists are reminded in the preface that although they love freedom they are not liturgical anarchists, and that their ancestors were convinced that "Standards of worship could not be fixed by the State; they had been determined by the Gospel."[92]

The page of acknowledgements indicates that the compilers

Chaplain, as E. R. Micklem was a former Chaplain of Mansfield College, Oxford, of which Huxtable was a member. Todd learned his Genevanism from J. S. Whale, another Mansfield man who became President of Cheshunt College, Cambridge. Particularly under the inspired liturgical leadership of Nathaniel Micklem, as Principal of Mansfield College, this one institution may be said to have provided in its College Chapel a standard of worship that led all the English Free Churches from 1933 onwards.

[89] *A Book of Public Worship*, Preface, p. xiii.
[90] *Ibid.*
[91] *Ibid.*, Preface, p. xiv.
[92] *Ibid.*, p. vii.

were well acquainted with the Reformed tradition outside their own denomination, for they made use of the Scottish Presbyterian sources of worship (*Euchologion*, and the Books of Common Order of 1928 and 1940), the service books of the American and English Presbyterian Churches, and of the Canadian Book of Common Order. Nor did they forget their own predecessors, as Hunter, Orchard, and Lloyd Thomas, as well as *The Book of Congregational Worship* of 1920, were laid under contribution.

Without question this is the worthiest modern directory of worship produced for the Congregational churches. As a directory, rather than a book of common prayer, it provides a theological structure for worship with an abundance of alternative prayers so that familiarity cannot breed contempt, nor capriciousness lead to congregational confusion. As a supplement to the five basic orders for Sunday worship, there is a valuable collection of ninety-three pages of "Additional Material for Public Worship" consisting of Scripture Sentences; Prayers of Adoration, Invocation, and Confession, with Assurances of Pardon; Prayers of Thanksgiving, Supplication, and for Special Graces; General Intercessions (in one Prayer, in Prayers for Special Subjects, in Prayers with Responses, and in Bidding Prayers); Prayers for Illumination, Dedications of the Offerings, Ascriptions of Glory, and Benedictions.

Furthermore, there are four excellent Orders for the Sacrament of Holy Communion, of which the first is the finest ever produced by Congregationalists and bears the mark of the influence of the Church of Scotland. The Prayer of Thanksgiving worthily commemorates the mighty acts of God in creation, incarnation, redemption, and resurrection, affirms the communion of saints, and includes an *epiklesis* or invocation of the Holy Spirit "to sanctify both us and these thine own gifts of bread and wine which we set before thee."[93] As in the Scottish rite the Words of Institution, with the Fraction, are not absorbed in the Prayer of Consecration, but set solemnly apart.

There are admirable Orders for the Sacrament of Baptism, one for the Baptism of Children and the other for the Baptism of Believers. The theology they express is that Baptism "is both an assertion of the individual application of the benefits of Christ's work, and the act of formal reception into the membership of the Church."[94] This is a great improvement upon preceding Congregational Baptismal rites which were hardly distinguishable from

[93] *Ibid.*, p. 37.　　　　　　　　[94] *Ibid.*, Preface, xix.

dedications. The covenant emphasis, characteristic of the Reformed and Puritan heritage, rightly informs the brief but impressive Order "for the Reception of Members into full Communion with the Church" which properly emphasizes the link with Baptism, and requires a profession of faith.

The service for the Ordination of Ministers, which has been approved by the denomination and is now in regular use, definitely requires the laying-on of hands (whereas this was left optional in the 1920 *Book of Congregational Worship* and in the 1936 *Manual for Ministers*). It also requires the solemn presentation of a Bible to the newly-ordained minister, a significant reminder that his authority is founded on the Gospel. The new Reformed emphasis is further stressed in the fourth requirement of the ordinand: "Do you promise to execute your charge with all fidelity, to preach the Word of God, to administer the Sacraments, to fulfil the pastoral office, and to live a godly life, adorning the doctrine of God our Saviour in all things?"[95]

One lack in the book, the absence of any services for the festivals of the Christian Year, was made good by the publication in 1951 of James M. Todd's *Prayers and Services for Christian Festivals*. This, too, availed itself of the chief Reformed sources in English, including the Church of Scotland's *Prayers for the Christian Year* and *Prayers for Use in Time of War*. It also made use of more Anglican sources than the earlier companion volume did, including *The Grey Book*, Eric Milner-White's *Daily Prayer*, and the Book of Common Prayer. This made available to Free Churchmen for the first time the famous Service of Nine Lessons and Carols which Bishop Frere had revived at Truro and Milner-White had popularized in the magnificent setting of King's College Chapel, Cambridge. There were services for Christmas Eve, Epiphany, for each day of Holy Week, Easter, Ascension Day, Whitsuntide, and a Watchnight Service. Furthermore, a collection of sentences and prayers for each festival was prepared for insertion into the five alternative orders of Sunday worship provided by *A Book of Public Worship*, together with short Orders of worship for use at Holy Communion on Christmas Day, Easter Day, and Whitsunday.

The two complementary volumes provided a great enrichment of Congregational worship. They represent a long overdue recognition on the part of concerned Congregationalists that twentieth century worship must fulfil five conditions. First, its variety must be

95 *Ibid.*, p. 202.

a "founded freedom"—that is, based upon a solid Biblical and theological structure. Secondly, that structure must be based upon the central Christian Sacrament, the Lord's Supper or Holy Communion. Within a Free Church tradition this is best recognized by making each service an Ante-Communion, and by providing several Orders of Holy Communion. *A Book of Public Prayer* provides four in full and a shorter order, while *Prayers and Services for Christian Festivals* adds three others. Thirdly, it is acknowledged by the publication of Todd's book that the Christian Year is a witness to the Gospel of the Incarnation, the multi-faceted significance of which is more fully apprehended by dividing it into festivals each with its own integrity. In the fourth place, in an ecumenical age, it is essential that the worshippers should transcend local congregational boundaries and understand that they are, in Forsyth's term, "the local outcrop" of the Holy Catholic Church. This is expressed in the traditional responses of the great Prayer of Thanksgiving in the Order of the Lord's Supper, and in a sense of the Communion of Saints. Finally, there is suitable provision, as there was not in the work of the Free Catholics, for the distinctive services of a single denomination, such as are provided in the services for Ordination and Induction to the Ministry, the Reception of Members into Full Communion, and the Admission of Deacons. Further, it is a great quality of these two volumes that they stress, less the dissidence of Dissent, than the basic unity of the Reformed tradition in worship.

There are two ways in which they might, however, be improved. In their zeal to do justice to the inevitable Biblical basis of worship, they have sometimes assumed that a catena of Scriptures of itself makes a prayer, forgetful of the need for phrases of convenient length and of the rhythms of speech and felicities of cadence that are essential in public prayer. Furthermore, while Biblical thought and a great deal of Biblical diction must be retained, there is an undue preponderance of archaisms.[96] The second defect is the singular absence of responsive prayers, except in one section of the General Intercessions. It is singular because the Congregational churches have insisted that the people, not the ministers alone, make up the community of the redeemed. Yet this service book,

---

[96] In *A Book of Prayer*, p. 47, the petition "*Suffer us* no longer to live unto ourselves . . ." is an example of archaism. A more modern translation of the Scriptures would lead to greater edification than the words (p. 137): "There hath no temptation taken you but such as is common to men." Above all one misses the vividness of Biblical metaphor and simile. Todd's book is almost free of such defects.

ignoring the modern Liturgical Movement's emphasis on the importance of the fullest participation of the laity, condemns them for the most part to be silent in public prayer.

Two recent denominational service books of great merit enable us to see two other Free Church denominations entering into their Reformed heritage with great confidence, while also acknowledging that heritage which they share with the Universal Church of Christ through the centuries. The first is *The Presbyterian Service Book for use in the Presbyterian Churches of England and Wales* and the other is the Baptist production, *Orders and Prayers for Church Worship: A Manual for Ministers*.

6. *Recent Presbyterian Worship*

The Presbyterian Church of England has a distinguished lineage in service books, dating from the famous Westminster *Directory* of 1645 which, for a brief and troubled fifteen years, displaced the Book of Common Prayer as the national formulary for worship. Among the English Free Churches, the Presbyterians claim the distinction of having produced the first official modern denominational service book in 1898. This was significantly revised in 1921, but used the same historic title of a *Director of Public Worship*. The title was reluctantly changed in 1948 only because the new service book was to be used in Wales as well as in England.

The particular interest of *The Presbyterian Service Book* of 1948 is that it combines within the same book two traditions of worship: the older, Puritan type of tradition which is still strong in Wales and the more liturgical tradition characteristic of Scottish and English worship. The Committee responsible for producing the new service book faced a double task: "Firstly, it sought to preserve what was most valuable in the forms of worship of both Churches, which had found expression on the one hand in the Directory of the English Church, and on the other in the freer tradition of the Welsh Church. Secondly, it sought to giver richer expression to the liturgical traditions of the Church Catholic and Reformed."[97] How was this to be done in the same book?

The Committee solved the problem by providing three orders for Sunday worship, the first of which was credal in character, the second non-credal, and the third more congenial to the Welsh tradition. In the same way it provided four orders for the celebration of Holy Communion. The first two were in Reformed liturgical

[97] Preface.

377

tradition, the third was in the Welsh Puritan tradition, and the fourth was an abbreviated order for the sick. The very considerable debt owed to the Church of Scotland for the liturgical orders is acknowledged. The Scottish influence is manifest in the three-fold prayers of Approach, Confession, and Petition in the first two orders of worship, in the first two orders for Holy Communion, and in the series of prayers for the major Christian festivals.

Where did the English Presbyterians obtain their zest for a worship both Reformed and also Catholic? There is no doubt that one major influence was that of the Iona Community, founded by the Rev. Sir George MacLeod.[98] This is a brotherhood of ministers and craftsmen bound together in a common devotional rule of life. For the three summer months their headquarters is the west-coast island of Iona, the birth-place of Scottish Christianity, where the members of the Community worship, study, learn the new techniques of evangelism, and share in the manual labour necessary to rebuild the Abbey of St. Columba.

MacLeod's theology centres on the Incarnation for the redemption of the spiritual and the material life of man in his totality as socio-politico-economic-cultural being. He is emphatic that the concept of social justice is implicit in the true understanding of Holy Communion, for "the Sacrament, whatever greater things it may declare, at least dictates to men how best to share their Bread. And what is the one remaining problem of this potentially plenteous earth but the problem of how to share the mercies that God would make available for all?"[99] Of chief significance for our purpose is MacLeod's insistence upon the absolute primacy of worship in the Christian life, because it comes before the service of men, because evangelism arises out of worship, and because the Church is the starting point of mission.[100] His understanding of worship is immensely dynamic.[101] No Presbyterian minister has more ardently encouraged the application of the insights of the Continental Liturgical Movement to the Reformed tradition than he, nor inspired more young ministers from his own and many other branches of the Church during their visits to Iona.

In consequence, several of the younger English Presbyterian ministers were the first English enthusiasts for the work of the Iona Community. They met for an annual conference on worship,

[98] See George F. MacLeod, *We shall re-build; the work of the Iona Community on Mainland and on Island.*
[99] *Ibid.*, p. 13.   [100] *Ibid.*, p. 23.   [101] See *ibid.*, pp. 29f.

and were called the "Parkgate" group because their first place of meeting was Parkgate in the Wirral, Cheshire. They concentrated their studies on such topics as the nature of the Sacraments, Eucharistic Sacrifice, and Ordination. Through retreats and the keeping of a Common Rule of devotion they kept alive their zeal for the reform of worship. Some of the members of this group were on the Committee which produced the 1948 book. The second important factor was the influence of the Scottish *Book of Common Order* of 1940. It was taken up with great zest by many English Presbyterian ministers, and the use of the First Order of Holy Communion "became the hallmark of the 'progressives.' "[102] For a great many ministers it still is the "norm." And, of course, it is to be found in the English Presbyterian service book.

It is important to notice the convergence of the liturgical ideals of the Congregational and Presbyterian ministers in England, which is so striking a feature of *A Book of Public Worship compiled for the use of Congregationalists* and of *The Presbyterian Service Book*, both of which appeared in 1948. The reasons are not far to seek. Both look back gratefully to Calvin's reformation in Geneva as the pattern of their churchmanship and worship. They were comrades-in-arms in the Westminster Assembly and shared in producing its famous *Directory*, as they have shared the ignominy and glory of the history of English Dissent. Both have benefitted from the splendid researches of the liturgiologists of the Church of Scotland in their attempt to create a Reformed Catholic worship for the twentieth century. Both have had their "ginger groups" of younger ministers dedicated to the promotion of a worthier worship in their own denomination, the "Church Order Group" in Congregationalism and the "Parkgate Group" in English Presbyterianism.

The growing sense of theological and liturgical unity between English Presbyterians and Congregationalists has led the two denominations to affirm a Covenant Relationship with each other in the hope that this may prove to be the penultimate step to organic unity. As a token of this Covenant they jointly publish each year a series of Meditations and Prayers for Holy Week.

[102] The information in this paragraph I owe to a lengthy and informative letter, of July 24, 1963, from the Rev. R. Aled Davies, Minister of St. Paul's Presbyterian Church, Croydon, the convener of the Presbyterian Church of England Committee on Public Worship and Aids to Devotion, to whom I am deeply grateful. For the latest revision of the Order for Holy Communion as celebrated in the General Assembly of the Church of Scotland, see the *Ordinal and Service Book for use in Courts of the Church*.

7. Recent Baptist Worship

The most intriguing example of the trend to a Reformed Catholic worship is a recent Baptist service book, *Orders and Prayers for Church Worship: A Manual for Ministers*. It shows a considerable theological and liturgical advance on its two predecessors: M. E. Aubrey's *Minister's Manual* and D. Tait Patterson's *The Call to Worship*. It is the work of Ernest A. Payne and Stephen F. Winward. The former is a distinguished historian of Nonconformity, now the General Secretary of the Baptist Union of Great Britain and Ireland, and, significantly, a member of the Central Committee of the World Council of Churches. This manual indicates that the most charismatic of all the English Free Churches, the Baptist, is fully abreast of all the developments of the modern Liturgical Movement, and equally concerned to express Reformed insights within the context and tradition of the Great Church of the centuries.

This may appear, on the surface, a sudden and surprising *volte face* on the part of the English Baptists. Certainly they are far more liturgically advanced than Baptists elsewhere in Europe or in the United States. But for many years they have included in their ranks rebels from the general trend of the "School of Spontaneity." Among these the names of F. B. Meyer, F. C. Spurr, Ruffell Laslett, H. Wheeler Robinson, A. C. Underwood, Hugh Martin, M. E. Aubrey, and more recently Neville Clark would have to be considered. The latter wrote an exciting volume, *Call to Worship* (1960).

The theme of this important essay is "the conviction that the recovery of the Liturgy is the most urgent need of the Free Churches at this time."[103] He offers a radical critique of the worst emphases in the Free Church tradition, including the unbalanced emphasis on preaching, the treatment of the Eucharist as an addendum, the looking for "a blessing" instead of making an offering, and the divorce of worship from life, resulting from the idea of worship as the edification of the elite instead of carrying out a representative action on behalf of a world for which Christ died. He argues for a worship which indissolubly unites Word and Sacrament, and that will be unmistakably corporate and congregational in character. Moreover, he has persuaded his own congregation, after the most careful instruction, to accept the way of renewal he pleads for. It is significant that so much of what Neville Clark hopes to see embodied in the worship of the Baptists is, in

103 Preface.

fact, provided for in *Orders and Prayers for Church Worship: A Manual for Ministers*, a most courageous publication.

A valuable introduction of fourteen pages provides a theology of worship, as dialogue between God and men, and an account of the two-fold origin of Christian worship combining "synagogue and Upper Room, scripture and sacrament, spoken word and "visible word"—which gives the complete pattern of Christian worship."[104] The influence of the Liturgical Movement is clearly seen in the statement that infrequent celebration of the Lord's Supper, or its relegation to an appendix, is to be deplored, and in the vigorous affirmation that "Christian worship is essentially eucharistic: it is to glory in Christ Jesus, incarnate, crucified, risen, exalted, coming in glory," and in the recognition that even when the Lord's Supper is not celebrated, the service of the Word should retain the pattern of Ante-Communion.[105] There is a firm insistence that the Holy Spirit is the agent in worship but that "he does not only act through 'inspired spontaneity.' "[106] Finally, the compilers desire a flexible liturgy: "In no sense is this book intended to be a Baptist equivalent of the Book of Common Prayer; it is intended rather to serve as a Book of Common Order."[107]

Their model has been the pattern of worship in the Church of Scotland. It is significant that while eight prayers are taken from Congregational sources, and several from the Book of Common Prayer and other Anglican sources, no less than thirty-eight prayers are borrowed from the Church of Scotland's Book of Common Order and eight from the same Church's *Prayers for the Christian Year*. The dependence upon the Scottish Rite is naturally and wisely fullest in the Order for the celebration of the Lord's Supper, for this is incomparably the best Reformed Rite in English-speaking lands, and has, in translation, been adopted for use in Calvin's cathedral church of St. Pierre in Geneva.[108]

It is in the central Prayer of Thanksgiving of the Communion Order that the fullest liturgical advance has been made. The *Sursum corda*, *Sanctus*, and *Benedictus qui venit*, are followed by the *anamnesis*, and the prayer concludes with an *epiklesis*, but unfortunately omits the note of oblation. Fraction and Libation are separated from the prayer so that their dramatic symbolism may be seen by the congregation. After Communion there is, rather un-

[104] *Orders and Prayers* . . . , Preface, p. x.
[105] *Ibid.*, pp. xi-xii. [106] *Ibid.*, p. xiv. [107] *Ibid.*, p. xv.
[108] W. D. Maxwell, *A History of Worship in the Church of Scotland*, p. 183.

happily, the choice between a read (or extempore) prayer of thanksgiving or a prayer for the Church Universal, including rejoicing in the communion of saints. The choice is unfortunate as the recognition of the communion of saints is an essential, not optional, element in the service. In fact, a general criticism would be that the eschatological element in the Eucharist is insufficiently stressed.[109]

The outstanding qualities of the book are precisely those which we discovered in *A Book of Public Worship compiled for the use of Congregationalists,* which it greatly resembles. The strong Scriptural basis of the Orders, the provision of much additional material to be placed in a theologically-structured service of Ante-Communion, the enhanced importance given to the Sacraments, the celebration of the chief festivals of the Christian Year including All Saints Day, and the place allowed for liturgical, extempore and silent prayer. It has one additional quality: a due recognition of the priesthood of all believers, which is clearly emphasized in the prayer before the laying-on of hands after Baptism: "Enable them as royal priests of Jesus Christ to bring others to Thee in prayer, and to take Thee to others in witness."[110] Yet, it too, fails to provide enough responsive prayers for the priesthood of the laity to become vocal.

Two other interesting characteristics of the book call for comment. One is that provision is made for the laying-on of hands, not only after Baptism and at the Ordination of ministers, but also in cases of sickness, as "was practised in apostolic times and by the early General Baptists of Britain."[111] The other is the all too rare recognition that unless there is family prayer in the homes, there cannot be satisfactory preparation for Sunday worship in Church. Therefore provision is made for prayers that may be helpful in the home.

8. *Recent Methodist Worship*

So far we have chronicled and evaluated the recovery of a Reformed Catholicity in Congregational, Presbyterian, and Baptist worship, but not in Methodist worship. Our difficulty is not any suspicion that such a reform has not taken place in Methodist worship in the last three decades, but the lack of official liturgical

---

109 Other rare infelicities are the colloquial "just" in the Exhortation of the Baptismal Order (p. 131), and the unwarrantable changing and weakening of the ending of Ignatius Loyola's famous prayer (p. 134).

110 *Orders and Prayers* . . . , p. 137.

111 *Ibid.*, Preface, p. xix.

documents to prove it. For this gap two reasons may be given. The impact of the Modern Liturgical Movement on England arrived too late to have any influence on the official *Methodist Book of Offices* of 1936, and the current negotiations between the Methodist Church and the Church of England would make a revision at present highly inopportune. But if we had a right to expect a fertile soil for such a movement towards a Reformed Catholicism it would be in English Methodism, with its joint Anglican and Free Church inheritance in worship, and its stressing of evangelical witness and Catholic sacramentalism. The renaissance of Luther studies in Methodism would also be a pointer in the same direction, as also the liturgical writings of J. E. Rattenbury, John Bishop, and John C. Bowmer, and the devotional writings of A. E. Whitham, notably *The Catholic Christ*.[112] Indeed, the fullest expression of the theological concept behind the liturgical movement is developed in the work of R. Newton Flew and Rupert Davies, entitled *The Catholicity of Protestantism*.

Fortunately there is more substantial evidence for the trend to Reformed Catholicism than has been hitherto indicated. This is chiefly to be found in the work of the important Methodist Sacramental Fellowship.[113] It was founded in 1935 shortly after the Methodist Union, its first members being "a group of young ministers who were distressed by the growing irreverence of our services and by the humanistic teaching of their day."[114] It came under suspicion for its "high" doctrinal and liturgical views but was cleared in a Conference investigation of 1938. Its Presidents have included A. E. Whitham, J. E. Rattenbury, and Donald Soper, in itself a sufficient claim for distinction. Its triple concern is: the re-affirmation of the historic Faith; the restoration of sacra-

[112] Whitham wrote (pp. 172-73): "But what I want to emphasize is not the necessity but the grace and kindness towards our infirmities of the Incarnation, the Church, the Sacraments. . . . If the Incarnation, Church and Sacraments mean anything, they do signify that we are not saved *from* the senses but *through* them, and we find God not in spite of the things of time and sense but through their hallowed ministry." Whitham wrote engagingly of the thrill of orthodoxy, the need to combine the evangelical and the sacramental in the Free Churches, the communion of saints past and present, the grace of God needing to be reflected in human charity, and of the gaiety that should characterize goodness.

[113] My information is derived from two letters from the Honorary Secretary, Dr. David Sharp of Felixstowe (August 25 and 29, 1957), and two pamphlets which he was kind enough to supply me with: A. S. Gregory, *The Methodist Sacramental Fellowship* (1954) and *What is the M.S.F.?* (5th edn., 1948). J. C. Bowmer refers briefly to its influence in *The Lord's Supper in Methodism*, 1790-1960, pp. 49-50.

[114] Pamphlet "In Defence of the M.S.F." by J. E. Rattenbury, p. 7 (cited by J. C. Bowmer, *op.cit.*, p. 49).

mental devotion; and the corporate reunion of believers.[115] It has from time to time been hinted that it is a coterie of sacerdotalists, but nothing could be further from the truth, for in 1939 "the membership stood at 320 in a proportion of one minister to two laymen."[116]

Each member is required to take a pledge, with God's help: "1. To say the Daily Office of prayer adopted by the Fellowship, or to observe some self-imposed discipline of daily devotion. 2. To receive the Holy Communion at least once a month after duly preparing myself. 3. To submit my mind humbly to the Faith of the Church as contained in Holy Scripture and expressed in the Nicene Creed. 4. To support with all loyalty the Methodist Church, and to help forward, as I can, both by prayer and service, the corporate reunion of all believers."[117] No one familiar with Wesley's own conviction of the central importance of the Sacrament, or his desire to restore "primitive Christianity," or his belief in daily devotional discipline, could suppose that the Methodist Sacramental Fellowship would not have gained his entire and hearty approval.

The Methodist Sacramental Fellowship has greatly helped to create an atmosphere favourable to reunion with the Church of England, and, more importantly, to retain in a well-organized and pragmatic denomination, devoted to evangelism and encouraging the vigorous witness of the laity as local preachers, a sense of the Holy Catholic Church as the communion of saints, and of Holy Communion as a "bounden duty and service" as well as the supreme privilege of the Church member. To the Fellowship must be attributed, in large degree, both the increasingly frequency with which the Sacrament is celebrated and the reverence with which it is received in contemporary English Methodism. Furthermore, the annual conferences of the Fellowship has brought to its meetings the rich insights of the modern Liturgical Movement, for its invited speakers have included Father Hebert and Dom Gregory Dix. It has also been in regular contact with parallel organizations in other denominations, such as the Church Service Society of the Church of Scotland, the Free Church Fellowship in the days of Nathaniel Micklem and Malcolm Spencer and its successor the Church Order Group represented by Hubert Cunliffe-Jones, and has encountered Orthodox spirituality in the person of Nicholas Zernov.[118]

[115] A. S. Gregory, *The Methodist Sacramental Fellowship*, pp. 8-9.
[116] *Ibid.*, p. 7.   [117] *What is the M.S.F.?*, p. 23.
[118] A. S. Gregory, *The Methodist Sacramental Fellowship*, p. 12.

While the Methodist Sacramental Fellowship has stressed two most significant parts of Methodism's inheritance, its Nicene faith and its Eucharistic heritage through the Wesleys, there has also been a re-appreciation of two of its distinctive ordinances, the Love-feast and the Covenant Service. The latter is now recognized as the standard observance of British Methodists each New Year and is, therefore, in no need of further attention, more particularly as the inclusion of part of it in the Clare College Manual for Holy Communion means that Anglicans are not likely to forget it either.

The revival of the Love-feast is a project dear to the heart of Frank Baker, as his book, *Methodism and the Love-Feast* amply proves. He suggests that the *agape* disappeared as Methodism became less of a group of revivalistic societies and more of a Church. The advantages of the love-feast were that at a simple meal of bread and water, the converts to the Christian way were able to encourage each other in fervent extemporary prayer and by recounting their testimonies of the goodness of God. Baker is disturbed that "despite the more careful ordering of our worship, in the matter of spontaneous spiritual utterance there has been nothing but decline—in extempore prayer, in prayer meetings, in bands and class meetings and society meetings, and, of course, in the love-feast."[119] But the wider interest of his book is his claim that this service is suitable for ecumenical gatherings for worship at the local level. It is most suitable for expressing unity amongst local congregations where intercommunion cannot yet be practised, as, for example, between Methodists and Anglicans. This was, in fact, the practice at Hilgay in Norfolk, in which the only two churches are Anglican and Methodist.

The Rev. G. I. F. Thomson, Rector of Hilgay, and the Rev. W. Morley Waite, the Methodist minister, shared with their congregations in a joint Agape in the Anglican church on Maundy Thursday evening, 1949. The broken bread was distributed by an Anglican church-warden and a Methodist local preacher. On Wednesday in Holy Week, 1951, another Agape was held at Hilgay, this time in the Methodist chapel, where the new Methodist minister was the Rev. John Lawson. A service was drawn up which was deeply ecumenical in the elements which composed it. The prayers were drawn from the Didache and the Agape of the Eastern Orthodox Churches, and part of the Litany was used to represent the Anglican and Roman traditions. The Methodist contribution

[119] P. 59.

consisted of the hymns for the love-feast, the extemporary prayer, and the offering of testimony. The common loaf was shared in the breaking of the bread and water was drunk, by representatives of the participating group only, from an old two-handled Methodist loving-cup.[120]

In some quarters it was welcomed as a pioneering break-through; in others it was criticized as glossing over the differences between the two denominations, and confusing the Agape and the Eucharist. Whatever may be thought of the ecumenical possibilities of this rite, one can sympathise with Baker for wishing to revive the deeply personal fellowship and charismatic character of worship in love-feasts or similar gatherings as a supplement to the dignified character of Eucharistic worship. The need for this was abundantly manifested in the House Church Communions provided by the present Provost of Southwark, Ernest Southcott, when Vicar of Halton. Moreover, it would be greatly to be lamented if the simplicity, spontaneity, and warmth of free prayer and the sharing of religious experience characteristic of the Puritan and Pietist traditions of devotion were to disappear as a result of the modern Liturgical Movement.[121] Indeed, the diminution of free prayer may in part be responsible for the attraction of some former Free Church members to the Pentecostalist Churches now mushrooming in growth.[122]

Even if the Methodist Church is to unite with the Church of England in the near future, it would be mistaken to suppose that all Methodist ministers would be entirely happy with the unrevised provisions of the Book of Common Prayer, for they are aware of the newer liturgical developments of our time. This is clearly the conviction of John C. Bowmer,[123] the historian of Methodist worship who offers an interesting series of conclusions relative to a revision of the Methodist rites. "There is," he writes, "no intrinsic merit in slavishly adhering to the forms of 1662."[124]

In any Methodist liturgical revision, he holds that much may be learned from *An Experimental Liturgy* and from the *Liturgy of*

---

[120] Details are given in the Appendix, pp. 74-78. Critiques are provided in *The Ecumenical Review* (Summer 1949); *The London Quarterly and Holborn Review* (April 1950); and *The Modern Churchman* (March 1950).

[121] Another Methodist minister aware of the importance of this side of the Methodist heritage is Gordon Wakefield, the author of *Puritan Devotion; its Place in the Development of Christian Piety*.

[122] See Horton Davies, *Christian Deviations*.

[123] *The Lord's Supper in Methodism, 1791-1960*, Chap. 6.

[124] *Ibid.*, p. 57.

the Church of South India,[125] especially in regard to the stress on the participation of all the people in the Eucharistic offering. He is also convinced of the rightness of the Church of Scotland's emphasis in its Communion Order on the manual Acts of Fraction and Libation, which he points out were rubrically required in *The Sunday Service of Methodists* until 1910. He argues for at least the placing of a chalice on the Communion Table, fearing that a germ-conscious people will not willingly give up its individual communion cups. In line with recent liturgical thinking he wishes to see a balance of Word and Sacrament in the Eucharistic celebrations, the provision of a free-standing Holy Table in new churches so that the Manual Acts can be performed in the sight of the people. He rightly wishes that more of the splendid Eucharistic hymns of John and Charles Wesley were revived. His conclusion is that the greatest need is for more instruction in the meaning of the Lord's Supper, and "it may be that this Sacrament which has been the greatest single dividing factor in Christendom shall yet become the means of achieving unity."[126]

Thus, there is no Methodist revision of worship to prove that the Methodist Church has, in fact, recovered the marks of a Reformed Churchmanship which is also sensitive to the Patristic heritage of the Universal Church as rediscovered in the Modern Liturgical Movement. But, as we have tried to show, the writings of Methodists in the related fields of theology and worship, and particularly the aims and interests of the Methodist Sacramental Fellowship, point strongly to a trend in the direction of an evangelical catholicism. And, after all, this would only be to tread in the footsteps of John Wesley himself.[127]

9. *The Summing Up*

In recounting the history of the three major trends—from charismatic spontaneity to Free Catholicism and on to the recovery of the Reformed heritage—the impression may have been given that the transition was a smooth one. That would, in fact, be a wholly erroneous impression. The claims of the proponents of each trend were often bitterly disputed by antagonists. The "School of Spontaneity" regarded the Free Catholics as traitors to Protestantism. The Free Catholics thought the latter no better than

[125] See T. S. Garrett, *Worship in the Church of South India.*
[126] Bowmer, *op.cit.*, p. 59.
[127] See the present author's *Worship and Theology in England, From Watts to Wesley and Maurice, 1690-1850*, Vol. III, Chap. VIII.

members of an Ethical Culture Society purveying, in Arnoldian phrase, "morality tinged with emotion." The Reformed Churchmen cried "a plague o' both your houses." Indeed, the antagonism between the advocates of a liberal and an orthodox theology, as between the enthusiasts for free or for liturgical prayer, continued throughout the period.[128]

The tension between the opposed viewpoints ran right through the denominations in the Free Churches, though it was most conspicuous in Congregationalism. The two opposing viewpoints were admirably embodied in the personalities of two well-matched historians of Congregationalism, Albert Peel (1887-1949), the founding editor of *The Congregational Quarterly*, and Bernard Lord Manning (1892-1941), Senior Tutor of Jesus College, Cambridge. In short, it might be described as a battle between the Quaker tendency and the Genevan emphasis on the interpretation of the Sacraments.

Peel's views were chiefly set forth in *Christian Freedom*, where he expressed his dismay that the Society of Friends might be excluded from the Ecumenical Movement because of its repudiation of the Christian Sacraments. His own doubts as to their Dominical institution were reinforced by Lietzmann's *Messe und Herrenmahl*. Peel felt that the Sacraments were obtruded by St. Paul into Christian practice on the analogy of the Gentile mystery religions of the first century. Furthermore, Peel held the view that symbols appeal only to primitive people and to immature minds. For him the natural development of the religion of the Spirit revealed by Christ was away from the use of outward symbols, and he conceived that the Spirit of Truth promised by Jesus demanded ethical obedience and not formal rite or external ceremonial.[129]

In complete contrast to Peel, Manning insisted that the Christian revelation was historically given and that it must be faithfully accepted rather than modernistically modified. The Sacraments, in his view, were given with the Gospel and the Church. He repudiated the notion that the Congregationalists were merely "an unspiritual reproduction of the Society of Friends."[130] In *Essays in Orthodox Dissent* he wrote ironically on this very point: "We have a doctrine of development which is the image of the Pope's.

---

[128] See Nathaniel Micklem, *The Box and the Puppets*.
[129] P. 81.
[130] *Essays in Orthodox Dissent*, p. 119.

Some of us are inclined to believe in a Spirit that takes the things of Christ to improve upon them. . . . We are disposed to set the rites of the Christian centuries beside those of the Old Testament, useful in their time, but now almost or quite outgrown. We look for an age of the Holy Ghost, when historic Christianity will become only a stage in our redemption. Some of us are almost emancipated from the Sacraments."[131] In such a war there could be no armistice.

These facts have been narrated, not to indicate that the battles between the schools are unending, but rather to show with what difficulties those who sought for improvements in the worship of the Free Churches had to contend. The present achievements are not the gains of the supine, but the rewards of courageous pioneers.

At this vantage of time, when so many liturgical gains have been consolidated, it is appropriate to consider their number and significance and how greatly they have changed the face of worship in the Free Churches.

In the first place, there is no longer any widespread prejudice against the use of set prayers, and there is in many places a welcome for liturgical forms, in the public worship of the Free Churches. The contrary was true at the beginning of this century. Sir John McClure was considered a radical when in 1919 he contended that so-called free prayer was more repetitive and didactic than the name implied; he even castigated it as "preaching with eyes shut."[132] B. M. Peake fourteen years later welcomed the Liturgical Movement because "Christianity is weary of individualism which weakens and divides; it is striving to escape the narrow bondage of the subjective into the freedom of the objective, the universal; from the limitations of the isolated individual to the fulness and strength of the great Community."[133]

It became increasingly recognized that liturgical forms had three advantages over free prayer. They made the preparation for worship less of a strain for the minister and they liberated the congregation from entire dependence upon his moods, feelings, and limitations. They provided a responsive element in devotions entirely suitable for denominations such as the Free Churches which had stressed throughout their history the importance of

[131] *Ibid.*, pp. 62-63.
[132] The Chairman's Address delivered in May 1919, and printed in *The Congregational Year Book* (1920), p. 56.
[133] "The Reform of Divine Worship," an article in *The Congregational Quarterly.*

the Reformed principle of the priesthood of all believers. Liturgical prayers also expressed the unity of the local congregation with the Great Church of the world and of the Christian centuries. Generally such prayers were accepted as a great relief after the prolix, diffuse, and repetitive extemporaneous effusions which congregations had often previously endured. The Free Catholics and the denominational service books have performed a useful service.

Today there is perhaps a serious danger that the revolt against spontaneity and free prayer has gone too far. For if the Free Churches were wholly to lose the gift of free prayer, as a supplement to liturgical prayer, they would have lost one of the gifts which they have to bring to the Universal Church. On the lips of a godly and affectionate pastor, who fully shares the hopes and fears of his flock, free prayer is, indeed, a means of grace. Its fervour, immediacy, and relevance to the needs of a local congregation complement the universal and objective qualities of a Liturgy. It is worth recalling the strength and conviction of the charismatic and Bible-centered worship of the seventeenth century Puritans and the eighteenth century Methodists which impressed thousands upon thousands with its unaffected sincerity and joy. Where it survives in village outposts it is still impressive today.[134]

The second gain for Free Church worship is the increasing use of the major festivals of the Christian Year: Advent to Pentecost, with daily services in Holy Week climaxed by the joy of Easter Day Communion. All the denominational service books make provision for these festivals celebrating the mighty acts of God consummated in Christ. Not only do they lead each year to disciplined meditation on the meaning of the Incarnation for the life of the Church and the world, but they have happily ousted many minor secular festivals that once pre-empted Christian interests in England and have become a commercial menace in the United States. In the high days of Puritanism there was a reaction against festivals, partly because the frequency of Saints' Days was an occasion for turning holy days into unholy holidays, but even more because for the Puritan each Sunday was in theory a Pentecost in which the Holy Spirit contemporized all the benefits of the Incarnation and the Atonement for God's covenanted people.

The present declension from Puritan practice in the Free Churches is to be justified as an accommodation to our human

---

[134] See *The Baptist Quarterly*, Vol. XIII (1949-1950), p. 105, for the account of a service conducted by laymen in a Methodist Chapel in a mining village in County Durham.

nature, which sees only in part and can therefore concentrate more readily on separate aspects of the multi-faceted meaning of the Incarnation. The beneficial discipline of Lent, once sneered at as a temporary term of committed discipleship in a year of comparative neglect, is now widely practised in the Free Churches. Holy Week, in particular, is a period when joint services between the local Free Churches are commonly held. Such festival occasions are to be welcomed because they are based upon that holy history which gives theological structure to the New Testament and the earliest creeds, and they prove to be a strengthening of the Christian faith and of spiritual life.

While the recitation of a creed in the Free Churches is not widespread at Sunday services, except in Communion Services in Presbyterian and Methodist churches, there is a much more positive attitude to creeds as summaries of belief, rather than as doctrinal tests. It is part of the decided return to theological orthodoxy in British theology. It is significant that the eminent Baptist Biblical scholar, H. Wheeler Robinson, considered as early as 1924 that the Independent wing of the Free Churches had been unwise in parading its independence of creeds. He was a little tired of ministers quoting Tennyson's half truth:

> There lives more faith in honest doubt,
> Believe me, than in half the creeds.

He preferred his own revised version:

> There lives more faith in honest creeds,
> Believe me, than in half the doubt.[135]

Nathaniel Micklem was not in the least singular in using the Apostles' Creed as a framework for his doctrinal introduction to Christianity in *The Creed of a Christian*, and the proof of the growing orthodoxy in belief of the Free Churches was signally demonstrated by Archbishop William Temple's invitation to Micklem to write a Lenten volume, *The Doctrine of our Redemption*. Any residual doubts about the wisdom of using the creeds in public worship spring from a conviction that the listing of historical and propositional statements about the nature of God is not a very lyrical activity. Indeed, as the perceptive Bernard Manning wrote: "Hymns are for us Dissenters what the Liturgy is for the Anglican. They are the framework, the setting, the

135 *The Baptist Quarterly*, Vol. II (1924-1925), p. 348.

conventional, the traditional part of divine service as we use it. They are, to adopt the language of the liturgiologists, the Dissenting Use. . . . We mark times and seasons, celebrate festivals, express experiences, and expound doctrines by hymns."[136] For this reason Congregationalists and Baptists have historically preferred to use covenants and hymns as substitutes for creeds, for they engage the heart and will in the joyful obedience of faith. But, as a basis for catechetical instruction and as warnings against recurrent heresies, the creeds fulfil a useful purpose. Their use in public worship, however, is as yet too infrequent, irregular, or unenthusiastic to be considered a major achievement.

The third positive gain in Free Church worship is a greatly enhanced appreciation of the Gospel Sacraments of Baptism and the Lord's Supper. It was not always thus. Many ministers in the Free Churches earlier in the century regarded the Sacraments as optional visual aids to preaching, or asserted with C. Ernest Watson that "our divine Master meant life to be sacramental in its common ways and not merely on set or formal occasions."[137] The neglect of infant Baptism was even more common, for as Kenneth Parry observed in 1933: "there are probably men who administer the Lord's Supper amongst us who have never been baptized. And there are certainly more than a few in the membership of our churches who were not baptized as children and have not been baptized as adults."[138] Even among the Baptists there was laxity in the requirement of Believers' Baptism for entrance to membership and Communion, for Principal A. C. Underwood of that denomination complained that it was occasionally administered "at a weeknight service, as though it needed to be tucked away in a corner."[139]

This is all very much *past* history for the present generation of Free Churchmen, and the new apprehension of the value of the Sacraments was gained by such pioneers as P. T. Forsyth. Today the Sacrament of the Lord's Supper is rarely an appendix to the preaching service for the pious few, administered in a perfunctory manner. It is now commonly regarded as the supreme privilege of church members to be guests at Christ's Holy Table and to partici-

[136] *The Hymns of Wesley and Watts*, pp. 133, 135.
[137] Article: "The Nature of the Church," in *The Congregational Quarterly*, Vol. VIII, No. 3 (July 1930), p. 344.
[138] Article, "Baptism: Congregational Theory and Practice," *The Congregational Quarterly*, Vol. XI, No. 4 (October 1933), p. 408.
[139] J. H. Rushbrooke, ed., *The Faith of the Baptists*, p. 14.

pate in the Lord's Supper. Every Free Church denomination, as we have seen, has a comprehensive and genuinely ecumenical order for Holy Communion in its official service-book, following the structure and intention of the historic liturgies of Christendom, emphasizing the meaning of this Sacrament as, at once, Sacrifice, Memorial, Communion, Thanksgiving, and anticipation of the eternal Messianic Banquet. Each rite has its great Prayer of Consecration or Blessing, complete with *Sursum corda*, *Sanctus*, *anamnesis*, *epiklesis* and oblation, together with a fitting emphasis on the great symbolic acts of Fraction and Libation. Such unity with the Universal Church of Christ in the chief Sacrament would have been unthinkable, even for the most sanguine of prophets, only fifty years ago. It is the greatest single achievement of the combined Liturgical and Ecumenical Movements.

Gone, too, is the old Memorialism which observed Communion as the memory of a crucified martyr and as primarily the badge of Christian fellowship. On all sides the Lord's Supper is interpreted as a communicating (and also, for Methodists, a converting) ordinance, that conveys to faith the blessedness of forgiveness and the assurance of eternal life. For many it is also the means of our incorporation into the mystical Body of Christ. For some its central act of divine blessing of human labour on the gifts of God prior to equal sharing is the anticipation of and impetus to a juster and more compassionate social order in the world community. For almost all it is a chief means of grace and its more frequent and more reverent celebration is greatly appreciated.

The former nominalism of the administration of Infant and Believers' Baptism has also largely disappeared, as worthier rites of initiation have been prepared in the official Service books of the Free Churches. This is recognized by all to be a Sacrament of the Church and therefore to be administered in the presence of the assembled Christian community. A further implication is that the parents (in the case of Infant Baptism) or believers (in the case of Adult Baptism) are required to give solemn affirmations of their faith and firm adherence to the Church, and this is, in fact, almost the universal practice.

The fourth gain is the great improvement in the solemnity of Ordination Services. We have seen that the Free Churches, with the exception of the Presbyterians, went through a period of anti-sacerdotal amateurishness,[140] when the Ordination of Ministers

---

140 It was typified by the rejection of dignity in dress as well as ceremonial, as

was rather perfunctorily treated. As an imitation of Quaker pan-sacramentalism weakened the appreciation of the historic Sacraments, so a kind of pan-vocationalism (when it was the fashion to "set apart" social workers to their office in special services) weakened the honour in which the historic ministry was held. Nowadays the ministry is held to be a gift of the ascended Lord to his Church. Consequently, as recent denominational service books show, the rite of Ordination is worthily administered with the laying-on of hands and the invocation of the Holy Spirit. The minister-elect is required to make a statement of faith and to offer solemn promises that he will be diligent in preaching God's Word, administering the Sacraments, and shepherding the flock. Usually there is a sermon in which minister and people are reminded of their responsibilities under God. These can be most moving and effectual in their combination of the Gospel's judgment and consolation.

What depth such a service can plumb is illustrated in Bernard Manning's ordination charge, which suffers greatly in condensation. He is speaking to the congregation of the hardships of the ministry. Then, with holy indignation rising, Manning reaches his tremendous climax, as sword-thrust follows sword-thrust into degenerate consciences:

"But what no young man who has put his whole life on the altar can expect—for until he has experienced it for he can not conceive it—is the coldness, the callousness, and the deadness of those to whom he looks for help, for support both in the work of the Church and in the daily quickening of his own spirit. The gates of hell, the whole world lying in the arms of the evil one, this will not daunt him; but it is when he sees the abomination of desolation standing where it ought not—indifference, worldliness, heartlessness in you the Body of Christ, it is then that the cold fear paralyses his soul, the fear that the whole business is a mockery and the shadow of a name. If this be Christ's Body, it is a dead body, and Christ is dead. You are still in your sins; then He is not risen. The faith is vain; and the man who has renounced all else to preach it is of all men most pitiable. Having preached to others

---

ministers preached in lounge suits (and occasionally flamboyant ties) to express the priesthood of all believers. One recalls the cartoon of Dr. R. F. Horton, distinguished minister of Lyndhurst Road Congregational Church, Hampstead, revealing him in complete nudity, from which the female members of his congregation shielded their eyes, while Horton asserted, "I will wear no clothes to distinguish myself from my brethren." A very considerable number of Free Church ministers wear a clerical collar and, when conducting worship, cassock, Genevan gown and bands.

he feels himself a castaway. In such an hour the Saviour can still save His servant, but do you envy the Church that plunges a man into that pit?"[141]

A fifth gain in Free Church worship is a better balance between Word and Sacrament. It is increasingly realized that the ideal towards which to work is a conjoint celebration of the Word and Sacrament each Sunday as in the Primitive Church. Even if this is a long way from attainment, fortnightly services of the Word and Sacrament are fairly common, especially in the metropolitan area. It is now recognized in the denominational service books that the weekly service on Sunday mornings should preserve the structure of the Liturgy, while stopping short of consecration and communion, relating it clearly to the fuller service of Word *and Sacrament* which is its climax and completion.

Of almost equal significance is the gradual realization that preaching and the celebration of the Sacrament reinforce each other powerfully. The values of a Sacramental Liturgy are its universality, its historicity, and its objectivity. These, apart from the proclamation of the Word, may seem antiquarian, generalized, abstract, and remote. Preaching, however, provides the necessary supplementation of particularity, contemporaneity, and existential subjectivity. Unrelated to Liturgy and Sacrament, preaching loses its effectiveness by the unbalanced exaggeration of its qualities. The Liturgy mediates the Gospel which preaching contemporizes.

In addition to these gains achieved during the present century, the Free Churches have not lost (with the possible exception of the charismatic factor now too much depreciated) their own distinctive emphases in worship. For them the authority of the Gospel[142] was and remains primary, to which all worship is the grateful response: the advent of a less philosophical and more Biblical theology in the Roman Catholic and Anglican Churches means only that others share it. Nor have the Free Churches lost the strong moral note which we found alike in Forsyth and Oman, their two chief theologians in this period. It was strongly asserted in the theology of the social gospel. It rings through the intercessory prayers, the offertory prayers, and the hymns of consecration. This was the reason why the footwashing episode from the Fourth Gospel (John 13:3-17) was included as a Post-Com-

---

[141] *A Layman in the Ministry*, pp. 156-57.
[142] P. T. Forsyth in the *Soul of Prayer*, p. 120, wrote: "And prayer in Christ's name is prayer inspired by His first interest—the Gospel."

munion lesson in the *Manual for Ministers*. Indeed, the conception of dedication is so all-pervasive that in the most recent Congregational service book there is even provision made for "The Dedication of a Bible"![143]

The authentic Nonconformist note was recently sounded by Principal John Marsh in his address as Chairman of the Congregational Union in 1963. He protested against making church life a religious ghetto: "We should think of the Church offering her worship to God most characteristically in all the life of the world, and of the sacramental, liturgical life we are privileged to share on Sundays as the means by which God has provided for our continual renewal in the attempt to be an obedient people of God in the world."[144] The concept of the Christian life as a covenant between God and His people is still effective in the Free Church tradition and its worship. The Methodists have, of course, an annual Covenant Service, and many Congregational churches and some Baptist churches recite the covenant pledges as new members are received into the full communion of the church, or at the anniversary services celebrating the foundations of their local congregations. Perhaps it is the sense of the local covenanted community which is most significantly missing in a Liturgy which rightly affirms the solidarity of Christians with the Church militant upon earth and triumphant in heaven. And it is this sense of a closely knit and integrated company of Christ which has been characteristic of the warmth of Free Church worship. This, too, must be even more carefully preserved when a more liturgical form of worship is adopted.

It may seem that a more optimistic picture of Free Church worship has been painted than the situation warrants. It is not claimed that congregations are large, or that the preaching is spell-binding, or that all ministers are liturgical enthusiasts. But it is claimed that amid the acute difficulties of preserving the Christian faith in a secular age (and the greater problems of communicating it to the outsider), the worship of the Free Churches today is a more faithful reflection of its heritage in Christ's Gospel than it has been at any time during this century, and that it is no longer the worship of sects but of part of the

[143] *A Book of Services and Prayers*, p. 111. This book is a declension from *A Book of Public Worship*, but its copious compilation of classical prayers, its provision of material for the Christian Year, and its comprehensive Eucharistic orders are proof of the immense liturgical advance since *Manual for Ministers*, p. 12.

[144] Published as *Theme with Variations* (1963).

Holy Catholic and Apostolic Church, as its ecumenical-type services of Word and Sacrament demonstrate.

At the same time, it would be dishonest not to indicate a few areas of remaining dissatisfaction. While all the denominational service books in their prefaces claim that they wish to supplement and not to supplant free prayer and the charismatic element in worship, their effect has been the contrary of their avowed intention. Many observers cannot but be disturbed that the gifts of free prayer and the capacity for silent meditation on God's Word seem to be dying out. The cultivation of these is essential if the practices of private prayer and family prayers are to be revived, and without these the renewal of Sunday worship will only be a shadow of what it might be. Along with this loss—so central to the Puritan and Pietist traditions of the Free Churches—is the increasing impersonality and lack of a sense of fellowship as God's covenanted people which the exclusive use of liturgical forms can produce. Finally, for churches which have given the laity so large a share in their government, there is an urgent need to use the gifted laity more prominently in sharing the leadership of worship with the ministry, and in giving them more frequent opportunity to instruct the congregation in the meaning of a Christian's calling in the world. Liturgical worship is intended to give the people a larger part in worship and the priesthood of all believers is negatived by the dominance of a single ministerial voice in lections, prayers, and sermon.

The most serious lack in the Free Church tradition, however, is of a daily discipline of corporate worship such as the Book of Common Prayer provides. It appears to be the single major factor which has caused former Free Church ministers to join the Church of England for that daily continuity in worship which their own denominations lacked.[145] The attempts by the Iona Community in Presbyterianism, the Church Order Group in Congregationalism, and the Methodist Sacramental Fellowship to set up a daily rule of life are witnesses to this profound need and to the temporary way in which it is being met.

All these questions about Free Church worship today are, however, more than counterbalanced by the very important advances made towards a worship that is deeply reverent, sacramentally rich, ecumenically comprehensive, and theologically faithful.

---

[145] See Dewi Morgan, ed., *They became Anglicans*, and Martin Thornton, *English Spirituality*, p. 4.

CHAPTER XI

THE WORSHIP OF THE SOCIETY OF FRIENDS

IF FREE CHURCH worship owes most to Calvin and Wesley, it has also, especially in the current century, acknowledged the attraction of Fox and his followers. The fascination of the worship of the Quakers is that it represents the most radical type of free corporate prayer and expresses the strongest protest against the restrictions of a liturgy and of sacerdotalism. It is a strenuous attempt to recover the important charismatic element in the worship of the apostolic Church.[1] It is a living commentary on the Johannine text "The Spirit bloweth where it listeth" and on the Pauline words "Likewise the Spirit also helpeth our infirmities, for we know not what we should pray for as we ought, but the Spirit maketh intercession for us." It is also a witness to the Divine initiative and prevenience in all religious experience and to the need for an expectant and prepared spirit to receive the intimations of the Holy Spirit.

In its quest for corporate mysticism it daringly claims to unite what has usually been separated in history. The mystic has been traditionally an isolated soul, representing the flight of the alone to the Alone, but Quaker mysticism aims to be a squadron in flight. Yet the Quaker mystics are also prophetic, as their witness against slavery and war amply demonstrates, so their corporate mysticism is also intra-mundane. Consequently, to maintain the metaphor, the squadron in flight touches down on the solid concrete of the runway.

Quaker worship has a peculiar relevance to twentieth century living conditions. Its emphasis on silence and meditation is most appropriate for what Aldous Huxley has called "the Age of Noise." At no other time in history does man seem to have been so assaulted by noise. The screaming of jet-engines in the skies, the blare of motor horns and the screeching of skidding tires in the streets, the ringing of the telephone in the office or home, and the competitive claims of radio, television, and stereophonic recording apparatus, demand silence for the preservation of sanity. The present

[1] Friedrich Heiler, *Prayer, A Study in the History and Psychology of Religion*, p. 308.

century has also seen the most persuasive statements of the Quaker viewpoint in a distinguished series of annual Swarthmore Lectures, subsequently published, and these have shown the significance of the predominantly silent Quaker Meetings as the dynamos of the Quaker testimony.

In addition, the contemporary philosophical movement of linguistic analysis, deriving from Wittgenstein, finds a parallel in the Quaker recognition of the inadequacy of our conventional verbal symbols to mediate the individual apprehension of the claim of God on the soul or the experience of the "inner light."[2] Moreover, in an expanding universe in which the writ of scientific law runs more extensively, contemplation is inevitably preferred to petitionary prayer, so that it is not surprising that distinguished scientists like Sir Arthur Eddington or Dr. Kathleen Lonsdale have found the worship of the Friends congenial. The Quakers claim, as will be seen, a further relevance for their worship in the present century, namely, that silent corporate meditation is the only type of prayer that will unite representatives of different religious faiths in their search for spiritual unity. Finally, both Anglicans and Free Churchmen increasingly allow a place for silent prayer in their forms of worship and thus pay a tribute to the importance of the Quaker concept of worship in the ecumenical movement.

1. The Modern Quaker Renaissance

Since George Fox's foundation of the Society of Friends in the Commonwealth of England in the seventeenth century, there have been many vagaries in its history and even in its worship. At the end of the seventeenth century and continuing through the eighteenth century the mystical trend was exaggerated to the extent of Quietism, and the prophetic witness was eliminated. In this situation passivity and an individualistic introversion were glorified. The nineteenth century brought about a dramatic reversal as Quakerism caught fire from the Evangelical Revival, and the mysticism was almost lost (not to mention the silence of meetings) in a passionate advocacy of preaching. The modern renascence of Quakerism dates from the latter part of the nineteenth century, and is chiefly attributable to the influence of two activistic Quakers who combined the mystical and prophetic strains of original

---

[2] Douglas V. Steere's *Where Words Come From*, a Swarthmore Lecture, is a brilliant and fascinating study of the art of listening to God and man at many levels.

Quakerism as in George Fox and his followers. These were Caroline Stephen, the gracious and cultured sister of Sir Leslie Stephen, and John Wilhelm Rowntree. The former was a convinced Friend, the latter a birthright Friend. Caroline Stephen was primarily the mystic and John Wilhelm Rowntree was primarily the prophet.

As an Anglican in an age of acute doubt, Caroline Stephen found it difficult to worship according to the Book of Common Prayer because the creeds and the traditional theology which that formulary expresses raised questions that reason stifled. The silent worship of the Society of Friends was the healing refuge that she needed: "What I felt I wanted in a place of worship was a refuge, or at least the opening of a doorway towards the refuge, from doubts and controversies; not a fresh encounter with them. Yet it seems to me impossible that anyone harassed by the conflicting views of truth, with which just now the air is thick, should be able to forget controversy while listening to such language as that of the Book of Common Prayer. It seems to me that nothing but silence can heal the wounds made by disputations in the region of the unseen."[3]

Its primary attraction lay "in the fact that it pledged me to nothing and left me altogether undisturbed to seek for help in my own way," but in time she came to recognize that silent worship had the additional benefit of a "strange subduing and softening effect upon my mind."[4] This is what Quakers commonly refer to as "tendering." In due time Caroline Stephen became the foremost interpreter in England of the Friends' way of worship and she had a lasting influence on several generations of Quaker university undergraduates in Cambridge while she was a member of the Meeting there.[5] She gladly testified that "Friends' Meetings have indeed been to me the greatest of outward helps to a fuller and fuller entrance into the Spirit from which they have sprung; the place of the most soul-subduing, faith-restoring, strengthening and peaceful communion, in feeding on the bread of life, that I have ever known."[6] Her influence was cast against any tendency to depreciate the royal priesthood of all believers by the possible introduction of a paid professional ministry on American Quaker lines.[7] She restored to the Quakers a conviction of the rightness of their seventeenth century heritage in a time of acute religious crisis.

---

[3] *Quaker Strongholds*, pp. 44-45.   [4] *Ibid.*
[5] Rufus M. Jones, *The Later Periods of Quakerism*, Vol. II, p. 969.
[6] *Quaker Strongholds*, p. 3.   [7] *Ibid.*, p. 110.

Her work was fully complemented by John Wilhelm Rowntree,[8] who, though a mystic, was less passive in his approach than she. He applauded Fox for having the courage to be logical, since many "other churches profess belief in inward guidance, but they dare not found their constitution on this belief."[9] The heritage of Quietism, forbidding any intellectual or spiritual preparation for worship, was rudely criticized by Rowntree. He was surely behind the conclusion of the Yearly Meeting on Ministry and Oversight which insisted: "True worship is intensely active. It consists in offering ourselves to God—body, mind, and soul—for the doing of His will."[10] He recommended that the children of Friends should be trained in Quaker schools and he was influential in the foundation of Woodbrooke Settlement in 1903 as a study centre for the social questions of the day. For him the preparation of mind and heart for Quaker worship and witness demanded a deep study of the Bible and of psychology.[11] The positive Christian basis of his message is seen in the peroration of his speech at a national Quaker Conference held in Manchester in 1895, when he asked, "Is there indifference to the Higher Life?" and answered:

"Then, O Christ, convince us by thy Spirit, thrill us with Thy Divine passion, drown our selfishness in Thy invading love, lay on us the burden of the world's suffering, drive us forth with the apostolic fervour of the early Church! So only can our message be delivered—'Speak to the children of Israel that they go forward.' "[12]

If Caroline Stephen emphasized the vertical dimension, then the chief importance of John Wilhelm Rowntree was that he linked it with the horizontal dimension of social service and thus prepared the way for the honourable witness of reconciliation and rehabilitation for which the twentieth century Quakers are renowned.

Since his time only one significant change has taken place in the arrangement of Quaker worship. Until 1924 those Friends who had a special gift in vocal ministry were recognized as "Ministers" and recorded as such in the annals of the Society. After this time no such distinction was recorded, and thus expression was given to the desire that the responsibility for vocal min-

8 See Evelyn Underhill's *The Mystics of the Church*, Chap. XIII, for a sympathetic study of Rowntree.
9 *Essays and Addresses*, p. 101.
10 *Worship and Ministry* (1899), the Epistle of the Yearly Meeting.
11 Gladys Wilson, *Quaker Worship*, pp. 89-90.
12 Rufus M. Jones, *op.cit.*, Vol. II, p. 975.

istry should be more widely shared among Friends. As a result, "more Friends do take part in vocal ministry now than formerly; but it has meant that most of their contributions are shorter than those of the earlier 'Ministers,' and that there is rarely any ministry in Meetings today which could accurately be described as preaching and little that could be called exposition."[13]

In general, three successive trends within twentieth century Quakerism may be noted, and each had its parallel in the theological movements of these years. The renaissance of Quakerism was correlated with the re-affirmation of mysticism in the first two decades of this century in the studies of Inge, Evelyn Underhill, and von Hügel. This was also the era of the "new Theology" or the "social Gospel" in which the social witness of the Friends was strengthened, especially during the years of the First World War. Finally, while it cannot be said that the Society, as a whole, has devoted itself to the study of Biblical theology or even to the Ecumenical Movement, it is significant that some of its contemporary exponents have noted these very needs.[14]

2. The Advantages of Corporate Silent Worship

From the days of Fox onward the Society of Friends has claimed that the chief advantage of its worship is that stress on inwardness and sincerity, instead of outward profession, which guards against hypocrisy in the Christian life. The claim is made in an unusually belligerent manner by John W. Graham, chiefly by criticizing the "professional prayers" of priests or clergy: "This vast and fruitful error comes from the original mistake in not realising that Prayer is an act of the Inward Man, something different from talking on demand or reading from a prayer book." He continues: "How real prayer can be produced on demand from a platform, or at a fixed point in a service I have never understood. All these devices, made for the help of human weaknesses, increase that weakness. Who can walk with permanent crutches?"[15] Harold Loukes avers that "there is still a need to be reminded that God is not limited by His own means. It is always possible to enjoy a ritual for the wrong reasons and not know one has missed the secret: to be moved by beauty and miss the beauty of holiness, to feed on language and miss the message. But if a man sits in silence with other worshippers, and nothing happens, he knows

[13] Gladys Wilson, op.cit., p. 89.
[14] Notably Douglas V. Steere, Thomas F. Green, and Gladys Wilson.
[15] The Quaker Ministry, p. 23.

that nothing has happened."[16] Thus, whether stated pugnaciously or pacifically, Quaker worship is first of all a protest against a worship of the lips without the life, a plea for uncoerced spontaneity in the response to the living God in prayer. But in this it does not differ radically from the Anabaptists, the Separatists, or the Puritans, who made the same plea for a sincere Spirit-led worship.

It is in the *corporate* practice of a predominantly silent worship that the distinctive characteristic of Quaker worship is found, and the word "corporate" has to be stressed so that this silent worship may be distinguished from the silence of Trappist monks or of Carthusians, each in his own cell. A constant claim is that this is productive of great serenity of soul, of an inward and healing calm of mind. The fact that this has been partly recognized to be true by many non-Quaker Christians must explain the great popularity among English-speaking Protestant congregations of Whittier's great hymn, "Dear Lord and Father of Mankind," with its closing verses:

> Drop Thy still dews of quietness,
> Till all our strivings cease:
> Take from our souls the strain and stress,
> And let our ordered lives confess
> The beauty of Thy peace.

> Breathe through the pulses of desire
> Thy coolness and Thy balm;
> Let sense be dumb, its heats expire:
> Speak through the earthquake, wind, and fire,
> O still small voice of calm.

Quakers believe that in their worship they find "the silence of eternity interpreted by love."[17]

That historian of modern spirituality and Quaker philosopher, Rufus M. Jones, declares that it is in the quiet that faith grows and faith produces serenity: "Religious faith when it takes us back to the true source of power removes from the mind the peril of bewildering unsettlement. It turns water to wine. It brings prodigals home. It turns sunsets to sunrises. It makes the impossible become possible. The master secret of life is the attainment of the

---

[16] *Friends Face Reality*, p. 119.
[17] Two lines from the second verse of the same hymn.

power of serenity in the midst of stress and action and adventure."[18] Certainly it does not strain the reason to believe that there is too much didacticism, and too many words, possibly too many dogmatic certainties in traditional Catholic and Protestant worship, whereas in corporate silent worship there is the intense relief of moving along at one's own speed of meditation, with the occasional incitation of the spoken ministry.

Another value claimed for corporate silent prayer is that the experience is subtly unitive, for "the group becomes fused into an organic whole through the empowering and enlightening action of the Spirit."[19] So great is this unitive power that Douglas Steere can report: "I have seen this silent worship level a group in which there was an ugly barrier separating two of its members, and I have seen it bring them to ask for forgiveness. I have seen it prepare members in a group to enter into holy obedience against their surface wills on matters in which the whole future course of their lives was at stake."[20] T. Edmund Harvey claims that corporate silent prayer is the most appropriate expression of the priesthood of all believers, whereas in the Free Church tradition the prayer of the minister is the expression of the aspiration of a single representative individual. The advantage of silent worship is that of being "the expression of the needs and longing of one who by a priestly act of the spirit puts himself alongside of his fellow-worshippers, enters in some measure into their spiritual condition, and, feeling their need as his own, prays not only for but with them, as one of them, and borne along by the spirit of prayer, raises with them the hands of a trusting child towards the unseen Father, in whose Presence all together stand."[21]

Several writers have expressed the conviction that silent prayer in a Quaker Meeting has a strongly egalitarian character.[22] No one has caught the distinctive atmosphere more vividly than Christopher Isherwood, the novelist and poet, in a recent work where he contrasts the febrile and frantic air of Hollywood with the recuperative quiet of a Philadelphia Quaker Meeting: "Never-

[18] Chap. 7, "Re-thinking Quaker Principles," in Herrymon Maurer, ed., *The Pendle Hill Reader*, p. 180.

[19] P. Edwall, E. Hayman, and W. D. Maxwell, eds., *Ways of Worship, The Report of a Theological Commission on Faith and Order*, p. 171, citation from the Committee on Christian Relationships of the Religious Society of Friends of Great Britain.

[20] *Prayer and Worship*, pp. 83-84.

[21] *Silence and Worship, A Study in Quaker Experience*, p. 51.

[22] Notably John Sykes, *The Quakers*, p. 261 and Howard H. Brinton, *Friends for 300 Years*, Chap. iv.

theless, the Silence, in its odd way, was coming to life. Was steadily filling up the bare white room, like water rising in a tank. Every one of us contributed to it, simply by being present. Togetherness grew and tightly enclosed us until it seemed that we must all be breathing in unison and keeping time with our heart-beats. It was massively alive and somehow unimaginably ancient, like the togetherness of Man in the primeval caves."[23]

As contrasted with the closed character of liturgical worship, the Quakers claim that their type of worship has a germinative quality—an openness to new possibilities of truth and insight. This group mysticism means, according to Howard H. Brinton, that the worshippers are like the spokes of a wheel, for the closer they come to the centre of all Life the nearer they are to each other, and in this unity they experience "the germinating silence of a Quaker Meeting sensitive to the emergence of new life and thought."[24]

A final claim made for Quaker worship is that by its avoidance of the aesthetic distractions of ceremonial and of the dulling repetitiveness of ritual, it leads to a realistic concern for the world. There is thus no temptation, it is asserted, to make worship an escape-hatch from social responsibility. This group-centred, life-affirming worship, built upon the interdependence of men recognizing their creaturehood, means that for Quakers "their customary face is towards the world" and that "their experience of Meeting sends them in search of it."[25]

These, then, are the values claimed for a silent group mysticism: an inwardness that avoids hypocrisy, the creation of serenity and recollectedness, an unitive egalitarianism that truly expresses the priesthood of all believers, an openness to the signals of new truth, and a stimulus to social service.

3. The Stages of Quaker Worship

Since the essential character of Quaker worship is that, unlike liturgical worship, it is utterly unpredictable, being dependent upon the sovereign freedom of the direction of the Holy Spirit, it is extraordinarily difficult to describe. The pattern of worship in one Meeting may be entirely different from that of another. The proportions of silence and vocal worship in any Meeting vary greatly.

[23] *The World in the Evening* (New York, Random House, 1954), p. 51.
[24] *Creative Worship*, p. 66.
[25] John Sykes, *The Quakers*, p. 49.

Nonetheless, many leading Quaker writers have attempted to show that it is appropriate to think of various stages or developments taking place in a session of Quaker worship, though, naturally enough, there are diversities in the description. Harold Loukes describes the Quaker Meeting in terms of a deepening of the vertical relationship with God and a deepening of the horizontal relationships between the worshippers.[26] John Sykes defines the separate stages as: settling down, meditative commitment, creativity, "centring down," and a climax of total stillness.[27] Both these accounts are, however, a little vague in their use of terms. Nonetheless, two of the stages they describe are familiar to all students of the Catholic contemplatives, for the "settling down" or concentrating of the attention is the first stage of meditation, and the "centring down" of the self from surface concerns to identity with the Divine will are essential preliminaries for the practice of mystical prayer.[28]

More precise are the analyses of Douglas Steere and Thomas F. Green, because they make fuller use of the familiar categories of traditional Catholic and Protestant prayer. Steere defines the stages as: Preparation, Confession, Adoration, Intercession, and Dedication.[29] Green uses the same categories but in a significantly different order: Adoration, Confession, Dedication, Thanksgiving, Intercession, and a return to Adoration. Green believes that Quaker worship should follow the pattern of the Lord's Prayer which begins and ends on the note of adoration. "It should begin with adoration—for the religious life is a response to a vision of greatness, not a grim drive towards moral virtues."[30]

Such definiteness in elaborating the stages of Quaker devotion may be anathema to other Quakers who might feel that this was to restrict the freedom of worship more subtly than a liturgy can. But it is significant that both Steere and Green are educators, rightly aware of the need of clarity and method in the instruction of the young. Professor Steere has a wide and deep knowledge of the history of Catholic and Protestant spirituality, and is actively engaged in ecumenical theological encounter. Green, the headmaster of Bootham, a distinguished Quaker public school in York, is a former Anglican. "I am deeply grateful," he has written, "for the religious training I received as a boy up to the age of twelve

[26] *Friends Face Reality*, pp. 121-24. [27] *The Quakers*, pp. 21-33.
[28] Evelyn Underhill, *Worship*, p. 310.
[29] *Where Words Come From*, p. 39. [30] *Preparation for Worship*, p. 17.

in a village school maintained by the Anglican Church. We learned by heart many psalms, passages from the prophets, the Gospels and the Epistles, and many of the prayers which voice in matchless language the needs of every man. Remembered passages, some, alas, fragmentary, are of inestimable value to me in our silent worship."[31] While Quaker worship has values to contribute to liturgical worship, it seems to be increasingly realized by Quaker leaders that traditional worship has an important theological structure to provide for corporate silent worship. Without an understanding of the discipline of mental prayer and of the Biblical revelation to which every type of *Christian* worship is a response, silent Quaker Meetings may degenerate into "nothing more than an unspoken exercise in the psychological game of free association—a succession of daydreams with a religious flavour."[32]

4. Quaker Self-Evaluation

It is a healthy sign in the Religious Society of Friends that thoughtful Quakers are far less defensive about their distinctive type of worship than they used to be, and are willing to recognize that it is open to abuse and in need of reformation.

Friends are no longer content to trust to the unprepared inspiration of spontaneity. The glorification of an impromptu ministry was, according to Rufus Jones, an encouragement of "passivity, not to say mental laziness and emptiness."[33] But what form should that preparation take? Thomas Green believes that the preparation should take a two-fold form—the practice of the techniques of mental prayer and the devotional study of the Bible. He warns that the emancipation of the Quakers from the Bible will lead to an inevitable and steady deterioration in the quality of worship, for "the Quaker, thrown upon his own resources, needs more than anyone a mind well stored with the passages of the Bible."[34] Moreover, he seems to question the wisdom of the traditional Quaker disregard of theological studies.[35] Douglas Steere pleads for a worship and ministry of members who "read and inwardly digest the Bible" and who are informed and "drawn down into the great Christian themes of the love, the joy, and the greatness of God; of suffering, sin, redemption, atonement and resurrection."[36] He even suggests that some of the younger Friends of today have been

---

[31] *Ibid.*, p. 18.   [32] *Ibid.*, p. 16.
[33] *The Later Periods of Quakerism*, Vol. II, p. 993.
[34] *Preparation for Worship*, p. 18.   [35] *Ibid.*, p. 5.
[36] *Where Words Come From*, pp. 64-65.

drawn into the Society by a passionate theological interest.

There is also an increasing recognition that the technique of silent, expectant worship is extraordinarily difficult to teach to children or to those familiar with the traditional Christian types of corporate prayer. T. Edmund Harvey admits that "it might be held that it would be as unreasonable to teach a child to swim by throwing him into a deep pool of water as to plunge him unprepared into a Quaker Meeting."[37] He further acknowledges that there is the need for an intermediate stage, which, in some cases, has led to the formation of special children's Meetings, in which the children are guided in their meditations and join in hymns. Thomas Hodgkin, in the same vein, recognizes that Quaker worship is "more fitted for those who have made some advance in the Christian life, than for those who are on the threshold," that it needs to be discreetly introduced and that it is not equally well suited to all mental types.[38] Thomas Green frankly admits the strain imposed on those who first attend a Quaker Meeting: "I well remember the first occasion I attended Meeting. After a quarter of an hour or so I felt intense fatigue of mind and body, and the remaining period was a prolonged agony of waiting. . . . Even now, after years of practice, I frequently find my powers of worshipping joyously are exhausted long before the prescribed period of an hour is over." He concludes with the wry observation: "At what varying speeds do the hands of our Meeting House clocks move!"[39]

The most serious criticisms of Quaker worship have yet to be advanced. Both Eric Hayman (who has since left the Society of Friends) and Thomas Green recognize that the absence of creeds, liturgies, sacraments, and of the keeping of the Christian Year, combined with Quakerism's historic indifference to theology, make it peculiarly susceptible to the *Zeitgeist*. The result is that there is a perpetual danger of the ethical dominating the religious motivation and of humanism supplanting devotion to God. Hayman sees this danger arising peculiarly in connection with the appeal that Quakerism makes in the modern world to a constituency wider than the bounds of the Christian Church, and in its becoming a kind of quiet parliament of all the religions.[40] He warns: "It seems that the discovery of a power of response in the human spirit, the realisation

37 *Silence and Worship*, pp. 56-57.
38 *The Fellowship of Silence*, p. 87.
39 *Preparation for Worship*, p. 12.
40 *Worship and the Common Life*, pp. 77-78.

of a window opening from the soul to eternity, leads some people irresistibly to the conclusion that a power discovered is a power possessed, and then that a power possessed is a power controlled and mastered by the possessor and even deriving from him."[41] Green recognizes the danger, but attributes its prevalence rather to the recovery in 1914 of the historic Quaker testimony to peace and reconciliation. Since that time Friends have been concerned with the unemployed in Britain, refugees from Nazi and Communist oppression, and famine-stricken villages in India. This has proved the sincerity of Quaker belief in the brotherhood of man, but only at the cost of neglecting the prior and primary sense of the Fatherhood of God which constituted them a religious society.[42] Ethics, which for historic Quakerism were theonomous, are becoming autonomous.[43]

Two other criticisms are made of Quakerism, but these are by no means generally accepted. One is Hayman's accusation that an isolationism is growing in Quakerism which insulates the Society of Friends from any desire for contact with the wider Christian Church.[44] It might be said, with more accuracy, that the Quakers will have to make a firm choice between association with the Ecumenical Movement on a firm Biblical and theological basis, and a non-theological immanentalism which might provide the basis for a unity between many religions and ethical humanists. Presumably Steere and Green would choose the first alternative, and perhaps Sykes would select the second.[45] Thomas Green asked a heterodox question which might point to a new style of Quaker architecture: "Is it a reprovable heresy to say that I have often found it easier to get free from the prison of self and catch a glimpse of the majesty of God in a cathedral built to His glory than in some of our drab Meeting Houses?"[46] It hardly seems likely that the Society of Friends would depart so far from their iconoclastic tradition as to build sanctuaries with traditional Christian symbols evocative of the meaning of the Incarnation.

Yet perhaps it is this very iconoclasm, which has amply served to make the historic protest against idolatry, which ought to be reconsidered. It is increasingly clear that in the history of Chris-

[41] *Ibid.*, p. 49.　　　　　　　　[42] *Preparation for Worship*, p. 8.
[43] *Ibid.*, pp. 5-6, where Green asserts: "I believe that future historians will discern at least a tendency in the thinking of many to replace religion by ethics."
[44] *Worship and the Common Life*, p. 144.
[45] This statement is made on the basis of pp. 29-30 and 261 of Sykes' *The Quakers, a new look at their place in society.*
[46] *Preparation for Worship*, p. 17.

tianity there have been two major means of communion with God, the spiritual and the sacramental. Surely they are complementary and not alternative? Evelyn Underhill, who was fully sympathetic to the qualities of Quaker worship and knew that many Catholic mystics had stressed the negative way and the claims of silence,[47] seems reasonable in claiming that the Quaker "exclusive mysticism, making an arbitrary distinction between sense and spirit, could never be adequate to the generous realities of an incarnational faith; or serve the religious needs of a creature poised between the worlds of spirit and sense, and participating in both."[48]

If Quakerism were able to take that step, without denying the importance of silent waiting in worship, or of a genuine interiority and sincerity in the approach to God, and thus find its way more fully into sharing the life of the Universal Church, the other branches would be more likely to take seriously the undoubted gifts which they would receive from the Religious Society of Friends. Thus the claims of both T. Edmund Harvey and Douglas Steere that Quakerism has much to teach the historic Church would be likelier of acceptance. Steere's suggestion is worth pondering, and therefore it is cited almost in full:

"How blessed any Protestant minister might feel if he could have the privilege of sitting for an hour in silent waiting with a little inner company of his congregation. . . . How that message might be clipped, how it might be refocussed, and upon occasion how it might be completely recast as he was swept by a deeper sense of both the needs of his group and of the abundance of God's power to meet the need. In such an experience how it might be charged with power!

"How helpful, too, it might be if this occasion might become the regular spring and source of his ministry, if ministry were required of him that week, or a place where one of the lay group sitting with him might from time to time be inwardly drawn to discharge the vocal ministry of the meeting and on that occasion relieve him of that exercise. If to this little group could in time be added the whole congregation who would all gather with him to wait in this way, with the freedom to minister shared still more widely, and the message come straight from a freshly touched mind and heart, is it impossible to see some, at least, of the steps

[47] A point also admitted by Violet Hodgkin in *Silent Worship: The Way of Wonder*, as she compared Quaker silence with that of Carthusian and Trappist monks.

[48] *Worship*, p. 312.

by which this Quaker treasure of a silent waiting ministry could be shared with the whole Free Church family?"[49]

To this query a two-fold answer may be given. The first is that in a remarkable way the Free Churches of England, at least, have recognized the need for silence in worship. This may be seen, for example, in the preface to *Orders of Worship for Use in Unitarian and Free Christian Congregations* (1932), where the editors write: "where there is worship, in spirit and in truth, moments of silence may be of very living and moving power."[50] In the Congregational *Manual for Ministers* (1936) it is specifically enjoined at the climax of the second Order for Holy Communion, when the elements are being received, that there shall be a short period of silence.[51] The Methodist *Divine Worship* (1935) deliberately makes room for "fervent petition and the silent adoration that asks nothing because it possesses all things in God."[52] W. E. Orchard in the Preface to *The Order of Divine Service* demands "that room shall be left both for freely uttered and for silent prayer, not only as existing alongside liturgical forms, but as their very crown and consummation."[53] The Church of Scotland (Presbyterian) customarily allows a period of silence in its prayers of thanksgiving for the faithful departed.[54] In the Church of England it is a frequent custom to have Bidding Prayers, requiring the silent response of the congregation. In all these ways it can be shown that the influence of the Quakers has been very considerable and is not likely to diminish.

Secondly, before it would be reasonable to ask Anglican and Free Church congregations to experiment further in the Quaker mode of worship, as Douglas Steere requests, it might be expected that Quakers would make a gesture of appropriating some of the features of Catholic and Protestant worship on occasion. But, first of all, the Friends themselves must determine whether their real future lies within the Christian orbit or in the direction of a wider religious and ethical syncretism. Certainly many responsible theologians would hold that a truly ecumenical worship must, because of the overwhelming preponderance of Roman Catholics,

---

[49] *Where Words Come From*, p. 67. The same suggestion is made by T. Edmund Harvey, *Silence and Worship*, p. 57.
[50] P. viii.   [51] P. 62.
[52] Introduction, p. 15. See also pp. 24, 26, 27, 39, 40, 59, 62, etc.
[53] P. 5.
[54] *The Book of Common Order*, pp. 22, 28, 35, etc. Provision is also made for a period of silence in the midst of prayers of intercession, as, for example, on pp. 28, 35, 108, etc.

Orthodox, Anglican and Lutheran Christians in the world, move towards a liturgical norm and form, but that within this context a regular place must be found for the immediacy, directness, and warmth of the charismatic elements of free and silent prayer. There is also a need for supplementing liturgical worship, especially among small groups, with occasions of free prayer and silent worship. Indeed, anything less would be to dishonour the varied ways in which men have found a living communion with God.

CHAPTER XII

UNITARIAN WORSHIP[1]

IF THE techniques of Quaker worship are radical, much of the religious thought in Unitarian worship is also radical. No religious communion in England has been more fertile in liturgical experimentation than the Unitarian. If its ancestry is traced back through English Presbyterianism it can point with pride to Richard Baxter's *Reformed Liturgy* of 1661 as the first attempt to provide a scriptural and comprehensive liturgy. If its origins are to be sought in eighteenth century Anglicanism, then they lead to the *Revision of the Liturgy* prepared by Theophilus Lindsey in 1774, itself deriving from Samuel Clarke's private manuscript revision of the Prayer Book.[2] But on either view it has a strong liturgical inheritance, and one which it has not entirely dissipated in the twentieth century. Like Methodism in this single respect, it has affiliations with both the Church of England and with Nonconformity. From the former it derives its appreciation of hallowed forms of prayer and from the latter the conviction that each new age requires its newly-devised prayers, convictions that in their opposition lead to friction.

The eighteenth century Biblical Unitarians did not object to a prayer book; on the contrary, they gave their attention to removing the more objectionable expressions of Trinitarianism in the Book of Common Prayer which they re-issued in theologically bowdlerised fashion. This was to put new wine in the old bottles. The nineteenth century Unitarians were, however, much more adventurous liturgically. Minister after minister of the Unitarian Church produced his own liturgy for his own congregation with astonishing enterprise and fertility of invention. But most were notable for effort rather than for achievement. The great exception was James Martineau's contributions to *Common Prayers for Christian Wor-*

[1] The author is happy to acknowledge the assistance given him on modern British Unitarian and Free Christian worship by the late Dr. E. Mortimer Rowe, from 1929 to 1949 the Secretary of the General Assembly of the British Unitarian and Free Christian Churches. Dr. Rowe generously lent copies of liturgical works and pamphlets long out of print and responded to requests for information by letters with generous alacrity. The author also acknowledges help from the Rev. Roger Thomas, Librarian of the Dr. Williams Library of London, and from the Rev. Dr. G. Stephen Spinks, former editor of *The Hibbert Journal*, now an Anglican clergyman.

[2] See the present author's *Worship and Theology in England*, Vol. III, *From Watts and Wesley to Maurice, 1690-1850*, Chap. IV.

ship. Here was choice new wine in the most delicately shaped new bottles. In unforgettable cadences he expressed a blend of Biblical faith and the insights of the day derived from the comparative study of religions, his deeply ethical sense, and from the love of nature and a conviction of the basic unity of mankind emanating from German and American versions of Transcendentalism.[3] Martineau therefore left to the twentieth century a heritage of historic techniques of prayer expressive of the newest insights into the ways of God and men. His influence was felt strongly in his own denomination, but also widely beyond it. It is significant that Martineau's prayers are included in John Hunter's *Devotional Services*, W. E. Orchard's *Divine Service*, *The Free Church Book of Common Prayer*, and the Congregational *Book of Services and Prayers*.

1. *The Anarchy of Eclecticism*

The Unitarian Church has not lacked intelligent and imaginative personalities in the present century, such as L. P. Jacks, the perceptive editor of the *Hibbert Journal* in its golden era and a gifted author, or J. Estlin Carpenter, the expert in the comparative study of religions, each of whom was Principal of Manchester College, Oxford. Both attempted the liturgical task. Jacks produced *Orders of Public Worship* in 1915 for the use of the Manchester College Chapel, "an inspired fusion of the Book of Common Prayer, Martineau's prayers, and of theistic mysticism."[4] A similar verdict might be passed on Estlin Carpenter's *Prayers in Public Worship and in College Chapel* of 1927, though here the inspiration was not as obvious. But neither man had Martineau's liturgical genius; their prayers lacked the balance, the concision, and above all the inevitability of diction that mark classical prayers. In any case, a denomination of highly developed individuals with a keen critical sense is hardly likely to produce or even to value a true liturgy which involves the suppression of idiosyncrasy for the attainment of genuinely *common* prayer.

In all honesty it must be acknowledged that for most of the Free Churches, and particularly for the Unitarians, the twentieth century has brought an ebbing of confidence. The decay of political and cultural liberalism, the disappearance of laissez-faire economics,

---

[3] See the present writer's *Worship and Theology in England*, Vol. IV, *From Newman to Martineau, 1850-1900*, pp. 267-81, for a study of Martineau's prayers.

[4] I take this description from the letter of the Rev. Dr. G. Stephen Spinks (August 3, 1963), a former Unitarian minister and *Hibbert Journal* editor, and the author of the intriguing *Psychology and Worship* (1963).

and the increasing standardisation of life in a social welfare state, have led to the depreciation of that radical independence of mind and prophetic love of freedom so characteristic of classical Unitarianism. In a century when it becomes a source for congratulation for any nation to have escaped from political authoritarianism and economic collectivism, while retaining a concern for social justice, those Communions are best able to survive which have either international ramifications like the Roman Catholic Church, or a national establishment like the Church of England, or a strongly connectional structure like the Methodist Church. It is far harder to command popular allegiance for a loosely-knit group of creedless congregations, such as the Unitarians, the Baptists, or the Congregationalists.

Moreover, as might be expected in the citadel of religious liberty which is Unitarianism, there were opposing trends, with different understandings of the meaning of their fellowship in the Unitarian and Free Christian Churches. Some, like William Whittaker of Manchester, were known as the "Christocentric Group" because they proclaimed the teaching and example of Christ as the basis of Unitarianism. Others, like J. M. Lloyd Thomas of the Society of Free Catholics, wanted to combine modernism in doctrine with the mystical and sacramental practices of the historic Church. A third group wanted to link Unitarianism with the monotheism of the great historic religions like Judaism and Islam in the hope of establishing a fellowship of world-wide theists. Others, again, were barely distinguishable from ethical humanists. Not only were there these different conceptions of the modern mission of Unitarianism, but they naturally resulted in different interpretations of worship. There the division was partly between those who loved liturgical worship and those who maintained that it was in the sermon and in the free prayer of the minister that the spirituality and freedom of Unitarianism were conserved. The inevitable result of these divergent viewpoints was that the anarchy of eclecticism overwhelmed Unitarian worship.

The divisiveness, accentuated by the maximum of local permissiveness, encouraged anarchy, and the chaos that ensued could be paralleled by the "Spontaneity School" in Congregationalism where some, like Orchard, were crypto-Catholics and others, like Peel and Snell, were crypto-Quakers.[5]

---

[5] The author can recall the almost complete loss of the sense of the numinous in Yorkshire Congregationalism. On one occasion, when praying with the choir

This chaotic eclecticism, especially in the years between the First and Second World Wars, could be documented in the experience of many Unitarian ministers. One of them, who naturally desires to remain anonymous, has painted a graphic picture of the situation, in letters and in an interview. When he became the newly-appointed minister of a historic Midlands Unitarian Chapel, with the classic lines and elegant austerity of the eighteenth century, he was surprised to find that the original oak Communion-table was now removed to a side position where it could be used to support ash-trays. In its place in the church was a most unsuitable red, baize-covered, trefoil Communion-table for which a fitted crochet table-cloth, costing many hours of labour, had been made by a devoted lady of the congregation. Utterly out of keeping with the classic simplicity of the building as the shoddy red-covered trinitarian table was, it had to remain. No one could have the heart to discard a really beautiful piece of handiwork made to cover it on Communion Sundays. The same informant tells me that he once visited a Unitarian church on the South coast of England which had three stained-glass windows. On one side was a window inscribed to "Faith"; on the other side a window inscribed to "Hope." In the apse, facing the congregation, was "Charity"—the War Memorial to those who had fallen in the First World War—without any apology or explanation of its incongruity.

It is, however, easier to criticize than to understand the causes of eclecticism. The critic can all too readily poke the finger of scorn at the disparities between theological affirmations and an eclectic symbolism which by its all-inclusiveness negates them. Yet it is often the very catholicity of symbolism which enables worshippers to break out of a theological prison by a leap of faith as well as of aesthetics. It may even be an unconscious protest against theological limitations. And there is no question that the Unitarian supporters of the Society of Free Catholics consciously urged that man was more than a logical mechanism, and that his spirit needed to be fed by the historic Christian symbols.

Yet it was from the very chaos of eclecticism that there arose a demand for ordered worship. The mantle of Martineau fell upon the shoulders of the Rev. J. M. Lloyd Thomas, founder of the

before entering the sanctuary, it was necessary to ask a youth to remove a still smoking cigarette which he was dangling from his lips. On another occasion he recalls an organist playing the "Baksheesh" section of Ketelby's "In a Persian Market" as an offertory voluntary. Casualness and even slovenliness were far from being limited to Unitarian gatherings for worship, as these Congregational cautionary incidents show.

Society of Free Catholics and the sensitive and most discriminating general editor of *The Free Church Book of Common Prayer*.[6] He recognized how easily spontaneity could degenerate into slovenliness and in the Old Meeting Unitarian Church in Birmingham, of which he was the minister, he set an example of worship that was both reverent and relevant.[7]

2. *The Reign of Law*

The success of Lloyd Thomas's book proved that Unitarians were ready to reconsider the provision of a denominational liturgy which would do for its day what Sadler and Martineau did for theirs in *Common Prayers for Christian Worship*. The clamant need was for a compilation of orders of worship which would express the aspiration of the denomination as a whole rather than the taste of its most advanced ministers. It became a matter of supreme importance to end the anarchy of eclecticism, to reform casualism, and to recover the sense of the numinous in worship.[8] One remaining difficulty, however, presented itself. That was the fact that while some congregations favoured a liturgical type of service, others were as decidedly supporters of free prayer. Hence the leaders of the denomination, and particularly its wise Secretary, Dr. E. Mortimer Rowe, prepared books of worship to satisfy the needs of both groups of congregations.

The reign of law was introduced by the preparation of three denominational compilations of worship, in each of which Dr. Rowe has taken the chief responsibility. The first to appear, in 1932, was *Orders of Worship for Use in Unitarian and Free Christian Congregations* which was shortly followed by the complementary volume, *A Book of Occasional Services* (1932). An anthology of prayers was prepared by Dr. Rowe and Professor Dorothy Tarrant under the title, *Prayers of Faith and Fellowship*, in 1952. As indicating the present character of Unitarian worship, it is interesting to note that of the 242 Unitarian congregations in England, seventy-five churches use a liturgical type of service and

[6] For a study of the Society of Free Catholics see Chap. x, Section 3.

[7] The Rev. Roger Thomas informs me that he was confirmed by the Rev. J. M. Lloyd Thomas in Manchester, but that the apostle of catholicity did not bother to ask him if he had been baptized (letter of August 20, 1963).

[8] Writing of this period of eclecticism, Dr. Stephen Spinks states: "As the years went by I discovered that Unitarianism was a highly tolerant and sometimes very companionable group of people huddled under a large umbrella labelled 'Free Churches' but whose individualistic forms of worship were often casual and non-reverential" (letter of July 29, 1963).

the rest prefer the free type of prayers.[9] It can be assumed that the worship books prepared in 1932 assist the worship of the former group, and that the one prepared in 1952 assists the worship of the latter group. The degree to which uninhibited individualism has been overcome is shown in an official report of the denomination, which amended Whitehead's famous definition of religion to read: "Thus religion is not only what a man does with his solitariness, but also what he does with his gregariousness."[10]

The preface to *Orders of Worship* tells, in condensed form, the story of Unitarian worship from Theophilus Lindsey to Martineau, and renews the latter's plea to make services "available for the voice of living piety" as the reason for the new compilation. Eight regular orders of worship for Sundays are provided and two of them maintain the legacy of the past. The seventh is a conflation of the famous ninth and tenth orders written by Martineau, and the eighth order is an adaptation of the Orders for Morning and Evening Prayer in the Book of Common Prayer. The other six orders are taken from a wide variety of sources including John Hunter's *Devotional Services*, the compilations of L. P. Jacks and J. Estlin Carpenter previously referred to, the Scottish *Book of Common Order* (1928), Dean Dwelly's *Acts of Devotion* and his *Services of Praise and Prayer for occasional use in Churches* (1924), Hugh Martin's *A Book of Prayers for Students* (3rd edition, 1921), Lloyd Thomas's *Free Church Book of Common Prayer*, and Plummer's compilation of *Devotions from Ancient and Mediaeval Services*. The sources are, therefore, most comprehensive.

The aim was to provide a definite structure and order for worship, but not at the cost of inflexibility.[11] Two admirable characteristics of the book are its provision of several responsive prayers or litanies and the place it makes for meditative silence. Hence the compilers write: "Provision is made in these Orders of Service for a large discretion on the part of the minister, in the alternative

---

[9] See *The Unitarian and Free Christian Churches Year Book of the General Assembly for 1963*, which lists those churches using a liturgy at one or both services on Sundays. Those chiefly in use are: *Orders of Worship, Ten Services of Public Prayer*, and *Seven Services for Public Worship* (p. 37). The *Seven Services*, edited by Bowie, appeared in 1900 and 1917. A better work was J. M. Connell's *Common Prayer in Nine Services*, which was prepared for the Unitarian congregation of Lewes, Sussex, was taken up by a few congregations, and is still in use.

[10] *A Free Religious Faith* (A Report presented to the General Assembly of the Unitarian and Free Christian Churches, 1945) p. 197.

[11] *Orders of Worship*, p. ix, reads: "While a common Order is preserved, in the main, throughout all the Services, the way is left completely open for variety within that order."

use of stated and other prayers, as also of the Litanies and Acts of Devotion. It is further recognised that where there is worship, in spirit and in truth, moments of silence may be of very living and moving power."[12] The latter was a decided innovation in Unitarian worship.

The number and variety of the Litanies and Acts of Devotion are impressive and wholly in conformity with the genius of the Free Church tradition's protest on behalf of the priesthood of all believers in prayer. The first order has a Litany of Thanksgiving, the second one of the Will of God, the third of Intercession, the fifth of Faith, the sixth of Supplication, while the Easter Day Service includes a Litany of Remembrance. Three additional Litanies are also included. Devotional Acts include an Act of Praise (fourth service), and, in the additional forms, Acts of Christian Discipleship, of Christian Remembrance, of Communion, and of Adoration. Furthermore, the orders for the seventh and eighth services include the Beatitudes, responsively affirmed, and the Great Commandments, with the response, "Write these words in our hearts, O Lord, we beseech Thee."[13]

Martineau's prayers clearly carry off the palm, especially his magnificent prayer of consecration, "Eternal God, who committest to us the swift and solemn trust of life," and his concise prayer for Faithfulness: "O GOD, thou hast set us in the train of many martyrs and holy men; and given us, as author and finisher of our faith, one who offered himself as a living and dying sacrifice. We are not our own, but thine. Freely may we crucify our shrinking will, surrender ourselves to the utmost claims of thy Spirit, and seek no peace but in harmony with thee."[14]

The clear serenity and noble obedience of Martineau's faith, the succinct and balanced phrasing, the Biblical content of his diction, and the clean and unrhetorical spirit of his prayers makes them incomparable. The dull didacticism of the "Litany of the Will of God" suffers badly by contrast.

Nonetheless, *Orders of Worship* is a definite advance on its predecessors (Martineau's *Ten Services* excepted) in the variety of its orders, in the rich provision of alternative responsive prayers, in the partial observation of the Christian Year, in the requirement of silent prayer before the concluding collect in each service, and the bidding prefaced to each short prayer in the central part of each service. The book sold over ten thousand copies in the first few

[12] *Ibid.*, p. viii.   [13] *Ibid.*, p. 93.   [14] *Ibid.*, p. 84.

years and contributed to the unification of Unitarian congregations. Its uniquely Unitarian qualities can be found negatively in the revisions in a monotheistic direction of the *Te Deum Laudamus* and the modification of the customary Trinitarian Benediction, and, positively, in some admirable prayers of thanksgiving for the "Glory of the Outward World"[15] and for human culture.[16]

A Book of Occasional Services was prepared by a committee of the Church's Ministerial Fellowship. The preface draws attention to two unique characteristics. It includes an Order of Thanksgiving for Women after Childbirth, which is "the first published attempt to provide such an order in conformity with present tendencies of Liberal Christian Thought."[17] It also bears in mind the need of laymen by providing specimen addresses for services of worship, which give an interesting summary of contemporary Unitarian teaching.

This brief volume consists of an ambiguously phrased "Service of Christening, Baptism, or Dedication of Children," forms for Thanksgiving After Childbirth, and for Dedication to Membership of the Church, as well as orders for the Administration of the Lord's Supper, Marriage, the Visitation of the Sick, and for the Burial or Cremation of the Dead. An unusual Appendix provides a brief anthology of poetry and some prose illustrating liberal religious thought, including excerpts from Tennyson, Whittier, Rabindranath Tagore, George Eliot, and Minot Savage, presumably for use as either private meditation or even for lections supplementing the Scriptures.[18]

The Liberal Christian emphasis on experience is strongly to the forefront in both the Orders for Baptism and the Lord's Supper. As the minister takes the child in his arms he is to say: "This water is an emblem of the purity which God desires in the souls of his children." Then he may use either of the two following formulae of Baptism: "A.B., I baptize thee in the name of God our Father, and in the spirit of his son, Jesus Christ" or, "A.B., In the spirit of Jesus we dedicate thee to his Father and our Father, his God and our God."[19] The address makes plain that the service is an act of thanksgiving, and a recognition of the duty of the parents and of the Church to share in the training of the child in the ways that lead to God.

---

[15] *Ibid.*, p. 167.   [16] *Ibid.*, p. 168.   [17] P. v.

[18] The supposition that all may be used for public reading is reinforced by the reference of p. 66 to Minot Savage's "Children in Heaven" as a suitable reading for the funeral of a child.

[19] *Ibid.*, p. 5.

The Order for the Administration of the Lord's Supper consists of fourteen elements. The Sentences of invitation are followed by the Lord's Prayer, the Collect for Purity, the Summary of the Commandments, a Prayer of Approach, a Scripture Lesson, an Address or Homily, the recital of the Words of Institution, the Delivery of the Bread, the Delivery of the Wine, a Silent Thanksgiving concluded with the *Gloria*, a Post-Communion Prayer, an optional Hymn, and the final Blessing. The two dominant aspects of the Communion Service are the emphasis on the commemoration of Christ's sacrifice, and the affirmation of discipleship. To that extent the doctrine may be regarded as Memorialist in character. This interpretation is clearly expressed in the Homily, which begins with the declaration that "In this service we commemorate a great friendship and a great sacrifice," and ends, "We should be one in this ministry of the Spirit, in our Christian discipleship, with all faithful men and women of every age and clime who have loved and served humanity in the spirit of Jesus Christ."[20] An identical emphasis marks the words with which the wine is delivered to the people: "In the presence of each other and before God, as a solemn testimony of our discipleship to Jesus Christ, let us take and drink this cup in remembrance of him."[21]

While there are those who might criticize this Communion Order from the standpoint of orthodox Christianity as failing to do justice to the Divinity of Christ, the objective accomplishment of the Atonement, or the eschatological banquet in eternity which should be foreshadowed by this rite, these criticisms are wholly inappropriate to an Unitarian rite, celebrated by those who, while rejecting the doctrine of the Holy Trinity, yet recognize Jesus as exemplar and supreme teacher. If the latter restriction be accepted, it can be seen that this is a moving tribute to Christ and a solemn pledge to follow his leadership.

Criticism may more appropriately be directed to the excessive subjectivity in the words of manducation which imply that it is more important to mention first the presence of participants than the presence of God, or to the words in the homily which state "To-day, whatever our perplexities or difficulties, we still acknowledge the truth and beauty of the Christian principle."[22] Surely a Communion Service is the occasion for the declaration of faith, rather than the confession of difficulty? That blight of so many Free Church services, didacticism, which so easily destroys the

[20] *Ibid.*, pp. 21-22.   [21] *Ibid.*, p. 23.   [22] *Ibid.*, p. 22.

mystical mood of aspiration, is also present in this Order.[23] None-theless, the final impression is that this service is a simple but moving testimony to the sacrifice of Christ, a reminder that it is those who follow him in ethical loyalty who are his genuine disciples, and a commemoration of the living and the departed as part of the great cloud of witnesses.

The Lord's Supper is not widely or frequently administered to Unitarian congregations. Some of the older Presbyterian founda-tions inherited the service, along with their silver Communion-plate, and celebrate the Sacrament quarterly or monthly for a minority of their present congregations. In Great Britain as a whole, however, the majority of Unitarian congregations has either discarded it, or never instituted it. Curiously enough, how-ever, it is always included in the programme of the Annual Meet-ings of the General Assembly, and attracts a large attendance of ministers and delegates. Several Unitarian ministers have objec-tions to celebrating the service as incompatible with a theism that denies the deity of Jesus Christ.[24]

A Book of Occasional Services deliberately omits any type of Ordination Service or Induction Service, and this was also the case in the Sadler and Martineau book, *Common Prayer for Chris-tian Worship* of 1861. If it is pointed out that this is incompatible with the title of "Reverend" commonly used by Unitarian ministers, it could be replied that this is merely a courtesy title and no more inconsistent than the practice of the famous Victorian Congrega-tionalist divine, R. W. Dale, who was ordained but refused to use the title. More seriously, it is probably a part of the consistent anti-sacramentalism which has characterized all Unitarians not of the Free Catholic type in the present century, and of the anti-sacer-dotalism which believes in a "meritocracy" rather than a hierarchy.[25]

The third official worship book to be published in this century by the Unitarians was *Prayers of Faith and Fellowship*, edited by Mortimer Rowe and Dorothy Tarrant. The book was intended to replace the 1910 *Prayers for Church and Home*, long out of print.

---

[23] Particularly in the longest Post-Communion Prayer on p. 25: "May we never forget the kindness that surrounds us in the present. . . ."

[24] I am indebted for the substance of this paragraph to Dr. Mortimer Rowe, as for much of my information on the present practices of the Unitarian and Free Christian Churches. The distinguished American Unitarian, Emerson, it may be recalled, resigned from the ministry because he felt it to be inappropriate to administer the Lord's Supper.

[25] See *Faith and Freedom*, Vol. XIII, No. 38 (Spring 1960), article by E. Mortimer Rowe, "The Historical Development of the Unitarian Ministry in England," pp. 61ff.

It was prepared with the needs of lay preachers prominently in mind, but also as an aid for private devotions. It was further "offered as a contribution to the enrichment of those congregations who do not desire complete liturgical services (such as are provided in *Orders of Worship*), but who prefer the simple and traditional Nonconformist pattern."[26] For that purpose the main contents were arranged in the form of an opening prayer followed by a group of three or four brief prayers in place of the usual prolix and comprehensive intercessory prayer of the minister in the Free Church tradition. With true psychological acumen the editors added that they considered the latter, "whether extempore or written . . . as a less helpful and inspiring type of utterance to-day in public worship."[27]

The sources of the prayers are chiefly those of the Unitarian tradition in Britain and America, so that "the book may be regarded as a treasury of Unitarian and Free Christian religious aspiration."[28] A multitude of nineteenth and twentieth century collections of prayers were carefully examined, and from them were chosen the most relevant and enduring prayers of Martineau, Sadler, Crompton Jones, Carpenter, Armstrong, Tarrant, and others. Specific acknowledgment is made of a prayer from Rauschenbusch's *Prayers for the Social Awakening*, for several prayers from the 1914 and 1937 prayerbooks of the American Unitarian Association, and for two prayers each composed by L. P. Jacks and Samuel A. Eliot. For the restrictive policy of limiting the collection to Unitarian devotions, with the exception of a few brief collects and the prayer of Rauschenbusch, it could be argued that this was an essential temporary measure to provide unity in a denomination suffering from an excess of eclecticism. Furthermore, it enabled the distinctive qualities of Unitarian worship to be observed in pure form. On the other hand, it could be held to be a most myopic policy in an ecumenical century when increasingly both hymn books and prayer books express an inter-confessional indebtedness. In one respect, however, the book broke new ground—in its liturgical "lend-lease" invigoration of English worship with the prayers of American Unitarianism, an example that could well be followed by other denominations.

Prayers of Faith and Fellowship provides a faithful mirror of the two predominant expressions of liberal theology in the twentieth

---

[26] *Prayers of Faith . . .* , p. v.
[27] *Ibid.*
[28] *Ibid.*, p. vi.

century: in the place given to mysticism and to the social gospel. The calm aspiration of mysticism and its longing for unity with God above the distractions of existence is finely matched with the prophetic concern for justice and compassion. The five evening prayers in this collection and several others breathe the serenity of mysticism, such as the one that pleads for "a heart at rest in the eternal love, and a spirit whose thirst is satisfied with the waters of eternal life."[29] The phrasing is often as felicitous as the spirit of the prayers. Indeed, the great quality of this volume is that it is almost wholly free of dreary didacticism. The emphasis of the social gospel is nobly expressed in five national prayers, with such typically fortifying petitions as the following: "let the need for action arouse us from our indifference to existing evils; let the need of endurance brace our powers and raise our hopes; let the fire of national trial burn up the overgrowth of our luxury, melt away our class-selfishness, fuse our cold hard prudence into a clear-sighted and self-forgetful energy, and make our whole people glow with a common faith in the right and a fervent trust in thee."[30]

At the same time the book is more than a mirror of fleeting twentieth century theological trends. It has three abiding qualities. In the first place, it advances beyond that genial vagueness which has sometimes characterized Unitarian devotions to a definite Christocentric reference in several of the prayers, as in those for Palm Sunday and Good Friday.[31] Secondly, the Unitarians have a strong sense of *pietas*, of the dependence of the living on the labours of their predecessors, which is given memorable expression in four prayers of commemoration.[32] Thirdly, there is the constant recognition that discipleship does not consist in the protestation of loyalty but in the performance of duty. These prayers are ethical through and through.

This conviction accounts for the reality and precision of the prayers of confession, in acknowledging before God that "when thou art nigh, we are weary of our selfish desires, our faithless cares, our unresisted temptations: wasted moments, and bitter words, and vain ambitions rise up in judgment against us: we lay at thy feet with shame the vows we have not kept, and the sorrows we have not sanctified."[33] It sounds through a Harvest Thanksgiving prayer: "May we never be satisfied to enjoy plenty so long as any are in want."[34] This insistence upon ethical honesty in religion

---

29 *Ibid.*, p. 83.   30 *Ibid.*, p. 103.   31 *Ibid.*, p. 95.
32 *Ibid.*, pp. 99-101.   33 *Ibid.*, pp. 70-71.   34 *Ibid.*, p. 97.

is not stilled even in the closing collects: "O God, may we who have united in worship be fruitful in good works, at one with all on earth who do thy will and one with thy great family in heaven."[35] Here is the authentic Unitarian utterance: "Let the voice of duty ring clear, and the word of conscience be unmistakable."[36]

Nevertheless, the book still suffers from two characteristic weaknesses of liberal theology. There is too much subjectivity and luxuriating in our own attitudes, as in the introspective words: "Yet in this transient moment of devotion we seek to awaken in ourselves some answering sense of humility and love."[37] Here we have the very nadir of Pelagianism in a "do-it-yourself" devotion! Not all the Christocentric references have the rootage in the Gospels of the prayers for Palm Sunday and Good Friday, which would give them objectivity and precision. Generalities do not provide the same ground of assurance in approaching God as do references to the example and teaching of Jesus of Nazareth. It is, for example better to pray "As disciples of the Man of Sorrows, may we steadfastly set our feet to go to our Jerusalem, responsive to all the counsels of thy will; seeking only strength to glorify the cross thou layest upon us, and prepared to be obedient unto death"[38] than to offer the petition, "May the spirit of Christ, the spirit of divine sonship and human brotherhood, be with us, and make us one in faith and love, now and evermore."[39]

3. An Evaluation

The Unitarians, though they have a rich tradition of liturgical worship, seem to have been plagued with the same trouble as were the Quakers in the twentieth century. That is whether their generous spirit and strongly humanitarian interests should lead them to move beyond the Christian orbit into the fellowship with all theists. This has tempted them to cast loose from the Christian historical tradition based upon a specific revelation, of which the Bible is the record and which is consummated in the life of Jesus the Messiah. Until the decision of either Communion is firmly made, whether to be theistic in general, or Christian in particular, their devotions are bound to be characterized by a degree of vagueness, with a consequent loss of power. A newer conception of the authority of the Bible, which conceives it as no longer an armoury

[35] *Ibid.*, p. 63.
[36] *Ibid.*, p. 20. See also the prayer on p. 11.
[37] *Ibid.*, pp. 88-89.
[38] *Ibid.*, p. 95, from the Palm Sunday prayer.
[39] *Ibid.*, p. 107.

of correct intellectual propositions about God but as the record of the Divine encounters with men, coupled with the recognition that theological orthodoxy has reflected more of the abstractness and speculation of Greek philosophy than of the concreteness of the historically given in the Hebrew understanding of God, should make it possible for those Unitarians and Quakers who deny the Incarnation but affirm the Messiahship of Christ to find a readier welcome in the ambit of the World Church than they did in past centuries. Certainly each denomination has its own insights into the nature of reality in worship to contribute to the Christian Commonwealth. It is interesting, too, that the Unitarians have been readier than any other denomination to concede the importance of the Quaker claim for the place of silence in corporate worship.

What, then, are the values within Unitarian worship which might prove an enrichment of traditional Catholic and Protestant worship? The Unitarians have always welcomed the discoveries of modern science and in this they have exhibited only one important facet of their recognition of the splendour and power of the Creator God. They have emphasized the significance of general revelation, and of the Divine inspiration in thinkers, poets, artists, writers, and philanthropists. They also have been among the first to acknowledge the spirituality of religious thinkers not of the Christian fold. All these insights would give a needed breadth and generosity to traditional Christian worship. In return, they would receive that concentration on the benefits of the historic revelation of Jesus Christ which leads to that adoration of God that stimulates the most sacrificial service in Christ's disciples. In addition, in the tradition of Free Church worship the Unitarians have continually kept alive the importance of responsive prayers stressing the part of the laity in worship. And, not least in importance, they have never allowed aestheticism or antiquarianism to deflect their witness to the need for intellectual and ethical integrity in worship.

CHAPTER XIII

CONCLUDING CRITIQUE

IN THIS epilogue it is proposed to present an evaluation of Christian worship in England in the middle of the seventh decade of the twentieth century, rather than to recapitulate the detailed conclusions of the preceding chapters. In previous volumes it would have been inappropriate to attempt such an assessment because Church traditions in worship were contrasted. In fact, the most that could be attempted in those pre-ecumenical centuries was to delineate the unconsciously complementary character of divergent modes of worship. In this Ecumenical Century, however, the Roman Catholic, Anglican, and Protestant traditions of worship have converged to a remarkable degree. In the first part of this critique there will be an attempt to assess the wide areas of agreement in worship. The second part of the critique will point to the remaining areas of disagreement and to the unsolved problems in worship.

I. AREAS OF AGREEMENT

In the twentieth century worship has come into its own. It is recognized to be integral to the life of the Church and, on the part of many scholars, to be the primary focus and expression of Christianity. In the eighteenth century the intellectual aspects of Christianity were dominant (and the Evangelical Revival did not so much answer the intellectual objections posed by Deism as ignore them). In the nineteenth century there was a violent revulsion from Rationalism to Romanticism and then Moralism, with the result that an exaggerated importance was given first to the aesthetic and then to the ethical aspects of Christianity at the expense of theology. In the twentieth century worship, theology, and ethics are seen to be three essential and inter-related aspects of the Christian life.

This balance was not, however, achieved in the earlier part of this century. The "social Gospel" asserted the ethical element as essential, to the depreciation of the aesthetic, and, to some degree, of the theological.[1] In reaction to this, the exponents of mysticism

---

[1] This immanental theology was superficial because it treated the historical foundation of Christianity lightly and excluded transcendence (and with it the holiness of God).

(von Hügel, Inge and Evelyn Underhill) almost neglected the aspect of social justice, though they did speak of the Divine charity, and they emphasized the aesthetic and ascetic aspects of Christian devotion. Gore and Temple, Forsyth and Oman, were forerunners of the balance which was to arrive finally in the Biblical-theological renaissance and the Liturgical Movement, as well as the concern to frame a "Christian Sociology" in the middle thirties.

1. *Worship as an Inclusive Category*

It is now realized that the Christian religion requires a cultus, a creed, and a code of conduct.[2] It can, indeed, be argued that the primacy of worship is partly due to its all-inclusiveness in providing for the needs of the nature of man-in-community. For worship ministers to his mind (creeds or confessions of faith, lections, and sermons), to his imagination and heart (sacraments, symbols, musical and visual art, hymns, prayers), and reinforces his will by a corporate discipline of inspiration and ethical instruction which is reaffirmed in the entire rite as a communal celebration of life's meaning.

2. *The Primacy of Worship as Encounter with God*

Even more important, however, is the recognition that in worship man's encounter with the living God is basal. The most significant empirical analysis which our century has provided of the distinctive character of religious experience is Rudolf Otto's *The Idea of the Holy*.[3] Here Otto attempts to define the *numinous*, while recognizing that his analysis destroys the complex reality by the very process of breaking it down into its component parts. (What Wordsworth said of poetical experience—"We murder to dissect"—can also be said of piety.) Otto finds in the sense of the numinous an important polarity of attraction and repulsion. The awe and love basic to man's experience of God is a *mysterium tremendum et fascinans*, a mystery which frightens and fascinates. It is the holiness of God which repels and His love which draws man near. Otto also insists that as religion develops it tends to

---

[2] The studies of such distinguished British anthropologists as Sir James Frazer, Tylor, Marett, Evans-Pritchard, Monica Wilson, and others (including E. O. James), encouraged the historians of Christian worship by demonstrating the importance of the cultus in non-Christian cultures.

[3] Professor Farmer has an admirable seven-fold analysis of man's apprehension of God in worship: as ontologically other, axiologically other, personal, giving all, demanding all, acting intimately within the individual's being, and a unique feeling-tone akin to awe (*Revelation and Religion*, Chaps. III and IV).

interpret the numinous less as eerie than as ethical. The glory of Christianity is that God makes the decisive approach to man in Jesus Christ in such fashion that He binds the world to Himself and Himself to the world. St. Augustine clearly sensed the polarity in the encounter with God, when he wrote: "What is that which gleams through me and smites my heart without wounding it? I am both a-shudder and a-glow. A-shudder in so far as I am unlike it, a-glow in so far as I am like it."[4] Almost fifteen hundred years later G. M. Hopkins expressed the same polarity as "lightning and love."[5] Theology, apart from that polarity regularly renewed in worship, and especially immanental theology, tends to sentimentalize God. Christian ethics, divorced from the experience of worship, loses its authority as it is no longer cosmically teleological.

Thus if worship includes the theological and the ethical, nevertheless its primary claim is that it mediates the sense of the numinous. It manifests, with ever-growing wonder, that the Ultimate has become intimate, the All-holy the All-loving too, in the Incarnation where "the Supreme became servant" (Temple) and in the Cross where Jesus Christ is "The Man for others" (Bonhoeffer), and His entire life demonstrates "the Humanity of God" (Barth). Worship is the response of the personality-in-community to this transforming Revelation, the homage of the Christian Community in the form of a celebration.

3. Worship and its Social Reference

Hitherto the vertical dimension has been stressed, but it is an important characteristic of worship in the twentieth century that it also emphasizes the horizontal direction of life. Biblical and liturgical theology insist that the Church is a new race. It is the People of God born not of flesh but of the Spirit, which transcends the centuries and overleaps the barriers of nationality, class, and culture. It is, moreover, not only a saved but a saving community, and as a saving community it is a serving community. While the Church is primarily a worshipping community, this is far from implying that it is a self-preserving society consisting of pious escapists.

The prophetic concern for a juster Christian social order has customarily been voiced from the pulpit, and it should be noted

[4] Confessions, XI, 9, para. 1. The translation is Professor H. H. Farmer's, as employed in his Revelation and Religion.
[5] In The Wreck of the Deutschland.

that the twentieth century Anglicans have succeeded to the prophetic role assumed by the "Nonconformist Conscience" in the nineteenth century. What is new in the twentieth century is the view that the Eucharist itself (in the interpretations of Archbishop Temple, Bishop J. A. T. Robinson, and Dom Gregory Dix) is a prophet, for it announces the Divine demand for sharing those resources which are the product of God's gifts and man's manufacture and distribution.

Furthermore, it has been realized with great clarity in our age that social service can easily degenerate into patronage, apart from that genuine humility which is a by-product of worship, and that true compassion which is an authentic response to Christ's Passion. The link between the Eucharist and social service is sacrifice, Christ's and that of His disciples. Intercession is completed by action.

We are not likely to establish the equality of men on any sociological basis. It is not a twentieth century Bill of Rights that is necessary; it is rather that man viewed from the religious perspective has a Bill of Wrongs. It is only as all human beings recognize themselves as forgiven and accepted sinners, that they stand shoulder to shoulder, or better, kneel together *coram Deo*. It is as shamed accomplices in the Christ-betraying and heartbreaking inequalities of the world that Christians go forth to serve their fellows, and not as experts. The note of social penitence is strong in the confessions and the intercessions of the twentieth century Church. Moreover, sermons on the Sacrament point out increasingly that the service of Holy Communion is a blue-print of a new world order, which is scandalized by the present world of haves and have-nots in which some eat cake and others furtively grab crusts from trash-cans.

4. *Worship as the Homage of the Whole People of God*

Increasingly in the present century we have come to realize that the Church is not properly defined as a hierarchical or sacerdotal society on the analogy of an army, with clerical officers and lay privates. Least of all is it to be defined as a worshipping society with clergymen as actors and the laity as mere spectators. It is, of course, still true that Churches in the Catholic tradition, with their emphasis on the apostolical succession, make much of the difference between the ordained and the unordained members of the Church; the Free Churches, by contrast, recognize that their ministers have a special function but insist that they do not have a superior status. It is, however, equally true that in Free Church worship the almost total monopoly of the minister's voice in the prayers has tended toward a virtual sacerdotalism, which denies the priesthood of all believers affirmed in their more democratic forms of Church government. The important point, however, is that in both the Catholic and Protestant traditions there is a new recognition that the Church is the whole People of God and that they must be given a fuller role in worship and in witness. Responsive prayers in the Roman Catholic and Anglican forms of worship have always provided this expression, but there has been an increasing concern to find other ways for liturgical participation on the part of the laity. It is now customary for them to take various parts in the worship, such as reading the lessons, or taking up the Communion Offertory (including the bread and wine with the alms), as an expression of the common priesthood of Christians. Above all, the stress on the vernacular in worship and the use of the Dialogue Mass are the most important recent Roman Catholic incentives to lay participation in the Liturgy. The Halton "House Church" experiment in the Church of England, making the dining-table in the home the temporary altar, and the inclusion of family prayers in the domestic Eucharist, are other aspects of the same concern that the Liturgy shall be the offering of worship by all God's people there present.

Perhaps the most striking proof of the new understanding that worship is *common* worship is the acceptance of the lessons of the Liturgical Movement by the Free Churches, even though this amounted to a revolution on the part of the heirs of the Puritan-Pietist tradition. The Presbyterian Church of England produced its pioneering revision of the Westminster Directory as its official denomination service-book in 1898, entitled *The Directory for Public Worship*, subsequently twice revised. The Congregationalists have produced three denominational service-books in this century, and the Baptists two, the latest being liturgically exceedingly advanced. The Methodists and the Unitarians, because of their Anglican lineage, have never entirely cut themselves off from the liturgical tradition. Coleridge's criticism was applicable in the nineteenth century, but is wholly outmoded today: "Many a proselyte has the Church gained from the Meeting-House through the disgust occasioned by the long-winded preaching prayers of the

431

Dissenting ministers, and the utter exclusion of the congregation from all active *share* in the public devotion."[6]

5. *Worship as Unitive*

This important trend from charismatic to liturgical worship on the part of denominations which had previously equated formality with insincerity may be an indication of a loss of confidence in their future, and indeed may jeopardize an important element in worship which the Free Church tradition exists to maintain for the coming Great Church—as will be argued later. A more sober, as well as generous evaluation, of this trend is that it represents the conviction that liturgical worship is unitive. It binds the Church of the past[7] with the Church of the present, and it is likelier to bind together the Christians of the future than is a charismatic form of worship. It is a sober recognition of the ecumenical possibilities inherent in liturgical worship which has led the English Free Churches to reconsider their ancient criticism of forms of prayer and, incidentally, to be less hostile to the episcopal form of the ministry. Such a decision is, of course, far from being unanimous, but it is significant that both liturgical worship and episcopacy were accepted by the Free Churches that joined with the Anglicans to form the Church of South India. That more variety is desirable within the structure of liturgical worship, and that no rite should be inalterable, are considerations which do not militate against the fact that a liturgical form of worship can be an important nexus of unity. It is also important to recognize that the Free Church service-books of the past two decades have approximated in their Orders for Holy Communion to the structure of the historic Consecration Prayer of the Western rites, and have incorporated several of its elements.[8]

6. *The Unity of Word and Sacrament*

A recognition of the desirability of liturgical worship, for its historic fidelity and its unitive power, need not imply any derogation of the traditional Protestant emphasis on the importance of

---

6 S. T. Coleridge, *Notes on English Divines*, Vol. II, p. 33.

7 G. K. Chesterton wittily argued that the Church "votes by tombstones." It is undeniable that historically the devotees of liturgical worship vastly outnumbered those practising charismatic worship in the primitive and mediaeval Church. Similarly, Roman Catholic and Orthodox Christians in combination greatly outnumber Protestant Christians.

8 See Huxtable *et alii*, eds., *A Book of Public Worship* . . . , and Payne and Winward, eds., *Orders and Prayers for Church Worship*.

the proclamation of the Word of God in the sermon. Indeed, while Protestants have reconsidered the value of the Sacraments,[9] Roman Catholics have rediscovered the value of preaching, with the result that there is now a conjoint emphasis on the interrelationship of Word and Sacrament.

How is this *rapprochement*, indeed re-marriage, of Word and Sacrament to be accounted for? It is due, at least in part, to an acknowledgment of the dangers inherent in their divorce in past centuries. The over-emphasis on preaching and the depreciation of prayers and sacraments in Protestantism has contributed to four very unfortunate results. As the element of adoration disappeared or was minimized in the Christian life, Christian faith became over-intellectualized. Thus what Jonathan Edwards called the "holy affections" no longer activated the imagination and the will, so that God's will was rather discussed than done. Again, as prayers and sacraments were depreciated, the cult of the popular preacher was magnified. (It should be noted that the twentieth century has not been an era of "spell-binders" in the pulpit.) Finally, an over-emphasis on preaching may well have accelerated the momentum towards splintering so characteristic of the history of Protestantism. Howard Hageman rightly poses the question: "Could the Reformed Churches have proved such fertile soil for the growth of sectarianism, producing one schism after another in their history, if every week they had reminded themselves that 'we being many are one bread and one body: for we are all partakers of that one bread'?"[10]

The *reductio ad absurdum* of this tendency is brilliantly satirized by Peter De Vries in his novel, *The Mackerel Plaza*. He depicts a Protestant Community church, "the People's Liberal," in a wealthy commuters' suburb in Connecticut, the minister of which is known for his taut and sophisticated sermons as the Hemingway of the pulpit. The hilarity of the novel's irony reaches its peak when the Rev. Mr. Mackerel conducts a group of visitors round the church "plant." They are shown the dining-area, kitchen, three parlours for committee and group meetings, as well as two baths on the ground floor. Proceeding upstairs, they are then shown the medical and neuro-psychiatric wings (indefinitely expandable), and the large all-purpose auditorium which can be used

[9] See Donald M. Baillie's *The Theology of the Sacraments* as to how far it is possible for a distinguished Presbyterian theologian to go in the Catholic direction in interpreting the Holy Communion as a sacrifice.
[10] *Pulpit and Table*, p. 115.

for drama, or as a dance-floor or gymnasium. Almost apologetically Mackerel finally observes: "There is a small worship area at one end. This has a platform cantilevered on both sides, with a free-form pulpit designed by Noguchi. It consists of a slab of marble set on four legs of four delicately differing fruitwoods, to symbolize the Four Gospels, and their failure to harmonize. Behind it dangles a large multi-colored mobile, its interdenominational parts swaying, as one might fancy in perpetual reminder of the Pauline stricture against those 'blown about by every wind of doctrine.' . . . Thus the People's Liberal is a church designed to meet the needs of today and to serve the whole man."[11]

Here can be seen the terrible revenge which falls upon those who make didacticism and up-to-date-ness ends in themselves, for the sermon has degenerated into a cultural lecture, and the obedience of faith into uninhibited idiosyncrasy. This is, of course, an extravaganza, but it points to the danger of preaching freed from worship and the sacraments, and both freed from Scripture. There was a period in the early part of this century in England when texts were used as pretexts, and when the chief Sacrament had become no more than a memorial to a heroic Jesus and a token of the allegiance of the pious.

There are equal dangers in the elevation of the Sacrament and the depreciation of the Word in preaching. The Sacrament alone, as the historic Reformers pointed out, could and did degenerate into an attempt to manipulate Divine power, a propitiatory sacrifice renewed instead of an acknowledgment of a gift received anew. It became a meritorious work to be chalked up on the credit side of a vast debit record, and a spectacle to be watched instead of an eucharistic action to be shared. It became the glorification of the priesthood and the depreciation of the role of the layman, and its introspective concentration on immolation eclipsed the holy joy of the Creation and the Resurrection. Moreover, the whole Liturgy was encased in an inalterable and sacrosanct rite of 1570 (Roman Catholic) or of 1661 (Anglican).

Dr. Karl Barth observed with justice that "one might say that the great temptation of Protestantism is Judaism, whereas the great temptation of Catholicism would be paganism."[12] If Protestants allowed worship to degenerate into didacticism, Catholics

---

[11] *The Mackerel Plaza* (Little, Brown and Company, Boston, 1958), p. 29.
[12] Reported in *The Christian Recorder* (an interdenominational weekly published in Standerton, Transvaal, South Africa), issue of April 26, 1963, giving as its source, *Réalités*, Paris.

permitted their spectator worship to become hopelessly fossilized until the arrival of the Modern Liturgical Movement. The former stressed ear-gate and the latter eye-gate.

Our century has seen the re-marriage of the Word and Sacrament, the Divine oracle and the Divine drama of salvation, in a conjoint emphasis on the Sermon and the Supper, the Pulpit and the Holy Table. It has recognized that the *verbum audibile* and the *verbum visibile* (to use St. Augustine's terminology) are mutually reinforcing channels or modes of the Divine encounter with humanity in worship. Already the results of this return to the pattern of the primitive Church can be seen in a piety which is Biblical, sacramental, and social.

It has also led the way to the ending of other baleful dichotomies. A comprehensive theology of the Word-made-*flesh* has provided a truer understanding of the nature of man as "ensouled body" instead of that "angelism" (Maritain's term) which depreciated the life of the senses and proposed that men should live as disembodied spirits. A genuine incarnationalism and sacramentalism have proved a spur to Catholic and Protestant concern for religious art and architecture, in which the Church of England has given the lead, with its encouragement of the work of Epstein, Henry Moore, Graham Sutherland, John Piper, Basil Spence, and others. Already there are signs in architecture (if not in art) that the Free Churches are overcoming their aesthetic iconoclasm as a result of their participation in the Ecumenical and Liturgical Movements. While they have never been great admirers of symbolism, there is no reason why they should be insensitive to the artists of the twentieth century, such as Picasso in *The Bombing of Guernica* or Georges Rouault in the *Miserere* series, who arouse a profound pity for or indignation over man's inhumanity to man.

A still further consequence can be seen in the increasing recognition that worship is a celebration of life, as thanksgivings recall the joys of "our creation, preservation, and all the blessings of this life," including the triumphs of technology and the divinely-donated insights of the visual and plastic arts, and the beauty, majesty and mystery of the universe opening out before us today in a vaster perspective. Much more, however, still needs to be done in this area.[13]

[13] Van Ogden Vogt in *The Primacy of Worship* has written: "Modern religion needs more expanded actions of praise. There is open opportunity for poetic compositions to celebrate the glory and goodness of life. In city churches, especially, the beauty and bounty of nature should have more frequent and ample

7. *The Recovery of the Christian Year*

Another consequence of the impact of an incarnational theology is the increasing use of the celebrations of the Christian Year by all Christian Communions in England, and not, as formerly, by the Roman Catholics and Anglicans alone. Three reasons account for this significant change. The first is the acknowledgment that the mystery of the Incarnation must be appropriated in episodic manner by distracted human personalities. What God deigns to impart of the mystery of His being and purpose for man is accommodated to man's Lilliputian personality in "God contracted to a span, marvellously made man" (Charles Wesley), and the Christian Year enables God's people to make this annually renewed pilgrimage into the mind and heart of God. Secondly, while men may guess that God's infinite wisdom permits Him to view the Incarnation as a simultaneous whole instead of as a succession of acts, we humans cannot do so. Similarly, a musical composer conceives the three movements of his symphony as an interrelated whole, yet it is necessary for the orchestra to play it and for the audience to listen to it as a succession of bars of music. Thus we learn the Divine Composer's intentions in the Incarnation, act by act, event by event, from the Advent to Pentecost. The Christian Year retells that narrative of transformation with appropriate pauses at the festivals. In the third place, the celebration of the Christian Year is the Church's ultimate defence against the ever-increasing encroachments of the world's calendar. It is the antidote to suffocation by secularism and choking by commercialism. National holidays as well as special days set apart for admirable humanitarian causes can crowd out the absolute claim of God in Christ in the Church. Thus the keeping of the Christian Year makes worship Christ-centred by its rootage in holy history remembered as the creative tradition that renews the corporate life of Christians. In short, the Christian Year is recognized on all sides as an important token of our continuing acknowledgment that the Church, triumphant in heaven[14] and militant on earth,

---

expression. And so many other factors of existence—man in his families, man in his vocational skills and loyalties, man in his civic achievements, man in his apprehensions and arts, man in his struggles for freedom—should be praised in festival and song" (p. 52).

[14] One important consequence of the Biblical-theological and Liturgical Renewal is that it has led to a reconsideration of the nature of the Church, and a rediscovery of the doctrine of the Communion of saints. It is not uncommon nowadays to hear prayers in the Free Churches which remember the faithful departed before

owes everything to the grace of God, which is both stimulus to adoration and propulsion to service.

II. AREAS OF DISAGREEMENT

Considerable as are the areas of agreement, as might be expected in the Ecumenical Century, yet too roseate a picture would have been presented if no reference were to be made to certain unsolved problems in worship which have generated considerable discussion in our period. This will involve the consideration of four important issues.

1. *Liturgical, Free and Silent Prayers*

The increasing recognition by the English Free Churches of the value of theological structure in worship, of the need for more responsive prayers, and, in short, of an increasingly liturgical type of worship is, it was argued, a revolution. It is not, however, an entire abandonment of the tradition of free prayer. While there is less confidence in the value of an entire dependence upon extemporary prayers, and especially of the so-called "long prayer" of intercession which customarily precedes the sermon, there is little indication that Free Churchmen would embrace a single inalterable Liturgy. In this connection it is important to realize that official Presbyterian, Congregational, and Baptist service-books provide *alternative forms* for Morning and Evening worship, as for the celebration of Holy Communion. By so doing, their compilers believe that they can preserve the fulness and fidelity of theological structure, along with such variability in the wording of prayers as will preserve freshness for minister and congregation and also prevent any "liturgical fundamentalism" or literalism. They hesitate to canonize any form of worship so as to give the impression that it is sacrosanct and inalterable. It is a natural expression of the Protestant principle which refuses to absolutize the finite. Furthermore, there is considerable feeling among Free Church ministers that a true doctrine of the Holy Spirit trusts that the Holy Spirit will lead God's people into fuller apprehensions of truth. Nor would they wish to deprive the leader of worship of the opportunity, within the framework of a liturgy, to pray for the particular needs of the gathered congregation as they have become known to him through pastoral visitation, with the immediacy and

God and pray that the congregation may follow their good example. This has been mediated to the Free Churches by the Church of Scotland.

intimacy of free prayer (whether this be prepared, as is customary, or entirely extemporary, which is becoming less common).

The general conclusion of the Free Churches in this matter has been aptly summed up by their greatest twentieth century theologian, P. T. Forsyth: "Public prayer, therefore, should be in the main liturgical, with room for free prayer. The more it really is common prayer, and the more our relations with men extend and deepen . . . the more we need forms which proceed from the common and corporate conscience of the Church."[15] The same writer was equally aware of the defect of even a great Liturgy such as the Book of Common Prayer, namely its tendency to canonize decorum and submissiveness of spirit in worship and life: "We shall think more of order than of effort, more of law than of life, more of fashion than of faith, of good form than of great power."[16]

As yet there seems to be no determined effort on the part of Anglicans to meet the need for the element of the charismatic and the spontaneous in worship to which the Free Church tradition in worship has witnessed. (The "House Church" experiment is a very great exception which proves the rule.) So, while Free Churchmen have come to agree with Anglicans that liturgical worship has very great advantages—notably its universal relevance, its objectivity and independence of ministerial moods and idiosyncrasies, and its ecumenical potentialities—there has been no comparable attempt to appreciate that tradition which Free Churchmen hold dear. Yet it is precisely that element of spontaneity, intimacy, and warmth in the worship of many modern forms of sectarianism in Christianity which has drawn many members away from "mainstream" Christianity. It has, for example, helped to account for the astonishing success of the Pentecostalist Movement.[17] A thoroughly ecumenical Church must seriously attempt to combine complementary qualities of worship in different traditions. The historic Churches stress order in worship, but all too often to the loss of ardour. Both are necessary.

If it cannot be said that there is an agreement to combine liturgical with free prayer, still less is there an over-all appreciation of the value of silent prayer. To be sure, Anglican bidding prayers usually include a short spell of silence after each bidding, but this results in a very "controlled" silence. Free Church orders of worship

15 *The Soul of Prayer*, p. 54.   16 *Ibid.*, p. 139.
17 See my *Christian Deviations: The Challenge of the Sects*, Chaps. I and VI.

often include a short period of silence, but this is only a minimal recognition of its role, and the congregation is not trained to use silence to the best advantage. Professor Paul Tillich's words warrant serious consideration: "Contemplation is the step-child in Protestant worship. Only lately has the liturgical silence been introduced into some Protestant Churches and, of course, there is no contemplation without silence."[18] While the Roman Catholic Church has in the religious orders a great tradition of contemplative prayer, it does not yet appear to have taught the laity to practice the art of corporate silence in the Mass. Thus the witness of the Society of Friends still holds in trust for the coming Great Church its own distinctive technique of worship.

It seems a tragedy that the Ecumenical Movement has not yet taught its constituent Churches that all three ways of approach to God are necessary in public worship.

There is another allied and unsolved problem. That is the need to provide a twentieth century discipline for private and familial piety. In part this is being met in the Roman Catholic and Anglican Churches by methods of spiritual discipline which derive from the rather legalistic and ascetic models of the Counter-Reformation, and in part in the Free Church tradition by manuals of prayer, such as John Baillie's fine *Diary of Private Prayer*. But the most disturbing fact is that until there is a discovery of suitable methods for private and family prayer which are Biblical in basis, contemporary in expression, and related to the pattern of public worship, we shall not see praying households of faith which are the essential prerequisite of a lively and expectant gathering of God's people for worship on Sundays. This is an important issue to which, as yet, little attention has been given in either denominational or ecumenical committees or commissions.

The family prayers of the seventeenth century Puritans, the eighteenth century Methodists, the nineteenth century Evangelical Anglicans and instructed Anglo-Catholics, were veritable dynamos of the Christian life. A viable twentieth century equivalent, expressive of the unity of the Universal Church, ought not be an impossibility.

2. *The Sacraments of Baptism and Holy Communion*

Two unresolved problems remain in connection with the under-

[18] *Systematic Theology*, Vol. III, p. 192.

standing of the two major Sacraments among different Christian Communions.

One problem is to preserve the emphasis on the Divine initiative in human salvation and on the Church as the community indwelt by the Holy Spirit, in Communions practising Infant Baptism, along with the emphasis of the Baptists and allied denominations on the necessity of expressing faith as a conscious and responsible commitment to Christ and His Church, which they insist is preserved only by the Baptism of Believers. This is still a knotty problem. Some part of the ground of disagreement has been covered, however, in that Churches practising paedo-baptism recognize that greater importance must be given to Confirmation, while Baptists have recognized the importance of Christian education in so-called services of Infant Dedication. Such a compromise, however, is no solution.

The remaining problem is that most of the Free Churches regularly open their Communion-services to members of any branch of Christ's Church, while Anglicans and Roman Catholics insist upon Confirmation in their own Church as the necessary precondition for receiving Holy Communion or Mass. For special ecumenical occasions individual Anglican Bishops are prepared to relax this prohibition, but such exceptions are few. This practice is defended by Anglicans on the ground that indiscriminate admission to Holy Communion masks the scandal of disunity by sentimentalism. The Free Church answer to this criticism is belligerently to accuse Anglicans of believing in "salvation by bishops" or, irenically, to insist that sharing in the Eucharist is itself a great impetus to reunion and a meaningful foretaste of the fruits of unity.

The most hopeful and promising sign in this area is that there is an astonishingly high level of agreement among Christian denominations in England on the meaning of the Holy Communion. This is all the more significant because historically this has so often proved to be the point of greatest contention among Christians. This agreement was high-lighted in the adoption, with a slight emendation, at the Lund Ecumenical Conference of the following definition:

"This dominical sacrament of Christ's Body and Blood, controlled by the words of institution, with the use of the appointed elements of bread and wine, is (a) a memorial of Christ's incarnation and earthly ministry, of His death and resurrection; (b) a sacrament in which He is truly present to give Himself to us, uniting us to Himself, to His eternal Sacrifice, and to one another; and (c) eschatologically, an anticipation of our fellowship with Christ in His eternal Kingdom."[19]

3. *Church Architecture and Art*

While there has been a remarkable renaissance of religious architecture and art in England in the twentieth century, it has raised as many new problems as it has solved. Among them is the extraordinary difficulty of finding satisfactory expressive symbols for Christianity in a secular age, which are neither uncommunicating stereotypes of the past nor broken forms. The situation is aggravated by the fact that the prevailing artistic modes of the twentieth century—naturalism, expressionism, and abstractionism —have no transcendent reference. There is the need for a re-mythologization of Christian art as well as of theology.[20]

In the realm of church architecture there has been a welcome rejection of neo-Gothicism, since this seems to be too obvious an admission of the irrelevance of the traditional Christian faith to contemporary culture. The problem has been to find an authentic Christian style in the twentieth century to replace the antiquarian one. Neither theologians nor architects have made up their minds whether to express numinosity or community. This is evident in the vacillation in modern church architecture between the stream-lined verticality which is the contemporary equivalent of Gothic, evocative of Divine mystery and majesty and of human aspiration, and the functional architecture stressing the central altar with the congregation gathered about it. Perhaps the clue may lie in a combination of asymmetry and intimacy, such as Le Corbusier attained in his masterpiece, Notre Dame du Haut, Ronchamp.[21]

4. *The Link between Worship and Evangelism*

It is a reflection of the loss of contact between the Church and the contemporary world that while the Church has probably become more fully aware of its essential nature as a worshipping community in the twentieth century, yet to the world outside it seems an excessively introverted institution. Its theology and its rites are, as it were, *romans à clef* to the Christian initiates and

---

[19] See the report edited by D. M. Baillie and John Marsh, *Intercommunion*, pp. 29-30.
[20] This is well argued by A. C. Bridge, *Images of God*.
[21] See G. E. Kidder Smith, *The New Architecture of Europe*, pp. 94-97.

deeply meaningful; to the outsider, however, they appear to be a code hardly worth the trouble of cracking. Despite the frenzied attempt to conduct large-scale preaching missions on the part of the Protestant Churches, and the preference for liturgical missions on the part of the Roman Catholics and the High Anglicans, and even after allowing for the promise of the para-liturgies devised by the Roman Catholic Church to meet the outsider half way, the link between worship and evangelism has yet to be found. Some very serious attempts to find a break-through are in progress, and many such experiments in Europe and in England are worthy of consideration.[22]

An equally discouraging consideration is that congregations using a charismatic type of worship appear to be likelier to produce energetic evangelists than those using liturgical forms. As has been observed before, order does not readily generate ardour.

This failure of communication, so dramatically evident in an England in which only one person in five regularly attends worship, has caused some theologians to call this the "post-Christian" age. It is a token of the bewilderment of Christian thinkers in a secular age. Two types of strategy have been advanced for meeting the situation. One is based on the belief that Christianity must be prepared to enter a new "Dark Age" for which the appropriate mode of Christian existence is withdrawal. For such a strategy a new monasticism seems most appropriate. (It is significant that there are Protestant monastic communities of the French and Swiss Reformed Churches and of the German Lutheran Church, while the Anglican Communion has had its own religious communities for over a century.) These will serve as miniature light-houses in a sea of secularism, ready to welcome the storm-tossed traveller. Then, when a secular world shall have become disillusioned with living as if God were dead, it is affirmed that it will call the Church to its aid. The other strategy believes that withdrawal is, in effect, abandonment. It prefers to find God in the heart of the secular, believing that the more the Church through its committed members is concerned to follow "The Man for others" in identification with the hardships of humanity, the more transparent will its witness to God become.

It is impossible to tell if either of these strategies is right. It would be rash to judge that the lively experimentation of the contemporary Church is a mark either of its present desperation or

[22] See Olive Wyon, *Living Springs.*

of its future vitality. The church historian can only point out that the prospects for the survival of Christianity were darker at the Crucifixion, or in 732 when the Moslem scimitars battered at the gates of Christian France, or on the eve of the sixteenth century Reformation, or in eighteenth century England before Wesley's Aldersgate Street experience, than they are today. The Church is, indeed, an anvil which has worn out many hammers.

Hopefulness for the future is ultimately grounded on faith in the Divine victory, but proximately on the signs of the times. Any prognosis of the future of the Christian Church would have to take account of four very healthy factors. The first, as we have tried to chronicle in this book, is the concentration on the adoration of God in the Modern Liturgical Movement, which is the Church's homage to His self-giving in Christ. The second is the striking expression of the same unitive love in the achievements of the Ecumenical Movement. The third is the massive theological attempt being made in our time to correlate Christianity and culture. The fourth is the ethical recognition that the Church is the servant people of God and that its place is precisely where human need is greatest. In today's world the Church cannot and ought not to compete with the clenched hand of power, but equally the folded hands of pietism are not enough. In the last analysis the pierced hands of compassion alone are adequate for the task and privilege of discipleship.

BIBLIOGRAPHY

1. SELECTED LITURGICAL TEXTS

(Arranged Chronologically by Denomination)

ANGLICAN

The Book of Common Prayer with the Additions and Deviations Proposed in 1928

Arnold, John Henry (ed.). *Anglican Liturgies* (Alcuin Club, London, 1939)

Wigan, Bernard (ed.). *The Liturgy in English* (London, 1962), containing a much wider selection of Anglican Liturgies than the previous volume, with later revisions, together with the Orders for Holy Communion of the Church of South India, the Church of Scotland and the English Congregationalists

BAPTIST

Aubrey, M. E. (ed.). *A Minister's Manual* (London, n.d.)

Patterson, D. Tait (ed.). *The Call to Worship, A Book of Services for the help and guidance of those who minister in the House of God* (London, 1930, revised edn., 1938)

Payne, Ernest A. and Winward, Stephen (eds.). *Orders and Prayers for Church Worship: A Manual for Ministers* (London, 1962)

CONGREGATIONALIST

Hunter, John (ed.). *Devotional Services for Public Worship* (London, 1882, 10th revised edn., 1920)

A Book of Congregational Worship (London, 1920)

Watson, C. Ernest (ed.). *The Rodborough Bede Book* (printed in Woodchester, Glos., 1930, for the use of the Congregational Church in Rodborough)

A Manual for Ministers (London, 1936)

A Book of Public Worship compiled for the use of Congregationalists (by John Huxtable, John Marsh, Romilly Micklem and James Todd, London, 1948)

Todd, James (ed.). *Prayers and Services for Christian Festivals* (London, 1951, a companion to the book listed immediately above)

A Book of Services and Prayers (London, 1959)

METHODIST

Divine Worship, approved by the Conference for Optional Use in Methodist Churches (London, 1935)

The Book of Offices, being the Orders of Worship authorized for use in the Methodist Church together with the Order of Morning Prayer (London, 1936)

PRESBYTERIAN

(English)

Directory of Public Worship (1898; largely revised in 1921)

447

Orchard, W. E. (ed.). *The Order of Divine Service for Public Worship, the administration of the Sacraments and other Rites and Ceremonies, and a selection from the Daily Office, compiled from ancient and modern devotions, together with an abridged and revised Psalter* (London, 1919)

Phillip, Eric (ed.). *Sacramental and other services* (Liverpool and London, 1927)

(English and Welsh)

The Presbyterian Service Book for use in the Presbyterian Churches of England and Wales (London, 1948)

(Scottish)

Prayers for Divine Service (1923, authorized by the Church of Scotland)

The Book of Common Order (1928, authorized by the United Free Church)

The Book of Common Order (1940, authorized by the new and expanded Church of Scotland after reunion)

Ordinal and Service Book for use in the Courts of the Church (1962, in which will be found the latest revision of the Order for Holy Communion as celebrated in the General Assembly of the Church of Scotland)

ROMAN CATHOLIC

Missale Romanum. Editio II juxta typicam Vaticanam amplificata I (New York, 1942)

Rituale Romanum. Desclée ed. (Romae, Typis Soc. S. Joannis Evangelistae, 1914)

UNITARIAN AND FREE CHRISTIAN

Sadler and Martineau (eds.). *Common Prayer for Christian Worship* (1862; revised edn., 1879 with new title, *Ten Services of Public Prayer*)

Jacks, L. P. (ed.). *Orders of Public Worship for use in the Chapel of Manchester College, Oxford* (1915)

Connell, J. M. (ed.). *Common Prayer in Nine Services* (1926, prepared for a congregation in Lewes)

Carpenter, J. Estlin (ed.). *Prayers in Public Worship and in College Chapel* (1927)

Thomas, J. M. Lloyd (general editor). *Free Church Book of Common Prayer* (1929)

Orders of Worship for use in Unitarian and Free Christian Congregations (1932)

A Book of Occasional Services (1932)

Rowe, E. Mortimer and Tarrant, Dorothy (eds.). *Prayers of Faith and Fellowship* (1952)

2. PERIODICALS

DENOMINATIONAL

BIBLIOGRAPHY

ANGLICAN

Anglican World
Church Illustrated
Church Times
Crockford
The Modern Churchman
Parish and People
Prism
Theology

BAPTIST

The Baptist Times
Baptist Quarterly
Transactions of the Baptist Historical Society
Yearbooks of the Baptist Union

CONGREGATIONALIST

Christian World
The Congregational Quarterly
Transactions of the Congregational Historical Society
The Yearbooks of the Congregational Union of England and Wales

METHODIST

The London and Holborn Quarterly Review
The Methodist Recorder
Minutes of the Methodist Conference
Transactions of the Wesley Historical Society

PRESBYTERIAN

The Church Service Society Annuals
The Coracle (Iona Community)
The Presbyterian Messenger
The Scottish Journal of Theology
Theology Today (Princeton, New Jersey)
Yearbooks of the Presbyterian Church of England

QUAKER

The Friend

ROMAN CATHOLIC

Downside Review
The Month
The Tablet

UNITARIAN

Faith and Freedom
The Hibbert Journal (interdenominational liberal quarterly)
Transactions of the Unitarian Historical Society
Yearbooks of the Unitarian and Free Christian Churches

449

INTERDENOMINATIONAL

British Weekly
Church History (Chicago)
The Ecumenical Review (Geneva; organ of the World Council of
    Churches)
Journal of Theological Studies
Journal of Ecclesiastical History
Studia Liturgica (Rotterdam; international and ecumenical liturgical
    review)

SECULAR

Architectural Design
Architectural Review
Daily Telegraph
Journal of the Royal Institute of British Architects
The Listener (organ of the British Broadcasting Corporation)
The Manchester Guardian
The Studio
The Times (of London)

3. SOURCES IN ENGLISH LITERATURE

Less direct use of English literature was made in this volume than
in its predecessors, because Christian thought and imagination played
a smaller role in an increasingly secularized century. Incidental references were made to the Jesuit poet, Gerard Manley Hopkins, whose
strangely modern poems conceived in the Victorian age were loosed by
Robert Bridges on the twentieth century sensibility, and to Wilfred
Owen whose realistic account of war—"the poetry is in the pity"—
provided a notable contrast with the chivalric and romantic mood of
Rupert Brooke.

Authors of pronounced Christian commitment often preferred to
express their convictions by indirection, such as Dorothy L. Sayers and
G. K. Chesterton in detective novels. The former's rippled with citations
from metaphysical poetry so as to deserve to be called "Who-Donne-its."
T. S. Eliot's subtle hints of Christianity's clue to the meaning of destiny
were expressed in *The Family Reunion* and *The Cocktail Party*.

It is particularly evident that Catholics and Anglo-Catholics, rather
than Protestants and Free Churchmen, with the exception of Edwin
Muir, found Christianity most stimulating to their imagination. This
may well be because the Incarnation (and its correlate the sacramental
principle) was central to the thought of the former, while the Atonement was central to the thought of the latter.

DRAMA

There has been a notable revival of poetic drama under Christian
    auspices in which the Church of England has taken the lead.
    T. S. Eliot's *Murder in the Cathedral*, Dorothy L. Sayers' *The Zeal
    of Thy House*, and Christopher Fry's *The Sleep of Prisoners* are
    three eminent examples. (See Gerald Weales, *Religion in Modern*

BIBLIOGRAPHY

English Drama, Philadelphia: University of Pennsylvania Press, 1961.)

Dorothy L. Sayers' *The Man Born to be King* (published 1953) is a dramatic radio cycle of plays regularly broadcast by the British Broadcasting Corporation in Holy Week, which presents Christology without docetism and with great realism.

POETRY

T. S. Eliot's *The Waste Land* and the *Hollow Men* are masterly evocations of the bitter disenchantment and *taedium vitae* of the first two decades of the century, while the *Four Quartets* mirror repentance and return.

Edwin Muir (with pared simplicity) and W. H. Auden (with far greater technical brilliance) walk the same path as Eliot, except that they have committed themselves to the social struggle.

Charles Williams, maker of subtle allegories, preserves a mediaeval sensibility in the modern world.

Dylan Thomas, a later and lesser Donne, reflects the civil war of sense and spirit and has produced some late poems in the metaphysical mode, reminiscent of Herbert.

NOVELS

The twentieth century offers some fascinating portraits of the difficulties of the ministry, ranging from the iconoclasm of W. Somerset Maugham in *Rain* and *Of Human Bondage*, and the polemical accounts of Anglo-Catholic priests in Compton Mackenzie's *The Altar Steps*, to the amused caricatures of Rose Macaulay's *The Towers of Trebizond*, and the sympathetic pictures of Pamela Hansford Johnson's *The Humbler Creation*, Rachel Trickett's *The Return Home*, and Alan Paton's *Cry the Beloved Country*. (See my *A Mirror of the Ministry in Modern Novels*, 1959.)

For an account of Roman Catholicism as it strikes two converts, see the well wrought novels of Graham Greene (especially the eschatological theme in *Brighton Rock* and *The Heart of the Matter* and the labyrinthine mode of grace brilliantly depicted in *The Power and the Glory*) and of that master of satire and eccentricity in character, Evelyn Waugh.

Christopher Isherwood's *The World in the Evening* was used for its subtle evocation of the cool tranquillity and unity of a Quaker meeting.

Peter de Vries' *The Mackerel Plaza* was used for its brilliant critique of a "culture-vulture" parson and for its indictment of a liberal accommodation of Christianity to the demands of the contemporary culture in a "community church."

James Baldwin's *Go Tell it on the Mountain* is a vivid reconstruction of the ardour of fundamentalist faith in an underprivileged social group, and throws light (by analogy) on the early background from which Stanley Spencer's paintings arose. Both novelist and artist are intellectually liberated from, but imaginatively captive to, such an intense religious upbringing.

451

4. BOOKS

(Except where otherwise indicated, all books were published
in London)

Abba, Raymond. *Principles of Christian Worship* (1957)

Abercrombie, Nigel J. *The Life and Work of Edmund Bishop* (1960)

Acts of the Convocations of Canterbury and York, 1921-60 (1961)

Addleshaw, G. W. O. and Etchells, F. *The Architectural Setting of Anglican Worship* (1948)

Ady, Cecilia M. *The English Church* (1940)

Allen, E. L. *Kierkegaard, His Life and Thought* (1935)

Anson, Peter F. *The Call of the Cloister* (1955)

———. *Fashions in Church Furnishings, 1840-1940* (1960)

———. *The Religious Orders and Congregations of Great Britain and Ireland* (Worcester, 1949)

Appleton, L. H. and Bridges, S. *Symbolism in Liturgical Art* (1960)

Argan, Guilio Carlo. *Henry Moore* (Torino, 1948)

Arnold, J. H. (ed.). *Anglican Liturgies* (1938)

Arnold, J. H. and Wyatt, E. G. P. (eds.). *Walter Howard Frere: a collection of papers on liturgical and historical subjects* (1940)

Attwater, Donald. *In the Beginning was the Word: a Plea for English Words in the Worship of the Roman Church* (1944)

Aulén, Gustaf. *Christus Victor* (1931)

Baillie, D. M. *God was in Christ, An Essay in Incarnation and Atonement* (1948, rev. edn., 1955)

———. *The Theology of the Sacraments* (1957)

Baillie, D. M. and Marsh, John (eds.). *Intercommunion* (1952)

Baillie, John and Martin, H. (eds.). *Revelation* (1937)

Baker, Frank. *Methodism and the Love-Feast* (1957)

Balleine, G. R. *A History of the Evangelical Party in the Church of England* (rev. edn., 1951)

Baptism and Confirmation: A Report submitted by the Church of England Liturgical Commission to the Archbishops of Canterbury and York in November 1958 (1959)

Baptism and Confirmation Today (1954) (The Report of the Joint Committee of the Convocations of Canterbury and York)

Baptist Hymn Book (1962) (The official denominational hymnbook of the British Baptists)

Barth, Karl. *Commentary on the Epistle to the Romans* (trans. E. C. Hoskyns, 1933)

Bate, H. N. (ed.). *Faith and Order* (1927) (Proceedings of the Lausanne Faith and Order Conference)

Batiffol, Pierre. *Histoire du Bréviaire Romain* (Paris, 1893)

Batsford, H. and Fry, C. *The Cathedrals of England* (1960)

Baumstark, Anton. *Comparative Liturgy* (rev. by Bernard Botte, ed. F. L. Cross, 1958)

Beauduin, Lambert. *Liturgy the Life of the Church* (trans. of *La Piété de l'Eglise*, 1914, now issued by Collegeville, Minnesota)

———. *Mélanges liturgiques receuillis parmi les oeuvres de Dom L. Beauduin, O.S.B.* (Louvain, 1954)

Beck, G. A. (ed.). *The English Catholics: 1850-1950* (1950)

Bedoyere, Michael de la. *Cardinal Bernard Griffin, Archbishop of Westminster* (1955)

———. *Christianity in the Market-Place* (1943)

———. *The Layman in the Church* (1954)

———. *The Life of Baron von Hügel* (1951)

["Begbie, Harold" pseud.] *Painted Windows, Studies in Religious Personality* (1922)

Bell, G. K. A. (ed.). *Documents of Christian Unity, Series I-III* (1924-1948)

———. *Randall Davidson, Archbishop of Canterbury* (2nd edn., 1938)

Bennett, Frank. *The Nature of a Cathedral* (London and Chester, 1925)

Bénoît, J-D. *Liturgical Renewal: Studies in Catholic and Protestant Developments in the Continent* (1958)

Benson, E. W. *The Cathedral: Its Necessary Place in the Life and Worship of the Church* (1878)

Benson, Louis F. *The Hymnody of the Christian Church* (New York, 1927, re-issued Richmond, Virginia, 1956)

Betjeman, John. *Collins Guide to English Parish Churches* (1958)

———. *Complete Poems* (1959)

———. *First and Last Loves* (1952)

Bevan, Edwyn. *Symbolism and Belief* (1938)

Biblical Doctrine of Baptism (Edinburgh, 1958) (A Study Document issued by the Special Commission on Baptism of the Church of Scotland)

Biedrzynski, R. *Kirchen unserer Zeit* (Munich, 1958)

Bishop, Edmund. *Liturgica Historica, Papers on the Liturgy and Religious Life of the Western Church* (Oxford, 1918)

Bishop, Edmund and Gasquet, F. A. *Edward VI and the Book of Common Prayer* (1890)

Bishop, John. *Methodist Worship in relation to Free Church Worship* (1950)

Black, Robert. *The Art of Jacob Epstein* (New York and Cleveland, 1942)

Booth, Charles. *Life and Labour of the People of London* (Third Series, 1902)

Bouyer, Louis. *Life and Liturgy* (1956)

Bowmer, John C. *The Lord's Supper in Methodism, 1791-1960* (1961)

———. *The Sacrament of the Lord's Supper in Early Methodism* (1951)

Boyd, Malcolm. *Crisis in Communication: A Christian Examination of the Mass Media* (New York, 1957)

Bradley, William L. *P. T. Forsyth, the man and his work* (1952)

Brémond, H. *Histoire Littéraire du Sentiment Religieux en France* (6 vols., Paris, 1923)

Brenner, Scott Francis. *The Art of Worship* (New York, 1961)
———. *The Way of Worship: A Study in Ecumenical Recovery* (New York, 1944)
Bridge, A. C. *Images of God* (1960)
Bridges, Robert (ed.). *The Yattendon Hymnal* (1899)
Briggs, Martin S. *Goths and Vandals* (1952)
———. *Puritan Architecture and its Future* (1946)
Brilioth, Yngve. *Eucharistic Faith and Practice, Evangelical and Catholic* (1930)
Brinton, H. H. *Creative Worship* (1931)
———. *Friends for 300 Years* (New York, 1952)
———. *Guide to Quaker Practice* (Wallingford, Pennsylvania, n.d.)
Brittain, Fred. *Bernard Lord Manning, A Memoir* (Cambridge, 1942)
Brown, C. K. F. *A History of the English Clergy, 1800-1900* (1953)
Brown, L. A. and Moore, L. T. *The Dual Purpose Church* (1952)
Brown, Robert McAfee. *P. T. Forsyth: Prophet for Today* (Philadelphia, 1952)
Buber, Martin. *I and Thou* (1937)
Buckle, Richard. *Epstein: Drawings* (1962)
———. *Jacob Epstein: Sculptor* (1963)
Burleigh, J. H. S. *A Church History of Scotland* (1960)
Burnet, George B. *The Holy Communion in the Reformed Church of Scotland, 1560-1960* (Edinburgh and London, 1960)
Butler, B. Christopher. *The Idea of the Church* (1962)
Butler, Cuthbert. *Benedictine Monachism* (1922)
———. *Western Mysticism* (1922)
Butterfield, Herbert. *Christianity and History* (1950)
Buttrick, George A. *Prayer* (New York and Nashville, 1942)

Cabrol, Fernand (ed.). *Peregrinatio Silviae* (1895)
Campbell, R. J. *Christianity and the Social Order* (1907)
———. *The New Theology* (1907)
———. *New Theology Sermons* (1907)
———. *A Spiritual Pilgrimage* (1917)
Carpenter, E. (ed.). *The Archbishop Speaks* (1958) (Speeches and addresses of Archbishop Geoffrey F. Fisher)
Carpenter, James. *Gore: A Study in Liberal Catholic Thought* (1960)
Carpenter, S. C. *Prophet and Priest . . .* (1953)
Casel, Odo. *Le Mémorial du Seigneur* (Paris, 1944)
———. *Le Mystère du Culte dans le Christianisme* (Paris, 1946)
Cavert, S. M. *The New Delhi Report* (1962)
Chapman, John. *Spiritual Letters* (1935; 1944 edn. with biography by Roger Hudleston)
Chesterton, G. K. *Autobiography* (1936)
———. *The Collected Poems of . . .* (1927)
———. *The Everlasting Man* (1925)
———. *Heretics* (1909)
———. *Orthodoxy* (1908)
Child, R. L. *The Blessing of Infants and the Dedication of Parents* (1946)

Church Hymnary (revised edition, 1927) (An important Presbyterian Hymnal used in the Church of Scotland and the other British and Commonwealth Churches of the Presbyterian Order)

Clark, Francis. *Eucharistic Sacrifice and the Reformation* (1960)

Clark, Henry W. *History of English Nonconformity* (2 vols., 1913)

Clark, Neville. *Call to Worship* (1960)

Clarke, B. F. L. *Church Buildings of the Nineteenth Century* (1938)

Clarke, W. K. Lowther. *A Hundred Years of Hymns Ancient and Modern* (1961)

———. (ed.). *Liturgy and Worship, A Companion to the Prayer Books of the Anglican Communion* (1932)

Clifford, John. *The Gospel of World Brotherhood according to Jesus* (1920)

———. *The Ultimate Problems of Christianity* (1906)

Collingwood, R. G. *The Principles of Art* (1938)

Collis, Maurice. *Stanley Spencer: A Biography* (1962)

Comper, J. N. *Further Thoughts on the English Altar, or Practical Considerations on the Planning of a Modern Church* (Cambridge, 1933)

———. *Of the Christian Altar and the Buildings which contain it* (1950)

———. *On the Atmosphere of a Church* (1947)

Congregational Praise (1951) (The official hymnal of the Congregational Union of England and Wales)

Constantini, Celso. *L'Istruzione de S'Officio sull' Arte Sacra* (Roma, 1952)

Cook, G. H. *The English Cathedral through the Centuries* (1957)

Cooper, Douglas (ed.). *The Work of Graham Sutherland* (1961)

Cope, Gilbert. *Symbolism in the Bible and the Church* (1959)

———. *Making the Building Serve the Liturgy* (1963)

Cope, G., Davies, J. G. and Tytler, D. A. *An Experimental Liturgy* (1958)

Cox, J. C. *English Church Fittings, Furniture and Accessories* (Oxford, 1915)

———. *Pulpits, Lecterns and Organs in English Churches* (Oxford, 1915)

Cozien, G. *L'oeuvre de Dom Guéranger* (Paris, 1933)

Crockford Prefaces: The Editor Looks Back (1947)

Cropper, Margaret. *Evelyn Underhill* (1958)

Cross, F. L. *Darwell Stone, Churchman and Counsellor* (1943)

——— (ed.). *The Oxford Dictionary of the Christian Church* (rev. edn. 1958)

Cunliffe, C. R. A. (ed.). *English in the Liturgy; a Symposium* (1956)

Dakin, A. *The Baptist View of the Church and Ministry* (1944)

Dale, A. W. W. *The Life of R. W. Dale of Birmingham* (1898)

Daniélou, Jean. *The Bible and the Liturgy* (South Bend, Indiana, 1956)

Dannatt, Trevor. *Modern Architecture in Britain* (1957)

Dark, Sidney. *Five Deans* (1928)

Davies, David Richard. *In search of myself; an autobiography* (1961)

———. *On to Orthodoxy* (1939)

Davies, Horton. *Christian Deviations* (3rd edn., London and Philadelphia, 1965)

———. *The English Free Churches* (rev. edn., 1962)

———. *A Mirror of the Ministry in Modern Novels* (New York, 1959)

———. *Varieties of English Preaching: 1900-1960* (London and Englewood Cliffs, New Jersey, 1963)

———. *Worship and Theology in England* (Vol. III: *From Watts and Wesley to Maurice, 1690-1850*; Vol. IV: *From Newman to Martineau, 1850-1900*; Princeton and London, 1961-1962)

———. *The Worship of the English Puritans* (1948)

Davies, John Gordon. *The Architectural Setting of Baptism* (1962)

Davies, Rupert. *Methodism* (1963)

Davies, Walford and Grace, Harvey. *Music and Worship* (1937)

Davis, Charles (ed.). *English Spiritual Writers* (1962)

Dearmer, Nan. *The Life of Percy Dearmer* (1940)

Dearmer, Percy. *Art and Religion* (1923)

———. *The Art of Public Worship* (1919)

———. *The Ornaments of the Minister* (1920)

———. *The Parson's Handbook* (Oxford, 1899, rev. edn., 1903; 6th edn. with additional matter, 1907)

———. *A Short Handbook of Public Worship* (Oxford, 1931)

———. *Songs of Praise Discussed* (1933)

De Blank, Joost. *The Parish in Action* (1955)

Deissmann, A. and Bell, G. K. A. (eds.). *Mysterium Christi* (1930)

Demant, V. A. *Christian Polity* (1936)

———. *Religion and the Decline of Capitalism* (1952)

———. *The Religious Prospect* (2nd edn., 1941)

Dictionary of National Biography and Supplements (1882—)

Dieci Anni di Architettura Sacra in Italia (Bologna, 1956)

Dillistone, F. W. *Christianity and Symbolism* (1955)

———. *The Structure of the Christian Society* (1951)

Dix, Gregory. *A Detection of Aumbries* (1942)

———. *The Shape of the Liturgy* (1945)

———. *The Theology of Confirmation in Relation to Baptism* (1946)

Doctrine in the Church of England (1938) (The Report of the Commission on Christian Doctrine appointed by the Archbishops of Canterbury and York in 1922)

Douglas, Winfred. *Church Music in History and Practice* (rev. Leonard Ellinwood, New York, 1962)

Driver, Christopher. *A Future for the Free Churches?* (1962)

Drummond, A. L. *The Church Architecture of Protestantism* (Edinburgh, 1934)

———. *The Churches in English Fiction* (Leicester, 1950)

———. *The Churches pictured by 'Punch'* (1947)

Dumoutet, E. *Le désir de voir l'Hostie* (Paris, 1926)

Dunkerley, R. and Headlam, A. C. (eds.). *The Ministry and the Sacraments* (1937)

Dwelly, F. W. *Acts of Devotion* (1923)
―――. *Services of Prayer and Praise for occasional use in Churches* (1924)

Edwall, P., Hayman, E., and Maxwell, W. D. (eds.). *Ways of Worship* (1951)
Edwards, David L. and Robinson, J. A. T. *The Honest to God Debate* (1963)
Ekström, Ragnac. *The Theology of Charles Gore, A Study in Modern Anglican Theology* (Lund, 1944)
Eliot, T. S. *The Idea of a Christian Society* (1939)
The English Hymnal (editions of 1906 and 1933) (An important Anglican hymnal)
Ensor, R. C. K. *England: 1870-1914* (Oxford, 1936)
Epstein, Jacob. *Epstein: An Autobiography* (1955)
Epstein, Kathleen. *Epstein at King's Lynn* (1963) (Annotated Exhibition brochure)
Every, George. *The Baptismal Sacrifice* (1959)
――― (ed.). *Herbert Kelly, S.S.M., No Pious Person* (1960)

Farmer, H. H. *God and Men* (1948)
―――. *The Healing Cross* (1941)
―――. *Revelation and Religion* (1954)
―――. *The Servant of the Word* (1941)
―――. *Things Not Seen* (1927)
―――. *Towards Belief in God* (1942)
―――. *The World and God* (1932)
Federer, K. *Liturgie und Glaube: eine theologie-geschichtliche Untersuchung* (Freiburg, 1950)
Fellowes, E. G. *English Cathedral Music from Edward VI to Edward VII* (1945)
Fénelon, François. *Spiritual Letters* (trans. by Sidney Lear, 1880, 1892, 1906)
Fifty Modern Churches (Incorporated Church Building Society, 1947)
Figgis, J. Neville. *The Gospel and Human Need* (1909)
Fison, J. E. *The Faith of the Bible* (1957)
Flemington, W. F. *The New Testament Doctrine of Baptism* (1948)
Fletcher, Joseph. *William Temple, Twentieth Century Christian* (New York, 1963)
Flew, R. Newton. *Jesus and His Church* (1938)
Flew, R. N. and Davies, R. E. *The Catholicity of Protestantism* (1950)
Forman, R. S. (ed.). *Great Christians* (1933)
Ford, D. W. C. *An Expository Preacher's Notebook* (1960)
Forsyth, Peter Taylor. *The Charter of the Church* (1896)
―――. *Christ on Parnassus* (1911)
―――. *The Church and the Sacraments* (1917)
―――. *Congregationalism and Reunion* (1919)
―――. *The Cruciality of the Cross* (1909)
―――. *Faith, Freedom and the Future* (1912)

Forsyth, Peter Taylor. *Intercessory Services for Aid in Public Worship* (London and Heywood, 1896)
———. *The Person and Place of Jesus Christ* (1909)
———. *Positive Preaching and the Modern Mind* (1907)
———. *Religion in Recent Art* (1887, 1905)
———. *The Soul of Prayer* (1916)
———. *Theology in Church and State* (1915)
———. *This Life and the Next* (1918)
———. *The Work of Christ* (1910)
Fortescue, Adrian. *Ceremonies of the Roman Rite Described* (1917, revised edn. of J. B. O'Connell, 1946)
——— (ed.). *The Divine Liturgy of . . . John Chrysostom* (1908)
Foss, Martin. *Symbol and Metaphor in Human Experience* (Princeton, 1949)
Foundations, a statement of Christian belief in terms of modern thought, by Seven Oxford men . . . (Intro. by B. H. Streeter, 1913)
Fox, Adam. *Dean Inge* (1960)
Fox, George. *Journal* (ed. N. Penney, Cambridge, 1911)
A Free Religious Faith (1945). (Report presented to the General Assembly of Unitarian and Free Christian Churches)
Frere, W. H. *English Church Ways* (1914)
———. *Principles of Religious Ceremonial* (1928)
———. *Studies in the Early Roman Liturgy* (3 vols., 1930-1935)
———. *The Use of Sarum* (2 vols., 1898-1901)
Frost, Maurice. *English and Scottish Psalm and Hymn Tunes* (1953)
Fuller, R. H. *What is Liturgical Preaching?* (1957)

Gammie, Alexander. *Preachers I have heard* (n.d., circa 1945)
Garbett, C. F. *The Claims of the Church of England* (1947)
———. *In an Age of Revolution* (1952)
Garrett, T. S. *Christian Worship* (1961)
———. *The Liturgy of the Church of South India, An Introduction to and Commentary on 'The Lord's Supper'* (Madras, 2nd edn., 1954)
———. *Worship in the Church of South India* (1958)
Gasquet, F. A. *Henry VIII and the English Monasteries* (2 vols., 1888-1889)
Gélineau, J. *La Sainte Bible traduite en français sous la direction de l'Ecole biblique de Jérusalem* (Paris, 1956; Engl. trans. Collins Fontana paperbacks, 1963)
George, A. R. *Communion with God in the New Testament* (1952)
Giedion, S. *Space, Time and Architecture* (3rd edn., Cambridge, Mass., and London, 1954)
Gill, Eric. *Autobiography* (1940)
———. *Christianity and Art* (Abergavenny, 1929)
———. *Letters of Eric Gill* (ed. W. Shewring, 1947)
———. *Sacred and Secular* (1940)
Gillman, F. J. *The Evolution of the English Hymn* (1927)

Gilmore, A. (ed.). *Christian Baptism, A Fresh Attempt to Understand the Rite in terms of Scripture, History and Theology* (1959)

Glazebrook, M. G. *The Faith of a Modern Churchman* (1918)

Glendenning, Frank (ed.). *The Church and the Arts* (1960)

Godfrey, F. M. *Christ and the Apostles, the Changing Forms of Religious Imagery* (1957)

Goodhart-Rendel, H. S. *English Architecture since the Regency* (1953)

Gore, Charles. *Anglo-Catholicism Today* (1925)

———. *The Body of Christ* (1901, 4th edn., 1931)

———. *The Church and the Ministry* (1888, 1919)

———. *The Incarnation of the Son of God* (1891)

———, et alii. *Lux Mundi* (1889)

———. *The New Theology and the Old Religion* (1907)

———. *The Reconstruction of Belief* (1. *Belief in God*, 1922; 2. *Belief in Christ*, 1922; 3. *The Holy Spirit and the Church*, 1924)

Graf, Ernest. *Anscar Vonier, Abbot of Buckfast* (1957)

Graham, John W. *The Quaker Ministry* (1925)

Grant, J. W. *Free Churchmanship in England, 1870-1940, with special reference to Congregationalism* (n.d. but ca. 1951)

Gray, James (ed.). *Studies on Baptism* (Birmingham, 1959)

Green, Thomas F. *Preparation for Worship* (1952)

Green, V. H. H. *Religion at Oxford and Cambridge: A History c. 1160-c. 1960* (1964)

Greene, T. M. *The Arts and the Art of Criticism* (Princeton, 1940)

Greenslade, S. L. *Schism in the Early Church* (1953)

Griffith, G. O. *The Theology of P. T. Forsyth* (London and Redhill, 1948)

Grigson, Geoffrey. *Henry Moore* (1944)

Grohmann, W. *The Art of Henry Moore* (trans. M. Bulloch, 1960)

Guardini, Romano. *Vom Geist der Liturgie* (trans. by A. Lane and published with another work as *The Spirit and the Liturgy*, London and New York, 1940)

Guyon, Madame. *Autobiography* (English trans. by Alpen, 1897)

———. *A Short and Easy Method of Prayer* (English trans. 1901)

Hageman, Howard. *Pulpit and Table* (Richmond, Virginia and London, 1962)

Hales, E. E. Y. *The Catholic Church in the Modern World: A Survey from the French Revolution to the Present* (1958)

Hamilton, H. A. *The Family Church in Principle and Practice* (1941, 3rd edn., 1960)

Hamilton, W. K. *Cathedral Reform. A Letter to Members of his Diocese* (1855)

Hammond, Peter. *Liturgy and Architecture* (1960)

——— (ed.). *Towards a Church Architecture* (1962)

Harnack, A. *Das Wesen des Christentums* (1900; trans. as *What is Christianity?* 1901)

Harries, John. *G. Campbell Morgan, The Man and his Ministry* (1930)

Harrison, A. W. *Church and Sacraments* (1935)

Harvey, J. *The English Cathedrals* (rev. edn., 1956)

Harvey, T. Edmund. *Silence and Worship, A Study in Quaker Experience* (1924)

Hauser, A. *The Social History of Art* (trans. S. Goodman, 2 vols., 1951)

Hay, G. *The Architecture of Scottish Post-Reformation Churches, 1560-1843* (1957)

Hayman, Eric. *Worship and the Common Life* (Cambridge, 1944)

Hazelton, Roger. *New Accents in Contemporary Theology* (New York, 1960)

Hebert, A. G. *The Form of the Church* (1944)

———. *Fundamentalism and the Church of God* (1957)

———. *Liturgy and Society: The Function of the Church in the Modern World* (1935)

———. *The Throne of David* (1941)

——— (ed.). *The Parish Communion, A Book of Essays* (1937; reissued 1939, 1944, 1954)

Hedley, J. C. *The Holy Eucharist* (1907)

Heenan, John C. *Cardinal Hinsley* (1944)

Heiler, Friedrich. *Prayer* (1932)

———. *The Spirit of Worship* (1926)

Henson, H. Hensley. *Ad Clerum* (1937)

———. *Bishoprick Papers* (1946)

———. *Church and Parson in England* (1927)

———. *The Creed in the Pulpit* (1912)

———. *Letters* (ed. F. E. Braley, 1950)

———. *Retrospect of an Unimportant Life: 1863-1939* (3 vols., 1942, 1943, 1950)

———. *Theology and Life* (ed. G. S. Stranks, 1958)

———. *Westminster Sermons* (1910)

Henze, Anton. *Contemporary Church Art* (London and New York, 1956)

Hervormde Kerkbouw na 1945 (The Hague, 1957)

Hicks, F. C. N. *The Fulness of Sacrifice* (1930, 3rd edn., 1946)

Higham, Florence. *Catholic and Reformed* (1962)

Hinchliff, P. B. *The Anglican Church in South Africa* (1963)

———. *The South African Liturgy* (1960)

Hitchcock, Henry Russell. *Architecture: Nineteenth and Twentieth Centuries* (Harmondsworth and Baltimore, 1962)

Hodgkin, Thomas. *The Fellowship of Silence* (ed. Cyril Hepher, 1920)

Hodgkin, Violet. *Silent Worship: The Way of Wonder* (1919)

Hodgson, Leonard (ed.). *The Second World Conference on Faith and Order* (1938) (Proceedings of the Edinburgh Conference)

Hodin, J. P. *Henry Moore* (Amsterdam, 1956)

Hofman, Werner. *Henry Moore, Schriften und Skulpturen* (Frankfurt A.M., 1959)

Homrighausen, E. G. (ed.). *J. H. Jowett* (New York, 1950)

Horder, Garrett (ed.). *Worship Song* (1905)

Hoskyns, Edwyn Clement. *Cambridge Sermons* (1938)
———. *The Fourth Gospel* (ed. F. N. Davey, 2nd edn., 1947)
Hoskyns, E. C. and Davey, F. N. *The Riddle of the New Testament* (1931)
Howell, Clifford. *Preparing for Easter* (1957)
Howson, J. S. (ed.). *Essays on Cathedrals* (1872)
——— (ed.). *A Week in Chester Cathedral* (London and Chester, 1872)
Hughes, Anselm. *The Rivers of the Flood: a personal account of the Catholic Revival in England in the twentieth century* (1961)
Hunter, Leslie S. *Church Strategy in a Changing World* (1950)
Huxley, Aldous. *On Art and Artists* (New York, 1960)
Hymns Ancient and Modern (1861, 1904, 1950) (A semi-official hymnal of the Church of England)

Inge, William Ralph. *Assessments and Anticipations* (1928)
———. *Christian Mysticism* (1899)
———. *Diary of a Dean, St. Paul's, 1911-1934* (1949)
———. *Faith and Knowledge* (2nd edn., Edinburgh, 1905)
———. *The Gate of Life* (1935)
———. *Goodness and Truth* (1958)
———. *God and the Astronomers* (1933)
———. *Labels and Libels* (New York, 1929)
———. *Outspoken Essays* (1st Series, 1919; 2nd Series, 1922)
———. *Personal Religion and the Life of Devotion* (1924)
———. *The Philosophy of Plotinus* (2 vols., 1918)
———. *Speculum Animae* (1912)
———. *Studies in English Mystics* (1907)
———. *Things New and Old* (1933)
———. *Vale* (1934)
Ireland, Geoffrey. *Epstein: A Camera Study of the Sculptor at Work* (1958)
Iremonger, F. A. *William Temple, Archbishop of Canterbury, His Life and Letters* (1948)
Ireson, G. W. *Church Worship and the Non-Churchgoer* (1945)

James, A. T. S. *A Cotswold Minister* (1940)
James, William. *The Varieties of Religious Experience* (1902)
Jasper, R. A. C. *Headlam, Life and Letters of a Bishop* (1960)
Jefferson, H. A. L. *Hymns in Christian Worship* (1950)
Jeffs, Ernest H. *Princes of the Modern Pulpit* (London, n.d.)
Jenkins, Daniel T. *Beyond Religion* (1962)
———. *Congregationalism* (1954)
———. *Equality and Excellence* (1961)
———. *The Nature of Catholicity* (1942)
———. *Tradition and the Spirit* (1954)
Jones, Alexander. *Unless some Man show me* (1951)
Jones, Cranston. *Architecture Today and Tomorrow* (New York, 1961)

Jones, Edgar DeWitt. *The Royalty of the Pulpit; A Survey and Appreciation of the Lyman Beecher Lectures on Preaching founded at Yale Divinity School 1871* (New York, 1951)

Jones, R. P. *Nonconformist Church Architecture* (1914)

Jones, R. Tudur. *Congregationalism in England (1662-1962)* (1962)

Jones, Rufus M. *The Later Periods of Quakerism* (vol. 2, 1921)

———. *Spiritual Reformers in the 16th and 17th Centuries* (1914)

Jordan, E. K. H. *Free Church Unity* (1956)

Jowett, J. H. *The Transfigured Church* (1910)

Joynson-Hicks, W. *The Prayer Book Crisis* (1928)

Julian, John (ed.). *Dictionary of Hymnology* (1890 etc.)

Jungmann, Joseph. *Missarum Solemnia* (Vienna, 1949; trans. *The Mass of the Roman Rite*, 2 vols., New York, 1951)

Jungmann, Joseph. *Public Worship* (trans. Clifford Howell, 1957)

———. *The Sacrifice of the Church* (trans. Clifford Howell, 1956)

Kemp, E. W. *The Life and Letters of K. E. Kirk* (1959)

Kepler, Thomas (ed.). *The Evelyn Underhill Reader* (1962)

Kirk, K. E. (ed.). *The Apostolic Ministry* (1957 edn. with new foreword by A. M. Farrer)

——— (ed.). *The Study of Theology* (1939)

———. *The Vision of God* (abridged edn., 1934)

Klauser, Theodor. *The Western Liturgy and its History: Some Reflections on Recent Studies* (trans. F. L. Cross, 1952)

Knowles, David. *The Monastic Order in England* (Cambridge, 1940)

———. *The Religious Orders in England* (Cambridge, 1948)

Knox, E. A. *Sacrifice or Sacrament?* (1914)

Knox, Ronald A. *The Belief of Catholics* (1927)

———. *Bridegroom and Bride* (1957)

———. *The Church in Bondage* (1914)

———. *Enthusiasm, A Chapter in the History of Religion* (Oxford, 1950)

———. *Essays in Satire* (1928)

———. *The Hidden Stream* (1953)

———. *In Soft Garments* (1942)

———. *Let Dons Delight* (1939)

———. *The Mass in Slow Motion* (1948)

———. *The Priestly Life: A Retreat* (1958)

———. *A Spiritual Aeneid* (1918)

———. *The Window in the Wall* (1956)

Koenker, E. B. *The Liturgical Renaissance in the Roman Catholic Church* (Chicago, 1954)

Korolevskij, C. *Liturgie en langue vivante; Orient et Occident* (Paris, 1955)

Kraemer, Hendrik. *The Christian Message in a Non-Christian World* (1938)

Küng, Hans. *The Council and Reunion* (1962)

Lampe, G. W. H. *The Seal of the Spirit* (1951)

Law, William. *Liberal and Mystical Writings* (ed. W. Scott Palmer, 1908)

Lawrence, Brother. *The Practice of the Presence of God* (English trans. 1906)

Leeming, Bernard. *The Principles of Sacramental Theology* (1956)

Lenwood, Frank. *Jesus—Lord or Leader?* (1930)

Lewis, Clive Staples. *Beyond Personality* (1944)

———. *Broadcast Talks* (1943)

———. *Christian Behaviour* (1943)

———. *The Pilgrim's Regress* (1933, rev. edn., 1944)

———. *The Problem of Pain* (1941)

———. *The Screwtape Letters* (1943)

———. *Surprised by Joy* (1955)

———. *Transposition and Other Addresses* (1949)

L'Hopital, Winifrede de. *Westminster Cathedral and its Architect* (2 vols., 1919)

Lightfoot, R. H. *History and Interpretation of the Gospels* (1935)

Lilley, A. L. *The Sacraments* (1928)

Lloyd, Roger. *The Church of England in the Twentieth Century* (2 vols., 1946, 1950)

Lloyd-Jones, Martyn. *Studies in the Sermon on the Mount* (2 vols., 1959-1960)

Lockhart, J. G. *Cosmo Gordon Lang, Archbishop of Canterbury* (1949)

Louden, R. S. *The True Face of the Kirk* (Edinburgh and London, 1963)

Loukes, Harold. *The Discovery of Quakerism* (1960)

———. *Friends Face Reality* (1954)

Luccock, Halford E. *The Best of Dick Sheppard* (New York, 1951)

McArthur, A. A. *The Christian Year and Lectionary Reform* (1958)

Macdonald, A. J. (ed.). *The Evangelical Doctrine of Holy Communion* (1930)

Mackintosh, Hugh R. *The Doctrine of the Person of Jesus Christ* (Edinburgh, 1912)

———. *Types of Modern Theology: Schleiermacher to Barth* (1937)

MacLeod, George F. *We shall rebuild: the work of the Iona Community on mainland and island* (Philadelphia, 1945)

Macquarrie, John. *The Scope of Demythologizing* (1960)

———. *Twentieth-century Religious Thought* (1963)

Maguire, Robert. *Programme and Idea* (New Churches Group Papers, 1962)

Maitland, C. *Dr. Leslie Weatherhead* (1960)

Major, H. D. A. *English Modernism: its Origin, Methods, Aims* (Cambridge, Mass., 1927)

Malvern, 1941 (1942) (Proceedings of the Archbishop of York's Conference)

Manning, Bernard Lord. *Church Union: The Next Step for Congregationalists* (1933)

463

Manning, Bernard Lord. *Essays in Orthodox Dissent* (1939)
———. *The Hymns of Wesley and Watts* (1942)
———. *A Layman in the Ministry* (1943)
———. *The Making of Modern English Religion* (1929)
———. *The Protestant Dissenting Deputies* (ed. O. J. Greenwood, Cambridge, 1952)
———. *Why not Abandon the Church?* (1939)
Manson, T. W. *The Church's Ministry* (1948)
Marchant, James (ed.). *The coming-of-age of Christianity* (1950)
—— (ed.). *Dr. John Clifford, C.H.: life, letters and reminiscences* (1924)
—— (ed.). *The Wit and Wisdom of Dean Inge* (1927)
Marsh, H. G. *The Origin and Significance of New Testament Baptism* (Manchester, 1941)
Martin, Hugh (ed.). *A Book of Prayers for Students* (3rd edn., 1921)
—— (ed.). *The Baptist Hymn Book Companion* (1962)
Martin, John R. T. *Christ our Passover: The Liturgical Observance of Holy Week* (1958)
Martin, W. B. J. *Acts of Worship* (New York and Nashville, 1960)
Martindale, C. C. *The Mind of the Missal* (1929)
Martineau, James. *Prayers in the Congregation and in the College* (1911)
Mascall, E. L. *Corpus Christi, Essays on the Church and the Eucharist* (1953)
———. *Theology and Images. A Critical Examination of Recent Scholarship* (1963)
———. *Up and Down in Adria* (1963)
Matheson, P. E. *Life of Hastings Rashdall* (1928)
Mathew, David. *Catholicism in England* (1936)
Matthews, W. R. and Atkins, W. M. (eds.). *A History of St. Paul's Cathedral* (1957)
Maufe, Edward. *Modern Church Architecture* (1948)
Maurer, H. and Trueblood, E. (eds.). *The Pendle Hill Reader* (New York, 1950)
Maxwell, William D. *The Book of Common Prayer and the Worship of Non-Anglican Churches* (1950)
———. *Concerning Worship* (1948)
———. *A History of Worship in the Church of Scotland* (1955)
———. *An Outline of Christian Worship, its Development and Forms* (1936)
May, Rollo (ed.). *Symbolism in Religion and Literature* (New York, 1960)
Mellor, Richard. *Modern Church Design* (1948)
Menzies, Lucy (ed.). *The Collected Papers of Evelyn Underhill* (1946)
Mesnard, Pierre. *Le Mouvement liturgique de Klosterneuberg* (Lyon, 1943)
Michell, G. A. *Landmarks in Liturgy* (1961)
Micklem, E. R. *Our Approach to God* (1934)

Micklem, Nathaniel (ed.). *A Book of Personal Religion* (1938)
———. *The Box and the Puppets, 1888-1953* (1957)
——— (ed.). *Christian Worship* (1936, reissued 1955, Oxford)
———. *Congregationalism and the Church Catholic* (1943)
———. *Congregationalism Today* (1937)
——— (ed.). *Officia Breva* (privately printed, n.d.)
———. *What is the Faith?* (1936)
Micklethwaite, J. T. *The Ornaments of the Rubrics* (1897)
Micklewright, F. H. A. *Sacraments for the Modern Man* (n.d., but ca. 1933)
Mills, Edward D. *The Modern Church* (1956)
———. *The New Architecture in Great Britain, 1946-1953* (1954)
Milner-White, E. and Smith, B. T. D. (eds.). *Cambridge Offices and Orisons* (1921)
Minchin, Basil. *The Celebration of the Eucharist facing the People* (1954)
———. *Covenant and Sacrifice* (1958)
———. *Everyman in His Ministry* (1960)
Moberly, R. C. *Atonement and Personality* (1901)
Moffatt, James. *The Presbyterian Churches* (1928)
Moorman, J. R. H. *A History of the Church in England* (1953)
Moore, Henry. *Heads, Figures and Ideas: A Sculptor's Notebook* (1958)
———. *Portfolio of Forty Drawings* (New York, 1946)
———. *Sculptures and Drawings* (intro. by Herbert Read, 3rd edn., 1949)
Morgan, Dewi (ed.). *They Became Anglicans* (1959)
———. *1662 and all that* (1961)
Morison, Stanley. *English Prayer Books, An Introduction to the Literature of Christian Public Worship* (Cambridge, 1943)
Moule, C. F. D. *Worship in the New Testament* (1961)
Mozley, J. K. (ed.). *G. A. Studdert Kennedy By His Friends* (1929)
———. *The Gospel Sacraments* (1933)
———. *Some Tendencies in British Theology, From the Publication of 'Lux Mundi' to the Present Day* (1951)
Mumford, Lewis. *The Culture of Cities* (New York, 1938)
———. *Technics and Civilization* (New York, 1934)
Murray, Gregory. *Accentual Cadences in Gregorian Chant* (Downside Abbey, Bath, 1958)
———. *The Authentic Rhythm of Gregorian Chant* (Bath, 1959)
———. *Gregorian Rhythm in the Gregorian Centuries* (Bath, 1957)
———. *Plainsong Rhythm* (Bath, 1956)

Neil, William. *The Rediscovery of the Bible* (1955)
Neill, Stephen (ed.). *Twentieth-Century Christianity, Modern Religious Trends* (1961)
Neumann, E. *The Archetypal World of Henry Moore* (trans. R. F. C. Hull, New York, 1959)

New Churches Illustrated (Incorporated Church Building Society, 1936)

Newbigin, J. Lesslie. *The Reunion of the Church* (1948)

Newman, John Henry. *Apologia pro vita sua* (1864)

———. *Meditations and Devotions* (1903)

Newton, Eric. *In My View* (1950)

Nichols, J. H. *A History of Christianity, 1650-1950* (New York, 1956)

Nicholls, William. *Jacob's Ladder: The Meaning of Worship* (1958)

Nicholson, Charles and Spooner, C. *Recent English Ecclesiastical Architecture* (2nd edn., ca. 1910)

Niebuhr, H. Richard. *The Kingdom of God in America* (2nd edn., Hamden, Conn., 1956)

Nuttall, G. F. and Chadwick, Owen. *From Unity to Uniformity (1662-1962)* (1962)

Nygren, Anders. *Agape and Eros: A Study of the Christian idea of love* (2 parts, 1937 and 1939, trans. respectively by A. G. Hebert and P. S. Watson)

Oldmeadow, E. *Francis Cardinal Bourne* (2 vols., 1940, 1944)

Ollard, S. L. *The Anglo-Catholic Revival, Some Persons and Principles* (1925)

Oman, John. *The Church and the Divine Order* (1911)

———. *Grace and Personality* (1917)

———. *The Natural and the Supernatural* (1931)

Orchard, W. E. *From Faith to Faith; an Autobiography of Religious Development* (1933)

———. *The New Catholicism and other sermons* (1917)

———. *Order of Divine Service for Public Worship, the Administration of the Sacraments and other Ceremonies* ... (1921)

———. *Sancta Sanctorum; Prayers for the Holy of Holies* ... (1955)

———. *The Temple: a Book of Prayers* (1928)

Otto, Rudolf. *The Idea of the Holy* (2nd edn., 1950)

Oulton, J. E. L. *Holy Communion and Holy Spirit, A Study in Doctrinal Relationships* (1951)

Parrinder, Geoffrey. *Worship in the World's Religions* (1961)

Parris, John. *John Wesley's Doctrine of the Sacraments* (1963)

Parry, K. L. and Routley, Erik. *Companion to Congregational Praise* (1953)

Parsch, Pius. *The Breviary Explained* (trans. Naydon and Hoegerl, St. Louis and London, 1952)

———. *The Church's Year of Grace* (3 vols., Collegeville, Minnesota, 1953)

Paton, David M. (ed.). *Essays in Anglican Self-Criticism* (1958)

Patrick, Denzil. *Pascal and Kierkegaard* (2 vols., 1947)

Patrick, Millar. *Four Centuries of Scottish Psalmody* (1949)

Payne, Ernest A. *The Baptist Union, A Short History* (1959)

———. *The Fellowship of Believers* (1944)

———. *The Free Church Tradition in the Life of England* (1944)

466

Payne, E. A. and Winward, S. (eds.). *Orders and Prayers for Church Worship* (1960)

Peck, W. G. *An Outline of Christian Sociology* (1948)

Peel, Albert. *Christian Freedom* (1937)

———. *These Hundred Years: A History of the Congregational Union, 1831-1931* (1931)

Pepler, C. *The English Religious Heritage* (1958)

Petre, M. D. *von Hügel and Tyrrell* (1937)

Phillips, C. H. *The Singing Church* (1945)

Phillips, C. S. *Hymnody Past and Present* (1937)

Phillips, C. S. *et alii. Walter Howard Frere, Bishop of Truro* (1947)

Pocknee, C. E. *Cross and Crucifix in Christian Worship and Devotion* (1962)

———. *Liturgical Vesture, Its Origins and Development* (1960)

Porritt, Arthur. *John Henry Jowett* (1924)

Prayer Book Revision in the Church of England; a Memorandum of the Church of England Liturgical Commission (1957)

Prestige, G. L. *The Life of Charles Gore* (1935)

———. *St. Paul's in its Glory, A Candid History of the Cathedral* (1955)

Proctor, F. and Frere, W. H. *A New History of the Book of Common Prayer* (1901)

Pullan, L. *Religion since the Reformation* (1923)

Purcell, William. *Woodbine Willie* (1962)

Pusey, E. B. *Remarks on the Prospective and Past Benefits of Cathedral Institutions* . . . (Oxford and London, 1833)

Quick, O. C. *The Christian Sacraments* (1927)

———. *The Doctrines of the Creed* (1938)

———. *Liberalism, Modernism and Tradition* (1922)

Rafferty, W. *Liturgy in the Parish* (1958)

Ramsey, Arthur Michael. *Durham Essays and Addresses* (1956)

———. *From Gore to Temple: The Development of Anglican Theology between Lux Mundi and the Second World War, 1889-1939* (London and New York, 1960)

———. *The Gospel and the Catholic Church* (1936)

———. *Image Old and New* (1963)

Ratcliff, E. C. *The Booke of Common Prayer of the Churche of England: Its making and revisions M.D. xlix-M.D. clxi* (1949)

———. *Three Commemorative Lectures delivered in Lambeth Palace* (1956)

Rattenbury, J. E. *The Eucharistic Hymns of John and Charles Wesley* (1948)

———. *Thoughts on Holy Communion* (1958)

———. *Vital Elements in Public Worship* (1936)

———. *Wesley's Legacy to the World* (1938)

Rauschenbusch, Walter. *For God and the People: Prayers of the Social Awakening* (New York, 1910)

467

Raven, Charles E. *The Creator Spirit* (1927)
Rawlinson, A. E. J. *Christian Initiation* (1947)
Read, Herbert. *Henry Moore, Sculptor* (1934)
———. *Icon and Idea: the Function of Art in the Development of Human Consciousness* (1955)
Reckitt, M. B. *Maurice to Temple: A Century of the Social Movement in the Church of England* (1947)
——— (ed.). *Prospect for Christendom* (1945)
Reed, Luther D. *Worship: A Study of Corporate Devotion* (Philadelphia, 1962)
Régamey, P. R. *Art Sacré au XXᵉ Siècle?* (Paris, 1952)
Reinhold, H. A. *Speaking of Liturgical Architecture* (South Bend, Indiana, 1952)
Relton, H. M. (ed.). *The New Prayer Book* (1927)
Report of the Cathedrals Commission (1961)
Report of the Royal Commission on Ecclesiastical Discipline (3 vols., 1906)
Reynolds, W. J. *A Survey of Christian Hymnody* (New York, 1963)
Richards, J. M. *An Introduction to Modern Architecture* (Harmondsworth and Baltimore, 1959)
Richardson, Alan, *et alii. Four Anchors from the Stern* (1963)
Richardson, R. D. *The Gospel of Modernism* (1933)
Roberts, R. Ellis. *H. R. L. Sheppard, Life and Letters* (1942)
Robinson, H. Wheeler. *The Life and Faith of the Baptists* (1927)
Robinson, John A. T. *The Body* (1961)
———. *Honest to God* (1963)
———. *In the End God* (1950)
———. *Liturgy Coming to Life* (1961)
———. *On Being the Church in the World* (1960)
Robinson, William. *A Companion to the Communion Service; a devotional Manual* (1942)
———. *What the Churches of Christ stand for* (Birmingham, 1926)
Roth, Cecil (ed.). *Jewish Art, An Illustrated History* (New York, 1961)
Rothenstein, Elizabeth. *Stanley Spencer* (1962)
Rothenstein, John. *Epstein: Arts Council Memorial Exhibition* (1961)
———. *Modern English Painters* (2 vols., 1952, 1956)
Rouse, Ruth and Neill, S. C. (eds.). *A History of the Ecumenical Movement, 1517-1948* (1954)
Rousseau, Olivier. *L'Histoire du Mouvement Liturgique* (Paris, 1945; Engl. trans. *The Progress of the Liturgy*, Westminster, Maryland, 1951)
Routley, Erik R. *The Church and Music* (1950)
———. *Church Music and Theology* (1959)
———. *English Religious Dissent* (Cambridge, 1960)
———. *The Gift of Conversion* (1957)
———. *Hymns and Human Life* (2nd edn., 1959)
———. *I'll Praise My Maker* (1951)
———. *The Man for Others* (1964)

———. *The Music of Christian Hymnody, A Study of the development of the hymn tune since the Reformation with special reference to English Protestantism* (1957)

———. *Music Sacred and Profane* (1960)

———. *Twentieth Century Church Music* (1964)

Routley, E. R. and Parry, K. L. *Companion to Congregational Praise* (1953)

Rowntree, John Wilhelm. *Essays and Addresses* (1905)

Rowse, A. L. *The England of Elizabeth* (1950)

Rupp, E. Gordon. *The Righteousness of God* (1953) (Study of Luther's Theology)

Rushbrooke, J. H. (ed.). *The Faith of the Baptists* (1926)

Sales, St. François de. *Introduction to the Devout Life* (Engl. trans. by A. Ross, 1925)

———. *Spiritual Letters* (Engl. trans. Sidney Lear, 1892)

———. *Treatise on the Love of God* (Engl. trans. W. J. Knox Little, 1901)

Sampson, Ashley (ed.). *Famous English Sermons* (Edinburgh and London, 1940)

Sanders, E. K. *Angélique of Port Royal* (1905)

———. *Fénelon, His Friends and Enemies* (1901)

———. *St. Chantal* (1918)

———. *Vincent de Paul* (1913)

Sangster, Paul. *Doctor Sangster* (1962)

Sangster, W. E. *The Craft of the Sermon* (1954)

———. *The Path to Perfection* (1943)

———. *Westminster Sermons* (2 vols., 1960, 1961)

Sayers, Dorothy L. *The Man Born to be King* (1953, 1962)

———. *The Mind of the Maker* (1941)

Schweitzer, Albert. *The Quest of the Historical Jesus* (Engl. trans., 1910)

Selden, John. *Table Talk 1689* (ed. E. Arber, Birmingham, 1868)

Selwyn, E. G. *An Approach to Christianity* (1925)

——— (ed.). *Essays Catholic and Critical* (1926)

Shands, A. R. *The Liturgical Movement and the Local Church* (1959)

Shepherd, Massey H. *The Eucharist and Liturgical Renewal* (New York, 1961)

——— (ed.). *The Liturgical Renewal of the Church* (New York, 1960)

———. *The Living Liturgy* (New York, 1946)

———. *The Reform of Liturgical Worship: Perspectives and Prospects* (New York, 1961)

Sheppard, H. R. L. *The Human Parson* (1924)

———. *Some of My Religion* (New York, 1936)

Shewring, Walter (ed.). *The Letters of Eric Gill* (1947)

Short, E. H. *The House of God* (4th edn., 1955)

Shuster, G. N. *The Catholic Spirit in Modern English Literature* (1922)

Simpson, James B. *The Hundredth Archbishop of Canterbury* (Arthur Michael Ramsey) (New York and Evanston, 1962)

Simpson, P. Carnegie. *Church Principles* (1923)

———. *The Evangelical Church Catholic* (1934)

———. *Recollections* (1943)

Simpson, W. J. Sparrow. *The History of the Anglo-Catholic Revival from 1845* (1932)

Sixty Post-War Churches (Incorporated Church Building Society, 1957)

Skilbeck, Clement O. *Illustrations of the Liturgy* (1912)

Slack, Kenneth. *The British Churches Today* (1961)

Smith, C. Ryder. *The Sacramental Society* (1927)

Smith, G. E. Kidder. *The New Architecture of Europe* (Cleveland and New York, 1961)

Smith, George D. (ed.). *The Teaching of the Catholic Church, A Summary of Catholic Doctrine* (2nd edn., 1952)

Smith, H. Maynard, *Frank, Bishop of Zanzibar* (1926)

Smith, R. Gregor. *The New Man: Christianity and Man's Coming of Age* (1956)

Smith, Richard Mudie (ed.). *The Religious Life of London* (1904)

Smyth, Charles H. *The Art of Preaching; a Practical Survey of Preaching in the Church of England, 747-1939* (1953)

———. *C. F. Garbett* (1959)

Söderblom, Nathan, *The Living God, Basal Forms of Religion* (1933)

Songs of Praise (1925, enlarged 1931)

Studdert-Kennedy, G. A. *Lies!* (n.d.)

———. *Rough Rhymes of a Padre* (1918)

———. *Rough talks by a Padre delivered to Officers and Men of the B.E.F.* (1918)

Southcott, Ernest W. *The Parish Comes Alive* (1956)

Spence, Basil. *A Phoenix at Coventry: The Building of a Cathedral* (1962)

Spinks, G. Stephens *et al. Religion in Britain since 1900* (1952)

Srawley, J. H. *The Early History of the Liturgy* (1913; rev. edn., Cambridge, 1949)

———. *The Liturgical Movement* (1954)

Staley, Vernon. *The Ceremonial of the English Church* (2nd edn., Oxford, 1900)

——— (ed.). *Hierurgia Anglicana* (3 parts, new edn., 1902-1904)

Steere, Douglas V. *Prayer and Worship* (New York, 1938)

———. *Where Words Come From, An Interpretation of the Ground and Practice of Quaker Worship* (1955)

Stephen, Caroline. *Quaker Strongholds* (4th edn., 1907)

Steuart, Benedict. *The Development of Christian Worship* (1953)

Stibbs, A. M. *Sacrament, Sacrifice and Eucharist* (1961)

Stone, Darwell. *History of the Doctrine of the Holy Eucharist* (2 vols., 1910)

Stott, John R. W. *Basic Christianity* (1958)

———. *The Preacher's Portrait* (1962)

Stranks, C. J. *Anglican Devotion* (1961)
——— (ed.). *Theology and Life* (1958)
Summerson, John. *Heavenly Mansions* (1949)
Sundkler, B. *The Church of South India: The Movement Towards Union, 1900-1947* (1954)
Sweeney, James Johnson. *Henry Moore* (New York, 1946)
Sykes, John. *The Quakers, a new look at their place in society* (1958)

Taylor, A. E. *The Faith of a Moralist* (2 vols., 1931)
Taylor, Michael J. *The Protestant Liturgical Renewal: a Catholic Viewpoint* (Westminster, Maryland, 1962)
Taylor, J. R. S. *et al. Baptism and Confirmation* (1947)
Temple, William. *Christianity and the Social Order* (1942)
———. *Christus Veritas* (1924)
———. *The Church and its Teaching Today* (1936)
———. *The Hope of a New World* (1940)
———. *Mens Creatrix* (1917)
———. *Nature, Man and God* (1934)
———. *Personal Religion and the Life of Fellowship* (1926)
———. *Readings in St. John's Gospel* (2 vols., 1939, 1940)
———. *Studies in the Spirit and Truth of Christianity* (1917)
The Theology of Christian Initiation (1948) (Report of a Theological Commission "appointed by the Archbishops of Canterbury and York to advise on the relations between Baptism, Confirmation and Holy Communion")
Thomas, J. M. Lloyd. *A Free Catholic Church* (1907)
Thompson, A. Hamilton. *The Cathedral Churches of England* (1928)
Thompson, Bard (ed.). *Liturgies of the Western Church* (Cleveland and New York, 1961)
t'Hooft, W. A. Visser (ed.). *The Evanston Report* (1954)
——— (ed.). *The First Assembly of the World Council of Churches* (1949)
Thornton, Lionel S. *Christ and the Church* (1956)
———. *The Common Life in the Body of Christ* (1942)
———. *Confirmation Today* (1946)
———. *The Dominion of Christ* (1952)
———. *The Incarnate Lord* (1928)
———. *Revelation and the Modern World* (1950)
Thornton, Martin. *English Spirituality* (1963)
Thurian, Max. *Joie du Ciel sur la Terre* (Neuchâtel, 1946)
Tillich, Paul. *The Protestant Era* (Chicago, 1948)
———. *Systematic Theology* (Vol. III, Chicago, 1963)
Todd, James M. (ed.). *Prayers and Services for Christian Festivals* (1951)
Tolles, F. B. *Quakers and the Atlantic Culture* (New York, 1960)
Tomkins, Oliver S. (ed.). *The Third World Conference on Faith and Order* (1953) (Proceedings of the Lund Conference)
Torrance, Thomas F. *Conflict and Agreement in the Church* (2 vols., 1959-1960)

Torrance, Thomas F. *Eschatology and the Eucharist* (1952)
Townsend, H. *The Claims of the Free Churches* (1947)
Townsend, W. T., Workman, H. B. and Eayrs, G. (eds.). *A New History of Methodism* (3 vols., 1909)
Travers, Martin. *The Celebration of High Mass* (1922)
———. *Pictures of the English Liturgy—Low Mass* (1916)
Trethowan, Illtyd. *Certainty, philosophical and theological* (1948)
———. *Christ in the Liturgy* (1952)
———. *An Essay in Christian Philosophy* (1954)
Tribe, F., Rees, A. H. *et al. Worship, its Social Significance* (1939)

Underhill, Evelyn. *The Essentials of Mysticism and other Essays* (1920)
———. *Immanence* (1912)
———. *The Life of the Spirit and the Life of Today* (1922)
———. *The Mystery of the Sacrifice* (1938)
———. *Mysticism* (1911)
———. *The Mystics of the Church* (1925)
———. *Worship* (1936)
Underwood, A. C. *A History of the English Baptists* (1947)

Van der Leeuw, Gerhardus. *Religion in Essence and Manifestation* (1938)
———. *Sacred and Profane Beauty* (New York, 1963)
Vidler, A. R. *The Church in an Age of Revolution, 1789 to the present day* (Vol. 5, Pelican History of the Church, Harmondsworth and Baltimore, Maryland, 1961)
———. *The Modernist Movement in the Roman Church* (Cambridge, 1934)
——— (ed.). *Objections to Christian Belief* (1964)
——— (ed.). *Soundings, Essays concerning Christian Understanding* (Cambridge, 1962)
———. *Windsor Sermons* (1958)
Vine, C. H. (ed.). *The Old Faith and the New Theology* (1907)
Vogt, Von Ogden. *The Primacy of Worship* (Boston, Mass., 1958)
von Hügel, Friedrich. *Essays and Addresses in the Philosophy of Religion* (2 vols., 1921, 1928)
———. *Eternal Life* (1912)
———. *The Mystical Element in Religion as studied in St. Catherine of Genoa and her friends* (2 vols., 1908)
———. *The Reality of God* (1931)
———. *Selected Letters, 1896-1924* (ed. B. Holland, 1933)
Vonier, Anscar. *The Collected Works of Abbot Vonier* (Vol. II; The Church and the Sacraments, 1952)

Wakefield, Gordon S. *Puritan Devotion, its place in the development of Christian piety* (1957)
Walsh, Chad. *C. S. Lewis, Apostle to the Skeptics* (New York, 1949)
Walton, Robert C. *The Gathered Community* (1946)

Wand, J. W. C. *A History of the Modern Church from 1500 to the Present Day* (1946)

Ward, Maisie. *Gilbert Keith Chesterton* (1944)

Ward, Marcus. *The Pilgrim Church* (1953)

Warschauer, J. *The New Evangel* (1907)

Watkin, E. I. *Catholic Art and Culture* (rev. edn., 1947)

———. *Roman Catholicism in England from the Reformation to 1950* (1957)

Watson, Philip S. *Let God be God* (1947) (Study of Luther's thought)

Waugh, Evelyn. *The Life of the Right Reverend Ronald Knox* . . . (1959)

Weales, Gerald. *Religion in Modern English Drama* (Philadelphia, 1961)

Wearmouth, R. F. *The Social and Political Influence of Methodism in the 20th Century* (1957)

Weatherhead, Leslie D. *In Quest of a Kingdom* (1943)

———. *The Key Next Door* (1960)

———. *Over His Own Signature* (1955)

———. *Personalities of the Passion* (1942)

———. *The Plain Man Looks at the Cross* (1945)

———. *Psychology in Service of the Soul* (1929)

———. *Psychology, Religion, and Healing* (1951)

———. *The Significance of Silence* (1945)

———. *That Immortal Sea* (1953)

Webb, C. C. J. *Religion and the Thought of Today* (1929)

———. *Religious Thought in England since 1850* (1933)

Webb, Geoffrey. *The Liturgical Altar* (1939)

Weinbach, Werner. *Der Barok als Kunst der Gegen Reformation* (Berlin, 1921)

Weltkirchen Lexikon Handbuch der Oekumene (Stuttgart, 1959)

Westbrook, F. B. *The Holy Communion Service* (1959)

Westminster Hymnal (rev. edn., 1940) (Official hymnbook of the Roman Catholic Church in Great Britain)

Weyres, Willy; Bartnung, Otto *et al. Kirchen: Handbuch fur den Kirchenbau* (Munich, 1959)

Whale, John Selden. *Christian Doctrine* (Cambridge, 1941)

———. *The Protestant Tradition* (Cambridge, 1955)

———. *Victor and Victim* (Cambridge, 1960)

———. *What is a Living Church?* (1937)

White, James F. *The Cambridge Movement: The Ecclesiologists and the Gothic Revival* (Cambridge, 1962)

Whitehead, A. N. *Science and the Modern World* (Cambridge, 1926)

Whitham, A. E. *The Catholic Christ* (1940)

———. *The Culture and Discipline of the Spiritual Life* (1938)

———. *The Pastures of His Presence* (1939)

Whitley, W. T. *A History of British Baptists* (1923)

Who's Who in Art (12th edn., Eastbourne, 1962)

Wickham, E. R. *Church and People in an Industrial City* (1957)

Wigan, Bernard (ed.). *The Liturgy in English* (1962)

Wilkinson, W. C. *Modern Masters of Pulpit Discourse* (London and New York, 1905)

Williams, Charles. *The Descent of the Dove* (1949)

——— (ed.). *The English Poems of John Milton* (see intro. essay of the World's Classics edn., 1940)

Williams, Daniel Day. *Interpreting Theology, 1918-1952* (1953; see also rev. edn., New York, 1959, entitled, *What Present-day Theologians are Thinking*)

Williams, N. P. and Harris, C. (eds.). *Northern Catholicism, Centenary Studies in the Oxford and Parallel Movements* (1933)

Williams, R. R. *Authority in the Apostolic Age* (1950)

Williams, T. Rhondda. *The New Theology—An Exposition* (1907)

Williams, U. Vaughan and Holst, I. *Heirs and Rebels* (1959)

Wilson, Gladys. *Quaker Worship* (1952)

Witte, Robert. *Das Katholische Gotteshaus* (Mainz, 1951)

Wood, H. G. *Belief and Unbelief since 1850* (Cambridge, 1955)

Woodforde, Christopher. *English Stained and Painted Glass* (1954)

Woodgate, M. V. *Father Benson of Cowley* (1953)

Woodward, G. R. (ed.). *Songs of Syon* (3rd edn., 1910)

Woolman, John. *Journal and Essays* (ed. A. M. Gummere, 1922)

Worship and Ministry (1899) (The Epistle of the Yearly Meeting of the English Society of Friends)

Wotherspoon, H. J. *The Religious Value of the Sacraments* (Edinburgh, 1928)

Wyon, Olive. *Living Springs, New Religious Movements in Europe* (1963)

INDEX

I. Index of Persons
II. Index of Places (and Churches)
III. Index of Topics

I. INDEX OF PERSONS

477

480

INDEX

493